what we say/
what we do

D0931597

Irwin Deutscher
Case Western Reserve University

Foreword by Charles Perrow
State University of New York
at Stoney Brook

what we say/
what we do
sentiments & acts

Scott, Foresman and Company
Glenview, Illinois   Brighton, England

To
Verda and Martha and Sara
Thank You

Library of Congress Catalog Card Number: 72-93708
ISBN 0-673-07806-x

Regional Offices of Scott, Foresman are located in Dallas, Texas;
Glenview, Illinois; Oakland, New Jersey; Palo Alto, California;
Tucker, Georgia; and Brighton, England.

Foreword

A number of subjects have suffered from a lack of concrete illustrations, engaging prose, and scientific candor; I think the sociological and the social-psychological methods courses, the general social psychology courses, and even the faster moving introductory sociology courses would be stimulated by this unusual volume. It is a well-guided tour through basic questions of methods and aims in sociology and social psychology, reprinting and carefully working over the classic studies from LaPiere to Milgram, utilizing positivists and ethnomethodologists, questioning but clarifying, and above all, sharing with us the trouble and excitement of doing sociology. An unusual number of topics and problems get covered in the process, and not, you finally realize, as "topics," but as illustrations and pieces of the puzzle of "saying" versus "doing," of words and deeds.

The book has some of the qualities of a detective story and of a drama. As a drama, it resembles a dialogue between the author and his friends and foes. It has those interior monologues we so rarely see in social science, where the principal character discusses his reasoning, thought processes, motivations, and values. It has a beginning, middle, and end that do not correspond to the economical, but quite ahistorical character of most scientific writing where the literature is reviewed and problems stated, the evidence presented and a conclusion reached. Instead, the beginning is an account of the author's confrontation with a nagging, persistent, and perhaps ultimately insoluble problem that faces every honest researcher—can we explain behavior by giving evidence of attitudes? The middle develops new leads an materials but never abandons the central characters of the first act. The end, in Pirandello fashion, leaves us with a feeling of illumination, but illumination of the essential paradoxes and difficulties—not the light that breaks on a heroic solution.

As a detective story, it takes up the question of accounting for the act, for behavior, in terms of motives, attitudes, words. Like the prosecutor when the evidence is circumstantial, we as social scientists probe attitudes and motives, and conclude they caused behavior. People who express antiblack or anti-whatever sentiments will act in that fashion, we assume. But are we right? Have we measured sentiments well? Do they guide behavior that much of the time? What about the setting, the intervening factors, the concrete stimulus? Have we interpreted the behavior correctly? What is the evidence, from the scores of respectable and even brilliant studies found in this book, that would support the current reasoning of social science? Our "common law" in this regard is basic to our enterprise as presently conceived and conducted; attitudes cause, or lead to, or influence behavior, and to predict or explain the latter we must determine the former. Hence the popularity of surveys; but should it be thus? As defense attorney, sorting out the evidence and attacking the imputations, Irwin Deutscher has his hands full, for many have volunteered that they killed Cock Robin. In the end, we are far from sure about the connection between all the words that are recorded and measured and the deed, but Deutscher has ruled several claimants out of court, introduced new suspects, specified conditions, and tried to make us all more honest men.

The reader is engaged throughout in the process of discovery. He learns early of weaknesses in the author's position—for the author reprints and discusses with candor those who have rebutted him. The reader then finds new pieces of information, on another level, and finds the author helping him in this discovery. At times one grows impatient— there are all those election predictions, for example, which do so well—only to find in the next section that it is in this kind of a situation that the juncture of sentiments and acts is best realized, but in predictions of drinking, or cheating, or discrimination, or crime, they may be so ill-joined as to reverse the findings. We will read, then, in an article he selects a resounding defense of the foundation of our research in questionnaires and interviews, demolishing the author's case. Then we see him patiently reconstruct the grounds of the reported research, examine the negative evidence (which, fortunately, keeps popping up in the flood of technical articles), and pose the problem in a novel light. We are no longer so sure about our methods; we are unsettled, made more cautious, and more respectful of the difficulties of doing decent, let alone brilliant, research. Then, from an unexpected direction, for example from laboratory experiments, we are encouraged that Deutscher's position and our embattled one might be made to converge after all. (He is not writing a sloppy paean for participant observation research and all that is "soft"; experimental studies, statistical tools, and hypothesis-testing are used and praised.) Some of the problems, at least, can be sorted out; triangulation is possible with several techniques. But we cannot take our methods for granted; we cannot ignore the impressive negative evidence; we cannot mindlessly continue to make the leap from words to deeds, sentiments to acts, attitudes to behavior. To do so is to distort the meaning of both sides, of attitudes as well as behavior. Between the conception and the act, the poet tells us, falls the shadow; that shadow should be one of the unique preoccupations of sociology.

One singular, and I believe quite unintentional, contribution of this book is that it provides an unobtrusive introduction to the bewildering land of ethnomethodology. This *enfant terrible* of sociology has deserved a much better introduction than it so far has received. It is an important position, even though it has severe limitations as Deutscher acknowledges, and it is a position that deserves to be explored in a nonconfrontational, nonabsolutist manner. This book succeeds in doing that because its concern is not with tearing down all sociological theory and sweeping the ground clean with a single-strawed broom, but is concerned with a problem for which ethnomethodology is able to provide some partial answers. It is also one of the remarkable feats of this book that you are not aware of the fact that you are receiving a gentle introduction to ethnomethodology until the final chapter when Deutscher, in his by-the-by manner, mentions this strand of sociological theory. I am quite certain that the book would not be certified as an approved text by the Central Committee of Ethnomethodologists, and were they concerned enough they would find many faults with it as an introduction. But that merely speaks to other battles than the ones that Deutscher is concerned with. I found it illuminated this area of sociological theory better than anything I have read before. But, I repeat, this was not Deutscher's intention; the road merely led by that place.

This book has several "firsts" to its credit, and one that I am particularly proud of is that it is the first in a series that I am editing—the Leading Edge Series. The series has two distinctions: it will focus upon new or continually unresolved problems that constitute some of the frontiers of our enterprise, and it will do so in a novel format with a concern for letting the student in on our developing areas. The social sciences seem to move forward in spurts and bulges within their established membranes. A "hot topic" attracts a number of investigators and in a few years it manages to reposition the neighboring topics and change our vectors. It is in these hot topics (or the relentless attempt to deal with apparently intractable problems, as in the case of this volume) that the student can get a sense of how a field works—the false starts, the antagonisms of identified positions, the warps that get built in early. The scholar who can survey this new area and judge it with both detachment and personal involvement is rare, but he has the chance to shape the leading edge and the direction of its cut.

The format I conceived of, so well exemplified in the easy-going, reflexive style of Deutscher, would use a historical, developmental outline that would alternate authors' comments and reprinted material in a dialogue format (rather than giving a brief introduction to a chapter full of dense articles written solely for other scholars). The author would devote as much space to discussing the material critically, and showing why it proved to be important at that time, as the selection itself would consume. In such a way the student learns how to read for himself, and learns something of the craft, as well as the substance, of the science. Finally, the author would point the ways in which he believed the area should best develop. He would be both engaged and reflective, supportive but critical.

In all these respects, this volume serves admirably as a model. I recommend the model to others. I find a good part of my craft to be exciting, controversial, baffling, and evolving over the years of circling and probing a basic issue. There is no reason that we cannot communicate this in our texts. This first item in the series will have succeeded if it encourages others to attempt that which Deutscher has done so well.

Charles Perrow
Stony Brook, Long Island

Preface

I suppose every problem has its beginning as an imperceptible itch in a scholar or a student. The itch may irritate until it has to be scratched or it may be ignored until it goes away. When one itches in an embarrassing spot, it is more genteel to suffer without scratching. In Chapter Two, I try to explain why the problem explored in this volume posed an awkward itch which was best ignored for as long as possible. It began, I think, in a graduate course on "Public Opinion" (circa 1951) at the University of Missouri. I may never forgive Professor Noel P. Gist for including on his reading list, and discussing in class, the LaPiere article which appears in Chapter Two. Although that may have been the beginning of this book, I managed to restrain the urge to scratch for another decade and a half.

In September 1965, I had the opportunity to address a plenary session of the Society for the Study of Social Problems. It was also a real opportunity to scratch before an influential and sympathetic audience. In this book I have drawn freely on the published version of that address ("Words and Deeds: Social Science and Social Policy," *Social Problems*, 13 [1966], 235–54). I have also used ideas and materials which were developed in a published comment, two articles, and two chapters in books, all of which I wrote while wrestling with the emerging subject of the present volume ("On Social Science and the Sociology of Knowledge: A Comment Inspired by Alex Carey's Critique of the Hawthorne Studies," *American Sociologist*, 3 [1968], 291–92; "Looking Backward: Case Studies on the Progress of Methodology in Sociological Research," *American Sociologist*, 4 [1969], 35–41; "Buchenwald, Mai Lai, and Charles Van Doren: Social Psychology as Explanation," *Sociological Quarterly*, 11 [1970], 533–40; "Asking Questions Cross Culturally: Some Problems of Linguistic Comparability," in *Institutions and the Person: Essays Presented to Everett C. Hughes*, edited by Howard S. Becker, Blanche Geer, David Riesman, and Robert S. Weiss [Chicago: Aldine Publishing Co., 1968], 318–44; "Public and Private Opinions: Social Situations and Multiple Realities," in *Social Contexts of Research*, edited by Saad Nagi and Ronald G. Corwin [New York: John Wiley and Sons, 1972], 323–99).

Immediately after delivering my address on "Words and Deeds," I embarked on two years of intensive reading and thinking about the relationship between what people say and what they do. This opportunity was provided by a Senior Postdoctoral Fellowship from the National Science Foundation (1965–66) and a Special Fellowship from the National Institute of Mental Health (1966–67). During the first year I was hosted by the Department of Sociology at the University of California, Berkeley, under the sponsorship of Herbert Blumer. The task I had set myself was to discover reasonable and empirically documented explanations for the sometimes discrepancy between words and deeds, of which I had taken note in my address. When I expressed my concern to Professor Blumer, he (figuratively) patted me on the head, and, as if speaking to a child, said, "Irwin, you know why there is a discrepancy." I didn't, but neither did I have the courage to admit it. Eventually, I came to understand what Blumer was talking about and that understanding is partially incorporated into Chapters Ten and Eleven. I am indebted to Professor Blumer for his encouragement and his inspiration.

Thanks are due to Charles Perrow for his careful critical reading of the manuscript and his detailed and constructive suggestions. Perrow and Scott, Foresman and Company had the imagination to provide an innovative format which I believe is ideal for the kind of material with which I am dealing. The creative intellectual contributions of Douglas Mitchell go far beyond the job specifications for a publisher's editor! I am also grateful to Johan Goudsblom, Derek Phillips, and Charles Hennon for their comments on the original draft, to Simhadri Yedla for his assistance in tracking down a great deal of obscure material, and to Linda McKenzie for secretarial help beyond what I had any right to expect.

The most useful critical feedback came to me during the course of a series of seminars out of which this book began to take shape. I am indebted to the graduate students and colleagues who participated in those seminars at Syracuse University, Case Western Reserve University, Ohio State University, and the University of Amsterdam. It is this new generation of sociologists who are taking off the old blinders and imagining a new sociology which, unlike the old, is conscious of its moral obligations, faithful to the world as we experience it, sensitive to the mistakes of history, and at the same time, scholarly, useful, and "relevant." May they invent that great sociology they dream of.

Irwin Deutscher

Contents

PART

TWO

Methods: The Credibility of Evidence

PART ONE What's the Problem?

1 The Biography of a Problem

This book is about the relationship between what people say and what they otherwise do. Although that statement is an oversimplification of the problem, it is a fair beginning. There is a slight improvement in the formulation offered by my nine-year-old daughter: "It is a book about hypocrites and people who complain about pollution and don't do anything about it." This, too, is an incomplete description. Hypocrisy is associated with simulation, deceit, or pretense—a conscious feigning of what one is not. I hope, however, that we may come to understand how men of integrity may *honestly* express concern about the condition of the environment while simultaneously polluting it. There is no further mention in this volume of the environment or its pollution. Nevertheless, this book does deal directly with that issue: the problem of what we say and what we do is endemic. The objects of saying and doing may be anything or anyone. Some of those objects will be considered explicitly; others, such as the environment, will remain implicit.

The title of this volume deliberately avoids the more traditional distinction, "attitudes and behavior," because of the connotational paraphernalia attached to these terms. Any dichotomy does an injustice to the problem; it is, in fact, necessary to draw much finer distinctions in order to make sense out of the great variety of frequently inconsistent evidence. There may be any number of sentimental orientations toward a given social object. As the evidence in Chapter Twelve suggests, values, norms, and beliefs are not necessarily related to one another. In like manner, there may be any number of action orientations toward the same object. Aware of the risks, I have chosen to avoid stylistic monotony by varying my terminology. I use "attitude," "sentiment," and "words" as if they were synonymous. They are not. In like manner I shift among "acts," "deeds," and "behavior." These terms also mask very different kinds of orientations.

In Chapter Two I will begin to address the problem directly. For the moment, I want to concentrate on the manner in which it has evolved. There is a customary style for reporting any research. That style of reporting generally moves with cool logic from the statement of the problem, through a review of literature, to a listing of hypotheses and their sources, a description of methods, a report of the data, and, finally, to a set of conclusions and, sometimes, recommendations (either for further research or for policy). With minor variations this is the way we generally report our findings. And, with minor variations, it is the way they are reported in this book. But this style of reporting should not be confused with the actual biography of any piece of research. Although each is guided by its own logic and, although each logic may be reasonable enough, the description of the process as it appears in writing may be very different from the process as it actually happened.

This is one example of the general problem addressed by this book: how people do research is not always the same as how they say they do it.[1]

Writers of methodology textbooks generally ignore this distinction of making discoveries and then verbalizing them, suggesting rather that the manner in which research is reported is the manner in which it ought properly to be conducted. This orthodoxy persists even in the face of blatantly irregular procedures which occasionally result in findings of such great importance that they must be incorporated into the standard literature of a field. Michael Polanyi reports that "when Einstein discovered rationality in nature, unaided by any observation that had not been available for at least fifty years before, our positivistic textbooks covered up the scandal by an appropriately embellished account of his discovery."[2]

In the Preface, I refer to an itch to examine the relationship between what men say and what they do. The irritant which caused that itch was Richard LaPiere's "Attitudes vs. Actions," which appears in Chapter Two. With a reading of that article and of the discussion which follows it, the source of my concern should become clear. At this point it is only important to know that I made my best effort to begin to find what I hope is an honest answer to what I am sure was an honest question: What, in fact, is the relationship between sentiments and acts? Furthermore, if there should be an occasional incongruity between the two, under what conditions is it likely to occur and how can it be explained?

I began by studying and thinking about LaPiere's paper. It deals with the relationship between racial prejudice and racial discrimination. But surely that is only one case (albeit an important one) of the more general issue of the relationship between what people say and what they otherwise do. Yet in my file there were references to less than half a dozen articles bearing on the problem. So my next step was to begin to identify and then to read the evidence. By mid-1971 my bibliography had grown from less than six items to 450 items. At this writing, I have read about two thirds of them and the bibliography continues to grow faster than I can read. The accretion, incidentally, is due in about even amounts to the discovery of older materials which I had overlooked and to an outburst of research reports, theoretical treatises, and methodological articles which has occurred in the late sixties and early seventies. After a long period of relative quiescence, the issue of "attitude vs. behavior" had again come to life.

1. Douglas Mitchell has suggested that "ancient theories of rhetoric were at pains to distinguish 'invention' and 'judgment,' for each of which they worked out elaborate (and fruitful) sets of arts and subdistinctions. Invention and discovery—the Latin *invenio* makes no distinction between them—were deliberate processes by which you got your bright idea; then the problem became one of how to formulate or 'dispose' it in reasoned, persuasive discourse (i.e., the process of judgment). The distinction of invention and judgment intersects, as you note, with that of deeds and words, but of course it's not a simple linear relationship. Invention is an art of discovering new (*verbal*) arguments as well as of uncovering new *things*; judgment is an art of appropriately *expressing* an invention, but is also the art of *testing* arguments, proving conclusions, and verifying statements. Hence, the plot would thicken with the introduction of further distinctions of form and matter, universal and particular, etc." (Personal communication, dated November 6, 1972.)

2. Michael Polanyi, *Personal Knowledge* (Chicago: University of Chicago Press, 1958), p. 11, as quoted in Melville Dalton, "Preconceptions and Methods in *Men Who Manage*," in *Sociologists at Work: Essays on the Craft of Social Research*, ed. Phillip E. Hammond (New York: Basic Books, Inc., 1964), p. 53. Dalton summarizes some of the leading philosophers of science on this subject (pp. 51–53). The Hammond volume consists of eleven research biographies or chronicles.

For some scholars a problem emerges over deciding what to include in a bibliography. I had no difficulties on this score. *Anything* which illustrates or considers the relationship between what people do and what they say is potential data as far as I am concerned: survey reports, congressional debates, ethnographies, newspaper columns, field studies, novels, laboratory experiments, academic polemics, personal anecdotes, etc. As I read, and considered, and as the bibliography grew, I began to classify the material into three major categories: empirical evidence, methodology and technique, and theory and concepts. The latter two categories became storage bins for material which the authors did not necessarily intend to deal with my problem, but which I found useful and relevant. (The pieces by Blumer and Garfinkel in Chapters Eleven and Thirteen are examples of such theoretical materials; Roth and Orne in Chapters Six and Eight illustrate methodological treatments which become relevant only after considerable exploration of the problem.) Much later, each of the three original categories was subdivided, one section dealing with the simple relationship between sentiments and acts, and the other dealing with the effects of a *change* in one on the other.

As I began to read the materials, the bibliography sometimes shrank as well as grew. Although I did not call it that at the time, I had already begun to "screen" for relevance and credibility. Some items, in spite of their seductive titles, turned out to have nothing to do with my problem. Others turned out to be unbelievable, regardless of their conclusions. This was the crude beginning of a process I would later come to think of as my *double screen*. If I were reporting my procedures in standard research style, I would probably begin with a discussion of the double screen, as if I had methodically planned my work in that manner. That might make a more reasonable narrative, but it would not be true. I will return to the double screen in a moment.

As I continued reading and taking notes, a retrieval technique began to emerge. It, too, was unplanned, although it could be reported in traditional style as a systematic procedure designed prior to the research. The technique for handling the wealth of materials I was exposed to closely parallels the procedures later described by Barney Glaser and Anselm Strauss.[3] The notes consisted of exact quotations with precise references, summaries of important findings and ideas, and notions of my own which occurred while reading the material. I gradually began to identify what seemed to be important sets of ideas and to make cross references and other identifying marks on the margins. It was out of this coding system that the major themes of this volume began to emerge. Some of these themes were pretested in papers presented at professional meetings or in occasional journal articles.[4]

The problem of making sense out of a wide variety of sometimes contradictory findings is an attribute of any research endeavor. I have already described the first step: scanning the literature in order to create a bibliography which provides a

---

3. Barney G. Glaser and Anselm L. Strauss, *The Discovery of Grounded Theory: Strategies for Qualitative Research* (Chicago: Aldine Publishing Co., 1967). Glaser and Strauss deal primarily with field observational data although they do mention the applicability of their methods to library research (see especially Chapter 7). A useful treatment of library research also appears in C. Wright Mills' "Appendix: On Intellectual Craftsmanship," in *The Sociological Imagination* (New York: Oxford University Press, 1959), pp. 195–226.

4. For example, I first began crystalizing the problem of conceptual confusion (Chapter Twelve) in a paper entitled "On Adding Apples and Oranges: Making Distinctions and Connections in Social Science," read at the annual meetings of the Midwest Sociological Society in 1967. Examples of themes which have appeared as articles can be found in the Preface.

reasonable sample of thinking and observations concerned with sentiments and acts. At the time, it seemed to me that the rest would be routine. I needed only to read the materials and determine the conditions under which the observations were made and then to tabulate the results. Surely when I counted up and sorted out the various conclusions, I would have quantitative evidence of the extent to which sentiments and acts are related under different conditions. I did, in fact, make an abortive effort in that direction. But the almost random hodgepodge of findings — sometimes entailing contradictions among studies exploring the same phenomena — in conjunction with the growing suspicion that the only clear relationship which was emerging was between the method employed and the conclusions reached, caused me to take a step back.

I have already mentioned my early discarding of materials which impressed me as blatantly incredible. At some point (I am not sure exactly when) it became clear to me that this procedure needed to be made more explicit and more systematic. I had discovered the need for what Hemingway has called a crap detector.[5] With few exceptions, however, it is difficult to make a clear-cut distinction between evidence which is and is not crap. Although there is a charm in Hemingway's earthy language, C. Wright Mills comes rather closer to the kind of screening that is necessary. Mills refers to a process he calls "discounting." He reminds us that an intelligent interpretation of historical data requires some knowledge of who wrote it, under what conditions, and why. When we understand this context, we can then properly discount the data. That means that rather than *discarding* much of what is reported as "crap," we instead *discount* it and interpret it; we do use it, but not necessarily with as much confidence or even in the same manner as the original author would have it.

We do, of course, routinely discount history or biography according to what we know about the author. If, for example, he provides us with an account of a battle, we would want to know, among other things, whether he was a soldier and, if so, was he a private or a general? Was he on the winning or the losing side? It is important to recognize that we attempt to locate biases and that we then take them into account by discounting the report to the degree and in the direction that seems appropriate. We do not discard reports merely because of biases or flaws of one sort or another. If we did, there would be no history. It is all presented by men who have some sort of a stake in the matters of which they write, who are located somewhere in their own society (and tend to see the world from that perspective), and whose work is more or less open to methodological criticism. This same observation can be made of all discourse, including social science research reports.

> Here sociologists can garner suggestions from critical historiography which attempts to locate (culturally and biographically) observers (e.g., Roman popes) of social events in order properly to discount their recorded observations. This method is aware of the differences of societal occurrences as seen and written of by variously situated reporters.[6]

5. The term is attributed to Hemingway by S. M. Miller who used it in an ad lib during an address at the annual meetings of the Ohio Valley Sociological Society, 1971.

6. C. Wright Mills, "Methodological Consequences of the Sociology of Knowledge," *American Journal of Sociology* 46 (1940): 316–30. Reprinted in *Power, Politics and People: The Collected Essays of C. Wright Mills,* ed. Irving L. Horowitz (New York: Ballantine Books, Inc., 1963), p. 467, n. 37.

Whether our data are derived from surveys, interviews, observations, laboratory experiments, or whatever, they require discounting (but rarely discarding). It is in this sense that nearly everything is admissible as evidence, but some evidence is more credible than others. I have no rules for the assessment of credibility, except, "do it." Inevitably different scholars will apply different criteria. To paraphrase both Hemingway and a bit of conventional wisdom, one man's meat is another man's crap.

I consider this process of discounting to be the first component of a *double screen* which all reports must pass through. It is primarily a methodological screen and it appears, in one form or another, in nearly every chapter of this book. There are some well-informed students of the relationship between attitude and behavior who suggest that once methodological problems are properly resolved, nearly all apparent discrepancies between what we say and what we do disappear. One may draw this implication from the fragment by Donald Campbell which introduces Chapter Nine. Howard Ehrlich is explicit on this matter, although he combines both elements of the double screen in his explanation: ". . . the evidence for inconsistency may be rejected on both methodological and conceptual grounds, and . . . there is no necessary incompatibility between a theory of attitudes and theories of interpersonal or intergroup behavior."[7] I concur in the observation that much of the variance is explained by methodological difficulties and still more is explained when conceptual problems are clarified. But, in addition, I will attempt to document the position that much of the variance can only be explained by the fact that, under many conditions, it can be empirically demonstrated that men do not act as they say they do. Some of the observed discrepancy between sentiments and acts is in fact more apparent than real; some of it is also very real.

Ehrlich has introduced the second component of the double screen. It may be that if we judge reports carefully on methodological grounds, discrepant findings will get sifted out and each one of the remaining studies will agree with the others. But this is unlikely. In my own research, the remaining evidence seemed to make more sense after methodological screening, but it was still far from coherent. Early in the game, I was inclined to treat with contempt critics who argued about what "attitudes" really are, or what "behavior" really is. I was willing to settle for comparisons between what people say and what they do. And when some critics reminded me that speech is behavior too, I shrugged impatiently at their petulance and snarled, "O.K., what people say and what they *otherwise* do!" And that is the way I proceeded.

The first time I seriously considered this issue in print, I wrote (using italics for emphasis): "We still do not know much about the relationship between what people say and what they do—attitudes and behavior, sentiments and acts, verbalizations and interactions, words and deeds. *We know so little that I can't even find an adequate vocabulary to make the distinction!*"[8] It was not until later, under pressure primarily from students who brought to my attention articles such as those by Rodman and Westie which appear in Chapter Twelve, that I realized the urgency of a *conceptual* as well as a methodological screen. It was then that I began to ask to

---

7. Howard J. Ehrlich, "Attitudes, Behavior, and the Intervening Variables," *American Sociologist* 4 (1969): 29. This article appears in full in Chapter Eleven.

8. Irwin Deutscher, "Words and Deeds: Social Science and Social Policy," *Social Problems* 13 (1966): 242.

what extent different studies are in fact addressing different issues under the same labels. Surely, if they are talking about different things, then their findings may be different but not at all inconsistent. By the time our information has filtered through the double screen—when it has been sorted for both credibility and for conceptual consistency—we can assume that the residual findings represent, in one way or another, the kinds of differences between sentiments and acts which actually occur among people in the various conditions which make up their everyday lives.

During the early period of my investigation, when I had begun to uncover convincing and disturbing evidence that people do not always do as they say and may sometimes do just the opposite, I found myself drifting toward a rather extreme behaviorist position. If we could not count on what people told us, then we had to be much more attentive to what they were doing. Perhaps what they did overtly was the only true evidence for social science. The implications of such a position troubled me even then, and, although I seemed to suggest it, I also tried to resist it.[9] I was assuming that actions speak louder than words. Gradually I came to realize that words may speak louder and more eloquently than actions. In the second bit of data presented in Chapter Two ("Fact and Factitiousness in Ethnic Opinionnaires"), Merton questions the assumption

> . . . that in one sense or another overt behavior is "more real" than verbal behavior. The assumption is both unwarranted and scientifically meaningless. . . . It should not be forgotten that overt actions may deceive; that they, just as "derivations" or speech reactions, may be deliberately designed to disguise or to conceal private attitudes. . . . The apriori assumption that verbal responses are simply epiphenomenal is to be accorded no greater weight than the assumption that words do not deceive nor actions lie.

This disillusionment was aided by my study of research which reported rigorous time sampling in the observation of what people were doing. It is possible, for example, to determine precisely the relative amount of time spent by nurses in different activities.[10] But it seemed to me not very helpful to know how much time nurses spent at the bedside or at the nursing station, if I didn't know why they were there and why they saw themselves doing whatever it was they were doing. There are very different purposes and consequences in changing sheets brusquely because it is time to change them and in changing sheets casually as a device to talk with the patient. Such "time and motion studies" did not seem to me helpful in understanding the relationship between what people say and what they do.

On the more positive side, I was led away from my initial behaviorist inclinations by the startling realization that when we asked people questions, they didn't always understand them as *we* intended and when we listened to their answers we didn't always understand them as *they* intended. In pursuing the relationship between language and conduct, I became increasingly aware that I was not on a lengthy tangent but on an issue of such great relevance to my problem that it re-

9. Ibid., p. 243.

10. Curt Tausky and Eugene B. Piedmont, "The Sampling of Behavior," *American Sociologist* 3 (1968): 49–51. For a technical critique of that article, see Sidney Rosen, "Independent Samples and Test-Retest Reliability," *American Sociologist* 3 (1968): 297.

quired serious study in its own right.[11] Although I may touch gently on language-related issues in this volume, especially in Chapter Seven, the subject deserves more extensive and independent treatment than can be afforded here.

The process of discounting involves an infinite regression, since the observations of the discounter must also be properly discounted. It is true that I have attempted to discount materials treated in this volume, but my own biases, from whatever source, must also be taken into account by the reader. *Argumentum ad hominem* is rightly viewed with disapproval in considering the merits of an issue, but in considering the works of a scholar, the man's location in his social world becomes a basis for interpretation and evaluation. This I take to be one of the central themes in Alvin Gouldner's *The Coming Crisis in Western Sociology*.[12] It is Gouldner's call for a "reflexive sociology" which is being echoed here. The close kinship between the present volume and Derek Phillips' *Knowledge from What* is reflected in a statement on his opening page: "In a book that raises many questions about the so-called objectivity of sociological research, it seems almost obligatory for me to provide some biographical information so that the reader can better understand my vantage point in doing this book. For it is my belief that, despite protestations to the contrary, the writer is always present in his narrative."[13] I believe this view to be correct. There is no such thing as a pure, objective, detached sociology. Sociology is done by sociologists whose own humanity inevitably interferes with what they do. With proper discipline, a sociologist may become inhumane, but he cannot become inhuman.

I was a resident graduate student at the University of Missouri during the years 1949–53. Those were the years when American sociology was full of hope. We studied Merton and Parsons (at first *The Structure of Social Action* and then with great anticipation the newly published *The Social System*) so that we could become part of the massive theoretical leaps we thought were occurring in our time. Lazarsfeld and Stouffer were bringing the new scientific methodology to life before our eyes (each volume of the American Soldier series made us more comfortable with the knowledge that our prescientific past was indeed being buried). Located as we were in the isolated Midwest, we were still heavily influenced by the already decaying Chicago school. The Yankee City series was read along with the American Soldier series. We suffered through Weber and Durkheim and Simmel in the manner of all sociology graduate students—then and now. But we also were exposed to Mead and Cooley and Dewey. And there were contemporary sociologists who were not so much in the "mainstream" of the great Eastern departments: Wirth, Burgess, Blumer, Hughes. Graduate students in places like Missouri got to know men like these

11. My consequent ruminations about language and social research can be found in "Asking Questions Cross Culturally: Some Problems of Linguistic Comparability," in *Institutions and the Person: Essays Presented to Everett C. Hughes*, eds. Howard S. Becker, Blanche Geer, David Riesman, and Robert S. Weiss (Chicago: Aldine Publishing Co., 1968), 318–44; "A Comment on Straus' Phenomenal Identity and Conceptual Equivalance," *Journal of Marriage and the Family* 31 (1969): 240–41; "Editor's Introduction: Language, Methodology, and the Sociologist," and "Asking Questions (and Listening to Answers): A Review of Some Sociological Precedents and Problems," both in *Sociological Focus: On Language and Conduct* 3 (1969–70): 1–12, 13–32.

12. Alvin W. Gouldner, *The Coming Crisis in Western Sociology* (New York: Basic Books, Inc., 1970).

13. Derek L. Phillips, *Knowledge from What: Theories and Methods in Social Research* (Chicago: Rand McNally and Co., 1971), p. xi.

at the small, folksy meetings of the Midwest Sociological Society. And they occasionally came to our campus where they talked sociology and drank beer until the wee hours with the handful of students who made up our graduate contingent.

Although the phenomenology of the Chicago pragmatists (they called it "Verstehen Sociology") was strong, it was not cultish, and it was tempered by a positivism with a Midwestern flavor. The hard logic of Ogburn and the experimental rigor of Chapin were not unrepresented. In fact I was impressed enough with the potentials for a new and sophisticated quantitative sociology that I pursued a Master's degree in statistics. My respect for elegant experimental design and the power of the evidence derived from it has never faded. Neither has my contempt for the persistent misapplication of statistics in the social sciences. I had the advantage of never being *trained* in sociology. The small group of dedicated and well-informed teachers in the department did their utmost, rather, to *educate* graduate students. They treated us like junior colleagues and, to my great bewilderment, frequently gave the impression that they wanted to learn from us. Like most graduate students, I learned much from my peers. We enjoyed each other; we enjoyed our poverty; we enjoyed sociology. Although it seems strange in retrospect, it never occurred to me at the time that I would eventually become a college professor. In fact, the present was so delightful that I never thought about the future at all.

The preceding pair of paragraphs are probably romanticized as are all reminiscences. Let the reader discount as best he can. I alluded to the early impact of LaPiere's paper in the Preface to this volume and will pursue it further in Chapter Two. My active concern about the relationship between sentiments and acts began on my first job. It stems directly from my dissatisfaction with the results of survey research methods I employed in attempting to obtain data from physicians and from the general public for monographs on public images of the nurse. I turned to depth interviews in my research on student nurses and on the postparental phase of the family cycle and, although there was some increase in my confidence in the soundness of my findings, I remained dissatisfied.

At that time I managed to defeat the problem by rationalizing it away. The rationalizations appear in two papers in which I argued essentially that we scientists know what we are doing and have to stick by our guns regardless of reactions of naive outsiders.[14] Unlike the questionnaire and interview studies, however, I was infused with a sense of high validity in the observational materials Peter New and I employed in the study of collective behavior during a tornado. A few years later the same participant-observation methods again yielded what seemed to me accurate and useful data.[15] My first effort to cope with the problem of empirically observable inconsistencies, although done in a primitive taxonomical manner, occurred as a result of our analysis of interviews with student nurses.[16]

14. Irwin Deutscher, "Physician's Reactions to a Mailed Questionnaire," *Public Opinion Quarterly* 20 (1956): 599–604; "The Stereotype as a Research Tool," *Social Forces* 37 (1958): 56–60.

15. Irwin Deutscher and Peter Kong-Ming New, "A Functional Analysis of Collective Behavior in a Disaster," *Sociological Quarterly* 2 (1961): 21–36; Irwin Deutscher, "The Gatekeeper in Public Housing," in *Among the People: Encounters with the Poor*, eds. Irwin Deutscher and Elizabeth Thompson (New York: Basic Books, Inc., 1968), pp. 38–50.

16. Irwin Deutscher and Ann Montague, "Professional Education and Conflicting Value Systems: The Role of Religious Schools in the Educational Aspiration of Nursing Students," *Social Forces* 35 (1956): 126–31.

For over a decade I was administratively responsible for a variety of re-search both at Community Studies, Inc., in Kansas City (now the Institute for Community Studies) and at the Syracuse University Youth Development Center. During the course of this work I grew increasingly concerned over the methodological sacrifices which are made in the name of fiscal or temporal economy: e.g., while research conducted over a period of time (longitudinal studies) is generally conceded to be superior to that conducted at only one point in time (cross-sectional studies), still, the former costs too much and takes too long. And I became uncomfortable about the high value placed on consistency (i.e., *reliability*) — sometimes at the cost of deter-mining whether or not we are consistently getting at what we intend (i.e., *validity*). During recent years I was disturbed, too, to find methodological decisions made more or less because of the requirements of existing technology: although we may not yet have developed appropriate tools, we do have others and so we will use them. And through all of this I became more and more suspicious of the tendency to mask our ignorance of the various kinds of relationships which obtain between the attitudinal and the behavioral dimensions by using operational definitions and op-erational assumptions. Such procedures eliminate definitional problems by defining the object of study in terms of the measuring device employed, e.g., "intelligence" is the score I receive on my intelligence test.

I have alluded to the distinction between training and education. Mills neatly puts his finger on what it means to be trained:

> Since one can be *trained* only in what is already known, training sometimes incapacitates one from learning new ways; it makes one rebel against what is bound to be at first loose and even sloppy. But you must cling to such vague images and notions, if they are yours, and you must work them out. For it is in such forms that original ideas, if any, almost always first ap-pear.[17]

In this volume, I have no intention of training anyone in anything. There is no body of information which I would like to convey. What I hope for is to make some slight dent in the trained incapacity we all acquire in our attempts to become educated. I do not believe that sociologists or social scientists in general know very much about the world or how it works or what can be done about it. But I do be-lieve that such knowledge is close at hand and that the primary requisite for it is to help a new generation of students to remove the blinders which so narrow the vi-sion of the rest of us. I suggest that, rather than building on what we know, they learn from our mistakes. Chapter Four focuses on this issue.

Like Phillips, I am appalled by the notion entertained by some radical soci-ologists that sociology is the tool of the establishment—some tool! Perhaps we are servants of the power structure, but hardly a useful tool for anyone. Phillips is sur-prised by the

> . . . apparent belief that sociologists actually know something that could be used *for* those in power and *against* [those not in power]. . . . I recog-nize that sociologists often lend legitimacy to the actions of the government

---

17. Mills, *The Sociological Imagination*, p. 212.

and ruling class, but that . . . radical sociologist[s] should share with the sociological elite the belief that sociologists possess some unique knowledge that can be put to the use of one or another segment of the society was unexpected by me.[18]

Let me illustrate our ignorance by pointing out what happens when two well-informed and sensitive sociologists attempt "an inventory of scientific findings" about human behavior. Berelson and Steiner's whole book is a disappointment to the student, largely because of their integrity. When such honest scholars attempt to list propositions, this is what sometimes happens: one "proposition" is the statement that "the lower classes presumably violate the law more frequently than the upper classes." This is immediately followed by the qualification, "In any case, they are more likely to get caught and punished." After musing over the possibility of recording bias, they conclude that "it is not at all clear what the fact is."[19] The fact is that they do not know; I do not know; and no one else knows. This isolated illustration may help clarify my reservations about "training."

In this chapter I have traced briefly the biography of my interest in the problem which this book employs as a point of departure. Inevitably my own professional and personal biography must be a part of it. These materials are provided as an aid to the reader so that he may better discount what I have to say. Credibility is a relatively simple matter in a volume such as this, since all of the raw data—the literature cited—is readily available for reanalysis. The particular format I have chosen presents some of that raw data in each chapter, not in the form of tabulations, but in the form of a selected sample of articles which seem to me to provide useful data in the construction of the ideas which emerge as the volume proceeds. Although I use the relationship between sentiments and acts as a point of departure or as a case in point, this problem entails most of the critical methodological and theoretical issues which confront contemporary social science.

It should be clear that if one is to understand the meaning of the evidence with which he deals, if he is to make the judgments required in order to assess credibility and conceptual clarity, if he is to put all of this together in an effort to explain what happens in a logical and empirically sound manner—if he is to do all of these things, then he has no choice but to attempt to live up to C. Wright Mills' mandate to "Be a good craftsman":

> Let every man be his own methodologist; let every man be his own theorist; let theory and method again become part of the practice of a craft. Stand for the primacy of the individual scholar; stand opposed to the ascendancy of research teams of technicians. Be one mind that is on its own confronting the problems of man and society.[20]

18. Phillips, *Knowledge from What*, p. xvi.
19. Bernard Berelson and Gary Steiner, *Human Behavior: An Inventory of Scientific Findings* (New York: Harcourt Brace Jovanovich, Inc., 1964), p. 488.
20. Mills, *The Sociological Imagination*, p. 224.

2 A Problem Found and Lost

The Temper of the Times and the Mystique of Science

There are three avenues through which social scientists can seek to understand human behavior: (1) we can observe it in process; (2) we can view the records men leave behind—written or otherwise artifactual; and (3) we can ask questions and listen to answers. There are different techniques for implementing these approaches and they may be employed in various combinations. Among sociologists, it is the last—the verbal approach—which is most commonly used.[1] We interview; we survey; we poll; we converse; we eavesdrop. Although we are often constrained to use verbal elicitation techniques, we are sometimes as interested in behavior or action as we are in verbalizations. Assuming the old-fashioned textbook definition of atttitudes as "tendencies to act," we frequently proceed to draw conclusions about the behavior of people on the basis of what they tell us. We assume that verbal responses reflect behavioral tendencies.

In his definitive volume on interviewing, Hyman makes this assumption explicit: "If one could wait around indefinitely," he writes,

> the natural environment would ultimately liberate behavior relevant to a given inference. However, practical limitations preclude such lengthy procedures. As Vernon puts it: "Words are actions in miniature. Hence by the use of questions and answers we can obtain information about a vast number of actions in a short space of time, the actual observation and measurement of which would be impracticable."[2]

---

1. For example, in 1965–66, over 90 percent of the research articles published in the *American Sociological Review* and the *American Journal of Sociology* used interviews or questionnaires as their primary data. See Julia Brown and Brian G. Gilmarten, "Sociology Today: Lacunae, Emphases and Surfeits," *American Sociologist* 4 (1969): 283–91.

2. Herbert Hyman et al., *Interviewing in Social Research* (Chicago: University of Chicago Press, 1954), pp. 17-18. The quotation is from P. E. Vernon, *The Assessment of Psychological Qualities by Verbal Methods*, Medical Research Council, Industrial Health Research Board, Report No. 83 (London: H. M. Stationery, 1938). This doubtful inferential process is frequently justified on the basis that private kinds of behavior are simply not observable. See, for example, Ira Riess' (Post-Kinsey and Pre-Masters and Johnson) *The Social Context of Premarital Permissiveness* (New York: Holt, Rinehart and Winston, 1967). It sometimes occurs without such justification, that is, when the behavior is more public, as in religious behavior. See J. E. Faulkner and G. DeJong, "Religiosity in 5-D: An Empirical Analysis," *Social Forces* 45 (1966): 246–254. The importance of distinguishing between public and private sentiments and behaviors is considered in Chapter Ten.

All of this, tempered with good judgment, reflects a basic assumption of contemporary social science. But ever since encountering Richard LaPiere's "Attitudes vs. Actions" as a graduate student, I have been haunted by the suspicion that this assumption may be untenable.

Employing methods which are equal if not superior to more recent research on the problem, LaPiere finds that what people say about a despised minority is not only unrelated to what they do when confronted with that minority; *it is inversely related.* People do the opposite of what they say—at least in this case. The evidence is powerful and the differences large. We will take a more detailed comparative look at LaPiere's methods in Chapter Four. Even if the analyst chooses to heavily discount this isolated bit of 1934 evidence, it cannot be discarded completely.

Richard LaPiere's quest has a history. It can be traced through a trilogy of his papers, the last of which is the one reproduced in this chapter. If such efforts can be thought of as originating at a specific point in time, LaPiere's probably began while he was attending a seminar with Malinowski at the London School in 1927.[3] During the course of that seminar, the term "verbalization" was employed to indicate a distinction between what informants may say and what may be the actual custom of the primitive society. Meanwhile, LaPiere was formulating a comparative survey of race prejudice in France and England.[4] Interested in the concept of "verbalization," he attempted to check his questionnaire findings against actual practices; this he accomplished by questioning hotel proprietors about their policy. The results left LaPiere satisfied at the time that he had found a fair concordance between verbal responses and, consequently, that his survey results were sufficiently valid.

Upon his return to the United States, he undertook a study of an Armenian community,[5] as a result of which, he writes, "I began again to doubt the certain value of verbal evidence." Perhaps as a result of this doubt, LaPiere reconsidered the evidence from his French study and realized that "at that time I overlooked the fact that what I was obtaining from the hotel proprietors was still a 'verbalized' reaction to a symbolic situation."[6] He had not compared verbal and nonverbal behavior. What he had done was to compare attitudes with self-reports of behavior. His concern resulted in a carefully designed and controlled experiment which consumed two years in the field and over ten thousand miles of driving and which culminated in "Attitudes vs. Actions."

LaPiere recorded the treatment a Chinese couple received in hotels, auto camps, tourist homes, and restaurants. *Of the 251 establishments approached, one auto camp refused to accommodate them.* Here then was an estimate of Caucasian-Oriental intergroup *behavior.* Allowing a time lapse of six months, a questionnaire was sent

---

3. I was fortunate to receive a lengthy communication from Professor LaPiere in which he reminisces about some of his early research experiences and about the general state of American sociology in the twenties and thirties. Many of my observations in this chapter are derived from that communication (dated October 23, 1964). Quotations attributed to LaPiere in this chapter, and not otherwise identified, are from this source. He has published a caustic satirical note along these lines as a "Comment on Irwin Deutscher's 'Looking Backward,'" *American Sociologist* 4 (1969): 41–42.

4. Richard T. LaPiere, "Race Prejudice: France and England," *Social Forces* 7 (1928): 102–11.

5. Richard T. LaPiere, "Type-Rationalizations of Group Antipathy," *Social Forces* 15 (1936): 232–37.

6. LaPiere, "Attitudes vs. Actions."

to each establishment. They were asked, "Would you accept members of the Chinese race as guests in your establishment?" *Only one "yes" response was received.* Here then was an estimate of Caucasian *"attitudes"* toward Orientals. Most important is the juxtapositioning of these two estimates: we have, in 1934, strong empirical evidence, not only that there may be no relationship between what people say and what they do, but that under some conditions there may be a high inverse relationship between the two.

LaPiere's conclusions are primarily theoretical and methodological. With scientific caution he restricts empirical conclusions to the empirical data and warns against careless generalization. He reminds us that the conventional questionnaire is a valuable tool for identifying such phenomena as political or religious *beliefs.* But, he continues, "if we would know the extent to which [an individual's belief] restrains his behavior, it is to his behavior that we must look, not to his questionnaire response."[7]

7. Ibid.

DATA:
Attitudes vs. Actions
RICHARD T. LAPIERE

By definition, a social attitude is a behavior pattern, anticipatory set or tendency, predisposition to specific adjustment to designated social situations, or, more simply, a conditioned response to social stimuli.[1] Terminological usage differs, but students who have concerned themselves with attitudes apparently agree that they are acquired out of social experience and provide the individual organism with some degree of preparation to adjust, in a well-defined way, to certain types of social situations if and when these situations arise. It would seem, therefore, that the totality of the social attitudes of a single individual would include all his socially acquired personality which is involved in the making of adjustments to other human beings.

But by derivation social attitudes are seldom more than a verbal response to a symbolic situation. For the conventional method of measuring social attitudes is to ask questions (usually in writing) which demand a verbal adjustment to an entirely symbolic situation. Because it is easy, cheap, and mechanical, the attitudinal questionnaire is rapidly becoming a major method of sociological

"Attitudes vs. Actions," by Richard T. LaPiere, from *Social Forces,* vol. 13 (October 1934–May 1935), pp. 230–37. Reprinted by permission of The Univeristy of North Carolina Press.
[1]See Daniel D. Droba, "Topical Summaries of Current Literature," *The American Journal of Sociology,* 1934, p. 513.

and socio-psychological investigation. The technique is simple. Thus from a hundred or a thousand responses to the question "Would you get up to give an Armenian woman your seat in a street car?" the investigator derives the "attitude" of non-Armenian males towards Armenian females. Now the question may be constructed with elaborate skill and hidden with consummate cunning in a maze of supplementary or even irrelevant questions yet all that has been obtained is a symbolic response to a symbolic situation. The words "Armenian woman" do not constitute an Armenian woman of flesh and blood, who might be tall or squat, fat or thin, old or young, well or poorly dressed—who might, in fact, be a goddess or just another old and dirty hag. And the questionnaire response, whether it be "yes" or "no," is but a verbal reaction and this does not involve rising from the seat or stolidly avoiding the hurt eyes of the hypothetical woman and the derogatory stares of other street-car occupants. Yet, ignoring these limitations, the diligent investigator will jump briskly from his factual evidence to the unwarranted conclusion that he has measured the "anticipatory behavior patterns" of non-Armenian males towards Armenian females encountered on street cars. Usually he does not stop here, but proceeds to deduce certain general conclusions regarding the social relationships between Armenians and non-Armenians. Most of us have applied the questionnaire technique with greater caution, but not I fear with any greater certainty of success.

Some years ago I endeavored to obtain comparative data on the degree of French and English antipathy towards dark-skinned peoples.[2] The informal questionnaire technique was used, but, although the responses so obtained were exceedingly consistent, I supplemented them with what I then considered an index to overt behavior. The hypothesis as then stated *seemed* entirely logical. "Whatever our attitude on the validity of 'verbalization' may be, it must be recognized that any study of attitudes through direct questioning is open to serious objection, both because of the limitations of the sampling method and because in classifying attitudes the inaccuracy of human judgment is an inevitable variable. In this study, however, there is corroborating evidence on these attitudes in the policies adopted by hotel proprietors. Nothing could be used as a more accurate index of color prejudice than the admission or non-admission of colored people to hotels. For the proprietor must reflect the group attitude in his policy regardless of his own feelings in the matter. Since he determines what the group attitude is towards Negroes through the expression of that attitude in overt behavior and over a long period of actual experience, the results will be exceptionally free from those disturbing factors which inevitably affect the effort to study attitudes by direct questioning."

But at that time I overlooked the fact that what I was obtaining from the hotel proprietors was still a "verbalized" reaction to a symbolic situation. The response to a Negro's request for lodgings might have been an excellent index of the attitude of hotel patrons towards living in the same hotel as a Negro. Yet to ask the proprietor "Do you permit members of the Negro race to stay here?" does not, it appears, measure his potential response to an actual Negro.

All measurement of attitudes by the questionnaire technique proceeds on the assumption that there is a mechanical relationship between symbolic and

[2]"Race Prejudice: France and England," *Social Forces*, September, 1928, pp. 102–111.

non-symbolic behavior. It is simple enough to prove that there is no *necessary* correlation between speech and action, between response to words and to the realities they symbolize. A parrot can be taught to swear, a child to sing "Frankie and Johnny" in the Mae West manner. The words will have no meaning to either child or parrot. But to prove that there is no *necessary* relationship does not prove that such a relationship may not exist. There need be no relationship between what the hotel proprietor says he will do and what he actually does when confronted with a colored patron. Yet there may be. Certainly we are justified in assuming that the verbal response of the hotel proprietor would be more likely to indicate what he would actually do than would the verbal response of people whose personal feelings are less subordinated to economic expediency. However, the following study indicates that the reliability of even such responses is very small indeed.

Beginning in 1930 and continuing for two years thereafter, I had the good fortune to travel rather extensively with a young Chinese student and his wife.[3] Both were personable, charming, and quick to win the admiration and respect of those they had the opportunity to become intimate with. But they were foreign-born Chinese, a fact that could not be disguised. Knowing the general "attitude" of Americans towards the Chinese as indicated by the "social distance" studies which have been made, it was with considerable trepidation that I first approached a hotel clerk in their company. Perhaps that clerk's eyebrows lifted slightly, but he accommodated us without a show of hesitation. And this in the "best" hotel in a small town noted for its narrow and bigoted "attitude" towards Orientals. Two months later I passed that way again, phoned the hotel and asked if they would accommodate "an important Chinese gentleman." The reply was an unequivocal "No." That aroused my curiosity and led to this study.

In something like ten thousand miles of motor travel, twice across the United States, up and down the Pacific Coast, we met definite rejection from those asked to serve us just once. We were received at 66 hotels, auto camps, and "Tourist Homes," refused at one. We were served in 184 restaurants and cafes scattered throughout the country and treated with what I judged to be more than ordinary consideration in 72 of them. Accurate and detailed records were kept of all these instances. An effort, necessarily subjective, was made to evaluate the overt response of hotel clerks, bell boys, elevator operators, and waitresses to the presence of my Chinese friends. The factors entering into the situations were varied as far and as often as possible. Control was not, of course, as exacting as that required by laboratory experimentation. But it was as rigid as is humanly possible in human situations. For example, I did not take the "test" subjects into my confidence fearing that their behavior might become self-conscious and thus abnormally affect the response of others towards them. Whenever possible I let my Chinese friend negotiate for accommodations (while I concerned myself with the car or luggage) or sent them into a restaurant ahead of me. In this way I attempted to "factor" myself out. We sometimes patronized high-class establishments after a hard and dusty day on the road and stopped at inferior auto camps when in our most presentable condition.

---

[3] The results of this study have been withheld until the present time out of consideration for their feelings.

In the end I was forced to conclude that those factors which most influenced the behavior of others towards the Chinese had nothing at all to do with race. Quality and condition of clothing, appearance of baggage (by which, it seems, hotel clerks are prone to base their quick evaluations), cleanliness and neatness were far more significant for person to person reaction in the situations I was studying than skin pigmentation, straight black hair, slanting eyes, and flat noses. And yet an air of self-confidence might entirely offset the "unfavorable" impression made by dusty clothes and the usual disorder to appearance consequent upon some hundred miles of motor travel. A supercilious desk clerk in a hotel of noble aspirations could not refuse his master's hospitality to people who appeared to take their request as a perfectly normal and conventional thing, though they might look like tin-can tourists and two of them belong to the racial category "Oriental." On the other hand, I became rather adept at approaching hotel clerks with that peculiar crab-wise manner which is so effective in provoking a somewhat scornful disregard. And then a bland smile would serve to reverse the entire situation. Indeed, it appeared that a genial smile was the most effective password to acceptance. My Chinese friends were skillful smilers, which may account, in part, for the fact that we received but one rebuff in all our experience. Finally, I was impressed with the fact that even where some tension developed due to the strangeness of the Chinese it would evaporate immediately when they spoke in unaccented English.

The one instance in which we were refused accommodations is worth recording here. The place was a small California town, a rather inferior auto-camp into which we drove in a very dilapidated car piled with camp equipment. It was early evening, the light so dim that the proprietor found it somewhat difficult to decide the genus *voyageur* to which we belonged. I left the car and spoke to him. He hesitated, wavered, said he was not sure that he had two cabins, meanwhile edging towards our car. The realization that the two occupants were Orientals turned the balance or, more likely, gave him the excuse he was looking for. "No," he said, "I don't take Japs!" In a more pretentious establishment we secured accommodations, and with an extra flourish of hospitality.

To offset this one flat refusal were the many instances in which the physical peculiarities of the Chinese served to heighten curiosity. With few exceptions this curiosity was considerately hidden behind an exceptional interest in serving us. Of course, outside of the Pacific Coast region, New York, and Chicago, the Chinese physiognomy attracts attention. It is different, hence noticeable. But the principal effect this curiosity has upon the behavior of those who cater to the traveler's needs is to make them more attentive, more responsive, more reliable. A Chinese companion is to be recommended to the white traveling in his native land. Strange features when combined with "human" speech and action seem, at times, to heighten sympathetic response, perhaps on the same principle that makes us uncommonly sympathetic towards the dog that has a "human" expression in his face.

What I am trying to say is that in only one out of 251 instances in which we purchased goods or services necessitating intimate human relationships did the fact that my companions were Chinese adversely affect us. Factors entirely unassociated with race were, in the main, the determinant of significant variations in our reception. It would appear reasonable to conclude that the "attitude" of the American people, as reflected in the behavior of those who are for pecuniary reasons presumably most sensitive to the antipathies of their white clientele, is anything but negative towards the Chinese. In terms of "social distance" we might conclude that native Caucasians are not averse to residing in the same hotels, auto-camps, and "Tourist Homes" as Chinese and will with complacency accept the presence of Chinese at an adjoining table in restaurant or cafe. It does not follow that there is revealed a distinctly "positive" attitude towards the Chinese, that whites prefer the Chinese to other whites. But the facts as gathered certainly preclude the conclusion that there is an intense prejudice towards the Chinese.

Yet the existence of this prejudice, very intense, is proven by a conventional "attitude" study. To provide a comparison of symbolic reaction to symbolic social situations with actual reaction to real social situations, I "questionnaired" the establishments which we patronized during the two year period. Six months were permitted to lapse between the time I obtained the overt reaction and the symbolic. It was hoped that the effects of the actual experience with Chinese guests, adverse or otherwise, would have faded during the intervening time. To the hotel or restaurant a questionnaire was mailed with an accompanying letter purporting to be a special and personal plea for response. The questionnaires all asked the same question, "Will you accept members of the Chinese race as guests in your establishment?" Two types of questionnaire were used. In one this question was inserted among similar queries concerning Germans, French, Japanese, Russians, Armenians, Jews, Negroes, Italians, and Indians. In the other the pertinent question was unencumbered. With persistence, completed replies were obtained from 128 of the establishments we had visited; 81 restaurants and cafes and 47 hotels, auto-camps, and "Tourist Homes." In response to the relevant question 92 per cent of the former and 91 per cent of the latter replied "No." The remainder replied "Uncertain; depend upon circumstances." From the woman proprietor of a small auto-camp I received the only "Yes," accompanied by a chatty letter describing the nice visit she had had with a Chinese gentleman and his sweet wife during the previous summer.

TABLE 1.   DISTRIBUTION OF RESULTS FROM QUESTIONNAIRE STUDY OF ESTABLISHMENT "POLICY" REGARDING ACCEPTANCE OF CHINESE AS GUESTS

Replies are to the question: "Will you accept members of the Chinese race as guests in your establishment?"

	Hotels, etc., Visited		Hotels, etc., Not Visited		Restaurants, etc., Visited		Restaurants, etc., Not Visited	
Total	47		32		81		96	
	1*	2*	1	2	1	2	1	2
Number replying.	22	25	20	12	43	38	51	45
No	20	23	19	11	40	35	37	41
Undecided: depend upon circumstances	1	2	1	1	3	3	4	3
Yes	1	0	0	0	0	0	0	1

*Column (1) indicates in each case those responses to questionnaires which concerned Chinese only. The figures in columns (2) are from the questionnaires in which the above was inserted among questions regarding Germans, French, Japanese, etc.

A rather unflattering interpretation might be put upon the fact that those establishments who had provided for our needs so graciously were, some months later, verbally antagonistic towards hypothetical Chinese. To factor this experience out responses were secured from 32 hotels and 96 restaurants located in approximately the same regions, but uninfluenced by this particular experience with Oriental clients. In this, as in the former case, both types of questionnaires were used. The results indicate that neither the type of questionnaire nor the fact of previous experience had important bearing upon the symbolic response to symbolic social situations.

It is impossible to make direct comparison between the reactions secured through questionnaires and from actual experience. On the basis of the above data it would appear foolhardy for a Chinese to attempt to travel in the United States. And yet, as I have shown, actual experience indicates that the American people, as represented by the personnel of hotels, restaurants, etc., are not at all averse to fraternizing with Chinese within the limitations which apply to social relationships between Americans themselves. The evaluations which follow are undoubtedly subject to the criticism which any human judgment must withstand. But the fact is that, although they began their travels in this country with

TABLE 2.   **DISTRIBUTION OF RESULTS OBTAINED FROM ACTUAL EXPERIENCE IN THE SITUATION SYMBOLIZED IN THE QUESTIONNAIRE STUDY**

Conditions	Hotels, etc.		Restaurants, etc.	
	Accompanied by investigator	Chinese not so accompanied at inception of situation*	Accompanied by investigator	Chinese not so accompanied at inception of situation
Total	55	12	165	19
Reception very much better than investigator would expect to have received had he been alone, but under otherwise similar circumstances	19	6	63	9
Reception different only to extent of heightened curiosity, such as investigator might have incurred were he alone but dressed in manner unconventional to region yet not incongruous	22	3	76	6
Reception "normal"	9	2	21	3
Reception perceptibly hesitant and not to be explained on other than "racial" grounds	3	1	4	1
Reception definitely, though temporarily, embarrassing ..	1	0	1	0
Not accepted	1	0	0	0

*When the investigator was not present at the inception of the situation the judgments were based upon what transpired after he joined the Chinese. Since intimately acquainted with them it is probable that errors in judgment were no more frequent under these conditions than when he was able to witness the inception as well as results of the situation.

considerable trepidation, my Chinese friends soon lost all fear that they might receive a rebuff. At first somewhat timid and considerably dependent upon me for guidance and support, they came in time to feel fully self-reliant and would approach new social situations without the slightest hesitation.

The conventional questionnaire undoubtedly has significant value for the measurement of "political attitudes." The presidential polls conducted by the *Literary Digest* have proven that. But a "political attitude" is exactly what the questionnaire can be justly held to measure; a verbal response to a symbolic situation. Few citizens are ever faced with the necessity of adjusting themselves to the presence of the political leaders whom, periodically, they must vote for — or against. Especially is this true with regard to the president, and it is in relation to political attitudes towards presidential candidates that we have our best evidence. But while the questionnaire may indicate what the voter will do when he goes to vote, it does not and cannot reveal what he will do when he meets Candidate Jones on the street, in his office, at his club, on the golf course, or wherever two men may meet and adjust in some way one to the other.

The questionnaire is probably our only means of determining "religious attitudes." An honest answer to the question "Do you believe in God?" reveals all there is to be measured. "God" is a symbol; "belief" a verbal expression. So here, too, the questionnaire is efficacious. But if we would know the emotional responsiveness of a person to the spoken or written word "God" some other method of investigation must be used. And if we would know the extent to which that responsiveness restrains his behavior it is to his behavior that we must look, not to his questionnaire response. Ethical precepts are, I judge, something more than verbal professions. There would seem little to be gained from asking a man if his religious faith prevents him from committing sin. Of course it does — on paper. But "moral attitudes" must have a significance in the adjustment to actual situations or they are not worth the studying. Sitting at my desk in California I can predict with a high degree of certainty what an "average" business man in an average Mid-Western city will reply to the question "Would you engage in sexual intercourse with a prostitute in a Paris brothel?" Yet no one, least of all the man himself, can predict what he would actually do should he by some misfortune find himself face to face with the situation in question. His moral "attitudes" are no doubt already stamped into his personality. But just what those habits are which will be invoked to provide him with some sort of adjustment to this situation is quite indeterminate.

It is highly probable that when the "Southern Gentleman" says he will not permit Negroes to reside in his neighborhood we have a verbal response to a symbolic situation which reflects the "attitudes" which would become operative in an actual situation. But there is no need to ask such a question of the true "Southern Gentleman." We knew it all the time. I am inclined to think that in most instances where the questionnaire does reveal non-symbolic attitudes the case is much the same. It is only when we cannot easily observe what people do in certain types of situations that the questionnaire is resorted to. But it is just here that the danger in the questionnaire technique arises. If Mr. A adjusts himself to Mr. B in a specified way we can deduce from his behavior that he has a certain "attitude" towards Mr. B and, perhaps, all of Mr. B's class. But if no such overt adjustment is made it is impossible to discover what A's adjustment would be should the situation arise. A questionnaire will reveal what Mr. A writes or says when confronted with a certain combination of words. But not what he will do when he meets Mr. B. Mr. B is a great deal more than a series of words. He is a man and he acts. His action is not necessarily what Mr. A "imagines" it will be when he reacts verbally to the symbol "Mr. B."

No doubt a considerable part of the data which the social scientist deals with can be obtained by the questionnaire method. The census reports are based upon verbal questionnaires and I do not doubt their basic integrity. If we wish to know how many children a man has, his income, the size of his home, his age, and the condition of his parents, we can reasonably ask him. These things he has frequently and conventionally converted into verbal responses. He is competent to report upon them, and will do so accurately, unless indeed he wishes to do otherwise. A careful investigator could no doubt even find out by verbal means whether the man fights with his wife (frequently, infrequently, or not at all), though the neighbors would be a more reliable source. But we should not expect to obtain by the questionnaire method his "anticipatory set or tendency" to action should his wife pack up and go home to Mother, should Elder Son get into trouble with the neighbor's daughter, the President assume the status of a dictator, the Japanese take over the rest of China, or a Chinese gentleman come to pay a social call.

Only a verbal reaction to an entirely symbolic situation can be secured by the questionnaire. It may indicate what the responder would actually do when confronted with the situation symbolized in the question, but there is no assurance that it will. And so to call the response a reflection of a "social attitude" is to entirely disregard the definition commonly given for the phrase "attitude." If social attitudes are to be conceptualized as partially integrated habit sets which will become operative under specific circumstances and lead to a particular pattern of adjustment they must, in the main, be derived from a study of humans behaving in actual social situations. They must not be imputed on the basis of questionnaire data.

The questionnaire is cheap, easy, and mechanical. The study of human behavior is time consuming, intellectually fatiguing, and depends for its success upon the ability of the investigator. The former method gives quantitative results, the latter mainly qualitative. Quantitative measurements are quantitatively accurate; qualitative evaluations are always subject to the errors of human judgment. Yet it would seem far more worth while to make a shrewd guess regarding that which is essential than to accurately measure that which is likely to prove quite irrelevant.

The Temper of the Times (Continued)

In LaPiere's work we find a line of continuity leading toward new theoretical insights into human behavior, new methods for attaining knowledge, and new kinds of evidence which could be used with confidence by policy makers bent on reducing some of the problems of the contemporary world. But that line of continuity has not been taken up by sociologists as a very important direction to follow. Some of the occasional efforts to proceed along this path are mentioned in Chapter Three as well as elsewhere in this volume. For the most part, though, social science proceeded in other directions.

LaPiere contends that no one has ever challenged his argument that what people say and what they do are not always in concordance.[8] "On the other hand," he writes, "it seems to have had no effect at all on the sociological faith in the value of data gathered via opinion, attitude, and other kinds of questionnaires. The 'Attitude vs. Action' paper was," he continues, "cited for years by almost everyone who wrote on attitudes or opinions as a sort of caution not to take their data too seriously; whereupon each author promptly ignored the caution and proceeded to assume that his data was indicative of what people would actually do in real-life circumstances."

LaPiere was certainly not alone; there were other voices crying in the wilderness. In the late Thirties some of the best young minds in American sociology were clearly concerned with the problem. Reading a paper at the 1938 meetings of the American Sociological Society, Robert K. Merton was critical of his own recently acquired survey data on attitudes toward Negroes. This paper was eventually published under the title, "Fact and Factitiousness in Ethnic Opinionnaires" and is included in this chapter. The paper gives the impression that Merton is desperately trying to report out a survey in traditional research style. It is his own good sense which compels him to expand his preliminary qualifications until his allotted space is nearly consumed. At that point, he tacks on a few tables and hastily concludes.[9]

Merton reflected on the possibility that Northerners treat Negroes less favorably than they talk about them and Southerners talk about Negroes less favorably than they treat them. Nearly thirty years later, with the "discovery" of de facto segregation and the invention of such euphemisms as "neighborhood schools" and "law and order," it became obvious to nearly everyone that at least one of these possibilities was reality; there was, in fact, a considerable discrepancy between the manner in which Northern whites related to blacks and the empty rhetoric they employed in chastising their Southern cousins. In 1938, Merton asked, "May we assume the amount and direction of spread between opinion and action to be relatively constant for members of different groups? To my knowledge," he continues, "no systematic research on this problem has been carried out."

8. This may or may not be correct, depending upon one's definition of a "challenge." The piece by Donald T. Campbell in Chapter Nine is, in my opinion, a challenge, although not an effective one. Any investigator who attributes observed discrepancies between sentiments and acts to methodological flaws or conceptual confusion is challenging LaPiere's conclusion.

9. All readers may not share my impression, but one of the liberties provided by the format of this book is that the "data" are here and anyone, including myself, is free to make his own judgments. I have wondered why this excellent article has remained so obscure. Merton has not included it in edited collections of his own work and I have not noticed it in any of the rash of patchwork collections which have glutted the academic market during recent years.

DATA:
Fact and Factitiousness
in Ethnic Opinionnaires
ROBERT K. MERTON

"For a desperate disease, a desperate cure"; therefore, if opinionnaires are to be used they must be discussed. This is a preliminary report on one phase of an extended study of opinions on ethnic groups. The major objectives are (1) to suggest certain lines of internal and external criticism of opinionnaire 'results' and (2) to present certain materials pertaining to group differences in the endorsement of a range of judgments about Negroes.[1]

It has been largely agreed for the last decade that the various 'attitude scales' introduced by L. L. Thurstone represent the most exact means of assaying group attitudes toward various social values. It is argued here that some of the procedures used in the scoring and interpretation of Thurstonian 'scales' involve methodological contradictions and sociological inadequacies. Although it is believed that this is true of the various Thurstonian opinionnaires (on War, Prohibition, Communism, 'the' Church, 'the' Negro, etc.), the present discussion is restricted to ethnic opinionnaires.

'Attitudes' of Religious Groups toward 'The' Negro.

The following tabulation is presented as an introductory basis for this discussion. The table summarizes results obtained through a printed opinionnaire concerning 'the' Negro which was administered to 679 college students registered in sociology courses at Harvard University, Radcliffe College, Pennsylvania State College, Tulane University, and Louisiana State University, at various times between October 1938 and October 1939.[2] The opinionnaire consists of thirty

"Fact and Factitiousness in Ethnic Opinionnaires," by Robert K. Merton, from *American Sociological Review*, vol. 5 (1940), pp. 13–27. Reprinted by permission of the author and the American Sociological Association. The original publication carries the following acknowledgment: "Read at the annual meeting of the American Sociological Society, Dec. 28, 1938. The writer is indebted to the Tulane University Council on Research for financial aid."
[1]Limitations of space preclude the extended discussion merited by each of the several points in question. Hence, the full evidence for various conclusions and inferences can be only imperfectly reported. The fault is not necessarily lessened by its admission.—Throughout the paper, certain terms have been consistently set off by inverted commas ('thus'). Terms thus qualified are to be read: so-called. This device lessens the likelihood of equivocation, of using the same term to denote two or more significantly different concepts.
[2]The opinionnaire (which is appended to this paper) is part of a larger test battery which is not treated here. I am indebted to the following persons for aid in administering these opinionnaires: at Harvard and Radcliffe, E. Y. Hartshorne, Logan Wilson, Edward Devereux and Dudley Kirk; at Pennsylvania State, Kingsley Davis and Gordon T. Bowden; at Louisiana State University, Edgar A. Schuler, T. Lynn Smith and M. B. Smith. The Harvard-Radcliffe sample was obtained between October 1–11, 1938 (except for retests which are not reported here); the Pennsylvania State sample, between February 18 and March 5, 1939; the Tulane-Newcomb sample on Sept. 30, 1939; the Louisiana State sample between Oct. 13–19, 1939.

statements about the Negro. It was adapted from a 'scale' constructed by I. D. MacCrone according to the Thurstone-Chave-Droba method of equal-appearing intervals.[3]

[3]See I. D. MacCrone, *Race Attitudes in South Africa*, chap. IX, New York, 1937. The original opinionnaire referred to the South African 'native' and the scale-values were based upon the judgments of 200 persons of European descent and 100 Bantu. Only those statements which were ordered similarly by both groups were included in the inventory. It will be noted that substitution of the term 'Negro' for the term 'the native' leads to a series of judgments which are substantially similar to those in the Hinckley-Thurstone 'attitude-toward-the-Negro scale.' The same assumptions underlie our adaptation of MacCrone's inventory and the use of 'generalized scales,' except that our adaptation involves the generalizing process to a lesser extent. See H. H. Remmers and E. B. Silance, "Generalized Attitude Scales," *J. Soc. Psychol.*, 5:298–312, 1934.

TABLE 1.   'MEAN SCORES' ON OPINIONNAIRES CONCERNING 'THE' NEGRO, ACCORDING TO SEX, COLLEGE, AND RELIGIOUS AFFILIATION OF SUBJECTS

Colleges	MALES																	
	Catholics			Protestants			Jews			None			Un-known			Total		
	N	MS	R[1]	N	MS	R	N	MS	R	N	MS	R	N	MS	R	N	MS	
Harvard	25	4.3	1	82	3.9	2	51	3.1	3	22	2.6	4	35	3.8		215	3.6	
Penn State	15	5.0	1	27	3.9	2	16	3.0	4	5	3.4	3	13	4.0		76	3.9	
Tulane	18	6.3	1	12	5.2	2	4	4.3	3	1	4.0	4	–	–		35	5.5	
L. S. U.	25	6.1	1	56	6.0	2	2	3.4	4	8	5.4	3	1	5.4		92	5.9	
Total	83	–	–	177	–	–	73	–	–	36	–	–	49	–		418	–	

Colleges	FEMALES																	
Radcliffe	21	4.4	1	40	3.4	$2\frac{1}{2}$	18	3.4	$2\frac{1}{2}$	5	2.7	4	5	3.9		89	3.6	
Penn State	6	4.8	1	24	3.5	2	3	3.1	3	1	3.0	4	3	4.1		37	3.7	
Newcomb	5	7.1	1	14	5.6	2	1	3.5	3	–	–	–	–	–		20	6.1	
L. S. U.	40	6.1	1	66	5.5	2	5	4.1	3	4	2.3	4	–	–		115	5.6	
Total	72	–	–	144	–	–	27	–	–	10	–	–	8	–		261	–	

CRITICAL RATIOS $\left(\dfrac{\text{diff.}}{\sigma \text{ diff.}}\right)$

Classes of Subjects Compared	"Northern" Subjects[2] (males and females)[3]	"Southern" Subjects[2] (males and females)[3]
Protestants versus Catholics	3.4	2.2
Protestants versus Jews	3.6	3.1
Protestants versus No Religious Affiliation	4.4	2.1
Catholics versus Jews	5.6	3.9
Catholics versus No Religious Affiliation	6.2	2.9
Jews versus No Religious Affiliation	1.8	0.7

[1]R is the rank order of religious groups according to an interpretation which will be presently criticized; MS is the 'mean score.'

[2]"Northern" subjects are: Harvard, Radcliffe, and Pennsylvania State subjects; "Southern" subjects are: Tulane, Newcomb and Louisiana State subjects.

[3]Inasmuch as the differences in means between males and females of the same geographical region and the same religious affiliation are insignificant, these groups have been combined in the computation of critical ratios.

The foregoing computations exhibit uniformities which appear to be statistically significant, despite the paucity of cases in some of the subgroupings. In all of the eight samples, the Catholics rank first in the endorsement of judgments 'unfavorable' to 'the' Negro. With almost equal regularity, the Protestants rank second; the Jews are usually third and those with no religious affiliation rank fourth (or 'least unfavorable'). The conventional indexes of statistical significance suggest that these are 'real' differences, particularly between the 'Northern' religious aggregates. (However, as the critical ratios indicate, the differences between the Jews and the 'non-religious' groups are anything but significant.) The consistency of these results is so pronounced that, despite occasionally insignificant differences between averages, there would appear some justification for proclaiming that "Catholics are least favorable toward the Negro whereas the nonreligious and Jews are most favorable, with the Protestants consistently between these extremes." In point of fact, conclusions of this general sort based upon the same kind of evidence are current in the literature on ethnic and racial attitudes.[4] When so based, such conclusions may be at once impugned.

Methodological Fallacies of the Thurstone Attitude Scales.

The basic objections to such a conclusion questions the meaning of summed or averaged scores of group responses to 'scales' using the Thurstone technique of construction. What do these 'averaged scores' denote? The usual answer is that they constitute an 'index' of the degree of 'favorableness' or 'unfavorableness' toward 'the' Negro. This answer is based on the conviction that the judgments which make up the inventory represent a 'linear continuum' and that the scale-values of endorsed judgments may be algebraically summed and averaged.[5] This assertion can be and has been challenged but, to my knowledge, the various criticisms have not been satisfactorily met.[6] The objections to the assumption of a linear continuum (involving additivity and determination of central tendencies) are of at least three interrelated kinds.

[4]*E.g.*, for sex differences in 'mean attitude scores,' see V. F. Sims and J. R. Patrick, "Attitude toward the Negro of Northern and Southern College Students," *J. Soc. Psychol.*, 7: 196–197, 1936.

[5]See the explicit statement of L. L. Thurstone and E. J. Chave on this point. "It is legitimate to determine a central tendency for the frequency distribution of attitudes in a group. Several groups of individuals may then be compared as regards the means of their respective frequency distributions of attitudes. The differences between the means of several such distributions may be directly compared because of the fact that a rational base line has been established." *The Measurement of Attitudes*, 82, Chicago, 1929.

[6]For basic methodological criticism of the Thurstonian assumption of a linear continuum, see the incisive papers by H. M. Johnson, "Pseudo-Mathematics in the Mental and Social Sciences," *Amer. J. Psychol.*, 48:342–351, 1936, and by Clifford Kirkpatrick, "Assumptions and Methods in Attitude Measurements," *Amer. Sociol. Rev.*, 1:75–88, 1936. See also Kirkpatrick's further papers on this subject cited therein, and the general methodological discussions of measurement by N. R. Campbell, *An Account of the Principles of Measurement and Calculation*, New York, 1928, and by Morris R. Cohen and Ernest Nagel, *An Introduction to Logic and Scientific Method*, chap. XV, New York, 1934. For a paper which purports to demonstrate the logical validity of such techniques of 'measurement' as those of Thurstone, see George A. Lundberg, "The Thoughtways of Contemporary Sociology," *Amer. Sociol. Rev.*, 1:703–723, 1936. Relevant to this discussion is the unpublished critique of Lundberg's paper read by R. K. Merton at the Eastern Sociological Conference, New Haven, April 18, 1936.

1. It can be shown that Thurstone's scale-values are not additive, inasmuch as his collections of statements do not have the 'group-property,' i.e., do not constitute closed systems.[7] To put this more concretely, let us examine Thurstone's assertion that "we may assign the scale-value to each of the statements that a subject has indorsed and then calculate their arithmetic mean."[8] Suppose (1) that a person, A, who is extremely unfavorable toward 'the' Negro, endorses Statement 6 ("I consider that the Negro is more like an animal than a human being") with a scale-value of 10.6. Suppose (2) that individual B is even more intensely unfavorable to 'the' Negro, and that he likewise endorses Statement 6 and also several other statements disparaging to Negroes (e.g., Statements 1, 2, 8 and 30, with scale-values of 10.3, 10.2, 9.7, and 8.8 respectively). B's 'score' (arithmetical mean) thus becomes 9.9 which is less 'unfavorable' than A's score of 10.6, which contradicts the hypothesis. The inevitable result of multiple endorsements of statements lying at either extreme of the 'scale' is a score which is less extreme than that obtained by endorsing *only* the limiting statements in the series. Given a finite number of statements, the 'score' of endorsed statements may thus become an inaccurate index of subjects' convictions concerning the value in question.[9]

2. That Thurstone's inventories do not constitute a linear 'scale' may be seen in another connection. Were the inventory a linear scale, endorsement of a statement with a given scale-value would involve "acceptance of all positions less extreme and in the same direction from the neutral position."[10] In other words, were the Thurstone inventory actually a 'scale,' in the strict sense, persons endorsing items graded as 'very unfavorable' might be assumed to endorse all statements involving slightly less depreciation of the social value in question. Likewise, endorsements of statements with scale-values of 8 and 10.3, let us say, would logically entail endorsement of all statements with scale-values falling between 8 and 10.3. This is a most elementary consideration. "No one could use a ruler on which he could not tell whether the point marked 7 would fall between 6 and 8 or whether it would have a capricious preference for some other point on the instrument."[11] In actual practice, however, as those who have used Thur-

---

[7]For a demonstration of this inadequacy, see Johnson, *op. cit.*, 349–350. For a brief discussion of the group-property, see Cassius J. Keyser, *Mathematical Philosophy*, chap. XII, New York, 1922.

[8]Thurstone and Chave, *op. cit.*, 64. In the Hinckley-Thurstone 'attitude-toward-the-Negro scale,' 'scores' are constituted by the median scale value. This is a difference which makes no difference to our argument. Likewise, the use of MacCrone's statements and scale-values, rather than Hinckley's, does not affect the *logical* basis of our discussion.

[9]For Thurstonian inventories which contain statements of the "A" and "E" types ('All,' 'No') this difficulty becomes readily apparent. The "A" proposition includes all the "I" propositions, yet the subject who endorses both the "A" statement and any or all of the "I" propositions will obtain a lower score than the subject who simply endorses the "A" statement. As Johnson suggests, "Perhaps the procedure should be worked over." *op. cit.*, 350.

[10]G. Murphy, L. B. Murphy and T. M. Newcomb, *Experimental Social Psychology*, 906, New York, 1937. The fact that Thurstone has chosen not to indicate a 'neutral' position on his 'scale' is irrelevant for, as he indicates, "The origin is arbitrarily assigned. We could have placed the origin in the middle of the scale, but that would necessitate dealing with negative class-intervals and nothing is statistically gained thereby." Thurstone and Chave, *op. cit.*, 63.

[11]Murphy, Murphy and Newcomb, *op. cit.*, 897.

stone's inventories can testify, there is no assurance that subjects will check all the statements with scale-values intermediate between the extremes of those actually endorsed. If this be a linear 'scale,' it is one belonging to a newly created species of scales.

3. Not unrelated to these considerations is the question of *interchangeability of units* in a measurable collection. The Thurstone units are not interchangeable, as can be illustrated by the following case. Individual *A* endorses Statement 6 ("I consider that the Negro is more like an animal than a human being") with a scale-value of 10.6 and also endorses Statement 25 ("I consider that the white man is neglecting to do his duty by not doing more to improve the lot of the Negro") with a scale-value of 2.8. By the Thurstone method of scoring, his score is 6.7. Individual *B* endorses Statement 24 ("I think that all the Negro needs to make him happy is the satisfaction of his material needs") with a scale-value of 6.7. In both cases, then, the score is 6.7. In what sense can we conclude that these two persons are equally 'favorable' (or equally 'unfavorable') to 'the' Negro? Interviews with various subjects who have identical 'scores' indicate that they will not readily substitute endorsement of one *set* of endorsed statements for another *set* of statements, even though the two sets result in identical or insignificantly different 'average scores.' If so, what is the denotation of 'equally favorable' scores? Can we conclude with such proponents of unalloyed operationalism as Lundberg that in this way "the term *attitude* would . . . have a very much narrower but a more definite meaning than at present?"[12] Narrower, perhaps, but hardly more definite, Thurstone *assumes* an interchangeability of judgments with identical scale-values which does not in fact exist. Statistical fiat does not make empirical fact.

In this connection, various investigators have maintained that these 'scales' are not designed to represent 'attitudes' pictorially. They assert that Thurstone's 'scales,' like scientific measuring instruments in general, do not measure *all* aspects of events. These instruments respond selectively to one aspect or property, e.g., 'favorableness,' just as the balance responds only to one property, weight. Hence, it is argued, criticisms which hold that Thurstone's 'scales' force complex attitudes into one dimension are wholly beside the point, since no scientific construct "attempts to cover all enumerable details of a class of phenomena."[13] To my mind, the analogy seems to be slightly misplaced. The fault of Thurstone's constructs is not their abstractness but their failure to constitute a continuum involving assignable magnitudes. Despite the complicated operations involved in the construction of these 'scales,' there is no introduction of *cardinal* numbers at any point. Thurstone's inventories are usable if they are treated for what they are: ordered series of statements concerning social values. In terms of certain criteria, they rank, but they do not 'measure,' opinions.

Sociological Inadequacies of the Thurstone Attitude Scale.

When we shift our attention from the inventory-as-a-whole to its component statements, several sociological assumptions come into view. In an effort to eliminate 'undifferentiating elements' from his 'scale,' Thurstone introduced such

[12]Lundberg, *op. cit.*, 711.
[13]L. L. Thurstone, *The Vectors of Mind,* 44–48, Chicago, 1935; see also Lundberg, *op. cit.*, 714.

criteria as 'ambiguity' (Q-value) and 'irrelevance.' To be sure, these criteria are necessary if the sole objective is to develop an instrument that will 'measure' a given property, but this very emphasis on linearity may obscure the sociological utility of including in an inventory some statements which, on the basis of these criteria, are not 'differentiating,' i.e., statements endorsed with equal frequency by persons with differentiated responses to other statements. In other words, if we abandon or modify the notion that these inventories 'measure' a single 'attitude,' opinions involving the coalescence of several cultural values may be included in the inventory, although conventional tests of reliability may lead us to designate these opinions as 'undifferentiating.' Otherwise, we rule out access to *those opinions which are shared* by most of our sample, irrespective of their differences about other opinions.

In the case of such opinions, we are no longer dealing with 'pure,' highly distilled opinions concerning 'the' Negro (as a 'pure' abstraction) but rather with complex opinions concerning Negroes within certain cultural contexts. Thus, using Thurstone's criteria, such statements as "I think that the Negro ought to be given every opportunity of education and development—just like the white man" would be discarded because they are endorsed by a large proportion of subjects with 'scores' lying near both extremes of the 'scale.' This statement would be suspect, for although our 'Northern' samples consistently endorsed it more frequently than did our 'Southern' samples, yet 45 percent of the latter also endorsed it. Apparently, then, this statement does not exclusively reflect 'attitudes' toward 'the' Negro, 'as such,' but involves also the 'halo-effect' induced by the prestige of 'universal education' as a cultural value in our society. Endorsement may thus be a resultant of opinions concerning 'the' Negro and of opinions concerning the cultural premise that "every American citizen has a right to an education." Thus, even though statements of this type are irrelevant by Thurstonian standards, frequency of endorsement can be adopted as a crude index of current opinions concerning Negroes-and-education as a value-complex. Combining separate tests of 'attitudes toward education' and 'attitudes toward the Negro' would no more provide an index of this opinion-configuration than combining encyclopedia articles on "France" and on "disease" would provide discussion of "the French disease." Otherwise stated, the effort to attain a linear scale should not be permitted to divert all attention from the sociologically and psychologically relevant question of opinion-configurations.[14] Group differentials in the endorsement or rejection of complex opinions constitute valuable descriptive data.[15]

[14] Clifford Kirkpatrick and Sarah Stone have evolved a 'belief pattern method' of appraising configurations of opinions. However, they also assert the 'unsatisfactory' nature of inventory-statements which are "ambiguous since either factual, evaluational or logical considerations may have motivated the acceptance or rejection of the statements." It may be suggested, however, that statements which are 'ambiguous' in terms of imputable motivation may nevertheless prove useful in ascertaining group differences in maintaining complex opinions. See Kirkpatrick and Stone, "Attitude Measurement and the Comparison of Generations," *J. Applied Psychol.*, 19:575, 1935.

[15] G. Murphy and R. Likert note "the importance of considering the qualitative significance of each item as well as the significance of the whole scales." *Public Opinion and the Individual*, 50–51, New York, 1938. See also Keith Sward's observation that 'mean scores' in rating scales are inadequate "except as the very roughest of devices." He finds that item-analysis contains an assortment of traits that are significant numerically and qualitatively." See his "Patterns of Jewish Temperament," *J. Applied Psychol.*, 19:410–425, 1935.

If opinionnaires are to serve as indexes of current opinion concerning social values, their component statements should be analyzed with reference to values besides those to which the inventory-as-a-whole is devoted. This assertion has implications for determining 'internal consistency' of an inventory by means of the association between each statement in the inventory and the total score. An item is said to be discriminating according to the extent to which it leads to differential responses by persons with markedly different total scores. It is further believed that nondiscriminating items should be discarded. Although this procedure is statistically impeccable,[16] it obscures fallacious assumptions by assuming a disputable 'logic of relations' between judgments involving social evaluations. Let us turn to cases.

The investigator who shelves his psychology and sociology while he deals with mathematical formulas will doubtless conclude that if a considerable proportion of subjects endorse both of the following statements, the 'internal consistency' is to this extent lessened.

"To my mind the Negro is so childish and irresponsible that he cannot be expected to know what is in his best interest" (scale-value = 8.4, i.e., 'unfavorable').

"I think that the Negro ought to be given every opportunity of education and development — just like the white man" (scale-value = 1.1, i.e., 'very favorable').

Endorsement by the same subjects of both these statements, rated as 'unfavorable' and 'favorable' respectively, will presumably cast suspicion on their reliability and validity.[17] A reconstruction of the implicit reasoning may be hazarded. If a person believes Negroes to be childish and irresponsible, he will scarcely favor their being given every opportunity of education. Hence, if the same subjects endorse both these judgments, they are not giving their 'real' opinions but are checking statements facetiously or at random. Or, it is inferred, the statements do not adequately reflect 'attitudes' toward the same entity, 'the' Negro. Both of these inferences contain a suppressed premise which, I suggest, is fallacious. This premise holds that subjects do not 'really' subscribe to 'logically' contradictory judgments. In making this assumption, the investigator is playing the role of logician rather than psychologist or sociologist. He is, in effect, tacitly assuming that these presumably incompatible assertions *should not* be endorsed by the same persons. Such a prejudgment minimizes the possibility of securing an adequate

[16]However, R. F. Sletto has demonstrated that "measurement of a single common variable cannot be safely inferred from the fact that items satisfy the criterion of internal consistency, as usually applied." See his "Critical Study of the Criterion of Internal Consistency in Personality Scale Construction," *Amer. Sociol. Rev.*, 1:61–68, 1936; and the valuable discussion of this paper by R. V. Bowers, *ibid.*, 69–74.

[17]The explicit relevant statement reads: "If we find considerable inconsistency [in endorsements], we might attribute it to the carelessness of the subjects in making their check marks more or less at random, or we might attribute it to defects in the statements themselves. . . . But the inconsistencies vary with the statement that is chosen as a basis of comparison with all the rest, and such differences are due primarily no doubt to defects in the statements themselves. We have so regarded them. . . ." Thurstone and Chave, *op. cit.*, 46–47.

representation of the inconsistencies of social judgments which in many instances actually obtain. This 'test of internal consistency' is based on a dubious rationalist assumption. In making this assumption, the investigator is using *norms* of logic, not facts of sociology.

Once we shift from the level of logical norms to the level of psycho-social fact, we observe that incompatible judgments are often made by the same person.[18] Thus, in the previous illustration, persons who subscribe to both the national democratic ideology — including the belief in education as a 'moral right' — and to the regional ideology which insists on the childishness and irresponsibility of the Negro, will readily and honestly endorse both statements. To assume, as Thurstone does, that persons hold rigorously consistent social opinions is to fly in the face of a store of clinical observations by psychologists, sociologists, anthropologists, and John Doe himself. It is not pertinent to our present problem to discuss the level on which these coexisting judgments are 'not consistent.' It is sufficient to indicate that Thurstone's criterion of 'irrelevancy' is loaded with assumptions which are contrary to fact; that here again mathematical technique has supplanted and obscured sociological considerations.[19]

A further mooted point in connection with opinionnaires is the relation of opinion to overt behavior. The current vogue of semanticism and Paretoism leads some to draw questionable inferences from these systems of thought and to urge that verbal responses are "really of minor importance." The metaphysical assumption is tacitly introduced that in one sense or another overt behavior is 'more real' than verbal behavior. This assumption is both unwarranted and scientifically meaningless. In some situations, it may be discovered that overt behavior is a more reliable basis for drawing inferences about future behavior (overt or verbal). In other situations, it may be found that verbal responses are a tolerably accurate guide to future behavior (overt or verbal). It should not be forgotten that overt actions may deceive; that they, just as 'derivations' or 'speech reactions' may be deliberately designed to disguise or to conceal private attitudes. The question of the relative 'significance' of verbal and overt responses must as yet be solved anew for each class of problems. The apriori assumption that verbal responses are simply epiphenomenal is to be accorded no greater weight than the assumption that words do not deceive nor actions lie. It is unnecessary to repeat additional considerations in this connection except to state, in company with Thurstone, Murphy, Likert and others, that the expression of opinion is itself a recurrent phase of social activity. Hence, reliable and valid opinionnaires may be useful even if unrelated to overt behavior.

Another issue in this controversy has not received adequate attention. It is not simply a question of whether or not overt behavior 'coincides' with expressed or endorsed opinions. This way of formulating the problem obscures one

---

[18]A paraphrase of an observation by Jean Piaget is pertinent. "For it is not by taking the ready-made schema of adult reasoning (and of explicit scientific . . . reasoning at that) and by submitting this schema to, say syllogistic tests so as to see whether the [subject] conforms to our practical and scholastic habits of thought, that we shall succeed in finding the true nature of [social opinions]." *Judgment and Reasoning in the Child,* 135, New York, 1928.

[19]A close reading of the method of constructing the criterion of 'irrelevance' shows that these invalid assumptions underlie the 'index of similarity.' See Thurstone and Chave, *op. cit.,* 46–56.

of its basic aspects, namely, may we assume the amount and direction of spread between opinion and action to be relatively constant for members of different groups? To my knowledge, no systematic research on this problem has been carried out.[20] It may be tentatively (and speculatively) suggested that the spread between opinion and action is not the same for different groups but that the 'differences in direction of spread' are relatively constant. Thus, the hypothesis may be advanced that 'the Northern index of *verbalized* tolerance' of Negroes is consistently *higher* than their 'index of *behavioral* tolerance' of Negroes. And, contrariwise, that 'the Southern index of *verbalized* tolerance' is consistently *lower* than their 'index of behavioral tolerance.' Put in less idiomatic but possibly more intelligible terms, it is possible that Northerners treat Negroes less 'favorably' than they talk about them and that Southerners talk about Negroes less 'favorably' than they treat them.[21] Or possibly the difference is one of degree rather than direction. In any event, setting the problem in these terms shifts the discussion from the question of correlation between opinion and action *in general* to comparisons of degree and direction of correlation in various groups. To be sure, these notions about possibly consistent group differences in spread between opinion and action are largely speculative at the present juncture.[22] But the very hypothesis emphasizes the need for caution in the use of 'attitude scores' derived from opinionnaires as indexes of predispositions to act in a determinate fashion toward a given value. Identical scores may well be associated with sharply diverging forms of overt behavior.

[20]Cf. Richard T. LaPiere, *Collective Behavior*, 49–50, New York, 1938.

[21]The terms 'favorable' and 'unfavorable' are suspiciously inexact and at times misleading. They should be interpreted within the context of considerations introduced in the next note.

[22]"Largely speculative," because the theory of social stereotypes suggests that such differences in spread may occur through the varying roles played by stereotypes in propositions and in overt behavior. Thus, 'Southerners,' when asked to respond to propositions about 'the' Negro may show an unequivocally 'unfavorable' and 'intolerant attitude,' although their relations with specific Negroes may involve a larger component of 'intimacy,' 'favorableness' and 'tolerance' than would be the case with 'Northerners' interaction with specific Negroes. In the proposition, there may be a response to a verbal stereotype, 'the Negro'; in behavior, there may be response to a concrete personality standing in a complex set of relations to the white, e.g., Herman-the-colored-handyman-who-has-been-with-the-family-for-years-and-knows-more-about-my-dahlias-than-I-do, etc. (John Dollard's speculations concerning the relative frequency and intensity of stereotypes of Negroes among Northern and Southern whites partly agree and partly disagree with these suggestions. See his *Caste and Class in a Southern Town*, 73, 84, 390, New Haven, Conn., 1937.) These suggestions indicate the vacuity of such one-dimensional terms as 'favorableness,' 'tolerance,' 'appreciation,' 'depreciation,' and the like. It would seem expedient to reassess the denotations of such crude abstractions, especially when one investigator can conclude that 'Northerners' have greater "*good-will*" toward 'the' Negro than 'Southerners'; while others conclude that "on the whole, a greater '*aversion*' was shown toward 'the' Negro by Northern than by Southern students"; and a third study informs us that Northern students are "more favorable" to 'the' Negro than are Southern students. Item-analyses of actual frequencies of endorsements of specific statements would do much to eliminate or to minimize such indulgence in verbalism. See C. W. Hunter, *A Comparative Study of the Relationship Existing Between the White Race and the Negro Race in the State of North Carolina and in the City of New York* (unpublished Columbia University M.A. thesis summarized by G. and L. B. Murphy, *Experimental Social Psychology*, 639–645, New York, 1931); D. Katz and F. H. Allport, *Students' Attitudes*, 102, Syracuse, 1931; Sims and Patrick, *op. cit.*, 194–195.

Regional Differences in Opinions Concerning 'The' Negro.

With these strictures in mind, we may now consider a preliminary report of regional differences in endorsement of statements about 'the' Negro. Some studies have assumed that student-subjects hold opinions which represent the mores of the region where they attend school. This assumption may or may not square with the facts; in any event, it should not be assumed without further ado that subjects represent the particular geographical region in which they are tested. Using the sixfold division into 'regions' developed by Odum,[23] we find considerable variations between our samples with regard to the percentages of subjects who have lived for the past decade in the same region as that in which their school is located. Thus, in the Harvard-Radcliffe sample, 68, or 21.6 percent had their residence outside the Northeastern region; of the Pennsylvania State sample, only 4, or 3.5 percent, derived from outside this region; of the Tulane-Newcomb sample, 5, or 9 percent, and of the Louisiana State University sample, 28, or 13.5 percent, had their homes outside the Southeastern region.[24] Thus, with respect to these samples, the assumption that the subjects' endorsements were those of persons living in the cultural region wherein their schools are located would lead to a significant error. The original data were reclassified according to the subjects' place of residence for ten years prior to 1938–39. This shifts the frequency distributions of endorsements to some extent and decreases the standard deviations.[25]

*   *   *

[At this point a page and a half classification and listing of response distributions is omitted along with a one-page chart, summarizing the classification and the percentages endorsing each of the 30 items which made up the opinionnaire. See pages 23–25 in the original. The full 30 item instrument along with the scale values for each item is included at the end of the original article on pp. 27–28. It has been omitted here.]

*   *   *

On the whole, fifty percent or more of our 'Northern' subjects subscribe to the 'democratic mores' which allege the right to equal opportunity for individual development, irrespective of race. These convictions are supported by a series of beliefs which deny the intrinsic inferiority of 'the' Negro. Contrariwise, Southern subjects largely assent to statements which endorse the current caste structure and justify their convictions by imputing inferiority to 'the' Negro. It should be noted, however, that the extreme statement which asserts that the Negro is more like an animal than a human is seldom endorsed by either Northerners or Southerners. It is the one item on which there is substantial agreement by both regional

---

[23]For an itemization of the states included in each of the six regions — Southeast, Southwest, Northeast, Middle States, Northwest, Far West — and a discussion of the criteria adopted in this classification, see Howard W. Odum, *Southern Regions of the United States*, 1–205, Chapel Hill, N. C., 1936.

[24]Fourteen cases in the Harvard-Radcliffe sample and four cases in the Pennsylvania State sample did not state their place of residence.

[25]Of course, when the research is designed with "practical objectives of college administration" in mind, breakdowns by residence are not necessary. See, e.g., Katz and Allport, *op. cit.*

groups, representing, as it were, an asymptotic nadir in the Southerners' imputation of inferiorities to the Negro.[26]

Two statements (14, 20) in the opinionnaire may be interpreted as expressions of ambivalence toward the caste-system. The Northern sample more often endorses one of these, and the Southern sample, the other; yet, even in the choice of ambivalent statements, there is a consistent difference. The Northern sample more often endorsed that ambivalent statement which implicitly weights more heavily a negative opinion concerning the caste-system; the Southern group more often assented to that ambivalent statement which weights more heavily a positive opinion concerning the caste-system. However, this difference should not be permitted to obscure the similarity: both groups are apparently subject to the conflict between co-existing democratic and caste ideologies. In all this, it should be remembered, we are dealing with opinions and not with overt behavior.

It should not be inferred from the foregoing discussion that the 'Northern' and the 'Southern' samples are wholly homogeneous in their respective opinions concerning the Negro. It can be shown that there are more or less consistent differences of opinion between subjects coming from different localities within the same general 'region.' Thus, in the 'Northeastern region,' on eight items the frequency of endorsement by Pennsylvania subjects is intermediate between the frequencies of Massachusetts and Louisiana subjects. Although only one of these differences between Massachusetts and Pennsylvania subjects is conventionally 'significant' — 26, with a C.R. of 3.7 — the fact that the Pennsylvanians are *consistently* intermediate between the Massachusetts and Louisiana subjects suggests that the Pennsylvanians are, in a sense, 'marginal' with respect to 'Northeastern' and 'Southeastern' opinion-inventories. As far as these results are concerned, then, we are not justified in treating Odum's 'Northeastern region' as reasonably homogeneous in opinions about the Negro. Pennsylvania subjects, although largely sharing the opinions of the Massachusetts sample, tend toward the 'Southeastern' configuration of opinions, in some respects. However, differences in frequency of endorsement by Pennsylvania and Louisiana subjects even with regard to these eight statements are conventionally significant (except for statement 14, with a C.R. of 2.4). For Statement 14, which is taken to express ambivalence toward the caste-system (with a dominant positive valence), the Pennsylvanians' frequency of endorsement more nearly approximates that of the Louisiana subjects. These data suggest that the populations of areas as extensive as Odum's regions may not have relatively similar distributions of opinions concerning the Negro (and, possibly, a range of other social values).

This report is admittedly incomplete. It is to be taken primarily as an in-

---

[26]In this connection should be noted Dollard's observation that some residents of 'Southerntown' were quite prepared to assert that "the Negro is a mere animal." Some nine percent of our Southern sample assented to this notion. This case incidentally illustrates the utility of opinionnaires; they help to establish, however crudely, the *relative frequency* of folk beliefs and thus serve as a check on observations of scattered cases. Opinionnaires do not supplant direct observations of opinions advanced in 'life-situations,' but they are a useful supplement, as Hortense Powdermaker has shown in her study of 'Southerntown.' See her *After Freedom*, 381–391, New York, 1939, also Dollard, *op. cit.*, 368–369. On page 387, Dollard remarks that not all Southern whites hold all of the 'defensive beliefs' which he itemizes, and adds that "it would be desirable, but it is impossible, to give a statistical delineation of the degree to which various attitudes are held."

dication of one way in which opinionnaire results may be legitimately employed without recourse to dubiously applicable mathematical operations. Further papers will check some of the hypotheses advanced here.

The Temper of the Times (Continued)

At about the same time as Merton, C. Wright Mills argued, "Perhaps the central methodological problem of the social sciences springs from recognition that often there is a disparity between lingual and social-motor types of behavior." Mills suggested that we need to know "how much and in what direction disparities between talk and action will probably go."[10] It is interesting that both of these young visionaries should identify the same problem as critical (in contrast to most of their more distinguished contemporaries), should do so at about the same time, and should suggest social-structural explanations. Merton speculates about "possibly consistent group differences in spread between opinion and action." That is, differences between Northerners and Southerners, or (presumably) men and women, the old and the young, whites and blacks, rural folk and urban, etc. Both Merton and Mills suspect that the location of people in particular strata of the society needs to be considered if one is to understand discrepancies between sentiments and acts. This is partly true, but Herbert Blumer employs a different perspective and, I think, with considerably more explanatory potential.

Blumer has been the most consistent spokesman for the point of view suggested by LaPiere's data. Since 1931 he has argued the logic of this position, in terms of theory,[11] in terms of method,[12] and in terms of substantive fields such as industrial relations and public opinion polling.[13] We will be attentive to his theoretical (i.e., explanatory) contribution in Part III. For the moment let us consider his conceptual argument. In his presidential address to the American Sociological Society in 1956, Blumer suggests that, not only do we know nothing about behavior or the relation between attitudes and behavior, but that we don't know much about attitudes either: "The thousands of 'variable' studies of attitudes, for instance, have not contributed to our knowledge of the abstract nature of an attitude; in a similar way the studies of 'social cohesion,' 'social integration,' 'authority,' or 'group morale' have done nothing, so far as I can detect, to clarify or augment generic knowl-

10. C. Wright Mills, "Methodological Consequences of the Sociology of Knowledge," *American Journal of Sociology* 46 (1940): 316–30, reprinted in *Power, Politics and People: The Collected Essays of C. Wright Mills*, ed. Irving L. Horowitz (New York: Ballantine Books, 1963), p. 467.

11. Herbert Blumer, "What Is Wrong with Social Theory," *American Sociological Review* 19 (1954): 3–10; "The Problem of the Concept in Social Psychology," *American Journal of Sociology* 45 (1940): 707–19; "Science Without Concepts," *American Journal of Sociology* 36 (1931): 515–33; "Sociological Implications of the Thought of George Herbert Mead," *American Journal of Sociology* 71 (1966): 535–44. Many of Blumer's theoretical and methodological essays are collected in Herbert Blumer, *Symbolic Interactionism: Perspective and Method* (Englewood Cliffs, N. J.: Prentice-Hall, Inc., 1969).

12. Herbert Blumer, "Sociological Analysis and the Variable," *American Sociological Review* 21 (1956): 683–90. Blumer's most recent and most comprehensive methodological statement appears as Chapter 1 in *Symbolic Interactionism*.

13. Herbert Blumer, "Sociological Theory in Industrial Relations," *American Sociological Review* 12 (1947): 271–77; "Public Opinion and Public Opinion Polling," *American Sociological Review* 13 (1948): 542–49.

edge of these categories."[14] Yet, in the closing lines of his address, after 25 years of persistence, Blumer acknowledges defeat with the wistful wish that people at least know what they are doing. He concludes, "In view, however, of the current tendency of variable analysis to become the norm and model for sociological analysis, I believe it important to recognize its shortcomings and its limitations."

Why have both the empirical evidence and the theoretical rationale been ignored? In Chapter Three we will see that there is adequate reason to suspect that behavior toward words about social or cultural objects (i.e., responses to questions) may not provide an adequate basis for imputing behavior toward the objects themselves (i.e., responses to the people or situations to which the words refer). Four decades ago LaPiere's explanation was couched in terms of economy and reliability: "The questionnaire," he observed, "is cheap, easy, and mechanical. The study of human behavior is time consuming, intellectually fatiguing, and depends for its success upon the ability of the investigator. The former method gives quantitative results, the latter mainly qualitative. Quantitative measurements are quantitatively accurate; qualitative evaluations are always subject to the errors of human judgment. Yet," he concludes, "it would seem far more worthwhile to make a shrewd guess regarding that which is essential than to accurately measure that which is likely to prove quite irrelevant."[15]

Others, like Mills, have assumed a more cynical explanation. Turning to the sources of research finance, he suggests that: "Many foundation administrators like to give money for projects that are thought to be safe from political or public attack, that are large-scale, hence easier 'to administer' than more numerous handicraft projects, and that are scientific with a capital S, which often only means made 'safe' by trivialization. Accordingly," Mills concludes, "the big money tends to encourage the large-scale bureaucratic style of research into small-scale problems as carried on by The Scientists."[16] These explanations have persisted and most of them remain as valid today as they were in the past, but I suspect that they reflect a deeper and perhaps more basic problem. It is possible that the apparent anomaly of acknowledging the correctness of one position while pursuing another can best be explained in terms of the sociology of knowledge.

Epistemology and Research Methods

The sociology of knowledge has to do with the way in which the temper of the times and the ideological milieu in which we are immersed affect the kinds of questions we ask, the kinds of answers which form a permissible range, and the kinds of methods we employ to seek those answers. It "is devoted to digging up the social roots of knowledge, to searching out the ways in which knowledge and thought are affected by the environing social structure."[17] We may indeed have some

---

14. Herbert Blumer, "Sociological Analysis and the Variable." This paper appears in full in Chapter Eleven of this volume.
15. LaPiere, "Attitudes vs. Actions."
16. C. Wright Mills, "IBM Plus Reality Plus Humanism = Sociology," *Saturday Review*, May 1, 1954, reprinted in Irving L. Horowitz, ed., *Power, Politics and People*, p. 570.
17. Robert K. Merton, *Social Theory and Social Structure* (Glencoe, Ill.: The Free Press, rev. ed., 1957), p. 440.

roots to dig in our attempt to understand the directions taken by American sociology during the last four decades. The perceptions of knowledge—notions of the proper or appropriate ways of knowing—which were fashionable during the late twenties and early thirties, when sociology had its choices to make, surely impinged upon those choices.

Men like LaPiere and Blumer and, later, Mills are arguing from a basically antipositivistic position at a time when a century or more of cumulative positivistic science was resulting in a massive payoff in our knowledge and control of physical forces. And sociology had its alternatives. L. L. Thurstone was giving birth to what was to become modern scale analysis. Emery Bogardus was translating some of these ideas into sociological scales of contemporary relevance. And men like George Lundberg and Stuart Chapin were creating the theoretical and methodological rationale for the new "science." Incisive critiques of the new sociology and the logic of its quantitative methods were plentiful. Merton, for example, in the article included in this chapter, raises serious questions about the logic of scaling (see the references cited in his footnote 9). But such basic issues have been assiduously avoided in favor of systematic improvement in scaling *technique*. Thus we have "advanced" from Bogardus to Guttman, without ever addressing the basic critique. If we listen to Richard LaPiere's recollections of the temper of the times it becomes apparent that logic may not have been the deciding factor. Here is the scene, and what it was like to live it, as painted by a man who was there. It is, of course, retrospective, perhaps distorted in some ways, certainly flavored by what has happened since, but nevertheless an eyewitness report by a deeply involved participant:

> As you no doubt learned in your first course on the history of sociology, American sociologists of the first two decades of this century were—with some few exceptions, of which Cooley is the only one that immediately comes to mind—just moralistic reformers in scientist's clothing. What you may not know, or at least not fully appreciate, is that well into the 1930's the status of sociology and hence of sociologists was abominable, both within and outside the academic community. The public image of the sociologist was that of a blue-nosed reformer, ever ready to pronounce moral judgments, and against all pleasurable forms of social conduct. In the universities, sociology was generally thought of as an uneasy mixture of social philosophy and social work. . . .
>
> Through the 1920's the department at Chicago was the one real center of sociology in the U.S.[18] It is my impression, one that I cannot document,

18. If somewhat less "real" by LaPiere's standards, there were, nevertheless, other centers. Anachronistic though it might be, the Sumner-Keller tradition at Yale apparently persisted into the late fifties. There was also what LaPiere refers to as Bogardus' "shabby little empire" in Southern California. In the Northwest, Lundberg was already creating a lively outpost and beginning to wonder, "Can Science Save Us?" There were a number of isolated but nonetheless distinguished sociologists located at various provincial outposts. From conversations with Robert Cooley Angell I get the impression that his uncle Charles was lonesome at Michigan and maintained close ties with G. H. Mead and the Chicago sociologists. I can understand how LaPiere, being the "Young Turk" that he was, chose to ignore the great amount of talent and activity carried out in the land grant colleges. Departments of rural sociology in the Midwest contained the kinds of reformers and activists to whom the young "scientists" most vehemently objected.

that most of the men who came out of the Chicago department during this time were fairly passive disciples of the "Chicago School" — mostly trained in the ideas of Park, if not by him — and that they went out to spread the good word with a strong sense of mission. . . . The men who were to shape sociology during the 1930's were, for the most part, products of one or two men departments (e.g., Columbia) of low status within their universities. They were therefore to a considerable degree self-trained and without a doctrinaire viewpoint, and they were exceedingly conscious of the low esteem in which sociology was held.

Such men, and I was one among them, were determined to prove — at least to themselves — that sociology is a science, that sociologists are not moralists, and that sociology deserves recognition and support comparable to that being given psychology and economics. It was, I think, to this end that toward the end of the 20's scientific sociology came to be identified with quantitative methods in sociology, and the latter in turn with reliance upon the questionnaire as the one valid tool of investigation. Keep in mind that our number was few, that we were widely scattered, and that the majority of well-established sociologists were products of or at least adherents to the Chicago School. What had we to offer; what had we to distinguish ourselves from the prescientific sociologists; what certainty that we too were not just moralists in disguise? Why, statistics, of course! Once this discovery had been made — and I suspect Stuart Chapin was as important in this as anyone else — the rest followed more or less automatically; and by the mid-thirties American sociologists were split into two antagonistic camps — the moralists, now usually described as "armchair theorists," and the scientists, whose distinguishing mark was the table of weights and measures.

About 1935 the scientists attempted an organizational purification of sociology proposing that membership in the ASS be limited to true sociologists and the rather considerable body of social workers, social reformers, and crack-pots be driven from our ranks. Like Luther, they discovered that it is impossible to reform from within, so they established the now long-defunct Sociological Research Association, with membership limited by charter to 100. By this time, the Chicago department had lost its homogeneity, and the conflict between quantitativists and qualitativists raged there as elsewhere. So some Chicago men were admitted to the inner circle — and so, for some reason, was I. But admission was by election, and before long the original criteria for membership was forgotten, and by 1940 the organization consisted of 50 or so self-defined great men who could agree upon nothing except that the supply of great men had been exhausted.[19]

Now as to my own uncertain part in all this. I was one of the Young Turks, and I shared with Lundberg, Bain, Stouffer, etc., the distaste for soci-

19. The Sociological Research Association is not as "defunct" as LaPiere believes (or hopes). It is, in fact, alive and well. I am acquainted with several of the elites who are members and I know one sociologist who rejected an invitation to join. Sitting next to a sixtyish sociologist of national repute at a dinner meeting, I learned that he and his fellow members of S.R.A. (whom he referred to as "supersociologists") now consider 125 a reasonable limit to their membership.

ology as it had been and the hurt of its lowly status. But unlike the majority of the rebels, I did not share their belief that the cure for bad sociology was quantification. I did set off in that direction. . . .[20]

LaPiere sees the history of American sociology between the two world wars as an effort, not to build knowledge, but to achieve respectability and acceptability. In terms of this goal, he believes we have been successful.[21] "For it has in considerable measure been sociological reliance on quantitative methods that has won for sociology the repute and financial support that it now enjoys. That in gaining fame sociology may have become a pseudo-science is another, and quite different, matter. Now that sociology is well-established, it may be possible for a new generation of Young Turks to evaluate the means through which sociology has won respectability."

It is possible to document a great sensitivity to public opinion on the part of sociologists who were seeking a bit more academic respect than, say, driver education has today. It becomes clear that this defensiveness of repute, persisted into the nineteen-forties when we examine an event which took place in 1947. The setting is the annual meeting of the American Sociological Society. The audience consists not only of sociologists, but also of other academicians such as psychologists and political scientists. Furthermore, it consists not only of academicians, but also commercial pollsters, market researchers, and others who find it useful to keep a finger on the pulse of public opinion. Herbert Blumer, reading his paper, "Public Opinion and Public Opinion Polling,"[22] is the villain in the drama. The heroic defenders of the discipline are two distinguished scholars: Julian Woodward and Theodore Newcomb.

In brief, Blumer issues a challenge to the empirical relevance of public opinion sampling procedures. His arguments tend to be logically and empirically unimpeachable. For example, he suggests that although each man may carry equal weight in an opinion poll, each man does not carry equal weight in influencing policy, implementing decisions, or otherwise acting on his opinion. It follows that, to the extent that we are interested in what is likely to happen at some future point in time, we ought to do something other than randomly sample the population. An alternative is to sample those who have the power and influence to effect the anticipated action or not to effect it. We should sample only those to whom the issues are salient, relevant, meaningful! In the present context, the substance of Blumer's remarks is unimportant. What is curious is that, within the context of the professional meetings, the discussants also treated the substance of Blumer's remarks as unimportant. The two discussants were indeed terribly distressed, but it was about something else.

Newcomb appears to miss Blumer's point. He allows that there are certainly bad pollsters as well as good ones: "Some of them, I suppose, do not even know

20. LaPiere was dissuaded from "that direction" by two experiences at the London School. The first was the Malinowski seminar referred to earlier in this chapter. The second was a serious study of statistics. I shared his second experience and its consequences a quarter of a century later. Why does the study of statistical theory sometimes lead to the rejection of quantitative methods as they are found in the social sciences?

21. For an elaboration of this view see Richard T. LaPiere, "Comment on Irwin Deutscher's 'Looking Backward.' "

22. Blumer, "Public Opinion," op. cit.

whether their respondents are archbishops or itinerant laborers."[23] The point is less what they are, than it is how influential they are and how salient the particular issue is to them. Cesar Chavez is an itinerant laborer, but his opinion is of a different order from that of some other itinerant laborers (even though it may be the same opinion). Because, I suspect, of his scientific blinders, Newcomb finds Blumer's argument about sampling elusive: "I wish [Blumer] had shown some inherent connection between sampling and failure to obtain adequate information." The question is not one of adequacy of information; it is one of relevance to action. Newcomb pounces and in doing so reveals what is really irritating him: "I happen to believe that Professor Blumer's stand is one which delays scientific progress."[24] As I read Blumer, this was in fact his intention. He had made a choice between attempting to understand human behavior or advancing that perspective which sociologists call "science." Newcomb goes on to draw analogies with "our older-brother sciences," but I would argue (and so too, I think, would Blumer) that they are no kin of ours.

Woodward appears to have a better grasp on what Blumer is trying to sell, but he won't buy. He does suggest that surveys could measure the intensity with which opinions are held, the affiliation of respondents, and the influence of respondents. Like Newcomb, however, it is the science and respectability dimension that bothers him. He is embarrassed by Blumer's comments and is worried about what others will think of sociology and sociologists:

> Unhappily this is exactly what people outside the academic world, and not a few in the other disciplines inside it, have come to expect of the sociologist. . . . It is perhaps permissible to call attention to the need that we sociologists pay attention to our own problem of mass communication and our own impact on public opinion. Fortunately very few of the practicing pollsters are here today . . . but . . . if they *were* present, these public opinion survey people, who so far owe very little to the sociologists . . . would hardly go away from the meeting convinced that they owe much more in the future. I am afraid Blumer's paper would increase, rather than narrow, the distance between practitioner and professor. . . . This is too bad. . . ."[25]

Blumer may be a prophet without honor. In a review of a public opinion textbook, published some seventeen years after the encounter I have just described, Angus Campbell recollects Blumer's comments with a touch of nostalgia and no little remorse: "It is curious," Campbell writes, "that Blumer's hopes for the functional analysis of public opinion have been so little realized. The ability to conduct effective research on the problems he would have selected seems to elude us. The direction research has actually taken has been heavily influenced by the methods available."[26] Blumer tells me that many years after their exchange, Newcomb wrote him a long letter in which he expressed his regret at not having better understood the issue at the time.

---

23. Theodore Newcomb, "Discussion," *American Sociological Review* 13 (1948): 550.
24. Ibid., p. 551.
25. Julian Woodward, "Discussion," *American Sociological Review* 13 (1948): 554.
26. See Angus Campbell's review of Lane and Sears, *American Sociological Review* 30 (1965): 633.

In those unhappy days we were an uneasy discipline, reaching simultaneously for knowledge and respectability. It may have been the very nature of our work which evoked an inherent contradiction between these two goals. Perhaps now that we have the security of respectability we can afford to take a more critical look at alternatives which were neglected at other times for reasons which are no longer cogent. Perhaps now we can begin again to achieve some understanding of the tenuous relationships between men's words and their actions. One strategic point of departure for such a reevaluation is an examination of some of the consequences of the choices we have made. In attempting to assume the stance of physical science, we have necessarily assumed its epistemology — its assumptions about the nature of knowledge and the appropriate means of knowing, including the rules of scientific evidence.

The requirement of clean empirical demonstration of the effects of isolated variables, in a manner which can be replicated, led us to create, by definition, such factors or variables. We knew that human behavior was rarely if ever directly influenced or explained by an isolated variable; we knew that it was impossible to assume that any set of such variables was additive (with or without weighting); we knew that the complex mathematics of the interaction among any set of variables, much less their interaction with external variables, was incomprehensible to us. In effect, although we knew they did not exist, we defined them into being. As Blumer's incisive critique of variable analysis (see Chapter Eleven) implies, uncontrolled catalytic agents may be expected to be the rule rather than the exception in social processes. If that is so, then research designed to capture those processes by controlling the relationship among preidentified variables, may lead us up a blind alley. That alley is all the more vicious because it is endless as well as blind. There are always other variables to consider and so we never discover that it is a dead end.

It is also true that the excellent tools we have been developing may not be appropriate for the job we need to do. The argument that, if our tools are inappropriate, we ought to select problems which fit them, is so specious that it is hardly worth comment. The point is that otherwise good tools may be doing the wrong job or unimportant jobs. The best of shovels is not very useful for chopping down trees and it is difficult to dig a hole with even the finest axe. I suspect we sometimes attempt such operations in social research.

We were not satisfied with creating variables. They had to be stripped of what little meaning they had in order that they might be operational, i.e., that they have their measurement built into their definition. One consequence then, was to break down human behavior in a way that was not only artificial but which did not jibe with the manner in which that behavior was observed. Having laid these foundations — and because the accretion of knowledge is a cumulative affair — we began to construct layer upon layer. As I mentioned earlier, in three decades we "advanced" from Bogardus to Guttman.[27] Merton suggests that the cumulative nature of science requires a high degree of consensus among scientists and leads, therefore, to

---

27. For Guttman's line of reasoning on the attitude-behavior issue, see Louis Guttman, "A Structural Theory for Intergroup Beliefs and Action," *American Sociological Review* 24 (1959): 318–28. This is closely related to the argument proposed by Campbell in his selection in Chapter Nine.

an inevitable enchantment with problems of reliability.[28] All knowledge, whether scientific or not, is cumulative and all men who think or write stand on the shoulders of those who have thought or have written before. Merton would, I hope, view this "inevitable consensus" and the resulting fascination with reliability as dysfunctional: that is, as an unintended consequence and one which is contrary to some of the accepted goals of science—the discovery of new perspectives, new methods, and new knowledge. Surely these cannot be attained when everyone is committed to agreeing with everyone else.

It does, nevertheless, appear that the adoption of the scientific model in the social sciences has resulted in an uncommon concern for methodological problems centering on issues of reliability and to the concomitant neglect of problems of validity. The cumulative nature of sociology and especially the issue of reliability and validity are the focal concerns of Chapters Four and Five. For the moment, I want only to introduce that issue. We have, in our pursuit of reliability, been absorbed in measuring the amount of error which results from inconsistency among interviewers or inconsistency among items on our instruments. We concentrate on consistency without much concern with what it is we are being consistent about or whether we are consistently right or wrong. As a consequence we may have been learning a great deal about how to pursue an incorrect course with a maximum of precision. It is not my intent to disparage the importance of reliability per se; it is the obsession with it to which I refer. As I observe in Chapter Five, zero reliability must result in zero validity. Without stable measurement we cannot get at what we intend. But the relationship is not linear, since infinite perfection of reliability (zero error) may also be associated with zero validity. That is, our measurement may be very stable, but still fail to get at what we intend. Whether or not one wishes to emulate the scientist and whatever methods may be applied in the quest for knowledge, we must make estimates of, allowances for, and attempts to reduce the extent to which our methods distort our findings. I hope this puts me on record as considering reliability a matter of serious concern. However, after the following paragraph the remainder of this book will be much more attentive to her neglected stepsister—validity.

It is because of the reliability issue that C. Wright Mills identifies the "disparities between talk and action" as "the central *methodological* problem of the social sciences."[29] Mills' plea for systematic investigations into the differences between words and deeds is based on the need for the "methodologist to build into his methods standard margins of error"—to learn how to apply the technique of discounting referred to in Chapter One. Just as Mills is concerned about reliability in the historical method, Hyman has documented the need for estimates of reliability in social-anthropological and clinical-psychiatric observations. He reminds us that the village of Tepotzlan as described by Oscar Lewis is quite different from the same village as it was described earlier by Robert Redfield. Hyman cites Kluck-

---

28. Merton, *Social Theory and Social Structure*, p. 448. One sociologist has attacked the verbal form of such consensus as an "immoral rhetoric." See Andrew J. Weigert, "The Immoral Rhetoric of Scientific Sociology," *American Sociologist* 5 (1970): 111–19.

29. Mills, "Methodological Consequences of the Sociology of Knowledge," p. 467 (italics added).

hohn's lament that "the limited extent to which ethnologists have been articulate about their field techniques is astonishing to scholars in other disciplines."[30]

One of the few positive consequences of our decades of "scientific" orientation is the incorporation into the sociological mentality of a self-consciousness about methods—regardless of what methods are employed. As a result, those few sociologists who bring ethnological field techniques to bear on their problems are constrained to contemplate methodological issues and to publish methodological observations. I have in mind specifically the continuing series of articles by Howard S. Becker and Blanche Geer.[31] Barney Glaser and Anselm Strauss have attempted to systematically codify and justify the procedures and the logic employed in such sociological field work.[32] Regardless, however, of the importance of reliability, there remains a danger that in our obsession with it, the goals—the purposes for which we seek knowledge—and the phenomena about which we seek knowledge, may become obscured.

One of the less desirable consequences of our neglect of the relationship between words and deeds has been the development of a technology which is inappropriate to the understanding of human behavior, and conversely, the almost complete absence of a technology which can facilitate our learning about the conditions under which people in various categories do or do not "put their monies where their mouths are." Under what conditions will people behave as they talk? Under what conditions is there no relationship? And under what conditions do they say one thing and behave in a manner exactly the opposite? In spite of the fact that all of these combinations have been empirically observed and reported (see Chapter Three), few efforts have been made to order such observations.[33] Perhaps of even

---

30. Hyman et al., *Interviewing in Social Research*, pp. 4–6. The citation to Clyde Kluckhohn is "The Personal Document in Anthropological Science," *Social Science Research Council Bulletin*, No. 53 (New York: Social Science Research Council, 1945).

31. See, for example, Howard S. Becker and Blanche Geer, "Participant Observation and Interviewing: A Comparison," *Human Organization* 16 (1957): 28–32, reprinted in Chapter Seven of this volume; Howard S. Becker, "Problems of Inference and Proof in Participant Observation," *American Sociological Review* 23 (1958): 652–60; Howard S. Becker and Blanche Geer, "Participant Observation: The Analysis of Qualitative Field Data," in *Human Organization Research*, eds., R. N. Adams and J. L. Preiss (Homewood, Ill.: Dorsey Press, 1960), pp. 267–89; Blanche Geer, "First Days in the Field," in *Sociologists at Work*, ed. Phillip E. Hammond (New York: Basic Books, Inc., 1964), pp. 322–44. For an elaboration of their methodology as applied to a specific area of research, see Howard S. Becker, Blanche Geer, and Everett C. Hughes, *Making the Grade: The Academic Side of College Life* (New York: John Wiley and Sons, Inc., 1968).

32. Barney G. Glaser and Anselm L. Strauss, *The Discovery of Grounded Theory: Strategies for Qualitative Research* (Chicago: Aldine Publishing Co., 1967).

33. In 1965, after my first systematic review of the literature, I discovered a few valiant efforts to make sense out of apparent inconsistencies between attitudes and behavior. These early, and generally unsatisfactory efforts, include A. J. Diekema, "Some Postulates Concerning the Relationship Between Attitudes and Behavior," paper read at the annual meetings of the Ohio Valley Sociological Society, 1965; Louis Guttman, "A Structural Theory for Intergroup Beliefs and Action," cited earlier in this chapter; Ulf Himmelstrand, "Verbal Attitudes and Behavior: A Paradigm for the Study of Message Transmission and Transformation," *Public Opinion Quarterly* 24 (1960): 224–50; Kiyoshi Ikeda, "Discriminatory Actions and Intergroup Attitudes: A Re-Examination," (ca. 1960), mimeo. Identifying the problem of apparent inconsistencies as one of the more important ones confronting social psychology, the Society for the Psychological Study of Social Issues devoted a full issue of the *Journal of Social Issues* (vol. 5, 1949) to consideration of that problem as it relates to intergroup relations. Although the intent of the editors was to encourage thinking and research, as far as I can determine their results were slim. See, for example, J. H. Mann, "The Relationship Between Cognitive, Affective and Behavioral Aspects of Racial Prejudice," *Journal of Social Issues* 49 (1959): 223–28.

greater importance, we do not know under what conditions a change in attitude anticipates a change in behavior or under what conditions a change in behavior anticipates a change in attitude. Again, both phenomena have been empirically observed and recorded. In Part III an attempt is made to begin to address this issue of microsocial change.

In Chapter One, I warned against misunderstanding my comments as a plea for the simple study of simple behavioral items. This would be a duplication of the same kinds of mistakes we have made in the simple study of simple attitudinal items. Overt action can be understood and interpreted only within the context of its meaning to the actors, just as verbal reports can be understood and interpreted only within the context of their meaning to the respondents. And in large part the context of each is the other. "Where but in social situations," asks Erving Goffman, "does speaking go on?"[34] But the fact remains that one of the methodological consequences of our recent history is that we are barely beginning to develop a technology for observing, ordering, analysing, and interpreting overt behavior — especially as such behavior relates to attitudes, norms, aspirations, opinions, values, and other sentiments. In Chapter One, I mentioned one abortive approach — the time and motion study — along with an illustration of its inadequacy. But if time and motion studies are inadequate because they leave one with no understanding of what the flow of action means to the actors, such understanding is not, in itself, adequate. For example, Roebuck and Spray[35] provide a description of sexual maneuvering in a cocktail lounge which reeks of validity. The credibility of their observational account with its rich sense of subtle interactional ploys, is unimpeachable. But what does one do with it? Implications and applications and relationships with other social phenomena are left to the reader to tease out. At best it is raw data. I submit that data, even very good data, cannot stand on its own.

The development of a new technology could take any number of directions. Ideally, we should seek to refine the model provided by LaPiere, whereby we obtain information from the same population on sentiments and acts under natural social conditions. Surely the kind of cleverness which creates situational apparati for the psychological laboratory could also create refined situational designs for research under conditions which have meaning for the actors. The theoretical and methodological rationalization of participant-observer field techniques begun by Becker and Geer and further systematized by Glaser and Strauss is a promising alternative. There may be as yet untapped possibilities in contrived laboratory experiments — if we can learn how to contrive them in such a way that their results are not denuded of any general meaning by the artificial specificity of the situations. If someday reliable and valid projective instruments are developed, we may have made a significant technological step forward. There has been considerable recent developmental work on instruments which facilitate self-reporting of overt behavior and allow comparisons to be made on the same people between sentiments and talk about behavior.[36]

Novel methodological innovations do lie buried in the literature. Kohn and Williams, for example, have suggested a method of deliberately introducing new

34. Erving Goffman, "The Neglected Situation," in *The Ethnography of Communication*, eds. John J. Gumperz and Dell Hymes (*American Anthropologist* 66 [part 2, 1964]: 134).

35. Julian Roebuck and S. Lee Spray, "The Cocktail Lounge," *American Journal of Sociology* 72 (1967): 388–95.

36. Robert H. Hardt and George E. Bodine, *Development of Self-Report Instruments in Delinquency Research* (Syracuse, N.Y.: Syracuse University Youth Development Center, 1964).

factors into natural situations for observational purposes.[37] This is a device for applying rigorous experimental controls to everyday life without creating unintended and undesirable reaction effects. Occasionally, a social psychologist devises a laboratory experiment with such diabolical cunning that the situation must surely appear real to his subjects. The article by Stanley Milgram in Chapter Eight is one such experiment. One group of psychologists has evolved a design which enables them to exploit the subject's definition of a dummy experimental situation, in order to distract him from the actual experiment, which appears as a natural event unrelated to the experiment. An example is provided by Himmelstein and Moore's piece in Chapter Ten.

There was a time earlier in this century when sociologists came to a crossroads. We could choose, on the one hand, to undertake neat orderly studies of measurable phenomena. This alternative carried with it all of the gratifications of conforming to the prestigious methods of pursuing knowledge then in vogue, of having access to considerable sums of monies through the granting procedures of large foundations and governmental agencies, of a comfortable sense of satisfaction derived from dealing rigorously and precisely with small isolated problems which were cleanly defined, of moving for forty years down one track in an increasingly rigorous, refined, and reliable manner, while simultaneously disposing of the problems of validity by the semantic trickery of operational definitions.

On the other hand, we could have tackled the messy world as we knew it to exist, a world where the same people will make different utterances under different conditions and will behave differently in different situations and will say one thing while doing another. We could have tackled a world where control of relevant variables was impossible not only because we didn't know what they were, but because we didn't know how they interacted with each other. We could have accepted the conclusion of almost every variant of contemporary philosophy of science that the notion of cause and effect (and therefore of stimulus and response or of independent and dependent variables) is untenable. We eschewed this formidable challenge. This was the hard way. We chose the easy way.

Yet the easy way provides one set of results and the hard way provides another. The easy way for Merton in 1938 would have been simply to present his survey findings in as sophisticated a manner as possible and to return for more data on additional samples if there were questions left unanswered. He chose instead to think about the potential impact of different group associations on the strength and direction of his findings and thus to seriously question their meaning. The easy way for Blumer in 1947 would have been to demonstrate his disciplinary loyalty by showing pollsters how his ingenuity could help them obtain better samples, rather than questioning the basic assumptions of polling methods. The easy way for La-Piere in 1934 would have been to conduct as rigorous as possible a survey of attitudes of hotel and restaurant managers towards Orientals. But this leads to a set of conclusions which are the opposite of what he finds when he does it the hard way, i.e., traveling thousands of miles in order to confront those managers with Orientals.[38]

37. Melvin Kohn and Robin Williams, "Situational Patterning in Intergroup Relations," *American Sociological Review* 21 (1956): 164–74.

38. Cook and Sellitz have examined the different results which may obtain by employing different methods of assessing attitudes—including both self-reports and behavioral observations. Stuart W. Cook and Claire Sellitz, "A Multiple Indicator Approach to Attitude Measurement," *Psychological Bulletin* 62 (1964): 36–58.

A short typescript paper by David Hanson reviews some of the literature on the relationship between attitudes and overt behavior.[39] He concluded that laboratory experimental studies such as those by Scott, King, and Janis, and by DeFleur and Westie[40] tend to show a positive correlation between attitudes and behavior, while observational field studies such as those by LaPiere, Kutner, and Yarrow, and by Saenger and Gilbert,[41] tend to show no such correlation. Although there are important exceptions to this rule,[42] it serves as a reminder that our choice of methods may not be unrelated to our conclusions. Let us turn from polemics to evidence. What observations can be found which reveal the empirical relationship between sentiments and acts? This is the central question of Chapter Three.

39. David J. Hanson, "Notes on a Bibliography on Attitudes and Behavior" (1965), unpublished paper. Although that was a graduate-student paper, Hanson's continuing ability to make sense out of what he reads is documented by his very neat challenge to me a few years later. See David J. Hanson, "Ideological Orientations and Sociological Facts," *American Sociologist* 4 (1969): 160.

40. W. A. Scott, "Attitude Change Through Reward of Verbal Behavior," *Journal of Abnormal and Social Psychology* 55 (1957): 72–75, and "Attitude Change by Response Reinforcement: Replication and Extension," *Sociometry* 22 (1959): 328–35; B. T. King and I. L. Janis, "Comparison of the Effectiveness of Improvised Versus Non-Improvised Role-Playing in Producing Opinion Changes," *Human Relations* 9 (1956): 177–86; Melvin L. DeFleur and Frank R. Westie, "Verbal Attitudes and Overt Acts: An Experiment in the Salience of Attitudes," *American Sociological Review* 23 (1958): 667–73 (included in Chapter Four of this volume).

41. LaPiere, "Attitudes vs. Actions"; Bernard Kutner, C. Wilkins, and P. B. Yarrow, "Verbal Attitudes and Overt Behavior Involving Racial Prejudice," *Journal of Abnormal and Social Psychology* 47 (1952): 649–52; Gerhart Saenger and Emily Gilbert, "Customer Reactions to the Integration of Negro Sales Personnel," *International Journal of Opinion and Attitude Research* 4 (1950): 57–76.

42. For example, a controlled laboratory study showing no relationship between attitude and behavior is reported in Michael Zunich, "Relationship Between Maternal Behavior and Attitudes Toward Children," *Journal of Genetic Psychology* 100 (1962): 155–65. (The scarcity of reports of experiments showing no relationship may be a function of publication policies of some psychology journals during the fifties and into the early sixties. These journals would not publish anything which did not report differences at a predetermined level of statistical significance. I will return to this source of distortion in the published literature in Chapter Eight.) On the other hand behavior under natural conditions which has been observed to conform to expressed attitudes is reported in Lawrence Cagle and Irwin Deutscher, "Housing Aspirations and Housing Achievement: The Relocation of Poor Families," *Social Problems* 18 (1971): 244–56.

3

Kansas Drinkers and Student Cheaters:

Bits of Evidence

And That's Only the Beginning

Linton Freeman, a former colleague, is inclined to make shocking utterances which, on second thought, turn out to make sense. I once heard him calmly announce to a gathering of busy, busy researchers that there should be an immediate national moratorium on all data gathering. He was at the time interested in such things as data banks and information retrieval systems; I could, therefore, understand the source of such a ridiculous notion, but of course neither I nor any of the other assembled sociologists could believe he was serious. Freeman was sensitive to the large amounts of unanalyzed and partially analyzed data on just about everything, gathering dust in files everywhere. It wasn't until a few years later, as I began to locate and read materials on the relationship between sentiments and acts, that I was willing to take Freeman's suggestion seriously.

I would still insist that when we are very clear about what we need to know it is then imperative to design research which will ferret out that specific bit of knowledge and to gather the necessary data. It may also at times be desirable to gather data for the purpose of verifying something which appears to be correct but which requires somewhat more evidence in order for us to be comfortable with it. There may be very good reasons for data gathering: the detection of temporal shifts, replication, validation, theory testing, theory building, or action research. Certainly, in the last case, in which research is undertaken in order to help bring about changes in a specific community, prison, school, hospital, or whatever, it is inconceivable to imagine any effective work without a considerable amount of data gathering in the specific setting. But as I have come more and more to suspect that a great deal of data gathering is ritual duplication—unnecessary, unproductive, and, mostly, not at all useful to anyone—I have had second thoughts about Freeman's shocking utterance.

I do not think it a contradiction to suggest that, on the one hand, there has been little attention paid to the problems raised by LaPiere in his pioneering study, and, on the other hand, there are a great deal of data available on that same issue. These statements can be consistent because, without any necessary awareness or concern for the problem of sentiments and acts, hundreds of observers have recorded information on how people behave, how they talk, and sometimes even on how they do both. The data are in the library, but they are "raw" data in the sense that the investigator must perform the analytic task of relating them to each other and to the problem which concerns him. It is doubtful that either of the two articles which appear in this chapter were intended to bear on the attitude vs. behavior is-sue. Yet both of them clearly do—as do many other pieces which will be referred to here. It is likely that there are sufficient data in the library to permit us to identify the nature of the relationship between sentiments and acts under a great variety of conditions. It is also likely that, once this is accomplished, certain important bits of research will be required in order to fill in the few pieces of the puzzle which are still missing. Many scholars will stubbornly insist on a considerable amount of verifi-cation before they are willing to accept some crucial observations. That, of course, is their privilege although I consider it a dull process which not only lacks the excite-ment of discovery, but doesn't always seem necessary anyway.

The trick, in this kind of research, is to locate empirical data which inform one on the relationship between what people say and what they otherwise do, re-gardless of the labels attached to these dimensions and regardless of the author's original intent. But why go to all this trouble, largely on the grounds of a primitive field study on a Chinese couple done during the Great Depression and the persis-tent polemics of Herbert Blumer? First of all, I personally consider the LaPiere study a masterpiece and I have gradually come to realize that Blumer makes very good sense. Others may disagree with both of these judgments. But it is difficult to dis-agree with the observation that LaPiere identified a problem of central importance to the understanding of human behavior and one which far transcends (1) American attitudes, (2) Chinese minorities, (3) relationships between restauranteurs and motel keepers with minority customers, (4) the decade of the thirties, or (5) problems of minority groups in general.

Let me document each of these five points: (1) There is reason to believe that interracial attitudes and behavior are not identical in nations other than the United States, for example, in Brazil.[1] (2) There is evidence, as Merton anticipated in Chapter Two, that sentiments about Negroes in Northern American communities do not coincide with behavior toward Negroes in those communities.[2] (3) Some research suggests that discrepancies between sentiments and acts regarding minorities extend to other kinds of exchanges such as those between department store clerks and cus-tomers or those involving housing.[3] (4) Data elicited during the decades of the fifties and the sixties appear to document the persistence of such inconsistencies in inter-racial attitudes and behaviors.[4] (5) Perhaps the most important point is that there are bits of empirical evidence indicating that this discrepancy between sentiments and acts is in no way limited to the arena of racial or ethnic relations. Let us consider this observation.

Anticipating Chapter Twelve, we should be aware that it is no matter of whimsy that the richest empirical observations on the relationship between what

---

1. R. Bastide and P. L. van den Berghe, "Stereotypes, Norms, and Interracial Behavior in São Paulo, Brazil," *American Sociological Review* 22 (1957): 689–94.

2. Wilbur B. Brookover and John B. Holland, "An Inquiry into the Meaning of Minority Group Attitude Expressions," *American Sociological Review* 17 (1952): 196–202.

3. Gerhart Saenger and Emily Gilbert, "Customer Reactions to the Integration of Negro Sales Personnel," *International Journal of Opinion and Attitude Research* 4 (1950): 57–76; Robin M. Wil-liams, Jr., *Strangers Next Door: Ethnic Relations in American Communities* (Englewood Cliffs, N.J.: Prentice-Hall, Inc., 1964).

4. See, for example, Lawrence S. Linn, "Verbal Attitudes and Overt Behavior: A Study of Racial Discrimination," *Social Forces* 43 (1965): 353–64 (reprinted in Chapter Four of this vol-ume).

people say and what they do are found in the study of (what is euphemistically called) intergroup relations. Confrontation by scholars with a public language of race relations which is frequently at odds with public behavior between races has led to a clear conceptual distinction between "prejudice" on the one hand and "discrimination" on the other. Once made, the conceptual distinction directs the investigator, in his observations, his analysis, and his conclusions, toward the fact that verbalizations and subjective states of mind are not necessarily related to objective actions toward others.

Without such an empirical and conceptual confrontation the social scientist is prone to ignore the possibility that people do not always do as they say and, in fact, may do the exact opposite. Sexual behavior provides an extreme case in point. To a degree, both talk about and public acts of sexual cohabitation are taboo in our society. However, under certain restricted social and cultural conditions some public sex talk is permissible and, in recent years, we have developed research techniques for tapping such talk. But public behavior in this substantive area, in contrast to race relations, is so uncommon that for all practical purposes it must be considered nonexistent. As a consequence, there is no confrontation with differences between what people say and what they do, although there may be a subliminal suspicion that such differences possibly exist. Nor is there a conceptual equivalent to the discrimination-prejudice distinction which can serve to direct the investigator toward understanding the relationship between sex talk and sex behavior. On the contrary, sex talk is assumed to reflect sex behavior for no better reason than the inaccessibility of behavioral observations. If it were possible to observe bedroom behavior (under more spontaneous conditions and with better sampling procedures than those employed by Masters and Johnson[5]), I wonder what would be the relationship between Kinsey's survey results and such observations? I don't know, nor does anyone else, but a contemporary novelist has a confused fictional respondent muse about a sex survey, "What do they expect of me? Do they want to know how I feel or how I act?"[6]

The piece by Warriner in this chapter suggests that it is necessary to be alert to differences between public and private sentiments and, by inference, public and private actions. We will return to this important dimension in Chapter Ten. In spite of the conceptual advantage offered to students of intergroup relations, there is evidence which suggests that the problem of sentiments and acts is endemic. It has been observed that trade union members talk one game and play another in much the same manner as people in an adult education program,[7] that urban teachers' descriptions of their classroom behavior are sometimes unrelated to the way teachers behave in the classroom,[8] that what rural Missourians say about their health

5. *Sex and Human Relationships*, ed. C. E. Johnson (Columbus, Ohio: Charles Merrill and Sons, 1970).

6. Irving Wallace, *The Chapman Report* (New York: Signet Books, 1961), pp. 106–7.

7. Lois Dean, "Interaction, Reported and Observed: The Case of One Local Union," *Human Organization* 17 (1958): 36–44; Eugene C. Hagburg, "Validity of Questionnaire Data: Reported and Observed Attendance in an Adult Education Program," *Public Opinion Quarterly* 32 (1968): 453–56.

8. Jules Henry, "Spontaneity, Initiative, and Creativity in Suburban Classrooms," *American Journal of Orthopsychiatry* 29 (1959): 266–79, reprinted in *Education and Culture: Anthropological Approaches*, ed. George D. Spindler (New York: Holt, Rinehart and Winston, 1963), pp. 215–33. See especially, p. 228.

behavior has little connection with their actual health practices (and a similar divergence appears elsewhere in the nation regarding tuberculosis),[9] that the moral and ethical beliefs of students do not conform to their behavior,[10] and that there is some lack of concordance among beliefs, behavior, and attitudes about smoking.[11]

Furthermore, it has been reported that small-time steel wholesalers mouth patriotism while undercutting the national economy in wartime,[12] that employers' attitudes toward hiring the handicapped are not reflected in their hiring practices,[13] that the behavior of mothers toward their children is unrelated to their attitudes toward them,[14] and that attitudes toward and participation in the Los Angeles Watts riots are discordant.[15] Pedestrians observed crossing an intersection against a "don't walk" light frequently informed an interviewer that they never engaged in such behavior and, even more frequently, expressed the sentiment that it is a naughty thing to do.[16]

Students of aging suspect that what older people have to say about retirement has little relationship to their behavior during that stage of the life cycle.[17] A pair of industrial psychologists, interested in assessing the current state of knowledge regarding the relationship between employee attitudes and employee performance, covered all of the literature in that area through 1954.[18] Treating various classes of studies separately, they find in every category "minimal or no relationship between employee attitudes and performance." In other words, what workers say about their work and how they evaluate it has nothing to do with how they act on the job. Perhaps now the reader can better understand why I see no contradiction in suggesting, on the one hand, a neglect of the problem of sentiments and acts, and on the other hand a plethora of available data. The parameters of the issue seem to me to have been adequately identified. In this case, at least, I would agree with

9. Edward Hassinger and Robert L. McNamara, "Stated Opinion and Actual Practice in Health Behavior in a Rural Area," *Midwest Sociologist* 1 (1957): 93–97; C. David Jenkins, "Group Differences in Perception: A Study of Community Beliefs and Feelings About Tuberculosis," *American Journal of Sociology* 71 (1966): 417–29.

10. Snell Putney and Russell Middleton, "Ethical Relativism and Anomia," *American Journal of Sociology* 67 (1962): 430–38; and "Religion, Normative Standards, and Behavior," *Sociometry* 25 (1962): 141–52.

11. D. J. Baer, "Smoking Attitudes, Behavior, and Beliefs of College Males," *Journal of Social Psychology* 60 (1966): 65–78.

12. Louis Kriesberg, "National Security and Conduct in the Steel Gray Market," *Social Forces* 34 (1956): 268–77.

13. Vera Meyers Schletzer et al., "Attitudinal Barriers to Employment," *Minnesota Studies in Vocational Rehabilitation: XI*, Industrial Relations Center, Bulletin No. 32 (Minneapolis, Minn.: University of Minnesota, 1961).

14. Michael Zunich, "Relationship Between Maternal Behavior and Attitudes Toward Children," *Journal of Genetic Psychology* 100 (1962): 155–65.

15. H. Edward Ransford, "Isolation, Powerlessness, and Violence: A Study of Attitudes and Participation in the Watts Riot," *American Journal of Sociology* 73 (1968): 581–91.

16. Lionel I. Dannick, "The Relationship Between Overt Behavior and Verbal Expressions as Influenced by Immediate Situational Determinants" (Diss., Syracuse University, 1969).

17. Leonard Z. Breen, "Retirement Norms, Behavior, and Functional Aspects of Normative Behavior," in *Processes of Aging*, eds. R. H. Williams, C. Tibbitts, and W. Donahue, vol. 2 (New York: Atherton Press, 1963), 381–88; William E. Henry and Elaine Cumming, *Growing Old: The Process of Disengagement* (New York: Basic Books, 1961)—see especially the section dealing with normative responses.

18. A. Brayfield and D. M. Crockett, "Employee Attitudes and Employee Performance," *Psychological Bulletin* 52 (1955): 396–428.

Freeman. There is no need to gather any more data describing the relationship between what people say and what they do.

All of these studies enjoy certain strengths and suffer certain weaknesses. The two examples which follow are selected not because of any necessary superiority, but because, in addition to illustrating the salience of the issue in areas unrelated to race relations, they will become useful documents in supplementing later chapters. Warriner suggests that Kansans who vote for prohibition may maintain and use well-equipped bars in their homes. He does not fall back upon simplistic explanations in terms of hypocrisy, but rather, suggests that the honest expression of opinion in a relatively public situation may be quite different from the equally honest expression of opinion in a relatively private situation. (This distinction among different kinds of social situations becomes central to the theory which begins to emerge in Chapter Ten.) Freeman and Ataöv illustrate the problem of inconsistencies in an area which students understand better than anyone else. It is a study, then, which not only serves our present purposes, but also provides student readers with an opportunity to read a piece of relevant research from the critical perspective of members of the group being studied. Finally, the Freeman and Ataöv data become useful as we move into our discussion of validity in Chapters Four and Five.

DATA:
The Nature and Functions of Official Morality
CHARLES K. WARRINER

I

In a clinical study[1] of The Village, a small rural community in Kansas, we discovered a systematic inconsistency between the public and private expressions of values about drinking alcoholic beverages. In public people affirmed an "official" morality which held that the drinking of alcoholic beverages was wrong, that The Village was a "dry" town, and that only "bums and other elements of the lower classes" drank. In observations of several thousand events we found no instance in which there was a public violation or rejection of this official morality. The general applicability of our observations was confirmed by a number of informants.

"The Nature and Functions of Official Morality," by Charles K. Warriner, from the *American Journal of Sociology*, vol. 64 (1958), pp. 165–68. Revised version of a paper read at the annual meeting of the American Sociological Society, Detroit, Michigan, September 1956. Reprinted by permission of the author and the University of Chicago Press.
[1]A report of this study is to be found in the author's "Leadership and Society" (microfilmed Ph.D. dissertation, University of Chicago Library, 1953).

This publicly expressed ideology was not, however, an indication of the private drinking behavior or of the personal sentiments and beliefs of the members of the community. For example, one of the leaders of The Village who had expressed the official morality most directly and forcefully during our first visit to the community was a regular though moderate drinker in his home and within his clique. Similarly, some members of the Women's Christian Temperance Union drank and served alcoholic beverages in their homes. Although some members of the community expressed personal moral beliefs consistent with the official morality, the majority did not feel that there was anything wrong with moderate drinking. Many of our informants recognized this inconsistency and typically expressed the idea that "this town is full of hypocrites; they vote dry and drink wet."

In most studies such an inconsistency is explained away by searching for some bias in the observational technique or by looking for some coercive, "distorting" factor in the milieu. Our thesis is that at least one class of these inconsistencies is real (i.e., is not a function of faulty observational techniques) and has been inadequately accounted for in the past. We propose that official morality[2] can be understood as a type of collective phenomenon and not as individual behavior, that its primary relevance is to the social system and not to the personal systems of the members, and that, because it is collective, it may have functions with respect to the community as a social system.[3]

II

Inconsistency between public morality and private behavior raises a question as to the nature of collective reality. We have frequently assumed that the term "collective" was merely a synonym for "common-individual" and that the collective was to be found only as it was reflected in the personality and personal behavior of individuals. This "pluralistic behavior" approach to the collective ignores the fact that persons, as actors in particular situations, may express beliefs or conceptions that they do not really believe. As isolated persons they know the ideology but do not believe it to be true, but as actors in particular collectivities they will act as if these same beliefs were true. The expression of the ideology occurs as a result of a variety of motivations which in effect define it as being "true" (i.e., appropriate) for a typically recurring situation—a particular social system. What is expressed in a particular context depends upon what is relevant and appropriate to that context.[4]

Our data on The Village show that there are a variety of these motivating sentiments. There were those who "really believed" in the official morality:

[2]"Official" in this case does not imply having a source in authority. As used here, it is more nearly synonymous with "collective," but we have retained the term "official" for its convenience.

[3]Our use of "social system" follows most directly the ideas of A. R. Radcliffe-Brown, *A Natural Science of Society* (Glencoe, Ill.: Free Press, 1957). See also Paul Meadows, "Models, Systems, and Science," *American Sociological Review*, XXII (February, 1957), 3–9.

[4]This formulation is consistent with the social-psychological theory represented in the work of Walter Coutu, *Emergent Human Nature* (New York: Alfred A. Knopf, 1949). For a fuller discussion of this view of collective reality see Charles K. Warriner, "Groups Are Real: A Reaffirmation," *American Sociological Review*, XXI (October, 1956), 549–54.

"drinking *is* immoral." Among those whose private sentiments were not consistent with the ideology, three different attitudes stand out. Some persons drink and accept drinking but are not sure that it is morally right. They support the official morality in their public behavior because "it might be true" as well as because it is supported by others. Another attitude stemmed from the belief that "others can't drink moderately" and that "I have a responsibility to keep temptation from being placed before them." This might be called "my brother's keeper" attitude. Still others supported the official morality in order to avoid conflict. As one informant expressed it: "Sure, I go along with that nonsense. It isn't worth fighting about. If you got up and said that there wasn't anything wrong with drinking a glass of beer now and then, you'd just get into a hell of an argument."

These and other sentiments and beliefs, combined in different ways in different individuals, support and give reality to a single collective fact. Because we find the collective "resides" in each person in a different way, we will discover it not by studying individuals but only by studying them as actors in collectivities.

The collective fact is that, whenever the members of the community acted within the context of the community, their behavior conformed to and expressed the explicit canons of the official morality.[5] Although people drank, they did so in their own homes, behind closed doors and drawn shades. They carefully disposed of their "empties." They seldom drank before going out, but, if they did, they disguised their breath with Sen-Sen or clove gum. They did not admit drinking, nor did they talk about it except with close friends. In effect, they conformed to the action prescriptions of the official morality. Furthermore, when acting as members of the community per se, they actively supported the official morality. For example, the town voted "dry" in the Kansas Repeal referendum, but, as far as we could tell from the data available, this dry vote heavily overrepresented the "drys" as measured by personal sentiments. Two informants who were known to drink reported that they had voted against Repeal to "keep it out of the hands of the bums."

III

The structural-functional point of view provides one vehicle for exploring the importance and relevance of this phenomenon. The functional hypothesis holds that a particular social form or process has consequences for the social systems in which it occurs — consequences that satisfy some "need" of the systems. We are thus interested in the *typically recurring* forms or processes and their *typically recurring* consequences in different instances of the relevant system.

Functions are not, however, simply consequences. Within the general functional hypothesis there is the additional hypothesis that "needs" of the social system are in some fashion the cause of or lead to the existence of the agent forms or processes whose consequences satisfy that "need." In most functional analyses "need" has been a logically necessary but a metaphysical, teleological device. It

---

[5]Implied here is the distinction between the community as a physical-ecological context for social life and the community as a social system. Events may occur within the geographical confines of a community without having any direct relevance to that community as a social organization.

is necessary, if possible, to turn this bit of metaphysics into empirically testable statements.[6]

We propose that the only way to accomplish this is to translate "need" into "predictable or emerging consequences" of particular and specified conditions of the system at a given time. "Need" is what happens to a (social) system as a consequence of the continuation of the factors operating at a particular time if no new factors or processes enter: a prediction to be made on the basis of adequate knowledge of previous cases.

However, to use this notion of need as a causal explanation, it is necessary to assume that in viable systems, such as biological or social ones, there are processes which in effect anticipate the consequences of any given conditions and initiate measures to vitiate those consequences. The nature of this "anticipation" must be specified and empirically demonstrated, otherwise "need" has no scientific meaning.

Can we, with the data and knowledge available, propose functional hypotheses concerning official moralities that meet the requirements and conditions outlined above? Our evidence indicated that the official morality did not exist when there was a high degree of consensus and homogeneity of personal sentiments about drinking. It arose and became strong as this homogeneity in the community broke down — as more and more people began to believe that drinking was acceptable.[7] One informant put it this way: "This has always been a dry town, but we never talked about how dry it was until some people started to think that drinking was okay. Before that we just took it for granted that people thought drinking was wrong."

The examination of the official moralities of wartime (such as those concerning the character of the enemy) and of those found in industrial and hospital organizations (such as those concerning the value of the product or service) suggests that official moralities arise when two conditions exist: (1) when members of the community or association hold opposing and contradictory *personal* beliefs or value judgments and (2) when this value dimension is thought to be highly important to the welfare of the group.

These conditions also define situations that are believed to be potentially disruptive to the social system. Any argument over the legitimacy of the war or the humanity of the enemy, if extended to a national scale during the war, is thought to be disruptive to the war effort. That such disruption is an inevitable consequence of conflicting beliefs is beside the point. It has already been shown that, in the dynamics of social life, if a thing is thought to be true we act as if it were true. Hence a belief that ideological conflict is a threat brings forth responses to it as a threat.

In The Village it was assumed that an extended argument over drinking

---

[6]That the "needs" of social systems require demonstration has been noted by others (cf. Philip Selznick, *TVA and the Grass Roots* [Berkeley, Calif.: University of California Press, 1949], p. 252).

[7]This change in attitudes toward drinking was concurrent with changes in other attitudes and corresponds to the period of increasing contact with the outside world. A greater mobility following the hard-surfacing of a county road made contact easier with several nearby cities and a large metropolitan center. At the same time there was an increasing "segmentalization" of life — a separation of family, clique, associational, and employment relations from each other and from the locality.

would have disrupted the community. There was already an uneasy peace between competing leadership groups in various associations in The Village,[8] and, because of this, it was assumed that argument involving important sentiments would spread to other areas of conflict of interest. In their terms such an argument would "split this town wide open."

Our evidence shows (1) that in this case and in similar illustrations personal values held by different members of the community are contradictory and of considerable importance to the members; (2) that the members of the community believe that a public discussion of these value differences would be disruptive to the community and would have threatening consequences; and (3) that the official moralities in these cases have the consequence of preventing such discussion at the level of the community.

Our data on these instances of official morality do not show whether belief in the disruptive consequences of such value conflicts is a valid one. If we assume, for the purposes of the argument, that it is valid—that empirical studies will show that unrestrained argument over such an issue under these conditions will lead to schism and disorganization of the social system—then we would propose the following hypothesis.

Official moralities function to maintain the equilibrium of the social systems in which they occur by preventing public argument between those with conflicting personal beliefs. The official morality, the agent of this consequence, is brought into existence and is in part sustained by the belief that such arguments do have deleterious consequences.

This belief is a necessary but not a sufficient factor in the development of official moralities. Since not everyone in a social system is likely to recognize this possibility and act upon it, other "causes" are important. Such multiple causation of the agent is important to understanding and predicting its character in any particular instance. Here we wish merely to show that this belief is a crucial factor and that its existence is sufficient to satisfy the requirement that we demonstrate the nature of the connection between "need" and the rise of the agent for satisfying that need—the nature of the "anticipation."[9]

Since our argument started with an assumption which cannot be tested by the data available, it is necessary to examine the implications of the alternate assumption that the belief in the disruptive consequences of the value conflict is a myth. If this belief does not state real consequences of the given conditions, then official moralities will make no difference in the degree of organization within the system. It will thus be necessary to seek other typically recurring consequences and, having found them, to show their relationship to the factors which give rise to the official morality.

The test of these hypotheses depends upon showing through the study of a sufficient number of cases (1) that the conditions specified do lead to disorganization if official moralities (or some other agent with similar functions) do not arise; (2) that official moralities do have the consequences claimed; and (3) that the recognition of the consequences is a necessary condition to the rise of official morality and, in effect, connects the "need" with the agent.

[8]For a fuller description of this situation see Charles K. Warriner, "New Ways in Old Places," *Adult Leadership*, IV (April, 1956), 8–9, 32.

[9]It is not necessary to assume that the "need" always brings forth this or any other agent for its satisfaction. Social systems do disintegrate, just as organisms die.

IV

We have shown that "official morality," like other collective phenomena, may have an immediate collective reality without being mirrored in the personalities of the individual members of the group and that it exists through certain attitudes which define it as true for particular situations.

Using an empirical definition for "needs," we developed the hypotheses that official moralities function to maintain the equilibrium of systems under conditions of predictable disorganization and that this "need" is anticipated and gives rise to the agent of its satisfaction through the recognition of the threat by some members of the society.

It is hoped that the definition of the phenomenon and the statement of the hypotheses will induce others to help collect data on a sufficient number of cases to provide an adequate test.

DATA:
Invalidity
of Indirect and Direct Measures
# of Attitude Toward Cheating

LINTON C. FREEMAN / TÜRKÖZ ATAÖV

Tests for the indirect assessment of attitudes have gained some currency in the literature of social psychology. They have been used primarily as indexes to behavior in situations where social pressures have been assumed to inhibit truthful response to direct questions. In such situations investigators have frequently assumed that responses to indirect questions provide more valid behavioral indexes than responses to direct questions. A few studies of the correlation between direct and indirect questions have been made (Campbell, 1953; Parrish & Campbell, 1953; Proshansky, 1943; Rankin & Campbell, 1955; Robinson & Rohde, 1946; and Sanford & Rosenstock, 1952), but although Campbell has questioned the validity of indirect questions as indexes to behavior, no systematic study of this question has been reported. The present study was designed in an attempt to examine the validity of several types of indirect questions and a direct question against the criterion of overt behavior.

Procedure

In attempting to test the validity of indirect questions it was considered desirable to select an area of behavior in which social pressures are known to operate, yet one which would be amenable to direct observation. Cheating on examinations by students is such an area; it was chosen for this study.

"Invalidity of Indirect and Direct Measures of Attitude Toward Cheating," by Linton C. Freeman and Türköz Ataöv, from the *Journal of Personality*, vol. 28 (1960), pp. 444–47. Reprinted by permission of the publisher. Copyright 1960, Duke University Press, Durham, North Carolina.

Ss were a group of 38 freshmen and sophomores enrolled in introductory sociology at Syracuse University.

Actual cheating on an examination was measured by a device similar to the one suggested by Hartshorne and May (1928). Fifteen ambiguous questions were introduced into the students' regular mid-term examination. Five of these were true-false, five were fill-in, and five were multiple choice. After the tests were administered, responses to these fifteen questions were recorded and the least popular answers were chosen as "correct." A key was prepared for the whole examination, and at the next class period the Ss were asked to score their own tests. The instructor was called from the room and a student was drafted to read the "correct" answers. The papers were collected and the presence of a changed answer constituted an instance of actual cheating.

Since "correct" answers had been determined according to the criterion of least (rather than zero) frequency, some of the original answers of some Ss were correct. In order to equalize opportunity to cheat, therefore, cheating was recorded in terms of type of answer changed rather than as an absolute frequency. Each S had "missed" at least two questions of each of the three question types, so each had an opportunity to cheat for every type of question. Scoring in this fashion produced a rank order of cheating. Fifteen Ss changed no answers at all, seven changed only one type, seven changed two types, and nine changed answers of all three types. These results constituted a Guttman scale with a coefficient of reproducibility of .94 (Kuder-Richardson reliability coefficient = .76). True-false answers were changed most frequently, multiple choice answers (which had to be circled) were least frequently modified, and fill-in items were intermediate.

After a delay of four weeks a different E was introduced to the class and presented the Ss with a questionnaire entitled, "Honor System Questionnaire." This title was selected in an effort to direct the Ss attention away from the intent of the inquiry. The "honor system" was, at the time, a topic of general interest and discussion at Syracuse.

The form consisted of 24 indirect items, six each of four types. The first six were apparently information questions concerned with factual data about the honor system. Questions of this error-choice type have been discussed by Hammond (1948). Examples of those used in the present study are the following:

> What is the percentage of students who cheat in an average college class with the honor system? a. one tenth; b. one fourth; c. one half; d. three fourths; e. over three fourths.
> What is the percentage of students who cheat in an average college class without the honor system? a. one tenth; b. one fourth; c. one half; d. three fourths; e. over three fourths.

Scoring of these items was based upon the assumption that Ss who inflated their estimates of the proportion of cheating were themselves cheaters. Two of these six items were dropped because of lack of variability among their answers. The remaining four formed a Guttman scale with a coefficient of reproducibility of .95 (Kuder-Richardson $r = .30$).

The second set of questions required the Ss to decide whether students described in ambiguous hypothetical situations were cheating or not.

Here, the question form was similar to the projective questions discussed by Getzels (1951).

For example:

One student makes an excuse to leave the room.
Cheating ———— Not cheating ————
One student is whispering to the student next to him.
Cheating ———— Not cheating ————

Scoring here was based upon the assumption that Ss who perceived cheating were themselves cheaters. Again two items were dropped for the reason of minimal variability and the remaining four scaled with a coefficient of reproducibility of .98 (Kuder-Richardson $r = .30$).

The third set of questions represented a type derived from Smith (1947). They described cheating in a series of contrived situations and required the Ss to decide whether such cheating had really occurred—whether the statement was fact or rumor. For example:

T———   F———   A set of students developed a code such that by coughing they were able to communicate the answers.
T———   F———   A student went to a magic shop and bought a piece of equipment which would allow him to make his notes appear and disappear at will.

The assumption in this case was that Ss who believed the contrived situations were cheaters. Two items which showed no variability were dropped and the remaining four scaled with a coefficient of reproducibility of .95 (Kuder-Richardson $r = .49$).

The fourth set of questions were similar to those developed by Rosenzweig (1945) and Murray and Morgan (1945); they involved argument completion. Ss were presented with six line drawings of pairs of people in interaction à la Rosenzweig's P-F scale. In each case one person was shown making a provocative remark about cheating. Ss were required to complete the conversation. For example:

A student says, "Boy, did I cheat on that exam!" Complete the discussion.
A student says, "When you guys cheat like that the rest of us don't have a chance . . ." Complete the discussion.

Responses to these items were independently evaluated by two clinical psychologists.[1] The intercorrelation between these ratings was tested by means of Chi-square. Chi-square was 1.76; it failed to achieve significance at the 5 per cent level. In view of this demonstrated lack of reliability these items were dropped from further analysis.

Finally, at the end of the task, the students were requested to turn their

[1]These responses were evaluated by F. N. Arnhoff of New York State Department of Mental Hygiene and N. Goldman of Syracuse University. The authors wish to express their gratitude for their help.

papers over and write either "yes" or "no" in answer to the direct question, "Have you ever cheated in an exam?" Of the 38 students 5 claimed not to have cheated and 33 admitted having cheated.

Results

Analysis was conducted on the basis of responses to the direct question, three types of indirect questions, and observed cheating behavior. Intercorrelations among these variables were computed by means of Kendall's *tau*. The results are summarized in Table 1.

TABLE 1   **INTERCORRELATIONS OF INDIRECT INDEXES AND ACTUAL CHEATING (KENDALL'S**Tau**)**

Actual cheating		Indirect indexes		
.10	Set 1			
.03	−.08	Set 2		
−.19	.10	−.03	Set 3	
−.13	−.13	.18	.20	Direct question

Table 1 reveals no appreciable amount of relationship between any of the pairs of variables studied. All of the observed correlations are small, five of the eight are negative, and none is significant at the 5 per cent level.

Discussion

On the basis of the results shown in Table 1, it must be concluded that neither the indirect items nor the direct question used in this study were of any utility whatsoever in predicting overt behavior. Such a result does not, of course, demonstrate any general lack of validity on the part of items of either type. It does suggest, however, that in some cases at least, the results provided by either direct or indirect items cannot be accepted as indexes to behavior. Although it is possible that other items might provide valid indexes, or that items of these types might be valid in other settings, the results of this study do imply that such assumptions are not necessarily true. Most of all, this study had demonstrated the need for further study of the validity of indirect attitude items rather than their acceptance on faith as indexes to behavior.

Summary

This study examined the relationship between overt behavior, a direct question, and three types of indirect attitude items on a sample of 38 Ss. Ss were ranked in terms of observed cheating, they were questioned both directly and indirectly about cheating, and the results were correlated. Since all correlations were insignificant, the results of this study cast some doubt upon the validity of either direct or indirect items for the assessment of certain types of overt behavior.

References

Campbell, D. T. *A Study of leadership among submarine officers*. Columbus, Ohio: The Ohio State Univer. Res. Found., 1953.

Getzels, J. W. The assessment of personality and prejudice by the method of paired direct and projective questions. Unpublished doctoral dissertation, Harvard Univer., 1951.

Hammond, K. R. Measuring attitudes by error-choice and indirect method. *J. abnorm. soc. Psychol.*, 1948, **43**, 38–48.

Hartshorne, H., & May, M. A. *Studies in the nature of character: I*. New York: Macmillan, 1928.

Murray, H. A., & Morgan, Christina, D. A clinical study of sentiments. *Genet. Psychol. Monogr.*, 1945, *I & II*, 1–309.

Parrish, J. A., & Campbell, D. T. Measuring propaganda effects with direct and indirect attitude tests. *J. abnor. soc. Psychol.*, 1953, **48**, 3–9.

Proshansky, H. A projective method for the study of attitudes. *J. abnorm. soc. Psychol.*, 1943, **38**, 383–395.

Rankin, R. E., & Campbell, D. T. Galvanic skin response to Negro and white experimenters. *J abnorm. soc. Psychol.*, 1955, **51**, 30–33.

Robinson, D., & Rohde, S. Two experiments with an anti-Semitism poll. *J. abnor. soc. Psychol.*, 1946, **41**, 136–145.

Rosenzweig, S. The picture-association method and its application in a study of reactions to frustration. *J. Pers.*, 1945, **14**, 3–23.

Sanford, F. H., & Rosenstock, J. Projective techniques on the doorstep. *J. abnorm. soc. Psychol.*, 1952, **47**, 3–16.

Smith, G. H. Beliefs in statements labeled fact and rumor. *J. abnorm. soc. Psychol.*, 1947, **42**, 80–91.

Sometimes Consistency

It would be a serious selective distortion of the existing evidence to suggest that all of it indicates an incongruence between what people say and what they do. Consumers sometimes do change their buying habits in ways that they say they will,[19] people frequently do vote as they tell pollsters they will, urban relocation populations may accurately predict to interviewers the type of housing they will attempt to obtain,[20] local party politicians do in fact employ the campaign tactics which they believe to be most effective,[21] and youngsters will provide survey researchers with

19. Harold H. Martin, "Why She Really Goes to Market," *Saturday Evening Post*, Sept. 28, 1963, 40–43.

20. Laurence T. Cagle and Irwin Deutscher, "Housing Aspirations and Housing Achievement: The Relocation of Poor Families," *Social Problems* 18 (1970): 243–56.

21. Richard T. Frost, "Stability and Change in Local Party Politics," *Public Opinion Quarterly* 25 (1961): 221–35.

reports of their own contact or lack of contact with the police which are borne out by police records.[22] The empirical evidence can best be summarized as reflecting wide variation in the relationships between sentiments and acts.

As a result of their review of all of the studies on employee attitudes and performance, Brayfield and Crockett observe, "The scarcity of relationships, either positive or negative, demonstrated to date even among the best designed of the available studies leads us to question whether or not methodological changes alone would lead to a substantial increase in the magnitude of the obtained relationships."[23] Having arrived at the point where they are able to question the assumption that a relationship must obtain between what people say and what they do, these authors can now question whether or not the failure to observe such a relationship is necessarily a consequence of the inefficiency of the measuring instruments.

This observation parallels that made by Warriner: "In most studies," he declares, "an inconsistency is explained away by searching for some bias in the observational technique . . . ." He continues, "Our thesis is that at least one class of these inconsistencies is real (i.e., is not a function of faulty observational techniques) and has been inadequately accounted for in the past." It seems to me that any research is open to methodological criticisms and that, for an investigator to attribute his findings to that source when he does not get what he expects, is something of a cop-out. One may, if he wishes, attribute any findings to methodological deficiencies—whether they suggest no relationship, an inverse relationship, or a positive relationship. What Brayfield and Crockett and Warriner are suggesting is that methodological faults do not account for all of the observations. They have applied one half of the double screen referred to in Chapter One, but it doesn't seem to them to screen out everything. This is an important breakthrough since it permits them, and us, to look at alternative explanations, including conceptual considerations. Let us explore what our existing conceptions about the nature of the social world would lead us to expect.

What Else Could You Expect?

Consider for a moment, some of the more popular conceptual frameworks entertained by social scientists. They all seem to suggest that no matter what one's theoretical orientation may be, he has no reason to expect to find congruence between sentiments and acts and every reason to expect to find discrepancies between them. This is true even of the varieties of balance theory, currently popular in social science. Functionalism in sociology and anthropology, and dissonance in psychology,[24]

22. Dramatic evidence of this is provided in Robert H. Hardt, "Juvenile Suspects and Violations: A Comparative Study of Correlates of Two Delinquency Measures" (Diss., Syracuse University, 1965), Table 8, pp. 73ff. See also, Maynard L. Erickson and Lamar T. Empey, "Court Records, Undetected Delinquency, and Decision Making," *Journal of Criminal Law, Criminology and Police Science* 54 (1963): 456–69; Harwin L. Voss, "Ethnic Differentials in Delinquency in Honolulu," *Journal of Criminal Law, Criminology and Police Science* 54 (1963): 322–27; Robert H. Hardt and George Bodine, *Development of Self-Report Instruments in Delinquency Research* (Syracuse, N.Y.: Syracuse University Youth Development Center, 1964), pp. 19–25.

23. Brayfield and Crockett, "Employee Attitudes and Employee Performance," p. 415.

24. Among psychologists, it is fashionable to tag any statement about the relationship between two variables and the experiments which test that relationship as a "theory." The little theories proliferated in this manner are usually identified by the name of the man who made the statement and who, frequently with his students, tested it. The name Heider is closely associated with "balance" theory, and the name Festinger with "dissonance" theory. Essentially, these seem to me to be two sides of the same coin. There are, of course, innumerable others.

may posit a drive or strain toward consistency but such an image of man and society must carry with it the assumption that, at any point in time, a condition of imbalance or dissonance or inconsistency obtains. A drive toward balance could not be a viable force unless we were constantly in a state of imbalance!

If one chooses, on the other hand, to work with such psychoanalytic concepts as the unconscious or the subconscious or the various defense mechanisms, then it must be assumed that people cannot themselves know how they might behave under specified conditions. Furthermore, such mechanisms as repression or rationalization suggest that respondents may not be able to tell an interviewer how they have behaved in the past. Turning to such dissimilar sociological ancestors as Charles H. Cooley and Emile Durkheim, we find that they built their concepts of man in society around the assumption that human nature requires social constraints. Under such conditions there is an inherent conflict between man's private self and his social self, hence the area of role theory is developed to help us understand some of the devices by which man is constrained to act appropriately in diverse social situations.

On the gross societal level (macro-sociological analysis), such concepts as social disorganization, anomie, and cultural lag suggest that people can be caught up in discrepant little worlds which make conflicting demands upon them.[25] The immigrant to a new world has been described as assuming new forms of behavior while clinging to older attitudes and beliefs. In the developing countries of Africa, the idea of cultural lag leads us to expect that the rapid acceptance of new behaviors may outrun, at least for a while, the rejection of old norms. Or perhaps behavioral changes may not be able to keep pace with the rapid acceptance of new norms. Either way, the outcome must be inconsistent attitudes and behaviors!

When we consider the behavior of groups smaller than societies, we frequently think in terms such as situational contingencies, the definition of the situation, public and private behavior, or reference-group theory—all of which relate what one does or what one says to the immediate context, both as it exists objectively and as it exists in the mind of the actor. Do we not expect attitudes and behaviors to vary as the definition of the situation is altered or as different reference groups are brought to bear? The symbolic interactionists have traditionally exhibited the greatest sensitivity to this problem in sociology. Among others, both Blumer and LaPiere have insisted that we act, either verbally or overtly, in response to the symbolic meaning the confronting object has for us in the given situation. A question put to me by an interviewer concerning how I feel about Armenian women forces me to respond to the words and to the interviewer; standing face-to-face with a real flesh-and-blood Armenian woman, I find myself constrained to act toward a very different set of symbols. Is there any reason to assume that my behavior should be the same in these two radically different symbolic situations?

25. One of the neatest expositions and applications of the social disorganization perspective appears in an undergraduate textbook (Robert E. L. Faris, *Social Disorganization*, [New York: The Ronald Press Co., 1948]). Merton's essay, "Social Structure and Anomie," along with the large amounts of research it has generated, is built around the notion of discrepancies between cultural goals and institutionalized means of achieving them (in Robert K. Merton, *Social Theory and Social Structure* [Glencoe, Ill.: The Free Press, rev. enl. edn., 1957], Chapters 4 and 5). William F. Ogburn's concept of cultural lag is sometimes thought to apply only to material objects and their adoption, but has a rich potential when applied to ideologies, norms, values, and beliefs (William F. Ogburn, "Cultural Lag as Theory," *Sociology and Social Research*, 61 [1957], reprinted in *William F. Ogburn on Culture and Social Change*, ed. O. D. Duncan [Chicago: University of Chicago Press, 1964], 86–95).

In his distinction between the psychology of prejudice and the sociology of intergroup relations, Arnold Rose has developed a vigorous symbolic interactionist argument regarding the theoretical and empirical independence of attitudes and behaviors.[26] Underpinning this conceptual framework is Herbert Blumer's interpretation of the social philosophy of George Herbert Mead.[27] From such a perspective, verbal behavior and overt behavior may be seen as different segments of a single act in process. Apparent inconsistencies can be conceptualized as resulting from errors in interpretation on the part of the actor, or from reinterpretation of the meaning of the act during the interval between the moment of verbal expression and the moment of overt behavior. This formulation also sensitizes the investigator to the possibility that the apparent inconsistency is a result of the actor's perception of the verbalization and the overt behavior as segments of two different acts; i.e., regardless of the investigator's intent, the word and the deed may be perceived by the actor as relating to different objects. Or, employing a distinction created by Rokeach, people may have attitudes toward objects and they may have attitudes toward situations and the two need not be related.[28]

One conceptual framework which we tend to neglect lies in the underdeveloped field of sociolinguistics. Although it may be many other things, sociolinguistics should also deal with an analysis of the meanings of verbal communications. As late as 1965, the central methodological role of language in social research continued to elude a gathering of some of the foremost sociolinguists in America.[29] There has indeed been a latent concern throughout the history of American sociology. It can be found in both Cooley's and Mead's fascination with the use of personal pronouns in the development of the social self, as well as in fragments of discontinuous work by sociologists like Everett Hughes, C. Wright Mills, Leonard Schatzman and Anselm Strauss, and James H. S. Bossard.[30] We have not been sufficiently concerned with whether people understood our questions as we intended or whether we understood their responses as they intended. Furthermore, as Mark Benney and Everett Hughes have put it, "The interview, as itself a form of social rhetoric, is not merely a tool of sociology but a part of its very subject matter."[31] More recently, the

26. Arnold M. Rose, "Intergroup Relations vs. Prejudice: Pertinent Theory for the Study of Social Change," *Social Problems* 4 (1956): 173–76.

27. Herbert Blumer, "Sociological Implications of the Thought of George Herbert Mead," *American Journal of Sociology* 71 (1966): 535–44.

28. Milton Rokeach, *Beliefs, Attitudes, and Values* (San Francisco: Jossey-Bass, Inc., 1970), pp. 128–129ff., especially Chapters 5 and 6.

29. Charles A. Ferguson, "Directions in Sociolinguistics: Report on an Interdisciplinary Seminar," *Social Science Research Council Items* 19 (1965): 1–4.

30. See, for example, "What's in a Name," Chapter 9 in Everett C. Hughes and Helen MacGill Hughes, *Where Peoples Meet: Racial and Ethnic Frontiers* (Glencoe, Ill.: The Free Press, 1952), pp. 130–44; C. Wright Mills' better-known essays, "Language, Logic, and Culture," "Situated Actions and Vocabularies of Motive," and "Methodological Consequences of the Sociology of Knowledge," appear in sequence with a less well-known piece entitled, "The Language and Ideas of Ancient China," in *Power, Politics, and People*, ed. Irving Louis Horowitz (New York: Ballantine Books, 1963), pp. 423–520; Leonard Schatzman and Anselm Strauss, "Social Class and Modes of Communication," *American Journal of Sociology* 60 (1955): 329–38; James H. S. Bossard, "Family Table Talk: An Area for Sociological Study," *American Sociological Review* 8 (1943): 295–301 and also by Bossard, "Family Modes of Expression," *American Sociological Review* 10 (1945): 226–37.

31. Mark Benney and Everett C. Hughes, "Of Sociology and the Interview: Editorial Preface," *American Journal of Sociology* 62 (1956): 137–42.

ethnomethodologists have contributed to a resurgent interest in everyday natural speech as sociological data.[32]

A linguistic perspective provides an untapped potential for understanding the relationship between what people say and what they do. What differences in meaning can be conveyed by different people with the same words? The eloquent black teen-age prostitute, Kitten, can find herself involved in a $100 misunderstanding only because she thinks she is listening to someone who speaks the same language.[33] The truth of the matter is that, unfortunately, she and her Babbitt-like white college sophomore protagonist employ the same vocabulary to speak different languages. Might this not also sometimes occur between interviewer and interviewee? In an address in 1965, I raised the question (only half seriously) of whether one could safely assume that the dichotomy between a negative response and an affirmative response was as easily translatable as it seemed to be: "Should we assume that a response of 'yah,' 'da,' 'si,' 'oui,' or 'yes' all really mean exactly the same thing in response to the same question? Or may there be different kinds of affirmative connotations in different languages?"[34] I have since discovered that this was a more serious question than I had thought. I learned, for example, that "a simple English 'no' tends to be interpreted by members of the Arabic culture as meaning 'yes.' A real 'no' would need to be emphasized; the simple 'no' indicates a desire for further negation. Likewise a nonemphasized 'yes' will often be interpreted as a polite refusal."[35]

As it happens, this problem is not restricted to exotic languages and cultures. It occurred to me that part of the conventional wisdom of American college men is that when a girl says "no" she may mean "yes." Even more revealing is David Riesman's finding that, in effect, there is something of the Arab (or college girl) in English-speaking American professors. Riesman personally interviewed survey respondents to the Lazarsfeld and Thielens teacher apprehension study. He asked the professors about their responses to precoded alternatives and concluded that, "It sometimes happens that people torn between 'yes' and 'no,' will answer in one direction and then add qualifications in the other, showing for example that their

---

32. See, for example, Garfinkel's use of dialogue as data in Harold Garfinkel, *Studies in Ethnomethodology* (Englewood Cliffs, N.J.: Prentice-Hall, Inc., 1967), pp. 24–31ff., 38–44; or Aaron Cicourel's concern for the relationship between legal and everyday uses of family terms in his "Kinship, Marriage, and Divorce in Comparative Family Law," *Law and Society Review* 1 (1967): 103–29; other examples are Jerry Jacobs, "A Phenomenological Study of Suicide Notes," *Social Problems* 15 (1967): 60–72; George Psathas and James M. Henslin, "Dispatched Orders and the Cab Driver," *Social Problems* 14 (1967): 424–43; Marvin B. Scott and Stanford M. Lyman, "Accounts," *American Sociological Review* 33 (1968): 46–62.

33. Robert Gover, *The One-Hundred Dollar Misunderstanding* (New York: Ballantine Books, 1963).

34. Irwin Deutscher, "Words and Deeds: Social Science and Social Policy," *Social Problems* 13 (1966): 249.

35. Edmund S. Glenn, "Semantic Differences in International Communication," *Etc.: A Review of General Semantics* 11 (1954): 163–80. See also, William H. Hunt, Crane W. Wilder, and John C. Wahlke, "Interviewing Political Elites in Cross-Cultural Comparative Research," *American Journal of Sociology* 70 (1964): 59–68. This research team was informed by an Austrian respondent that "every 'yes' has its 'however,' and every 'no' its 'if.'" They also report that "it was not possible to find a French equivalent for 'may or may not' as a check-list response" (p. 66).

'yes' doesn't quite mean 'yes,' and may even lean toward 'no.'"[36] I would suggest that it may be impossible to accurately translate most words in any language to any other language.

Words are fragments of linguistic configurations; they mean nothing in isolation from the configuration. We have a great deal to learn from linguistics if we can bring ourselves to view language from the perspective of the symbolic interactionist and the ethnomethodologist—as social and cultural symbolism. Clearly, I have developed a certain respect for the explanatory power of the symbolic interactionist perspective. The basis for this respect is developed in Chapters Ten and Eleven. I do not believe that I held (much less understood) this position when I began the present exploration in 1964. It came to appear to me as one of the more reasonable and empirically correct modes of explanation as I tried to make sense out of the morass of data I was drowning in. It is, however, not my purpose at this point to urge anyone's conversion to a symbolic interactionist perspective. I will be satisfied if the reader will agree that no matter what his perspective, there is no basis for assuming consistency between what people say and what they do.

Let me suggest that, as an intellectual exercise, you take whatever other conceptual frameworks you may be partial to or comfortable with and determine whether or not they permit you to assume that you can expect people to act in accordance with their words. Meanwhile, I will return to Brayfield and Crockett, who helped me earlier with the transition from method to theory: "Foremost among [the] implications," of their review of research, "is the conclusion that it is time to question the strategic and ethical merits of selling to industrial concerns an assumed relationship between employee attitudes and employee performance."[37] It is but a slight extension of this conclusion to question the strategic and ethical merits of selling anything to anyone or to any establishment, based on the dubious assumption that what people say is related directly to what they do. For example, if we had only LaPiere's verbal data to go on, surely we would suggest to minority peoples that they are unlikely to find food or lodging on a cross-country auto trip. His behavioral indicators lead to no such recommendation. It seems clear to me that there are implications in all this for the role of social science research in policy recommendations. Research aimed at evaluation or demonstration frequently tends to make precisely the assumption which I have been challenging: that what people say is a predictor of what they will do.

There is a body of folk-wisdom encased in such aphorisms as: "The proof of the pudding is in the eating," "Put up or shut up," "Talk is cheap," and others. These suggest that in the common sense world of the man in the street, everyday life may be governed in part by a rule which implies doubt as to the probability or the intention of others acting as they speak. If there is an "Ah, ha!" quality about all this, then I suspect that that is what sociology is all about. It is true that the common sense world of the sociologist is not the same as the common sense world of the man in the street. But it is not at all clear which of the two incorporates the most effective methodology for understanding and dealing with recurrent problems of human interaction and social processes.

---

36. David Riesman, "Some Observations on the Interviewing in the Teacher Apprehension Study," in *The Academic Mind*, eds. Paul F. Lazarsfeld and Wagner Thielens, Jr. (Glencoe, Ill.: The Free Press, 1958), p. 277n.

37. Brayfield and Crockett, "Employee Attitudes and Employee Performance," p. 421.

This I take to be the central theme of ethnomethodology, as Harold Garfinkel has named it. The position deserves to be considered with respect. Under incessant needling by a group of prominent sociologists, Garfinkel makes it clear that he intends no irony in his choice of terms.[38] He contrasts ethnomethodology with such fields as ethnobotany or ethnoastronomy which, he suggests, are ironic. By this he means that the ethnoastronomer (or whatever) studies the curious (perhaps naive and certainly "unscientific") manner by which primitive peoples explain the workings of the solar system and the celestial universe. This primitive folk knowledge is evaluated and judged by the standards of Western science. It is essentially an ethnocentric procedure whereby we see how close the simple folk have guessed the truth as we know it to be. Ethnomethodology, in contrast, assumes that the man in the street governs his everyday relations with others by a set of rules. It is these rules which, taken for granted though they may be, constitute an effective methodology for human relations. I suspect that sociologists have been remiss in not being more attentive to the fact that every man must indeed be his own social scientist if he is to survive at any level in a human society.

I suspect, furthermore, that we need to make a more deliberate effort to discover what everyman knows but takes for granted in negotiating his everyday life with others. The more orthodox symbolic interactionists deliberately involve themselves in the little worlds they study precisely in order to discover that "Ah, ha!" quality of those worlds—to render their social processes and perspectives explicit.[39] The ethnomethodologist, although operating on some of the same assumptions for the same purposes, takes a somewhat different methodological stance. Since members of little social worlds are seen as behaving according to rules which they take for granted, the researcher must maintain a certain distance in order to avoid being seduced into those taken-for-granted worlds. Only by maintaining a degree of detachment—as a stranger—can the investigator perceive what members routinely assume.

But why do I fuss so? Science is a cumulative affair and sociology is young. Given time to build a body of knowledge, we will discover our mistakes, rectify them, and systematically move ahead. Yet, as I have suggested in Chapter Two, it sometimes seems that we aren't getting anywhere. This may be a myopic view, but in Chapter Four we will examine more closely, using a case-study approach, the "progress" we have been making in understanding the relationship between sentiments and acts.

38. *Proceedings of the Purdue Symposium on Ethnomethodology*, eds. Richard J. Hill and Kathleen Stones Crittenden (Purdue, Indiana: Institute for the Study of Social Change, Department of Sociology, Purdue University, 1968), pp. 7–17ff.

39. The better collections of illustrations of what symbolic interactionists do include: *Human Behavior and Social Processes: An Interactionist Approach*, ed. Arnold M. Rose (Boston: Houghton Mifflin Company, 1962); *Institutions and the Person: Essays Presented to Everett C. Hughes*, eds. Howard S. Becker, Blanche Geer, David Riesman, and Robert S. Weiss (Chicago: Aldine Publishing Company, 1968); *Pathways to Data: Field Methods for Studying Ongoing Social Organizations*, ed. Robert W. Habenstein (Chicago: Aldine Publishing Company, 1970).

4   A Cumulative Science?

The Test of Time

My first careful reading and comparison of available literature on the so-called attitude-behavior problem left me with an uneasy feeling. I began pondering the possibility that we weren't getting anywhere: research done in the fifties left me with the
impression that I was not being informed much beyond what I had learned from
LaPiere's 1934 article. As is likely to happen with such disturbing thoughts, this one
was tucked away in a dark corner where it would not offend me — but not for long.
In 1965 Lawrence Linn published the paper included in this chapter. That paper
provided an opportunity to undertake at least a partial test of our cumulative knowledge about sentiments and acts. Since there is a great deal of research being conducted on a great many problems in the social sciences, it cannot be assumed that
progress will proceed apace in all fields. No one empirical test can reflect on all of
social science, but it is necessary to start somewhere, and I had found what seems to
me to be a propitious starting place.

      The LaPiere piece was published in the mid-thirties and up until Linn's
1965 article, the only clearly comparable and credible piece of research had been
Melvin DeFleur and Frank Westie's 1958 article. Linn provided the third point on a
time line. Obviously these three studies are far from identical and, as the reader can
see for himself, in some important ways not even comparable. On the other hand,
we could not have learned anything about continuity in knowledge if all we had
were replications, since, in that case, each study would simply duplicate the errors
(or truths) of the previous one. (This point will be developed in our discussion of
validity and reliability in Chapter Five.) What makes these three studies useful for
our purposes is, first, that each represents an acceptable degree of craftsmanship for
its time. They are not straw men, but are, rather, reasonable exemplars of sociological research. Second, it is fortuitous that they are well spaced over a thirty-year
period.

      There are four other important qualities which these three studies share.
Most important is the fact that each deals with the relationship between verbal
expressions and overt acts, and in each, both the word and the deed are recorded for
the same population. Furthermore, each employs the same substantive problem situation: dominant-group attitudes and acts toward a minority. In addition, each is an
empirical study which attempts to rigorously design and control the research situation. Finally, all three of them employ the same style of reporting the problems, the
methods, and the results, and all three are published. For these reasons I felt that the
opportunity had presented itself to test my uneasy hunch about progress in research. The test is only partial, to be sure, but it is nevertheless an improvement
over the hunch.

In late 1965 I had the opportunity to subject the three articles to a detailed analysis and, at a professional meeting in the spring of 1966, I read the resulting paper. It was later distributed in mimeograph form and I used it as a basis for parts of some of my graduate seminars for several years. With the emergence of the *American Sociologist* as a lively forum for methodological debate under the editorship of Raymond Mack, and at the urging of a group of graduate students, I sent the paper to that journal in 1968. It was published early in 1969.[1] The remainder of this chapter and much of Chapter Five is based on that 1969 article. But there have been modifications, largely as a result of the extensive and thoughtful feedback which followed its publication.[2] The most comprehensive critique came from a group of Illinois psychologists and is included in Chapter Five. What follows, then, is an analysis of three cases that provide an opportunity to improve upon my guess about the extent to which we have been progressing methodologically in the kind of social research which is the concern of this volume. Let us examine the progress of three decades of sociological pursuit of answers to the same question.

1. Irwin Deutscher, "Looking Backward: Case Studies on the Progress of Sociological Research," *American Sociologist* 4 (1969): 35–41.
2. Leonard Gordon, "Letter: On Attitude-Behavior Correlations," *American Sociologist* 4 (1969): 250–51; William L. Ewans, "Letter: Looking Backward Through a Glass Darkly," *American Sociologist* 4 (1969): 251; Carlo L. Lastrucci, "Looking Forward: The Case for Hard-Nosed Methodology," *American Sociologist* 5 (1970): 273–75; Icek Ajzen, Russell K. Darroch, Martin Fishbein, and John A. Hornik, "Looking Backward Revisited: A Reply to Deutscher," *American Sociologist* 5 (1970): 267–73 (reprinted in Chapter Five of this volume).

DATA:
Verbal Attitudes and Overt Acts:
An Experiment on the Salience of Attitudes
MELVIN L. DEFLEUR / FRANK R. WESTIE

In the face of the steady stream of studies of the verbal dimension of attitudinal behavior, the paucity of investigations of the overt-action correlates of such verbal behavior is indeed striking. Those who have conducted attitude research are not surprised by this one-sided emphasis: overt acceptance-avoidance acts are extremely difficult to isolate and measure. One source of this difficulty lies in the fact that few, if any, standardized situations or instruments have been developed enabling the investigator to quantify, on a positive-negative continuum, an accep-

"Verbal Attitudes and Overt Acts: An Experiment on the Salience of Attitudes," by Melvin L. DeFleur and Frank R. Westie, from *American Sociological Review*, vol. 23 (1958), pp. 667–73. Reprinted by permission of the authors and the American Sociological Association.

tance or avoidance act for a set of subjects, with other conditions held constant.[1]

The present paper reports an attempt to develop an instrument which can readily be used in an interview situation for measuring the "salience" of a person's attitudinal orientations. It also explores the use of reference groups by subjects whose attitudinal salience is being measured. The term *salience* can be defined as the readiness of an individual to translate his (previously expressed verbal) attitude into overt action in relation to the attitude object. The relationship between inner conviction and overt behavior has frequently been discussed in connection with the validity of measures of verbal attitudes. In a thorough summary of the literature, Green[2] comments on this view of attitude measurement validity, pointing out that the validity of an attitude scale is actually the extent to which it truly represents behavior within a particular *attitude universe*. He distinguishes between a verbal attitude universe, from which attitude scale items are drawn, and an action attitude universe, consisting of a variety of overt behavior forms regarding the attitude object. Validity in the measurement of an attitude is the problem of determining the degree to which it measures behavior within its appropriate universe; it is not necessarily a problem of determining the extent to which it predicts behavior from one universe to another. In line with this view, the purpose of the present study is not to develop a device for "validating" other attitude instruments. Its aim rather is to provide a simple device which can be used as an "action opportunity" for a subject to give public and overt testimony of his acceptance or rejection of a Negro in a specific action context.

Studies of Inconsistency

Earlier studies indicate that a person's verbal acceptance or rejection of minority groups may be quite unrelated to what he actually does or would do in overt interaction situations. For example, in company with a couple from China, LaPiere[3] made an extensive tour of the Pacific Coast and transcontinental United States during which they were accommodated by over 250 restaurants, hotels, and similar establishments. Refusal of service by virtue of the racial characteristics of the Chinese occurred only once. But when LaPiere sent each establishment a letter and questionnaire requesting a statement of its policy regarding accommodating Chinese clients, over 90 per cent of the replies noted that they adhered to a policy of non-acceptance of such minority group members. In these cases, the overt act reversed the stated intention.

In a more recent study of overt behavior or action attitudes by Lohman and Reitzes[4] 151 residents of an urban neighborhood were located who were also

[1]There have been several attempts to develop *hypothetical situations tests* as measures of what subjects thought they might do in hypothetical situations which were described to them. Such statements of belief are not conceptually different from other forms of verbal behavior with which verbal attitudes are measured. See, e.g., A. C. Rosander, "An Attitude Scale Based Upon Behavior Situations," *Journal of Social Psychology*, 8 (February, 1937), pp. 3–15. Also: C. Robert Pace, "A Situations Test To Measure Social-Political-Economic Attitudes," *Journal of Social Psychology*, 10 (August, 1939), pp. 331–344.

[2]Bert F. Green, "Attitude Measurement," in Gardner Lindzey, editor, *Handbook of Social Psychology*, Cambridge, Mass.: Addison-Wesley, 1954, Vol. I, Chapter 9.

[3]Richard T. LaPiere, "Attitudes vs. Actions," *Social Forces*, 13 (December, 1934), pp. 230–237.

[4]Joseph D. Lohman and Dietrich C. Reitzes, "Deliberately Organized Groups and Racial Behavior," *American Sociological Review*, 19 (June, 1954), pp. 342–348.

members of a particular labor union. Two conflicting norms regarding behavior toward Negroes prevailed in these two collectivities. The urban neighborhood was predominantly white and was resisting Negro penetration; a property owners association (of which the subjects were members) had been organized for this purpose. In this behavioral area, that is, with respect to having a Negro for a neighbor, the subjects uniformly acted in an anti-Negro manner. However, the 151 subjects also belonged to a labor union with a clear and well implemented policy of granting Negroes complete equality on the job. Here, then, with the same subjects and the same attitude object, were two seemingly opposite action forms. An explanation of this situation in terms of individual verbal attitudes would be inadequate. The authors show that each of the formal organizations (the union and property owners association) provided the individual with a set of well formulated reasons and justifications for his actions in each of these spheres. Clearly, action attitudes may be determined to a considerable degree by the extent to which the individual is actually or psychologically involved in social systems providing him with norms and beliefs which he can use as guides to action when *specific* action opportunities arise.

In studying attitude salience, then, it may be predicted that individuals faced with the necessity of making an action decision with regard to Negroes will partially determine the direction of this action by consideration of the norms and policies of social groups which are meaningful to them. Ordinarily, we do not expect subjects to be involved in such well defined groups, with clearly specified policies regarding action toward Negroes, as those studied by Lohman and Reitzes. Norms and guides to action in more ordinary situations are more likely to be derived from family, friends, or other persons used as reference groups. For this reason, the present paper includes a probe into the reference groups invoked in an action decision made by subjects regarding public involvement with Negroes.

In the larger program of experiments, of which the present report is a part, the subjects were studied from the standpoint of the relationship between three dimensions of their attitudinal behavior: verbal, autonomic-physiological, and overt. There were three phases to this research: attitude testing, a laboratory session in which the subjects' autonomic-physiological responses to race stimuli were recorded, and a post-laboratory interview. This paper, however, is concerned only with the relationship between the verbal and overt dimensions and draws its data largely from the post-laboratory interview.

The Summated Differences Scales[5] were administered to 250 students in introductory sociology classes. From the 250 cases, two smaller groups were selected for more intensive study. The distribution of total scores was determined,

[5]This device employs the principle of eliciting a response to a white person of a given occupational status and then, many pages later, a response to a Negro of the same occupational status, each portrayed in the same hypothetical relationship with the respondent. Numerical differences between the responses to whites and to Negroes are then summed. For example, in one item the respondent is asked to respond (from "strongly agree" to "strongly disagree" in five possible categories) to the statement "I believe I would be willing to have a *Negro Doctor* have his hair cut at the same barber shop where I have mine cut." Later, after approximately 200 items have been interposed, he is asked to respond to the statement, "I believe I would be willing to have a *White Doctor* have his hair cut at the barber shop where I have mine cut." Thus, a respondent may "strongly disagree" to one of these propositions and "agree" to the other. The wide separation between the white and Negro of identical occupation by interposing a great many items provides a concealment

and from those scoring in the top quartile (indicating the greatest verbal rejection of Negroes) 23 subjects were selected on the basis of eight criteria (noted below). These individuals were carefully matched, by the method of frequency distribution control, with 23 subjects scoring in the lowest quartile (indicating the least verbal rejection of Negroes). The matching process reduced the size of the original group substantially, but 46 subjects were thus carefully selected for their similarity on eight characteristics of their social background. The frequency distributions of the groups were matched according to age, sex (half of each group was male), marital status, religion, social class, social mobility experience, residential history, and previous contact with Negroes. For convenience, we refer to that group showing the greatest verbal rejection of Negroes as the "prejudiced group," and their counterparts at the opposite end of the verbal scales as the "unprejudiced group."

Method

After each subject had completed a laboratory session in which his autonomic responses to race relations stimuli were recorded,[6] he was conducted to an interview room where a variety of questions, devices, and situations were presented to him regarding his feelings about Negroes. Shortly before the end of this hour-long post-laboratory interview the subject was presented with what may be called an "overt action opportunity." In the laboratory session, and in earlier phases of the interview, each subject had viewed a number of colored photographic slides showing interracial pairings of males and females. Some of these

factor. The ability of the respondent to remember how he responded earlier is greatly reduced by this control. The difference between the responses is given a numerical value indicating differential acceptance of the white and Negro of the same occupational status in this particular relationship with the respondent. A total of eight occupational categories are involved and a large variety of activities. In all, over 500 responses are elicited from a given subject. The respondent's total score is simply the summated numerical differences between his responses to whites and Negroes of similar occupation in a variety of relationships with the respondent. The total score indicates the extent to which the respondent regards Negroes as objects to be accepted or rejected as compared to whites.

The reliability coefficients of the scales were derived through testing and retesting 99 undergraduate students of Indiana University. The time interval between the test and retest was five weeks. The reliability coefficients were as follows:

Scale I   Residential: $r = .95$
Scale II   Position: $r = .95$
Scale III Interpersonal-Physical: $r = .80$
Scale IV   Interpersonal-Social: $r = .87$
Combined Scores: $r = .96$

For a detailed discussion of this device, see Frank R. Westie, "A Technique for the Measurement of Race Attitudes," *American Sociological Review*, 18 (February, 1953), pp. 73–78.

[6]These autonomic responses to racial stimuli are described in some detail in a paper forthcoming in the *Journal of Abnormal and Social Psychology*. Briefly, they consist of galvanic skin responses and changes in finger blood volume occurring when prejudiced and unprejudiced subjects viewed photographic slides portraying Negroes and whites of both sexes shown singly and in all possible pairs. The results indicate that attitudinal responses include changes in the autonomic system which differ for types of subjects classified as prejudiced and unprejudiced.

slides portrayed a well-dressed, good looking, young Negro man paired with a good looking, well-dressed, young white woman. Others showed a white man similarly paired with a Negro woman. The backgound for all of the slides consisted of a table, a lamp, and a window with a drapery, giving an effect not unlike that of a living room or possibly a dormitory lounge. The persons in the photographs were seated beside each other in separate chairs, and were looking at one another with pleasant expressions. The photographer and models had been instructed to strive for a portrayal of cordiality, but not romance.[7] Each of the 46 subjects had given projective interpretations of "what was happening" in these pictures.

To present the overt action opportunity, the interviewer told each subject that another set of such slides was needed for further research. The subject was first asked if he (or she) would be willing to be photographed with a Negro person of the opposite sex, a request which elicited a wide variety of responses, as well as considerable hesitation in many cases. A number indicated willingness, but others refused categorically to be so photographed. Then, regardless of his (or her) stated position, the subject was presented with a mimeographed form and informed that this was "a standard *photograph release agreement*, which is necessary in any situation where a photograph of an individual is to be used in any manner." The photograph release agreement contained a graded series of "uses" to which the photograph would be put (see Figure 1), ranging from laboratory experiments, such as they had just experienced, to a nationwide publicity campaign advocating racial integration. They were to sign their name to each "use" which they would permit.[8]

In American society, the affixing of one's signature to a document is a particularly significant act. The signing of checks, contracts, agreements, and the like is clearly understood to indicate a binding obligation on the part of the signer to abide by the provisions of the document. The signing of the document in the present study took on additional significance due to the involvement of the racial variable.

The problem of the validity and reliability of this device as a measure of the salience of a subject's attitude toward Negroes can be only partially answered at present. Various approaches to establishing the validity of measuring instruments have been discussed in the literature.[9] The question of acceptable criteria of validity for a particular instrument has received many answers, and the entire issue is currently a controversial one. Such validating techniques as the "known groups" method are unacceptable for measures of salience because the evidence for validity rests upon comparisons of groups on the basis of known *verbal* attitudes. Correlating the instrument with other measures of overt acceptance-avoidance acts would be a useful method, but no standardized instruments exist for such a task.

[7]This effort to avoid romantic and sexual connotations was made so that the slides could be used as projective devices in another phase of the research. In spite of these efforts, female subjects tended to "see" these situations as romantic.

[8]In all cases, it was emphasized to the subject that he was free to terminate his participation in the experiment at any time. He was told that he could do so without prejudice on the part of the interviewer, and that he would remain anonymous in this decision. No subject took advantage of this opportunity.

[9]See, e.g., Harold Gulliksen, "Intrinsic Validity," *The American Psychologist,* 5 (October, 1950), pp. 511–517.

If the items in an instrument are a reasonably good representation of the items characterizing the attitudinal universe, many investigators would say that the scale is valid by definition, that is, it has *face validity*. The term *intrinsic validity* has been used by Gulliksen to describe this situation.[10] A method which he suggests for at least a preliminary approach to validating an instrument is to employ a group of "experts" to evaluate the items selected for a measuring device.

In a modified version of Gulliksen's procedure, the series of "photograph usages" was submitted in random order to eight judges, who were sociolo-

[10]*Ibid.*

Figure 1. Photograph Authorization

The directors of the experiment you just participated in need more photographs like you saw on the screen (with Negroes and whites posed together). If you will volunteer to pose for such photographs, please indicate the conditions under which you will allow these pictures to be used by signing the "releases" below. You may sign *some of them, all of them* or *none of them as you see fit.* (It is standard practice to obtain such a signed release for any kind of photograph which is to be used for some purpose.)

If you are not interested in participating in this phase of the study, you are absolutely free to do as you wish. If you do not want to commit yourself in any way on this matter, it is perfectly all right and we will respect your decision. Whatever you do, your decision will be held in the strictest confidence.

I will pose for a photograph (of the same type as in the experiment) with a Negro person of the opposite sex with the following restrictions on its use:

1. I will allow this photograph to be used in laboratory experiments where it will be seen only by professional sociologists.

    Signed . . . .

2. I will allow this photograph to be published in a technical journal read only by professional sociologists.

    Signed . . . .

3. I will allow this photograph to be shown to a few dozen University students in a laboratory situation.

    Signed . . . .

4. I will allow this photograph to be shown to hundreds of University students as a teaching aid in Sociology classes.

    Signed . . . .

5. I will allow this photograph to be published in the *Student Newspaper* as part of a publicity report on this research.

    Signed . . . .

6. I will allow this photograph to be published in my home town newspaper as part of a publicity report on this research.

    Signed . . . .

7. I will allow this photograph to be used in a nation-wide publicity campaign *advocating racial integration.*

    Signed . . . .

gists of faculty status. The judges were asked to rate the usages, ranking first the use to which they felt the prejudiced person would least object. There was almost complete agreement among their rankings: only one judge reversed the order of a single adjacent pair in the 618 pair-judgments. In the eyes of presumably competent specialists, then, the items of the instrument represent an ordered sample of acts which prejudiced persons would object to in regularly increasing degrees.

The items in the instrument were designed and arranged so that they represent a cumulative series, thereby providing an obvious possibility for scaling. This was not undertaken, however, with the present version of the instrument due to the relatively small number of scale items and subjects. Nevertheless, the response patterns show almost complete transitivity: in only three of the 46 cases were there irregularities in the cumulative feature of the instrument. (In these three instances subjects did not sign an item lower on the scale, selecting one with a higher rank.) This pattern is a rough indication that the reproducibility would be rather good if the items were to be scaled. Such evidence of transitivity, of course, gives only a partial answer to the question of reliability, just as the judgments of experts meet only partially the validity problem.

The subjects uniformly perceived the behavioral situation posed for them as a highly realistic request, and many clearly exhibited discomfort at being caught in a dilemma. Wishing to cooperate with the interviewer, they nevertheless preferred to be uninvolved in a photograph with a Negro of opposite sex. There were a few, of course, who were quite willing to sign the agreement and did so without hesitation.

Verbal Prejudice and Overt Acts

The purpose of creating this situation was to provide the subjects opportunity to give public and overt testimony of their acceptance or rejection of Negroes. But the data so obtained also allow a test of the hypothesis that individuals with negative or positive verbal attitudes will act in accord with those attitudes in an overt situation.

The results of the photographic release agreement and its relationship to the verbally elicited attitudinal category of the subjects are given in Table 1. Subjects were classified as falling above or below the mean level of endorsement. The distribution was such that the mean and median fell at identical points.

In this situation, there was clearly a greater tendency for the prejudiced

TABLE 1. **RELATIONSHIP BETWEEN RACE ATTITUDES AND LEVEL OF SIGNED AGREEMENT TO BE PHOTOGRAPHED WITH NEGRO**

| | | Subject Attitude | |
		Prejudiced	Unprejudiced
Signed level of agreement	Below $\overline{X}$	18	9
	Above $\overline{X}$	5	14
		Chi square $= 7.264$ $p<.01$	

persons than the unprejudiced to avoid being photographed with a Negro. The relationship is significant, suggesting some correspondence in this case between attitudes measured by verbal scales and an acceptance-avoidance act toward the attitude object. In spite of the statistical significance, however, there were some prejudiced persons who signed the agreement without hesitation at the highest level, as well as some unprejudiced persons who were not willing to sign at any level. Thus, the relationship between these verbal and overt attitudinal dimensions, while significant, is not a simple one-to-one correspondence. These findings are consistent with much of the earlier research, some of which is described above. The factors which account for this seeming inconsistency need careful exploration.

One possibility of explaining the inconsistency in the present study is to assume that prejudiced subjects who signed at the higher levels and unprejudiced persons who refused to sign were misclassified by the original measurement of verbal attitudes. But this explanation is suspect due to the fact that the individuals used as subjects represent the extremes (upper and lower quartiles) of the verbal attitude distribution. While this does not eliminate the possibility of error, of course, it reduces it considerably. The inadequacy of an explanation on the basis of error alone is also suggested by the distribution in Table 1. Fourteen of forty-six subjects (almost one-third) show behavior patterns in opposition to their verbally elicited attitudes—this is too large a proportion to attribute to measurement errors. The latter, moreover, theoretically are cancelled out by errors in the opposite direction.

The lack of a straight-line relationship between verbal attitudes· and overt action behavior more likely may be explained in terms of some sort of social involvement of the subject in a system of social constraints, preventing him from acting (overtly) in the direction of his convictions, or otherwise "legitimizing" certain behavorial patterns. These channelizing influences on behavior have received theoretical attention in terms of such concepts as "reference groups," "other directedness," and "significant others."

Reference Groups

Reference groups were cited earlier as possibly an important influence upon the direction of behavior of individuals confronted with action opportunities regarding attitude objects. This possibility accounts for our hypothesis that the act of signing the photograph agreement involves a conscious consideration of reference groups. Thus the subjects were asked, immediately following their response to the document, "Was there any particular person or group of people (other than the interviewer) who came to mind when you decided to sign (or refused to sign) this document? That is, are there people whom you felt would approve or disapprove?" (Since the entire interview was recorded on tape for later study, it was possible to examine carefully the responses to this question.) The majority of the subjects needed little or no prompting for presumably they had certain key groups or individuals clearly in mind when they made their decisions.

Sixty reference groups were identified as being influential in the decision-making of the 46 subjects regarding the signing of the photographic release. Nearly three-fourths of them (71.8 per cent) invoked some type of reference group when faced with this problem, while the remaining fourth (28.2 per cent) apparently made an "inner-directed" decision. Perhaps significantly, *all* of those who did cite a reference group mentioned some type of peer group, while only a third referred to the family. In all cases the subjects were able to state whether these groups would approve or disapprove of their posing for such a photograph.

Riesman (among others) has discussed the peer group as an important source for behavioral cues and has described the "other-directed" personality, presumably on the increase in American middle class society, as a type for which the peer group operates as a predominant director of behavior.[11] Earlier research, for example the Bennington study,[12] has shown that campus groups function as important influences on attitudes. The present findings are consistent with these conclusions.

In summary, verbally expressed attitudes were significantly related to the direction of the action taken by subjects regarding being photographed with a Negro of the opposite sex. On the other hand, a third of the subjects behaved in a manner quite inconsistent with that which might be expected from their verbal attitudes. Whatever the direction of this action, however, it was a *peer-directed* decision for the majority, with the subjects making significant use of their beliefs concerning possible approval or disapproval of reference groups as guides for behavior.

Conclusions

The present findings have at least two implications for further research. First, in order to analyze the relationship between the verbal and action dimensions of attitudes, it may be necessary to add to attitude scales a systematic categorization of the system of social constraints within which individual behavior ordinarily takes place. Thus, analysis of the beliefs of an individual about the attitudes, norms, and values held by his reference groups, significant others, voluntary organizations, peer groups, and the like may be essential for better prediction of individual lines of action with the use of verbal scales. This would represent a more distinctly sociological approach.

Second, a systematic development of standardized *overt action opportunities* may be necessary before an individual can be accurately classified on a positive-negative continuum concerning a particular attitude object. That is, standardized opportunities for subjects to make overt acceptance-avoidance acts may provide quantitative assessment of the *salience* of attitudes by classifying overt non-verbal action toward an attitude object. The photograph authorization reported here is a crude attempt to classify such action. Further studies of salience could be based on overt action opportunities in small group settings. For example, individuals could be observed and their behavior categorized when given actual opportunities, say, for physical contact with a Negro, to be seen in public with a Negro in primary group settings, or to use physical facilities used by Ne-

---

[11]David Riesman, *The Lonely Crowd*, New Haven: Yale University Press, 1950, *passim.*
[12]Theodore M. Newcomb, "Attitude Development as a Function of Reference Groups: The Bennington Study," reprinted in E. E. Maccoby, T. M. Newcomb, and E. L. Hartley, editors, *Readings in Social Psychology*, New York: Henry Holt, 1958, pp. 265–275.

groes. Such behavioral settings could provide standarized ways of measuring the action attitudes of subjects placed in such contexts. They could also provide methods for validating measuring instruments such as the one described in this paper.

Methods which require elaborate or cumbersome physical facilities would have limited utility in the practical measurement of attitude salience. Measuring instruments such as the photograph authorization have the advantage of portability. If it can be shown that these measures correlate highly with overt action in standardized small group behavioral situations, their validity can be established more firmly.

Further advances in the prediction of overt behavior from attitude measuring instruments may require both systematic measures of the social anchorages of individual psychological orientations and careful studies of their translation into overt social action. These would probably help to clarify the often perplexing relationship between the verbal and overt action dimensions of attitudinal phenomena.

DATA:
Verbal Attitudes and Overt Behavior:
A Study of Racial Discrimination
LAWRENCE S. LINN

The present study is concerned with the relationship between verbal attitudes as expressed through response items on an attitude questionnaire and subsequent overt behavior.[1] It is incorrect to assume that the response to a verbal question (printed or oral) necessarily reveals an attitude which would become operative in the situation depicted in the question. This study will examine the utility of attitude measurements as a means for predicting future behavior. Since considerable funds are expended on attitude research each year and since such research constitutes a large bulk of the social science enterprise, it is essential to make clear what relevance such data have and what kind of restrictions must be

"Verbal Attitudes and Overt Behavior: A Study of Racial Discrimination," by Lawrence S. Linn, from *Social Forces*, vol. 43 (1965), pp. 353–64. Reprinted by permission of The University of North Carolina Press. The author of this article is indebted to David Mechanic for his valuable advice and criticism in the designing and carrying out of this study and to Michael Hakeem, Gerald Marwell, and William H. Sewell for their criticisms of the text. The work reported here was supported by an NIMH training program in social psychology (Grant #2N-7413).

[1]One of the most diversely defined concepts in social psychology is attitude. Not only are there vast differences concerning what properly constitutes an attitude, but there has been developing a large literature debating how attitudes should be measured. Both of these topics have been thoroughly discussed in a recent article by Melvin DeFleur and Frank Westie, "Attitude as a Scientific Concept," *Social Forces*, 42 (October 1963), pp. 17–31, so that a long theoretical analysis of the problems of defining and measuring attitudes will not be dealt with in this paper. This is not to say that they will be ignored; they will be discussed, but relevant only to issues that are raised in this research.

placed on their application. This is not to say that there are no verbal attitudes which correlate highly with behavior. But, if the goal of a research project is to predict behavior on the basis of verbal attitudes, evidence must be cited showing the probability of accurate prediction and the degree of validity in generalizing from an attitude to behavior.[2]

The present study will examine the relationship between expressed racial attitudes and overt behavior, looking at the level of precision and accuracy that can be obtained in predicting behavior from attitude scores based on written verbal responses. It will also be of interest to examine how people will account for discrepancies between their expressed attitudes and their behavior if and when discrepancies exist. But, before turning to a discussion of the empirical findings of this study, it would be beneficial to review the studies done in the past on the relationship between attitudes and action, paying particular attention to the following three variables: (1) the *method* of attitude and behavior measurement, (2) the *prevalence* of discrepant behavior between attitude and action, and (3) the *direction* of the discrepant behavior.

The first study which examined the relationship between human behavior and expressed attitudes was the classical study by LaPiere.[3] LaPiere traveled through the United States with a Chinese couple, stopping at many hotels, motels, and restaurants, but they were refused service only once. In a follow-up study, he mailed questionnaires to the proprietors of the establishments visited in order to find out if members of the Chinese race would be accepted as guests. Approximately 93 percent of the restaurants and 92 percent of the sleeping places indicated that they would not accept or accommodate Chinese people. A control group of other restaurants and hotels were also sent questionnaires, and almost identical results were obtained. This study clearly shows a large discrepancy between expressed attitudes and overt behavior but in a *positive* direction. In other words, although the hotel and restaurant owners expressed a verbal policy of discrimination, when confronted face-to-face with the situation, they did not discriminate. However, it must be pointed out that the LaPiere study has certain methodological problems which reduce the validity of the results and which make a comparison of attitudes and action less credible. First, the questionnaire which he used to measure attitudes toward the Chinese dealt with general prejudice indices and was *not* necessarily comparable to the behavioral situation in the study. Secondly, LaPiere's presence with the couple probably had a considerable biasing effect. Much different results would have been obtained had the couple gone across the country alone. Nevertheless, the study, even with its problems, does demonstrate a considerable discrepancy between expressed attitudes and overt behavior.

A more recent study by Kutner, Wilkins, and Yarrow[4] seems to substan-

---

[2]Robert K. Merton has pointed out that it should not be assumed that overt behavior is intrinsically any "more real" than verbal behavior nor should it be considered as more "truthful." Overt actions do not necessarily reflect verbal attitudes and may deliberately conceal or disguise them. In fact, there are times when it may be valuable to know a person's verbal opinion even if it is not directly related to his behavior . . . . See Merton, "Fact and Factitiousness in Ethnic Opinionaires," *American Sociological Review*, 5, (1940).

[3]Richard LaPiere, "Attitude vs. Action," *Social Forces*, 13 (December 1934), pp. 230−37.

[4]Bernard Kutner, Carol Wilkins, and Penny Yarrow. "Verbal Attitudes and Overt Behavior Involving Racial Prejudice," *Journal of Abnormal & Social Psychology*, 47 (1952), pp. 649−52.

tiate LaPiere's findings that attitude scores alone are not sufficient predictors of behavior and that racially discriminatory behavior may be less likely to occur in a face-to-face situation. In their study, two white women and one Negro woman entered 11 restaurants in a fashionable community and were served in a normal manner. Two weeks later, letters were sent to each establishment inquiring about reservations for a social affair. Included in the letter was the sentence, "Since some of them are colored, I wondered whether you would object to their coming?" Seventeen days after the letters were sent out, no replies had been received, and thus telephone calls were made repeating parts of the letters. In eight of the 11 cases, the managers denied receiving the letters. In a control phone call made a day later, no reference to the racial character of the group was made, and all but one restaurant accepted the reservation of the party. Thus, this study, like the La-Piere study, demonstrates a substantial discrepancy between verbal attitudes and subsequent overt behavior involving racial prejudice. Again, it should be noted that the discrepancy is in the *positive* direction, moving from a conservative, prejudicial attitude position to a more liberal behavioral one.

There are further lines of evidence which demonstrate the discrepancy between verbal attitudes and overt behavior. Saenger and Gilbert,[5] when testing the hypothesis that anti-Negro prejudice in white department store customers would not lead to discrimination against Negro sales personnel or the stores employing them, found that there was no tendency in prejudiced individuals to avoid dealing with Negro clerks. Minard,[6] in examining the attitudes and behavior of white coal miners toward Negroes within the same mine and outside it, found that racial integration and equality only existed within the work roles of the mine. Outside the job, the two races occupied different status levels in almost every situation. In the Saenger and Gilbert study, the discrepant behavior was again in the positive direction. In the Minard study the direction is less clear, but it appears that the discrepancies in behavior ran in both directions.

Fishman,[7] in his introduction to a study of the Negro's entrance into Bridgeview, a New Jersey suburb near New York City, found a clear discrepancy between expressed attitudes and actual behavior that ran in both the positive and negative directions. He found that many people who, for the most part, had negative attitudes toward the Negro nevertheless remained in an interracial community which was progressively becoming more Negro. Yet, others who had positive attitudes toward Negroes moved away.

DeFleur and Westie[8] have also studied the relationship between attitude and action. After the administration of a prejudice scale to a group of college students, those scoring high and low were recalled as subjects and given a projective test in which each was shown slides of pairs of Negro and white men and women in various social situations. At the end of the projective test session, each S was

[5]Gerhart Saenger, and Emily Gilbert. "Customer Reactions to the Integration of Negro Sales Personnel," *International Journal of Opinion Attitude Research*, 4 (1950), pp. 57–76.

[6]R. D. Minard. "Race Relationships in the Pocahontas Coal Field," *Journal of Social Issues*, 8 (1952), pp. 29–44.

[7]J. Fishman, "Some Social and Psychological Determinants of Inter-Group Relations in Changing Neighborhoods: An Introduction to the Bridgeview Study," *Social Forces*, 40 (October 1961), pp. 42–51.

[8]Melvin DeFleur and Frank Westie, "Verbal Attitudes and Overt Acts: An Experiment on the Salience of Attitudes," *American Sociological Review*, 23 (1958), pp. 667–673.

asked to pose with a Negro person of the opposite sex. The *Ss* were then given a standard photographic release agreement which consisted of a graded series of situations in which the photograph might be used. The *S* was asked to sign his name to each release. The relationship between the amount of prejudice expressed on the questionnaire and the level of signed agreement to be photographed with a Negro is shown below.

signed level of agreement	prejudiced	non-prejudiced
Below mean	18	9
Above mean	5	14
$X^2 = 7.264$ $p = .01$		

Although DeFleur and Westie found the relationship between attitude and action statistically significant, it was not found to be a linear relationship. Fourteen students, about 30 percent of the sample, showed discrepant behavior. DeFleur and Westie considered these 14 cases to be too many to be attributed to measurement error and therefore suggest that the lack of a linear relationship may be explained by an intervening variable related to social involvement.

Even though the DeFleur and Westie study is methodologically superior to its predecessors, there are still problems of the reliability and validity of attitude measurement. For example, *Ss* in their study were chosen on the basis of high and low prejudice scores on Summated Difference Scales. In this technique the *S* is asked many questions which involve him in a hypothetical relationship with both a Negro and a white of the same occupation. The *Ss* are scored according to the total number of racial discrepancies for each occupational category. This method of attitude assessment actually may not measure the same attitude objects or situational variables involved in the willingness to pose for a picture with a Negro in various social situations. Therefore, in attempting to improve attitude measurement, the present study will use attitude objects (items on the questionnaire) identical to the behavior observed (the signing of photographic releases). Since all the past studies have lacked a reliable or precise attitude measurement that validly could be related to the observed behavior, it is important to see if a linear relationship might exist when direct comparisons between attitude and behavior can be made in a more credible manner. If discrepant behavior continues to exist even after refinements have been made, then, as has been suggested, it might be beneficial to look for intervening variables which would account for the *Ss* discrepancies.

A second improvement built into the design of the present study involves making the experimental situations more credible. This was, in part, accomplished by the fact that the *Ss* did *not* know that they were subjects in a psychological experiment and also by the use of Negro experimentors. The effect of their presence will be discussed later in the paper, but here it might be pointed out that besides making the situation more real, their presence should also serve to intensify the *Ss* attitudes towards Negroes.

A final advantage of the present study is the use of a post-test interview. This interview session will serve as a check on the validity of the behavior-measuring instrument (the photographic releases) and hopefully will give insight into some of the social-psychological aspects of the *Ss* behavior.

Thus, the concern of the present study is to examine the relationship between racial attitudes and overt behavior looking at (1) the level of consistency between the two phenomena, which implies (2) the ability to predict behavior accurately on the basis of attitude scores, and (3) the existence of intervening variables such as peer or family reference groups which would account for any discrepant behavior.

Therefore, the present study will examine and test the following hypothesis:

> Individuals with either positive or negative verbal attitudes do not necessarily act in accord with those attitudes in an overt situation, even when the measuring instrument apparently taps the same attitude objects that are involved in the behavior.
>
> A. This implies that attitudes may often be poor indicators of behavior and that their use in this direction must be carefully restricted.
>
> B. The accuracy of an attitude scale as an indicator of behavior can be determined by empirical research and is necessary in determining the validity of the instrument.

Method

Subjects. All of the *Ss* in the present study were females enrolled in introductory courses in sociology at the University of Wisconsin. An attitude questionnaire was administered to ten discussion sections and scattered among the total number of questions were 14 items concerning attitudes toward Negroes. The 14 questions were used by the present study to construct the following two attitude scales:

Scale I

1. I would be willing to pose with a Negro of the opposite sex if the picture were to be used in laboratory experiment work where it would be seen only by professional sociologists and psychologists.

2. I would be willing to pose with a Negro of the opposite sex if the picture were to be published in a professional journal and read only by professional sociologists and psychologists.

3. I would be willing to pose with a Negro of the opposite sex if the picture would be shown to a few dozen university students in a laboratory situation.

4. I would be willing to pose with a Negro of the opposite sex if the picture were to be used as part of a projective personality test to be used widely by psychologists and sociologists to measure peoples' attitudes.

5. I would be willing to pose with a Negro of the opposite sex if the pic-

ture were to be published in the student newspaper in my own university as part of a campus-wide campaign for racial integration by an organization like the NAACP.

6. I would be willing to pose with a Negro of the opposite sex if the picture were to be published in my hometown newspaper as part of a publicity campaign by an organization like the NAACP for racial integration.

7. I would be willing to pose with a Negro of the opposite sex if the picture were to be used in a brochure of an organization like the NAACP and circulated in a nationwide campaign for racial integration.

Scale II

8. I don't mind going to a racially integrated school, Negroes and whites mixed together.

9. I wouldn't mind living in a neighborhood where there were some Negroes integrated into the community.

10. I wouldn't mind if a Negro lived next door to me in my home community.

11. I wouldn't mind if a Negro family lived in the same building in which I lived.

12. I wouldn't mind attending a party in which there were both Negro and white couples.

13. If I were unattached, I would have no objection to dating a Negro person of the opposite sex.

14. If I were in love, I would have no objections to marrying a Negro of the opposite sex.

Design and procedure. Four weeks after the administration of the attitude questionnaire, it was announced to each of the classes sampled that:

> Two student representatives of the Psychological Testing Company, Boston, Mass., will be interviewing students on campus during the next ten days. They are interviewing Wisconsin students who may be interested in helping to develop a new semi-projective personality test. Participation is completely voluntary, and not all of you will be asked to take part at the same time . . . .

> The interview session will take about 15 minutes. The names of those who are asked to help construct the test have been given to your teacher along with an appointment sign-up schedule. If your name is on the list, and, if you desire to participate, sign up now or after class for a time that is convenient to you.

The students who were asked to volunteer were all of the 18 and 19 year old girls who had previously responded to the attitude questionnaire. The girls who signed up for interview appointments were told to wait in chairs outside the Psychological Testing Company office until called. The white *E* greeted the *S* and ushered her into the office, introducing himself and *E'* (a light-skinned Negro) as representatives of the Psychological Testing Company. The *S* was seated directly opposite the two *Es*. In the first part of the interview, the *Es* discussed the general plans of the "Test Construction Program." The Ss were shown the TAT test as a model for construction and given a short lecture on the construction, purpose, and use of projective personality tests. The second phase of the interview became more specific:

> (Dialogue—E', light-skinned Negro). What the company is interested in developing is a set of cards which will be used similarly to the TAT that you have just seen, but with pictures of people of different races who will portray various social situations. The number of people in each picture will vary, but the focus of attention of each one will be on a racially integrated couple, a Negro and a white. The subject matter of the pictures will be typical social scenes like playing cards or chess, studying together, dancing, or sipping a coke. . . .

> (Dialogue—E, white). More specifically, we have asked you here today to see if you would be willing to help us with our test construction program and if you would therefore be willing to pose for a photograph with a Negro of the opposite sex of the type that has just been described to you. If you are interested in helping us construct the test, we would like you to indicate the conditions under which you will allow the pictures to be used. This is formally done by the signing of these photographic releases. The signing of a photographic release agreement is standard procedure and is necessary in any situation in which a photograph of an individual is used in any professional way. You may sign some of them, all of them, or none of them as you see fit. . . .

If the S signed any of the releases, E' set up an appointment on a future date for taking the photograph. The S was told that the photo appointment would take only 15 minutes and that she should wear neatly-appearing school clothes.

For the final phase of the interview, the Ss were asked to talk to a representative of the National Association for the Advancement of Negro Rights (NAANR), a dark-skinned Negro (E''). After introductions were made, E'' explained to the S what the NAANR was and why they were interested in the photographs, explaining that they would be interested in them for various campaigns and publicity programs for racial integration. The S was then asked to sign three more photographic release agreements. The four photographic release agreements which E' presented to the S were identical to the first four items in Scale I which the S had previously completed four weeks ago. The three releases which E'' presented to the S were identical to the remaining three items in Scale I.

The Ss who were supposedly to have their pictures taken returned individually several days later for their appointments. They were met by the white E at the Pyschological Testing Company office and were asked to come and sit down for a minute so that some details could be ironed out before posing for the pictures. The S was seated and asked if she had changed her mind about participating in the program. After answering the question, the S was then told that the "construction program" was an experiment, was given some explanation, and finally interviewed about the entire situation. The content of the interview and the results of the information gained from it will be reported in another section of the paper. Also, Ss who refused to sign any of the releases were contacted by telephone, told that the "construction program" was an experiment, and asked to return for an interview.

Results and Discussion

Relationship Between Attitude and Action

Degree of relationship. As has been discussed, past studies examining racial attitudes and overt behavior have found varying relationships between the two variables. For example, the studies by LaPiere, Kutner, and others have shown that, when people who have racially prejudiced attitudes are placed in a situation calling for overt action, they fail to behave in a discriminatory fashion. Although the magnitude of the results of these studies was impressive, the methodological problems inherent in each study were so large that a more careful analysis of the problem was necessary. DeFleur and Westie attempted such a study using an experimental laboratory approach in examining the problem. They found that racial attitudes were *positively* related to behavior at the .01 level of confidence. Yet, in spite of the statistical significance, almost one-third of the cases were clear instances of discrepant behavior. The present study devised a means of measuring racial attitudes (Attitude Scale I) in which direct comparison can be made from the attitude scores to the overt behavior observed. An attitude score ranging from 0–7 was compiled for each S, showing the degree of willingness to pose for a photograph with a Negro in a social situation. Similarly, a comparable behavior score was compiled for each person, indicating the *signed* level of agreement to pose for a photograph with the Negro. Mean and median scores were compiled for both attitude scales (I and II) and the scale of overt behavior. (See Table 1.) Notice that for both attitude scales, the mean and the median are considerably higher than for the behavioral scale, showing a marked difference between attitude and overt behavior. Focusing more closely on discrepant behavior, 59 percent of the total sample (N = 34) was found to have discrepant scores of *two* or more (out of a possible 7), and 65 percent of this group had scores showing *three* or more discrepancies. More significant relationships can be seen in Table 2, where the responses have been divided into three categories for each variable — low (score of 0–2), medium (score of 3–5), and high (score of 6–7) willingness to pose for a photograph with a Negro for the attitude variable and low (score of 0–2), medium (score of 3–5), and high (score of 6–7) level of signed agreement to pose for such a photograph. A chi-square test was run on Table 2, and an r correlation was run on the two variables. Neither test showed the variables to be significantly related, thus confirming the hypothesis that individuals with either positive or negative verbal attitudes do not necessarily act in accord with those attitudes in an overt situation even when the measuring instru-

TABLE 1. **THE MEAN AND MEDIAN SCORES FOR THE 34 SUBJECTS ON TWO ATTITUDE SCALES AND A BEHAVIOR SCALE**

Scale	Mean	Median	N
Attitude Scale I	4.9	5.5	34
Behavior Scale.	2.8	2.5	34
Attitude Scale II	4.3	5.0	34

ment apparently taps the same attitude objects involved in the observed behavior.[9]

   Direction of discrepant behavior. Thus far, the present study has shown that there is no linear relationship between expressed attitudes and overt behavior and that, in fact, 52 percent of the *Ss* in the sample showed behavior which was inconsistent with previously expressed attitudes. The purpose of this section is to analyze and discuss the direction of these discrepant cases. In Table 2, the marginal totals clearly show that, whereas 50 percent of the respondents verbally expressed a high willingness to pose for a photograph with a Negro, only 24 percent of the respondents showed a high level of signed agreement to pose for such a photograph. By the same token, whereas only 18 percent of the respondents verbally expressed a low willingness to pose with a Negro, 52 percent of the respondents, when confronted with the actual situation, expressed a low level of signed agreement. Of the 18 cases showing discrepant behavior in Table 2, 89 percent (16 cases) were discrepant in a "negative" direction. By negative it is meant that more liberal, less prejudiced attitudes were originally expressed, but, when the individual was confronted with the real situation, his behavior became more discriminatory than his attitudes had formerly indicated. Only *two Ss* in the present study deviated from their expressed attitudes in a "positive" direction. How can the negative direction of the discrepant behavior be accounted for in the present study? What factors might be attributed to its cause?

   Some of the directional disparity—but certainly not all of it—might be due to more valid, reliable, and precise measurement of variables. Of more importance, however, in the present study is the cultural milieu of the *S*. That is, the *Ss* were college students attending a large midwestern university which has a reputation for being politically and racially liberal. Within this climate of university liberalism, it is a social and cultural norm held by most faculty and students to take a liberal position on racial integration. Liberal attitudes toward the Negro

TABLE 2.   **THE RELATIONSHIP BETWEEN THE SCORES ON ATTITUDE SCALE 1, SHOWING THE LEVEL OF WILLINGNESS TO POSE FOR A PHOTOGRAPH WITH A NEGRO OF THE OPPOSITE SEX AND THE SIGNED LEVEL OF AGREEMENT TO POSE FOR SUCH A PHOTOGRAPH. (N = 34)**

	Overt Behavior				
Verbal Attitude	**High level of signed agreement (6–7)**	**Medium level of signed agreement (3–5)**	**Low level of signed agreement (0–2)**	**Total**	**% of N**
High level of willingness (6–7)	7 (41%)	3 (18%)	7 (41%)	17	(50%)
Medium level of willingness (3–5)	1 (9%)	4 (36%)	6 (55%)	11	(32%)
Low level of willingness (0–2)	0	1 (17%)	5 (83%)	6	(18%)
Totals	8 (24%)	8 (24%)	18 (52%)	34	(100%)

$X^2 = 7.26$ with 4 degrees of freedom; not significant.

[9]It should be pointed out that the Chi-square test and *r* correlations are both very sensitive to sample size. The relatively small sample size in the present study probably accounts for the lack of statistical significance. Regardless, the major concern here is to point out that more than 50 percent of the *Ss* of the study showed behavior which was discrepant with their previously expressed attitudes.

are, in most circles, not only criteria for social approval but a sign of intellectual maturity—a sign of a "liberal education." It is therefore not surprising that 50 percent (17) of the Ss expressed highly liberal racial attitudes and 32 percent (11) expressed attitudes that fell within the middle range. In other words, the skewed distribution of attitude scores toward the liberal direction is at least in part due to the students' playing, or attempting to play, their social role of the liberal college student. However, this role of "racial liberalism" with its associated constellation of attitudes is quite contradictory to the way in which most people have been socialized into our society. Contrary to the university atmosphere, most segments of American society and the norms associated with them do *not* see racial integration as being socially acceptable; in fact, integration is probably more often viewed as something either to fear or to avoid on a personal level. The present study therefore suggests that discrepant behavior in a negative direction is partially due to a breakdown of *unstable* attitudes which are part of a social role that has never been behaviorally put to test. Further evidence for and development of this position will be presented later in the paper.

The salient effect of Negro experimenters and its effect on action. Both of the Negroes used in the present study were intelligent and impressive college graduates. However, in spite of their attractiveness, the Ss were very conscious of their race. For many of them, the experimental situation provided the first actual face-to-face contact with a Negro. This situation became very stressful for some, producing strong feelings of uncertainty. Three of the Ss never kept their appointments to have their pictures taken even though they had signed photographic releases. These three Ss could not be recontacted, and they refused to respond to several telephone messages. Three other girls who signed release agreements refused to have their pictures taken, saying that they had changed their minds and did not want to participate.

TABLE 3.   **THE RELATIONSHIP BETWEEN PREJUDICE SCORES ON ATTITUDE SCALE II AND THE LEVEL OF SIGNED AGREEMENT TO POSE FOR A PHOTOGRAPH WITH A NEGRO. (N = 34)**

	Overt Behavior				
Verbal Attitude	High level of signed agreement (6–7)	Medium level of signed agreement (3–5)	Low level of signed agreement (0–2)	Total	% of N
Low prejudice (5–7)	7 (30%)	6 (27%)	10 (43%)	23	(68%)
High prejudice (1–4)	1 (10%)	2 (18%)	8 (72%)	11	(32%)
Totals	8 (24%)	8 (24%)	18 (52%)	34	(100%)

$X^2 = 3.79$ with 2 degrees of freedom; not significant.

It is interesting that on the attitude questionnaire only *two Ss* were not willing to pose for a photograph with a Negro no matter how the picture would be used, but, when confronted with the actual situation, *twelve Ss* refused to sign any of the releases. The act of refusing to sign any of the photographic releases in the presence of a Negro, while at the same time holding more liberal attitudes, appeared to be a confusing and stressful situation for the S. Several girls, at the time they were asked to sign the releases, explained in an almost remorseful tone, "I want to . . . but I can't!"

Of course, the *Ss* level of involvement with a Negro in the present study is much different than allowing a Negro to take a room in a motel, allowing him to eat in a restaurant, working with him in a coal mine, or buying merchandise from him in a department store. Posing for a photograph with a Negro of the opposite sex, in which the photograph would be used in the situations depicted in the present study, involves an extremely high degree of personal social involvement, much greater than that required in the situations depicted in other studies. In summary, however, it can be said that the use of Negro experimenters in the present study seems to have served its purpose. It heightened the *Ss* attitudes toward the Negro in general and made the situation more credible and immediate.

Attitudes as predictors of behavior. This final section discussing the relationship between attitude and action will examine the reliability and validity of the racial attitude as a predictor of behavior as found in the present study. Again looking at Table 2, which shows the relationship between scores from Attitude Scale I and the subsequently observed overt behavior, it can be said that imprecise and unreliable prediction occurs only for *Ss* who hold more liberal attitudes (high and medium willingness to pose). For those *Ss* who expressed prejudiced attitudes (low willingness to pose), their behavior in all but one case was consistent. The same trend was found when Attitude Scale II was used as a predictor of overt behavior. As shown in Table 3, a total of 70 percent of the predictions made for *Ss* with *low* prejudice attitudes were inaccurate. However, for *Ss* with *high* prejudice attitudes, 72 percent behaved consistently with their attitudes, making prediction of behavior for this group reasonably accurate.

Therefore, it is apparent from the findings shown in Tables 2 and 3 that *Ss* with racial prejudiced attitudes can be expected to behave in accord with those attitudes; prediction of overt behavior for *Ss* with liberal racial attitudes can be made no better than by chance; and, finally, that *Ss* who exhibit racially discriminatory behavior may actually hold to liberal attitudes as often as not.

Post-Test Interview

There were two major functions which the post-test interview session was to serve in the present study: (1) as a validity-check on the measurement of behavior and (2) as a means of gaining insight into the *Ss* perceptions and feelings about the experimental situation.

Validity check. In the present study, appearance or non-appearance for the "picture taking" session was a means of checking the precision, reliability, and validity of the photographic release agreement as a measure of behavior. That is, it is possible that, even though a *S* has signed an agreement to have her photograph released, she may refuse to have her picture taken (not keeping her appointment) or she may change her mind on how the pictures are to be used. Thus, one of the reasons for having *Ss* return for a picture posing session rather than ending the experiment immediately after signing the releases was to correct for measurement error. In fact, it was found that corrections had to be made for six cases, 18 percent of the total sample. Of these six cases, three never showed up for their appointments or responded to any subsequent phone messages. The other three changed their minds about participating.

A second means for checking the validity of the study was to ask the Ss if they had any knowledge that they were participating in a psychological experiment, and secondly, if the experimental situation seemed credible. Of the 29 Ss interviewed, only one thought that the present study was an experiment. All 29 Ss felt that the situation was credible.

Persuasion, salience, and the effect of Negro experimenters. One of the goals of the research design was to make the situation as credible and realistic as possible without persuading or forcing the Ss into behavior which was against their wishes. As has already been pointed out, all Ss indicated that the situation was credible, but the question still remains, had they been persuaded into making a decision to sign (or not sign) the photographic releases? Out of the 29 Ss interviewed, only four indicated that they had felt persuaded and not in full control over the decision to sign or not to sign the release agreements.

Yet, although most of the Ss did not feel that they had been persuaded, it was interesting that 38 percent of the sample (11 cases) felt that the presence of a Negro had "bothered" them. Some students indicated that the presence of the Negro had an effect on their action; others found his presence made the decision to sign the releases more "uncomfortable." For example:

> I didn't know if I should sign or not. I really couldn't visualize the consequences. Yes, I was aware of the fact that there was a Negro present. I couldn't look at him but only at you (white E) when I told you I wouldn't sign the releases. It was really a very embarrassing type of situation. What could he (the Negro E) be thinking of me?

> I felt a little pressured. The presence of a Negro made it a little uncomfortable. If I didn't sign, it made me not look like a good American. I thought the pictures were too much like dating, and I don't like that. I really felt guilty for not doing my part.

> You *want* to say yes, but because he is a Negro there are strong social pressures. It was like I was discriminating against him to his face.

The majority (62 percent) of the Ss reported that they were not bothered or influenced in a negative way. In fact, some Ss commented that the presence of a Negro made the situation more real. For example:

> The presence of a Negro really had no effect in my signing the releases, but he made the situation seem more important, just his being there. The Negro being right there showed that he felt it was important and thus you wanted to help him.

Discrepant behavior: how the Ss explain it. As has been pointed out earlier, 59 percent of the sample were found to have two or more discrepant responses between their verbal attitudes and overt behavior. In the process of interviewing, these Ss were confronted with their differing attitudes and action scores and asked, "How would you account for your discrepant behavior?" Most of the responses could be classified into a single category. Essentially, this group of *Ss* saw the signing of the photographic releases as being a different, more "real" situation than answering questions on a questionnaire. Yet, the questionnaire response was also seen as representing "what I *should* or *would like* to do" and the signing of releases as being "what I *could* or *had to* do." For example:

> I don't really know how I feel until I'm actually confronted with the situation. You *think* you should act one way, but you're not sure and probably won't.

> In the questionnaire I wasn't faced with the real thing. It (the signing of the releases) *should* be done, but I can't. Those were my desires, but I couldn't do them. I had to think of my parents and of my hometown.

> When it comes down to it, I guess I back down. I hadn't given another thought to the questionnaire, but the face-to-face situation made me back down. It was nice to think I'd be willing!

> At that time (time of the questionnaire) I was thinking of what I *should* do, but when confronted with the situation, I thought more deeply about participating. I was worried about other people and what they would think. I was not worried for myself.

> On the questionnaire it seemed all right but when it came to the *real* thing, it seemed "scary." It wouldn't have been so bad for a large group picture. Did anybody else do what I did?

Discrepant behavior: an analysis and its relationship to reference group theory. DeFleur and Westie in trying to explain the lack of a straight-line relationship between attitudes and action suggest that a conscious consideration of reference groups intervenes and is responsible for making the decision to act or not to act consistently with one's attitudes. They therefore conclude that the decision to pose or not to pose for a photograph with a Negro was a peer-directed one. The present study recognizes the importance of reference groups in the decision-making process but believes that they are more inclusive than peers alone and furthermore should be seen as antecedent rather than intervening variables. In other words, reference groups influence the individual by being part of his normative system which reflects the attitudes and norms of the society in which he lives, as well as his community, family, friends, and school. Prejudice and discrimination are the products of learning the customs, beliefs, values, and norms of these various social groups and institutions. Thus, the group, whether community, family, or friendship, becomes the agent of attitude formation for the individual through the processes of interaction, identification, or association. The forces which account for an individual's behavior are far greater than just his immediate referents. In fact, quite often people will behave in ways contrary to their peers. Therefore, prejudice and discrimination as conceived by the present study are products of experience and learning which have occurred throughout one's lifetime. Several sociologists have described the process as follows:

> Prejudices are generally acquired slowly and over a period of time. The child acquires his ethnic and racial attitudes as he learns other social lessons, from adults, from his peers, and from his life experiences. . . .[10]

> Few parents actually teach their children to be prejudiced; however, their own attitudes and behavior, their restrictions on the playmates of their children, and the tendency to stereotype all individuals of a given racial or religious group with certain physical, behavioral, and mental characteristics results in a pattern of prejudice which their children imitate. It is not the parents' attitudes alone, but the whole home influence that is responsible for the development of prejudice.[11]

Thus, for the most part, the values and norms of the general society do *not* foster the nature and degree of integration as depicted in the present study. These values, which often characterize the Negro as being dirty, dangerous, and dumb, may be learned, overtly or covertly, within the context of the family, the community or the school. These values of racial prejudice and the associated norms of segregation and discrimination are part of what is taught and what is learned in our society.

FIGURE 1. **FREQUENCY OF RESPONSES TO ATTITUDE SCALE 1.**

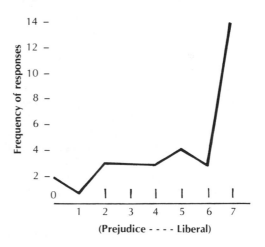

(Prejudice - - - - Liberal)

[10]M. Vosk, "Correlates of Prejudice," *Review of Educational Research*, 23 (1953), pp. 353–361.

[11]Elizabeth Hurlock, *Child Development* (3d ed.; New York: McGraw-Hill Book Co., 1956), p. 290.

On the other hand, within the university community there exists a "sub-culture" in which the prevailing values and norms appear to be quite opposite of those of the general society. As has already been mentioned, in this "subculture" it is the social norm to take a liberal position on racial integration. Figure 1 shows this skewed distribution of attitude scores toward the liberal direction, quite contrary to what might be expected from society in general.

Thus far, two antecedent variables have been introduced which are thought to explain the lack of a straight-line relationship between verbal attitudes and overt actions: (1) that racial prejudice and/or racial discrimination have been either overtly or covertly the prevailing norm in the general society and (2) that the social norm in the "university subculture" is one advocating racial liberalism, a norm which conflicts with the norms of the general society. But a third and most crucial variable which must be added in order to account for the behavior in the present study as well as in the past ones is the concept of social involvement. The level of social involvement is determined by the amount of interaction with the attitude object, the degree of visibility of this interaction, who views it, and what consequences, positive or negative, might arise.

Hopefully, by relating these three variables together, it will be possible to arrive at one possible explanation for discrepant behavior in both a positive and negative direction.

The *Ss* in the present study as well as in the DeFleur and Westie study were young college girls who had only recently been exposed to the norms and values of the liberal university subculture. As has been shown, a large number of them, when asked to indicate their attitudes toward Negroes in a questionnaire, had already begun to play their university social role as a racial liberal. The questions asked the *Ss* if they would be willing to pose for a photograph with a Negro of the opposite sex which would be used in situations with varying degrees of visibility, seen by various kinds of audiences, and having different kinds of potential consequences. Posing for a picture with a Negro which eventually will be published is a situation with a high degree of social involvement, especially when compared with the situations depicted in other studies, such as serving a Negro in northern restaurants or working with Negroes in a coal mine.

However, for many of the *Ss*, the role of a racial liberal had been discussed or thought about only on a symbolic or hypothetical level and had rarely, if ever, been put to empirical test. Most of the *Ss* had no chance to test their attitudes with overt action in real situations. Thus, they had no way of reinforcing, modifying, or possibly even rejecting the validity or stability of their attitudinal position. The present study provided a very clear opportunity for *Ss* with racially liberal attitudes to act overtly in the direction of their convictions, but it was interesting, yet not unusual, to find that a large number of girls were unable to act in this way. The explanation offered by the present study suggests that the *Ss* were confronted with two sets of conflicting roles; that the overt behavior which resulted (various degrees of discrimination) was due to the stronger role, the more stable and comfortable role, the more imprinted, tested, and experienced role becoming operative and dominant over the weaker one. But, this process of the "differential association" between two opposing sets of norms and associated roles was dependent upon the required level of social involvement with the attitude object. Therefore, the following hypothetical statement can be made in explaining when and why discrepant behavior occurs: The level of consistency between racial attitudes and racial behavior is a function of the stability of the attitude position and of the degree of social involvement required between the individual and the attitude object. Therefore, the following types of propositions can be made:

1. Discrepant behavior in a negative direction (racially liberal attitudes which are inconsistent with subsequent discriminatory behavior) will increase if the liberal attitudes represent an *un*stable position (the lacking of actual experience and reality-testing) and if the level of social involvement with the attitude object is high.

2. Discrepant behavior in a positive direction (racially prejudiced attitudes which are inconsistent with subsequent behavior which is non-discriminatory) will increase if the level of social involvement is low and if the prejudiced attitudes have not been overtly tested. Both of these propositions assume that the measurements of attitude and behavior can be validly compared.

Looking Backward

In the analysis of Linn, the most recent case, I will establish the criteria which emerged as I read these three articles comparatively and will then judge each of the other two according to those same criteria. Linn "is concerned with the relationship between verbal attitudes as expressed through response items on an attitude questionnaire and subsequent behavior." The investigator is interested ultimately in achieving prediction of behavior from written attitude scores. Recall that the attitude of his female subjects is obtained by asking them if they would be willing to pose for hypothetical photographs with Negro men. A graded series of conditions under which the pictures would be used, ranging from strictly scientific use to propaganda, provides a "scale" from which an estimate of prejudice is made. Selected subjects are asked at a later point if they would be willing to cooperate with a psychological testing agency by permitting their photos actually to be taken with Negroes. Under these supposedly real conditions, the subjects are asked to sign a series of photographic releases, that series being graded along the same lines as the conditions in the attitude scale. As the author puts it, "attitude objects (items on the questionnaires) [are] identical to the behavior observed (the signing of photographic releases)."

This cleverly indirect technique for establishing the relationship between attitude and behavior suffers from at least five types of defects. The first of these is the emphasis on prediction.

Criterion 1: Prediction

Prediction is a primitive scientific notion that assumes a direct, uninterrupted, straight-line flow of behavior. The idea of such simple cause and effect relationships between two variables has by and large been discarded in the philosophy of science. Among social scientists, however, the idea sometimes survives as what Weigert has called "The Magical Rhetoric of Methodology." According to Weigert, "A common designation of magic is the attribution of empirical efficaciousness to minutely observed rites without understanding the causal link between rite and effect."[3] Some introductory textbooks do continue to retain in their definition of science the criterion of "prediction and control." Prediction is, in fact, as closely related to magic as it is to science. One may accurately predict without ever understanding why the prediction works. Malaria, for example, could be related to the presence of stagnant water in warm climates and effectively brought under control without any knowledge of the particular breed of mosquito that carried it, much less of what that mosquito carried. This is effective and valuable social action in the public health arena; it has nothing to do with science. Nehemiah Jordan puts it this way:

> Imagine the green man from Mars coming in his space ship and giving us the gift we have all been looking for — the perfect computer. The computer is an unopenable black box with two slots, one for inputting the questions and the other for outputting empirical predictions to observable events. Perfect prediction is observed. Does this toll the death knoll for science? Not at all. The scientists of the existing disciplines will be compelled to try to figure out why the predictions are correct. And a new science will undoubtedly develop to try to answer the most burning question of them all. The name of this science will be a Graeco-Latin neologism which will mean: "How the hell does this damn black box work?"[4]

Herbert Blumer has argued repeatedly that prediction of a later phase of a social act is not possible solely on the basis of knowledge of an earlier phase. As Blumer points out, the act is a process in constant development: it is being constructed. The earlier dimension tapped (for example, attitudes toward Dingbats) does not determine any later dimension that may be tapped (for example, overt action toward a Dingbat). The determination is made during the course of the intervening period and may be heavily influenced by factors in the immediate situation in which the act or attitude is called forth. This position seems reasonable and seems to conform to the experience of everyday life, and it encapsulates Blumer's overall reaction to attempts to understand the relationship between sentiments and acts. In his own words:

> The general remark that I would like to make refers to the whole task of seeking to make predictions of overt conduct on the base of some alleged initial and initiating agent of that conduct. Essentially, all schemes of explanation and prediction which we have in sociology presuppose the formula of initiating agents leading to and causing a prescribed form of overt behavior. Yet, as you know, I believe on the basis of Mead's scheme that this formula is fundamentally in error. It is in error because of the fact that that overt conduct is a late stage in the development of the act. Between the initiating agent and the overt expression the act is built up. In this construction of the act the individual is engaged in defining what confronts him in his situation and is engaged in the process of making indications to himself

---

3. Andrew J. Weigert, "The Immoral Rhetoric of Scientific Sociology," *American Sociologist* 5 (1970): 116.

4. Personal communication, ca. 1966. Jordan develops this and related themes systematically in Chapter 15 in Nehemiah Jordan, *Themes in Speculative Psychology* (London: Tavistock Publications, 1968).

in doing so. It is out of this process that he shapes his overt behavior. In other words, how he acts overtly is formed primarily out of what he takes into account and how he molds what he takes into account. The deficiencies of essentially all schemes, including that which reasons from attitude to overt behavior, lie in the failure to accommodate this intervening process of constructing the act. I do not know whether there is much likelihood, given the temper of contemporary thought, for sociologists to see this simple and obvious point.[5]

As we shall see in Chapter Eleven, Blumer may have been overly pessimistic in 1966. In the years since that time there has been an increasing tendency among some sociologists to be more attentive to the process which intervenes between the expression of a sentiment and the performance of an act.[6]

The fact remains that science is concerned with "input" and "output" only in marginal ways. Its central concern is understanding "why" and "how" — what goes on *inside* the black box! If prediction is closely akin to magic, I suspect that control is more nearly a problem of politics. The most effective and economic means of controlling human behavior is probably through coercion — whether military or otherwise and whether real or threatened. Moral questions aside, it is both expensive and inefficient to attempt to apply social science to the control of human behavior.

The point of this discussion of prediction is that any study which takes it to be a major goal of research is confusing science and magic. Clearly one of the several available devices for confirming either a magical or a scientific claim is the predic-

5. Personal communication, March 29, 1966.

6. See, for example, Gordon H. DeFriese and Scott Ford, "Verbal Attitudes, Overt Acts and the Influence of Social Constraints in Interracial Behavior," *Social Problems* 16 (1969): 493–505; James M. Fendrich, "A Study of the Association Among Verbal Attitudes, Commitment and Overt Behavior in Different Experimental Situations," *Social Forces* 45 (1967): 347–55; James M. Fendrich, "Perceived Reference Group Support: Racial Attitudes and Overt Behavior," *American Sociological Review* 32 (1967): 960–70; H. Edward Ramsford, "Isolation, Powerlessness and Violence: A Study of Attitudes and Participation in the Watts Riot," *American Journal of Sociology* 73 (1968): 581–91; Lyle G. Warner and Melvin L. DeFleur, "Attitude as an Interactional Concept: Social Constraint and Social Distance as Intervening Variables Between Attitudes and Action," *American Sociological Review* 34 (1969): 153–69; Seymour S. Bellin and Louis Kriesberg, "Relationship Among Attitudes, Circumstances and Behavior: The Case of Applying for Public Housing," *Sociology and Social Research* 51 (1967): 453–69; Lawrence T. Cagle and Irwin Deutscher, "Housing Aspirations and Housing Achievement: The Relocation of Poor Families," *Social Problems* 18 (1970): 244–56; Howard J. Ehrlich, "Attitudes, Behavior, and the Intervening Variables," *American Sociologist* 4 (1969): 29–34 (reprinted in Chapter Eleven of this volume); Harry E. Allen, Clifford E. Simonsen, and Harold J. Vetter, "Attitudes and Behavior: A Test," paper read at the annual meetings of the Ohio Valley Sociological Society, 1971; Stan L. Albrecht, Melvin L. DeFleur, and Lyle G. Warner, "Attitude-Behavior Relationships: A Re-Examination of the Postulate of Contingent Consistency," *Pacific Sociological Review* 15 (1972): 149–68. Most of these papers would be found wanting by Blumer since they do not generally adopt a symbolic interactionist perspective. All of them do, however, pay serious attention to the role of events which may intervene in the process between the expression of a sentiment and the performance of an act. For a contemporary critique of such studies from a behavioral modification perspective, see Donald L. Tarter's work, including "Toward Prediction of Attitude-Action Discrepancy," *Social Forces* 47 (1969): 398–405; "Attitude: The Mental Myth," *American Sociologist* 5 (1970): 276–78; "Pragmatic Sociology: Sociology and the Behavior Modification Movement," *L.S.U. Journal of Sociology* 1 (1971): 20–37.

tive test. If I say unto you that the sun will be blotted out at high noon tomorrow because the Gods are displeased, and if it is blotted out, my magic has been put to a predictive test and has passed. If I inform you that there will be a total eclipse of the sun at precisely noon tomorrow because my calculations indicate that the moon will pass between the earth and the sun at that moment, and if there is a total eclipse, my science has been put to a predictive test and has passed. It is a legitimate and persuasive test, but it is not legitimately a primary concern of scientific research.

Criterion 2: The Sample

Linn's Sample is small and select—too small and too select! It consists of thirty-four eighteen- and nineteen-year-old girls enrolled in an introductory sociology course at a state university. The selectivity is compounded by the fact that only volunteers from among those who took the attitude test were exposed to the behavior test. The investigator concedes that his subjects have had few or no contacts with members of the minority group during their young lives, therefore leaving some doubt as to the salience of the research situation to them. I see nothing wrong with either a small sample or a homogeneous one, but it ought to be at least large enough to allow the intended statistical operations. As we shall see below, this is not the case. And it ought to be homogeneous according to characteristics of people who make a difference when we generalize to others like them. It isn't very helpful to accumulate a body of valid knowledge about eighteen-year-old female sociology students in a state university—especially when they are both naive and powerless. In terms of Blumer's argument about public opinion (Chapter Two), we may pose the question: How appropriate or relevant is it to ask or observe anything with this particular public? They have no influence, no understanding, no experience, no sensitivity, and no importance in relation to the particular situation being studied.

Criterion 3: Experimental Design

I am particularly taken with the power of evidence derived from a study which incorporates experimental controls. Such a study need not, of course, be constructed under synthetic laboratory conditions, but to me the important kind of control (from among many types) is the one that provides a comparison between those who do and do not receive the experimental treatment.[7] In Linn's case, the question unanswered by the lack of such controls is, to what extent were the girls who took the behavioral test influenced by the fact that they had previously taken an attitudinal test regarding this same matter. This is a question of reactivity and it is, in my opinion, a very important one. His questionnaire items dealing with photo releases must have seemed unusual even to questionnaire-conditioned undergraduates. It is possible that they not only remembered them, but that they thought about them and, in Blumer's terms, had begun constructing an act which terminated when they were confronted with the behavioral test. This is what I mean when I say that the behavioral test may have been influenced by the attitudinal test. Although it may

7. For a clear delineation of the logic of experimental design and the kinds of conclusions which can appropriately be drawn from different kinds of designs, see Donald T. Campbell, "Factors Relevant to the Validity of Experiments in Social Settings," *Psychological Bulletin* 54 (1957): 297–312.

not always be possible to avoid such reactivity if one wishes to expose subjects to similar stimuli at different points in time, experimental controls would at least permit us to estimate how much reactivity is present. In this case, what would be the difference between the subjects and a matched group of girls who had not taken the original attitudinal test? If we knew that Linn's design was not reactive, we could have much greater confidence in his conclusions. Since we do not know that, we must continue to entertain considerable doubt and to discount the study heavily.

Linn could also have strengthened the explanatory power of his study by controlling for sex and race (and possibly other variables which he had reason to believe were relevant). In submitting samples of black males, black females, and white males to the attitudinal and the behavioral tests, it would become possible to obtain estimates of the amount of variance attributable to sex, race, and interaction between them.

Criterion 4: Assumptions Related to Scaling and Scalability

Linn had to make several assumptions about the scalability of his seven items in the two presumed scales. In transforming the noun, "a scale," into a verb, "to scale," Louis Guttman achieved not only a technical, but also a methodological innovation. He created a new way of thinking about how you go about accumulating evidence. Campbell achieves much the same end in his contribution to Chapter Nine. Linn, however, does not entertain questions about the way in which responses to one item on his "scale" relate to responses on other items. In effect he fails to employ the verb form introduced by Guttman and retains instead the older noun-type notion employed by Bogardus in his social distance scales. There is no evidence whether or not or to what degree these seven items do, in fact, form a scale.

Related to the above issue is the question of how large a discrepancy between ratings on the attitude scale and on the behavior scale can be assumed to represent an inconsistency. Linn reports that 59 percent of the girls had discrepancies of two or more intervals between attitude and behavior. A two-point discrepancy on a seven-point scale is not necessarily indicative of gross inconsistency. Finally, there is empirical evidence that unit intervals at one end of an attitude scale are not necessarily the same size as their presumed equivalents at the other end of the scale. Reanalyzing data from several previously published studies, Jordon concludes that "in these experiments a 'positive attitude' or 'positive affect' does not have an effect upon 'measured behavior' oppositely equivalent to the effect of a 'negative attitude' or 'negative affect.' The universal symmetry underlying present-day thinking on the subject is questionable."[8] Jordan denounces as unjustifiable the custom of finding an arithmetic average of attitude ratings that includes both positive and negative ratings. Linn's evidence, based on his scales, seems not very powerful.

Criterion 5: Statistical Treatment

There are numerous assumptions required by the statistical procedures employed by Linn without any evidence that these assumptions are met: sampling assumptions, assumptions about the populations, assumptions of additivity, as-

---

8. Nehemiah Jordan, "The 'Asymmetry' of 'Liking' and 'Disliking': A Phenomenon Meriting Further Reflection and Research," *Public Opinion Quarterly* 29 (1965): 315.

sumptions related to the size and symmetry of the scale intervals, and in the case of his coefficient of correlation, assumptions about linearity. This latter assumption is clearly not met! A cursory review of the theoretical underpinnings of the various statistical procedures employed by Linn suggests that this is only the beginning of his failure to meet assumptions. I do not mean to be picky on this issue and there is already extant a large body of literature related to the misuse of statistics in social science research, but in my mind there are two types of statistical assumptions. One is the ideal type which makes logical sense and which we strive to approximate. The requirement for a normal distribution that underlies some procedures is an example. Obviously, one is unlikely to encounter a normal distribution when dealing with empirical social data. The ideal-type assumption simply warns us that if the curve is of a very different type, we ought to consider other techniques. It has been demonstrated that a high degree of skewness can be tolerated in applying techniques which ideally require a normal curve.[9]

There is, however, another type of assumption which needs to be taken much more literally. This I think of as a mathematical assumption. For example, in applying the Analysis of Variance, it must be assumed that cell frequencies are equal or proportional to one another. If they are not (or if we do not take steps to simulate that assumption) then our results are such that one and one does not add up to two. It is intolerable to breach that kind of assumption. This is precisely what Linn does when he applies a correlation technique which assumes linearity to a relationship which he knows to be nonlinear.

Linn also encounters considerable loss of degrees of freedom resulting from his grouping of data and from other computational procedures. Of even greater importance, the use of the statistics he selects is questionable. One of these is a 3 × 3 Chi-square analysis. Interpretation of a 2 × 2 matrix is difficult enough; the 3 × 3 is much more problematic. In Linn's analysis, frequencies of less than five would be expected in seven of the nine cells. Although there is nothing magical about the number five, it is a customary procedure to limit Chi-square analysis to tables in which at least five observations are expected to occur in each cell. This seems to me a reasonable enough custom since large differences in the Chi-square

---

9. The distinction between two basic types of assumptions first occurred to me when I encountered Snedecor's experiments with controlled agricultural plots. He describes the effects of deliberate departures from normality in Chapter 11 of his *Statistical Methods*. For an updated version see George W. Snedecor and William G. Cochran, *Statistical Methods* (Iowa City, Iowa: Iowa State University Press, 1967). Further evidence can be found in L. C. H. Tippett, *Statistical Methods in Industry* (London: British Iron and Steel Federation, 1943); C. Eisenhart, "The Assumptions Underlying the Analysis of Variance," *Biometrics* 3 (1947): 1–21; W. G. Cochran, "Some Consequences When the Assumptions for the Analysis of Variance Are Not Satisfied," *Biometrics* 3 (1947): 22–37; J. O. Irwin, "Mathematical Theorems Involved in the Analysis of Variance," *Journal of the Royal Statistical Society* 94 (1931): 284ff. The issue as related to educational research is treated in A. D. Rosander, *Elementary Principles of Statistics* (New York: D. Van Nostrand Co., 1951). Rosander summarizes the case as follows:

> The use of the z or F distributions for purposes of testing statistical hypotheses requires that the variate be distributed as the normal probability curve. It has been shown that some departure from normality has no appreciable effect upon the results of the tests. Both Snedecor and Tippett point out that departure from normality does not seem to be of any great importance in the types of practical problems which they encounter. Tippett states that randomization and replication are much more important in experimental design than is a normal distribution of the variate (p. 573).

can result from relocation of a single observation when very small frequencies are expected. This problem is most serious in small matrices, with the likelihood of distortion decreasing as the number of degrees of freedom increases.

The other statistic employed by Linn is the simple Pearsonian Coefficient of Correlation. As I mentioned above, this is questionable under conditions where the author has already posited nonlinearity and where two variables are correlated that by definition are limited in their fluctuations to a range between one and seven. What would be a random or chance coefficient under these conditions? Certainly not zero! On the basis of tests employing the Chi-square and the Pearsonian coefficient, Linn concludes that "neither test showed the variables to be significantly related, thus confirming the hypothesis that individuals with either positive or negative verbal attitudes do not necessarily act in accord with those attitudes in an overt situation. . . ." In what seems to be a direct contradiction to this conclusion Linn states in a footnote that if his sample had been larger, the differences would probably have been significant. By the time I have finished discounting Linn's research, I conclude that, no matter what his findings, they are not very credible. If he has not already done so, the reader should take note of the nit-picking quality of some of these criticisms. They are nit-picking in the sense that they have to do with problems of technique which are endemic to sociological research—problems we have by and large learned to live with. What is important is not so much that Linn or DeFleur and Westie (like nearly everyone else) can be taken to task on these grounds, but that it is possible to avoid such troublesome distortions of the empirical world— as we shall see! Sociological research does not *have* to be incredible. A second aside to the reader has to do with the need to treat the Linn (and the DeFleur and Westie) study with the respect it deserves. I am deliberately presenting a one-sided analysis in this chapter, ignoring many of the unique positive qualities of these studies. Furthermore, if the reader should mistakenly be inclined to view either Linn or DeFleur and Westie contemptuously, he will find in Chapter Eleven that they laid the most important groundwork for future research. Linn is cited in most recent research as one of the first to draw attention to the need to look at intervening processes rather than at the simple attitude-behavior relationship. DeFleur and his associates have continued to contribute more than any other group of sociologists to the understanding of this problem.

Having established the criteria of judgment in the analysis of Linn's 1965 article, let us look back of the DeFleur and Westie undertaking which preceded Linn by seven years. They, too, address themselves to the relationship between verbal attitudes and overt acts, and Linn's design closely parallels theirs. But the two studies are sufficiently different so that they cannot be considered replications. It is therefore legitimate to attribute any convergence in conclusions to the validity of the studies rather than to the fact that they find the same things because they proceed in the same manner (as would be true in a replication). DeFleur and Westie were methodologically oriented. They observe that "in the face of the steady stream of studies of the verbal dimension of attitudinal behavior, the paucity of investigations of the overt-action correlates of such verbal behavior is indeed striking." Their major goal is the development of standardized situations or instruments "enabling the investigator to quantify, on a positive-negative continuum, an acceptance or avoidance act for a set of subjects, with other conditions held constant."

Their behavioral test, you will recall, is identical with that employed later by

Linn: a request to have the subject's picture taken with a Negro and to sign a graded series of releases for the use of the picture. The identity ends here. In the DeFleur-Westie study, the attitudinal dimension is derived from an occupational social-distance scale that asks for acceptance or rejection of a large number of occupations when the incumbents are white and when they are Negro. The sum of the differences of ratings of Negroes and whites provides a prejudice score. Extreme prejudiced and unprejudiced group quartiles were identified, and a multi-factor matching procedure resulted in matched samples of 23 prejudiced and 23 unprejudiced undergraduate sociology students. Measures of attitude toward and behavior toward the minority group were available for 46 subjects. Using the five criteria employed in the analysis of the Linn study, what kinds of progress can be detected during the seven-year period which separates these two articles?

Criterion 1: Prediction

Coupled with their determination to reduce apparent methodological difficulties in sociological research, DeFleur and Westie explicitly reject the notion of prediction as a central concern. They observe that "the relationship between these verbal and overt attitudinal dimensions, while significant, is not a simple one-to-one correspondence." There is a clear awareness here that it is unreasonable to assume simple prediction from one variable to another. There remains, nevertheless, the implicit assumption of a direct, if nonlinear, relationship between an independent and a dependent variable—the notion of cause and effect: "Further advances in the prediction of overt behavior from attitude measuring instruments may require. . . ." Although their stance may not fully meet the requirements of Criterion 1, the authors of this older research seem to me more sophisticated in this respect than their descendant.

Criterion 2: The Sample

Although the DeFleur-Westie sample was small, it was larger than Linn's later sample—46 subjects compared to 36. In the earlier study the sexes are equally represented and the introduction of a matching procedure reduces the probability of self-selective differences between prejudiced and unprejudiced volunteers. Although DeFleur and Westie's midwestern university (Indiana) is further south than Linn's (Wisconsin) and has a less liberal tradition, the salience of the questions to the subjects remains problematic, especially in terms of the perceived consequences of their responses. The notion of demand characteristics in research with students was not articulated by Orne until 1962. Even though there was good reason to suspect that the behavior of students in experiments was more a consequence of being in an experiment than of anything else, DeFleur and Westie may be excused for being insensitive to this possibility, but by 1965, Linn ought to have been more aware of this problem. The possibility of student expectations and felt obligations as subjects in research conducted by their professors is one which demands attention (see Orne in Chapter Eight). Although still defective, it seems to me that the sampling procedures employed by DeFleur and Westie in 1958 were superior to those employed by Linn in 1965.

Criterion 3: Experimental Design

Like Linn, DeFleur and Westie are essentially lacking in experimental controls. Some controls are implicit in this earlier study since both sexes are represented and other matching factors appear equally in both the prejudiced and the unprejudiced groups (quartiles). Although in this respect the earlier study has a potentially superior design, neither piece of research attempts to control for any effect it may have created when it administered the original verbal test. With the benefit of hindsight (as well as a lesson learned from LaPiere's 1934 study), we can see how both sets of investigators could have greatly improved the power of their evidence by subjecting an untreated control group to the behavioral test.

Criterion 4: Assumptions Related to Scaling and Scalability

The conclusions of both Linn and DeFleur and Westie are based upon reflections of differences between attitude and behavior on scales constructed for the purpose of estimating those two dimensions and the differences between them. DeFleur and Westie, unlike Linn, treat the issue of scalability self-consciously. In this earlier study, the derivation of the rank order of the scale is described and its validity argued on the basis of a high rate of agreement among a panel of expert judges. Although no scale analysis is possible because of sample limitations, high transitivity is reported: only three irregularities in the cumulative feature of the instrument occur in the forty-six cases. Extreme prejudiced and unprejudiced scorers are used in the earlier study and the subjects are classified behaviorally according to whether or not they signed the releases at a level above or below the mean of the total sample. As a result of these procedures in classifying both attitude and behavior, DeFleur and Westie do not encounter a problem found in Linn's later work — the need to arbitrarily assume that a two point discrepancy on the scales reflects inconsistency. By scaling criteria, the earlier study appears to be superior to the later one.

Criterion 5: Statistical Treatment

Unlike Linn, DeFleur and Westie employ no correlation analysis. This means that they did not need to make as many assumptions as Linn would later require. This superior assumptional parsimony may, however, be nullified by their need to assume that differences in rating the Negro and white occupations are additive, and by the loss of additional degrees of freedom consequent to computing the mean level at which photographic releases were signed. The application of Chi-square analysis by DeFleur and Westie in 1958 is clearly more sophisticated than its use by Linn in 1965. In spite of their larger sample, the earlier investigators hold their Chi-square down to a 2×2 matrix which is easily interpreted and they manage to achieve sufficient expected frequencies in each cell. Although Ajzen and his colleagues find a computational error in this Chi-square, it seems to make no difference in the conclusions (see the selection by Ajzen et al. in Chapter Five).

On the basis of the Chi-square analysis, DeFleur and Westie reach the opposite conclusion from what Linn was to come up with seven years later: "In this situation, there was clearly a greater tendency for the prejudiced persons than the unprejudiced to avoid being photographed with a Negro. The relationship is significant, suggesting some correspondence in this case between attitudes measured by verbal scales and an acceptance-avoidance act toward the attitude object." This conclusion is followed immediately by a qualification: "In spite of the statistical significance, however, there were some prejudiced persons who signed the agreement without hesitation at the highest level, as well as some unprejudiced persons who were not willing to sign at any level. Thus the relationship between these verbal and overt attitudinal dimensions . . . is not a simple one-to-one correspondence."

In spite of the fact that the probability is 99 out of 100 that the distribution in the Chi-square table is attributable to something other than chance (presumably to the relationship between attitude and behavior), the fact remains that 30 percent of the cases are deviant: 14 of the 46 subjects were either prejudiced people who showed a high level of willingness to sign releases or unprejudiced people who showed an unwillingness to sign releases. As we shall see in Chapter Nine, these two types of inconsistency are very different and require special treatment. Certainly the DeFleur-Westie evidence, reported in 1958, is weak and inconclusive, but the disturbing observation to me is that it seems more credible than the 1965 study.

LaPiere's article precedes DeFleur and Westie by twenty-four years and is thirty-one years older than Linn's. Let us look all the way back. You will remember that LaPiere, like the others, seeks to document the relationship between verbal attitudes and overt acts toward members of a minority racial group. In this case the minority group is Chinese rather than black. LaPiere employs Chinese confederates who seek to obtain services from entrepreneurs who are actually operating businesses. Two hundred and fifty-one such behavioral observations were made and the acceptance-avoidance results recorded. From among these, 128 attitude observations were obtained by allowing a six-month time lapse and then sending each of the entrepreneurs a questionnaire in which he was asked if he would service Chinese people in his establishment. Let us expose LaPiere to the five criteria used to evaluate the other two studies.

Criterion 1: Prediction

Linn, it will be recalled, is committed to a primitive notion of prediction. In DeFleur and Westie we found a deliberate effort to set aside that notion, although many of its concomitant assumptions remained. LaPiere openly challenges the theoretical tenability of posing a causal relationship between attitude and behavior toward the same object. Attitude and behavior, he suggests, are discrete phenomena that are theoretically independent of each other. He argues throughout the last two pages of his article that it is unreasonable to posit a prediction of behavior on the basis of attitudes. For example, "Only a verbal reaction to an entirely symbolic situation can be secured by the questionnaire. It may indicate what the responder would actually do when confronted with the situation symbolized in the question, but there is no assurance that it will."

Even without LaPiere's precedent, Linn should have suspected this, since his girls told him as much. As one of Linn's respondents with an unprejudiced attitude explained to him (when asked why she did not show up for her photograph): "I wanted to but couldn't." It seems to me that LaPiere, back in 1934, had a clearer grasp of this issue than either of the experimenters who followed him over the next thirty years. In spite of his efforts, however, he, like the rest of us, finds it difficult not to think in the causal terms with which we have all been so deeply imbued.

Criterion 2: The Sample

LaPiere's sample consists not of 34 or 46 captive undergraduates, but of 128 mature adults engaged in the conduct of responsible business. The number is not only larger but the probability of self-selectivity is considerably less. Linn and De-Fleur-Westie both coerced their total samples to participate in the verbal dimension of the study (at least neither investigator reports any refusals of students to cooperate with that phase of the study), but both permitted voluntary withdrawal from the overt behavior test. LaPiere's study, on the other hand, is designed to coerce the total sample to participate in the behavioral test (every entrepreneur is confronted with an acceptance-avoidance choice) but permits voluntary refusal to respond to the verbal test. With this difference in mind and also the fact that the DeFleur-Westie sample was reduced by the matching procedure as well as by noncooperation, the percentages of voluntary withdrawal between these two earlier studies can be compared. (Linn reports only that the girls were told that "participation is completely voluntary." There is no indication of how many subjects did not volunteer. We know only that the students who had previously responded to the attitude questionnaire "were asked to volunteer.")

In the DeFleur-Westie study, the combined loss resulting from the matching procedure, the use of only extreme quartiles, and voluntary withdrawal was 81.6 percent (these three sources are indistinguishable in their report). In contrast, LaPiere lost a total of 49 percent. To the extent that rates of voluntary withdrawal of subjects provide an index of self-selectivity, LaPiere appears less self-selective in his sample than the investigators who followed him. The universe from which this oldest sample is drawn also represents an improvement in sampling procedure over its two descendants. We no longer have undergraduate students for whom the verbal dimension is of doubtful salience. The LaPiere sample is drawn from a population that must make choices both in terms of intent and in terms of action—choices they perceive as having real consequences in the conduct of their daily activities. It is my impression that LaPiere's 1934 sample and his sampling procedures inspire greater confidence than those of either Linn or DeFleur and Westie.

Criterion 3: Experimental Design

The great power of LaPiere's design is that, unlike the other two, it permits the use of a nontreated sample for control purposes. A sample of establishments which had not been tested on the behavioral dimension, and which was matched with the experimental sample by quality and geographic locale, received the same verbal inquiry. The distribution of responses from both treatment and control groups was nearly identical. This control of the effect of the treatment itself represents a methodological superiority over both of the later studies. If there is a moral to be drawn from this, it is that laboratories don't necessarily make experiments and field studies may be experimental.

Criterion 4: Assumptions Related to Scaling and Scalability

Since LaPiere allows only an acceptance or a rejection—a dichotomous choice—on both the overt-action dimension and the verbal-attitude dimension, the problems of scaling, scalability, arbitrary assignments of the number of discrepancy units that are assumed to indicate an inconsistency, computations of means, grouping of data, use of only extreme scorers, and the many assumptions that must accompany these techniques are all eliminated from his pioneer work. This represents clear superiority over the later studies in assumptional parsimony.

Criterion 5: Statistical Treatment

Assumptional parsimony is an impressive achievement since the fewer assumptions we are required to buy in order to accept the conclusions, the greater the credibility of those conclusions. This assumptional parsimony is carried still further in the analytic techniques employed by LaPiere. The need to make unsubstantiated statistical assumptions no longer exists and the loss of degrees of freedom resulting from computational procedures is eliminated. Of the 251 establishments confronted with the acceptance-avoidance choice of action, *all but one chose to accept.* Of the 128 responding to the verbal test, *only one chose an unqualified acceptance* (over 90 percent of the establishments chose to reject on the verbal test, with the remaining providing qualified responses). The visible weight of this evidence regarding the inconsistency of attitude and behavior vis-à-vis a racial minority is so overwhelming that neither statistical approximations nor probability estimates are required to interpret the results. The ambiguity in conclusions of the two later studies, resulting largely from high frequencies of deviant cases, disappears in LaPiere's work. This time the data permit only one clear-cut conclusion regarding the hypothesis. The difference in credibility between the oldest study and the two more recent ones is massive.

Conclusions: What Validates What?

Recapitulating, the DeFleur and Westie study, as judged by five broad criteria, appears methodologically superior to the later study by Linn. But it is the oldest study, by LaPiere, which uniformly has the highest credibility. To the extent that the analysis of these three studies is correct, we may have suffered a methodological regression during the thirty-one-year time lapse covered by them. We cannot, however, overlook the fact that LaPiere's work dealt with Chinese while the other two were concerned with blacks. Whether prejudice and discrimination toward Chinese in the 1930s was of the same nature as those postured toward Negroes in the fifties and sixties remains a moot question (and, incidentally, a question not entertained by either Linn or DeFleur and Westie). There are, however, several field studies dealing with attitudes and behaviors toward blacks that appear to validate LaPiere's Chinese study.[10] Theoretical bases for the independence of prejudiced attitudes and discriminatory acts have also been persuasively put forth.[11]

10. See, for example, Joseph Lohman and Dietrich Rietzes, "Deliberately Organized Groups and Racial Behavior," *American Sociological Review* 19 (1954): 342 – 48 (reprinted in Chapter Ten of this volume); Bernard C. Kutner, C. Wilkins, and P. B. Yarrow, "Verbal Attitudes and Overt Behavior Regarding Racial Prejudice," *Journal of Abnormal and Social Psychology* 47 (1952): 649 – 52; Gerhart Saenger and Emily Gilbert, "Customer Reaction to the Integration of Negro Sales Personnel," *International Journal of Opinion and Attitude Research* 4 (1950): 57 – 76; Melvin Kohn and Robin Williams, "Situational Patterning in Intergroup Relations," *American Sociological Review* 21 (1956): 164 – 74.

11. Arnold M. Rose, "Intergroup Relations vs. Prejudice: Pertinent Theory for the Study of Social Change." *Social Problems* 4 (1956): 173 – 76.

Linn's study is superior in some respects to that of DeFleur and Westie. For example, Linn relates attitude and behavior more directly to the same object and, by carrying the photography farce a step further than DeFleur and Westie, he confronts his subjects more directly with the overt action decision. On the other hand, Ajzen and his colleagues question the whole photography process (see Chapter Five). Linn also introduces a different dimension into his analysis as a result of his attention to the direction of discrepancy between attitude and behavior—a question raised many years before by Merton (see Merton's contribution to Chapter Two). It is also true that Linn's design does not suffer from the use of extreme samples as does the DeFleur-Westie one. The modest Chi-square which results from the later study would likely not have been significant had the total sample been included. Linn must also be credited for debriefing his subjects and presenting some of the rich comments obtained through that procedure. I am, however, unable to find the two later studies superior to the pioneer project in any respect. It is possible that another analyst, employing other criteria, could identify ways in which the LaPiere study suffers in comparison with the two later ones. Linn believes that his study is superior to the other two and states that "the DeFleur and Westie study is methodologically superior to its predecessors . . . ," including LaPiere.

Although they acknowledge the existence of the LaPiere study, DeFleur and Westie offer no criticism of it. Linn, you will recall, chooses to attack LaPiere on two fronts:

> . . . It must be pointed out that the LaPiere study has certain methodological problems which reduce the validity of the results and which make a comparison of attitudes and action less credible. First, the questionnaire which he used to measure attitudes toward the Chinese dealt with general prejudice indices and was *not* necessarily comparable to the behavior situation in the study. Secondly, LaPiere's presence with the couple probably had a considerable biasing effect. Much different results would have been obtained had the couple gone across the country alone.

Thumbing back through LaPiere's article, I find these two criticisms difficult to understand. He reports that every establishment that had been confronted by the Chinese couple received the question: "Will you accept members of the Chinese race as guests in your establishment?" It seems to me that, if you are going to ask a question, that is about as close to the behavioral situation as you can get! The fact that half the subjects also were asked questions about other ethnic groups for comparative purposes does not alter the response distribution (compare columns 1 and 2 in LaPiere's Table 1). The influence of the investigator's role on the phenomena he is studying presents a persistent problem in social research. LaPiere was aware of this and made a deliberate effort to control for experimenter effect by remaining out of sight and forcing the Chinese to conduct negotiations alone whenever possible. His behavioral data are classified according to the presence or absence of the investigator and are so reported (see his Table 2). There is no denying that this is an important problem and, despite LaPiere's valiant efforts to exercise control over it, it remains uncertain to what extent experimenter effects persist in his study. But the fact is that neither DeFleur and Westie nor Linn report an effort to control for this potential effect; LaPiere does.

Surely another analyst could, and probably would, come up with criteria of judgment different from the kind I employ here. Clearly, I have not attempted a balanced examination. I have been asking the extent to which an older study was as good or better than more recent ones. This seems to me the critical test of the assumption of cumulative progress in the creation of knowledge. This one test—and I must acknowledge that it is limited—offers no evidence to confirm that assumption. In fact it suggests the possibility of regression. *Even those severest critics who sharply disagree with my analysis reach essentially the same conclusion:* "A thorough methodological analysis of the three case studies does not seem to indicate a regressive trend in methodology—although *there is no indication of a significant advance either.*" (Icek Ajzen et al., in Chapter Five of this volume, italics added.)

I did not review a mass of comparable studies and deliberately select only those that would prove my point. To the contrary, I took the best sequence available at the time and worked with it. When I began the undertaking I was not at all certain that my initial disturbing impression was correct. It makes little difference to me how one reaches the conclusion that we may not have been making much progress over the past several decades. However arrived at, it should be a matter for social scientists to worry over. I submit, as one possible explanation for our lack of progress, that it may be a consequence of decisions made during earlier decades, largely in terms of scientific respectability. We may now be reaping the fruits of choices seeded out of the temper of those times. Those seeds and those times were discussed in Chapter Two.

The research cited in footnote six in this chapter provides some hopeful indication that, since 1965, this situation may be improving. In Chapter Ten we will consider that possibility. Discussions with Melvin DeFleur who, with his students and colleagues has provided important leadership in exploring this problem, leads me to believe that he is aware of and sensitive to most of the issues raised in the present critique and that his future research will attempt to deal with them. The relative amount of confidence we are able to have in these three studies raises questions about validity tests based upon independent verification (convergent validity) in contemporary sociology. In Chapter Five, we will use this analysis as a launching pad for a consideration of the problem of validity and its cousin, reliability. As we shall see, the question of what validates what is a sticky one even under the best of conditions. In order to make optimal use of our credibility screen and to aid in properly discounting the evidence being considered, Part II will concentrate on methodological issues.

PART TWO

Methods: The Credibility of Evidence

5 How Do We Know We Know?

The Validity Problem

The problem of validity has tended to receive short shrift in the social sciences. At least, this appears to be true when we compare it to the attention devoted to the problem of reliability. Following the customary distinction, the concept of validity addresses itself to the truth of an assertion made about something in the empirical world. The concept of reliability, on the other hand, focuses on the degree of consistency in observations obtained from the devices we employ: interviewers, schedules, tests, documents, observers, informants. Although it is possible to create an abstract mathematical relationship between validity and reliability, the relationship between the two concepts is asymmetric; i.e., measurement can be consistently in error as well as consistently correct and therefore a high degree of reliability can be achieved anywhere along the continuum between absolute invalidity and absolute validity.

The paradigm may be expressed as follows: when reliability is high, validity may be either high or low, but when reliability is low, validity must be low. Cases of low reliability associated with high validity must be attributed either to chance or to a hidden (unrecognized and unintended) dimension of reliability in the instrument. It follows that any mathematical formula which expresses validity as a direct function of reliability, or vice versa, must be in error. Whenever I suggest this formulation, students inevitably raise the question of the unique historical event, a problem which also concerns Weigert.[1] The reliability of observations of events which do not repeat themselves is an important matter—as is the validity of reports of those observations. Such an event may range anywhere from a large-scale encounter which no one alive remembers (say, the War of 1812) to a small-scale exchange of action or conversation (of the type reported by Whyte in *Streetcorner Society* or Leibow in *Talley's Corner*). Such events do happen only once, but there are ways of checking both the reliability and the validity of reports on them. The concept of inter-rater reliability, generally applied to comparisons of ratings by different raters of a test or coding system, is equally applicable to different observers of an historical event. It is also possible to apply the notion of test-retest reliability (comparisons of ratings on a test or coding system at different times) to historically embedded events,[2] but this procedure has peculiar problems even when applied to a standardized test.

1. Andrew J. Weigert, "The Immoral Rhetoric of Scientific Sociology," *American Sociologist* 5 (1970): 115–16.
2. Rhonda K. Cassetta, "Stranger in the Family," in *Among the People: Encounters with the Poor*, eds. Irwin Deutscher and Elizabeth J. Thompson (New York: Basic Books, Inc., 1968), pp. 294–315.

The notion of test-retest or any other reliability measure involving a time sequence is antithetical to social science since it must make the incorrect assumption that human thought and behavior is static, and therefore, that any change in response is a reflection of either instrument error or deception. Such recorded changes are, in fact, more likely to reflect shifts in sentiment or behavior on the part of the respondent. For this reason, I will restrict the concept of reliability to procedures which have no time component, e.g., inter-rater, inter-item, interviewer, informant, or observer reliability. If this is not done, then the distinction between reliability and validity becomes even fuzzier than it is otherwise. If I administer an instrument designed, for example, to measure prejudice, and then readminister the same instrument to the same population a second time, how do I interpret whatever differences appear? Assuming the logic of test-retest reliability, my interpretation is that the instrument is not stable—that I get different results from different administrations to the same people and that therefore there is something defective in the technique. On the other hand, the very same differences can be construed as valid reflections of rapid and subtle changes in attitudes. This second interpretation suggests that, rather than being defective, the instrument is extremely sensitive.

The fuzziness in the distinction derives largely from the fact that whether one is dealing with the idea of validity or with the idea of reliability depends on one's purpose and perspective.[3] If, on the one hand, the investigator is interested in the internal consistency of an instrument—a question of reliability—then he may randomly split the items into two sets and compare them for uniformity of results. If, on the other hand, he is interested in whether one half of the items on the same instrument can provide substantiating or confirmatory evidence that the other half are in fact getting at what is intended, then we have a test of validity. This is indeed an uncomfortable kind of relativity with which to live. Appalled by the absurdity of it all, Weigert coins what he refers to as his mock-serious "barbaric term 'valiability.' " One of the things that bothers Weigert is Campbell and Fisk's conclusion that reliability and validity can be conceptualized as a continuum:[4] "As you move away from reliability, you do not approach validity!"[5] Clearly, such a continuum perverts the distinction between the ideas of reliability and validity.

Weigert throws up his hands in disgust, describing the concept of validity as "an untenable naiveté."[6] I cannot argue that he is incorrect, but although we may entertain the same conclusion, I am more hopeful than he. I believe that the ideas of validity and reliability taken together provide the basis for determining credibility. Unless we can cope in a satisfactory way with the question, "How believable is the evidence?" then we are permanently mired down. There can be no progress without consideration of that question and I view the concepts of reliability and validity, however fuzzy (or "naive"), to be the best available hooks on which to hang that essential question. But it must be conceded that the confusion between these two concepts has not been fully considered here. For example, a further qualification to the paradigm describing the relationship between the two needs to be added. It

3. It was Joseph Gutenkauf, in a seminar, who first convinced me of this relativity. Later, I discovered essentially the same logic employed in Donald T. Campbell and D. W. Fiske, "Convergent and Discriminant Validation by the Multitrait-Multimethod Matrix," *Psychological Bulletin* 56 (1959): 81–105.

4. Ibid.

5. Weigert, "The Immoral Rhetoric of Scientific Sociology," p. 115.

6. Ibid., p. 115.

must be allowed that every reliable indicator is also a valid indicator of *something!* In other words, if a measure is highly consistent then it is reflecting a consistency in something in the empirical world. Here we identify the essentially subjective nature of the idea of validity: when the paradigm suggests the coupling of high reliability with low validity, *that means validity in terms of what the investigator intends to observe.* Our observation is not valid unless it matches our intentions, unless it addresses that object in the empirical world about which we are curious. If it reflects some other object then, for all its reliability, it is valid only in relation to that other object. It has no or low validity for our purposes.

Having laid this definitional groundwork, let me return to what I referred to in Chapter Two as our "obsession with reliability." Clearly, I believe that we have tended to neglect validity and to be over-attentive to problems of reliability. The sources of our "enchantment with reliability," as Merton more graciously put it, can be at least partially identified. First, reliability is in fact an important issue meriting serious attention. We are indeed faced with serious problems not only of instability in our measuring instruments but of instability of the populations we are attempting to measure. This dual instability compounds our problems, since we cannot always be certain of the extent to which discrepant readings on our instruments are a result of instrument error and the extent to which they are a result of the innate cussedness of our research subjects, who frequently insist on changing their minds—changing both their sentiments and their actions—and therefore changing their responses to our delicately balanced instruments. Robert Redfield and Oscar Lewis, for example, provide radically different pictures of the same little Mexican village—Tepotzlan. To what extent is the difference attributable to differential reliability in the two observers and to what extent does it result from the flow of historical events? Furthermore, if the problems with interviewers described by Julius Roth (Chapter Six) are widespread, then serious reliability problems remain for us to deal with.

Since it is not possible, except by chance alone, to obtain high validity in conjunction with low reliability, this is a problem of no mean importance. One reason, then, for our concentration on problems of reliability is that they are central to our successful pursuit of knowledge about human behavior. Clues to a second source of our concern with problems of reliability can be found, I believe, in the sociology of knowledge. Harking back to some of the evidence presented in Chapter Two, it seems that during the 1930s those sociologists who were most committed to objective empirical research embarked upon a crusade to achieve scientific respectability for the discipline, which at that time suffered considerable contempt both within the universities and outside. This crusade manifested itself in an effort to purify sociology of its association with do-gooders, on the one hand, and, on the other, a self-conscious pursuit of methodological rigor along lines analogous to what was perceived as The Scientific Method. Problems of reliability were amenable to attack within this framework. A body of technology already existed and could easily be developed further. We know now how to measure reliability and we know how to improve it and, most important, we can obtain clear, convincing, and reproducible evidence of the precise extent to which our methodological refinements increase our confidence in the reliability of our data. We can measure our improvements in measurement and we can measure them well and that is a very satisfying accomplishment—one upon which a scientist in any discipline can look with pleasure and approval.

The most critical source of our obsession with reliability may be the fact that we have been able to concentrate on it while simultaneously neglecting validity because we have developed certain concepts that encourage us to do so. The idea of the operational definition is a device precisely designed to eliminate the problem of validity. When we define the object of our interest to be the phenomenon our instrument is measuring, we need no longer worry about validity. Etzioni provides an example of how operational definitions can divert us from our intended purposes:

> Lewis Richardson sought to discover whether an increase in armaments increases or decreases national security. As armaments cannot be totaled, he used, instead, sums spent on arms. As security cannot be neatly quantified, he used the number of casualties in the wars that followed periods of arming. Thus, rather than answer the question he set out to answer—one of vital importance—he discovered how much it costs to kill a soldier.[7]

More recent conceptual innovations that achieve the same end as the operational definition are such notions as "intrinsic validity," "construct validity," and "face validity."[8] There have been a variety of efforts to classify types of validity (as Ajzen et al. suggest in their section of this chapter), but such taxonomical games provide no solutions. Another analyst has put it nicely: "The pretentiousness involved in such phrases as 'face validity' for common sense, and 'group validity' for authoritative opinion, and 'construct validity' for logical consistency is patently rhetorical."[9]

I have suggested three possible explanations for our obsession with reliability. Although they may be plausible in that they help us to understand why we have not concentrated on the problem of validity, they do not obviate the need for an independent verification that our conclusions do indeed reflect the empirical phenomena we claim—i.e., that they are valid. I find the idea of convergent validity a useful one under some conditions. Webb and his colleagues borrow the concept of "triangulation" from celestial navigation in order to argue that independent sources of information can confirm (validate) one another, even though each of those sources may have certain weaknesses:

> Once a proposition has been confirmed by two or more independent measurement processes, the uncertainty of its interpretation is greatly reduced. The most persuasive evidence comes through a triangulation of measurement processes. If a proposition can survive the onslaught of a series of imperfect measures, with all their irrelevant error, confidence should be placed in it. Of course, this confidence is increased by minimizing error in each instrument and by a reasonable belief in the different and divergent effects of the sources of error.[10]

7. Amatai Etzioni, "Communication: Mathematics for Sociologists?" *American Sociological Review* 30 (1965): 943. In Chapter Twelve, we shall again consider the problems created by operational definitions.

8. H. Gulliksen, "Intrinsic Validity," *American Psychologist* 5 (1950): 511–17; L. J. Cronbach and P. E. Meehl, "Construct Validity in Psychological Tests," *Psychological Bulletin* 52 (1955): 281–302.

9. Weigert, "The Immoral Rhetoric of Scientific Sociology," p. 115.

10. Eugene J. Webb, Donald T. Campbell, Richard D. Schwartz, and Lee Sechrest, *Unobtrusive Measures: Nonreactive Research in the Social Sciences* (Chicago: Rand McNally & Company, 1966), p. 3.

As we shall see when we consider the question of "what validates what," the triangulation solution is only partial. That is, when our multiple sources agree, its usefulness is different from conditions under which those sources disagree. There are several criteria of validity, but much of the remainder of this chapter hinges on what I consider to be the relatively viable notion of convergent validity. The idea of triangulation as reflected in the quotation above will be central to part of my analysis in Chapter Eight, where two very different studies with very different strengths and weaknesses are used to help answer the question, "Can the weaknesses of one be the strengths of the other?" For the moment, I will employ the data and analysis presented in Chapter Four as a basis for considering the logic of convergent validity.

Unlike Weigert I have considerable respect for "common sense," and the notion of convergent validity is one we commonly employ in our everyday pursuit of confirmation of events in the world around us. We seek validation of questionable impressions by searching for an independent source — hopefully one which has a different set of defects from the original source. If we find several such witnesses, reports, or observations which are in accord and, if we do not find independent observations which are contradictory, then we feel more secure in the truth of our impressions. That is convergent validation. That is what Webb et al. mean by "triangulation." That is the kind of behavioral rule which I suspect the ethnomethodologist seeks in his efforts to tease out the methodology applied by the ordinary member of society in his own pursuit of successful interaction and in his own effort to make sense of the empirical world.

Recall that the three studies analyzed in Chapter Four were all concerned with the general problem of the relationship between what people say and what they do. Furthermore they all focused on the same substantive expression of that problem — the relationship between a dominant and a minority group. They were conducted by different investigators, in different places, with different subjects, at three points in time. None of those studies is a rigorous replication of the others although two of them are similar in technique and instrumentation. It should be recognized that this similarity weakens the power of the validity test, since, to the extent that different studies replicate each other's methods, concordance between their results must be viewed as evidence of reliability rather than of independent validation. In such a replication we have evidence only that the same methods obtain the same results when employed by different investigators. We have evidence of validity just to the extent that the investigators employ methods that are mutually independent.

The analysis in Chapter Four suggests that the degree of confidence we can have in the conclusions of a study is related to factors independent of their temporal sequence: it is possible that in some important respects the oldest study may be the "best" and the most recent one, the "worst." Any application of a time-sequence logic to the idea of convergent validity is questionable. With the current state of our methods, we cannot assume that a later study necessarily validates or invalidates an earlier one. It would indeed be an error to assume that Linn's 1965 study could either validate or invalidate LaPiere's 1934 study under any conditions. If Linn is correct in his challenges to LaPiere's methods, then the LaPiere study would have to be treated as if it did not exist. It would make no difference whether there was agreement or disagreement between the Linn and the LaPiere findings. With LaPiere's study completely discounted, any relationship between the two sets of findings must be attributed to chance and the Linn study then becomes the baseline for future efforts at validation. To achieve validation we need to obtain evidence by means of at least two independent methods, both of which are tenable. It is not enough to simply observe that they both reach the same conclusions—as Linn and LaPiere do.

One group of distinguished scholars appears to deny the possibility of comparing studies undertaken from widely different perspectives. In what may be a gentlemanly avoidance of the issue, the members of a symposium attempting to relate field studies and laboratory experiments in social psychology have offered the following solution: without denigrating either type of evidence, they conclude that the findings based on these two types of studies are simply not "commensurate."[11] I believe otherwise. In the attempt to analyze such different studies comparatively, the trick, it seems to me, is not to accept them on the terms of the original investigator; rather, it is necessary to provide one's own unifying perspective. When this is done such studies do become commensurate. In Chapter Eight I shall apply this principle to a rigorous laboratory experiment and a clever field study.[12]

I closed Chapter Four with the comment that the question of what validates what is a sticky one even under the best of conditions. Let us pursue that comment. When two credible studies agree, the evidence is clear: they are valid. But what if they disagree? Which of the two is "invalid"? Campbell, for example, is able to show a correlation of +.90 between the morale rankings of submarine crews as measured on an "expensive and extensive" questionnaire and as ranked by informants who knew all the crews.[13] Since the two methods provide independent answers to the same question and those answers are nearly identical, we have evidence that our information is valid. But let us suppose that Campbell's comparative research had resulted in a low or negative correlation. What then? Perhaps one source of data is valid; perhaps the other one is; perhaps neither of them is. *It would appear that although we can achieve evidence of convergent validity when there is agreement, we are unable with this method to demonstrate where the source of invalidity lies when there is disagreement.*

It might be argued that, if we have three or more independent tests and if the three are of equal credibility, and if there is agreement between two and disagreement with the third, then we can assume that the third is invalid—that the majority rules. The three studies analyzed in the preceding chapter provide an example of one hypothetical difficulty with such a democratic position. Let us suppose that Linn and DeFleur-Westie had agreed with each other and had reached radically different conclusions from LaPiere (which, fortunately, they did not). We would then have considered LaPiere invalid—largely on the basis of the fact that he had been outnumbered and on the basis of our faith in "progress." That is, we would assume that the more recent the investigation, the more refined are its methods,

11. "Narrowing the Gap Between Field Studies and Laboratory Experiments in Social Psychology: A Statement by the Summer Seminar," SSRC Items, 8 (New York: Social Science Research Council, 1964).

12. Raymond L. Gorden, "Interaction Between Attitude and the Definition of the Situation in the Expression of Opinion," *American Sociological Review* 17 (1952): 50–58; B. H. Raven, "Social Influence on Opinions and the Communication of Related Content," *Journal of Abnormal and Social Psychology* 58 (1959): 119–28.

13. Donald T. Campbell, "The Informant in Quantitative Research," *American Journal of Sociology* 60 (1955): 339–42.

hence the more confidence we can place in its conclusions. It has been demonstrated in Chapter Four that this faith in Progress may be unwarranted.

It is also possible that when the results of two independent tests disagree, neither is valid. Employing as their criteria the ultimate evidence of behavioral validity—direct observation of the behavior in question—Freeman and Ataöv (see Chapter Three) find no correlation between direct and indirect indexes of the behavior and no correlation between either index and the behavior itself. This study of student cheating also suggests the disturbing possibility that independent observations may agree while both are in error. Suppose Freeman and Ataöv had found a high correlation between their direct and indirect measures, and suppose they had no observation of the behavior itself? We would have assumed convergent validity and we would have been wrong. Their neat little validation study suggests one solution to the validity-testing problem: the problem of validity is reduced when we have direct observation of the actual phenomenon we are attempting to approximate with our measuring instruments. Freeman and Ataöv have such a direct observation and so does LaPiere. This argument is elaborated by Becker and Geer in Chapter Seven.

LaPiere, you will remember, records direct observations of behavior under actual conditions of social interaction that are a real segment of the flow of everyday behavior of the actors. Statements such as this are not intended as denials of the "reality" of any observed behavior—including the behavior of students in experimental situations (such as those reported by Linn and DeFleur and Westie). I have already allowed that any reliable observation must be a valid indicator of something. It may be possible to derive valid conclusions from experiments with students, but those conclusions would relate to the behavior of subjects under experimental conditions (this is an interesting methodological phenomenon in its own right which will be addressed in Chapter Eight). Only LaPiere's work, however, permits valid conclusions regarding the behavior of members of a dominant group toward members of a minority group.

Validity poses a serious problem when we use instruments designed to provide estimates of hypothetical behavior. If, instead, our data consist of direct behavioral observations, the problem of validity is reduced to the extent that inferences are less necessary. We then become free to concentrate on important problems of reliability. Thus, in the case of LaPiere, we know that he observed what he intended to observe, but we are not certain how accurately he observed it. It is not a difficult task to determine the extent to which different observers will make the same observations. Replication becomes an important and legitimate pursuit under these conditions, rather than the meaningless game it is under conditions where validity is indeterminate. As Ehrlich and Rinehart[14] have demonstrated in their analysis of a highly reliable stereotype-measuring instrument which has been a standard tool since 1933, we can be consistently wrong and, as a consequence, consistently misunderstand human behavior.[15]

14. Howard J. Ehrlich and J. W. Rinehart, "A Brief Report on the Methodology of Stereotype Research," Social Forces 43 (1965): 564–75.

15. Being misunderstood, especially when dealing with so muddled a problem as reliability and validity, is a perennial problem. In the process of developing the position on validity expressed in the last few paragraphs, I have frequently found my comments interpreted as supportive of a behavioristic methodological stance. As I mentioned in Chapter One, this oc-

Direct behavioral observations reduce and may even eliminate problems of validity, but only if the concern of the investigation is the behavior being observed. Thus, if one is evaluating a program designed to change behavior and if that behavior is directly observable, then behavioral indicators are called for. But these qualifications are important since sometimes the behavior in question is not directly observable and, even more often, programs may be designed to do something other than have a direct effect on behavior. They may intend rather, to propagandize, to educate, to brainwash, to persuade, or to otherwise alter not so much what people do as what they think or believe or say. Such programs call for appropriate nonbehavioral indicators if they are to be properly evaluated. Furthermore, the relationship between attitudinal change and behavioral change remains elusive. It may be that under some conditions the most effective means of altering behavior is to first induce an attitudinal change.

But more to the point is what the term "behavioral observation" refers to. I have already indicated my dissatisfaction with the kind of fragmentation which occurs with time-and-motion studies such as the one reported by Tausky and Piedmont.[16] I have also suggested that there is a persuasive ring of credibility to participant observational reports such as the one provided by Roebuck and Spray[17] — although I had some reservations about the relevance of these "true" observations. But whether our observations are behavioral or attitudinal, we cannot afford, as scientists, to limit ourselves to input and output. As the discussion of prediction in the preceding chapter suggests, this is magical thinking. Regardless of the nature of our indicators, our primary concern is to build knowledge and this is done by focusing attention on what goes on inside the little black box — on the process of change — rather than focusing on the outcomes produced by certain stimuli.

In Chapter Two I referred to the need for a new technology of behavioral observations — one which observed, recorded, and made sense out of the social pro-

---

curred following the publication of my original statement in 1966 ("Words and Deeds: Social Science and Social Policy," *Social Problems* 13 [1966]: 235–54). I attempted to clarify and elaborate that statement in a 1969 article, but the misunderstanding persisted ("Looking Backward: Case Studies in the Progress of Methodology in Sociological Research," *American Sociologist* 4 [1969]: 35–41). In his introduction to a collection of papers on evaluation research, Francis Caro cites me as arguing "in favor of direct behavioral measures because they pose fewer validity problems than do procedures designed to provide estimates of hypothetical behavior" (Francis G. Caro, "Evaluation Research: An Overview," in *Readings in Evaluation Research*, ed. Francis G. Caro [New York: Russell Sage Foundation, 1971], p. 23). Donald Tarter, an articulate proponent of operant conditioning techniques in sociological research, would like to completely eliminate the mentalistic concept of attitude. He suggests that I support this proposal since I have argued that by observing behavior we can "reduce the problem of validity of our measuring instruments to negligible proportions and concentrate on the important problem of reliability" (Donald E. Tarter, "Attitude: The Mental Myth," *American Sociologist* 5 [1970]: 278). The quotes are accurate, but their interpretation is not. I hope that the following paragraphs will help clear this matter up. Incidentally, Tarter's position on operant conditioning is considered in Chapter Twelve.

16. Curt Tausky and Eugene B. Piedmont, "The Sampling of Behavior," *American Sociologist* 3 (1968): 49–51. For a critique of this paper, based on somewhat different grounds, see Sidney Rosen, "Letters: Independent Samples and Test-Retest Reliability," *American Sociologist* 3 (1968): 297.

17. Julian Roebuck and S. Lee Spray, "The Cocktail Lounge," *American Journal of Sociology* 72 (1967): 388–95.

cess of which the act is a part.[18] Sometimes that process and that act can be very simple. If we are concerned with student cheating on examinations, it is clear that the most valid indicator is the act itself: Freeman and Ataöv watch students cheat! This is the implication of Becker and Geer's analysis in Chapter Seven. When you remove yourself from direct knowledge of the phenomena and attempt to obtain reports or estimates by indirection, you become vulnerable to a variety of distorting influences. As the statistician would say, you lose degrees of freedom. Dealing with the more common and complicated social processes with which many social sciences are concerned, Becker and Geer insist that "participant observation can . . . provide us with a yardstick against which to measure the completeness of data gathered in other ways, a model which can serve to let us know what orders of information escape us when we use other methods."[19] What they are suggesting is a standard for gauging validity. Criminologists have always been aware of the distortions which occur in statistics on crime as one moves from crimes committed, to crimes reported, to criminals apprehended, to criminals convicted, to prisoners. Each of these population samples represents the loss of a degree of freedom and an increasing selective distortion in the residue. In the end, studies of prisoners are not very valid bases for inferences about criminals. The moral is, stay close to where the action is, whether that action be lingual, attitudinal, or behavioral.

This reference to criminal statistics brings us back once more to the observation that any reliable data must be a valid reflection of something. At this point, however, we shift perspectives from small, independent studies to larger sets of data frequently gathered and reported for official or public purposes. The traditional problem with statistics in criminology is that there have been no reliable data available on criminals, in part because many crimes are not reported and many criminals are either never identified or never apprehended. Criminologists have therefore sometimes used data such as those provided by the FBI on crimes reported to the police or data on incarcerated criminals. When such data are used as indicators of crime, they are not valid. However, when such data are used as indicators of reported offenses or prison populations, they are indeed valid—to the extent that they are reliable. The classic case remains Emile Durkheim's use of nineteenth-century suicide statistics.[20] Let us examine his interpretation of these data.

Durkheim's analysis suggests a remarkable stability in suicide rates within nations and within certain populations such as urban and rural or married and nonmarried or religious denominations. His data also suggest a high degree of stability through time. Furthermore, he observes that there are considerable differences

18. The notion of "unobtrusive measures" introduced by Webb et al., cited in footnote 10, provides useful clues to such a new technology. They argue that physical traces are nonreactive, i.e., not influenced by the process of being observed. Thus the differential wear of steps in a public building is a nonreactive indicator of differential use of that building or the presence of empty liquor bottles in trash is a nonreactive indicator of liquor consumption. This notion can be imaginatively applied to any number of areas of social research.

19. Howard S. Becker and Blanche Geer, "Participant Observation and Interviewing: A Comparison," *Human Organization* 16 (1957): 28 (reprinted in Chapter Seven). A well-informed "Comment" by Martin Trow, with a rejoinder by the authors, follows the article (pp. 33–40). For a collection of Becker's papers on method, see the first part of Howard S. Becker, *Sociological Work: Method and Substance* (Chicago: Aldine Publishing Co., 1970).

20. Emile Durkheim, *Suicide: A Study in Sociology* (Glencoe, Ill.: The Free Press, 1951). The original French edition was published in 1897.

in suicide rates among and between such populations and that these differences are relatively stable. The importance of these observations has been widely acknowledged among sociologists. There has also been considerable criticism. One of the most common critiques is the argument that the data available to Durkheim were crude and unreliable and therefore the conclusions he draws from those data are questionable. But, as we have seen, reliability is essentially a matter of consistency or stability, and that is precisely what is most remarkable about Durkheim's data. They are, in fact, highly reliable. Since we are proceeding on the assumption that any reliable data provide a valid indicator of something, the important question about Durkheim's suicide data becomes, "What are they a valid indicator of?"

In a highly critical vein, Jack Douglas suggests that what Durkheim is working with is the recording of norms of officials who are reflecting nothing more or less than what they perceive to be the values of the community. This is the basis for his argument that all such official data are social constructions of reality.[21] It is also the basis for suspicion of official data on the part of conscientious scientific analysts. Bernard Beck warns that "most of these officially and semiofficially generated statistics are untrustworthy and misleading . . . ."[22] There is, however, a more constructive note in Garfinkel's observation that there are "Good Organizational Reasons for 'Bad' Clinic Records."[23] There are many examples of the validity of consistent data when their consistency is properly identified. A study of 1000 New York schoolchildren during the 1930s is informative. They were selected as a sample of children who had not yet had their tonsils removed and were submitted to a panel of physicians for diagnosis. Roughly 40 percent of the children were diagnosed as needing their tonsils removed. The remainder were again submitted to a panel of physicians and, again, about 40 percent of them were diagnosed as needing their tonsils removed. The procedure was repeated until there were no longer sufficient numbers of remaining children. The percentage remained constant through each surviving cohort.[24]

What these data suggest is that the question of how many people "really" need their tonsils out or "really" kill themselves is essentially unanswerable, except within the limits of a collective judgment about tonsils or suicide. It may be that there was a dimension to Durkheim's notion of a "collective conscience" which

21. Jack D. Douglas, *The Social Meaning of Suicide* (Princeton: Princeton University Press, 1967).

22. Bernard Beck, "Cooking Welfare Stew," in *Pathways to Data: Field Methods for Studying Ongoing Social Organizations*, ed. Robert W. Habenstein (Chicago: Aldine Publishing Company, 1970), p. 27.

23. This is the title of Chapter 6 in Harold Garfinkel, *Studies in Ethnomethodology* (Englewood Cliffs, N.J.: Prentice-Hall, Inc., 1967), 186–207. See also John L. Kitsuse and Aaron V. Cicourel, "A Note on the Use of Official Statistics," *Social Problems* 11 (1963): 131–39.

24. *Physical Defects: Pathways to Correction* (New York: American Child Health Association, 1934). This is a crude report of the findings of an obscure study which I have not read. I am indebted to Alexander Rysman for the reference. In a personal communication, Rysman informs me that there is evidence that rates of surgery in the U.S. are higher than in England because there are more surgeons in the U.S., i.e., "the amount of surgery is a function of the number of surgeons." See John P. Bunker, "Surgical Manpower," *New England Journal of Medicine* (January 15, 1970): 135–44. Rysman also refers to Milton Roemer's argument that the amount of hospitalization is a function of the number of hospital beds. See Alexander Rysman, "Ill?" in *Social Problems in a Revolutionary Age*, ed. Jack Douglas (New York: Random House, forthcoming).

even he did not recognize. Durkheim proceeded as if his data did indeed reflect the rates at which people took their own lives. He attributed differences in rates largely to differences in social constraints. What is suggested by the ethnomethodological perspective (which is what we have been reviewing) is that the differences in rates are indeed a creature of the collective conscience—so much so that they may have little to do with the rates at which people "really" kill themselves. I believe that Douglas, in his otherwise excellent critique of Durkheim, is essentially making this argument, although he fails to get it across in his eagerness to destroy The Master. Durkheim's data, I submit, provide valid information on official and public norms about how many people of what types ought to be killing themselves. It is no different from data which inform us of professional norms about how many children ought to have their tonsils out.

Many of the observations made in this and the preceding chapter are not likely to find common agreement among contemporary social scientists. It may be helpful to provide some exposure to contrary views. One of the best statements criticizing the viewpoint I have been presenting is by a group of University of Illinois psychologists. The reader should be aware that any apparent non sequiturs in the following critique may be attributable to changes I have made as I restated my ideas. Let us listen to the other side.

DATA:
Looking Backward Revisited: A Reply to Deutscher
ICEK AJZEN / RUSSELL K. DARROCH / MARTIN FISHBEIN / JOHN A. HORNIK

In a recent article, Irwin Deutscher (1969) takes a backward look at three studies dealing with the attitude-behavior relationship in order to demonstrate a lack of progress in social science methodology. Essentially, Deutscher argues that progess in social science research has been delayed or blocked by (1) a failure to consider the problem of validity, and (2) a primary concern with prediction. He tries to support these arguments by analyzing three studies (those of LaPiere, 1934; DeFleur and Westie, 1958; and Linn, 1965), and he concludes that "we have suffered a dramatic methodological regression during the thirty-one-year time lapse covered by them." Finally, he argues that because of this methodological regression it becomes almost impossible to know "what validates what." Convergent validation by means of independent methods cannot be seriously considered since "with the current state of our methods, we cannot assume that a later study necessarily validates or invalidates an earlier study."

The present paper is a response to Deutscher on all of these points. More specifically, we hope to show that (1) the social sciences have been concerned with the validity problem, (2) Deutscher's treatment of "prediction" is

"Looking Backward Revisited: A Reply to Deutscher," by Icek Ajzen, Russell K. Darroch, Martin Fishbein, and John A. Hornik, from The American Sociologist, vol. 5 (1970), pp. 267–72. Reprinted by permission of the American Sociological Association and the authors.

inadequate, (3) there is no basis for the pessimistic evaluation of current methodology in the social sciences, and (4) there is a great deal of convergent validation, at least with respect to the area of discourse selected by Deutscher, namely the attitude-behavior relationship.

Validity

Deutscher claims that the social sciences have been so obsessed with the reliability problem that they have almost completely neglected the problem of validity. To anyone familiar with the vast body of literature on the validity problem, this statement is, at best, somewhat surprising. Further, for someone as concerned with validity as Deutscher seems to be, it is also surprising to find that he completely confounds three different aspects of validity: the validity of measurement instruments or test validity, and both the internal and the external validity of experimental designs.

Test validity refers to the question of whether we are measuring what we think we are measuring. Deutscher, in a beautiful example of confused reasoning, not only dismisses the operational definition as a device that tends to obscure the problem of validity, but, in the same vein, rejects such notions as "intrinsic validity," "construct validity," and "face validity." According to Deutscher, all of these notions "assure us that we may be content with the validity of an instrument if the items of which it is composed appear reasonably to represent the object of our interest," and he cites Cronbach and Meehl (1955) as a basis for this assertion. It should be noted, first, that Deutscher's concern is clearly with Bergman's (1951) explicit form of operationalism, an outmoded formulation that has long since been replaced by a more liberal form allowing multiple reductions and showing considerable interest in the question of appropriateness and validity of definitions (Kaplan, 1964). Second, to any reader familiar with the logic of Cronbach and Meehl's validating methods, the notion that construct validity is tied solely to item content and thus is equivalent in some way to face validity must come as a surprise. Third, since Deutscher seems willing to regard convergence as an acceptable method of validation, his rejection of construct validity is even less understandable since convergent validity is *one* of the aspects of construct validity discussed by Cronbach and Meehl.

Deutscher's discussion of test validity, however, is completely irrelevant to his subsequent methodological critique in which he raises a question concerning the degree to which a research finding of a relationship (or lack of a relationship) between two variables is valid. Here, as Campbell and his associates (Campbell, 1957, 1969; Campbell and Stanley, 1963) have pointed out, two distinct types of validity are involved: (1) internal validity, or the question "Did in fact the experimental treatments make a difference in this experimental instance?" and (2) external validity, or "the question of *generalizability:* To what populations, settings, treatment variables, and measurement variables can this effect be generalized?"

Not only have Campbell and his associates made this distinction, they have provided a list of fifteen factors jeopardizing internal and external validity. This list provides a very useful guide for the experimenter and clearly shows a great concern with achieving a high degree of validity within our experimental designs. Deutscher, however, essentially dismisses the whole question of internal validity by rejecting the notion of cause and effect as a legitimate concern of science; it may therefore be worthwhile to consider this question before continuing our discussion of validity.

Prediction

To varying degrees, Deutscher criticizes the studies he reviewed for their "primary concern with prediction, a primitive scientific notion that assumes a direct, uninterrupted, straight-line flow of behavior. The idea of such simple cause-and-effect relationships between two variables has been by and large discarded in the philosophy of science."

This astounding statement is footnoted by some anecdotes about the futility of prediction on the grounds that "one may accurately predict without ever understanding why the prediction works." Deutscher further "supports" this statement by referring to Herbert Blumer's assertion that "prediction of a later phase of a social act is not possible on the basis of knowledge of an earlier phase." Thus, according to Deutscher, not only is prediction impossible, it is unscientific. While it is true (and hardly new) that prediction is possible without understanding why the prediction works, it is also true that there can be no understanding without at least some degree of predictability. Whether or not the task of science is to further understanding, there is always the need for objective criteria of the "goodness" of any proposed theoretical account. Although prediction is by no means the only, and is perhaps not the best, criterion, it is one that has proved useful.

But what is even more amazing than Deutscher's rejection of prediction is his equation of prediction with cause and effect. Deutscher's own argument that prediction is possible without understanding is testimony to the fact that the demonstration of predictability *does not* imply anything about cause and effect. Similarly, Deutscher seems to have no argument with the search for simple relationships among variables *even though* a statistical relationship usually implies some degree of predictability but does not imply anything about causality. Indeed, none of the studies reviewed by Deutscher could have had (as he implies) an objective of confirming or disconfirming a causal relationship since all three were correlational in nature. As Deutscher correctly observes, the purpose of each of the studies was to investigate the relationship between some paper-and-pencil measure and some observation or indicant of behavior. While it may be true that the authors of the papers that he refers to were primarily interested in the degree to which they could predict behavior from attitude, they could just as well have been interested in the degree to which they could predict attitude from behavior. Deutscher thus falsely accuses the studies of being concerned with cause and effect because he fails to distinguish between prediction and causal relations.

It should be noted that had the studies been directed at exploring causal hypotheses, many of Deutscher's concerns with the question of validity would have been answered. It is only in the context of experimental or quasi-experimental designs (not correlational ones) that causal hypotheses can be investigated, and, as pointed out above, we do have adequate guidelines for examining those factors that threaten internal and external validity.

Indeed, while Deutscher claims that there is no place for the study of causal relations in science, we would argue that science often progresses through such undertakings. Understanding of a phenomenon is usually attempted by proposing some explanation, by building a theory. In a theory, the scientist can propose any number of constructs and any kind of relationship among the constructs. The relationship may or may not imply cause and effect. Whatever the theoretical structure, however, it is the scientist's task to provide evidence for his theory. In the context of a scientific theory, then, the question of prediction or causal relationships becomes a question of the methodology required to substantiate the theory; it ceases to be a meta-theoretical question regarding the legitimacy of postulating causal relationships.

To summarize briefly, up to this point we have tried to show that (1) the social sciences have not neglected the validity problem; indeed, one has merely to look at the works of Cronbach and Meehl (1955), Lovinger (1957), and Campbell and Fiske (1959) on test validity and Campbell and his associates (Campbell, 1957, 1969; Campbell and Stanley, 1963; Winch and Campbell, 1969) on the validity of experimental designs to realize that the validity problem is one that has received considerable attention in the literature; and (2) Deutscher's objection to prediction is speculative, meta-theoretical, and based on a failure to distinguish between prediction and causal relationships.

Let us now turn to the question of whether social science methodology has progressed or regressed, as indicated by the three studies selected by Deutscher. Before doing this, however, certain points should be made.

First, it would appear unwise to rest our judgment of the state of current methodology in the social sciences on an examination of a single subject (the attitude-behavior relationship) and, within that area, on a limited selection of three studies. However, since this has been the approach taken by Deutscher, we shall reply to his arguments within these restrictions.

Second, since the three studies reviewed by Deutscher are correlational in nature, the whole question of internal validity and the concern with testing causal relations becomes irrelevant. Indeed, the only questions about validity that can be raised relate to test validity and external validity or the question of generalizability. That is, in the context of a correlational study we face two major problems of validity: (1) Are our tests measuring what we think they are measuring? and (2) If these measures are indeed valid, to what populations, settings, and measurement variables can the observed relationship between these two measures be generalized? It is worth noting that to a large extent Deutscher's primary concerns are with this latter question of external validity. He also asks another question that may or may not be viewed as properly falling under the rubric of validity: If these measures are valid, have we applied appropriate statistical analyses to study the degree of relationship between them?

Methodology: A Reanalysis

Deutscher's methodological criticism of three studies in the attitude and behavior domain (Linn, 1965; DeFleur and Westie, 1958; LaPiere, 1934) attempts to show that the state of the behavioral scientist's art in this area has not only failed to advance but has regressed since LaPiere. While some of Deutscher's criticisms are correct and appropriate, he has at times overstated his case. In addition, he has overlooked several important flaws in each of the studies and has made a few errors in his evaluation of the methods of data analysis employed in them. He has also failed to realize that the three studies may not be readily comparable.

Deutscher begins his methodological analyses with a consideration of Linn's (1964) study, and, among other things, he criticizes the study because Linn's sample is "small (34) and select (female students)" and because this selectivity is additionally compounded by Linn's use of volunteers. While Deutscher is correct in questioning the possible selection bias involved in using only volunteers, his opposition to the use of a homogeneous subject population (female students) overlooks the advantage of such a sample in decreasing variability due to extraneous factors (a practice quite common to laboratory research). Further, it should be noted that selecting a sample from a homogeneous population will only weaken the external validity, not the internal validity, of a study (Campbell and Stanley, 1963).

As to sample size, a small sample is not necessarily bad; it may actually provide a more conservative test of the investigator's hypotheses because it demands a stronger relationship in order to obtain a standard level of statistical significance. Had Linn used a larger sample and found the same trends in his data, it is likely that his results would have been significant. Deutscher's comments on sample size and correlations suggest that he does not fully understand the relationship between sample size and statistical significance. One problem concerning sample size that does exist in the Linn study (and that was correctly identified by Deutscher) is that the application of the chi-square is inappropriate since the expected frequencies for seven of nine cells are less than five. According to most standards, expected frequencies of this size violate one of the main assumptions of the test.

This, however, is the only assumption of the test that is not met. Deutscher's statement that "numerous assumptions are required by the statistical procedures without evidence that these assumptions are met" is groundless. The failure to demonstrate scalability of test items does not violate the statistics' assumptions because only nominal categories are required. However, it may be argued that Linn's statistical treatment could be improved. If we can assume that the data is ordinal, Linn could have made use of available non-parametric correlational techniques. Although Linn had computed a correlation coefficient, he failed to report it. A reanalysis of the data given by Linn yields a gamma coefficient of .54, which, although not statistically significant (p > .05), suggests that some 50 per cent of the variance in the data is accounted for by the relationship between attitude and behavior (Goodman and Kruskal, 1954). Thus the discrepancy between these variables may be smaller than Linn indicates. He also did not report the correlation between his two measures of attitude, and this could be of interest.

Deutscher's argument that the Linn study "incorporates no form of control group" fails to recognize that this study employs a correlational design and not a true experimental design (see Campbell and Stanley, 1963). In correlational studies, subjects serve as their own controls, and therefore Deutscher's criticism is inappropriate.

As in the case with the Linn study, Deutscher's discussion of the study by DeFleur and Westie (1958) makes incorrect criticisms of the size and selection of their sample. Subjects in their study were selected from the top and bottom quartiles of scores on an attitude scale (a summated differences scale) and they were matched on eight socio-economic and experiential variables; they did not volunteer. Neither this selection nor the size of the sample threatens the internal validity of the study, although it may lack external validity. However, as mentioned above, Deutscher does not distinguish between these two types of validity.

The suggestion that the questionnaires used may have been reactive is a point well taken. However, as this is also a correlational design, our comments concerning control groups made with regard to the Linn study again apply. The study does not demand a control group in the sense suggested by Deutscher, although such a group would answer a question concerning the reactivity of the questionnaire.

Deutscher's observation that DeFleur and Westie achieve some parsimony in the number of assumptions required because they do not use correlational analysis seems to be irrelevant. Indeed, if the data meet the assumptions of a more powerful statistical test, one can only lose information by failing to use (or rejecting the use of) such a test. However, we agree with Deutscher that the use of chi-square in the DeFleur and Westie study is acceptable since the expected values in each cell are greater than five. Unfortunately, Deutscher fails to notice that the chi-square computed by DeFleur and Westie is in error, because for 1 degree of freedom (as in their 2-by-2 table, p. 671) the chi-square test of association calls for the use of Yates's correction for continuity (Hays, 1963). Recomputing that statistic yields a value of 5.72 which is somewhat less than the 7.26 reported by the original authors. The recomputed value still yields a significant result, but at the .02 rather than the .01 level. Also, it would have been helpful if they had reported the mean used in determining their categories for the chi-square table.

There are several other comments that pertain to both the Linn and the DeFleur and Westie studies. First, neither study determined subjects' feelings about having their picture taken under any circumstances; casual observation (one of the authors is a photographer) leads us to suspect that several of the subjects in each study may not have signed any level on the release form simply because they did not want to be photographed. Second, the releases did not distinguish between two possible types of behaviors: (1) whether or not the Ss would be photographed with a black, and (2) the minimal *use* to which Ss would allow such a photograph to be put. Linn and DeFleur and Westie only used the second of these measures even though the first measure may have been more appropriate to their theoretical concerns and some of their analyses. Our comment is that the studies should have been designed so that the act of photographing the subject with a black actually occurred.

Finally, Deutscher observes that "voluntary withdrawal (i.e., refusal to participate) in Study Y [DeFleur and Westie's study] was 81.6 per cent; in Study Z [LaPiere's study] it was 49.0 per cent." Careful reading of the DeFleur and Westie article assures us that they did not report *any* refusals to participate. We are forced to conclude that Deutscher calculated the percentage of "volunteers" as follows:

$$100 \times \frac{\substack{46 \text{ laboratory } Ss \\ (\text{matched: 23 upper, 23 lower quartiles})}}{250 \; Ss \text{ in the original attitude survey}} = 18.4\%$$

Then he concluded that 81.6 per cent of the subjects refused to participate! De-Fleur and Westie selected a subset of the larger group; they did *not* ask for volunteers. Such gross misrepresentation of the data seems less than desirable.

Apart from his ubiquitous comments about the nature of the cause-and-effect relationship between attitudes and behavior, Deutscher treats LaPiere's study as the high point in the history of the investigation of this relationship. Apparently enamoured by the field nature of the study, he overlooks many of its difficulties. At least two of his criticisms of Linn and DeFleur and Westie also apply to LaPiere. First, the 49 per cent refusal rate on LaPiere's questionnaire is a real refusal rate, not a statistical creation like Deutscher's 81.6 per cent rate for the DeFleur and Westie study. While a 51 per cent return rate on a mailed questionnaire is fairly good, it still presents the usual difficulties of unknown selection bias. Second, Deutscher implies that the use of "128 mature adults engaged in the conduct of responsible business" is a great advance over the use of laboratory subjects. We fail to understand why the external validity of a relationship based on observations drawn from a population that is homogeneous with respect to age and education is necessarily weaker than one based on a population that is homogeneous with respect to occupation. LaPiere's study clearly suffers from some of the defects Deutscher has found in the researches of Linn and DeFleur and Westie. However, these are not the only problems of the LaPiere study that Deutscher has chosen to overlook.

The description of the attitude object and the situation is sufficiently incomplete and ambiguous in the letter-questionnaire that it probably constituted a very different stimulus from the actual Chinese couple. The relationship LaPiere found might have been different if the question had been worded, "Would you accept a young, well-dressed, well-spoken, pleasant, self-confident, well-to-do Chinese couple accompanied by a mature, well-dressed, well-spoken . . . educated European gentleman as guests in your establishment?" Furthermore, many of the respondents may have regarded the questionnaire not as an opportunity to speculate on what they would do in such a situation but as a convenient opportunity to avoid any possible trouble. Thus, the responses may not be honest expressions of intention. In addition, LaPiere had no way to determine if the person who responded to the questionnaire was the same person who had served him and the Chinese couple in the actual situation. Particularly in larger establishments, the person serving the Chinese couple and the person who responded to the questionnaire may not have been the same. Further, there may have been a number of changes in personnel during the six months between the observations of behavior and the questionnaire. A related problem is that the reliability of the attitudinal and behavioral measures would decrease over six months. Since the strength of the relationship between the two measures, separated in time, depends partly upon their separate test-retest reliabilities, the long time lag may be a problem. However, no reliability data were reported.

Deutscher chastises Linn and DeFleur and Westie for their carelessness about demand characteristics while praising LaPiere for his "valiant effort" to remain out of the behavioral situation. Inspection of LaPiere's data reveals, however, that he remained outside of the situation on only 14 per cent of the occasions. Finally, while Deutscher claims that LaPiere's study uses a control group, he again fails to recognize that it is still a correlational design. At best, the control group could only show that the behavior probably did not influence responses on the questionnaire; it provides no information concerning the influence of attitude on behavior.

A thorough methodological analysis of the three case studies does not seem to indicate a regressive trend in methodology — although there is no indication of a significant advance either. Inferring a regression or advance in the history of method in social science on the basis of a comparison of only three studies is of questionable value anyway. Furthermore, there are a number of differences between the measures used in the three studies, and this suggests that it may not be possible to make a meaningful comparison between their outcomes. It seems that three, and not two, variables have been investigated, and it is useful to distinguish between them. The first variable is attitude toward an object (A_0) which is the amount of positive or negative affect toward the object. The second is the behavioral intention (BI) which is the degree to which a person *intends to engage in* a particular behavior with respect to the attitude object. The third is the behavior (B) that a person *actually engages in* with respect to the given attitude object.

Reviewing the measures used in the three studies cited by Deutscher, it is apparent that each study employed different subsets of these three variables. Linn first obtained a general measure of attitude toward Negroes (A_0) and an indication of the individual's willingness to release a hypothetical photograph with a Negro for various purposes (BI). One week later he asked volunteers from the first group of subjects to sign a series of photographic releases. While the act of signing may be viewed as a behavior, it can more adequately be viewed as an indication of the subject's willingness to release a hypothetical photograph (BI) since the signing *preceded* the photography (which was never done).[1] A behavioral observation (B) was made on those subjects who had indicated any willingness to release a photograph by asking them to return at a later time to be photographed and then observing whether or not they showed up.

DeFleur and Westie first obtained a general measure of attitude toward Negroes (A_0) and then asked a selected sample of subjects to sign a series of photographic releases. In the context of this study also, the releases indicated only a willingness to release hypothetical photographs and again the study must be regarded as measuring behavioral intention (BI). It did not include a measure of behavior. LaPiere employed a measure of behavioral intention (that is, to serve a Chinese couple) and a measure of actual behavior. No measure of attitude (as defined above) was included at any point in his study. This discussion is summarized in Table 1. Further, a consideration of the relationships investigated in each of these studies demonstrates a lack of comparability between them. That is, Linn investigated the relationship between S's intention to sign photographic releases at T_1 with his intention (or signing) at T_2 (that is, BI_1 with BI_2). DeFleur and Westie considered the relationship between a general attitude measure and intention to sign (or actual signing of) photographic releases (that is, A_0 with BI_2). LaPiere was concerned with the relationship between people's intentions to admit Orientals to their establishments and the actual acceptance or rejection behavior that occurred (that is, BI with B). Given the partial overlap between the variables and the

---

[1]It is worth noting that these two behavioral intention measures are identical for all practical purposes. The relatively low relationship between them can be interpreted in two ways: (1) that the instrument has low reliability and/or (2) that there were differences in the conditions under which the two measurements were taken.

lack of any overlap in the relationships investigated by the studies, it seems un-likely that any particular benefit can be derived from arguing that the studies are comparable and therefore validate or invalidate each other.

TABLE 1. **SUMMARY OF VARIABLES MEASURED IN THREE STUDIES**

Author	Attitude toward an Object (Ao)	Behavioral Intention (BI)	Behavior (B)
Linn (1965)	X	X_1 X_2	(X)
DeFleur and Westie (1958)	X	X_2	..
LaPiere (1934)	..	X	X

An "X" indicates that a measure of the variable was obtained.

The "(X)" under the behavior column for Linn in Table 1 represents the fact that only those subjects who signed the release (twenty-two out of thirty-four) were asked to return to have their pictures taken and that little use was made of this observation in the presentation of results. It is worth noting that sixteen of the twenty-two actually did show up for their appointments, indicating that there is some relationship between verbal expression of intention and behavior, although Linn and Deutscher choose to ignore this. If Linn had requested *all* subjects to return to be photographed (that is, if he had asked those subjects who refused to sign any release to come back if they changed their minds), he might have found an even stronger relationship between intention and behavior. In the absence of such data, we propose the following conservative, but suggestive, analysis. Assum-ing that as many as three of the twelve nonsigners had showed up (if all subjects had been asked to do so), we have the data necessary to compute a phi co-efficient. This computation yields a value of .70 (p < .01), which offers some ad-ditional support for the conclusion that there is some relationship between behav-ioral intention and behavior in this situation. (Linn's report does not provide data on the relationship between his attitude measure and behavior.) Of course, the relationship between verbal expression of intention and behavior is not perfect, and to expect it to be so would be naive.

Another difference between the studies that may make a substantial dif-ference in the obtained relationships is that different norms are appropriate to the situations. In the Linn study, the norms that were relevant for the students might have been the values of their parents or peers; DeFleur and Westie have evidence (perhaps artifactual due to the demand characteristics of the interview question) that suggests that peers' norms were most salient. In the LaPiere study it is likely that norms of hospitality and courtesy (recall that the "subjects" were hotel and restaurant employees) strongly influenced the respondents' behavior. Further sup-port for the importance of norms and attitudes as codeterminants of behavior appears in the recent writings of Ehrlich (1969), Fishbein (1967), and Warner and DeFleur (1969).

Convergent Validation

Based on his review, Deutscher reaches the conclusion that due to the poor methodology in the social sciences different studies cannot be taken to validate or invalidate each other; that is, there can be no evidence of convergent validity. However, as we have seen, Deutscher's case against the methodology of the three studies is overstated. Indeed, as far as the relationship between attitudinal-type variables and behavior is concerned, it appears possible to draw with reasonable confidence a conclusion based on a far greater number of studies than the three reviewed by Deutscher (for example, Kutner, et al., 1952; Saenger and Gilbert, 1950; Mann, 1959; Fendrich, 1967; Newton and Newton, 1950; Potter and Klein, 1957). Festinger (1964) and McGuire (1969) have concluded that there is a rather low relationship between a person's verbal report of his attitude and his actual behavior toward the object of the attitude. At the same time there does seem to be some evidence for a strong relationship between measures of specific behavioral intentions and behavior (Ajzen, 1969; Ajzen and Fishbein, 1969; Dulany, 1967; Fishbein, 1967). Recent publications (Fishbein, 1967; Warner and DeFleur, 1969; Ehrlich, 1969) indicate a renewed interest in these problems, and this interest takes as its starting point the low degree of relationship usually found between attitude and behavior.

While there are many other objections that could be made about various statements in the Deutscher paper (for example, his argument that "the ultimate evidence of validity [is] direct observation of the behavior in question") we feel that we have already spent too much time "looking backward." For the sake of progress in the social sciences, we hope that less effort will be expended in "looking backward" through distorted lenses and that more effort will be directed toward taking constructive steps forward.

References

Ajzen, Icek
    1969   Prediction and Change of Behavior in the Prisoner's Dilemma. Unpublished doctoral dissertation. University of Illinois, Urbana.
Ajzen, I., and M. Fishbein
    1969   "The prediction of choice behavior in the prisoner's dilemma game." Paper presented at 41st annual meeting of the Midwestern Psychological Association.
Bergman, G.
    1951   "The logic of psychological concepts." Philosophy of Science 18 (April):93 – 110.
Campbell, D. T.
    1957   "Factors relevant to the validity of experiments in social settings." Psychological Bulletin 54 (July):297 – 312.
    1969   "Reforms as experiments." American Psychologist 24 (April):409 – 429.
Campbell, D. T., and D. W. Fiske
    1959   "Convergent and discriminant validation by the multitrait-multimethod matrix." Psychological Bulletin 56 (March):81 – 105.
Campbell, D. T., and J. C. Stanley
    1963   "Experimental and quasi-experimental designs for research on teaching." In N. L. Gage (ed.), Handbook of Research on Teaching. Chicago: Rand McNally.
Cronbach, L. J., and P. E. Meehl
    1955   "Construct validity in psychological tests." Psychological Bulletin 52 (July):281 – 302.

DeFleur, M. L., and F. R. Westie
    1958   "Verbal attitudes and overt acts: an experiment on the salience of attitudes." American
             Sociological Review 23 (December):667–673.
Deutscher, I.
    1969   "Looking backward: case studies on the progress of methodology in sociological re-
             search." American Sociologist 4 (February):35–41.
Dulany, D. E.
    1967   "Awareness, rules, and propositional control: a confrontation with S-R behavior the-
             ory." In D. Horton and T. Dixon (eds.), Verbal Behavior and S-R Behavior Theory. En-
             glewood Cliffs, N.J.: Prentice-Hall.
Ehrlich, H. J.
    1969   "Attitudes, behavior, and the intervening variables." American Sociologist 4 (February):
             29–34.
Fendrich, J. M.
    1967   "A study of the association among verbal attitudes and overt behavior in different ex-
             perimental situations." Social Forces 45 (March):347–355.
Festinger, L.
    1964   "Behavioral support for opinion change." Public Opinion Quarterly 28 (October):
             404–417.
Fishbein, M.
    1967   "Attitude and the prediction of behavior." In M. Fishbein (ed.), Readings in Attitude
             Theory and Measurement. New York: Wiley.
Goodman, L. A., and W. H. Kruskal
    1954   "Measures of association for cross classifications." Journal of the American Statistical
             Association 49 (December):732–764.
Hays, W. L.
    1963   Statistics for Psychologists. New York: Holt, Rinehart and Winston.
Kaplan, Abraham
    1964   The Conduct of Inquiry. San Francisco: Chandler.
Kutner, B., C. Wilkins, and P. R. Yarrow
    1952   "Verbal attitudes and overt behavior involving racial prejudice." Journal of Abnormal
             and Social Psychology 47 (July):649–652.
LaPiere, R. T.
    1934   "Attitudes vs. action." Social Forces 13 (December):230–237.
Linn, L. S.
    1965   "Verbal attitudes and overt behavior: a study of racial discrimination." Social Forces
             43 (March):353–364.
Lovinger, J.
    1957   "Objective tests as instruments of psychological theory." Psychological Reports 3,
             Monograph Supplement 9 (December):635–694.
McGuire, W. J.
    1969   "The nature of attitudes and attitude change." In G. Lindzey and E. Aronson (eds.), The
             Handbook of Social Psychology. 2nd edition. Reading, Pa.: Addison-Wesley.
Mann, J. H.
    1959   "The relationship between cognitive, behavioral and affective aspects of racial preju-
             dice." Journal of Social Psychology 49 (May):223–228.
Newton, N., and M. Newton
    1950   "Relationship of ability to breastfeed and maternal attitudes toward breastfeeding."
             Pediatrics 5 (December):869–875.
Potter, H. W., and H. R. Klein
    1957   "On nursing behavior." Psychiatry 20 (January):39–46.
Saenger, G., and E. Gilbert
    1950   "Consumer reaction to the integration of Negro personnel." International Journal of
             Opinion and Attitude Research 4 (Spring):57–76.
Warner, L. G., and M. L. DeFleur
    1969   "Attitude as an interactional concept: social constraint and social distance as interven-
             ing variables between attitudes and action." American Sociological Review 34 (April):
             153–169.
Winch, R. F., and D. T. Campbell
    1969   "Proof? No. Evidence? Yes. The significance of tests of significance." American Sociol-
             ogist 4 (May):140–143.

The Last Word

It is tempting to exploit the opportunity to get in the last word by dwelling on many of the details of the above critique. I have done my best to resist that temptation and to touch here on only a few points. Some of those points are extremely important. For example, in the Illinois psychologists' critique there appears, for the first time in this book, a clear indication of the nature of the conceptual problem. It comes not, as one might expect, from the use of different verbal dimensions, but from the use of different behavioral ones. In Chapter Twelve I shall dwell on the many discrete phenomena we lump together as "attitudes," along with the fact that we do likewise with "behavior."

In their critique, especially in their discussion of Table 1, Ajzen and his fellows point out a distinction between "behavioral intention" and "actual behavior." This is a distinction which one encounters in the empirical world: there are many people who do intend to get into public housing but they never actually get in, and there are many people who do intend to brush their teeth, but they never actually get around to it. In like manner there are soldiers who do not intend to go over the hill, but they end up doing so anyway.[25] I first learned the importance of this kind of distinction from LaPiere. In reflecting on his earlier comparative study of prejudice in France and England, he comments in "Attitudes vs. Action" that "at that time I overlooked the fact that what I was obtaining from the hotel proprietors was still a 'verbalized' reaction to a symbolic situation." The Illinois psychologists and LaPiere are clear on this distinction. It is curious that neither Linn nor DeFleur and Westie take note of it. Until we understand better the conditions under which behavioral intention is related to actual behavior, we cannot assume that studies dealing with these two perspectives are equivalent or comparable. Thus, the three studies I chose to compare might have reached different conclusions because they were studying different relationships.

The Illinois critics object to my assertion that validity has been a neglected issue. Actually, my statement is a relative one, suggesting only that validity has been neglected as compared to reliability, but that is a minor point. They do cite a number of references (and there are others) which wrestle with the logic of validity and sometimes suggest methodological devices for dealing with it. In considering their comments, it occurred to me that the problem is not so much that social scientists have been inattentive to validity (as I suggested) as that they have not done much about it. The literature they cite is largely hortatory, urging colleagues to be more attentive to the problem. I submit that there was practically no concern in the social sciences for validity issues prior to the mid-1950s and that there has been little since that time. My observation is derived from my reading of empirical studies. But of greatest importance is my impression that the vast literature on reliability has exerted considerable influence on the design and reporting of research. The vast literature on validity, if there be such, has not to any large degree found its way into the design and reporting of research.

---

25. Lawrence T. Cagle and Irwin Deutscher, "Housing Aspirations and Housing Achievement: The Relocation of Poor Families," *Social Problems* 18 (1970): 244–56; Louis Kriesberg and Beatrice R. Treiman, "Preventive Utilization of Dentists' Services Among Teenagers," *Journal of the American College of Dentists* (March 1962): 28–45; Harry E. Allen, Clifford E. Simonsen, and Harold J. Vetter, "Attitudes and Behavior: A Test," paper read at the annual meetings of the Ohio Valley Sociological Society, 1971.

All of this has to do with an important phenomenon which the critique amply illustrates but the critics seem unaware of: what men say may not always be related to what they do. The rhetoric of science and the behavior of scientists do not seem to coincide when it comes to matters of validity. It is also true rhetoric that Bergman's formulation of the operational definition is acknowledged to be outmoded. Most reputable social scientists would accept this. It is equally true, however, that Bergman's formulation of the operational definition is still widely used.[26] While I will allow that it is rhetorically correct that prediction is unrelated to cause and effect, my reading of the products of social scientists, however, suggests otherwise. For the moment I will concede that, rhetorically, none of the three studies I reviewed "could have had . . . an objective of confirming or disconfirming a causal relationship since all three were correlational in nature." Ajzen fails to compare his true rhetoric with the fact that all three of the studies clearly imply exactly that objective. Perhaps my critics and I sometimes talk past each other because they are attentive to *what is said about research*, while I am attentive to *what is done in research*.

The psychologists conclude that my objection to prediction[27] is "speculative, meta-theoretical, and based on a failure to distinguish between prediction and causal relationships." All of this is correct! I am speculating (perhaps the most important and the most useful procedure in that chain of activities which make up science); my objective is in part meta-theoretical (I checked the prefix, "meta," in my desk dictionary and I rather like the idea of being a "meta-theoretician"); finally, it is precisely in the confusion of prediction with causal relations that I find my argument. Although I don't believe it correct to suggest that I confuse them, they are indeed frequently confused. Correlation analysis, in the sense which Ajzen et al. use that term, has nothing to do with explanation and is atheoretical. Because it only describes, it cannot make any cumulative or abstract contribution to knowledge. In taking such a position, they completely discount a great deal of what I believe is very important evidence. Clearly, there are many kinds of research which they would call correlational, but which I find useful—as useful and as credible as some experimental analyses.

Actually, the distinction made by the critics between "correlational studies" (such as the three analyzed in Chapter Four) and those with the objective of confirming a causal relationship seems to me neither clear nor useful. Correlation techniques are employed in theoretically grounded research to provide a partial test of causal or directional hypotheses. When we correlate cigarette smoking with lung cancer, it is in order to accumulate evidence of the extent to which smoking may cause cancer. Very few of the studies finding a relationship between attitude and behavior do not either state or imply a causal relationship between the two—sometimes one way and sometimes the other. It would be difficult to find any study dealing with attitudinal and behavioral change which fails to suggest causality. This being the state of affairs, it is unwise to suggest (as the Illinois group does) that one

---

26. I have dealt with the matter of operational definitions in Chapter Four and will pursue it further in Chapter Twelve. It should be clear that I concur that Bergman's 1951 (like P. W. Bridgman's 1927) formulation of the operational definition is outmoded (why would reasonable social scientists ever have accepted it as à la mode?). But that it "has long since been replaced" by anything else is a statement I cannot agree with.

27. The theoretical grounds underlying my irritation with "prediction" are developed in Chapter Eleven.

need not be concerned with (external) validity in correlation studies. If they can tell us nothing beyond themselves, then they can tell us nothing.

I do, nevertheless, find sound experimental evidence to be the most credible of all. The fact that LaPiere did introduce some controls into his work adds immensely to its credibility and the fact that neither Linn nor DeFleur and Westie did so (although both might have and should have) detracts immensely from theirs. Surely it is inappropriate to excuse them from such rigor (as Ajzen does) by tacking the appellation "correlational" to their work. The desirability of controls is further documented by the comments of one of the critics who is a photographer. He suggests that there may be a sizable proportion of people who resist having their photograph taken under any conditions. Thus it is impossible to determine how many refusals are a result of racial bias and how many are generalized reactions to the camera. This is an important point which had not occurred to me.

It follows that the closer the observation to the empirical phenomenon, the greater the probability of validity (other things being equal). Each step away from that direct observation requires an assumption about the relationship between the indirect indicator or estimate and the phenomenon itself. Howard Becker and Blanche Geer's work articulates the logic of this position in Chapter Seven, while Freeman and Ataöv provide clear evidence in Chapter Three. Sometimes our assumptions are technical ones required to rationalize statistical procedures. Sometimes they are logical assumptions required in order to make inferential jumps. An example from criminology, employed earlier in this chapter, is to the point. There is a selective loss in validity which occurs in the study of criminals as one moves further away from the criminal act itself. It is possible to operationally define prisoners "for our purposes" as criminals, but in fact very little an investigator may learn about prisoners is likely to be true of criminals. I submit this as an analogue to what happens with statistical devices. They provide estimates of and confidence limits to what we would find in the empirical world *if we could approach it directly.* Thus, the fewer statistics required to substantiate the findings, the fewer assumptions, and the greater parsimony. For these reasons I fail to understand the critics' argument that one would be remiss if he were not to use every statistical technique whose assumptions his data appeared to meet. It seems to me that if it is not essential that we make innumerable statistical assumptions, we ought to abide by the rule of parsimony. Incidentally, one assumption which usually must be made in dealing with someone else's analysis is that there are no computational errors. If there are no computations this assumption is unnecessary. Ajzen and his colleagues did discover such an error in the DeFleur-Westie Chi-square.

It is true that I am "enamored" of field studies, especially (but not exclusively) those which incorporate elements of experimental design. It is equally true that I am skeptical of most laboratory experiments with human subjects (regardless of their so-called internal validity). The grounds for this skepticism will be spelled out in Chapter Eight. My critics, on the other hand, seem quite taken with evidence derived from laboratory experiments with students (homogeneous groups reduce unwanted variation). It seems to me more important to discover how grown-ups behave in everyday life. But this, I suppose, is a matter of taste. What concerns me is their failure to recognize that conclusions regarding the relationship between attitude and behavior may be related to the setting in which the research takes place. This problem is touched on in Chapter Two. For documentation, the reader (and the critics) are referred to the two sets of studies which are cited in the opening paragraph of Ajzen's concluding section. Note that the set which suggest a relationship consist for the most part of laboratory experiments while their set suggesting no relationship are nearly all field studies. It makes a difference how the study is done; methods (not "good" or "bad," but "different") may explain some of the lack of convergent validity.

There is nothing wrong with evidence from the laboratory (much of the argument in this book is based on such evidence) as long as it passes the double screen. The test of credibility holds of course for any source of evidence as does the conceptual test. We should admit as evidence almost anything which has an empirical base and makes sense: field studies, surveys, experiments, novels, ethnographies, biographies, histories, philosophies, and well-grounded polemics. Independent convergence among such various data is, in fact, independent, while if one restricts legitimacy to only one of these sources of evidence, identical sources of errors (sources derived from the method) occur in all of the studies. This is hardly independent convergence.

Ajzen and his colleagues assert that "a small sample is not necessarily bad." This is true. An informed analysis of a single case can provide highly credible evidence. Of course, it is generally better if there are two cases, since we then have a basis for comparison. But three is probably best because it provides the points necessary to establish the type of curve (if any) with which we are dealing. As a matter of fact, the selection of a probability sample is an irrelevant ritual in theoretical research.[28] I do suspect, however, that my basis for this position is quite different from that of the critics. They argue that a small sample may be superior since, "it may actually provide a more conservative test of the investigator's hypotheses because it demands a stronger relationship in order to obtain a standard level of significance." Knowingly treading on the dangerous grounds of the Type I–Type II error bind (see Chapter Eight),[29] I nevertheless translate this to mean that a small sample is likely to encourage conclusions that are contrary to what is found in the empirical world. The English word "conservative" is, in my opinion, inappropriately used by social psychologists in this context. In effect, since the demands are more stringent for us to reach any given level of significance, and since conclusions are frequently based upon that level, conclusions based upon excessively small samples may be in error in that they do not represent what is found in the universe from which the sample is drawn. Linn acknowledges that he would have reached opposite conclusions with a larger sample. It does not take a very great inflation of sample size for the same thing to occur with the DeFleur-Westie data. In this sense, their samples seem to me to be "too small." What kind of knowledge do we have when conclusions are reversible depending on the size of the sample?

In order to make progress methodologically we must be able to assess

---

28. Elaborations of this position can be found in Hans Zetterberg, *On Theory and Verification in Sociology* (Totowa, N.J.: The Bedminster Press, 3rd enl. ed., 1965), 128–30; Barney Glaser and Anselm Strauss, *The Discovery of Grounded Theory: Strategies for Qualitative Research* (Chicago: Aldine Publishing Company, 1967), pp. 62–65; Amitai Etzioni, *The Active Society: A Theory of Societal and Political Processes* (New York: The Free Press, 1968), p. 48, and the final footnote on that page.

29. The bind results from the fact that an excessively large sample is likely to do the same thing. It is supposedly necessary to make an arbitrary decision as to whether the investigator wishes to risk falsifying a true hypothesis or accepting a false one. I am not certain that it is necessary to risk either.

where we have been and to identify where we still need to go. Such historical analyses or retrospective longitudinal studies enable us to make reasonable judgments
on what is required in the near future. The unfortunate choice of an antihistorical
closing sentence by the Illinois psychologists seems to me to reflect both an anti-intellectual and an unscientific perspective: "For the sake of progress in the social sciences, we would hope that less effort would be expended in 'looking backward'
through distorted lenses, and more effort would be directed at taking constructive
steps forward." All history is "distorted" (or selective) by the perspective and position of the historian. It may be that there are more useful distortions than mine, but
it cannot be that we can afford to refuse to examine our progress. I do, nevertheless,
take their advice and include in Chapter Eleven a section entitled, "Looking Forward."

A sense of history might have constrained my critics from chastising me for
not referring to two articles which were published after the article they criticize.
Furthermore, if they were more attentive to looking backward, they would not have
attributed to Bergman (1951) an invention of Bridgman's (1927)[30] or to Campbell and
associates (1957, 1963, 1969) a distinction discovered by Louis Guttman in 1950. I
think too, that in my particular analysis, the dangers from unrecognized distortion
are much less than in most research, since my raw data (the three studies) are readily available for independent evaluation. The critics do find serious flaws in these
studies which I overlooked and their conclusion, which seems something of an
understatement, is acceptable to me: "Thorough methodological analysis of these
three studies does not seem to indicate a regressive trend in methodology." But,
they continue, "there is no indication of a significant advance either." Although I
am not dissuaded of the impression that we may have been in reverse, I am satisfied
with their conclusion. It should be of interest to social scientists that there are two
recent independent empirical analyses which suggest that we did not improve
methodologically over a recent thirty-year period. That is convergent validity!

---

30. P. W. Bridgman, *The Logic of Modern Physics* (New York: Macmillan Company, 1927). See
p. 5 for the heart of the matter.

6

Anyone May Lie a Bit, Cheat a Bit, and Try to Be Helpful

Getting in Our Own Way

The importance of learning how to discount evidence as part of our screening process was broached in the opening chapter of this book. To what extent can we accept different kinds of evidence as credible? Although C. Wright Mills has dressed it up in modern language, this is not a new problem. It dates back, in fact, to the origins of modern sociology. It was Herbert Spencer's 1874 statement which appears to have fed Mills' concern: "From the intrinsic natures of its facts, from our own natures as observers of its facts, and from the peculiar relation in which we stand towards the facts to be observed, there arise impediments in the way of Sociology greater than those in the way of any other science."[1] Spencer proceeds to wrestle with such very contemporary issues as "objectivity" and "reactivity" in the social sciences. It is precisely such issues which we continue to address one hundred years later in this and the following two chapters.

Although I have allowed almost any source—including fiction, poetry, and journalism—legitimacy as "evidence," I do lean most heavily on survey research findings, laboratory experimental reports, and the results of participant-observational field studies. Chapters Six, Seven, and Eight are designed to sensitize us to some of the credibility problems typical of those three sources. Martin Trow, meanwhile, reminds us in his critique of Becker and Geer's advocacy of participant observation that every cobbler thinks leather is the only thing.[2] I have already confessed to being "enamored" of field studies and to being "taken with" the quality of evidence derived from experimental design. I also have reservations about the validity of much of what is reported on the basis of large-scale surveys. But the fact is that leather is not the only thing and for certain purposes it may be a very poor material; I have referred to the possibility that we sometimes try to chop down trees with shovels because we have no axes and our shovels are very good (Trow's more dainty metaphor is that of scalpel and forceps).

Common to all of these methods is the problem of reactivity. Interviewers and respondents are human beings engaged in an interactive encounter. The resulting protocol is a product of that interaction. This is sometimes called "interviewer effect" and, as we shall see, efforts are made to minimize it. Participant observers are present in the situations which they observe and their very presence alters the

---

1. Herbert Spencer, *The Study of Sociology* (New York: D. Appleton and Company, 1874), p. 72. Spencer's complete essay, "The Class Bias," is reprinted in *Images of Man: The Classic Tradition in Sociological Thinking*, ed. C. Wright Mills (New York: George Braziller, Inc., 1960), 48–64.
2. Martin Trow, "Comment on 'Participant Observation and Interviewing: A Comparison,'" *Human Organization* 16 (1958): 35.

social nature of that situation. This is sometimes called "observer effect" and efforts are made to deal with it too. Finally, the fact that subjects in an experiment know that they are taking part in an experiment and usually know who the experimenter is introduces those kinds of reactivity sometimes referred to as "experimental effect" and "experimenter effect." This is the central problem which Webb and his colleagues address in their essays on "unobtrusive measures."[3] Their solution is two pronged. First they suggest that, when possible, certain nonreactive indicators be used, such as empty liquor bottles in the trash, worn steps in the library, or nose prints on the museum exhibit. Such indicators are not created in interaction with the researcher, but it is also true that they are not always available. I have referred several times to the private nature of sex behavior in our society and thus to the difficulty of making behavioral observations in this sensitive area. Webb et al. provide clues to procedures for beginning to measure at least some aspects of sexual behavior. The clever methodologist must begin by first asking himself, "What objective traces are left by such behavior?" — as the heavy use of a stairway can be verified by the wearing of the steps.[4]

The second prong to their solution lies in the process of triangulation which we discussed in relation to validity. If, for example, we have convergence in the conclusions from a survey, an experiment, and a field study — each with its own peculiar form of reactivity — then they become collectively more credible. This is the logic which I shall illustrate in Chapter Eight in considering the question, "Can the weaknesses of one be the strengths of the other?" Reactivity seems to me nearly endemic in social research. Precisely how much it distorts our findings and under what conditions remains debatable, and there are indeed many social scientists who deny that it deserves any serious attention.[5] Nevertheless, I will adopt the position that as long as a reasonable doubt exists, reactivity must be seriously considered.

Earlier in this volume, I quoted Benney and Hughes' observation "that the interview, as itself, a form of social rhetoric, is not merely a tool of sociology but a part of its very subject matter."[6] The same can, of course, be said of experimental or observational studies. Their point is that there are some things social scientists do understand about human interaction and that those things pertain as well to interaction between interviewer and respondent as they do to any other kind of interaction. That the psychological experiment can be viewed in the same manner is clearly reflected in the subtitle employed by an experimenter in reporting his experiment

3. Eugene J. Webb, Donald T. Campbell, Richard D. Schwartz, and Lee Sechrest, *Unobtrusive Measures: Nonreactive Research in the Social Sciences* (Chicago: Rand McNally & Company, 1966).

4. While cleaning cesspools in suburban Long Island in the summer of 1949 (one of the few occupations then available to a college graduate with a major in philosophy), I was impressed with the number of condoms found in the sewage of a large apartment house, the mailboxes of which carried only Irish surnames. This might be taken as an unobtrusive measure of the use of birth control by Roman Catholics. However, it requires the assumption that all persons with Irish surnames are Catholic. Furthermore, there is no indication of the distribution among apartments; conceivably all of the condoms could have come from a small minority of tenants.

5. See, for a starter, Robert A. Gordon, "Letter: Amongst Competent Sociologists?" *American Sociologist* 4 (1969): 249–50. Gordon's letter contains a number of references to critiques of some of the work I will cite in this chapter. Gordon's position will receive further consideration in Chapter Thirteen.

6. Mark Benney and Everett C. Hughes, "Of Sociology and the Interview: Editorial Preface," *American Journal of Sociology* 62 (1956): 138.

with experiments: "The Psychological Experiment as a Social Interaction."[7] It is this simple suggestion—that the few things we think we do know as social scientists ought to be applied to our own activities as social scientists—which lies at the heart of Julius Roth's contribution to this chapter.

7. Neil Friedman, *The Social Nature of Psychological Research: The Psychological Experiment as a Social Interaction* (New York: Basic Books, Inc., 1967).

DATA:
Hired Hand Research
JULIUS A. ROTH

Case I

After it became obvious how tedious it was to write down numbers on pieces of paper which didn't even fulfill one's own sense of reality and which did not remind one of the goals of the project, we all in little ways started avoiding our work and cheating on the project. It began for example when we were supposed to be observing for hour and a half periods, an hour and a half on the ward and then an hour and a half afterwards to write up or dictate what we had observed, in terms of the category system which the project was supposed to be testing and in terms of a ward diary. We began cutting corners in time. We would arrive a little bit late and leave a little bit early. It began innocently enough, but soon boomeranged into a full cheating syndrome, where we would fake observations for some time slot which were never observed on the ward. Sam, for example, in one case, came onto the ward while I was still finishing up an assignment on a study patient and told me that he was supposed to observe for an hour and a half but that he wasn't going to stay because he couldn't stand it anymore. He said he wasn't going to tell anyone that he missed an assignment, but that he would simply write up a report on the basis of what he knew already about the ward and the patients. I was somewhat appalled by Sam's chicanery, and in this sense I was the last one to go. It was three or four weeks after this before I actually cheated in the same manner.

It was also frequent for us to miss observation periods, especially the 8 to 9:30 a.m. ones. We all had a long drive for one thing, and we were all chronic over-sleepers for another. For a while we used to make up the times we missed by coming in the next morning at the same time and submitting our reports with the previous day's date. As time went on, however, we didn't bother to make up the times we'd missed. When we were questioned by our supervisor about the miss-

"Hired Hand Research," by Julius A. Roth, from *The American Sociologist*, vol. 1, no. 1 (November 1965), pp. 190–96. Reprinted by permission of the author and the American Sociological Association. This paper was initially prepared for The Columbia University Seminar on Content and Method in The Social Sciences, December 14, 1965.

ing reports, we would claim that there had been an error in scheduling and that we did not know that those time slots were supposed to be covered.

There were other ways we would cheat, sometimes inadvertently. For example, one can decide that one can't hear enough of a conversation to record it. People need to think fairly highly of themselves, and when you think that you're a cheat and a liar and that you're not doing your job for which you are receiving high wages, you are likely to find little subconscious ways of getting out of having to accuse yourself of these things. One of the ways is to not be able to hear well. We had a special category in our coding system, a question mark, which we noted by its symbol on our code sheets whenever we could not hear what was going on between two patients. As the purgatory of writing numbers on pieces of paper lengthened, more and more transcripts were passed in with question marks on them, so that even though we had probably actually heard most of the conversations between patients, we were still actually avoiding the work of transcription by deceiving ourselves into believing that we could not hear what was being said. This became a good way of saving yourself work. If you couldn't hear a conversation, it just got one mark in one column of one code sheet, and if you wrote down an elaborate conversation lasting even ten minutes, it might take you up to an hour to code it, one hour of putting numbers in little blocks. In the long run, all of our data became much skimpier. Conversations were incomplete; their duration was strangely diminishing to two or three minutes in length instead of the half-hour talks the patients usually had with each other. We were all defining our own cutting off points, saying to ourselves, "Well, that's enough of that conversation." According to the coding rules, however, a communication can't be considered as ended until the sequence of interaction has been completed and a certain time lapse of silence has ensued.

In order to ensure the reliability of our coding, the research design called for an "Inter-Rater Reliability Check" once every two months, in which each of the four of us would pair up with every other member of the team and be rated on our ability to code jointly the same interaction in terms of the same categories and dimensions. We learned to loathe these checks; we knew that the coding system was inadequate in terms of reliability and that our choice of categories was optional, subjective, and largely according to our own sense of what an interaction is really about, rather than according to the rigid, stylized, and preconceived design into which we were supposed to make reality fit. We also knew, however, that our principal investigators insisted on an inter-rater reliability coefficient of .70 in order for the research to proceed. When the time came for another check, we met together to discuss and make certain agreements on how to bring our coding habits into conformity for the sake of achieving reliability. In these meetings we would confess our preferences for coding certain things in certain ways and agree on certain concessions to each other for the duration of the check. Depending on what other individual I was to be paired with, for example, I had a very good idea of how I could code in order to achieve nearly the same transcriptions. We didn't end it there. After each phase of a check, each pair of us would meet again to go over our transcriptions and compare our coding, and if there were any gross discrepancies, we corrected them before sending them to the statistician for analysis. Needless to say, as soon as the reliability checks were over with, we each returned to a coding rationale which we as individuals required in order to do any coding at all — in order to maintain sanity.

Case II

There didn't appear to be too much concern with the possibility of inconsistency among the coders. Various coders used various methods to determine the code of an open-end question. Toward the end of the coding process, expediency became the keynote, leading to gross inconsistency. The most expedient method of coding a few of the trickier questions was to simply put down a "4." (This was the middle-of-the-road response on the one question that had the most variation.) If the responses were not clear or comprehensible, the coder had two alternatives: on the one hand, he could puzzle over it and ask for other opinions or, on the other hand, he could assign it an arbitrary number or forget the response entirely.

In the beginning, many of us, when in doubt about a response, would ask the supervisor or his assistant. After a while, I noted that quite often the supervisor's opinion would differ when asked twice about the same response and he would often give two different answers in response to the same question. One way the supervisor and his assistant would determine the correct coding for an answer would be to look at the respondent's previous answers and deduce what they should have answered—thereby coding on *what they thought the respondent should have answered*, not on the basis of what he *did* answer. One example that I distinctly remember is the use of magazines regularly read as reported by the respondent being used as a basis on which to judge and code their political views. This, in my opinion, would be a factor in some of the cases, such as the reading of an extreme leftist or extreme rightist magazine, but to use magazines such as *Time* or *Reader's Digest* to form any conclusions about the type of person and his views, I feel is quite arbitrary. Furthermore, I feel questionnaires should be used to see *if* consistent patterns of views exist among respondents and it is not the coder's job to put them in if the respondents fail to!

Some of the coders expected a fixed pattern of response. I, not being sure of what responses meant in a total political profile, treated each response separately—which I feel is the correct way of coding a questionnaire. Others, as I learned through their incessant jabbering, took what they thought was a more sophisticated method of treating an interview. A few would discuss the respondent's answers as if they took one political or social standpoint as an indicator of what all the responses should be. They would laugh over an inconsistency in the respondent's replies, feeling that one answer did not fit the previous pattern of responses.

The final problem leading to gross inconsistency was the factor of time. The supervisor made it clear that the code sheets had to be in to the computation center by Saturday. This meant that on Saturday morning and early afternoon the aim of the coders was to code the questionnaires as quickly as possible, and the crucial factor was speed, even at the expense of accuracy. The underlying thought was that there were so many questionnaires coded already (that were *assumed* to be coded consistently and correctly) that the inconsistencies in the remainder would balance themselves out and be of no great importance. I found myself adapting to this way of thinking, and after spending two or three hours there on Saturday morning, I joined in the game of "let's get these damn things out already." It did indeed become a game, with the shibboleth, for one particularly vague and troublesome question, "Oh, give it a four."

Case III

One of the questions on the interview schedule asked for five reasons why parents had put their child in an institution. I found most people can't think of five reasons. One or two—sometimes three. At first I tried pumping them for more reasons, but I never got any of them up to five. I didn't want (the director) to think I was goofing off on the probing, so I always filled in all five.

Another tough one was the item about how the child's disability affected the family relationships. We were supposed to probe. Probe what? You get so many different kinds of answers, I was never sure what was worth following up. Sometimes I did if the respondent seemed to have something to say. Otherwise I just put down a short answer and made it look as if that was all I could get out of them. Of course, (the director) *did* list a few areas he wanted covered in the probing. One of them was sex relations of the parents. Most of the time I didn't follow up on that. Once in a while I would get somebody who seemed to be able to talk freely without embarrassment. But most of the time I was afraid to ask, so I made up something to fill that space.

Then there was that wide open question at the end. It's vague. Most people don't know what to say. You've been asking them questions for about an hour already. Usually you get a very short answer. I didn't push them. I'd write up a longer answer later. It's easy to do. You have their answers to a lot of other questions to draw on. You just put parts of some of them together, dress it up a little, and add one or two bits of new information which fit in with the rest.

Any reader with research experience can probably recall one or more cases in which he observed, suspected, or participated in some form of cheating, carelessness, distortion, or cutting of corners in the collection or processing of research data. He probably thought of these instances as exceptions—an unfortunate lapse in ethical behavior or a failure of research directors to maintain proper controls. I would like to put forth the thesis that such behavior on the part of hired data-collectors and processors is not abnormal or exceptional, but rather is exactly the kind of behavior we should expect from people with their position in a production unit.

The cases I have presented do not constitute proof, of course. Even if I presented ten or twenty more, my efforts could be dismissed as merely an unusually industrious effort to record professional dirty linen (or I might be accused of making them up!) and not at all representative of the many thousands of cases of hired researching carried out every year. Rather than multiply examples, I would like to take a different tack and examine the model we have been using in thinking about research operations and to suggest another model which I believe is more appropriate.

The ideal we hold of the researcher is that of a well-educated scholar pursuing information and ideas on problems in which he has an intrinsic interest. Frequently this ideal may be approximated when an individual scholar is working on his own problem or several colleagues are collaborating on a problem of mutual interest. Presumably such a researcher will endeavor to carry out his data-collection and processing in the most accurate and useful way that his skills and time permit.

When a researcher hires others to do the collecting and processing tasks of his research plan, we often assume that these assistants fit the "dedicated scientist" ideal and will lend their efforts to the successful conduct of the over-all study by carrying out their assigned tasks to the best of their ability. As suggested by my examples, I doubt that hired assistants usually behave this way even when they are junior grade scholars themselves. It becomes more doubtful yet when they are even further removed from scholarly tradition and from the direct control of the research directors (e.g., part-time survey interviewers).

It seems to me that we can develop a more accurate expectation of the contribution of the hired research worker who is required to work according to somebody else's plan by applying another model which has been worked out in some detail by sociologists — namely, the work behavior of the hired hand in a production organization. First, let us look at one of the more thorough of these studies, Donald Roy's report on machine shop operators.[1]

Roy's workers made the job easier by loafing when the piece rate did not pay well. They were careful not to go over their informal "quotas" on piece rate jobs because the rate would be cut and their work would be harder. They faked time sheets so that their actual productive abilities would not be known to management. They cut corners on prescribed job procedures to make the work easier and/or more lucrative even though this sometimes meant that numerous products had to be scrapped. Roy's calculations show that the workers could have produced on the order of twice as much if it had been in their interest to do so.

But it is *not* in their interest to do so. The product the hired hand turns out is not in any sense his. He does not design it, make any of the decisions about producing it or about the conditions under which it will be produced, or what will be done with it after it is produced. The worker is interested in doing just enough to get by. Why should he concern himself about how well the product works or how much time it takes to make it? That is the company's problem. The company is his adversary and fair game for any trickery he can get away with. The worker's aim is to make his job as easy and congenial as the limited resources allow and to make as much money as possible without posing a threat to his fellow workers or to his own future. The company, in turn, is placed in the position of having to establish an inspection system to try to keep the worst of their products from leaving the factory (an effort often unsuccessful — the inspectors are hired hands, too) and of devising some form of supervision to limit the more extreme forms of gold-bricking and careless workmanship.

Almost all the systematic research on "restriction of output" and deviation from assigned duties has been done on factory workers, office clerks, and other low prestige work groups. This is mostly because such work is easier to observe and measure, but also because much of this research has been controlled in part by those in a position of authority who want research done only on their subordinates. However, there is evidence to indicate that work restrictions and deviations in the form of informal group definitions and expectations are probably universal in our society. They can be found among business executives and in the professions, sports, and the creative arts. They are especially likely to crop up when one is working as a hired hand, and almost all productive activities have their hired hand aspects. A professor may work hard on scholarly tasks of his own choosing and perhaps even on teaching a course which he himself has devised,

[1]Donald Roy, "Quota Restriction and Goldbricking in a Machine Shop," *American Journal of Sociology*, 57 (March 1952), pp. 427–442.

but he becomes notoriously lax when he is assigned to a departmental service course which he does not like—spending little or no time on preparation, avoiding his students as much as possible, turning all the exams over to a graduate assistant, and so on.

"Restriction of production" and deviation from work instructions is no longer regarded by students of the sociology of work as a moral issue or a form of social delinquency. Rather, it is the expected behavior of workers in a production organization. The only problem for an investigator of work practices is discovering the details of cutting corners, falsifying time sheets, defining work quotas, dodging supervision, and ignoring instructions in a given work setting.

There is no reason to believe that a hired hand in the scientific research business will behave any different from those in other areas of productive activity. It is far more reasonable to assume that their behavior will be similar. They want to make as much money as they can and may pad their account or time sheet if they are paid on that basis, but this type of behavior is a minor problem so far as the present discussion is concerned. They also want to avoid difficult, embarrassing, inconvenient, time-consuming situations as well as those activities which make no sense to them. (Thus, they fail to make some assigned observations or to ask some of the interview questions.) At the same time they want to give the right impression to their superiors—at least right enough so that their material will be accepted and they will be kept on the job. (Thus, they modify or fabricate portions of the reports in order to give the boss what he *seems* to want.) They do not want to "look stupid" by asking too many questions, so they are likely to make a stab at what they think the boss wants—e.g., make a guess at a coding category rather than having it resolved through channels.

Even those who start out with the notion that this is an important piece of work which they must do right will succumb to the hired-hand mentality when they realize that their suggestions and criticisms are ignored, that their assignment does not allow for any imagination or creativity, that they will receive no credit for the final product, in short, that they have been hired to do somebody else's dirty work. When this realization has sunk in, they will no longer bother to be careful or accurate or precise. They will cut corners to save time and energy. They will fake parts of their reporting. They will not put themselves out for something in which they have no stake except in so far as extrinsic pressures force them to. Case No. I is an excerpt from the statement of a research worker who started out with enthusiasm and hard work and ended with sloppy work and cheating when she could no longer escape the fact that she was a mere flunky expected to do her duty whether or not it was meaningful. The coders in Case II soon gave up any effort to resolve the ambiguities of their coding operation and followed the easiest path acceptable to their supervisor. In this case, the supervisor himself made little effort to direct the data-processing toward supplying answers to meaningful research issues. We must remember that in many research operations the supervisors and directors themselves are hired hands carrying out the requests of a client or superior as expeditiously as possible.

Many of the actions of hired hand researchers are strikingly analogous to restrictive practices of factory operatives. Interviewers who limit probing and observers who limit interaction recording are behaving like workers applying "quota restriction," and with interacting hired hands informal agreements may be reached on the extent of such restrictions. To fabricate portions of a report is a form of goldbricking. The collusion on the reliability check reported in Case I is strikingly similar to the workers' plot to mislead the time-study department. Such similarities are no accident. The relationship of the hired hand to the product and the process of production is the same in each case. The product is not "his." The production process gives him little or no opportunity to express any intrinsic interest he may have in the product. He will sooner or later fall into a pattern of carrying out his work with a minimum of effort, inconvenience, and embarrassment — doing just enough so that his product will get by. If he is part of a large and complex operation where his immediate superiors are also hired hands with no intrinsic interest in the product and where the final authority may be distant and even amorphous, quality control of the product will be mechanical and the minimal effort that will get by can soon be learned and easily applied. The factory production situation has at least one ultimate limitation on the more extreme deviations of the hired hands: the final product must "work" reasonably well in a substantial proportion of cases. In social science research, on the other hand, the product is usually so ambiguous and the field of study so lacking in standards of performance, that it is difficult for anyone to say whether it "works" or not.

What is more important is the effect of the hired hand mentality on the *nature* of the product. Workmen not only turn out less than they could if it were in their interest to maximize production, but often produce shoddy and even dangerous products.[2] In the case of research, the inefficiency of hired hands not only causes a study to take longer or cost more money, but is likely to introduce much dubious data and interpretations into the process of analysis. Our mass production industrial system has opted to sacrifice individual efficiency and product quality for the advantages of a rationalized division of labor. The same approach has been applied to much of our larger scale scientific research and the results, in my opinion, have been much more disastrous than they are in industrial production with little of the compensating advantages.

When the tasks of a research project are split up into small pieces to be assigned to hired hands, none of these data-collectors and processors will ever understand all the complexities and subtleties of the research issues in the same way as the person who conceived of the study. No amount of "training" can take the place of the gradual development of research interests and formulations on the part of the planner. Since the director often cannot be sure what conceptions of the issues the hired hands have as a result of his explanations and "training," he must make dubious guesses about the meaning of much of the data they return to him. If he attempts to deal with this difficulty by narrowly defining the permissible behavior of each hired hand (e.g., demand that all questions on a schedule be asked in a set wording), he merely increases the alienation of the hired hand from his work and thus increases the likelihood of cutting corners and cheating. As he gains in quantity of data, he loses in validity and meaningfulness.[3]

[2] I want to emphasize once again that in a business setting, supervisors and executives, as well as production line workmen, participate in aspects of the hired hand mentality. None of them may have an intrinsic interest in the quality of the product. (See, for example, Melville Dalton, *Men Who Manage,* New York: John Wiley and Sons, Inc., 1959, especially Chapters 7, 8, and 9.) The same is the case in much large-scale research.

[3] In this discussion I am assuming there *is* some one (or a small group of colleagues) who has initially formulated the research problem or area of concern because of intrinsic interest and curiosity. In much of our social science research, we do not have even this saving grace and the research is formulated and carried out for various "political" reasons. In such cases, we cannot count on having anyone interested enough to try to turn the accumulations of data into a meaningful explanatory statement.

I do not want to give the impression that the hired hand mentality with its attendant difficulties is simply a characteristic of the large-scale on-going research organization. We may find it at all size levels, including the academic man hiring a single student to do his research chores. The argument may be advanced that assignment of specified tasks by the director of a study is essential to getting the job done in the manner that he wants it done. My answer is that such assignments are often not effectively carried out and it is misleading to assume that they are.

Let me illustrate this point. A researcher wants to do a study of the operation of a given institution. He has some definite notion of what aspects of behavior of the institutional personnel he wants information about and he has some ideas about the manner in which he will go about analysing and interpreting these behaviors. He finds it possible and useful to engage four trained and interested assistants. Let me outline two ways the study might be conducted:

A.   Through a series of discussions, general agreement is reached about the nature of the study and the manner in which it might be conducted. Some division of labor is agreed upon in these discussions. However, none of the field workers is held to any particular tasks or foci of interest. Each is allowed to pursue his data-collection as he thinks best within the larger framework, although the field workers exchange information frequently and make new agreements so that they can benefit from each other's experience.

B.   The director divides up the data-collection and processing in a logical manner and assigns a portion to each of the assistants. Each field worker is instructed to obtain information in all the areas assigned to him and to work in a prescribed manner so that his information will be directly comparable to that of the others. The director may use a procedural check such as having each assistant write a report covering given issues or areas at regular intervals.

Which is the preferred approach? Judging from my reading of social science journals, most research directors would say Method B is to be preferred. Method A, they would maintain, produces information on subjects, issues, or events from one field worker which is not directly comparable to that collected by another field worker. They would also object that if each field worker is permitted to follow his own inclinations even in part, the total study will suffer from large gaps. These accusations are quite true — and, I would add, are an inevitable result of dividing a research project among a number of people. What I disagree with, however, is the assumption that Method B would not suffer from these defects (if indeed, they should be regarded as defects). It is assumed that the assistants in Method B are actually carrying out their assigned tasks in the manner specified. In line with my earlier discussion of the behavior of hired hands, I would consider this highly unlikely. If the information produced by these assistants is indeed closely comparable, it would most likely be because they had reached an agreement on how to restrict production. And, whether the study is carried out by Method A or by Method B, gaps will occur. The difference is that the director of Study A — assuming he had succeeded in making his assistants into collaborating colleagues — would at least know where the gaps are. The director of Study B would have gaps without knowing where they are — or indeed, that they exist—because they have been covered over by the fabrications of his alienated assistants.

It is ironic that established researchers do not ascribe the same motivating forces to their subordinates as they do to themselves. For many years research scientists have been confronting those who pay their salaries and give them their grants with the argument that a scientist can do good research only when he has the freedom to follow his ideas in whatever way seems best. They have been so successful with this argument that university administrations and research organization directorates rarely attempt to dictate—or even suggest—problems or procedures to a researcher on their staff, and the more prominent granting agencies write contracts with almost no strings attached as to the way in which the study will be conducted. Yet research directors fail to apply this same principle to those they hire to carry out data-collection and processing. The hired assistant's desire to participate in the task and the creative contribution he might make is ignored with the result that the assistants' creativity is applied instead to covertly changing the nature of the task.

There has been very little discussion in our journals and our books on research methods on the relationship of the hired hand to the data collected. Whatever discussion there *has* been can be found in the survey interview field where there have been some studies of the effect of such demographic factors as age, sex, and race, sometimes measured personality traits, on "interviewer bias." The nature of the interviewer's status in a research organization is seldom discussed in print. The problem of interviewer cheating, although a common subject of informal gossip, is seldom dealt with openly as a serious problem. When Leo Crespi published an article twenty years ago in which he expressed the worry that cheating was seriously affecting the validity of much survey data,[4] those who responded (mostly survey organization executives) stated reassuringly that few interviewers cheated and that they had pretty effective ways of controlling those who did.[5] If the analysis offered in this paper is correct, the first part of this reassurance is almost certainly wrong. The low-level flunky position which most interviewers occupy in survey organizations[6] should lead us to expect widespread deviations from assigned tasks. The survey executives who responded give no convincing evidence to the contrary. As for the second part of the assertion, their descriptions of their control measures indicate that they can hope to block only the cruder, more obvious, and repeated forms of cheating. The postal card follow-up will catch the interviewer who does not bother to contact his respondents at all. Spot-check follow-up interviewing may eventually catch the interviewer who makes contacts, but fabricates demographic data (to fill a quota sample) or completes only part of the interview and fills in the rest in a stereotyped manner later on. (Even here, many of his interviews may be used before he is detected.) However, from the cases of hired hand interviewing which I am familiar with, I would say such crude cheating is not the most common form of cutting corners on the job.

[4]Leo Crespi, "The Cheater Problem in Polling," *Public Opinion Quarterly*, Winter 1945–1946, pp. 431–445.

[5]"Survey on Problems of Interviewer Cheating," *International Journal of Opinion and Attitude Research*, 1 (1947), pp. 93–107.

[6]Julius A. Roth, "The Status of Interviewing," *The Midwest Sociologist*, 19 (December 1956), pp. 8–11.

Far more common is the kind found in Case III where the interviewer makes his contact, obtains a fairly complete interview, but leaves partial gaps here and there because he found it time-consuming, embarrassing, or troublesome, felt threatened by the respondent, or simply felt uncertain about how the study director wanted certain lines of questioning developed. With a little imagination, such gaps can be filled in later on in a way that is very unlikely to be detected in a follow-up interview. If, for example, a supervisor in Case III had returned to the respondents and asked them whether the "five reasons" listed on their interview form were accurate reflections of their opinion, probably most would have said yes, and the few who objected to one or two of the reasons could have been dismissed as the degree of change that one expects on re-interview.[7]

Some gimmicks for catching cheaters may even put the finger on the wrong person. Thus, one approach to detecting cheating is to compare the data of each interviewer to the group averages and to assume that if one deviates markedly from the group, he is cheating or doing his work improperly. This reasoning assumes that cheating is exceptional and will stand out from the crowd. I have already suggested that the opposite is often the case. Therefore, if the cheaters are working in the same direction (which is readily possible if they have reached an informal agreement or if the question is of such a nature as to suggest distortion in a given direction), it is the "honest" person who will deviate. In the study alluded to in Case III, for example, one of the interviewers always left spaces open on the "five reasons" item. At one point the director reprimanded him for not obtaining five responses "like the rest of the interviewers." The director preferred to believe that this man was not doing his job right than to believe that all the rest were making up responses.

Large survey organizations have at least made some attempts to control the cruder forms of cheating. In most studies using hired hands, even this limited control is absent. The academic man with one or a few assistants, the research organization study director with one or a few small projects, usually has no routine way of checking on the work of his assistants. If he duplicates much of their work or supervises them very closely, he may as well dispense with their services. If he gives them assignments without checking on them closely, he is in effect assuming that they are conducting their assignment more or less as directed and is accepting their products at face value. This assumption, I assert, is a dubious one. And since it is a common practice nowadays to farm out much of one's research work—quite often to accumulate research grants only to hire others to do the bulk of the work—the dubious nature of hired hand research is a widespread problem in small as well as large scale research, in surveys, in direct observation, and in various forms of data processing.

I do not want to suggest, however, that the major failure of hired hand research is the lack of control of cheating. Rather, the very fact that we are placed in a position of having to think up gimmicks to detect cheating is in itself an ad-

[7]I have even heard the argument that it makes no difference if perceptive interviewers make up parts of the interview responses with the help of information from other responses because their fabrications will usually closely approximate what the subject would have said if he could have been prompted to answer. But if we accept this argument, a large portion of the interview should have been eliminated to begin with. It means we already claim to know the nature of some of the relationships which the study is purportedly investigating.

mission of failure. It means that we are relying for an important part of our research operation on people who have no concern for the outcome of the study. Such persons cannot have the kind of understanding of the data-collection or data-processing procedures which can come only with working out problems in which the researcher has an intrinsic interest and has gone through a process of formulating research questions and relevant ways of collecting and processing data.

I can hear the objection that much social science cannot be done without hired hands. But we should at least be aware of the doubtful nature of some of the information collected in this way and construct our data-collection and processing in such a way as to reduce the encouragement of cheating and restriction of production as much as possible. (See Crespi's list of "ballot demoralizers."[8]) More important, however, I believe the need for hired hands has been greatly exaggerated. Why, for example, must we so often have large samples? The large sample is frequently a contrivance for controlling various kinds of "errors" (including the "error" introduced by unreliable hired hands). But if the study were done on a much smaller sample by one person or several colleagues who formulated their own study and conducted it entirely by themselves, much of this error would not enter in the first place. Isn't a sample of fifty which yields data in which we can have a high degree of confidence more useful than a sample of five thousand where we must remain doubtful about what it is that we have collected? Often a large-scale study tries to do too much at one time and so ends up as a hodge-podge affair with no integration of ideas or information ever taking place because it is, in effect, *nobody's* study. How often have you read the report of a massive study expending large amounts of money and employing large numbers of people where you were disappointed at the paucity of the results, especially when compared to a far smaller project on a similar issue conducted entirely by one or a few people?

Let me repeat that I am not singling out large-scale operations as the only villains. The current structure of professional careers is such that often small studies are turned over to hired hands. We tend to be rated on how many studies we can carry on at the same time rather than on how thoroughly and carefully we can carry through a given line of research. Soon we find that we do not have time for all of the projects we have become involved in and must turn some over to others of lower professional status. This might not be so bad if we were willing to turn over the research work wholeheartedly. We might simply act as entrepreneurs to funnel funds to others and to provide them with appropriate clearance and an entrée to research settings. We can then leave the specific formulation of the problem and procedure (and the credit for doing the work) to the person we have helped out. Such is often done, of course. However, there are many instances in which the senior researcher believes those he has hired cannot be trusted to formulate their own plans, or professional career competition convinces him that he cannot "afford" to give up any of his studies to others. In such cases he is likely to maintain a semblance of control by mechanically structuring a research plan and making assignments to his assistants. This, as I have indicated, is the way to the hired hand mentality with its attendant distortions of research data.

What is a hired hand? So far I have been talking as if I knew and as if the

[8]Leo Crespi, *op. cit.*, pp. 437–439.

hired hand could readily be distinguished from one who is not. This, of course, is not true. The issue is a complex one and information on it is, by its very nature, not very accessible. It is a crucial question which deserves study in its own right as part of the more general study of the process of "doing research."

Let me attempt a crude characterization of hired hand research, a characterization which hopefully will be greatly refined and perhaps reformulated with further study. A hired hand is a person who feels that he has no stake in the research that he is working on, that he is simply expected to carry out assigned tasks and turn in results which will "pass inspection." Of course, a hired assistant may not start out with the hired hand mentality, but may develop it if he finds that his talents for creativity are not called upon and that his suggestions and efforts at active participation are ignored.

From specific examples from the research world and by analogy from research on hired hands in other occupational spheres, I am convinced that research tasks carried out by hired hands are characterized, not rarely or occasionally, but *typically*, by restricted production, failure to carry out portions of the task, avoidance of the more unpleasant or difficult aspects of the research, and outright cheating. The results of research done in part or wholly by hired hands should be viewed as a dubious source for information about specific aspects of our social life or for the raw material for developing broader generalizations.

Of course, this leaves open the question of what constitutes a "stake in the research" and how one avoids or reduces the hired hand mentality. Again, I have no specific answers and hope that issue will receive much more attention than it has up to now. A stake may mean different things in various circumstances. For graduate students, a chance to share in planning and in writing and publication may often be important. For interviewers or field workers, the determination of the details of their procedure may be crucial. In an applied setting, the responsibility for the practical consequences of the research findings may be most important.[9]

It would also be worthwhile to examine the conditions which make for hired hand research. Here again, I have little specific to say and this subject, too, needs much more investigation. However, I will suggest a few factors I consider important.

Size: Hired hands can be found in research staffs of all sizes from one on up. However, it is clear that when a very small number of researchers are working together, there is a greater possibility of developing a true colleagueship in which each will be able to formulate some of his own ideas and put them into action. The larger the group, the more difficult this becomes until the point is probably reached where it is virtually impossible, and the organization must be run on the basis of hierarchical staff relations with the lower echelons almost inevitably becoming hired hands.

Subordination: If some members of the research group are distinctly subordinate to others in a given organizational hierarchy or in general social status, it will be more difficult to develop a true colleague working relationship than

---

[9]The "human relations in industry" movement has given us some useful suggestions about the circumstances which alienate workers and executives, and also ways in which industrial employees may be given a real stake in their jobs. See, for example, Douglas McGregor, *The Human Side of Enterprise*, New York: McGraw-Hill Book Co., 1960, Part 2.

if their status were more closely equal. The subordinate may hesitate to advance his ideas; the superordinate might be loath to admit that his lower-level co-worker be entitled to inject his ideas into the plans. Formal super-subordinate relationships can of course be muted and sometimes completely overcome in the course of personal contact, but certainly this is an initial, and sometimes permanent, basis for establishing hired hand status.

Adherence to Rigid Plans: If a researcher believes that good research can be done only if a detailed plan of data-collection, processing, and analysis is established in advance and adhered to throughout, he has laid the basis for hired hand research if he makes use of assistance from others who have not participated in the original plan. Sticking to a pre-formed plan means that others cannot openly introduce variations which may make the study more meaningful for them. Any creativity they apply will be of a surreptitious nature.

In their research methods texts, our students are told a great deal about the mechanics of research technique and little about the social process of researching. What little is said on the latter score consists largely of Pollyannaish statements about morale, honesty, and "proper motivation." It should be noted that appeals to morality and patriotism never reduced goldbricking and restriction of production in industry, even during the time of a world war. There is no reason to believe that analogous appeals to interviewers, graduate students, research assistants, and others who serve as hired hands will be any more effective. If we want to avoid the hired hand mentality, we must stop using people as hired hands.

Glaser and Strauss state that we regularly "discount" aspects of many, if not most, of all scientific analyses we read because we consider the research design onesided, believe that it does not fit the social structure to which it was generalized, or that it does not fit in with our observations in an area where we have had considerable experience.[10]

I would like to suggest another area in which we might consistently apply the "discounting process." When reading a research report, we should pay close attention to the description of how the data was collected, processed, analyzed, interpreted, and written up with an eye to determining what part, if any, was played by hired hands. This will often be a difficult and highly tentative judgement, requiring much reading between the lines with the help of our knowledge of how our colleagues and we ourselves often operate. However, we can get hints from such things as the size of the staff, the nature of the relationship of the staff members, the manner in which the research plans were developed and applied, the organizational setting in which the research was done, mention made of assignment of tasks, and so on. If there is good reason to believe that significant parts of the research have been carried out by hired hands, this would, in my opinion, be a reason for discounting much or all of the results of the study.

Getting in Our Own Way (Continued)

Roth reminds us that we know from a number of studies in industry as well as in other kinds of organizations that workers tend to develop their own set of norms

[10]Barney Glaser and Anselm L. Strauss, "Discovery of Substantive Theory: A Basic Strategy Underlying Qualitative Research," *American Behavioral Scientist,* 8 (February 1965), pp. 5–12.

regarding production—independent of whatever norms may be set by management. He leans on Donald Roy's research in a machine shop to illustrate his point. Why should we expect that what we know occurs in other kinds of organized work does not also happen in the work of social scientists? If this process of informal norm-setting occurs among other kinds of hired help, then surely it must also occur among the hired help we employ on our large scale research projects. Roth documents his logic with three case studies. I doubt that he has in the least overstated his case. Since the publication of his paper, I have asked students to consider it and suggested it as a possible topic for a term paper. Every time I have done this, the result has been either a confirmatory tale told by a graduate hired hand in seminar or a detailed term paper further documenting the process described by Roth.

It is true that in some ways Roy's evidence is not as direct a parallel as Roth would have it. Interviewers, for example, unlike industrial workers, frequently get paid on a piecework basis, rather than receiving an hourly or weekly rate. They get so much per interview and they have no basis in fact or precedent for suspecting rate reductions if output is too high. It is most unlikely that an interviewer's rate would be changed after a study was fielded. Furthermore, since interviewers are frequently isolated from one another, it is difficult for norms to develop regarding what is "too high" an output. To the extent that interviewers work alone, without contact with other interviewers, collective norms are unlikely either to develop or to be transmitted.[8] Nevertheless, Roth's point on hired hand research is well taken. There is every reason to suspect a great deal of fraud in the filling out of questionnaires—not so much on the part of the respondent, as on the part of the presumably dedicated people who administer those instruments. This is as true of advanced graduate students as it is of part-time workers recruited from the community.

But Roth also spells out a solution to the problem he has identified: if we treat our co-workers as colleagues and fellow "pros," then they will act that way; if we treat them like employees, then they will act that way. It would seem that in spite of our obsession with reliability over the past few decades, we still are far from having the problem under control. The "Hired Hand" thesis applies to any kind of large-scale research project which employs assistants in any capacity—as interviewers, coders, bibliographers, technicians, statistical clerks, etc. Aside from the distance this kind of organized research creates between an investigator and his data, it also strips him of his intellectual independence. He can no longer (as Mills advised) be his own theorist and his own methodologist. It is to survey research that Roth primarily addresses his thesis. Let us consider the peculiar vulnerability of this and other kinds of research which depend on conversations for their data.

The Problem with Talking to People: Surveys and Interviews

At the time I began earnestly pursuing the relation between what people say and what they do, I was most familiar with data derived from surveys or from interviews in depth. My most extensive research experience had been with those two sources of data and I thought I understood the strengths and weaknesses of reports based on such information. In the process of learning that people did not always act

---

8. Robert Bogden reports an exception. He has described with considerable insight (in a term paper, Syracuse University, 1968) the manner in which a clerk or secretary can establish informal production norms for survey interviewers when they are isolated from one another.

as they talked, I also learned that utterances or acts made among intimates seemed likely to vary from those made in public or among different publics.[9] We know from our everyday experiences that different opinions on the same subject can be elicited from the same people in different situations. Such opinions may at times be inconsistent with each other, but regardless of such apparent inconsistency, all such opinions may be valid. All of them may be real opinions. An attitude which is likely to be expressed under conditions of actual social interaction is real and becomes a public opinion when it is expressed. As for our private opinions — basic, consistent, internalized orientations toward objects — they rarely have an opportunity to find expression as public opinions or as actions.[10]

In a sense, then, such private opinions are rarely "real." Exceptions occur in situations where people can express themselves collectively with anonymity or in confidence among intimates. This public opinion then may be congruent with the private opinion. James Reston,[11] for example, once observed of Lyndon Johnson that "he is confusing what men say to the pollsters with what they say to their friends." Furthermore, the President "knows what his aides say to him personally, but he does not know what they say to their wives." More than most men, a president with long congressional experience should understand that men can hold to many honest opinions — opinions which are contingent upon the context within which they are called forth.[12] Thus, in 1964 when United States congressmen were considering a sizable increase in salary for themselves, a Republican attempt to eliminate the pay increase was thwarted by a vote of 125 to 37. Yet, minutes later when the bill was voted on, a demand for a roll call succeeded, and the pay increase was overwhelmingly defeated.[13] Congressional voting behavior reflected one opinion as long as that behavior remained anonymous. But these same men immediately reversed their votes when they knew they would be held individually accountable for them.

9. Some of the ideas presented below and in Chapters Seven and Nine were originally developed in a paper entitled "Public vs. Private Opinions: The 'Real' and the 'Unreal,'" read at the annual meetings of the Eastern Sociological Society in 1966. Helpful comments on that paper came from Lawrence Cagle, Lionel Dannick, Edward Sagarin, Alphonse Sallett, and Elbridge Sibley. I have applied these same arguments supported by this same evidence to a consideration of the question of how assurances of confidentiality impinge on the kinds of information received by social researchers in "Public and Private Opinions: Social Situations and Multiple Realities" in Saad Z. Nagi and Ronald G. Corwin, eds., The Social Contexts of Research (New York: John Wiley and Sons, 1972), 323–49.

10. For a divergent perspective, see Milton Rokeach, "Attitude Change and Behavior Change," Public Opinion Quarterly 30 (1966–67): 530–50. Rokeach has incorporated all of this material into his Beliefs, Attitudes, and Values (San Francisco: Jossey-Bass, Inc., 1970).

11. From his column appearing in the San Francisco Examiner and Chronicle, on May 1, 1966 under the title, "The Price Mr. Johnson Pays."

12. President Kennedy appears to have been more aware of this than President Johnson. Robert F. Kennedy reports in Thirteen Days that "to keep the discussions from being inhibited and because he did not want to arouse attention, he [President Kennedy] decided not to attend all the meetings of our committee. This was wise. Personalities change when the President is present, and frequently even strong men make recommendations on the basis of what they believe the President wishes to hear." Such situational constraints are not limited only to presidents in Washington, D.C. Streetcorner men in that same city have been observed to talk one way about women when in the company of their fellows, but to act very differently when in the company of women. See Elliot Liebow, Tally's Corner (Boston: Little, Brown and Company, 1967), p. 145.

13. For a detailed report of the proceedings see The Congressional Record, 88th Congress, Second Session, vol. 110, no. 45, Washington, D.C., March 12, 1964. For additional commentary see Congress and the Nation, 1964–1965 (Washington, D.C.: Congressional Quarterly Service, 1965), p. 1491.

If exceptions to the reality of private opinions occur in such anonymous collective situations, they also can occur when people have the opportunity to express themselves individually with anonymity as in such cases as nose-picking, voting, masturbating, the purchase of certain items of consumer goods, cheating one's self at solitary games[14] — or responding to a survey interview. As the case of the congressmen suggests, such private acts and opinions cannot be assumed to have any relationship to public acts or opinions. Paradoxically, then, one of the few instances in which an attitude is unlikely to be translated into an opinion or an act in any social context is when it is elicited in a rigorously controlled interview situation by highly trained interviewers employing a technically high quality instrument. This is not to deny the "reality" of interaction in an interview situation. I suggest only that the situation is so meticulously constructed and carefully managed by one party in pursuit of a clear goal (to obtain a completed interview) that it is difficult to imagine any routine social situation which resembles the formal interview. In short, responses to formal interviews inform us about behavior in a formal interviewing situation and little else. The conditions where such data may be otherwise informative are considered later in this chapter.

So brash a statement demands explanation! Current research-interviewing technology assumes the desirability of sterile conditions in the interview situation: neither the interviewer nor the instrument should act in any way upon the situation. The question, ideally, should be so put and so worded as to be unaffected by contextual contaminations. The interviewer must be an inert agent who exerts no influence on response by tone, expression, stance, or statement. The question must be unloaded in that it does not hint in any way that one response is more desirable or more correct than any other response. It must be placed in the sequence of the instrument in such a way that the subject's response is not affected by previous responses. The respondent is provided with maximum assurances of anonymity and the implied guarantees of protection from sanctions. *In effect, the respondent is urged to reveal his most private opinions on an object without relating it to any other objects, or placing it in any context, with the assurance that the interviewer doesn't care what he says and no one else will ever know he said it.*[15] We are confronted then with the paradoxical argument that we obtain an "unreal" opinion when a person is provided with the opportunity to state what he "really" thinks.

The interview is structured in such a way as to maximize the opportunity to elicit a private opinion. The facts of social life are that real utterances of opinion always are public in the sense that they occur in the presence of others. They never occur in isolation and one must always consider the consequences of having uttered them. In real life, there is neither anonymity nor guarantee against possible sanctions. Public opinions are always uttered in a particular context, both in the sense of assessing the impact they are likely to have on others who are present and in the sense of resulting in part from, and being influenced by, what has immediately preceded their utterance in the flow of the action. Consequent overt behavior toward the object of the opinion also takes place in a social context and is as much con-

---

14. Such cheating can occur not only in the obvious instances of solitaire or checkers but in self-deprivational games such as those involving smoking, drinking, dieting, or narcotics. Even in such relatively private acts there is, in a Meadian sense, a public quality in that interaction occurs between the "I," the "me," and the "generalized other."

15. In our discussion of Kent Marquis' work below, we shall see some evidence of a new awareness of the absurdity of this position.

strained by others and by the actor's interpretation of the situation at the time as is the utterance of an opinion. Real expressions of attitude and overt behavior rarely occur under the conditions of sterility which are deliberately structured for the interview situation.

The survey methodologist views his instruments, his interviewers, and the interview situation as potentially contaminating elements. Nearly every volume of the *Public Opinion Quarterly* contains research notes and articles designed to help the pollster and survey researcher reduce the amount of variance in his results which is attributable to interviewer effect, instrument construction, and external features of the interview setting. Efforts are made to elicit opinions which are more purely "private" by using knowledge about situational effects for the purpose of removing or reducing those effects. In contrast to the approach of the social psychologist (see Chapter Seven), this is a strangely negative role of knowledge: the student of public opinion seeks to learn how people express their opinions and their behavior under real (public) conditions in order to alter those conditions in such a way that they become unreal and thus facilitate his elicitation of private opinions.

At least one of the more sophisticated students of attitude and opinion research is clearly aware of this paradox. Herbert Hyman writes:

> . . . The general aim of modern opinion and attitude research has been to provide a situation in which the subject's "true" attitude can come out unhindered by any social barriers. Now there is perfectly good justification for being interested in the world of private, unhindered attitudes, but if our intent is to predict from test results to behavior, we should realize that the private attitudes revealed under test conditions may never be expressed in the more normal situations of everyday life.[16]

Although one's public opinions toward any given object may vary with the context in which they are called forth, and will usually vary from one's private opinion (for any "sane" person), it has been suggested that in mass society the discrepancies grow even greater. Riesman and Glazer, for example, argue that in an increasingly other-directed society, public opinion is something different from what it may have been in a tradition-directed or inner-directed society where a man presumably was an atom with an opinion of his own.[17] Again we are confronted with a paradox: it is precisely in those societies where rigorous efforts to assess public opinions are most likely to be perceived as necessary and most likely to occur that the opinions they elicit are least likely to be real. It follows from the discussion so far that in more gemeinschaft–folk-type societies there is less likelihood of divergence between public and private opinions.[18] These societies are hospitable to fewer publics, en-

16. Herbert Hyman, "Inconsistencies as a Problem in Attitude Measurement," *Journal of Social Issues* 5 (1949): 38.

17. David Riesman and Nathan Glazer, "The Meaning of Opinion," *Public Opinion Quarterly* 12 (1948–49): 631–48.

18. This does not imply that the introduction of rigorous interviewing techniques into such societies is appropriate. To the contrary, the diffusion of American techniques into other societies may be most inappropriate for reasons I have discussed elsewhere. See my "Asking Questions Cross-Culturally: Some Problems of Linguistic Comparability," in *Institutions and the Person: Essays Presented to Everett C. Hughes*, eds. Howard S. Becker, Blanche Geer, David Riesman, and Robert S. Weiss (Chicago: Aldine Publishing Company, 1968), 318–40.

compassing a limited variety of perspectives, and thus contain a narrower range of public opinions. Is it coincidental that social control is greater and naughty behavior less in such societies?

Our consideration of survey and interview data has been focused on validity issues: to what extent do we get what we intend when we ask people questions and record their answers? Roth, you will recall, does not contend with the validity or the appropriateness of the methods. To the contrary he raises questions about reliability and suggests solutions in order to improve our confidence in such research. Survey methodologists have, in fact, been most sensitive to issues of reliability. They constantly seek ways to reduce response variance attributable to such phenomena as interviewer effect and the ambience of the interview, including the external features in the setting in which it takes place.[19] As Hyman put it, the general aim of modern opinion and attitude research has been to provide a situation in which the respondent's "true" attitude can come out unhindered by any social barriers. Survey researchers have learned that the type of pairing of interviewer and respondent can strongly influence the data obtained. Methodological studies by survey organizations suggest that people express different opinions to different kinds of interviewers (in terms of age, sex, and race) in different kinds of situations (alone vs. with others, at home vs. in the office, etc.). Such variation is seen as technical interference with reliability; it messes up consistency. From this perspective, the survey researcher finds such situational effects on interview outcome utterly abhorrent. His purpose in studying them is to find ways of eliminating or at least reducing them.

But studies of this kind of "distortion" can provide a wealth of information if they are interpreted as providing opportunities for reclamation rather than opportunities for garbage disposal. Hyman, perhaps in a weaker moment, has implied as much:

> Up to now, experiments providing data on the influence of the loaded question, the factor of anonymity, the group membership of the interviewer, the position of the question in a context of related questions, etc. have been regarded mainly as guides to the technician in the field of polling. In addition to the *practical* value of such experiments for technicians, there is the implicit *theoretical* value for the student of inconsistencies between attitudes and behavior. The interview or test situation can be regarded as a miniature social situation in which certain forces may hinder the expres-

19. For a comprehensive summary of studies of response bias see C. F. Cannell and R. L. Kahn, "Interviewing," in *Handbook of Social Psychology*, vol. II, eds. G. Lindzey and E. Aronson (Reading, Mass.: Addison-Wesley Co., Inc., 1968). See also L. Bouman, T. Rogers, S. Lipson, A. Cantor, and C. Weiss, "A Bibliography on Respondent-Interviewer Interaction in the Research Interview," Bureau of Applied Social Research (New York: Columbia University, n.d.). For a consideration of problems related to interviewing poor people and the intrusion of such factors as social distance and rapport into the interviewer-respondent relationship, see Carol H. Weiss, "Validity of Welfare Mothers' Interview Responses," *Public Opinion Quarterly* 32 (1968–69): 622–33. See also, earlier in that same volume of *Public Opinion Quarterly*, Barbara Snell Dohrenwerd, John Colombotos, and Bruce P. Dohrenwerd, "Social Distance and Interviewer Effects." A summary of Weiss' observations can be found in her "Interaction in the Research Interview: The Effects of Rapport on Response," Bureau of Applied Social Research (New York: Columbia University, 1970). For evidence that the interaction in the interview situation is a reality *sui generis*, see Derek L. Phillips and Kevin J. Clancy, "Response Biases in Field Studies of Mental Illness," *American Sociological Review* 35 (1970): 503–15.

sion of the attitude. We can understand the problem of inconsistency if we re-examine such experiments and conceive of them as analogies to the way real life situational factors operate to influence the expression of attitude.[20]

I have been able to locate only a few examples of efforts in this direction. Although they are reported twenty years apart, two of them are concerned with utilizing knowledge of interviewer effect and both deal with surveys of black communities. During the Second World War, it was suspected that there might be some underlying discontent among Negroes with the Roosevelt administration and that this discontent could affect the 1944 elections in ways not revealed by the polls. On the basis of earlier National Opinion Research Center studies, Williams and Cantril[21] knew that Negroes respond differently to Negro and to white interviewers. They reasoned that Negroes were likely to hide race-sensitive opinions from white interviewers. Their study was designed to measure the extent of such opinions. Race-sensitive responses were to be identified by differences obtained when one half of the Harlem sample was interviewed by whites and the other half by Negroes. They concluded from this survey that the suspected underlying discontent did not exist and therefore would not distort predictions based on the polls.

The second study attempting to make use of knowledge of interviewer effect took place in an Illinois college town in the 1960s.[22] Bindman reports a wide range of discrepancies when black respondents previously interviewed by whites are reinterviewed by blacks. He is aware that such data are ordinarily interpreted as reflections of low reliability, but he recognizes that this interpretation is based on the assumption that there is only one "correct" answer. Bindman sees the discrepancies for what they are: different kinds of responses to different kinds of interviewers. As a result of both his reinterviews and the cross-interviewing similar to that of Williams and Cantril, Bindman is able to add new dimensions to his analysis. These are two examples of how "reliability" knowledge can be put to work for informative or theoretically relevant purposes. The thesis developed in Chapter Nine is based in part upon this kind of evidence.

Using knowledge of interviewer effect and controlling it in order to obtain new knowledge is only one of several means of obtaining "real" opinions. I have argued elsewhere for the employment of popular stereotypes in the deliberate creation of loaded questions. In a survey of public images of the nurse, four independent tests of validity provided convergent evidence that the opinions elicited by stereotyped — i.e., loaded — questions were real.[23] At that time I observed that some of the better methodology texts grudgingly acknowledged — parenthetically, in foot-

20. Herbert Hyman, "Inconsistencies as a Problem in Attitude Measurement," pp. 40–41.

21. Frederick Williams and Hadley Cantril, "The Use of Interviewer Rapport as a Method of Detecting Differences Between 'Public' and 'Private' Opinion," *Journal of Social Psychology* 22 (1945): 171–75. These authors use the terms *public* and *private* opinion in the opposite manner from which I have employed those terms in this chapter.

22. Aaron M. Bindman, "Interviewing in the Search for 'Truth,'" *Sociological Quarterly* 6 (1965): 281–88.

23. Irwin Deutscher, "The Stereotype as a Research Tool," *Social Forces*, 37 (1958), 56–60. Robert E. Mitchell suggests that leading questions can be used to help reduce the effect of the notorious courtesy bias in Southeast Asia polls. See his "Survey Materials Collected in the Developing Countries: Sampling, Measurement and Interviewing Obstacles to Intra- and International Comparisons," *International Social Science Journal* 17 (1965): 681.

notes, or as an afterthought—that "a 'loaded' question is not *necessarily* undesirable . . ."[24] In this chapter, I am suggesting the obverse: "unloaded" or objective questions are not *necessarily* undesirable. In describing the nurse survey, I wrote:

> We asked "leading" questions and we asked "loaded" questions, because we were seeking neither superficial information nor testing the respondent's knowledge. We literally desired to "lead" the respondent into revealing his "loaded" feelings, rather than to obtain simpering clichés.[25]

Aurbach and his associates have reported the provocative manner in which deliberately loaded questionnaires (creating both positive and negative valences) can be used to establish opinion baselines in survey research.[26] Helson and his associates, in their petition-signing experiment, use the same model in the laboratory (see Himelstein and Moore in Chapter Ten).[27] A rich bank of empirical data providing leads to understanding the manner in which companions influence behavior lies dormant in the methodological literature of survey research. Constructive reinterpretation of these data is needed if they are to enrich knowledge by complementing data provided from other sources.

Marquis displays the kind of ingenuity which recognizes that what are traditionally viewed as dangerous biasing tactics can provide useful hints for the improvement of interviews.[28] Marquis is dealing with what he calls "facts" (presumably in distinction from attitudes or opinions or beliefs). Even when seeking to obtain the most straightforward kind of health information, it becomes clear that "interviewing persons about facts is not necessarily similar to interrogating computer memories or retrieving data from written record sources. One essential difference is that the personal interview relies heavily on verbal transactions between human beings."[29] Marquis' point of departure is the observation of gross underreporting when interview reports of sickness and medical service utilization are compared to information contained in medical records. In a controlled survey experiment, Marquis finds that the application of operant conditioning in the form of gentle reenforcement (anathema to the traditional survey interviewer) significantly increases the amount of accurate health information obtained. Most importantly, he recognizes the broader implications of his relatively small finding: "The presence or absence of the kind of social reinforcement used in this research is only one small part of a wide variety of interviewer behaviors which can be systematically varied in the household interview setting."[30]

24. "The Stereotype as a Research Tool," pp. 56–57. This particular quotation is from Leon Festinger and Daniel Katz, *Research Methods in the Behavioral Sciences* (New York: The Dryden Press, 1952), p. 347 (italics added).

25. "The Stereotype as a Research Tool," p. 57.

26. Herbert A. Aurbach, John R. Coleman, and Bernard Mausner, "Restrictive and Protective Viewpoints of Fair Housing Legislation: A Comparative Study of Attitudes," *Social Problems* 8 (1960): 118–25.

27. H. Helson, R. R. Blake, and J. S. Mouton, "Petition-Signing as an Adjustment to Situational and Personal Factors," *Journal of Social Psychology* 48 (1958): 3–10. Himelstein and Moore's follow-up experiment (reprinted in Chapter Ten) provides an example of an instance in which deliberate unloading was desirable.

28. Kent H. Marquis, "Effects of Social Reinforcement on Health Reporting in the Household Interview," *Sociometry* 33 (1970): 203–15.

29. Ibid., p. 203.

30. Ibid., p. 213.

This chapter would be incomplete without reference to the fact that even if survey research and polling were to begin to elicit real *individual opinions*, the major problem of reality in *collective opinions* would remain (in terms of the likelihood of collective action following their expression). This issue was raised by Blumer in 1947 and remains unanswered. At that time Blumer argued that "if public opinion is to be studied in any realistic sense its depiction must be faithful to its empirical character."[31] Blumer's analysis rests essentially on the observation that, although every man may carry equal weight in the voting booth, every man does not carry equal weight in collective actions undertaken in a society. The opinions of the president of the United States and myself carry equal weight at the ballot box; there is, however, considerable disparity in the weight we carry in the formation of national policy. Blumer argues that "current sampling procedure forces a treatment of society as if society were only an aggregation of disparate individuals . . . . Certainly the mere fact that the interviewee either gives or does not give an opinion does not tell you whether he is participating in the formation of public opinion in the society."[32] Eighteen years later, Angus Campbell writes that "it is curious that Blumer's hopes for the functional analysis of public opinion have been so little realized."[33] In Chapter Two we considered the comments of Blumer's discussants. It appeared that in 1947 we were unable to cope with his carefully developed argument, largely because we were so defensive about our scientific reputation.[34] Perhaps now we can give it the serious attention it deserves.

I am not attempting to argue that current public opinion polling and survey methods are never valid. In my discussion of loaded questions and, earlier, of essentially "private" acts, I have suggested that, on occasion, current methods are appropriate. Sometimes private opinions may have real consequences. Blumer points out that there are conditions under which every man's opinion does have equal weight:

> . . . Many actions of human beings in a society are of this nature — such as casting ballots, purchasing toothpaste, going to motion picture shows, and reading newspapers. Such actions, which I like to think of as mass actions of individuals, in contrast to organized actions of groups, lend themselves readily to the type of sampling that we have in current public opinion polling. In fact, it is the existence of such mass actions of individuals which explains, in my judgment, the successful use in consumer research of sampling such as is employed in public opinion polling.[35]

Blumer provides a rationale for the use under certain conditions of the sterile, anonymous, unloaded, individual-oriented questionnaire. In a critique of public opinion research Nehemiah Jordan makes the same observation: "This is why the concrete act of voting is closely related to behavior evoked in public opinion research — the psychological field of the polling booth is obviously very similar to the

---

31. Herbert Blumer, "Public Opinion and Public Opinion Polling," *American Sociological Review* 13 (1948): 543.

32. Ibid., p. 546.

33. In a book review in the *American Sociological Review* 30 (1965): 633.

34. Discussions by Theodore Newcomb and Julian Woodward follow the Blumer paper, *American Sociological Review* 13 (1948): 549–54.

35. "Public Opinion and Public Opinion Polling," p. 547.

psychological field evoked by the public opinion poll."[36] In my own efforts to understand the frequent lack of concordance between attitude and behavior, I have been struck by the fact that there is congruence in the very areas where Blumer suggests there should be: "Consumers sometimes do change their buying habits in ways that they say they will [and] people frequently do vote as they tell pollsters they will. . . ."[37] In the preceding chapter, the Illinois psychologists provided us with one clue to understanding the discrepancy which is sometimes reported between attitudes and acts: there are different kinds of attitudes and different kinds of acts. Studies which use these same terms may, in fact, be referring to very different phenomena. A second explanation appears for the first time in this book in the preceding paragraphs. Blumer points out that we can expect behavior to relate to sentiments when both are elicited under the same conditions — in the same kind of situation — or, in Jordan's terms, when the two fields are the same. It follows that when a verbalization is elicited in one situation (e.g., private) and a behavior is elicited in another (e.g., public), we may expect them to be different. In Part III such explanations along with others will be considered in detail. Let us continue in Part II to consider the basis for judging credibility of the various kinds of evidence which will be employed in Part III.

In this discussion of credibility issues related to surveys and interviews, I have barely touched on the psychological literature dealing with such phenomena as "acquiescence response sets" (the inclination to go along with anything) and "social desirability" (the inclination to answer "right").[38] These are problem areas which bridge the research of survey sociologists, psychological testers, and attitude researchers. It is my impression that the psychologist engaged in experimental work does not share the survey interviewer's abhorrence of such "interference." Nor does he study such things in order to learn how to eliminate them. The psychologist seems rather more curious about how such phenomena enter into the behavior of his subjects. Problems of credibility in experimental research will be considered in Chapter Eight. In the following chapter, however, we will consider the role of language in the verbal exchanges we call surveys and interviews. It is possible to consider language as a source of distortion which must be eliminated, but it is also possible to consider language as a most revealing and helpful tool — if we can come to understand its nuances. Although language may get in the way when we conduct formal interviews or administer questionnaires, advocates of participant observation suggest that it becomes most useful when it is considered in the context of whatever action is occurring.

36. Nehemiah Jordan, "Some Critical Thoughts Concerning Public Opinion Polls," Hudson Institute Discussion Paper HI-188-DP (Feb. 8, 1963), 4.

37. Irwin Deutscher, "Words and Deeds: Social Science and Social Policy," *Social Problems* 13 (1966): 235–54.

38. For a discussion of these two concepts, the distinction between them, and evidence relating their operation to both personality tests and attitude scales, see James Bentley Taylor, "What Do Attitude Scales Measure: The Problem of Social Desirability," *Journal of Abnormal and Social Psychology* 62 (1961): 386–90. See also footnote 19, above.

7 Speaking in Tongues:

Language and Social Research

Although social scientists do not always recognize it, it is impossible to deal with survey and interview situations without considering language. These are situations which by definition require linguistic exchanges. In this chapter we will consider the survey and the interview from a linguistic perspective, first exploring the problems which arise with language when it is lifted out of its conventional social context (as in the survey or interview). We will then consider the extent to which participant observation resolves our problems by being attentive to language within its conventional contexts. Finally, we will consider the price which must be paid in seeking solutions in this direction. What are the weaknesses and limitations of the method of participant observation? Let us begin by pursuing the problem of reactivity from a somewhat different angle.

Speaking out of Context: Questionnaires and Formal Interviews

One type of reactivity is found outside of the relationship between the investigator and his objects of investigation. It lies in what G. H. Mead would call the conversation between the "I" and the "me" as it occurs in the investigator himself. He interacts with his data in a variety of ways which produce subtle changes in the outcome. I think of this as a reactivity of the scientist qua scientist, and some aspects of it transcend social science to include all scientific endeavors. Aaron Cicourel[1] articulates this problem in terms of language, either oral or written, which he sees as the instrument through which nearly all of our data are filtered. We devise things to say to our subjects or respondents and we listen to what they say in return (either to us or to each other or to our confederates). In privately considering such linguistic exchanges and making sense out of them, we pass our data through a filter, being attentive to some of them and inattentive to others. But this is not the only linguistic filter which permits some data to pass through and strains out others. Usually our data are forced through a second and finer filter: the coding process. That is, in our efforts to make sense out of the data we translate them into a more managable form

1. Aaron V. Cicourel, "Language as a Variable in Social Research," *Sociological Focus* 3 (1969–70): 43–52.

involving sets of categories. The choices we make in creating those categories and the further decisions we make when we place data in categories are another kind of linguistic filter. Our data then require translation both in their reception and in their classification. And this is not the end of it. Cicourel suggests that in the reporting of research findings we need to consider—here we encounter yet a third filter— language as a critical variable in producing research results. Cicourel also raises the disturbing question of what does not pass through these three filters and how such information can be recovered.

Sociolinguists such as Cicourel and Bruce Anderson point out that translation problems exist even when the investigator is a native speaker of the language in which he conducts his research. This is a consequence of the existence of various dialects or speech variations within any society. Unless both participants to an interaction are fluent in the same specific speech variation, it becomes difficult for them to fill in the meanings they would consider "obvious" in interacting with their own kind. This is the issue that Anderson addresses in a series of papers.[2] Translation problems arise whenever different kinds of people are required to deal with the same question. Both Anderson, from a more positivistic perspective, and Cicourel, from a more phenomenological perspective, identify the same issue as critical and frequently overlooked in sociological methodology. Such convergence is one bit of evidence of the importance of the issue: increased sensitivity to the relevance of language in domestic research is seen as urgent regardless of the theoretical orientation of the sociologist.

If reactivity is ubiquitous in social research, so, too, is the definitional problem of a research encounter. This is actually a variety of reactivity since it involves the researcher as an active agent, but it is a more social variety than the kinds usually considered. Whenever a person finds himself in a social situation it becomes imperative for him to muster some reasonable definition of what is happening so that he may appropriately engage in the encounter. The investigator may define himself as engaging in an encounter with a "subject" or a "respondent" and the situation as one which advances man's knowledge of himself. But the other person also needs to satisfy himself as to what is happening. It can by no means be assumed that he automatically shares the investigator's definition of the situation. He may see himself as the victim (e.g., "I'm not telling any white interviewer anything he can use to put down black children"). On the other hand, he may see himself as the beneficiary (e.g., "It's about time you people got around to finding out what us middle Americans think"). Or he could define the situation as one requiring courtesy to an uninvited guest (e.g., "I don't understand what you want, but do come in and have a cup of tea"). Obviously there are any number of possible definitions. The discussion which follows focuses on the interview, but these linguistic problems are encountered in any kind of research which requires that an account be given by the researcher to the objects of his research.[3]

Benney and Hughes define an interview, in part, as a relationship between

2. R. Bruce W. Anderson, "Hidden Translation Problems in Mono-Cultural Research," *Sociological Focus* 3 (1969–70): 33–42. See also his "On the Comparability of Meaningful Stimuli in Cross-Cultural Research," *Sociometry* 30 (1967): 124–36.

3. For a consideration of what kinds of statements require explanation and what constitutes a satisfactory account, see Marvin B. Scott and Stanford M. Lyman, "Accounts," *American Sociological Review* 33 (1968): 46–62.

two people where both parties behave as though they are of equal status for its duration, whether or not this is actually so. This kind of fiction is obviously going to come off better in some cultures than in others, among some segments of a society than in others, and among some mixes of individuals than in others. In their words:

> Anthropologists have long realized—if not always clearly—that the transitory interview, held with respondents who do not share their view of the encounter, is an unreliable source of information in itself . . . . Equally, the climate which makes widespread interviewing possible in the West today is itself relatively novel.[4]

The kind of cultural climate which tolerates a situation like an interview is "a fairly new thing in the history of the human race."[5] The interview is most generally seen as an encounter with a stranger. There are wide variations in prescribed forms of interaction and language with a stranger. As we shall see below, there are equally wide variations in such particular concepts as "privacy," "security," and those matters which are considered to be of an intimate or personal nature.

The Southeast Asian cultural value of "courtesy" has been described in detail by Emily Jones.[6] This "important and pervasive value" defines the interview situation in a manner which has a large potential for distorting supposedly "comparable" data. It can act as a deterrent to obtaining reliable information—either in response to formal questions or in an interviewing situation which is more open. From the perspective of the respondent, it is a cultural obligation to see to it that the interviewer is not distressed, disappointed, or offended in any way. And, to further complicate matters, should the interviewer be a product of this same culture, then he is likewise obliged not to distress, disappoint, or offend his respondents. This amiable definition, however, has its advantages as well as its drawbacks. For example, "To ask personal questions is well within the bounds of courteous behavior."[7]

Many different definitions of the interview situation may be subsumed under the gross cultural value which leads to courtesy bias. Mitchell suggests that a courtesy or hospitality bias is common in Asia everywhere from Japan to Turkey:

> The direction of the courtesy bias is different in different countries. For example, the humility of the Japanese is said to lead them to under-evaluate their own achievements, class positions, and the like. On the other hand, some researchers in the Middle East claim that respondents there tend to exaggerate their achievements, class position, knowledge of the world, and extent to which they are modern rather than traditional. In prac-

4. Mark Benney and Everett C. Hughes, "Of Sociology and the Interview: Editorial Preface," *American Journal of Sociology* 62 (1956): 142.
5. Ibid.
6. Emily L. Jones, "Courtesy Bias in South-East Asian Surveys," *International Social Science Journal* 15 (1963). The elements of the code are listed on p. 71. References to the South-East Asian value of "courtesy" all predate the decade of social and cultural destruction wreaked by the United States on that once gentle corner of the world. Although it is unlikely that such a value as "courtesy to strangers" has survived, it remains a useful historical example for our purposes.
7. Ibid.

tical terms, this means that the type of question-wording appropriate in Japan and the West would be inappropriate in Turkey and Iran.[8]

If courtesy is highly valued in some parts of the world, one might anticipate that the opposite would be true in other parts. There are certainly ethnocentric societies (and ethnic groups within societies), where all outsiders—including interviewers—are considered fair game for deception. Such a "sucker" bias is described by the Keesings in a study of elite communications in Samoa.[9]

Although it may well be within the bounds of courtesy to ask personal questions in Southeast Asia, most other peoples set limits. Hunt reports that "even native French persons asked to help in translating interview questions could think of no discreet way to ask respondents their religious views."[10] Lerner remarks on the basis of his interviews with Frenchmen that the French equate security with privacy. It follows that if they permit a breach of their privacy for interviewing purposes, they view this as a self-breach—a violation of their personal security. His problem was not a matter of the validity of data obtained but a matter of obtaining it in the first place: "Most refusals were based squarely upon the feeling that such an interview was an unwarranted intrusion into their personal affairs."[11] Lerner found that the trick was to get a Frenchman started, "but, once started how they talked!"[12]

Both Lerner and Hunt report types of resistance among Frenchmen which differ from the typical American survey experience. The traditional survey check-list or yes-no type of questions were regarded with suspicion by both Austrians and Frenchmen: "A relatively high proportion could not be persuaded to answer in the customary and familiar form used in almost all American surveys."[13] Europeans described such questions as "too brutal" and suggested that they smacked of American gimmickry. This differential definition is further confounded by the observation that the French regard as silly, frivolous, and unworthy of attention any question which requires a respondent to play a role (e.g., "What would you do if . . ."). Lerner interprets this within a culture-personality framework:

8. Robert E. Mitchell, "Survey Materials Collected in the Developing Countries: Sampling, Measurement and Interviewing Obstacles to Intra- and International Comparisons," *International Social Science Journal* 17 (1965): 681. In addition to Jones, Mitchell cites Mary R. Hollsteiner, *The Dynamics of Power in a Philippine Municipality* (Quezon: Community Development Research Council, University of the Philippines, 1963).

9. Felix M. Keesing and Marie M. Keesing, *Elite Communications in Samoa: A Study of Leadership* (Stanford: Stanford University Press, 1956), cited by Mitchell, "Survey Materials," pp. 681–82. In a personal communication Robert Weiss has pointed out the relationship between the "sucker bias" and the process of "putting someone on." The respondent defrauds the interviewer by acting, for example, as someone the interviewer might imagine him to be. Weiss' observation can be extended to include the "courtesy bias" as well, since it, too, is a form of "put-on."

10. William H. Hunt, Wilder W. Crane, and John C. Wahlke, "Interviewing Political Elites in Cross-Cultural Comparative Research," *American Journal of Sociology* 70 (1964): 66.

11. Daniel Lerner, "Interviewing Frenchmen," *American Journal of Sociology* 62 (1956): 193.

12. Ibid., pp. 187–88.

13. Hunt et al., "Interviewing Political Elites," p. 65. Evidence of the consequences of such differential definitions is found in the proportion of completed forms returned from two subsamples who were asked to mail them. The request was met by 97 percent of the California legislature and by 62 percent of the lower Austrian legislature (p. 65).

Such questions are handled with greater facility by people . . . who are closer than the French are to other-directed personalities, and who, having a less stable or less rigid conception of themselves and their proper conduct in the world, show a more supple capacity for rearranging their self-system upon short notice.[14]

Lerner relates this observation to an earlier experience interviewing in the Middle East, where he found that the "traditionalists" were unable to answer such questions as "What would you do if you were president of Syria?" The "moderns," on the other hand, had no difficulty responding to questions which required them to take the role of a newspaper editor, the leader of their country, or a resident of another country.[15] *There are then cultural differences in both those things people are able to talk about and those things they are willing to talk about.* We have already noted the inability to make discreet inquiries about religion among Frenchmen. This is also the case in Moslem Pakistan but not so in Hindu India. The Almond-Verba five-nation study reports that Italians seem reticent about political topics.[16] Middle-class Americans prefer not to be too specific about their incomes. And there are people who consider sex talk taboo.

In some African areas, as well as in other parts of the world, there is a reluctance to talk about dead children and the number of people in a household . . . . In the Middle East there is a reluctance to discuss ordinary household events, and Chinese businessmen in any country are reported to be especially secretive about any and all facets of their work and personal lives. In many countries, respondents are reticent about political topics in general and party preference in particular. On the other hand, it is by no means clear that family planning is nearly as sensitive an issue in the developing countries as might be expected.[17]

But the overriding cross-cultural problem remains that of differences in definitions of what must be perceived as an alien social situation by most people of the world—certainly by the less cosmopolitan and the more poorly educated. The American has had sufficient routine exposure to polls and surveys, both as consumer and respondent, to feel that he knows what they are. The same assumption cannot be made regarding other peoples in other societies. The study of the evolving social relationship between interviewer and respondent in various cultures is in itself an important sociological undertaking. It is, of course, not to problems of cross-cultural research that this book addresses itself. Let us consider the implications of our discussion so far for the kinds of talking research we do at home. If sentiments are expressed, it is usually a verbal process.

14. Lerner, "Interviewing Frenchmen," p. 191.
15. Ibid.
16. Gabriel Almond and Sidney Verba, *The Civic Culture* (Princeton, N.J.: Princeton University Press, 1963), Chapter 2, cited by Mitchell, "Survey Materials," p. 671.
17. Mitchell, "Survey Materials," p. 675. Mitchell considers a number of related problems not covered in this chapter, including the difficulty in obtaining comparable sampling frames in different societies, the differential accessibility of the sexes as respondents in survey research in different countries, and the problem of intrasocietal ethnic differences. For example, his secondary analysis of marginal tabulations in several Southeast Asian surveys reveals large differences in Chinese and Indian responses, especially in the proportion of "no response."

When Benney and Hughes suggest that the interview as a form of social rhetoric is not merely a tool of sociology but part of its very subject matter, they are reminding us that the peculiar thing about human interaction is its symbolic nature and, in large part, the symbols employed are linguistic ones. It is possible that many of the kinds of errors in translation and interpretation—the semantic slip-ups—which occur in cross-lingual situations also occur between interview and interviewee within our own society. In his unique analysis of the interviewing process in a domestic survey, Riesman identifies many of the communication problems we have reviewed above. Like some European legislators and Middle East traditionalists, some American academicians appear to reject "role-playing" questions: they are "too 'iffy' to make sense."[18] Yet these very types of questions which met resistance in one kind of college proved to be "just what the doctor ordered" in another kind.[19] What I referred to in Chapter Three as Riesman's discovery of a bit of the Arab in American professors, suggests not only that "yes" may mean "no," but also that there may be degrees of "yesness" and "noness." If this is true, then one cannot assume a simple dichotomy and, furthermore, one cannot assume a symmetrical scale with "no" and "yes" at points equidistant from the center. Asymmetry in scale distributions points up the fact that what appears to be a strong "no" is not necessarily as strong as a strong "yes."[20]

Critics of surveys in the developing countries have argued that there may be no "public opinion" in those countries or that "opinion" may be restricted only to certain areas.[21] This is the logic Herbert Blumer applied to the domestic scene so many years ago and which we reviewed in the previous chapter. It has been empirically verified for one "developing country" by Converse who found that even issues considered to be salient to wide segments of the American population had relatively small publics.[22] The Blumer thesis on public opinion is further documented by Riesman: "We see here one of the problems of a national survey, namely, that coverage and comparability mean that the same questions will be asked of those who are virtually 'know nothings' and those who could write a book on each theme."[23] He concludes that "on a national survey there is always danger in the assumption that we are in fact one country, and that issues relevant to one part of the population are or could become meaningful to another."[24]

Throughout his analysis of an American national survey, Riesman is sensitive to the role of "politeness" as it enters into the interview situation—a phenomenon reminiscent of the Southeast Asia "courtesy bias" discussed earlier. Finally, he provides us with an illustration of the manner in which "cultural" differences between an English-speaking interviewer and respondent can impinge upon the inter-

18. David Riesman, "Some Observations on the Interviewing in the Teacher Apprehension Study," in Paul F. Lazarsfeld and Wagner Thielens Jr., *The Academic Mind* (Glencoe, Ill.: The Free Press, 1958), p. 275, n. 12.

19. Ibid., p. 316, n. 55.

20. Nehemiah Jordan, "The 'Asymmetry' of 'Liking' and 'Disliking': A Phenomenon Meriting Further Reflection and Research," *Public Opinion Quarterly* 29 (1965): 315–22.

21. Mitchell, "Survey Materials," pp. 672–73; Gabrielle Wuelker, "Questionnaires in Asia," *International Social Science Journal* 15 (1963): 35–47.

22. Phillip E. Converse, "New Dimensions of Meaning for Cross-Section Sample Surveys in Politics," *International Social Science Journal* 16 (1964): 19–34.

23. Riesman, "Some Observations,"p. 360.

24. Ibid., pp. 365 and 375–76, n. 9.

view situation on the domestic scene. The case in point is the inability of a northern faculty member in a southern college to accurately take the role of his southern
interviewer:

> "Southern charm" is . . . a two-way street. Interviewers who might, in old
> Southern fashion, emphasize their kin connections to gain entrée, might
> also evoke the gallantry of otherwise fearful administrators and respon-
> dents; this was perhaps especially likely where an apparently well-born in-
> terviewer could talk to the intellectual elite with freedom from demagogic
> clichés on the race question: class pride, in the South especially, can link
> Jeffersonian traditions of academic freedom to good manners in expressing
> such traditions. Obviously enough, such nuances of communication might
> well be lost on a City College graduate teaching his first year of anthropolo-
> gy at a state-controlled institution in the Deep South.[25]

This example provides an instance of what are essentially social structural
interferences with communication in a presumably monolinguistic situation (are
such interferences of the same order as those which obtain as a result of cultural differences between an Englishman and an American?). It appears, then, that it is possible that there are types of lingual interference which operate not only cross culturally, but which also derive from social-structural differences within a given society.
Furthermore, there may be microscopic interferences resulting from the particular
situations in which people find themselves. Definitions from all of these levels can
enter into the construction of the interaction between interviewer and interviewee.
Riesman describes his college professor respondents as very American in their willingness to trust strangers and their unwillingness to "play it close to the chest," as
well as in their consequent fear of having talked too much.[26] Riesman sees these as
cultural attributes — related to the American character. It remains for the analysts of
interviews with Arkansans following a disaster to draw clear *social-structural* distinctions in the definition of the interview situation. The meaning of the interview for
middle-class respondents is posed like this:

> Although the interviewer is a stranger, an outsider, he is a well spoken,
> educated person. He is seeking information on behalf of some organiza-
> tion, hence his questioning not only has sanction but sets the stage for both
> a certain freedom of speech and an obligation to give fairly full informa-
> tion. . . . At the very least he has had some experience in talking to educated
> strangers . . . . So he becomes relatively sensitive to communication *per se*
> and to communication with others who may not exactly share his view-
> points or frames of reference.[27]

In contrast, the lower-class person infrequently meets a middle-class person
in a situation anything like the interview:

25. Ibid., p. 332.
26. Ibid., p. 281.
27. Leonard Schatzman and Anselm Strauss, "Social Class and Modes of Communication,"
American Journal of Sociology 60 (1955): 336–37.

Here he must talk at great length to a stranger about personal experiences, as well as recall for his listener a tremendous number of details. Presumably he is accustomed to talking about such matters and in such detail only to listeners with whom he shares a great deal of experience and symbolism, so that he need not be very self-conscious about communicative technique. He can, as a rule, safely assume that words, phrases, and gestures are assigned approximately similar meanings by his listeners. But this is not so in the interview or, indeed, in any situation where class converses with class in non-traditional modes.

Cicourel sees the interview situation in Goffmanesque terms as a managed performance on the part of both actors, where, regardless of social class or other structural differences, "each seeks to bargain with the other implicitly about what will be tolerated, how each seeks to convey or blur some image of themselves, their relative interest in each other as persons, and so on."[28] His sensitivity to linguistic and paralinguistic nuances of interaction and the manner in which they enter into the interview "findings" provokes him into designing an alternate strategy to conventional survey interviewing. This strategy, derived from the phenomenology of Alfred Schutz, leads to a concentration on the routine grounds for making sense of communication. What is not said becomes as important as what is said. Linguistic codes and their switching become data. Standard techniques such as the "probe" (e.g., "What do you mean by that?") are prohibited since they strip the respondent of "the kind of vague or taken for granted terms and phrases [he] characteristically uses as a competent member of the society."[29]

Although primitive, this approach provides a refreshing glimpse of language and its use in the interview as a central datum. From Cicourel's perspective, formal precoded instruments become anathema, imposing a role of passive compliance upon the respondent—compliance to the preconceived categories of those who write the questions. Although the problems of measurement reactivity are clearly present in the interview, their very recognition as such reduces their problematic aspects. Recall that one of the major solutions offered by the authors of *Unobtrusive Measures* was to avoid verbal indicators. Cicourel and the ethnomethodologists are committed to treating conversations as data in themselves. It becomes possible, then, to view the interview as an exchange in which one or another variety of reality is negotiated or socially constructed by the interviewer and the respondent.[30]

Evidence concerning the great varieties of classification and categories employed in different languages alerts us to the possibility that problems of the same order may arise within a language community.[31] It is possible, as Schatzman and Strauss suggest, that the lower-class respondent "cannot talk about categories of

28. Aaron V. Cicourel, "Fertility, Family Planning and the Social Organization of Family Life: Some Methodological Issues," *Journal of Social Issues* 23 (1967): 57–81.

29. Ibid.

30. For the general argument, see Thomas J. Scheff, "Negotiating Reality: Notes on Power in the Assessment of Responsibility," *Social Problems* 16 (1968), 3–17 (reprinted in Chapter Thirteen of this volume).

31. For a brief discussion of distinctions and classifications along with a number of references, see my "Asking Questions Cross-Culturally," in *Institutions and the Person: Essays Presented to Everett C. Hughes*, eds. Howard S. Becker, Blanche Geer, David Riesman, and Robert S. Weiss (Chicago: Aldine Publishing Company, 1968), pp. 318–40.

people or acts because, apparently, he does not think readily in terms of classes."[32] On the other hand these same scholars are aware that, as middle-class observers, they may be unable to recognize lower-class classifications. The latter explanation seems more credible. Jordan's secondary analysis of previously published scales does suggest that sometimes the categories imposed by an investigator are unlike those in the minds of the subjects.[33] In order to detect the scales people may carry around in their heads, Hamblin has followed a lead from psychophysics. He suggests that social scientists employ ratio measures which are based on whatever ranges or intervals are used by respondents.[34]

Researchers need to keep in mind the fact that communication styles do vary, as, for example, among the social classes. Schatzman and Strauss are convinced, on the basis of transcripts of interviews, that lower-class respondents are interpersonally incompetent—relatively unable to take the role of the other. Cohen and Hodges appear to verify this position and conclude that "interview and questionnaire techniques are more likely, when applied to lower class respondents than when applied to respondents in the other strata, to produce caricatures. . . ."[35] In commenting on the lack of any visible signs of role-taking ability in the interviews of lower-class people, Cohen and Hodges concede that this does not deny its existence and remind us of the "peasant shrewdness" of the lower classes as, for example, in their "conning" ability.[36]

A solution to this field communication problem is suggested by Basil Bernstein who also suspects a class link between verbal fluency and role-taking ability. The middle class switches easily between an "elaborated" coding of English and a "restricted" code, while the lower classes are limited to the restricted code. Bernstein provides a clue to methods of tapping lower-class communication channels when he observes that "in restricted codes, to varying degrees, the extraverbal channels become objects of special perceptual activity; in elaborated codes it is the verbal channel."[37] It would seem to follow, then, that in order to successfully interview users of restricted codes the field worker must shift his detection devices from verbal indicators to nonverbal indicators. The semantics of the situation, which is what the field worker seeks to grasp, are revealed through communications channels other than those based on vocabulary or syntax. One survey expert masterfully understates the issue: "Since those who prepare questionnaires are typically from the middle and upper classes, the instruments they produce are likely to be somewhat inappropriate for large segments of the population."[38]

It should be clear by now that the interview is in fact a peculiar situation.

32. Schatzman and Strauss, "Social Class," p. 333.

33. Jordan, "The 'Asymmetry' of 'Liking' and 'Disliking.'"

34. Robert L. Hamblin, "Ratio Measurement and Sociological Theory: A Critical Analysis," (St. Louis: Washington University, 1966), mimeo. Hamblin's argument appears in part in more readily available form in "Ratio Measurement for the Social Sciences," Social Forces 50 (1971): 191–214 and in "Mathematical Experimentation and Sociological Theory: A Critical Analysis," Sociometry 34 (1971): 423–52.

35. Albert K. Cohen and Harold M. Hodges, "Characteristics of the Lower Blue-Collar Class," Social Problems 10 (1963): 333.

36. Ibid., p. 332.

37. Basil Bernstein, "Elaborated and Restricted Codes: Their Social Origins and Some Consequences," in The Ethnography of Communication, eds. John J. Gumperz and Dell Hymes, Part 2 of the American Anthropologist 66 (1964): 63.

38. Mitchell, "Survey Materials," pp. 678–79.

Possibilities of distortion arising out of differential definitions of that situation have been discussed. This section took Aaron Cicourel's more recent work as its point of departure. An earlier statement of his seems helpful as we bring our discussion of language to a close. Cicourel is interested in "how conversational materials and their properties become transformed when they become interviews, questionnaires, and written reports. . . . Interviews and questionnaires," he says, "usually are removed from the actual conditions of social interaction in which conversations occur . . . and therefore [are] in doubtful correspondence (seldom established empirically) with the actual activities to which the interview and questionnaire items refer."[39] That "doubtful correspondence" between verbal statements and overt actions is, of course, what we are all about in this book. What specifically concerns Cicourel is the variation in degree of management of verbalizations under various conditions. And if there is any doubt about the ability and inclination of ordinary people to shift their style of speaking along with the context in which the speech occurs, Labov's data on New Yorkers should dispel it. His tables show a consistent shift among all social classes toward more phonetic "correctness" as the context shifts from informal conversation ("casual speech") to the interview ("careful speech") and finally to highly formalized contexts (reading style and word lists).[40]

It would appear that a great deal remains to be learned about how to communicate with those we seek to understand. In our interviews and questionnaires we may more frequently talk at them than talk with them. Certainly the nonverbal dimensions of language require considerably more attentiveness than they have received so far.[41] It is remarkable that social scientists have managed to so great a degree to avoid consideration of the methodological implications of language. The unique quality of human conduct is its symbolic mediation through language, and our basic tools are lingual. Sociologists generally understand that this is the heart of George Herbert Mead's imagery of human nature. This discussion assumes that the language a man speaks cannot be divorced from his behavior, "for language, in the full, is nothing less than an inventory of all the ideas, interests, and occupations that take up the attention of the community."[42] As Kenneth Burke would have it, "the names for things and operations smuggle in connotations of good and bad—a noun tends to carry with it a kind of invisible adjective, and a verb an invisible adverb."[43] The Hughes sum it up this way: "There is generally a great deal in a name, as Juliet plainly knew. Often it is more than a pointer; it points with pride, or with the finger of scorn."[44]

The alternative proposed by some sociologists to the transitory verbal exchange known as an "interview" is participant observation. This technique provides an opportunity to interview in context—such that the invisible adjectives and

39. Aaron V. Cicourel, "Kinship, Marriage, and Divorce in Comparative Family Law," *Law and Society Review* 1 (1967): 103–29.

40. William Labov, "The Effect of Social Mobility on Linguistic Behavior," in *Explorations in Sociolinguistics*, ed. Stanley Lieberson, special issue of *Sociological Inquiry* 36 (1966): 186–203.

41. For an application of paralinguistics to social research see Alan D. Grimshaw, "Some Problematic Aspects of Communication in Cross-Racial Research in the United States," *Sociological Focus* 3 (1969–70): 67–85.

42. Roger W. Brown, *Words and Things* (Glencoe, Ill.: The Free Press, 1958), p. 60.

43. Kenneth Burke, *Permanence and Change: An Anatomy of Purpose* (Los Altos, Calif.: Hermes Publications, 1954), p. 244.

44. Everett C. Hughes and Helen MacGill Hughes, "What's in a Name," Chapter 9 in *Where Peoples Meet: Racial and Ethnic Frontiers* (Glencoe, Ill.: The Free Press, 1952), pp. 130–44.

adverbs become visible—where things are happening and the interview is a part of them. It also presents us with a world in which what people say is intimately related to what they are doing, although perhaps not consistently so from the perspective of the naive outsider. Two of the strongest proponents of participant-observational field methods spell out their rationale in the following article.

DATA:
Participant Observation and Interviewing:
A Comparison
HOWARD S. BECKER / BLANCHE GEER

The most complete form of the sociological datum, after all, is the form in which the participant observer gathers it: An observation of some social event, the events which precede and follow it, and explanations of its meaning by participants and spectators, before, during, and after its occurrence. Such a datum gives us more information about the event under study than data gathered by any other sociological method. Participant observation can thus provide us with a yardstick against which to measure the completeness of data gathered in other ways, a model which can serve to let us know what orders of information escape us when we use other methods.[1]

By participant observation we mean that method in which the observer participates in the daily life of the people under study, either openly in the role of researcher or covertly in some disguised role, observing things that happen, listening to what is said, and questioning people, over some length of time.[2] We want, in this paper, to compare the results of such intensive field work with what might be regarded as the first step in the other direction along this continuum: the detailed and conversational interview (often referred to as the unstructured or undirected interview).[3] In this kind of interview, the interviewer explores many facets of his interviewee's concerns, treating subjects as they come up in conversation, pursuing interesting leads, allowing his imagination and ingenuity full rein as he tries to develop new hypotheses and test them in the course of the interview.

"Participant Observation and Interviewing: A Comparison," by Howard S. Becker and Blanche Geer. Reproduced by permission of the Society for Applied Anthropology from *Human Organization*, vol. 16, no. 3 (1957), pp. 28–32.
[1]We wish to thank R. Richard Wohl and Thomas S. McPartland for their critical reading of an earlier version of this paper.
[2]Cf. Florence R. Kluckhohn, "The Participant Observer Technique in Small Communities," *American Journal of Sociology*, 45 (Nov., 1940), 331–43; Arthur Vidich, "Participant Observation and the Collection and Interpretation of Data," *ibid.*, 60 (Jan., 1955), 354–60; William Foote Whyte, "Observational Field-Work Methods," in Marie Jahoda, Morton Deutsch, and Stuart W. Cook (eds.), *Research Methods in the Social Sciences* (New York: Dryden Press, 1951), II, 393–514, and *Street Corner Society* (Enlarged Edition) (Chicago: University of Chicago Press, 1955), 279–358.
[3]Two provisos are in order. In the first place, we assume in our comparison that the hypothetical interviewer and participant observer we discuss are equally skilled and sensitive. We assume further that both began their research with equally well formulated problems, so that they are indeed looking for equivalent kinds of data.

In the course of our current participant observation among medical students,[4] we have thought a good deal about the kinds of things we were discovering which might ordinarily be missed or misunderstood in such an interview. We have no intention of denigrating the interview or even such less precise modes of data gathering as the questionnaire, for there can always be good reasons of practicality, economy, or research design for their use. We simply wish to make explicit the difference in data gathered by one or the other method and to suggest the differing uses to which they can legitimately be put. In general, the shortcomings we attribute to the interview exist when it is used as a source of information about events that have occurred elsewhere and are described to us by informants. Our criticisms are not relevant when analysis is restricted to interpretation of the interviewee's conduct *during the interview,* in which case the researcher has in fact observed the behavior he is talking about.[5]

The differences we consider between the two methods involve two interacting factors: the kinds of words and acts of the people under study that the researcher has access to, and the kind of sensitivity to problems and data produced in him. Our comparison may prove useful by suggestive areas in which interviewing (the more widely used method at present and likely to continue so) can improve its accuracy by taking account of suggestions made from the perspective of the participant observer. We begin by considering some concrete problems: learning the native language, or the problem of the degree to which the interviewer really understands what is said to him; matters interviewees are unable or unwilling to talk about; and getting information on matters people see through distorting lenses. We then consider some more general differences between the two methods.

Learning the Native Language

Any social group, to the extent that it is a distinctive unit, will have to some degree a culture differing from that of other groups, a somewhat different set of common understandings around which action is organized, and these differences will find expression in a language whose nuances are peculiar to that group and fully understood only by its members. Members of churches speak differently from members of informal tavern groups; more importantly, members of any particular church or tavern group have cultures, and languages in which they are expressed, which differ somewhat from those of other groups of the same general type. So, although we speak one language and share in many ways in one culture, we cannot assume that we understand precisely what another person, speaking as a member of such a group, means by any particular word. In interviewing members of groups other than our own, then, we are in somewhat the same posi-

---

[4]This study is sponsored by Community Studies, Inc., of Kansas City, Missouri, and is being carried out at the University of Kansas Medical Center, to whose dean and staff we are indebted for their wholehearted cooperation. Professor Everett C. Hughes of the University of Chicago is director of the project.
[5]For discussion of this point, see Thomas S. McPartland, *Formal Education and the Process of Professionalization: A Study of Student Nurses* (Kansas City, Missouri: Community Studies, Inc., 1957), 2–3.

tion as the anthropologist who must learn a primitive language,[6] with the important difference that, as Icheiser has put it, we often do not understand that we do not understand and are thus likely to make errors in interpreting what is said to us. In the case of gross misunderstandings the give and take of conversation may quickly reveal our mistakes, so that the interviewee can correct us; this presumably is one of the chief mechanisms through which the anthropologist acquires a new tongue. But in speaking American English with an interviewee who is, after all, much like us, we may mistakenly assume that we have understood him and the error be small enough that it will not disrupt communication to the point where a correction will be in order.

The interview provides little opportunity of rectifying errors of this kind where they go unrecognized. In contrast, participant observation provides a situation in which the meanings of words can be learned with great precision through study of their use in context, exploration through continuous interviewing of their implications and nuances, and the use of them oneself under the scrutiny of capable speakers of the language. Beyond simply clarifying matters so that the researcher may understand better what people say to each other and to him, such a linguistic exercise may provide research hypotheses of great usefulness. The way in which one of us learned the meaning of the word "crock," as medical students use it, illustrates these points.

I first heard the word "crock" applied to a patient shortly after I began my field work. The patient in question, a fat, middle-aged woman, complained bitterly of pains in a number of widely separated locations. When I asked the student who had so described her what the word meant, he said that it was used to refer to any patient who had psychosomatic complaints. I asked if that meant that Mr. X, a young man on the ward whose stomach ulcer had been discussed by a staff physician as typically psychosomatic, was a crock. The student said that that would not be correct usage, but was not able to say why.

Over a period of several weeks, through discussion of many cases seen during morning rounds with the students, I finally arrived at an understanding of the term, realizing that it referred to a patient who complained of many symptoms but had no discoverable organic pathology. I had noticed from the beginning that the term was used in a derogatory way and had also been inquiring into this, asking students why they disliked having crocks assigned to them for examination and diagnosis. At first students denied the derogatory connotations, but repeated observations of their disgust with such assignments soon made such denials unrealistic. Several students eventually explained their dislike in ways of which the following example is typical: "The true crock is a person who you do a great big workup for and who has all of these vague symptoms, and *you really can't find anything the matter with them.*"

Further discussion made it clear that the students regarded patients primarily as objects from which they could learn those aspects of clinical medicine not easily acquired from textbooks and lectures; the

[6]See the discussion in Bronislaw Malinowski, *Magic, Science, and Religion and Other Essays* (Glencoe: The Free Press, 1948), 232–8.

crock took a great deal of their time, of which they felt they had little enough, and did not exhibit any interesting disease state from which something might be learned, so that the time invested was wasted. This discovery in turn suggested that I might profitably investigate the general perspective toward medical school which led to such a basis for judgment of patients, and also suggested hypotheses regarding the value system of the hospital hierarchy at whose bottom the student stood.

At the risk of being repetitious, let us point out in this example both the errors avoided and the advantages gained because of the use of participant observation. The term might never have been used by students in an ordinary interview; if it had, the interviewer might easily have assumed that the scatological term from which it in fact is descended provided a complete definition. Because the observer saw students on their daily rounds and heard them discussing everyday problems, he heard the word and was able to pursue it until he arrived at a meaningful definition. Moreover, the knowledge so gained led to further and more general discoveries about the group under study.

This is not to say that all of these things might not be discovered by a program of skillful interviewing, for this might well be possible. But we do suggest that an interviewer may misunderstand common English words when interviewees use them in some more or less esoteric way and not know that he is misunderstanding them, because there will be little chance to check his understanding against either further examples of their use in conversation or instances of the object to which they are applied. This leaves him open to errors of misinterpretation and errors of failing to see connections between items of information he has available, and may prevent him from seeing and exploring important research leads. In dealing with interview data, then, experience with participant observation indicates that both care and imagination must be used in making sure of meanings, for the cultural esoterica of a group may hide behind ordinary language used in special ways.

Matters Interviewees Are Unable or Unwilling to Talk About

Frequently, people do not tell an interviewer all the things he might want to know. This may be because they do not want to, feeling that to speak of some particular subject would be impolitic, impolite, or insensitive, because they do not think to and because the interviewer does not have enough information to inquire into the matter, or because they are not able to. The first case — the problem of "resistance" — is well known and a considerable lore has developed about how to cope with it.[7] It is more difficult to deal with the last two possibilities for the interviewee is not likely to reveal, or the interviewer to become aware, that significant omissions are being made. Many events occur in the life of a social

[7]See, for example, Arnold M. Rose, "A Research Note on Interviewing," *American Journal of Sociology*, 51 (Sept., 1945), 143–4; and Howard S. Becker, "A Note on Interviewing Tactics," *Human Organization*, 12:4 (Winter, 1954), 31–2.

group and the experience of an individual so regularly and uninterruptedly, or so quietly and unnoticed, that people are hardly aware of them, and do not think to comment on them to an interviewer; or they may never have become aware of them at all and be unable to answer even direct questions. Other events may be so unfamiliar that people find it difficult to put into words their vague feelings about what has happened. If an interviewee, for any of these reasons, cannot or will not discuss a certain topic, the researcher will find gaps in his information on matters about which he wants to know and will perhaps fail to become aware of other problems and areas of interest that such discussion might have opened up for him.

This is much less likely to happen when the researcher spends much time with the people he studies as they go about their daily activities, for he can see the very things which might not be reported in an interview. Further, should he desire to question people about matters they cannot or prefer not to talk about, he is able to point to specific incidents which either force them to face the issue (in the case of resistance) or make clear what he means (in the case of unfamiliarity). Finally, he can become aware of the full meaning of such hints as are given on subjects people are unwilling to speak openly about and of such inarticulate statements as people are able to make about subjects they cannot clearly formulate, because he frequently knows of these things through his observation and can connect his knowledge with these half-communications.

Researchers working with interview materials, while they are often conscious of these problems, cannot cope with them so well. If they are to deal with matters of this kind it must be by inference. They can only make an educated guess about the things which go unspoken in the interview; it may be a very good guess, but it must be a guess. They can employ various tactics to explore for material they feel is there but unspoken, but even when these are fruitful they do not create sensitivity to those problems of which even the interviewer is not aware. The following example indicates how participant observation aids the researcher in getting material, and making the most of the little he gets, on topics lying within this range of restricted communication.

A few months after the beginning of school, I went to dinner at one of the freshman medical fraternities. It was the night non-resident members came, married ones with their wives. An unmarried student who lived in the house looked around at the visitors and said to me, "We are so much in transition. I have never been in this situation before of meeting fellows and their wives."

This was just the sort of thing we were looking for—change in student relationships arising from group interaction—but I failed in every attempt to make the student describe the "transition" more clearly.

From previous observation, though, I knew there were differences (other than marriage) between the non-residents and their hosts. The former had all been elected to the fraternity recently, after house officers had gotten to know them through working together (usually on the same cadaver in anatomy lab). They were older than the average original member; instead of coming directly from college, several had had jobs or Army experience before medical school. As a group they were somewhat lower in social position.

These points indicated that the fraternity was bringing together in relative intimacy students different from each other in background and experience. They suggested a search for other instances in which dissimilar groups of students were joining forces, and pointed to a need for hypotheses as to what was behind this process of drawing together on the part of the freshmen and its significance for their medical education.

An interviewer, hearing this statement about "transition," would know that the interviewee felt himself in the midst of some kind of change but might not be able to discover anything further about the nature of that change. The participant observer cannot find out, any more than the interviewer can, what the student had in mind, presumably because the student had nothing more in mind than this vague feeling of change. (Interviewees are not sociologists and we ought not to assume that their fumbling statements are attempts, crippled by their lack of technical vocabulary, to express what a sociologist might put in more formal analytic terms.) But he can search for those things in the interviewee's situation which might lead to such a feeling of transition.

While the participant observer can make immediate use of such vague statements as clues to an objective situation, the interviewer is often bothered by the question of whether an interviewee is not simply referring to quite private experiences. As a result, the interviewer will place less reliance on whatever inferences about the facts of the situation he makes, and is less likely to be sure enough of his ground to use them as a basis for further hypotheses. Immediate observation of the scene itself and data from previous observation enable the participant observer to make direct use of whatever hints the informant supplies.

Things People See Through Distorting Lenses

In many of the social relationships we observe, the parties to the relation will have differing ideas as to what ought to go on in it, and frequently as to what does in fact go on in it. These differences in perception will naturally affect what they report in an interview. A man in a subordinate position in an organization in which subordinates believe that their superiors are "out to get them" will interpret many incidents in this light though the incidents themselves may not seem, either to the other party in the interaction or to the observer, to indicate such malevolence. Any such mythology will distort people's view of events to such a degree that they will report as fact things which have not occurred, but which seem to them to have occurred. Students, for example, frequently invent sets of rules to govern their relations with teachers, and, although the teacher may never have heard of such rules, regard the teachers as malicious when they "disobey" them. The point is that things may be reported in an interview through such a distorting lens, and the interviewer may have no way of knowing what is fact and what is distortion of this kind; participant observation makes it possible to check such points. The following is a particularly clear example.

Much of the daily teaching was done, and practical work of medical students supervised, in a particular department of the hospital, by the house residents. A great deal of animosity had grown up between the particular group of students I was with at the time and these residents, the students believing that the residents would, for various malicious reasons, subordinate them and embarrass them at every opportunity. Before I joined the group, several of the students told me that the residents were "mean," "nasty," "bitchy," and so on, and had backed these characterizations up with evidence of particular actions.

After I began participating daily with the students on this service, a number of incidents made it clear that the situation was not quite like this. Finally, the matter came completely into the open. I was present when one of the residents suggested a technique that might have prevented a minor relapse in a patient assigned to one of the students; he made it clear that he did not think the relapse in any way the student's fault, but rather that he was simply passing on what he felt to be a good tip. Shortly afterward, this student reported to several other students that the resident had "chewed him out" for failing to use this technique: "What the hell business has he got chewing me out about that for? No one ever told me I was supposed to do it that way." I interrupted to say, "He didn't really chew you out. I thought he was pretty decent about it." Another student said, "Any time they say anything at all to us I consider it a chewing out. Any time they say anything about how we did things, they are chewing us out, no matter how God damn nice they are about it."

In short, participant observation makes it possible to check description against fact and, noting discrepancies, become aware of systematic distortions made by the person under study; such distortions are less likely to be discovered by interviewing alone. This point, let us repeat, is only relevant when the interview is used as a source of information about situations and events the researcher himself has not seen. It is not relevant when it is the person's behavior in the interview itself that is under analysis.

Inference, Process and Context

We have seen, in the previous sections of this paper, some of the ways in which even very good interviews may go astray, at least from the perspective of the field observer. We turn now to a consideration of the more general areas of difference between the two methods, suggesting basic ways in which the gathering and handling of data in each differ.

Since we tend to talk in our analyses about much the same order of thing whether we work from interviews or from participant-observational materials, and to draw conclusions about social relations and the interaction that goes on within them whether we have actually seen these things or only been told about them, it should be clear that in working with interviews we must necessarily infer a great many things we could have observed had we only been in a position to do so. The kinds of errors we have discussed above are primarily errors of inference, errors which arise from the necessity of making assumptions about the relation of interview statements to actual events which may or may not be true; for what we have solid observable evidence on in the first case we have only secondhand reports and indices of in the second, and the gap must be bridged by inference. We must assume, when faced with an account or transcription of an interview, that we understand the meaning of the everyday words used, that the interviewee is able to talk about the things we are interested in, and that his account will be more or less accurate. The examples detailed above suggest that these assumptions do not always hold and that the process of inference involved in interpreting interviews should always be made explicit and checked, where possible, against what can be discovered through observation. Where, as is often the case, this is not possible, conclusions should be limited to those matters the data directly describe.

Let us be quite specific, and return to the earlier example of resident-student hostility. In describing this relationship from interviews with the students alone we might have assumed their description to be accurate and made the inference that the residents were in fact "mean." Observation proved that this inference would have been incorrect, but this does not destroy the analytic usefulness of the original statements made to the fieldworker in an informal interview. It does shift the area in which we can make deductions from this datum, however, for we can see that such statements, while incorrect factually, are perfectly good statements of the perspective from which these students interpreted the events in which they were involved. We could not know without observation whether their descriptions were true or false; with the aid of observation we know that the facts of the matter are sometimes quite different, and that the students' perspective is strong enough to override such variant facts. But from the interview alone we could know, not what actually happened in such cases, but what the students thought happened and how they felt about it, and this is the kind of inference we should make. We add to the accuracy of our data when we substitute observable fact for inference. More important, we open the way for the discovery of new hypotheses for the fact we observe may not be the fact we expected to observe. When this happens we face a new problem requiring new hypothetical explanations which can then be further tested in the field.

Substitution of an inference about something for an observation of that thing occurs most frequently in discussions of social process and change, an area in which the advantages of observation over an extended period of time are particularly great. Much sociological writing is concerned, openly or otherwise, with problems of process: The analysis of shifts in group structure, individual self-conception and similar matters. But studies of such phenomena in natural social contexts are typically based on data that tell only part of the story. The analysis may be made from a person's retrospective account, in a single interview, of changes that have taken place; or, more rarely, it is based on a series of interviews, the differences between successive interviews providing the bench marks of change. In either case, many crucial steps in the process and important mechanisms of change must be arrived at through inferences which can be no more than educated guesses.

The difficulties in analyzing change and process on the basis of interview material are particularly important because it is precisely in discussing changes in themselves and their surroundings that interviewees are least likely or able to give an accurate account of events. Changes in the social environment and in the self inevitably produce transformations of perspective, and it is characteristic of such transformations that the person finds it difficult or impossible to remember his former actions, outlook, or feelings. Reinterpreting things from his new perspective, he cannot give an accurate account of the past, for the concepts in which he thinks about it have changed and with them his perceptions and memories.[8] Similarly, a person in the midst of such change may find it difficult to describe what is happening, for he has not developed a perspective or concepts which would allow him to think and talk about these things coherently; the earlier discussion of changes in medical school fraternity life is a case in point.

Participant observation does not have so many difficulties of this sort. One can observe actual changes in behavior over a period of time and note the events which precede and follow them. Similarly, one can carry on a conversation running over weeks and months with the people he is studying and thus become aware of shifts in perspective as they occur. In short, attention can be focused both on what has happened and on what the person says about what has happened. Some inference as to actual steps in the process or mechanisms involved is still required, but the amount of inference necessary is considerably reduced. Again, accuracy is increased and the possibility of new discoveries being made is likewise increased, as the observer becomes aware of more phenomena requiring explanation.

The participant observer is both more aware of these problems of inference and more equipped to deal with them because he operates, when gathering data, in a social context rich in cues and information of all kinds. Because he sees and hears the people he studies in many situations of the kind that normally occur for them, rather than just in an isolated and formal interview, he builds an ever-growing fund of impressions, many of them at the subliminal level, which give him an extensive base for the interpretation and analytic use of any particular datum. This wealth of information and impression sensitizes him to subtleties which might pass unnoticed in an interview and forces him to raise continually new and different questions, which he brings to and tries to answer in succeeding observations.

The biggest difference in the two methods, then, may be not so much that participant observation provides the opportunity for avoiding the errors we have discussed, but that it does this by providing a rich experiential context which causes him to become aware of incongruous or unexplained facts, makes him sensitive to their possible implications and connections with other observed facts, and thus pushes him continually to revise and adapt his theoretical orientation and specific problems in the direction of greater relevance to the phenomena under study. Though this kind of context and its attendant benefits cannot be reproduced in interviewing (and the same degree of sensitivity and sense of problem produced in the interviewer), interviewers can profit from an awareness of those limitations of their method suggested by this comparison and perhaps improve their batting average by taking account of them.[9]

[8]Anselm L. Strauss, "The Development and Transformation of Monetary Meanings in the Child," *American Sociological Review,* 17 (June, 1952), 275–86, and *An Essay on Identity* (unpublished manuscript), *passim.*

[9]We are aware that participant observation raises as many technical problems as it solves. (See, for instance, the discussions in Morris S. Schwartz and Charlotte Green Schwartz, "Problems in Participant Observation," *American Journal of Sociology,* 60 (Jan., 1955), 343–53, and in Vidich, *op. cit.*) We feel, however, that there is considerable value in using the strong points of one method to illuminate the shortcomings of another.

Speaking in Context: Participant Observation

Perhaps because I am "enamored" with it, I am inclined to emphasize the more advantageous attributes of participant observation in this volume. It is also true that its weaknesses are more easily recognizable than the subtler flaws of our more conventional methods. Nevertheless, let us consider some of the problems inherent in participant observation — problems which must be surfaced if we are to manage our discounting effectively. In some quarters participant observation is viewed as an extension of ancient ethnographic techniques which have long since been replaced by more reliable scientific methods. Although I believe this position is absurd, no method can be accepted without proper discounting and judgments of credibility. There is little question of validity in field studies since they occur where the action is. There is, however, a very real problem with reliability. Whether these studies report the lives of Irish cornerboys in Boston, poor black men in Washington, D.C., Indians in Tepotzlan, or the admissions officer in a public housing project, they remain observations of unique events, usually by a single observer, and not subject to replication. How do we know that the observer did in fact observe what he reports? Furthermore, how do we know that what one observer honestly reports is the same as what another equally honest observer might report? Selective perception resulting from preconceptions or other blinding perspectives can affect what we see and hear as well as how much we see and hear.

It may be argued that, as a protective corrective, the field worker ought to embark on his enterprise without preconceptions — without even reading the relevant literature until he has had a chance to immerse himself in "reality." This is the position taken by Glaser and Strauss[45] but it seems to me self-deluding. I cannot erase my background and preconceptions on command. I must and will carry them with me into whatever situation I set out to study. Furthermore, I like to think they are useful — that I needn't start from scratch every time I seek to learn something. I doubt that this procedure is worth trying even if it is thought to be possible. Becker and his colleagues use small teams working closely together, primarily to permit collection of more and different sorts of data, but also as checks on each other. Although this may enhance reliability a bit, the fact is that in their study of a medical school Becker, Geer, Hughes, and Strauss rarely observed the same events.

If other techniques are open to the criticism that the method itself is permitted to select out and guide the kinds of problems studied, so, too, is participant observation. Surely there are big and important problems which are simply inaccessible through participant observation.[46] It is also true that nature does not always provide us with an ongoing act of the type we are curious about. There may be nothing available to participate in or to observe. Does this mean that we simply avoid the problem? Furthermore some kinds of activity are socially defined as private and thus may never be available for observation even though we know they occur frequently. Laud Humphreys' study of outhouse homosexuals is the exception to this rule.[47] As with the interview or the laboratory experiment, reactivity remains

45. Barney G. Glaser and Anselm L. Strauss, *The Discovery of Grounded Theory: Strategies for Qualitative Research* (Chicago: Aldine Publishing Co., 1967).

46. See Martin Trow, "Comment on 'Participant Observation and Interviewing: A Comparison,'" *Human Organization* 16 (1957): 33–35.

47. Laud Humphreys, *Tearoom Trade: Impersonal Sex in Public Places* (Chicago: Aldine Publishing Company, 1970).

something of a problem in this type of field work. To the extent that the field worker participates in the process he observes, he becomes a part of the action and, to that extent, he alters the outcome. Things might not be the same if he were not around. This is as true of the unobtrusive observer who "fades into the woodwork" as it is of the observer who assumes some routine role in the situation.[48]

There are, in participant-observational procedures, ethical problems which are potentially more dangerous than their counterparts in other kinds of research. Although the experimental subject may be deceived about the nature of the experiment, he does know that he is involved in an experiment (and that, as we shall see in Chapter Eight, is part of the problem with experiments). But sometimes the subjects in participant-observational studies do not know they are involved in research and therein lies deception of a different order.[49] At another level is the problem posed by the intensity of participant-observational work. It is extremely demanding of the observer, usually requiring him to do everything a normal participant would do during the course of a day and, in addition, requiring him to observe, remember, record, and analyze—sometimes well into the night. This procedure requires not only a high level of technical skill, but also a certain amount of talent.

Furthermore, as I mentioned above, participant observation is practical only within limited settings. The action must be localized in an establishment or some other specific social context. As Trow has pointed out, this method is useless in dealing with important problems involving dispersed publics. Trow also raises a point which is rarely understood by advocates of participant observation. Because the method provides access to the inside, it is assumed that all of the inside dope and inner feelings of participants will become exposed. But as the ethnomethodologists understand so well, there are many important things which insiders act on but which they take for granted. There are other important things which are simply taboo for insiders to discuss with one another, although a stranger on a bus or an interviewer might have access to such data:

> Ordinary social life may well inhibit the casual expression of sentiments which are actually or potentially important elements in the explanation of the social phenomena under study. And participant observation is a relatively weak instrument for gathering data on sentiments, behaviors, relationships which are normatively proscribed by the group under observation.[50]

Although we have concentrated in this and the preceding chapter on interviews and questionnaires and on participant observation, much talking also happens in the doing of a laboratory experiment. In many respects our discussion of language can be extended to cover the experimental procedures discussed in the chapter which follows.

48. James Scoggins, for example, has observed emergency room intake by sitting quietly in a corner while, at the other extreme, I have worked as an office boy in a public housing admissions office while observing intake procedures there. In either case our presence must somehow alter the situation. (James Scoggins, "Gatekeepers: Those Who Know," term paper, 1971; Irwin Deutscher, "The Gatekeeper in Public Housing," in *Among The People: Encounters With the Poor*, eds. Irwin Deutscher and Elizabeth Thompson [New York: Basic Books, Inc., 1968], pp. 38–50).
49. Filstead has collected six good papers dealing with ethical problems in field studies. See William J. Filstead, *Qualitative Methodology: Firsthand Involvement With the Social World* (Chicago: Markham Publishing Company, 1970), Part Six.
50. Trow, "Comment," p. 34.

What Can You Believe Nowadays?

For the first time in this book, we begin a chapter with data rather than with discussion. The barbaric hell devised for experimental purposes by Milgram represents one of the most credible experiments in the literature. Orne, on the other hand, raises questions which he believes cast doubt on the credibility of any laboratory experiment because of the very nature of the enterprise. Let the reader make his own assessment.

DATA:
Group Pressure and Action Against a Person
STANLEY MILGRAM

A great many variations of a paradigm provided by Asch (1951) show that there is an intelligible relationship between several features of the social environment and the degree to which a person will rely on others for his public judgments. Because it possesses merits of simplicity, clarity, and reconstructs in the laboratory powerful and socially relevant psychological processes, this paradigm has gained widespread acceptance as a basic technique of research on influence processes.

One feature that has been kept constant through the variations on Asch's work is that verbal judgment has been retained as the end product and basic index of conformity. More generally, a *signal* offered by the subject as representing his judgment has been the focus of study. Most often the signal has taken the form of a verbal pronouncement (Asch, 1956; Milgram, 1961), though mechanical devices which the subject uses to signal his judgment have also been employed (Crutchfield, 1955; Tuddenham & MacBride, 1959).

A distinction can be made between *signal conformity* and *action conformity* in that the immediate consequence of the former is purely informational; the subject states his opinion or reports on his perception of some feature of the environment. Action conformity, on the other hand, produces an immediate effect or alteration in the milieu that goes beyond a contribution of information. It refers

Stanley Milgram, "Group Pressure and Action Against a Person," *Journal of Abnormal and Social Psychology,* vol. 69, no. 2 (1964), pp. 137–43. Copyright © 1964 by the American Psychological Association, and reproduced by permission. The original bears the following acknowledgment: "This research was supported by Grant NSF G-17916 from the National Science Foundation. My thanks to Taketo Murata of Yale University for computational and statistical assistance."

to the elicitation of a *deed* by group forces, the induction of an act that is more than communicative in its effect. The act may be directed toward the well being of another person (e.g., a man is induced by group pressure to share bread with a beggar) or it may be oriented toward nonsocial parts of the environment (a delinquent is induced by gang pressure to throw a rock at a shop window).

There is little reason to assume a priori that observations made with regard to verbal conformity are automatically applicable to action. A person may pay lip service to the norms of a group and then be quite unwilling to carry out the kinds of behavior the group norms imply. Furthermore, an individual may accept and even promulgate a group standard at the verbal level, and yet find himself *unable* to translate the belief into deeds. Here we refer not to the distinction between overt compliance and private acceptance, but of the relationship between a genuinely accepted belief and its transformation into behavior.

The main point of the present experiment is to see if a person will perform acts under group pressure that he would not have performed in the absence of social inducement. There are many particular forms of action that can be inserted into a general group-pressure experimental design. One could study sorting IBM cards, or making paper cutouts, or eating crackers. Convenience makes them attractive, and in several valuable experiments investigators have used these tasks to good advantage (Frank, 1944; French, Morrison, & Levinger, 1960; Raven & French, 1958). But eventually social psychology must come to grips with significant behavior contents, contents that are of interest in their own right and are not simply trivial substitutes for psychologically meaningful forms of behavior. Guided by this consideration, a relatively potent form of action was selected for shaping by group pressure. We asked: Can a group induce a person to deliver punishment of increasing severity to a protesting individual? Whereas Asch and other have shown in what manner group pressure can cause a person to pronounce judgments that contradict his thinking, the present study examines whether group pressure causes a person to engage in acts at variance with his uninfluenced behavior.

Method

The details of subject recruitment, subject composition, experimenter's introductory patter, apparatus, and learning task have been described elsewhere (Milgram, 1963) and need only be sketched here.

Subjects consisted of 80 male adults, ranging in age from 20 to 50 years, and distributed in equal numbers, ages, and occupational statuses in the experimental and control conditions.

Procedure for Experimental Condition

General. The basic experimental situation is one in which a team of three persons (including two confederates) tests a fourth person on a paired-associate learning task. Whenever the fourth party makes a mistake the team punishes him with an electric shock. The two confederates suggest increasingly higher shock levels; the experimenter observes in what degree the third member of the team (a naive subject) goes along with or resists the confederates' pressure to increase the voltage levels.

Details. Four adults arrive at a campus laboratory to participate in a study of memory and learning. On arrival each subject is paid $4.50. The experimenter explains that a variety of roles must be performed in the experiment, and that to make role assignments fairly, subjects are to draw printed slips from a hat, each slip designating a particular experimental role. Actually, three of the adults are confederates, and only one naive subject is tested each hour. The drawing is rigged so that the naive subject is always assigned the position, Teacher 3, and Confederate B is always the Learner. The role assignments, which the subjects read from the drawn slips, are as follows:

Role title	Participant	Task
Teacher 1	Confederate C	First, you will read word pairs to the learner. Then you will read a stimulus word along with four possible answers.
Teacher 2	Confederate A	When the learner gives his answer, your task is to indicate whether he is correct or incorrect. When he has erred you will provide him with the correct answer.
Teacher 3	Naive subject	Whenever the learner gives an incorrect answer, you will administer punishment by activating a shock generator.
Learner	Confederate B	Your task will be to learn a list of word pairs read to you by Teacher 1.

The experimenter explains that the purpose of the experiment is to study the effects of punishment on memory in a context of "collective teaching." Confederate B is taken to an adjoining room and in full view of the others is strapped into an electric-chair apparatus. The experimenter explains the nature of the learning task to the Learner and, passing over a remark made by the Learner concerning a mild heart condition, takes the three teachers to the main experimental room.

They are seated before an imposing shock generator whose essential feature is a horizontal line of 30 lever switches, labeled 15–450 volts, in 15-volt increments. Verbal designations are spread along the line of switches reading: Slight Shock, Moderate Shock, Strong Shock, Very Strong Shock, Intense Shock, Extreme Intensity Shock, and Danger: Severe Shock.

The experimenter restates that the Learner is to be tested on a paired-associate learning task (see Milgram, 1963, for details). Teachers are told that the Learner must be shocked each time he errs in the learning task. The experimenter explains how the level of shock is to be determined:

> Now the amount of punishment given on any trial is decided by the teachers themselves. Each of you will suggest a shock level. And the shock actually administered will be the lowest level suggest by any of the three teachers. In order to the keep the experiment running smoothly, give suggested levels in this order: Teacher 1, submit your bid first; Teacher 2, submit your bid second; and Teacher 3, submit your bid third. Remember you can stick to one level or raise or lower your level as you desire, but on any trial, the punishment administered will be the lowest level suggested by any teacher on that trial.

Thus the naive subject finds himself in a position in which, on any trial, he can effectively control the maximum shock administered to the Learner, e.g., the ground rules of the experiment would permit him to hold the shock level down to 15 volts throughout the laboratory session. On the other hand he may go along with or move in the direction of the group choice. It is the naive subject who actually administers the shock by depressing the appropriate lever on the generator (i.e., he always emerges from the rigged drawing as Teacher 3).

The three teachers each have their roles spelled out for them again, and there remains only the task of giving each a sample shock from the generator before the experiment gets under way.

Behavior of Teachers 1 and 2 (Confederates). According to a prearranged schedule the two confederates at the shock generator call for a one-step increase in the shock level each time the Learner errs. On the first error they both call for Shock Level 1 (15 volts); on the twentieth error they both call for Shock Level 20 (300 volts), and so forth. Their constant unanimity is rendered credible by having Teacher 1 play a somewhat domineering, and Teacher 2 a somewhat submissive type. The confederates, played by adult actors, appear indifferent to the complaints of the Learner.

Behavior of the Learner. According to a prearranged schedule the Learner responds to the learning task by providing answers in the proportion of three wrong answers to each correct one. There are a total of 40 trials, 30 of them being critical (occasions when the Learner answers incorrectly).

The Learner's responses are not limited to providing answers. As the shocks administered to him become stronger, he grunts, protests, and demands to be let out of the experiment. Each complaint of the Learner is, in fact, prerecorded on magnetic tape, and is coordinated to a specific shock level. The protests and expressions of discomfort follow spontaneously the administration of an electric shock.

The Learner indicates no discomfort until the 75-volt shock is administered, at which time there is a slight grunt in response to the punishment. Similar reactions follow the 90- and 105-volt shocks, and at 120 volts the Learner shouts to the experimenter that the shocks are becoming painful. Painful groans are heard on the administration of the 135-volt shock, and at 150 volts the Learner cries out that he wants to be released from the experiment, complaining of a heart disturbance. Cries of this type continue with generally rising intensity, so that at 180 volts, the Learner cries out "I can't stand the pain," and by 285 volts his response to the shock is clearly an agonized scream. At 300 volts the victim shouts in desperation that he will no longer provide answers to the memory test, and so forth through 450 volts. In other words, increases in shock level are met by increasingly severe reactions from the person being punished.

It is to be remembered that this is merely a *potential* series of responses. If a shock no higher than the 75-volt level is administered, only a grunt is heard. As a point of procedure, protests were not repeated at the same shock level, e.g., after the first grunt was used in response to Shock Level 75, no further complaints were introduced until and if a higher shock level were used.

Experimental measures. The principal experimental measure, therefore, is the level of shock administered by the subject on each of the 30 critical trials. The shock levels were automatically recorded by an Esterline-Angus event recorder wired directly into the shock generator, providing us with a permanent record of each subject's performance.

Postexperimental session. An interview and debriefing session were held immediately after each subject's performance. A variety of background measures was obtained, as well as qualitative reactions to the experimental situation.

Control Condition

The purpose of the control condition is to determine the level of shock the naive subject administers to the Learner in the absence of group influence. One naive subject and one confederate (the Learner) perform in each session. The procedure is identical to that in the experimental condition, except that the tasks of Confederates A and C are collapsed into one role handled by the naive subject. References to collective teaching are omitted.

The naive subject is instructed to administer a shock each time the Learner errs, and the naive subject is told that as teacher he is free to select any shock level on any of the trials. In all other respects the control and experimental procedures are identical.

Results

Figure 1 shows the mean shock levels for each critical trial in the experimental and control conditions. It also shows a diagonal representing the stooge-group's suggested shock level on each critical trial. The degree to which the ex-

FIGURE 1. **MEAN SHOCK LEVELS IN EXPERIMENTAL AND CONTROL CONDITIONS OVER 30 CRITICAL TRIALS.**

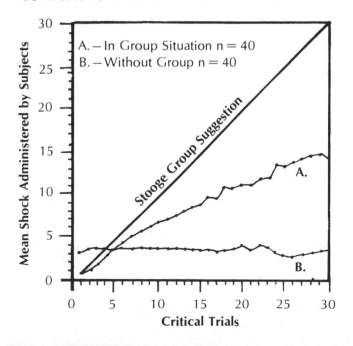

perimental function moves away from the control level and toward the stooge-group diagonal represents the effects of group influence. Inspection indicates that the confederates substantially influenced the level of shock administered to the Learner. The results will now be considered in detail.

In the experimental condition the standard deviation of shock levels rose regularly from trial to trial, and roughly in proportion to the rising mean shock level. However, in the control condition the standard deviation did not vary systematically with the mean through the 30 trials. Representative mean shock levels and standard deviations for the two conditions are shown in Table 1. Hartley's test for homogeneity of variance confirmed that the variances in the two conditions were significantly different. Therefore a reciprocal-of-the-square root transformation was performed before an analysis of variance was carried out.

As summarized in Table 2, the analysis of variance showed that the overall mean shock level in the experimental condition was significantly higher than that in the control condition ($p < .001$). This is less interesting, however, than the differing slopes in the two conditions, which show the group effects through the course of the experimental session.[1] The analysis of variance test for trend confirmed that the slopes for the two conditions differed significantly ($p < .001$).

Examination of the standard deviations in the experimental condition shows that there are large individual differences in response to group pressure, some subjects following the group closely, others resisting effectively. Subjects were ranked according to their total deviation from the confederates' shock choices. On the thirtieth critical trial the most conforming quartile had a mean shock level of 27.6, while the mean shock level of the least conforming quartile was 4.8. Background characteristics of the experimental subjects were noted: age, marital status, occupation, military experience, political preference, religious affiliation, birth-order information, and educational history. Less educated subjects (high school degree or less) tended to yield more than those who possess a college degree ($X^2_{df=1} = 2.85$, $p < .10$). Roman Catholic subjects tended to yield more than Protestant subjects ($X^2_{df=1} = 2.96$, $p < .10$). No other background variable measured in the study was associated with amount of yielding, though the number of subjects employed was too small for definite conclusions.

The shock data may also be examined in terms of the *maximum* shock administered by subjects in the experimental and control conditions, i.e., the highest single shock administered by a subject throughout the 30 critical trials. The information is presented in Table 3. Only 2 control subjects administered shocks beyond the tenth voltage level (at this point the Learner makes his first truly vehement protest), while 27 experimental subjects went beyond this point. A median test showed that the maximum shocks administered by experimental subjects were higher than those administered by control subjects ($X^2_{df=1} = 39.2$, $p < .001$).

[1]On the first four trials the control group has a higher mean shock than the experimental group; this is an artifact due to the provision that in the experimental condition the shock actually administered and recorded was the lowest suggested by any member of the group; when the subject called for a shock level higher than that suggested by the confederates, it was not reflected in the data. (This situation arose only during the first few critical trials.) By the fifth critical trial the group pressure begins to show its effect in elevating the mean shock level of the naive subjects.

TABLE 1   REPRESENTATIVE MEAN SHOCK LEVELS AND STANDARD DEVIATIONS IN
THE EXPERIMENTAL AND CONTROL CONDITIONS

Trial	Experimental condition		Control condition	
	Mean shock level	SD	Mean shock level	SD
5	4.03	1.19	3.35	2.39
10	6.78	2.63	3.48	3.03
15	9.20	4.28	3.68	3.58
20	11.45	6.32	4.13	4.90
25	13.55	8.40	3.55	3.85
30	14.13	9.59	3.38	1.89

TABLE 2   ANALYSIS OF VARIANCE OF SHOCK LEVELS ADMINISTERED IN THE EXPERI-
MENTAL AND CONTROL CONDITIONS

Source	df	SS	MS	F
Total between individuals	79	966,947.1	12,239.8	
Between experimental conditions	1	237,339.4	237,339.4	25.37*
Between individuals	78	729,607.7	9,353.9	
Within individuals	2,320	391,813.5	168.9	
Between trials	29	157,361.7	5,426.3	96.04*
Trials × Experimental conditions (Trend)	29	106,575.4	3,675.0	65.04*
Remainder	2,262	127,876.4	56.5	

*$p < .001$.

The main effect, then, is that in the experimental condition subjects were substantially influenced by group pressure. When viewed in terms of the mean shock level over the 30 critical trials, as in Figure 1, the experimental function appears as a vector more or less bisecting the angle formed by the confederates' diagonal and control slopes. Thus one might be tempted to say that the subject's action in the experimental situation had two major sources: it was partly determined by the level the subject would have chosen in the control condition, and partly by the confederates' choice. Neither one nor the other entirely dominates the average behavior of subjects in the experimental condition. There are very great individual differences in regard to the more dominant force.

Discussion

The substantive contribution of the present study lies in the demonstration that group influence can shape behavior in a domain that might have been thought highly resistant to such effects. Subjects are induced by the group to inflict pain on another person at a level that goes well beyond levels chosen in the absence of social pressure. Hurting a man is an action that for most people carries considerable psychological significance; it is closely tied to questions of conscience and ethical judgment. It might have been thought that the protests of the victim and inner prohibitions against hurting others would have operated effec-

TABLE 3. **MAXIMUM SHOCK LEVELS ADMINISTERED IN EXPERIMENTAL AND CONTROL CONDITIONS**

Verbal designation and voltage indication	Number of subjects for whom this was maximum shock	
	Experimental	Control
Slight Shock		
15	1	3
30	2	6
45	0	7
60	0	7
Moderate Shock		
75	1	5
90	0	4
105	1	1
120	1	1
Strong Shock		
135	2	3
150	5	1
165	2	0
180	0	0
Very Strong Shock		
195	1	0
210	2	0
225	2	0
240	1	0
Intense Shock		
255	2	0
270	0	0
285	1	0
300	1	0
Extreme Intensity Shock		
315	2	0
330	0	0
345	1	0
360	2	0
Danger: Severe Shock		
375	0	1
390	0	0
405	1	0
420	2	0
XXX		
435	0	0
450	7	1

tively to curtail the subject's compliance. While the experiment yields wide variation in performance, a substantial number of subjects submitted readily to pressure applied to them by the confederates.

The significance of yielding in Asch's situation is sometimes questioned because the discriminative task is not an issue of self-evident importance for many subjects (Bronowski).[2] The criticism is not easily extended to the present

[2]J. Bronowski, personal communication, January 10, 1962.

study. Here the subject does not merely feign agreement with a group on a perceptual task of undefined importance; and he is unable to dismiss his action by relegating it to the status of a trivial gesture, for a person's suffering and discomfort are at stake.

The behavior observed here occurred within the framework of a laboratory study presided over by an experimenter. In some degree his authority stands behind the group. In his initial instructions the experimenter clearly legitimized the use of any shock level on the console. Insofar as he does not object to the shocks administered in the course of the experiment, his assent is implied. Thus, even though the effects of group pressure have been clearly established by a comparison of the experimental and control conditions, the effects occurred within the context of authoritative sanction. This point becomes critical in any attempt to assess the relative effectiveness of *conformity* versus *obedience* as means of inducing contravalent behavior (Milgram, 1963). If the experimenter had not approved the use of all shock levels on the generator, and if he had departed from the laboratory at an early stage, thus eliminating any sign of authoritative assent during the course of the experiment, would the group have had as powerful an effect on the naive subject?

There are many points of difference between Asch's investigation and the procedure of the present study that can only be touched upon here.

1. While in Asch's study the *adequate* response is anchored to an external stimulus event, in the present study we are dealing with an internal, unbound standard.

2. A mispoken judgment can, in principle, be withdrawn, but here we are dealing with action that has an immediate and unalterable consequence. Its irreversibility stems not from constraints extrinsic to the action, but from the content of the action itself: once the Learner is shocked, he cannot be unshocked.

3. In the present experiment, despite the several sources of opinion, there can be but a single shock level on each trial. There is, therefore, a competition for outcome that was not present in the Asch situation.

4. While in the Asch study the focus of pressure is directed toward the subject's judgment, with distortion of public response but an intermediary stage of influence, here the focus of pressure is directed toward performance of action itself. Asch's yielding subject may secretly harbor the true judgment; but when the performance of an action becomes the object of social pressure, there is no comparable recourse to a covert form. The subject who performed the act demanded by the group has yielded exhaustively.

5. In the Asch situation a yielding subject engages in a covert violation of his obligations to the experimenter. He has agreed to report to the experimenter what he sees, and insofar as he goes along with the group, he breaks this agreement. In contrast, in the present experiment the yielding subject acts within the terms of the "subject-experimenter contract." In going along with the two confederates the subject may violate his own inner standards, and the rights of the Learner, but his relationship with the experimenter remains intact at both the manifest and private levels. Subjects in the two experiments are faced with different patterns of social pressure and violate different relationships through social submission.

References

Asch, S. E. Effects of group pressure upon the modification and distortion of judgment. In H. Guetz-
    kow (Ed.), *Groups, leadership, and men*. Pittsburgh: Carnegie Press, 1951.
Asch, S. E. Studies of independence and conformity: I. A minority of one against a unanimous major-
    ity. *Psychol. Monogr.*, 1956, **70** (9, Whole No. 416).
Crutchfield, R. S. Conformity and character. *Amer. Psychologist*, 1955, **10**, 191–198.
Frank, J. D. Experimental studies of personal pressure and resistance. *J. gen. Psychol.*, 1944, **30**, 23–
    64.
French, J. R. P., Jr., Morrison, H. W., & Levinger, G. Coercive power and forces affecting conformity.
    J. abnorm. soc. Psychol., 1960, **61**, 93–101.
Milgram, S. Nationality and conformity. *Scient. American*, 1961, **205**, 45–51.
Milgram, S. Behavioral study of obedience. *J. abnorm. soc. Psychol.*, 1963, **67**, 371–378.
Raven, B. H., & French, J. R. P. Legitimate power, coercive power, and observability in social influ-
    ence. *Sociometry*, 1958, **21**, 83–97.
Tuddenham, R. D., & MacBride, P. The yielding experiment from the subject's point of view. *J. Pers.*,
    1959, **27**, 259–271.

DATA:
On the Social Psychology
of the Psychological Experiment:
With Particular Reference to
Demand Characteristics and Their Implications
MARTIN T. ORNE

> It is to the highest degree probable that the subject['s] . . . general attitude of
> mind is that of ready complacency and cheerful willingness to assist the investiga-
> tor in every possible way by reporting to him those very things which he is most
> eager to find, and that the very questions of the experimenter . . . suggest the
> shade of reply expected . . . . Indeed . . . it seems too often as if the subject
> were now regarded as a stupid automaton. . . .
>
> A. H. Pierce, 1908[1]

Since the time of Galileo, scientists have employed the laboratory experiment
as a method of understanding natural phenomena. Generically, the experimental
method consists of abstracting relevant variables from complex situations in

Martin T. Orne, M.D., Ph.D., "On the Social Psychology of the Psychological Experiment: With Particular Reference to Demand Characteristics and Their Implications," *American Psychologist*, vol. 17, no. 11 (Nov. 1962), pp. 776–83. Copyright © 1962 by the American Psychological Association, and reproduced by permission. This reprinted version includes editorial emendations and updated references introduced at Dr. Orne's request. The
article in the form in which it was originally published bears the following acknowledg-
ments:
    "This paper was presented at the Symposium, 'On the Social Psychology of the Psycho-
logical Experiment,' American Psychological Association Convention, New York, 1961.
    "The work reported here was supported in part by a Public Health Service Research
Grant, M–3369, National Institute of Mental Health.
    "I wish to thank my associates Ronald E. Shor, Donald N. O'Connell, Ulric Neisser, Karl
E. Scheibe, and Emily F. Carota for their comments and criticisms in the preparation of this
paper."
[1]See reference list (Pierce, 1908).

nature and reproducing in the laboratory segments of these situations, varying the parameters involved so as to determine the effect of the experimental variables. This procedure allows generalization from the information obtained in the laboratory situation back to the original situation as it occurs in nature. The physical sciences have made striking advances through the use of this method, but in the behavioral sciences it has often been difficult to meet two necessary requirements for meaningful experimentation: reproducibility and ecological validity.[2] It has long been recognized that certain differences will exist between the types of experiments conducted in the physical sciences and those in the behavioral sciences because the former investigate a universe of inanimate objects and forces, whereas the latter deal with animate organisms, often thinking, conscious subjects. However, recognition of this distinction has not always led to appropriate changes in the traditional experimental model of physics as employed in the behavioral sciences. Rather the experimental model has been so successful as employed in physics that there has been a tendency in the behavioral sciences to follow precisely a paradigm originated for the study of inanimate objects, i.e., one which proceeds by exposing the subject to various conditions and observing the differences in reaction of the subject under different conditions. However, the use of such a model with animal or human subjects leads to the problem that the subject of the experiment is assumed, at least implicitly, to be a *passive responder* to stimuli — an assumption difficult to justify. Further, in this type of model the experimental stimuli themselves are usually rigorously defined in terms of what *is done* to the subject. In contrast, the purpose of this paper will be to focus on what the human subject *does* in the laboratory: what motivation the subject is likely to have in the experimental situation, how he usually perceives behavioral research, what the nature of the cues is that the subject is likely to pick up, etc. Stated in other terms, what factors are apt to affect the subject's reaction to the well-defined stimuli in the situation? These factors comprise what will be referred to here as the "experimental setting."

Since any experimental manipulation of human subjects takes place within this larger framework or setting, we should propose that the above-mentioned factors must be further elaborated and the parameters of the experimental setting more carefully defined so that adequate controls can be designed to isolate the effects of the experimental setting from the effects of the experimental variables. Later in this paper we shall propose certain possible techniques of control which have been devised in the process of our research on the nature of hypnosis.

Our initial focus here will be on some of the qualities peculiar to psychological experiments. The experimental situation is one which takes place within the context of an explicit agreement of the subject to participate in a special form of social interaction known as "taking part in an experiment." Within the context of our culture the roles of subject and experimenter are well understood and carry with them well-defined mutual role expectations. A particularly striking aspect of the typical experimenter-subject relationship is the extent to which the subject will play his role and place himself under the control of the experimenter. Once a subject has agreed to participate in a psychological experi-

---

[2]Ecological validity, in the sense that Brunswik (1947) has used the term: appropriate generalization from the laboratory to nonexperimental situations.

ment, he implicitly agrees to perform a very wide range of actions on request without inquiring as to their purpose, and frequently without inquiring as to their duration.

Furthermore, the subject agrees to tolerate a considerable degree of discomfort, boredom, or actual pain, if required to do so by the experimenter. Just about any request which could conceivably be asked of the subject by a reputable investigator is legitimized by the quasi-magical phrase, "This is an experiment," and the shared assumption that a legitimate purpose will be served by the subject's behavior. A somewhat trivial example of this legitimization of requests is as follows:

A number of casual acquaintances were asked whether they would do the experimenter a favor; on their acquiescence, they were asked to perform five push-ups. Their response tended to be amazement, incredulity and the question "Why?" Another similar group of individuals was asked whether they would take part in an experiment of brief duration. When they agreed to do so, they too were asked to perform five push-ups. Their typical response was "Where?"

The striking degree of control inherent in the experimental situation can also be illustrated by a set of pilot experiments which were performed in the course of designing an experiment to test whether the degree of control inherent in the *hypnotic* relationship is greater than that in a waking relationship.[3] In order to test this question, we tried to develop a set of tasks which waking subjects would refuse to do, or would do only for a short period of time. The tasks were intended to be psychologically noxious, meaningless, or boring, rather than painful or fatiguing.

For example, one task was to perform serial additions of each adjacent two numbers on sheets filled with rows of random digits. In order to complete just one sheet, the subject would be required to perform 224 additions! A stack of some 2,000 sheets was presented to each subject — clearly an impossible task to complete. After the instructions were given, the subject was deprived of his watch and told, "Continue to work; I will return eventually." Five and one-half hours later, the *experimenter* gave up! In general, subjects tended to continue this type of task for several hours, usually with little decrement in performance. Since we were trying to find a task which would be discontinued spontaneously within a brief period, we tried to create a more frustrating situation as follows:

Subjects were asked to perform the same task described above but were also told that when finished with the additions on each sheet, they should pick up a card from a large pile, which would instruct them on what to do next. However, every card in the pile read,

> You are to tear up the sheet of paper which you have just completed into a minimum of thirty-two pieces and go on to the next sheet of paper and continue working as you did before; when you have completed this piece of paper, pick up the next card which will instruct you further. Work as accurately and as rapidly as you can.

Our expectation was that subjects would discontinue the task as soon as they realized that the cards were worded identically, that each finished piece of

[3]These pilot studies were performed by Thomas Menaker.

work had to be destroyed, and that, in short, the task was completely meaningless.

Somewhat to our amazement, subjects tended to persist in the task for several hours with relatively little sign of overt hostility. Removal of the one-way screen did not tend to make much difference. The postexperimental inquiry helped to explain the subjects' behavior. When asked about the tasks, subjects would invariably attribute considerable meaning to their performance, viewing it as an endurance test or the like.

Thus far, we have been singularly unsuccessful in finding an experimental task which would be discontinued, or, indeed, refused by subjects in an experimental setting.[4, 5] Not only do subjects continue to perform boring, unrewarding tasks, but they do so with few errors and little decrement in speed. It became apparent that it was extremely difficult to design an experiment to test the degree of social control in hypnosis, in view of the already *very high degree of control in the experimental situation itself.*

The quasi-experimental work reported here is highly informal and based on samples of three or four subjects in each group. It does, however, illustrate the remarkable compliance of the experimental subject. The only other situations where such a wide range of requests are carried out with little or no question are those of complete authority, such as some parent-child relationships or some doctor-patient relationships. This aspect of the experiment as a social situation will not become apparent unless one tests for it; it is, however, present in varying degrees in all experimental contexts. Not only are tasks carried out, but they are performed with care over considerable periods of time.

Our observation that subjects tend to carry out a remarkably wide range of instructions with a surprising degree of diligence reflects only one aspect of the motivation manifested by most subjects in an experimental situation. It is relevant to consider another aspect of motivation that is common to the subjects of most psychological experiments: high regard for the aims of science and experimentation.

A volunteer who participates in a psychological experiment may do so for a wide variety of reasons ranging from the need to fulfill a course requirement, to the need for money, to the unvoiced hope of altering his personal adjustment for the better, etc. Over and above these motives, however, college students tend to share (with the experimenter) the hope and expectation that the study in which they are participating will in some material way contribute to science and perhaps ultimately to human welfare in general. We should expect that many of the characteristics of the experimental situation derive from the peculiar role relationship which exists between subject and experimenter. Both subject and experimenter share the belief that whatever the experimental task is, it is important, and that as such no matter how much effort must be exerted or how much discomfort must be endured, it is justified by the ultimate purpose.

---

[4]Tasks which would involve the use of actual severe physical pain or exhaustion were not considered.

[5]This observation is consistent with Frank's (1944) failure to obtain resistance to disagreeable or nonsensical tasks. He accounts for this "primarily by S's unwillingness to break the tacit agreement he had made when he volunteered to take part in the experiment, namely, to do whatever the experiment required of him" (p. 24).

If we assume that much of the motivation of the subject to comply with any and all experimental instructions derives from an identification with the goals of science in general and the success of the experiment in particular,[6] it follows that the subject has a stake in the outcome of the study in which he is participating. For the volunteer subject to feel that he has made a useful contribution, it is necessary for him to assume that the experimenter is competent and that he himself is a "good subject."

The significance to the subject of successfully being a "good subject" is attested to by the frequent questions at the conclusion of an experiment, to the effect of, "Did I ruin the experiment?" What is most commonly meant by this is, "Did I perform well in my role as experimental subject?" or "Did my behavior demonstrate that which the experiment is designed to show?" Admittedly, subjects are concerned about their performance in terms of reinforcing their self-image; nonetheless, they seem even more concerned with the utility of their performances. We might well expect then that as far as the subject is able, he will behave in an experimental context in a manner designed to play the role of a "good subject" or, in other words, to validate the experimental hypothesis. Viewed in this way, the student volunteer is not merely a passive responder in an experimental situation but rather he has a very real stake in the successful outcome of the experiment. This problem is implicitly recognized in the large number of psychological studies which attempt to conceal the true purpose of the experiment from the subject in the hope of thereby obtaining more reliable data. This maneuver on the part of psychologists is so widely known in the college population that even if a psychologist is honest with the subject, more often than not he will be distrusted. As one subject pithily put it, "Psychologists always lie!" This bit of paranoia has some support in reality.

The subject's performance in an experiment might almost be conceptualized as problem-solving behavior; that is, at some level he sees it as his task to ascertain the true purpose of the experiment and respond in a manner which will support the hypotheses being tested. Viewed in this light, the totality of cues which convey an experimental hypothesis to the subject become significant determinants of subjects' behavior. We have labeled the sum total of such cues as the "demand characteristics of the experimental situation" (Orne, 1959a). These cues include the rumors or campus scuttlebutt about the research, the information conveyed during the original solicitation, the person of the experimenter, and the setting of the laboratory, as well as all explicit and implicit communications during the experiment proper. A frequently overlooked, but nonetheless very significant source of cues for the subject lies in the experimental procedure itself, viewed in the light of the subject's previous knowledge and experience. For example, if a test is given twice with some intervening treatment, even the dullest college student is aware that some change is expected, particularly if the test is in some obvious way related to the treatment.

The demand characteristics perceived in any particular experiment will vary with the sophistication, intelligence, and previous experience of each experimental subject. To the extent that the demand characteristics of the experiment

[6]This hypothesis is subject to empirical test. We should predict that there would be measurable differences in motivation between subjects who perceive a particular experiment as "significant" and those who perceive the experiment as "unimportant."

are clear-cut, they will be perceived uniformly by most experimental subjects. It is entirely possible to have an experimental situation with clear-cut demand characteristics for psychology undergraduates which, however, does not have the same clear-cut demand characteristics for enlisted army personnel. It is, of course, those demand characteristics which are perceived by the subject that will influence his behavior.

We should like to propose the heuristic assumption that a subject's behavior in any experimental situation will be determined by two sets of variables: (a) those which are traditionally defined as experimental variables and (b) the perceived demand characteristics of the experimental situation. The extent to which the subject's behavior is related to the demand characteristics, rather than to the experimental variable, will in large measure determine both the extent to which the experiment can be replicated with minor modification (i.e., modified demand characteristics) and the extent to which generalizations can be drawn about the effect of the experimental variables in nonexperimental contexts (the problem of ecological validity [Brunswik, 1947]).

It becomes an empirical issue to study under what circumstances, in what kind of experimental contexts, and with what kind of subject populations, demand characteristics become significant in determining the behavior of subjects in experimental situations. It should be clear that demand characteristics cannot be eliminated from experiments; all experiments will have demand characteristics, and these will always have some effect. It does become possible, however, to study the effect of demand characteristics as opposed to the effect of experimental variables. However, techniques designed to study the effect of demand characteristics need to take into account that these effects result from the subject's *active* attempt to respond appropriately to the *totality* of the experimental situation.

It is perhaps best to think of the perceived demand characteristics as a contextual variable in the experimental situation. We should like to emphasize that, at this stage, little is known about this variable. In our first study which utilized the demand characteristics concept (Orne, 1959b), we found that a particular experimental effect was present only in records of those subjects who were able to verbalize the experimenter's hypothesis. Those subjects who were unable to do so did not show the predicted phenomenon. Indeed we found that whether or not a given subject perceived the experimenter's hypothesis was a more accurate predictor of the subject's actual performance than his statement about what he thought he had done on the experimental task. It became clear from extensive interviews with subjects that response to the demand characteristics is not merely conscious compliance. When we speak of "playing the role of a good experimental subject," we use the concept analogously to the way in which Sarbin (1950) describes role playing in hypnosis: namely, largely on a nonconscious level. The demand characteristics of the situation help define the role of "good experimental subject," and the responses of the subject are a function of the role that is created.

We have a suspicion that the demand characteristics most potent in determining subjects' behavior are those which convey the purpose of the experiment effectively but not obviously. If the purpose of the experiment is not clear, or is highly ambiguous, many different hypotheses may be formed by different subjects, and the demand characteristics will not lead to clear-cut results. If, on the other hand, the demand characteristics are so obvious that the subject becomes fully conscious of the expectations of the experimenter, there is a tendency to lean over backwards to be honest. We are encountering here the effect of another facet of the college student's attitude toward science. While the student wants studies to "work," he feels he must be honest in his report; otherwise, erroneous conclusions will be drawn. Therefore, if the subject becomes acutely aware of the experimenter's expectations, there may be a tendency for biasing in the opposite direction. (This is analogous to the often observed tendency to favor individuals whom we dislike in an effort to be fair.)[7]

Delineation of the situations where demand characteristics may produce an effect ascribed to experimental variables, or where they may obscure such an effect and actually lead to systematic data in the opposite direction, as well as those experimental contexts where they do not play a major role, is an issue for further work. Recognizing the contribution to experimental results which may be made by the demand characteristics of the situation, what are some experimental techniques for the study of demand characteristics?

As we have pointed out, it is futile to imagine an experiment that could be created without demand characteristics. One of the basic characteristics of the human being is that he will ascribe purpose and meaning even in the absence of purpose and meaning. In an experiment where he knows some purpose exists, it is inconceivable for him not to form some hypothesis as to the purpose, based on some cues, no matter how meager; this will then determine the demand characteristics which will be perceived by and operate for a particular subject. Rather than eliminating this variable then, it becomes necessary to take demand characteristics into account, study their effect, and manipulate them if necessary.

One procedure to determine the demand characteristics is the systematic study of each individual subject's perception of the experimental hypothesis. If one can determine what demand characteristics are perceived by each subject, it becomes possible to determine to what extent these, rather than the experimental variables, correlate with the observed behavior. If the subject's behavior correlates better with the demand characteristics than with the experimental variables, it is probable that the demand characteristics are the major determinants of the behavior.

The most obvious technique for determining what demand characteristics are perceived is the use of postexperimental inquiry. In this regard, it is well to point out that considerable self-discipline is necessary for the experimenter to obtain a valid inquiry. A great many experimenters at least implicitly make the demand that the subject not perceive what is really going on. The temptation for the experimenter, in, say, a replication of an Asch group pressure experiment, is to ask the subject afterwards, "You didn't realize that the other fellows were confederates, did you?" Having obtained the required, "No," the experimenter breathes a sigh of relief and neither subject nor experimenter pursues the issue further.[8] However, even if the experimenter makes an effort to elicit the subject's

---

[7]Rosenthal (1961) in his recent work on experimenter bias, has reported a similar type of phenomenon. Biasing was maximized by ego involvement of the experimenters, but when an attempt was made to increase biasing by paying for "good results," there was a marked reduction of effect. This reversal may be ascribed to the experimenters' becoming too aware of their own wishes in the situation.

[8]Asch (1952) himself took great pains to avoid this pitfall.

perception of the hypothesis of the experiment, he may have difficulty in obtaining a valid report because the subject as well as he himself has considerable interest in appearing naive.

Most subjects are cognizant that they are not supposed to know any more about an experiment than they have been told and that excessive knowledge will disqualify them from participating, or, in the case of a postexperimental inquiry, such knowledge will invalidate their performance. As we pointed out earlier, subjects have a real stake in viewing their performance as meaningful. For this reason, it is commonplace to find a pact of ignorance resulting from the intertwining motives of both experimenter and subject, neither wishing to create a situation where the particular subject's performance needs to be excluded from the study.

For these reasons, inquiry procedures are required to push the subject for information without, however, providing in themselves cues as to what is expected. The general question which needs to be explored is the subject's perception of the experimental purpose and the specific hypotheses of the experimenter. This can best be done by an open-ended procedure starting with the very general question of, "What do you think that the experiment is about?" and only much later asking specific questions. Responses of "I don't know" should be dealt with by encouraging the subject to guess, use his imagination, and in general, by refusing to accept this response. Under these circumstances, the overwhelming majority of students will turn out to have evolved very definite hypotheses. These hypotheses can then be judged, and a correlation between them and experimental performance can be drawn.

Two objections may be made against this type of inquiry: (a) that the subject's perception of the experimenter's hypotheses is based on his own experimental behavior, and therefore a correlation between these two variables may have little to do with the determinants of behavior, and (b) that the inquiry procedure itself is subject to demand characteristics.

A procedure which has been independently advocated by Riecken (1958) and Orne (1959a) is designed to deal with the first of these objections. This consists of an inquiry procedure which is conducted much as though the subject had actually been run in the experiment, without, however, permitting him to be given any experimental data. Instead, the precise procedure of the experiment is explained, the experimental material is shown to the subject, and he is told what he would be required to do; however, he is not permitted to make any responses. He is then given a postexperimental inquiry as though he had been a subject. Thus, one would say, "If I had asked you to do all these things, what do you think that the experiment would be about, what do you think I would be trying to prove, what would my hypothesis be?" etc. This technique, which we have termed the pre-experimental inquiry, can be extended very readily to the giving of pre-experimental tests, followed by the explanation of experimental conditions and tasks, and the administration of postexperimental tests. The subject is requested to behave on these tests as though he had been exposed to the experimental treatment that was described to him. This type of procedure is not open to the objection that the subject's own behavior has provided cues for him as to the purpose of the task. It presents him with a straight problem-solving situation and makes explicit what, for the true experimental subject, is implicit. It goes without saying that these subjects who are run on the pre-experimental inquiry conditions must be drawn from the same population as the experimental groups and may, of course, not be run subsequently in the experimental condition. This technique is one of approximation rather than of proof. However, if subjects describe behavior on the pre-inquiry conditions as similar to, or identical with, that actually given by subjects exposed to the experimental conditions, the hypothesis becomes plausible that demand characteristics may be responsible for the behavior.

It is clear that pre- and postexperimental inquiry techniques have their own demand characteristics. For these reasons, it is usually best to have the inquiry conducted by an experimenter who is not acquainted with the actual experimental behavior of the subjects. This will tend to minimize the effect of experimenter bias.

Another technique which we have utilized for approximating the effect of the demand characteristics is to attempt to hold the demand characteristics constant and eliminate the experimental variable. One way of accomplishing this purpose is through the use of simulating subjects. This is a group of subjects who are not exposed to the experimental variable to which the effect has been attributed, but who are instructed to act *as if* this were the case. In order to control for experimenter bias under these circumstances, it is advisable to utilize more than one experimenter and to have the experimenter who actually runs the subjects "blind" as to which group (simulating or real) any given individual belongs.

Our work in hypnosis (Damaser, Shor, & Orne, 1963; Orne, 1959b; Shor, 1959) is a good example of the use of simulating controls. Subjects unable to enter hypnosis are instructed to simulate entering hypnosis for another experimenter. The experimenter who runs the study sees both highly trained hypnotic subjects and simulators in random order and does not know to which group each subject belongs. Because the subjects are run "blind," the experimenter is more likely to treat the two groups of subjects identically. We have found that simulating subjects are able to perform with great effectiveness, deceiving even well-trained hypnotists. However, the simulating group is not exposed to the experimental condition (in this case, hypnosis) to which the given effect under investigation is often ascribed. Rather, it is a group faced with a problem-solving task: namely, to utilize whatever cues are made available by the experimental context and the experimenter's concrete behavior in order to behave as they think that hypnotized subjects might. Therefore, to the extent that simulating subjects are able to behave identically, it is possible that demand characteristics, rather than the altered state of consciousness, could account for the behavior of the experimental group.

The same type of technique can be utilized in other types of studies. For example, in contrast to the placebo control in a drug study, it is equally possible to instruct some subjects not to take the medication at all, but to act as if they had. It must be emphasized that this type of control is different from the placebo control. It represents an approximation. It maximally confronts the simulating subject with a problem-solving task and suggests how much of the total effect could be accounted for by the demand characteristics — assuming that the experimental group had taken full advantage of them, an assumption not necessarily correct.

All of the techniques proposed thus far share the quality that they depend upon the active cooperation of the control subjects, and in some way utilize his thinking process as an intrinsic factor. The subject does *not* just respond in these control situations but, rather, he is required *actively* to solve the problem.

The use of placebo experimental conditions is a way in which this problem can be dealt with in a more classic fashion. Psychopharmacology has used such techniques extensively, but here too they present problems. In the case of placebos and drugs, it is often the case that the physician is "blind" as to whether a drug is placebo or active, but the patient is not, despite precautions to the contrary; i.e., the patient is cognizant that he does not have the side effects which some of his fellow patients on the ward experience. By the same token, in psychological placebo treatments, it is equally important to ascertain whether the subject actually perceived the treatment to be experimental or control. Certainly the subject's perception of himself as a control subject may materially alter the situation.

A recent experiment (Orne & Scheibe, 1964) in our laboratory illustrates this type of investigation. We were interested in studying the demand characteristics of sensory deprivation experiments, independent of any actual sensory deprivation. We hypothesized that the overly cautious treatment of subjects, careful screening for mental or physical disorders, awesome release forms, and, above all, the presence of a "panic (release) button" might be more significant in producing the effects reported from sensory deprivation than the actual diminution of sensory input. A pilot study (Stare, Brown, & Orne, 1959), employing pre-inquiry techniques, supported this view. Recently, we designed an experiment to test more rigorously this hypothesis.

This experiment, which we called Meaning Deprivation, had all the *accoutrements* of sensory deprivation, including release forms and a red panic button. However, we carefully refrained from creating any sensory deprivation whatsoever. The experimental task consisted of sitting in a small experimental room which was well lighted, with two comfortable chairs, as well as ice water and a sandwich, and an optional task of adding numbers. The subject did not have a watch during this time, the room was reasonably quiet, but not soundproof, and the duration of the experiment (of which the subject was ignorant) was four hours. Before the subject was placed in the experimental room, 10 tests previously used in sensory deprivation research were administered. At the completion of the experiment, the same tasks were again administered. A microphone and a one-way screen were present in the room, and the subject was encouraged to verbalize freely.

The control group of 10 subjects was subjected to the identical treatment, except that they were told that they were control subjects for a sensory deprivation experiment. The panic button was eliminated for this group. The formal experimental treatment of these two groups of subjects was the same in terms of the objective stress—four hours of isolation. However, the demand characteristics had been purposively varied for the two groups to study the effect of demand characteristics as opposed to objective stress. Of the 14 measures which could be quantified, 13 were in the predicted direction, and 6 were significant at the selected 10% alpha level or better. A Mann-Whitney U test has been performed on the summation ranks of all measures as a convenient method for summarizing the overall differences. The one-tailed probability which emerges is $p = .001$, a clear demonstration of expected effects.

This study suggests that demand characteristics may in part account for some of the findings commonly attributed to sensory deprivation. We have found similar significant effects of demand characteristics in accounting for a great deal of the findings reported in hypnosis. It is highly probable that careful attention to this variable, or group of variables, may resolve some of the current controversies regarding a number of psychological phenomena in motivation, learning, and perception.

In summary, we have suggested that the subject must be recognized as an active participant in any experiment, and that it may be fruitful to view the psychological experiment as a very special form of social interaction. We have proposed that the subject's behavior in an experiment is a function of the totality of the situation, which includes the experimental variables being investigated and at least one other set of variables which we have subsumed under the heading, demand characteristics of the experimental situation. The study and control of demand characteristics are not simply matters of good experimental technique; rather, it is an empirical issue to determine under what circumstances demand characteristics significantly affect subjects' experimental behavior. Several empirical techniques have been proposed for this purpose. It has been suggested that control of these variables in particular may lead to greater reproducibility and ecological validity of psychological experiments. With an increasing understanding of these factors intrinsic to the experimental context, the experimental method in psychology may become a more effective tool in predicting behavior in nonexperimental contexts.

References

Asch, S. E. *Social psychology.* Englewood Cliffs, N. J.: Prentice-Hall, 1952.

Brunswik, E. *Systematic and representative design of psychological experiments with results in physical and social perception.* (Syllabus Series, No. 304) Berkeley: Univer. California Press, 1947.

Damaser, Esther C., Shor, R. E., & Orne, M. T. Physiological effects during hypnotically-requested emotions. *Psychosom. Med.,* 1963, **25,** 334–343.

Frank, J. D. Experimental studies of personal pressure and resistance: I. Experimental production of resistance. *J. gen. Psychol.,* 1944, **30,** 23–41.

Orne, M. T. The demand characteristics of an experimental design and their implications. Paper read at American Psychological Association, Cincinnati, 1959.   (a)

Orne, M. T. The nature of hypnosis: Artifact and essence. *J. abnorm. soc. Psychol.,* 1959, **58,** 277–299.   (b)

Orne, M. T., & Scheibe, K. E. The contribution of nondeprivation factors in the production of sensory deprivation effects: the psychology of the "panic button." *J. abnorm. soc. Psychol.,* 1964, **68,** 3–12.

Pierce, A. H. The subconscious again. *J. Phil., Psychol., scient. Meth.,* 1908, **5,** 264–271.

Riecken, H. W. A program for research on experiments in social psychology. Paper read at Behavioral Sciences Conference, University of New Mexico, 1958.

Rosenthal, R. On the social psychology of the psychological experiment: With particular reference to experimenter bias. Paper read at American Psychological Association, New York, 1961.

Sarbin, T. R. Contributions to role-taking theory: I. Hypnotic behavior. *Psychol. Rev.,* 1950, **57,** 255–270.

Shor, R. E. Explorations in hypnosis: A theoretical and experimental study. Unpublished doctoral dissertation, Brandeis University, 1959.

Stare, F., Brown, J., & Orne, M. T. Demand characteristics in sensory deprivation studies. Unpublished seminar paper, Massachusetts Mental Health Center and Harvard University, 1959.

Subjects Are People Too

The survey methodologist uses knowledge of situational effects on interaction primarily as an emetic for decontaminating his instruments and purifying the situation.

Many social-psychology laboratory experiments reflect interest in essentially the same problem, but the psychologists assume a more positive stance toward their subject. Rather than attempting to remove contaminating effects in order to create private behavior, the psychologists attempt to *add* contaminations under controlled conditions in order to achieve a better understanding of public behavior. Like socio-logical field studies and survey research, this body of literature is nevertheless se-verely circumscribed as a source of evidence. But its limitations are not all of the same order. Some psychologists are themselves aware of the artificiality of the situa-tions and the contrived nature of the interaction typical of experiments in social psychology.[1] In his contribution to this chapter, Stanley Milgram insists that "even-tually social psychology must come to grips with significant behavior contents that are of interest in their own right and are not simply trivial substitutes for psycho-logically meaningful forms of behavior." Milgram deplores the use of such tasks as sorting IBM cards, making paper dolls, or eating crackers—all of which have been employed in experiments conducted by his colleagues. When I refer to the artificiali-ty of many experimental setups, I mean that they are inauthentic or simulated: such experiments do not deal with what they intend, but with an approximation of some element of the intended phenomenon. It is in this sense that they are artificial—in the same sense in which the interview frequently obtains "unreal" or private opin-ions. In both cases, our results may be largely artifacts of our procedures. But it is also true that, just as the interview is a "real" form of interaction in its own right, so, too, is the experiment. If one intends to study the behavior of students in situations which they themselves define as experimental, there is no better place to do it than in an experiment. The work of Friedman and Rosenthal[2] is of this order as is Orne's report in this chapter.

Even more basic to the social-psychological experiment is the underlying determination to perceive the research "subject" as an "object." Unfortunately peo-ple are not simply inert reactors to external pressures; they are actors who frequently enter into the construction of the act and sometimes even initiate action on their own. It is possible to find an occasional psychologist pleading with his fellows as Orne does. In describing his efforts to identify samples of more and less suggestible experimental subjects, he reports that he was unable to find a task boring enough to make subjects give it up in a reasonable length of time. In a thoughtful discussion, Orne concludes that "the experimental situation is one which takes place within the context of an explicit agreement of the subject to participate in a special form of so-cial interaction known as 'taking part in an experiment.' . . . Once a subject has agreed to participate in a psychological experiment, he implicitly agrees to perform a very wide range of actions on request without inquiring as to their purpose and

1. Apparently psychology, too, had its voices in the wilderness during the thirties. For an example see Saul Rosensweig, "The Experimental Situation as a Psychological Problem," *Psy-chological Review* 40 (1933): 337–54. Although one could never guess it from the title of their article, Irwin Silverman and Arthur D. Shulman suggest that much the same thing was hap-pening in psychology that I have described in sociology in Chapter Two. See their "A Concep-tual Model of Artifact in Attitude Change Studies," *Sociometry* 33 (1970): 97–107.

2. Robert Rosenthal, *Experimenter Effects in Behavioral Research* (New York: Appleton-Centu-ry-Crofts, 1966); Neil Friedman, *The Social Nature of Psychological Research: The Psychological Experiment as a Social Interaction* (New York: Basic Books, Inc., 1967). Two scholars have made a constructive effort to reconsider the issue of "realism versus artificiality." Their approach is to consider the question, What is it that makes an experiment "realistic"? See Thomas E. Drabek and J. Eugene Haas, "Realism in Laboratory Simulation: Myth or Method," *Social Forces* 45 (1967): 337–46.

frequently without inquiring as to their duration." It is precisely this concern for the subject as an active agent from which Campbell's long history of interest in reactivity derives. "Any measurement procedure," he states, "which makes the subject self-conscious or aware of the fact of the experiment can be suspected of being a reactive measurement."[3] In spite of such admonitions, it does not appear that most social psychologists are aware of the need to view the experiment itself as a form of interaction. Even though persuasive experimental evidence is added to the earlier admonition, resistance based on counter-evidence persists.[4]

In spite of such serious shortcomings, the experiment has, nevertheless, superior credibility to survey research in several respects. First, there is usually some theoretical framework to guide it and to make it coherent. It, unlike many survey reports, is unlikely to result in a random assortment of "facts" which presumably speak for themselves. Second, through experimental controls, the experiment, by definition, must create loaded situations for study rather than sterile ones. This permits us to determine more precisely the effect of specified interventions. We have some estimate of what things would have been like had there been no intervention. Clearly not everything that happens in a laboratory is an experiment and sometimes experimental design is implemented through survey research. Finally, as I have indicated before, methodological conclusions drawn from experiments are more likely to be interpreted in terms of a positive contribution to understanding human behavior than are methodological discoveries in survey research.

As is also true of surveys and field studies, the experimental literature provides hundreds of reports from which one can pick and choose. The experiments with which we shall be mainly concerned are those having to do, in one way or another, with interpersonal influence. It is important to note that some of these have been designed to study the consequences of group pressures on overt behavior or action as well as on opinion or attitude. Among these, there are a few which have managed to create experimental situations involving relatively meaningful behavior. Some of the best examples of this type of experiment are found in the work which takes Helson's notion of adaptation-level as a point of departure. Helson considers the various components of the situation, including the actor's personality, social constraints, and the meaning of the object toward which the attitude or behavior is directed. The experimental setup employed by Helson and others is such that the actual experiment is viewed by the subject as an extraneous incident occurring during the course of what he believes to be the experiment. The article in Chapter Ten by Himmelstein and Moore provides an example. Milgram's work seems to me to be uniformly credible. But not everyone agrees—especially Martin Orne whose work appears back to back with Milgram's in this chapter.

Milgram has published a considerable number of reports in addition to the one included here, some of which employ his terrible electrical shocking machine and some of which do not. In a 1968 paper he describes an experiment which is less subtle than the one here. In the later study, the naive subject is actively supported by the experimenter in administering increasing voltage to the "learner." The ques-

---

3. Donald T. Campbell, "Factors Relevant to the Validity of Experiments in Social Settings," *Psychological Bulletin* 54 (1957): 298–99.
4. For examples of such resistance and such counterevidence see David J. Hanson, "Letter: Ideological Orientations and Sociological Facts," *American Sociologist* 4 (1969): 160, and Robert A. Gordon, "Letter: Amongst Competent Sociologists?" *American Sociologist* 4 (1969): 249–50.

tion addressed in this study is that of obedience to authority.[5] He does find that subjects—this time adult working males in New Haven—throw excessive voltage into learners, in spite of personal qualms, as long as the experimenter keeps supporting their actions. In order to assure himself that it is the authority of the person rather than the authority of Yale University to which his subjects are responding, Milgram repeats the experiment in a rather shabby downtown office in Bridgeport. The results, although somewhat less impressive, continue to hold up. This article is followed by four critiques and a rejoinder.[6] For the most part, the critics find Milgram's work enchanting. But this is not the case for Orne and Holland. Although Masserman is also critical—largely on the grounds that after all this is only an experiment and it doesn't really tell us much about what happens in everyday life—neither his logic nor his evidence are as persuasive as those presented by Orne and Holland. Let us consider what they find problematic with what is probably one of the most credible sets of experiments available.

Orne and Holland argue that it is not possible to generalize Milgram's results beyond the laboratory; they question the success of the deception required in this and other experiments which con naive subjects; they say that in an experiment people will do whatever they are told to do by the experimenter; they do not believe that anything can be learned about the outside world from an experiment as long as the subject knows that he is participating in an experiment—regardless of whether he knows its purpose or anything else about it. The essential argument is summed up as follows:

> . . . the agreement to participate in an experiment gives the E *carte blanche* about what may legitimately be requested. In asking the S to participate in an experiment, the E implicitly says, "Will you do whatever I ask for a specified period of time? By so doing you may earn a fee, contribute to science, and perhaps even learn something of value to yourself. In return I promise that no harm will befall you. At the completion of the experiment you will be no better or worse off than you are now and though you may experience temporary inconvenience, this is justified by the importance of the undertaking." A corollary to this agreement is that the S may not ask why certain things are required of him. He must assume that these actions are legitimate and appropriate for the needs of the experiment.[7]

All of this is an extension and application to Milgram of the argument presented by Orne in the paper reprinted in this chapter. Although the point is unde-

---

5. Stanley Milgram, "Some Conditions of Obedience and Disobedience to Authority," *International Journal of Psychiatry* 6 (1968): 259–76.

6. Ibid., pp. 277–95. The critiques are by Milton Erikson, Amitai Etzioni, Jules Masserman, and Martin T. Orne and Charles H. Holland. A short reply to them all by Milgram follows.

7. Martin T. Orne and Charles H. Holland, "On the Ecological Validity of Laboratory Deceptions," *International Journal of Psychiatry* 6 (1968): 291. Orne's thinking is clarified in what he considers to be more adequate statements of his position in Martin T. Orne, "Hypnosis, Motivation, and the Ecological Validity of the Psychological Experiment," in *Nebraska Symposium on Motivation*, eds. W. J. Arnold and M. M. Page (Lincoln: University of Nebraska Press, 1970), pp. 187–265, and in Martin T. Orne, "Demand Characteristics and the Concept of Quasi-Controls," in *Artifact in Behavioral Research*, eds. R. Rosenthal and R. Rosnow (New York: Academic Press, 1969), pp. 143–79.

niably an important one, it seems to me that its application to Milgram's work is less than persuasive. I should say, it did seem that way until I read their evidence! Holland replicated Milgram's work and, in interviewing his subjects during a debriefing, found that "three quarters of the Ss run in the analog of Milgram's situation indicated that they did not really believe the deception when carefully questioned after the experiment."[8] Now the dilemma for the analyst is that both Milgram and Orne inspire a high degree of confidence in their work and the problem of discounting therefore becomes knotty. In the end it is a matter of judgment. Were Holland's respondents simply afraid to appear foolish and gullible? What other problems have not been considered here? We cannot be certain, but at this point I will continue to assign high credibility to Milgram's work. Others must make their own decisions.

The Asch model (see Chapter Eleven, p. 281), which I suppose is the ancestor of Milgram's design, is clever and innovative and has been widely employed in experimental social psychology. But the use of confederates as a standard component of such experiments must inevitably create problems, especially when the subjects tend to be sophisticated undergraduates. Surely, if subjects suspect the presence of a confederate when they participate in an experiment, then the very purpose of the experiment must be sabotaged. This is as true when there is in fact no confederate or when the subject suspects the wrong person as it is when the subject is correct in his suspicions. Just as the respondent's definition of the interview situation impinges on the interaction which takes place, so, too, does the subject's definition of the experimental situation. And there is evidence that deceived subjects do not behave in the same way as undeceived subjects.[9] Martin has pursued this problem by staging various "experiments" before a class and then determining who, in the experimental situation, is likely to arouse suspicion as a possible confederate. Although his work tells us little about actual suspicion by participants in experiments, the fact that 79 to 98 percent of the members of his classes suspected the presence of a stooge in the four experiments they viewed is worth taking note of.[10]

Even Sherif's classic discovery of the autokinetic effect in the early thirties — endlessly replicated, duplicated, varied, and extended since that time — is being questioned as a consequence of the new sensitivity to reactivity. Sherif discovered that when no point of reference is provided, subjects tend to establish norms — their judgments converge — as to the direction and extent of movement of a spot of light in a darkened room.[11] In two experiments reported in 1970, Alexander and his colleagues provide evidence that the autokinetic effect may be largely a consequence of expectations created by the laboratory situation. They point out that "the laboratory setting itself generates expectations for patterned and orderly stimulus experiences," and that "stability, regularity, and logical purpose are associated with

8. Orne and Holland, "Ecological Validity of Laboratory Deceptions," p. 291. See C. H. Holland, "Sources of Variance in the Experimental Investigation of Behavioral Obedience" (diss., University of Connecticut, 1967).

9. Lawrence J. Stricker, Samuel Messick, and Douglas N. Jackson, "Evaluating Deception in Psychological Research," *Psychological Bulletin* 71 (1969): 343–51.

10. J. David Martin, "Suspicion and the Experimental Confederate: A Study of Role and Credibility," *Sociometry* 33 (1970): 178–92.

11. The most succinct and readily available report of Sherif's original work can be found in Muzafer Sherif, "Group Influences Upon the Formation of Norms and Attitudes," in *Readings in Social Psychology*, eds. E. Maccoby, T. Newcomb, and E. Hartley (New York: Henry Holt and Co., 1958).

[Sherif's] design and conduct of the experiment and presentation of experimental stimuli."[12] Their experiments, in which they deliberately redefine the situation for subjects, tend to support their contention.

There is another serious weakness of experimental work which tends to impugn the credibility of the kinds of conclusions I will begin to draw from it in Chapter Ten. It is a weakness which is at least partly shared by field studies that tend to reach the same conclusions. The observation which is most important in all of these studies is that there is something other than personality, social structure, and culture which appears to account for a large segment of the variance in human behavior: It is the actor's perception of the situation in which he finds himself—and especially his perception of others in that situation—which appears to provide much of the material from which he constructs his own line of action. To paraphrase Erving Goffman, where else but in a social situation does action take place?[13] But it is the central concept of David Riesman's *The Lonely Crowd*[14] which suggests the serious weakness I am addressing.

Riesman delineated societies and eras which he described as other-directed, inner-directed, and tradition-directed. Societies may vary in the extent to which members' thoughts and actions are guided by their contemporaries (rather than by internalized constraints). There is also the suggestion that generations may vary in this respect, and the implication that in a mass society some segments may be more or less other-directed than other segments or strata. Riesman's thesis generally follows the tradition of the national character or personality and culture schools. Most of the literature we will review as evidence of the extent to which the company one keeps is related to the behavioral choices one makes is based on experiments and observations of Americans, nearly all middle class, and frequently youthful college students. Do people in other parts of the world behave like Americans? Do lower- or upper-class Americans behave like middle-class ones? Do middle-aged and older people behave like youngsters? There is considerable evidence that, at least in some respects, the answer to all of these questions is "No!" It is not safe, then, to conclude that the tendency of people other than middle-class American college students is to alter their behavior so as to bring it more into line with what they perceive others around them to approve of. We will consider the evidence related to this issue in Chapter Ten.

Systematic Distortion: The Ubiquitous Type I Error

It has been suggested that laboratory experiments are simulated substitutes for reality, frequently dealing with trivia, and generally lacking any real consequences for

---

12. C. Norman Alexander, Jr., Lynne G. Zucker, and Charles L. Brody, "Experimental Expectations and Autokinetic Experiences: Consistency Theories and Judgmental Convergence," *Sociometry* 33 (1970): 112.

13. Goffman actually asks where else but in a social situation does *speech* take place? See Erving Goffman, "The Neglected Situation," in *The Ethnography of Communication*, eds. John G. Gunperz and Dell Hymes, Part 2 of the *American Anthropologist* 66 (1964): 133–36.

14. David Riesman and Reuel Denny, *The Lonely Crowd: A Study of the Changing American Character* (New Haven: Yale University Press, 1950).

the actors. The likelihood of subjects playing a game called "being in an experiment" seems high. Clearly these experiments tend to be isolated fragments unrelated to anything that is otherwise happening in the flow of everyday activity of the subjects (except that many undergraduates, especially psychology majors, understand that to be in an experiment is an expected part of the general process leading to college graduation). Finally, there are many population biases in these studies, including nationality, social class, and age. But that is not the end of it. As an outside reader of occasional doctoral dissertations in psychology at various institutions and as a poker-playing crony of a number of psychologists in various parts of the United States, I became aware of a rather strange criteria for "successful" research in contemporary psychology.

It seemed (at least during the fifties and sixties) that in order for a dissertation to be accepted in psychology, it must first of all be designed to test one or more null hypotheses (a peculiar restriction in itself) and, furthermore, it must provide statistical evidence for the rejection of those null hypotheses (technically, it must find no evidence to support the hypotheses). This norm distressed me on the grounds that if a student had sound theoretical reasons for expecting certain outcomes and if he did his research well, it seemed all the more remarkable that things did not turn out as he expected them to. It is under such conditions that important theoretical and methodological discoveries are made. My friends in psychology generally pooh-poohed such reasoning pointing out that when the student found no significant differences it was most likely because he had originally misinterpreted his basic theory, had chosen to test untenable theories, or had goofed up methodologically—in his design, his technique, or his analysis. To these psychologists, an acceptable dissertation was one which reported significant differences in the expected direction. An unacceptable dissertation was one which did not find significant differences in the expected direction. Another argument used by the psychologists was that publication policy of some of their journals required statistical significance at specified levels before an article could be considered by the editorial readers. I don't think I ever really believed that. At any rate, I was unable to make a dent in the thinking of these scholars and they, of course, had little influence on mine.

Generally, the scholar assesses available evidence, judges its credibility, and draws conclusions on the extent of its usefulness. We cannot, however, properly discount research which we have not seen, and editors of professional journals are the gatekeepers of most of what we see. It is in this respect that an observation documented by David Bakan and others becomes troublesome.[15] Some editors of psychology journals have in fact used a specific confidence level at which the null hypothesis must be rejected as a criterion of eligibility for publication. This not only assumes that a null hypothesis is a necessary prerequisite to knowledge, but that the rejection of that hypothesis at, say, the $p < .05$ level is a predeterminant of what is and is not good research. For at least one editor that level was not considered adequate. Bakan cites an editorial by Arthur W. Melton, written as he stepped down after twelve years as editor of the *Journal of Experimental Psychology*:

15. See Chapter 1 in David Bakan, *On Method: Toward a Reconstruction of Psychological Investigation* (San Francisco: Jossey-Bass, Inc., Publishers, 1968). This subject has not escaped the attention of sociologists. See, for example, David Gold, "Statistical Tests and Substantive Significance," *American Sociologist* 4 (1969), 42–46.

In editing the Journal there has been a strong reluctance to accept and publish results related to the principal concern of the research when those results were significant at the .05 level, whether by one- or two-tailed test. This has not implied a slavish worship of the .01 level, as some critics may have implied. Rather, it reflects a belief that it is the responsibility of the investigator in a science to reveal his effect in such a way that no reasonable man would be in a position to discredit the results by saying that they were the product of the way the ball bounces.[16]

Although Bakan appears to recognize the consequences of such a policy, he makes it clear that he considers it neither necessary nor desirable to change it: "It is important to point out that I am not advocating a change in policy in this connection."[17] But let us consider the implications of such an editorial policy. If 100 investigators test the hypothesis that there is no relationship between, say, group pressure and the actions of an individual and 99 of these investigators find no difference at the .01 level, while one of them does find differences large enough to permit rejection of the hypothesis, it is the lone man whose research is eligible for publication. The ninety-nine need not bother to send their papers to the journal. It is then the findings of a minority of investigators which get into print even though all of the 100 studies may have been conducted in identical ways. This suggests something more than the lack of publication of certain important studies or the occasional publication of results which are, in fact, in error. It suggests a systematic distortion of knowledge since, in our example, the adoption of the .01 level of confidence means that out of every 100 experimental trials, differences as large as those observed can be expected to occur once *as a result of chance alone.* We need not even consider the likelihood that in these "publish or perish" times a young experimenter, itching for a promotion, may run his experiment until he does get publishable (significant) results—even if he has to run 100 trials.

In short, the disturbing conclusion I must reach is that such an editorial policy systematically selects out conclusions which are in error; it publishes the one chance finding and deliberately rejects the 99 correct ones. But what of verification? The answer is clear. Of the 100 studies which attempt to replicate the study, 99 fail to verify while one does so at the .01 confidence level. Again it is only this last one which is eligible for publication. The incorrect conclusion is confirmed, and we move ahead with greater confidence in our knowledge. All of this does not mean that research published in journals with such a policy must all be rejected out of hand. In fact, *if we carefully follow the dictates of probability theory, we can safely assume a high level of confidence in the reverse of all published findings under such an editorial policy.* However, even if I depended exclusively upon such journals for my

---

16. Arthur W. Melton, "Editorial," *Journal of Experimental Psychology* 64 (1962): 553–54. An unanticipated consequence of an editorial policy such as Melton's is that it provides a rationale for precisely the kind of discrediting it was designed to avoid. One research team, for example, argues that the frequently observed significant differences between attitude and behavior are a spurious artifact of that policy. They believe that investigators finding a relationship between the two variables are unlikely to get their results published because journal editors consider such findings "unexciting" and "not worthy of publication." See C. A. Insko and J. Schopler, "Triadic Consistency: A Statement of Affective-Cognitive Consistency," *Psychological Review* 74 (1967): 361–76.

17. Bakan, *On Method,* p. 9.

sources of information, I could not apply this principle of reciprocal conclusions, since authentic and inauthentic findings are randomly mixed. Fortunately, I am not that dependent upon any one source of data and thus am free to consider each article as a case in itself, without the need to apply probability theory to a large sampling of articles.

All of this is, nevertheless, of serious concern to me since much of the evidence on which I base the arguments in Chapter Ten is derived from psychology journals, some of which did have such an editorial policy. Fortunately, it seems to me that there is enough evidence from other sources (with their own peculiar kinds of weaknesses) to provide a degree of convergent validity. I remain confident in my tentative conclusions in spite of this great weakness in one source of evidence.

Can the Weakness of One Be the Strength of the Other?

The criticisms in Chapters Six, Seven, and Eight are not meant to discourage or to induce a cynical "to-hell-with-all-of-their-data" reaction. It is important that we understand the potential weaknesses and limitations of data derived from any source, so that we may use it in a sensible manner. In other words, very little is so useless that it should be thrown away, but most is so circumscribed that it must be appropriately discounted. There is also a useful device for treating data so that it becomes part of a cumulative, credible body, rather than having to stand on its own weak two feet. This chapter closes with an illustration of how different sources of error (different weaknesses) may, taken together, enhance our confidence in their conclusions. What I hope to demonstrate is that two wrongs *can* make a right. This is one version of what Webb et al. have called "triangulation." Let us see if the strengths of one may be the weaknesses of the other.[18]

This illustration consists of a comparison of a study conducted in the laboratory by a psychologist and one conducted in the field by a sociologist.[19] Raven, the psychologist, employs the Asch design in an experiment with undergraduate subjects aimed at determining the effects of group pressure in changing attitudes. His subjects are volunteers who express an interest in the subject of racial attitudes. With the use of confederates Raven creates a number of situations which lead him to conclude that 1) a member of the group who has deviant attitudes tends to select and distort the content of what he communicates so as not to be rejected by the group and then 2) to select and distort what he perceives so that it tends to be more and more in line with group norms and, 3) seeing more evidence to support the group norm, he brings his attitudes into conformity with those of the group.

There are striking parallels between this laboratory simulation and Gorden's field study of a cooperative rooming house. Gorden, a member of the co-op,

18. From time to time I have received useful suggestions from graduate students in making this comparison. Among them are David Brogi, Anthony Gold, Carlton A. Hornung, David S. Hunt, Melody H. Lewis, Charles L. Shull, Burton Silver, Henry J. Travers, Jr., Norman L. Weiner, and Esther Young.

19. Raymond L. Gorden, "Interaction Between Attitude and the Definition of the Situation in the Expression of Opinion," *American Sociological Review* 17 (1952): 50–58, and B. H. Raven, "Social Influences on Opinions and the Communication of Related Content," *Journal of Abnormal and Social Psychology* 58 (1959): 119–28.

administered a political questionnaire to his fellow members on the pretext that he needed to try it out. Later, in the presence of other co-op members, parallel political questions were informally raised by Gorden. In both of these studies "private opinions" are first elicited and the subjects are later confronted with the need to express themselves publicly. Gorden notes "an acute awareness of the presence of the other members of the group when they are asked to express their opinion. Confused efforts to appear nonchalant, efforts to escape the situation, and attempts to prevent others from hearing one's response are all telltale signs of the awareness of pressure."[20]

Raven and Gorden are both interested in the way in which members of a group who are aware of their own deviant attitudes alter those attitudes to preserve their group affiliation. Pursuing the problem independently and employing very different methods, they reach identical conclusions. Taken by itself, either study has enough weaknesses to leave its conclusions in doubt. But, because the weaknesses of one are the strengths of the other, they provide, in combination, highly credible evidence in support of the hypothesis they share. What we have is something like an error-canceling process. For example, Raven's laboratory work contains all of the kinds of potential reactivity which occurs when students define themselves as "participating in an experiment." They know what an experiment is and they know what the experimenter is. Gorden's field study, on the other hand, takes place in a natural setting where people are going about their everyday routines. He not only observes subjects relating to their fellows, but he employs interviewing techniques. He is part of the scene; the subjects know him in other contexts. The kinds of reactivity likely to occur under these conditions are problematic in equal measure to Raven's, but *they are very different*. There is a difference in the types of discounting which must take place in considering the credibility of these two studies.

Raven's subjects are homogeneous and they are selective in the sense that he deliberately removes those subjects who are suspected of being "suspicious." Gorden's population is heterogeneous; it is also selective but in different ways. What kinds of relatively isolated (and mobile?) people are found living in boarding houses? At any rate his subjects are varied in age, occupation, and race. Raven has a segmented experience to observe—one of no great import to the participants either before or after. In contrast, Gorden's study involves an affect-laden issue which transcends the research situation and has real consequences for the participants. Although Raven's study is clearly more reliable (reproducible, objective, standardized in its technique), Gorden's is clearly more valid, dealing with a live issue among an ongoing social entity rather than simulating both the issue and the group. In general Gorden has a relatively loose study while Raven remains in tight control of the situation and of his subjects.

There is, of course, a residue of problems which both studies share, such as the lack of experimental controls or the imposition of arbitrary scales created by investigators but not necessarily reflecting the categories employed by subjects. What this residue means is that these studies must still be discounted to a degree. But what is most important is that taken together they become far more credible than either of them standing alone. This, I submit, is because the strengths of one are in large part the weaknesses of the other. Both of these studies conclude that when opinion becomes public rather than private, it is likely to change radically. Further-

20. Gorden, "Interaction Between Attitude and Definition," p. 57.

more, they both note that the change is in the direction of conformity to the perceived group norms. In Chapter Ten we will consider other evidence pointing in the same direction, but my point for the moment is that I find these studies taken together highly credible.

Many such instances of convergence lie buried in the literature. We have only to seek them out. Hovland, although he identifies seven specific methodological artifacts which tend to bring about opposite results, nevertheless concludes that it is "quite apparent . . . that a genuine understanding . . . requires both the survey and the experimental methodologies. At the same time there appear to be certain inherent limitations of each method. . . ."[21] In 1954 the participants in a summer seminar discussing the possibility of narrowing the gap between field studies and laboratory experiments in social psychology arrived at some pessimistic conclusions. They suggest that a different orientation toward theory results in "noncorrespondence" between field and laboratory findings: "Conclusions reached through the two methods will not necessarily agree nor even be related. Field workers tend to talk a different dialect from that used in laboratories, and field and laboratory results are less often contradictory than incommensurable."[22] In view of some of the relationships and parallels suggested in this chapter and in view of increasing sensitivity to their own weaknesses on the part of some investigators in both disciplines, it may be that the situation is more hopeful a decade or so later.

In the past three chapters, I have made no effort to be exhaustive in enumerating the types of vulnerability different methods are susceptible to. It should be clear that any approach has certain built-in deficiencies. It should be equally clear that any approach has certain built-in advantages. Some problems are better addressed with some approaches than with others and some investigators are happier when working in some media than in others. It is also true that the categories I have chosen are based on common-sense usage of such terms as field studies, experiments, surveys, and interviewing. Such common-sense categories lack a certain precision when we begin working seriously with them. It is not only possible, but desirable to impose the logic of experimental design on survey or participant-observational work. That being the case, they cannot be and, in fact, are not logically distinct categories. They have nevertheless proved useful hooks on which to hang our discussion. In Chapter Nine, our final venture into the methodological dimension, we shall turn to a series of arguments which suggest, with considerable merit, that much of what we see as discrepancies between sentiments and acts is more apparent than real.

21. Carl J. Hovland, "Reconciling Conflicting Results Derived from Experimental and Survey Studies of Attitude Change," *The American Psychologist* 14 (1959): 14.

22. "Narrowing the Gap Between Field Studies and Laboratory Experiments in Social Psychology: A Statement by the Summer Seminar," *Social Science Research Council Items* 8 (December 1954), 38–39.

The Logic
of Our Procedures

DATA:
Pseudoinconsistency
in the Attitude Literature
DONALD T. CAMPBELL

The allegation [is made here] . . . that verbal report is in some circumstances a mode of diagnosing dispositions also manifest in overt behavior. This viewpoint contrasts strikingly with the prevailing tenor of the social-attitude literature, which emphasizes the inconsistency between verbal attitude expression and overt action. Thus Logan et al. [p. 82], in a discussion of the use of verbal report in a context similar to the present paper, cite the classic LaPiere study, purportedly showing the undependability of verbal-questionnaire reports in predicting discriminatory behavior toward Chinese upon the part of restaurants and lodging places. Thus Harding et al. devote a 2,400-word section, "Relationships among Intergroup Attitudes and Intergroup Behavior," to emphasizing the inconsistency shown in the literature. A whole issue of *The Journal of Social Issues* [Chein et al.] has been devoted to the subject, with similar conclusions. By and large, this literature has confused correlational inconsistency with situational threshold differences, and has thus exaggerated the inconsistency present.

On an arithmetic test of four items, the child who gets only two items correct is not necessarily regarded as less consistent than the child who gets all right or all wrong. If he gets the two easiest right and the two hardest wrong, he is equally consistent. On intelligence we today think in terms of a continuum, and can conceive of consistent mediocrity. Similarly, . . . we can regard honesty as something people have in degree, rather than as an all-or-none trait. A person of intermediate degree can be just as consistent as a person of extreme position, and his attitude can be determined from his behavior just as well. Inconsistency does, of course, occur, but from the type of analysis presented by May and Hartshorne and popularized by Guttman, one can distinguish between consistent mediocrity and inconsistent scatter. For intelligence and honesty, we have achieved dimensionality in our thinking. For more emotion-laden topics, such as standing up for civil rights, we have not. If a university president protects a pacifist professor but fires an atheist, we call him inconsistent. If he protects a pacifist and an atheist, but fires a Communist, we accuse him of backing down under pressure. Conceptually, we have the notion of a total nondefendant of professors' rights and a total defender of professors' rights, and lack any concept of genuine mediocrity which would *in consistency* produce defense in a situation of low threshold and firing in another situation with a higher threshold value.

In terms of the scale-analysis model, let us examine the classic cases of inconsistency. In LaPiere's study, he and the Chinese couple were refused accommodation in .4 per cent of places stopped. The mailed questionnaire reported 92.5 per cent refusal of Chinese. The first thing we note is that the two diagnostic situations have very different thresholds. Apparently it is very hard to refuse a well-dressed Chinese couple traveling with a European in a face-to-face setting, and very easy to refuse the Chinese as a race in a mailed questionnaire. We can see easily why this would be so. But there is as yet no evidence of inconsistency. Inconsistency would be represented by persons who refused face to face and accepted by questionnaire. There is no report that such cases occurred. The fact that 92 per cent of the cases were mediocre in their Sinophilia, having enough to get over the low hurdle but not enough to get over the high hurdle, is irrelevant to the problem of inconsistency, but rather speaks only as to the heights of the hurdles.

Minard's casual comments on the Pocahontas coal miners involves two items which can be diagramed as in Fig. 1. His report clearly indicates that the settings of mine and town have markedly different situational thresholds for non-discriminatory reactions of white miners, only 20 per cent being friendly in town, 80 per cent being friendly in the mines. He reports no instances of true inconsistency, i.e., being friendly in town and hostile in the mines. From this point of view, and considering the long-standing model of the Bogardus social distance steps, Harding et al. [p. 1032] are clearly wrong to conclude that the middle 60 per cent are persons "whose overt behavior provides no clue as to their attitudes." Their behavior clearly indicates that they have consistently middling attitudes. The two items, mine and town, correlate perfectly, using any index not biased by uneven item marginals (i.e., tetrachoric correlation or phi-over-maximum-phi).

Merton's four "ideal types" of consistent and inconsistent liberalism are open to a similar interpretation. A verbal item, perhaps "Are you in favor of segregation?" might have a threshold of 50 per cent. One behavioral item, refusing to eat with a Negro at a businessmen's luncheon club, might be one in which it would be hard to show prejudice, perhaps only 10 per cent doing so. Another behavioral item, refusing to rent one's house to Negroes, might have a very high threshold for the liberal response, 90 per cent showing prejudice. If this were the situation, and if all persons were perfectly consistent, one would have these four types, using Merton's labels:

1. The "all weather liberal," who shows nondiscriminatory behavior in all three settings (10 per cent)
2. The "fair weather liberal," showing liberalism in words and at the luncheon, but not on the house rental (40 per cent)
3. The "fair weather illiberal," showing discrimination in words and in house rental but not at the luncheon (40 per cent)
4. The "all weather illiberal," who discriminates on all three (10 per cent)

FIGURE 1. **MINARD'S DATA ON MINER'S ATTITUDES TOWARD NEGROES.**

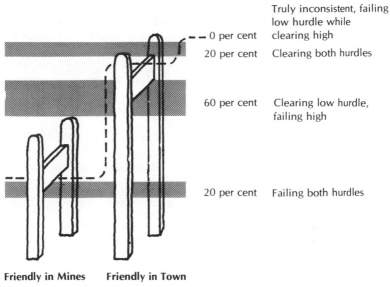

Truly inconsistent, failing
low hurdle while
clearing high

0 per cent

20 per cent   Clearing both hurdles

60 per cent   Clearing low hurdle,
failing high

20 per cent   Failing both hurdles

Friendly in Mines   Friendly in Town

Of this typology, Harding et al. [p. 1034] say, "Types 2 and 3 represent the extreme case of no dependence of behavior on attitudes." This is clearly un-called for if no nonscale types occur (such as renting to Negroes while speaking out for segregation, etc.). If all cases are accounted for by the four types, then the three items correlate perfectly, and one can predict as well from the verbal item to either one of the behavioral items as one can from one behavioral item to the other.

Thus in the literature there has been a stubborn confusion of the fact that verbal behaviors and overt behaviors have different situational thresholds with the fact of consistency. Once this is clarified, we can look to correlational evidence of consistency. Of course, the Minard and Merton examples actually *exaggerate* this consistency. Between two measures of response strength in the animal labo-ratory, the correlations are far from perfect. Two social actions hypothesized to tap the same disposition will correlate far less than unity in practice, as will also one verbal statement and one overt response, or two verbal statements. The de-gree of correlation is, for the most part, yet to be discovered. Where the overt act of joining an ideological group has been correlated with verbal reports on own attitudes, the relationships found have been obvious and very high, as in compari-sons of church members with organized atheists, conscientious objectors with ROTC members, etc. [Murphy et al.]. Probably the validity of attitude tests will be found higher than that of the more complex personality-trait measures when checked against overt behavior. In such studies, the unreliability and invalidity of overt-behavior measures should also be remembered and measured, and in no case should a single overt behavior be regarded as the criterion of a disposition. It would certainly be expected . . . for situations in which there are not special inhibitory dispositions affecting actions or words (for those situations in which the respondents are naïve or cooperating) that a positive diagnostic correlation will be obtained. Remembering that the average interitem correlation for a good verbal attitude test or intelligence test is as low as .20 or lower, we must not expect high correlations between attitude tests and *single* behavioral items.

References

Borgardus, E. S. *Immigration and race attitudes.* Boston: Heath, 1928.
Chein, I., Deutsch, M., Hyman, H., & Jahoda, M. (Eds.) Consistency and inconsistency in intergroup relations. *J. soc. Issues,* 1949, **5** (3), 1–63.
Guttman, L. The basis for scalogram analysis. In S. A. Stouffer, L. Guttman, E. A. Suchman, P. F. Lazarsfeld, S. A. Star, & J. A. Clausen, *Measurement and prediction.* Princeton, N.J.: Princeton Univer. Press, 1950. Pp. 60–212.
Harding, J., Kutner, B., Proshansky, J., & Chein, I. Prejudice and ethnic relations. In G. Lindzey (Ed.), *Handbook of social psychology.* Reading, Mass.: Addison-Wesley, 1954. Pp. 1021–1061.
LaPiere, R. T. Attitudes vs. actions. *Soc. Forces,* 1934, **13**, 230–237.
Logan, F. A., Olmstead, D. L., Rosner, B. S., Schwartz, R. D., & Stevens, C. M. *Behavior theory and social science.* New Haven, Conn.: Yale Univer. Press, 1955.
May, M. A., & Hartshorne, H. First steps toward a scale for measuring attitudes. *J. educ. Psychol.,* 1926, **17**, 145–162.
Merton, R. K. Discrimination and the American creed. In R. M. MacIver (Ed.), *Discrimination and national welfare.* New York: Institute for Religious and Social Studies, 1949. Pp. 99–126.
Minard, R. D. Race relationships in the Pocahontas coal field. *J. soc. Issues,* 1952, **8**, (1), 29–44.
Murphy, G., Murphy, L. B., & Newcomb, T. M. *Experimental social psychology.* (Rev. ed.) New York: Harper, 1937.

What Is an Inconsistency?

Our text in this concluding note on methods concentrates on the trenchant fragment with which Donald Campbell leads off this chapter. Campbell submits that the logic of literature suggesting an "inconsistency" is faulty. There is in fact no inconsistency between attitude and behavior if one will just look at the discrepancy from a proper perspective. Campbell tenders a literally "methodological" solution to the relationship between sentiments and acts — one which addresses itself to the logic of our procedures and to the manner in which we think about our data. There is a certain elegance about this and it does provide a partial explanation. On the other hand, it by no means resolves all or even most of the problematic aspects of the relationship between what people say and what they otherwise do. After considering Campbell's (and related) arguments, we will turn to some of the more technical explanations suggesting that observed discrepancies between sentiments and acts are more apparent than real.

Late in World War II, Louis Guttman invented a new way of thinking about the relationship between items on a test or a questionnaire, or what had previously been referred to by the noun *a scale.* Guttman converted the noun into a verb and in so doing converted an arbitrary set of presumably related items into a process, one which not only determines more precisely their empirical relationship, but which tests that precision through predicting responses on each item in the given set from responses to other items. He called this process "scale analysis"[1] and its logic is the logic employed by Campbell in his metaphor of high hurdles and low hurdles. Campbell reasons that "apparently, it is very hard to refuse a well-dressed Chinese couple traveling with a European in a face-to-face setting, and very easy to refuse the Chinese as a race in a mailed questionnaire." Note, and store away, that Campbell is dealing with two factors here: (1) the personal confrontation vs. the impersonal mailed questionnaire, and (2) the specific Chinese couple vs. the abstract or generalized "Chinese race." Campbell does not develop the second factor, but in Chapter Twelve Westie does. It is factor number one on which Campbell concentrates his analytic skills.

It seems to me that the explanation quoted from Campbell above is not dissimilar from that tendered by LaPiere in Chapter Two. The only difference lies with the example, LaPiere suggesting that it is considerably different to find oneself face-to-face with a flesh and blood Armenian woman than it is to respond to items on a social distance scale about Armenians. There is a difference between those two examples and their shared explanation, on the one hand, and another example proffered by LaPiere. He suggests that a university professor when questioned about the likelihood of his visiting a French whorehouse during a Parisian tour would undoubtedly offer an honest and emphatic demurral (and I imagine that was true in the thirties if not in the seventies). But, LaPiere asks, how is anyone including the professor himself able to determine how he would in fact behave in Paris (presumably after a few bottles of champagne) when actually confronted with the opportunity? This example poses a problem and suggests an explanation very different from the two ethnic illustrations. It is a kind of situation which suggests that discrepancies or "inconsistencies," although they may sometimes be more apparent than real, can also be very real. We will return to this matter when we consider the relationship between bad company and naughty behavior in Chapter Ten.

Both Campbell and LaPiere explain the "inconsistency" in terms of different definitions of different situations. Then they part company. LaPiere is willing to settle for the word "different" in describing the discrepancy. Campbell adds a value dimension, suggesting that observed differences fall on a continuum which is the result of some choices being "harder" than others. Campbell converts the apparent discrepancy into a "harder" to "easier" scale. Life is full of thresholds: questions that are too hard to answer, situations that are too difficult to face, hurdles that are too high to jump. There is nothing inconsistent about failing to pass these thresholds while simultaneously answering easy questions, facing routine situations, or jumping low hurdles. By this criterion, LaPiere has no evidence of inconsistency. In Campbell's terms, "The fact that 92 per cent of the cases were mediocre in their Sinophilia, having enough to get over the low hurdle but not enough to get over the

---

1. Louis Guttman, "The Cornell Technique for Scale and Intensity Analysis," *Educational and Psychological Measurement* 7 (1947): 247–79; Louis Guttman, "The Problem of Attitude and Opinion Measurement," in Samuel A. Stouffer et al., *Measurement and Prediction* (Princeton: Princeton University Press, 1954), pp. 46–59; Louis Guttman, "The Basis for Scalogram Analysis," ibid., pp. 60–212. There are some scholars who believe that Guttman scaling has been misleading, but the argument is generally in terms of a partisan appeal for factor analysis. This is the position taken by Scarr in his examination of the relationship between an obligation and a hypothetical action. See Harry A. Scarr, "Measures of Particularism," *Sociometry* 27 (1964): 429.

high hurdle, is irrelevant to the problem of inconsistency, but rather speaks only as to the heights of the hurdles."

What is very likely to attract the attention of scientists is the observation of a departure from normal expectations: an inconsistency, an anomaly, an irregularity, an incongruity. These are the kinds of discoveries which create questions worth pursuing. This is the kind of impetus which drove LaPiere through a series of studies to his classic "Attitudes vs. Actions." Consider, in this light, Campbell's pique: "Harding et al. [as well as LaPiere] *are clearly wrong* to conclude that [many of their subjects] are persons 'whose overt behavior provides no clue as to their attitudes,' " (italics added). What Campbell has done is to carry LaPiere's (and Harding's) explanation far enough with the logic of scale analysis that he no longer needs to view the situation as anomalous. He has done his scientific work in clarifying an apparent inconsistency. But those who provided him with his point of departure were in no sense "wrong." They were merely antecedent to Campbell, in one of those rare cumulative sequences in building social science knowledge. Campbell has not removed from the empirical realm the fact observed by his predecessors: people frequently do not act in accord with their sentiments! That empirical fact remains. What is different is that we are now beginning to understand it.

Although the "inconsistency" has been removed in the mind of the scientist (as a result of his understanding it), that same observable "inconsistency" remains in the empirical world. These two facts are hardly incongruent, although a bit of verbal exorcism might illuminate their compatibility: perhaps we should reserve the term *inconsistency* for our preliminary observations of a discrepancy and, upon discovering reasonable explanations, magically alter the reference so that, at that point in the development of knowledge, it becomes, not a pumpkin, but a "difference." Students, including myself, are inclined to see behaviorists and phenomenologists at opposite poles. But this is not always a correct perception. Two self-styled behaviorists provide the same phenomenological interpretation of an "inconsistency" as I have. Kendler and Kendler remark that the terms *consistent* and *inconsistent* "are judgments made by the scientist about the social behavior he observes. . . . They refer to the responses the psychologist makes to the behavior he is observing."[2] The question then becomes, Whose social reality are we talking about?

Part of the vulnerability of Campbell's argument lies in the fact that it is often difficult and sometimes impossible to objectively determine what is "hard" and what is "easy." Although there may be a degree of shared intersubjectivity in the definition of these matters, that consensus can vary from group to group. In short, what is hard and what is easy is not always as clearly defined as it is, say, among questions on a school test. And even there not all students would agree as to which questions are harder than others. In the instance of racial attitudes and behaviors, the hurdles might in fact be reversed! For example, a southern restauranteur (or a northern school superintendent) who sincerely holds an egalitarian ideology can be governed in his behavior by fear of losing his customers (or his job) if he practices what he preaches. It is "hard" for such functionaries to voice prejudice, but it is "easy" for them to turn blacks away from their restaurants or schools.

The possibility of interchangeability of hurdles is also illustrated by Minard's study of Appalachian miners (referred to by Campbell) and Lohman and Reitz-

2. Howard H. Kendler and Tracy S. Kendler, "A Methodological Analysis of the Research Area of Inconsistent Behavior," *Journal of Social Issues* 5 (1949): 27.

es' study of Chicago union men (reprinted in Chapter Ten). Although both of those studies describe men who work under egalitarian conditions while living in discriminatory communities (with norms of the situation governing their relationships with Negroes), it is also conceivable that people may live in an egalitarian community while working under discriminatory conditions (with the norms of the situation still governing their relationship with Negroes). In the latter case, the workers would more likely reject Negroes at work and accept them at home in contrast to the finding of those two studies. The hurdles become reversed.

All of this is not to say that Campbell's logic does not reflect what sometimes happens empirically. One of Linn's subjects tried to explain how such hurdles occurred in his study. Speaking of having her picture taken with a black man, she says, "On the questionnaire it seemed all right but when it came to the real thing, it seemed 'scary.' "[3] The high and low hurdles are clearly identified. Louis Guttman published empirical verification of Campbell's argument four years before that argument was made.[4] Guttman suggests that each different orientation to a given social object (beliefs, norms, anticipatory behavior, overt action) can be regarded as a subuniverse and that the different facets of this subuniverse need to be examined in terms of their interrelationships. To demonstrate his reasoning, Guttman reorders a set of correlation coefficients reported in a study of interracial behavior in Brazil.[5]

The nearly perfect scales which emerge from Guttman's analysis provide empirical verification of Campbell's argument. Using the terms "weak" and "strong" (rather than hard and easy), Guttman reports that

> A common meaning for the ordering can be suggested: they show in each case a progression from a weak to a strong form of behavior of the subject vis-à-vis Negroes. "Belief" is weaker than "overt action" in being passive rather than active. Referring to the behavior of "subject's group" is weaker than the subject referring to "himself," insofar as the subject's relations with Negroes are concerned. "Comparative" behavior is weaker than "interactive" behavior since it does not imply social contact; a comparison is more passive than interaction.
>
> Accepting this interpretation of the orderings within facets, we can say that the ordering of the subuniverses themselves also runs from weakest to strongest. "Stereotype" [belief] is the weakest form of intergroup subuniverse. "Personal Interaction" [overt action] is the strongest form, while the other two subuniverses are intermediate in strength, in the indicated order [norms being weaker than hypothetical interaction].[6]

3. Lawrence Linn, "Verbal Attitudes and Overt Behavior," reprinted in Chapter Four.

4. Louis Guttman, "A Structural Theory for Intergroup Beliefs and Action," *American Sociological Review* 24 (1959): 318–28.

5. Roger Bastide and Pierre van den Berghe, "Stereotypes, Norms, and Interracial Behavior in São Paulo Brazil," *American Sociological Review* 22 (1957): 689–94. Those coefficients are reproduced in Chapter Twelve.

6. Guttman, "A Structural Theory for Intergroup Beliefs and Action," pp. 320–21. Although I have retained his usage of "norms" to refer to "ought" statements, I will generally use the term "value" in reference to such statements, reserving "norm" to refer to statements reflecting the subject's perception of what other people believe. What Guttman refers to as "stereotype" is clearly a personal belief on the part of the subject. Guttman is of course constrained in part by the terminology employed by Bastide and van den Berghe.

The scaling thesis is not the only important point made by Campbell in the brief segment which leads off this chapter. In Chapter Two, Merton was attentive not only to the amount of discrepancy but to its direction, suggesting that among different groups the discrepancy might be in different directions. Campbell is explicitly concerned with the sorting out of two different types of "inconsistency," only one of which he would allow as "real" inconsistency. If we know the order of the hurdles as a result of our scale analysis, then certainly we no longer can think of those who jump low hurdles and miss high ones as "inconsistent." We can, however, take note of the inconsistency of those who jump the high ones while missing the low ones—those who do the hard thing while failing to accomplish the easy one or, in Guttman's terms, those who betray the strongest subuniverse while remaining loyal to the weakest. The matrix which illuminates these two kinds of differences between sentiments and acts, in any area of human behavior, looks like this:

		Expresses Sentiment?	
		Yes	No
Performs Act?	Yes	X_1	Y_2
	No	Y_1	X_2

The two X cells are easily recognizable as consistent ones. In X_1, people who express an affirmative sentiment ("I think white men are groovy") can be observed performing concordant acts (grooving with white men). In X_2, people who express a negative sentiment ("I think white men are dangerous") can be observed performing concordant acts (avoiding white men). Although these two cells share the virtue of concordance or consistency, we recognize that they represent radically different empirical phenomena. What we sometimes fail to recognize is that the same is true of the two Y cells. In the case of Y_1, we have Merton's example of the Northerner who talks a good line about racial equality while practicing discrimination. In the case of Y_2, we have his example of the Southerner who mouths prejudice while practicing less discrimination than his Northern counterpart. I choose this example from Merton's discussion deliberately because it illustrates again that there are limits to the application of Campbell's logic (there is nothing wrong with the logic itself). When we have our hurdles properly ordered, we may comfortably discard one of the Y cells as involving no inconsistency. But, in other cases we must stop short by simply recognizing that the two Y cells represent very different kinds of inconsistency. Which of Merton's two Y cases is a "real" inconsistency and which is spurious?

The identification of different kinds of orientations to a social object and their clear delineation from one another is a first essential step in the solution of our conceptual problem. The extent to which and the manner in which those orientations relate to one another is the next step. This is the problem addressed in Chapter Twelve. It was first broached by Ajzen et al. in Chapter Five. In their Table 1, they sort out attitude toward an object from "behavior" and both of these from "behavioral intention." They suggest that differences in the findings of the three studies considered may be attributable to differences among these three types of orientations since they are not uniformly tapped by all three studies. Such a question must remain unanswered until we know something about the relationship among these three orientations. If any two of them are highly correlated, then we may assume that they are interchangeable for analytic purposes. If they are not correlated or if they are negatively correlated then we can assume no such thing. If they scale, as Campbell and Guttman suggest they may, then we can determine one from the others within reasonable limits. These are matters which we will consider further in Chapter Twelve.

Before leaving Campbell's illuminating suggestion that apparent inconsistencies may dissolve if we examine them properly, it may be equally illuminating to consider the reverse of that situation. If some *apparent inconsistencies* can be explained in this manner, we ought to be sensitive to the possibility that some *apparent consistencies* may obscure real, underlying inconsistencies. That we can sometimes be deceived by apparent uniformity is illustrated by Donald Roy's study of a machine shop. This is the same research which Julius Roth puts to work in Chapter Six.[7] A naive observer (perhaps a time-and-motion-study man) examining the behavior of Roy's machine-shop workers would note that frequently they do not appear to be doing anything. They smoke, they horse around, they hang out in the lavatory, they gossip around their machines, etc. A somewhat more sophisticated observer might note that the men refer to the jobs they are doing at such times as "stinkers" or as "gravy." An even more meticulous observer would consider that these two words, referring to jobs which the men appear to neglect in the same manner, are not synonyms, but antonyms.

It takes a participant observer like Roy to come to recognize how these names are used to designate different kinds of jobs and how those designations, in turn, have different consequences—in spite of the apparent similarity of the workers' behavior. They do indeed loaf on a "stinker" job. They do so because the job is so difficult that no matter how hard they work, they figure they cannot exceed their minimum day's wages anyway: so, why bother to work at all? The consequence of such a definition is that the day's production quota is not nearly met. A "gravy" job, on the other hand, is one where the men do not work most of the day because it is so easy that they can make what they consider to be a reasonable day's maximum in a few hours. These two different definitions, resulting in apparently similar behavior, have two very different consequences for production. The lesson is that we ought to suspect apparent consistency as much as we suspect apparent inconsistency.

Methodology as Theory: Are Observed Inconsistencies More Apparent Than Real?

There are other, somewhat less methodological and more technical, efforts to explain observed inconsistencies between sentiments and acts as artifacts of how we do our research. Since these do in fact explain some of what, up to this point, we have thought of as "discrepancy," they are actually partial *theories*. They illuminate in part our understanding of the relationship between what people say and what they do. It is in this sense that methodology becomes theory. In attempting to order the observations made by contributors to a collection of papers he has edited, Chein

7. Donald Roy, "Quota Restriction and Goldbricking in a Machine Shop," *American Journal of Sociology* 57 (1952): 427–42.

makes a distinction between "surface inconsistency" and "real inconsistency." The former, which at the beginning "looks like an inconsistency no longer seems to be one when we get to know enough about what is going on; the inconsistency vanishes under adequate inspection."[8] I take Campbell's analysis to be an example of how to dissolve such apparent inconsistency. Chein's point in making the distinction is that in properly identifying a surface inconsistency as such, "we have in the very process of doing so, resolved it. . . ." This argument encompasses not only the pure methodological reasoning of Campbell and Guttman, but also, and at the other extreme, the process of doing badly what we ought to know how to do well. In its most candid form, this suggests that some research is simply incompetent technically, and thus its findings need to be completely discounted. Observed differences may be more apparent than real, then, because they are spurious artifacts of improper research technique.

Tittle and Hill provide a comparative analysis of fifteen studies of attitude and behavior, many of which have been mentioned in this volume. One of the bases for their classification is the type of attitude measure used. Their analysis shows a clear relationship between the kind of measure and the kind of resulting relationship between attitudes and behaviors.[9] They then proceed to report their own study of voting attitudes and behaviors which incorporates four different types of attitude measure (Likert, Guttman, Thurstone, and Semantic Differential): "The degree of interrelationships of the several attitude measures varied considerably. . . . This points up the fact that various methods of measuring the same characteristic may result in the ordering of individuals quite differently. Presumably the variation is accounted for by error factors intrinsic to the measurement techniques."[10] They believe that their data show that the degree of correspondence observed between attitude and behavior is partly a function of the techniques employed. Howard Ehrlich carries this argument from the measurement of attitudes to the measurement of behaviors.

Ehrlich argues in his contribution to Chapter Eleven that one of the technical difficulties lies in an inconsistency in the developmental stage of our measurement techniques. "While the operations for attitude scale construction are relatively well standardized, the operations for observing and recording behavior, particularly in natural settings, are generally unstandardized. . . ."[11] In the opening section of their contribution to Chapter Four, DeFleur and Westie make the same point. Ehrlich continues with the observation that "while the items of attitude scales are presumably a representative set of statements from the attitude domain studies, most behavioral units selected for study have been chosen on a nonsystematic or *ad hoc* basis."[12] Ehrlich concludes that at least some of the observed discrepancies can be attributed to the differential rigor in measurement of the two dimensions. It would,

8. Isador Chein, "The Problems of Inconsistency: A Restatement," *Journal of Social Issues* 5 (1949): 53–54.

9. Charles R. Tittle and Richard J. Hill, "Attitude Measurement and Prediction of Behavior: An Evaluation of Conditions and Measurement Techniques," *Sociometry* 30 (1967); see especially Table 1, p. 203.

10. Ibid., p. 208.

11. Howard J. Ehrlich, "Attitudes, Behavior, and the Intervening Variables," *American Sociologist* 4 (1969): 29 (reprinted in Chapter Eleven of this volume).

12. Ibid.

however, seem a reasonable extension of this logic to suggest that some of the research which reports consistency between sentiments and acts needs also to be discounted on the same grounds. Actually, Ehrlich believes that the attitude dimension is also sorely wanting in that it "has been demonstrated to be seriously imprecise and unreliable." His conclusion on methodological grounds is that we need to suspend judgment regarding the relationship between attitudes and acts. When he completes the double screen, by considering the conceptual problem, he concludes that our knowledge in this area is "untenable." Ehrlich screens out everything, but does leave us with some hopeful suggestions for new directions in research. Most of his paper focuses on the problem of what's in between attitudes and behaviors. We shall return to that subject and to Ehrlich's recommendations in Chapter Eleven.

The state of the art, technical incompetence, or other method-related factors, can be used to discredit any research of which one may disapprove or with which one may disagree. A capable critic can find serious shortcomings in even the best of research and this is not an uncommon device in efforts to support the contention that there is or is not a certain kind of prevailing relationship between sentiments and acts. Clearly, such criticism is necessary and appropriate and much of Part II of this volume has concentrated on alerting the student to certain bases for judging the procedural soundness of research in this area. But the argument that research findings are methodological artifacts can also be a cop-out. It is true that those reports that are utterly incredible do not tell us anything. It is equally true that few studies fall in that category. In the closing section of Chapter Eight, I suggested that there is a peculiar mathematics involved in adding the results of weak studies. Rather than a simple addition of weakness piled on weakness, the mathematics is more nearly analogous to the logic of the solution of simultaneous equations where unknown variables are identified by using sets of equations, none of which permits the identification by itself. The coupling of different kinds of incredibility may provide credible conclusions, for the strengths of one may indeed be the weakness of the other.

Campbell is right. Some kinds of observed discrepancies between sentiments and acts can be understood as matters of degree in terms of the logic of scaling. It would be a mistake, however, to assume that this represents a complete or satisfactory solution to the problem. In Part III we shall learn not only that many discrepancies of the type noted in Chapter Three may be very real, but we shall also consider why this is so.

PART THREE

Theory: A Hatful of Explanations

10 The Social Situation:

Does Bad Company Cause Naughty Behavior?

Public and Private Opinion

In Chapter Six we considered some of the methodological literature in survey research. That literature suggests that the mix between interviewer and respondent can effect the outcome of the interview: people talk differently to people of other races, other ages, and other sexes than themselves. They do not necessarily lie when not speaking with their own kind. It is more precise to say that their perspectives, their definitions of the situation, shift ever so subtly as the relationship between interviewer and interviewee is varied. It appears that people express different opinions depending on who is asking and under what conditions. We have opinions we express in private and they are not necessarily the same as those we express in public. Furthermore, the opinion we express in one public is not necessarily the same as that we express in a different public.[1] When we examine field and laboratory observations of overt behavior or action, this same kind of variation persists. This is suggested in our discussion of methods in Chapters Seven and Eight. Part II, then, serves as a springboard for the thesis developed here. In this chapter we will document some of the polemical aspects of the earlier methodological discussions and pursue further the differences between sentiments and acts displayed under different conditions.

In Part I, we considered such old saws as "actions speak louder than words," "the proof of the pudding is in the eating," "put your money where your mouth is," etc. Let us now consider another kind of conventional wisdom. While working as a part-time juvenile probation officer, I was impressed by the frequency

---

1. In fact, what I sometimes refer to as "private opinion" is no more than an opinion expressed in a more restricted public (e.g., in an interview, in the family, among close friends, in the executive suite, "just between us girls," among the president's advisors, etc.). Although I will continue to employ the term "private opinion" for rhetorical purposes, it should be clear that what is usually referred to is an opinion expressed in those publics which members of a society define as "in private." An authentic "private opinion" would be one never shared — never spoken or acted upon — and therefore of no social consequence. My usage is consistent with that employed in some of the recent research reviewed in Chapter Eleven. Current investigators make the distinction between private and public on the grounds of threatened "disclosure" of the opinion to significant others.

with which parents insisted that their boys were really good boys, but had gotten in with the wrong crowd; other boys—bad ones—had led their youngsters astray. Juvenile judges shared the premise of evil companions. Conditions of probation and parole inevitably prohibit association with certain categories of people. Contact with known criminals is sufficient grounds for the revocation of adult parole. Most impressive was the juvenile judge's great reluctance to use an important legal correctional option always available to him. He would institutionalize a boy only as a last resort *because* of the kinds of naughty boys with which this would throw him into close and continuing contact.

I suspect that most of us have experienced the application of this kind of conventional wisdom at the hands of "understanding" parents, friends, or associates. At a time when I was directing an interdisciplinary social science organization and had behaved in a manner frowned upon by the administration, a university vice-president shook his head sympathetically, and said, "Surrounded by the kind of staff you have, I can understand how you would be influenced." I have always regretted not having had the presence of mind to respond in kind. Such popular notions seem to suggest an ignorance of the importance attributed by psychologists, sociologists, and anthropologists to the behavioral constraints imposed by "personality," "social structure," and "culture." Such concepts suggest relatively stable forces built up over a long period of time which constrain people to talk and to act and to think in certain ways. Except for a few "deviants," these same forces compel us not to talk or think or act in other ways. Conventional wisdom, then, does not seem in accord with social-scientific knowledge. My interest in the folk knowledge of parents, judges, and university vice-presidents is derived from the general concern of this book: How come people talk or act one way at one time and then talk or act another way at another time? Could it be that they find themselves thrust among evil companions at one time, while being immersed in good company at another? Let us consider the evidence.

Evidence can be derived from a variety of independent sources. If there is one common feature in all of the American community studies—from Middletown, to Yankee City, to Elmtown—it is the finding that people vary their opinions and their actions with the context in which they are observed. Recall Warriner's study of a small Kansas community (Chapter Three). He observes, on the one hand, a public affirmation of what he terms "official morality," i.e., it is wrong to drink alcoholic beverages. On the other hand, he finds that "the majority did not feel that there was anything wrong with moderate drinking." A decade later wide variations in public and private morality in another small Kansas community are reported by Wayne Wheeler.[2] It is important to note, in view of our discussion of methodology as theory in Chapter Nine, a reminder provided by Warriner: "In most studies such an inconsistency is explained away by searching for some bias in the observational technique or by looking for some coercive, 'distorting' factor in the milieu."

Warriner's insistence that the inconsistency is not a methodological artifact is crucial. He is suggesting that the findings are not distorted by the instruments. Instead, peoples' views are distorted by their interpretation of the situation in which those views are called forth. A man can publicly support public morality by

2. Wayne Wheeler, "Backstage With Swedeholm's Youth," *Review of Religious Research* 5 (1963): 1–5.

advocating prohibition and at the same time approve of drinking in the limited circle of his friends. Both of these sentiments are real in that social situations occur repeatedly in which they are expressed and both are followed by consistent action: the same man votes for prohibition and consumes alcohol at home. Although these two acts appear inconsistent with each other, they are perfectly consistent with that man's public opinions vis-à-vis the two different publics to which they refer: his circle of close acquaintances and "people in general." The only way we ever learn this man's private opinion is through his response to a perfect interviewer, with a perfect questionnaire, in a perfect interviewing situation. But for what purpose would we want to elicit this private opinion? The respondent's real opinions are those which are manifested in the real situations in which he finds himself.

The irrelevance of private attitudes for conduct is documented in Stanton Wheeler's study at a reformatory for male felons. His data suggest considerable private support among inmates for conventional values. But this support is not acted upon. In like manner, custodial officers reveal private opinions which are more like those of inmates than the inmates perceive them to be. Inmates are in constant contact with one another and feel the need to conform to what they believe the expectations of others to be:

> Thus, the inmate is under pressure to conform to the expectations he perceives other inmates to hold. His perception of group opinion rather than his private feelings should serve as a model for overt conduct. So long as he perceives most inmates to be opposed to staff norms, his public behavior is likely to take the form of a conspicuous show of hostility toward the staff.[3]

The degree of influence persons in an interaction situation will be able to exercise is subtly altered by the actor's definitions of those other persons. Miller et al. report a study suggesting that perceived ability of others to reward has a greater effect on the actor's behavior than comparative perceptions of the ability of others to punish.[4] It is little wonder then, that prisoners should be more influenced by their comrades than by the guards. That the power of others in the situation is related to their influence is also evidenced by a study reporting the offense rates of military trainees to be related to the offense rates of their immediate superiors.[5] A further bit of evidence is provided by Stephen Cole who documents the crucial influence of colleagues in the decisions of teachers to involve themselves in a strike.[6] The volatility of sentiments — their vulnerability to external influences — is documented in a final illustration from an attitude experiment conducted by a pair of psychologists. Everything in their two trials is exactly the same, except the designation of the sponsor. In one case, subjects are informed that the sponsor is "The Institute for Propaganda Effects"; in the other, the sponsor is identified as "The Institute for the Study of Communication and Information Processing." Silverman and Shulman report

3. Stanton Wheeler, "Role Conflict in Correctional Institutions," in *The Prison*, ed. Donald R. Cressey (New York: Holt, Rinehart and Winston, 1961), pp. 229–59.

4. Norman Miller, Donald C. Butler, and James A. McMartin, "The Ineffectiveness of Punishment Power in Group Interaction," *Sociometry* 32 (1960): 24–41.

5. John P. Hymes and Sheldon Blackman, "Situational Variables in Socially Deviant Behavior," *Journal of Social Psychology* 65 (1965): 149–53.

6. Stephen Cole, "Teacher's Strike: A Study of the Conversion of Predisposition into Action," *American Journal of Sociology* 74 (1969): 506–20.

"highly significant differences in attitude change scores" resulting from the change in sponsor designation.[7] Although less dramatic, Milgram finds a similar effect when he shifts sponsorship from Yale University to the deliberately shabby surroundings of the "Research Associates of Bridgeport." Full obedience of the experimenter's commands drops from 65 percent to 48 percent of subjects under this condition.[8]

The ease with which people in a complex society can hold contradictory sentiments in insulated compartments, with no manifestations of dissonance or anomie, has been observed by field researchers among widely diverse publics. Robert Coles combines longitudinal observations with informal interviewing, visiting his subjects' homes "week after week, until it has come to pass that I have known certain families for many years." Coles' families describe themselves as George Wallace's "average man on the street." Let them speak for themselves:

> Sometimes I'd like to tell every colored person I see to go back to Africa. Half of them are on welfare. They don't want to work. Their kids steal. Meanwhile, those fancy rich people and the college professor crowd go slumming and pat on the head every colored kid they see. . . . Sometimes I wonder what's happening to this country. When I was a kid we had this terrible Depression. Well, now we're better off—or are we? . . . I believe this country is made for the rich. The tax laws are written for them, and they hire those high-priced lawyers who can get you out of anything. It's the little guy who suffers; it's the little guy who works like a dog and keeps the country going. I'll tell you, I feel sorry for the colored person. They've had an awful time in this country. Sometimes I wonder how I'd feel if I was colored. Sometimes I stop and think: They do the dirty work in this country—just like I do [ellipses in original].[9]

So much for race and poverty, but as Coles shows, those who call themselves "hawks" on the Vietnam war can be as tormented by that war as any "dove." He reports a conversation with a factory worker a few days after the funeral of his son who had been killed in the war:

> How are we to make sense of this? I read in the paper that a lot of our best people—the college students, the professors, and the doctors and the lawyers—I read they are against the war. . . . But it's our kids who go off and die. It's up to my sons to fight. It's people like us who bail the country out of its messes. We have to lose our sons because Presidents and their clever-type advisers make mistakes and aren't honest enough to admit it. I hate this war. The sooner it ends, the better. But I hate the people who spit at the flag and insult the country. I ask you: how can a man believe that his son's life was wasted? The people I see on television knocking this country don't have to ask themselves a question like that [ellipses in original].[10]

7. Irwin Silverman and Arthur D. Shulman, "A Conceptual Model of Artifact in Attitude Change Studies," *Sociometry* 33 (1970): 97–107.

8. Stanley Milgram, "Some Conditions of Obedience and Disobedience to Authority," *International Journal of Psychiatry* 6 (1968): 270–72.

9. Robert Coles, "The 'Average Man' Might Fool You," *Life*, 7 May 1971, p. 4. This magazine fragment is from a book by Coles and Jon Erikson entitled *The Middle Americans* (Boston: Little, Brown and Co., 1971).

10. Ibid.

Kriesberg describes such compartmentalization among steel distributors who participated in the gray market during the Korean War. "All of the men in the gray market agreed with the government that national security was a prime consideration and the nation faced a dangerous threat to its security." According to Kriesberg, some of these men neatly sort their evaluations into one compartment and their conduct into another:

> Inconsistencies are not perceived, and if they are pointed out, the rejoinder is, 'that's too deep for me.' However, this shifting of perspectives from context to context cannot be regarded only as a way of escaping from the strain of conflicting obligations. The same inconsistencies, vagaries, and compartmentalizations are to be found among those who did not engage in activities they felt were condemned by the government.[11]

Both Coles and Kreisberg imply that compartmentalization occurs all of the time. People compartmentalize consistent as well as inconsistent fragments of their social lives. It is a normal process to hold diverse opinions about an object—some of which may be contradictory. This must certainly be true of French Catholic Communist workers as revealed in Lipset's description of their voting behavior.[12] In my own research with student nurses, I was impressed by their ability to simultaneously assimilate the cold impersonal professional orientation and the warm, personal, helping orientation. Montague and I found compartmentalization to be "more common than the acceptance of one set of institutional values and the rejection of the other."[13]

In an abortive attempt to measure the extent of opposition to fair housing legislation, Rose found so much inconsistency in response that he was forced to abandon the effort: "The chief finding that emerged from our questioning was that we could not, in fact, measure the extent of the opposition, as we got almost as many different results as we had approaches to the question."[14] He observes that "a given individual may hold a number of attitudes toward the same object, perhaps applicable to different segments, but logically incompatible if they should be confronted with each other in the same setting." The most significant finding that emerged from this study, according to Rose, was that most of the expressed attitudes were contradicted by other expressed attitudes or by reports of behavior. Westie, in his contribution to Chapter Twelve, reports considerable inconsistency among Americans who voice agreement with the values of the American Creed but are inclined to devalue blacks when situations are specified. Among the types of resolutions of this contradiction is compartmentalization. Westie's interviewers took special note of inconsistent responses and probed respondents unmercifully about them: "Of the 293 inconsistencies noted, respondents admitted approximately 42 per cent . . . and recognized but denied about the same number. . . . Nearly 16 per

---

11. Louis Kriesberg, "National Security and Conduct in the Steel Gray Market," *Social Forces* 34 (1956): 274.

12. S. M. Lipset, "Democracy and Working-Class Authoritarianism," *American Sociological Review* 24 (1959): 482–501.

13. Irwin Deutscher and Ann Montague, "Professional Education and Conflicting Value Systems: The Role of Religious Schools in the Educational Aspirations of Nursing Students," *Social Forces* 35 (1956): 126–31.

14. Arnold M. Rose, "Inconsistencies in Attitudes Toward Negro Housing," *Social Problems* 8 (1961): 286–92.

cent of the inconsistencies remained unseen even after extensive probing." Perhaps of even greater importance is the fact that about a quarter of the explanations elicited in this manner, were *explanations of consistencies!* The compartmentalization observed by Westie involves a conscious disconnection of the apparently inconsistent sentiments; like Kriesberg's gray marketeers, people are aware of them but see no relationship.[15]

The two classic field studies of compartmentalization are those by Minard[16] and by Lohman and Reitzes. The following study by Lohman and Reitzes helps explain the difficulty Arnold Rose reports in his open-housing research. Like Minard, Lohman and Reitzes demonstrate empirically the manner in which the situation is defined differently for the same individuals in different settings — at home and at work. Their data suggest that white union members can be egalitarian and accepting of blacks at work while simultaneously exhibiting prejudice and rejection of blacks in their neighborhood: "The majority of the individuals studied were consistent in exhibiting what appeared to be an ambiguous and contradictory pattern in their identification with both the community and the union with regard to the race relations pattern." Those who persist in ignoring the locale in which an interview takes place or a questionnaire is filled in, ought to consider these findings.

15. Another type of resolution identified by Westie is "repression," which is distinguished from compartmentalization on the basis of awareness or consciousness. For my purposes, the distinction is not necessary; both types are compartmentalization.

16. R. D. Minard, "Race Relationships in the Pocahontas Coal Field," *Journal of Social Issues* 8 (1952): 29–44.

DATA:
Deliberately Organized Groups and Racial Behavior
JOSEPH D. LOHMAN / DIETRICH C. REITZES

This paper analyzes race relations in a neighborhood situation of a large city. The analysis is centered on the deliberately organized collectivities of the neighborhood and the role of these collectivities in mobilizing individuals and in providing a framework for action.

The observed actions, of a sample of 151 residents of the neighborhood toward Negroes as neighbors, were analyzed. This analysis was made in relation to an intensive background study of the neighborhood itself. The 151 individuals within the neighborhood selected for study were all members of a labor union with a clear, implemented policy of granting Negroes complete equality on the job. The neighborhood in which they were residents and of which they were an organic part, however, was strongly anti-Negro with respect to the movement of Negroes into the neighborhood. The majority of the individuals studied were con-

"Deliberately Organized Groups and Racial Behavior," by Joseph D. Lohman and Dietrich C. Reitzes, from *American Sociological Review*, vol. 19 (1954), pp. 342–48. Reprinted by permission of Dietrich C. Reitzes and the American Sociological Association.

sistent in exhibiting what appeared to be an ambiguous and contradictory pattern in their identification with both the community and the union with regard to the race relations pattern.

It follows that this individual behavior cannot be understood in terms of individual attitudes in either case but does become intelligible when examined in the perspective of deliberately organized groups. Seen against the background of the organizational structuring of the individuals as members of the neighborhood group and on the other hand as members of an organized work group (union) this seemingly paradoxical behavior becomes understandable.

The study of the neighborhood indicated that in the center of the organizational pattern of the community was the deliberately organized property owners' association, called the Civic Club. This Civic Club can be considered a key factor in explaining the action of individuals toward Negroes as neighbors.

The role of the Civic Club is indicated by the following comment made by its president: "Now we generally don't talk about that freely, but actually the main purpose of the club is to keep up the bar against the colored element moving in here. That was the purpose when it was first organized and that is still the purpose today." This was further substantiated by the club's secretary-treasurer who had been in office for about twenty years and controlled the club thoroughly. He said: "Of course we are interested in keeping this community white. We are not intolerant but just like to protect our homes and interests. We have had several intrusions but all of them have been eliminated by direct action of the club."

The Civic Club represented itself as the voice of the people of the community. In letters to officials and newspapers the club always purported to represent and express the sentiments of *all* the inhabitants. This claim, however, was unfounded. It is more accurate to state that the club formulated the sentiments and gave direction to the actions of a large portion of the population on certain issues, namely those dealing with the residential neighborhood.

The community had a population of about 10,000. During the years 1946–49 the club had a paid membership of about 300 families. Attendance records showed, however, that a very small proportion of the members actually attended meetings. At two meetings the attendance was 75 persons, at two meetings it was between 40 and 49, at twenty-seven meetings it was between 30 and 39, at eight meetings between 20 and 29, and at five meetings the attendance was below 20 persons. Furthermore the club was actually controlled by a small clique. This clique formulated club policies, drew up resolutions, and acted in the name of the club.

The operations of the club must be understood on two levels: the direct actions of the club, and the actions of the club in influencing the activities of other community organizations where Negroes were involved.

On the first level the club acted directly to prevent Negroes from moving into the neighborhood. As the president stated: "People here know that we exist and they will turn to us as soon as a problem comes up — it gives them a feeling of security to know that the club is there." Another official stated: "Let something happen and they come running to us. Let one Negro move within ten blocks, and they come saying to us, 'What are you going to do about it?' 'Why did you let this happen?' "

Even more important is the second level of activity. As far as the Negro question is concerned, there was general agreement among people who are familiar with the community that the Civic Club intentionally provided the initiative for all other community organizations. One of the board members indicated in an interview that the club made a definite effort to have the key people of the various other organizations as active members and officers. A detailed study of the active members of the club revealed that the Civic Club had been successful in establishing ties with all the other community organizations. Consequently the influence of the club was actually greater than is indicated by its actual membership. By being in the center of the organizational structure of the community, the club was able to define and structure any situation which involved Negroes as neighbors.

Through this organizational structuring and definition the Civic Club was able to mobilize individuals in terms of the specific interests of the individuals in the situation. In the community situation these interests centered around property values and social acceptance. The Civic Club's definition of the situation — rejection of Negroes as neighbors — provided the individual with well formulated statements, reasons, and justification for specific actions in specific situations involving the individual's interests in the neighborhood stiuation.

The same individual in a different context, for example, at work, with a corresponding organizational structuring of the specific situation, acts in terms of this definition of the situation by another deliberately organized collectivity. In neither case does the individual act out any abstract generalized attitudes toward Negroes, which could become important only when the deliberate definition is absent. In modern society, however, the major and significant areas of social life, namely those centered around jobs, business and the community, are increasingly characterized by the presence of organized interest groups.

The interviews indicated the validity of the above approach. We selected for interviews 151 industrial workers who lived in the neighborhood studied and who belonged to the union studied. Their names and addresses were obtained from the union files. Two locals of the union were involved. In the case of one local we interviewed all the members who lived in the neighborhood. In the case of the other local a union staff member selected a random sample for us. We attempted to interview all individuals whose addresses we obtained. One hundred and fifty-one interviews were actually conducted. In 51 cases we were either unable to locate the person or unable to obtain an interview. A detailed study of these 51 cases did not disclose anything that would indicate that they were significantly different from the interviewed group.

After the interviews were completed we extracted from each interview all available information relating to the person's involvement in the community, his rejection of Negroes in the community, his identification with the union and his acceptance of Negroes on the job. Each case was then judged "high," "medium," or "low" in each of these areas. We then constructed tables to indicate the association between these areas.

Three tables and a list of criteria used in making the judgments accompany this paper. Table 1 indicates a significant association between involvement in the neighborhood and rejection of Negroes in the neighborhood. Table 2 indicates a significant association between identification with the union and acceptance of Negroes on the job. Table 3 indicates no association between rejection of Negroes in the neighborhood and acceptance of Negroes on the job.

TABLE 1. RELATIONSHIP BETWEEN INVOLVEMENT IN COLLECTIVE EXISTENCE OF THE NEIGHBORHOOD AND REJECTION OF NEGROES IN NEIGHBORHOOD*

Rejection of Negroes in Neighborhood	Involvement in the Collective Existence of the Neighborhood			
	High	Medium	Low	Total
High	56	9	3	68
Medium	8	36	18	62
Low	1	8	12	21
Total	65	53	33	151

Chi-square = 79.90
T = .41

*Criteria for judging involvement of individual in the collective existence of the neighborhood.

The major consideration in judging an individual in this area is the degree to which he is exposed to the collective existence of the neighborhood. The following factors should be taken into consideration: (1) Expression of likes or dislikes for the community and reasons; (2) Length of time lived in neighborhood; (3) Community newspapers read and evaluation of them; (4) Membership in organizations, frequency of attendance, leadership positions held; (5) Church attendance and membership in church organizations, frequency of attendance, leadership positions held; (6) Knowledge of community organizations, particularly of the Civic Club; (7) Informal social contacts of the individual in neighborhood, social clubs, friends in neighborhood, relationship with neighbors; (8) Home ownership.

Guides for judgment

High: Indication of high degree of involvement with neighborhood and receptiveness of individual to collective influences of neighborhood. This involvement can be through a number of the above factors or through a few intensive contacts.

Medium: Mild involvement indicated by few contacts or by lack of interest in neighborhood.

Low: Indications of indifference to what goes on in neighborhood by having minimum contacts; or indications that interests are definitely outside neighborhood.

Criteria for judging rejection of Negroes in neighborhood by individuals (guides for judgment).

High: Very strong expression of rejection of Negroes as neighbors and listing of reasons for rejection, such as: property values drop, crime increases, Negroes are dirty, Negroes are diseased, Negroes are lazy; accompanied by indication that individual is favorably inclined toward some action to keep Negroes out of neighborhood.

Medium: Expressed rejection of Negroes but vague as to reasons for it.

Low: Indifference to the presence of Negroes in neighborhood or acceptance of Negroes in neighborhood.

The major consideration in judging an individual in this area, is the individual's degree of involvement in union activities. The following factors should be taken into consideration: (1) (a) If the individual began work about 1942 — time interval between starting to work and joining union; (b) If the individual began to work before 1942—time interval between 1942 and joining the union; (2) Reasons given by individual for joining the union; (3) Expression of feeling that union has helped him; specific instances of help; (4) Attendance at meetings; (5) Offices held; (6) Expression of satisfaction or dissatisfaction with union and reasons. (In view of the clearly defined union position in regard to Negroes, an individual's dissatisfaction because he considers the union weak, should influence a high rating, as opposed to a lower rating for dissatisfaction with the union because it interferes with the individual's freedom of activity.)

Guides for judgment

High: Indication of strong involvement in union activities and receptiveness of the individual to the union's definition of the situation. Particularly important would be strong feeling that union has been helpful and ability to give specific instances of help.

Medium: Indications of moderate involvement in union activities—qualified approval of union, moderate feeling that union has been helpful.

Low: Indications of indifference or rejection of union. Denial that union has been helpful.

Criteria for judging acceptance of Negroes in work situation (guides for judgment).

High: Positive statement in regard to Negroes in work situation—in the plant and in the union.

Medium: Passive acceptance of Negroes in work situation—expression of sentiment that nothing can be done about Negro workers combined with absence of strong anti-Negro statements.

Low: Strong anti-Negro statements and suggestions that Negroes should be removed.

TABLE 2. **RELATIONSHIP BETWEEN INVOLVEMENT IN UNION ACTIVITIES AND ACCEPTANCE OF NEGROES AT WORK***

Acceptance of Negroes at Work	Involvement in Union Activities			
	High	Medium	Low	Total
High	45	19	2	66
Medium	7	47	13	67
Low	0	6	12	18
Total	52	72	27	151

Chi-square = 86.45
T = .53

*Criteria for judging involvement in union activities.

TABLE 3. **RELATIONSHIP BETWEEN REJECTION OF NEGROES IN NEIGHBORHOOD AND ACCEPTANCE OF NEGROES AT WORK**

Acceptance of Negroes at Work	Rejection of Negroes in Neighborhood			
	High	Medium	Low	Total
High	31	25	10	66
Medium	26	32	9	67
Low	11	5	2	18
Total	68	62	21	151

Public and Private Opinion (Continued)

At the end of Part II, I pointed out the apparently anomalous perspective of two rather extreme behaviorists who remind us that consistency is a creature of scientists and has no relation to how the man in the street may perceive the situation.[17] The evidence does suggest that this is frequently the case. This is also a central theme of the ethnomethodological argument. On this issue the extremes of positivism and phenomenology seem to meet (and that is convergence worth noting!). Jack Douglas, for example, builds on Harold Garfinkel's position that

> . . . sociologists and other outsiders often see social actions as involving moral conflict because they assume the actors are (or *should* be) attending to certain abstract morals in a "rational" way, whereas there are generally understood, situated meanings or common-sense criteria of rationality specifying the appropriate processes of inference. However, it is also most important to note that most of us live highly compartmentalized moral lives: we have *situated moral and other meanings* for many different types of situations and feel relatively little need to relate the situations to each other via abstract meanings.[18]

Although the behaviorists say it more clearly and succinctly, the argument is the same and, more important, it is made on the same grounds. Despite the cautionary lessons proposed in Part II, such inconsistencies are not to be easily dismissed as reflecting deception on the part of respondents or technical inefficiency on the part of our instruments. Anticipating both the behaviorists and the ethnomethodologists by several decades, Robert Merton observed that internal tests of consistency assume rationality—that people never really hold inconsistent attitudes—and he concludes that "in making this assumption, the investigator is using *norms* of logic, not *facts* of sociology" (see Merton, Chapter Two).

I do not mean to imply that people holding discordant views or behaving in ways other than their verbalizations indicate are always able to mobilize so neat a psychological separater as compartmentalization. To the contrary, this situation, when the person is confronted with it, can create considerable stress. The convergence of Gorden's findings with those of Raven was discussed toward the close of Chapter Eight. Gorden's study of members of a cooperative rooming house reveals the stress which people undergo when they feel constrained to modify private opinions (i.e., previously elicited in an anonymous interview) in the presence of their fellow co-op members. Gorden notes "an acute awareness of the presence of the other members of the group when they are asked to express their opinion. Confused efforts to appear nonchalant, efforts to escape the situation, and attempts to prevent others from hearing one's response are all telltale signs of the awareness of pressure.[19] Nevertheless, these individuals did tend to alter their private opinions to conform to their conception of the group norm when giving their public opinion.

17. Howard H. Kendler and Tracy S. Kendler, "A Methodological Analysis of the Research Area of Inconsistent Behavior," *Journal of Social Issues* 5 (1949): 28.

18. Jack D. Douglas, "The General Theoretical Implications of the Sociology of Deviance," in *Theoretical Sociology: Perspectives and Developments* (New York: Appleton-Century-Crofts, 1972).

19. Raymond L. Gorden, "Interaction Between Attitude and the Definition of the Situation in the Expression of Opinion," *American Sociological Review* 17 (1952): 50–58.

Milgram reports much the same kind of reaction when his laboratory subjects find themselves behaving in ways contrary to their beliefs: "Persons were observed to sweat, tremble, stutter, bite their lips, and groan as they found themselves increasingly implicated in the experimental conflict."[20] In that paper Milgram describes an "obedient" subject who consistently insists that he will not hurt the victim and he will not continue, yet while talking in this manner, he proceeded to the highest shock level on the generator: "He displayed a curious dissociation between word and action."[21] In their own way, these studies by Gorden, Raven, and Milgram parallel the findings of Wheeler in his work on committed felons.[22] The major difference is that the former set of investigators induce stress by entrapment of their subjects. Wheeler, on the other hand, demonstrates how stress is avoided by conformity to perceived expectations and suppression of private opinions.

Even under the deliberately designed conditions of fantasy characteristic of controlled experiments, there is no evidence that attitude, or opinion, or behavior remain stable through time or under changing conditions.[23] These experiments are so designed that their results can be interpreted as evidence that people react almost immediately to adapt themselves to perceived social constraints. The only conclusion I can draw from this body of literature is that, like the sociological field studies and the methodological investigations in survey research, it suggests that actors can harbor real attitudes which can be contravened in such a way that within a short period of time they become different—although still "real"—as a consequence of redefinitions of the situation by the actor. Much of this psychological research is concerned with the concept of "compliance" and is designed to investigate compliant behavior. Some of Kelman's earlier work and later investigations by Goldstein and McGinnies provide examples.[24] That the effect of group pressure toward conformity in the experimental situation rapidly erodes—presumably as a consequence of exposure to other groups and other pressures—has also been documented.[25] This provides convergence of experimental observations with field observations such as those by Lohman and Reitzes.

Some of the laboratory experiments have been designed to study the consequences of group pressures on behavior as well as on opinion change. Among these a few have even managed to create experimental situations involving relatively meaningful behavior. Such studies clearly demonstrate that private opinion has nothing to do with overt behavior in a "real" situation, i.e., one which involves other people and which has meaning to the subject. The evidence from the field studies, like the evidence from the laboratory, suggests that one's private opinion is

20. Milgram, "Some Conditions of Obedience and Disobedience to Authority," p. 268.

21. Ibid., p. 269. (This subject is quoted at length in the closing section of this chapter.)

22. Stanton Wheeler, "Role Conflict."

23. There is the disturbing possibility that only a selective set of experiments ever get published. The bias resulting from publication policies in some journals, as well as prevailing norms in psychology, militate against publication of findings of "no difference." See Chapter Eight for a discussion of this problem.

24. Herbert C. Kelman, "Compliance, Identification, and Internalization: Three Processes of Attitude Change," *Journal of Conflict Resolution* 2 (1958): 51–60, and Irwin Goldstein and Elliott McGinnies, "Compliance and Attitude Change Under Conditions of Differential Social Reinforcement," *Journal of Abnormal and Social Psychology* 68 (1964): 567–70.

25. See William A. Watts and William J. McGuire, "Persistence of Induced Opinion Change and Retention of the Inducing Message Contents," *Journal of Abnormal and Social Psychology* 68 (1964): 233–41.

not likely to be the same as his public opinion, that one can hold a number of public opinions simultaneously, and, incidentally, that there is no necessary relationship between any kind of opinion about an object and subsequent behavior toward that object. And that is one answer to the key question addressed by this book. Referring to only a single area of interaction, Kohn and Williams suggest that

> There is now abundant research evidence of situational variability in intergroup behavior: an ever-accumulating body of research demonstrates that allegedly prejudiced persons act in a thoroughly egalitarian manner in situations where that is the socially prescribed mode of behavior, and that allegedly unprejudiced persons discriminate in situations where they feel it is socially appropriate to do so.[26]

I suppose I might have taken their word for it in 1956 and saved myself a great deal of trouble. But then, I do not expect many social scientists to take my word for it even with an additional fifteen-year accumulation of evidence including much from fields other than inter-group relations. We will continue to bring critical evidence to bear in the closing section of this chapter as I try to spell out the implications of this remarkable convergence of some highly credible evidence.

Implications: Toward a Situational Sociology

It is over a decade since Dennis Wrong challenged "The Over-Socialized Conception of Man in Modern Society."[27] Reacting to a determinism which pervaded the social sciences and which seemed to be seeping into popular currency, Wrong asked if man were in fact as constrained by a monolithic culture as we social scientists would have it. A few years later Harold Garfinkel referred more bluntly to the models of men constructed by the various social sciences: he called them "judgmental dopes." The cultural dope and psychological dope are, respectively, the man in the sociologist's society and the man in the psychologist's society (see Garfinkel in Chapter Thirteen). Although both Wrong and Garfinkel have, in my opinion, properly identified one of the most critical issues in contemporary social science, their solutions are not so clear. Wrong appears to have opted hopefully for an image of man free to construct his lines of action as he sees fit. Garfinkel, on the other hand, seems to be working his way toward an image of man constrained in his most microscopic relationships by an indelibly imprinted set of taken-for-granted rules. The evidence we have been sampling, converging from a variety of sources, suggests to me a somewhat different solution to the problem posed by Wrong and Garfinkel.

As I have suggested above, some of the laboratory experiments have been designed to study the consequences of group pressures on behavior as well as opinion change. Some of the best examples of this type of experiment are found in the work which takes Helson's notion of adaptation level as a point of departure. These

26. Melvin Kohn and Robin M. Williams, Jr., "Situational Patternings in Intergroup Relations," *American Sociological Review* 21 (1956): 264–74.

27. Dennis H. Wrong, "The Oversocialized Conception of Man in Modern Society," *American Sociological Review* 26 (1961): 183–93.

experiments illustrate a wide range of the phenomena we are discussing. Helson considers the various components of the situation, including aspects of the actor's personality, social constraints, and the meaning of the object toward which the attitude or behavior is directed. The Himelstein and Moore article which follows is typical of the experimental setup employed in these studies. The actual experiment is viewed by the subject as an extraneous incident occurring during the course of what he believes to be the actual experiment. The device is to have a student (confederate) wander into the experimental setting during an interlude and solicit the subject's signature on a petition in the presence of another confederate who has been instructed either to agree or refuse to sign the petition. Although Orne would question the kind of atmosphere created by "being in an experiment" (whether or not the subject is wise to precisely which set of activities comprise that experiment), there is no reason for the subject to suspect that the petition is anything but "real."

DATA:
Racial Attitudes and the Action of Negro- and White-Background Figures as Factors in Petition-Signing
PHILIP HIMELSTEIN / JAMES C. MOORE

A. Statement of the Problem

Helson's (2) theory of adaptation-level has been demonstrated to be a useful framework for understanding the role of social pressures upon behavior. According to this theory, S's behavior in a particular situation is determined by the relative weights assigned by him to the stimulus immediately confronting him, the background stimuli, and residuals from past experience. Included in the third category are beliefs, attitudes, traits, and cultural determinants. In a recent study employing the adaptation-level paradigm, Helson, Blake, and Mouton (3) studied petition-signing as an adjustment to situational and personal factors. In this experiment, a confederate responded to the petition-bearer according to prearranged instructions. After the confederate had either signed or refused to sign the petition in full view of S, S was then requested to sign the petition. In this instance, the confederate's behavior would form the background, while the petition is the immediate stimulus. Another aspect of this study was concerned with personal factors (residuals), namely, S's tendency toward submission. The conclusion of this study was that petition-signing represents not so much the inner convictions of the individual as it does the situational factors brought to bear upon the individual.

In the study by Helson, Blake and Mouton, two petitions were employed. These were termed "positive" or "negative" petitions because of the de-

"Racial Attitudes and the Action of Negro- and White-Background Figures as Factors in Petition-Signing," by Philip Himelstein and James C. Moore, from The Journal of English Psychology, vol. 61 (1963), pp. 267–72. Reprinted by permission of The Journal Press and the authors.

grees to which they attracted signatures in the absence of background factors. The positive petition, which had elicited 96 per cent signing, elicited only 30 per cent when the confederate refused to sign. The negative petition, which had elicited only 15 per cent signing, was signed by 33 per cent when the confederate signed. From this study, it is quite apparent that the relative strength or weakness of a petition can be manipulated by the confederate's behavior toward the petition.

The purpose of the present study is to explore a particular attribute of the confederate as a factor in influencing S's behavior in a petition-signing situation. The study by Lefkowitz, Blake, and Mouton (4) suggests that the status of the background figure may influence whether or not Ss perform the same act as this figure. The attribute selected for examination was the race or color of the confederate, with attitudes toward Negroes serving as the residual factor. It was hypothesized that, among college students with a white southern background, attitudes toward a Negro confederate would be reflected in S's reaction to a petition after the confederate had either signed or refused to sign the petition. The specific hypothesis to be tested is that, for white Ss with high scores on a scale measuring prejudice toward Negroes, the behavior (signing or not signing) would tend to be the reverse of that of the Negro confederate and the same as that of the white confederate.

B. The Experiment

1. Subjects

The Ss for this experiment were drawn from elementary classes in psychology, sociology, and government. To avoid problems in sex differences, the Ss were all males. All were white and native Arkansans.

2. Procedure

The first phase of the study consisted of collecting information about attitudes toward Negroes from the Ss. This phase was conducted in the classroom, and consisted of the administration of a nine-item attitude scale adapted from the *Authoritarian Personality* (1). A previous study with this scale revealed that samples of college students from Northern states score lower (i.e., are less prejudiced toward Negroes) than do Southern students, thus indicating construct validity for the attitude scale.[1] The scales were administered to the entire class, both male and female, and Ss were led to believe that the test administration constituted a complete study. The Ss for the later phases of this study were then dichotomized into high- and low-prejudice groups, on the basis of the relationship of the S's score to the median of the sample.

At a later date, a person other than the administrator of the attitude scale approached the students in class and requested volunteers for an experiment. Since participation in psychological experiments is required of all students in general psychology, these Ss are not "free volunteers." Appointments were then made for the male Ss and these Ss were instructed to report individually to a specified room in the Psychology Building at the scheduled hour.

[1]G. Maranell, Personal Communication, 1960.

When the S arrived for his appointment, he found another student (actually an experimental assistant) already seated in the room. As soon as S was seated, E entered and explained that the previous S had not yet finished, and then departed. On a signal, another assistant, with a petition, entered from another door, explained the purpose of the petition and requested the assistant to sign. The assistant signed or refused according to a prearranged sequence. The petition-bearer then requested the S to sign the petition, and recorded his response. This phase of the study is similar in most respects to the procedure employed by Helson, Blake, and Mouton (3). The S was then requested by E to accompany him to the experimental room, where he was given a Semantic Differential form to complete. Since the purpose of the task was to make the actual experimental condition seem realistic, the Semantic Differential was discarded after S left the room.

Within the framework of the above procedure, half of the Ss encountered a Negro waiting his turn in the waiting room, while half shared the waiting room with a white assistant. Approximately 100 Ss took part in this experiment. The background conditions can be summarized as follows:

W – Pos: White confederate signs the petition.
W – Neg: White confederate refuses to sign the petition.
N – Pos: Negro confederate signs the petition.
N – Neg: Negro confederate refuses to sign the petition.

The petition employed in this study contained a proposal to extend the library hours on Saturday evening until eight o'clock. This was chosen because it represented an issue on which there should not be strong approval or disapproval. To determine a neutral point for the petition, students were requested to sign the petition without reference to a background of the assistant's behavior. The "neutral" Ss were chosen at random on the campus and presented with the petition. Under this condition, 74 per cent signed the petition.

C. Results

The specific hypotheses to be tested are that low-prejudice individuals would tend to react to the petition in the same manner as the Negro assistant, while high-prejudice individuals would tend to do the reverse. The results of this analysis are summarized in Table 1. In general, the results indicate that both low- and high-prejudice Ss tend to be strongly influenced by the behavior of the confederate and to about the same extent. When the confederate, white or Negro signs the petition, it is highly unlikely that S will refuse.

It is less clear as to what is taking place when the confederate refuses to sign the petition. In this instance, it appears that low-prejudice Ss tend to sign after seeing the Negro refuse, and to refuse to sign when the white confederate refuses. The high-prejudice Ss, on the other hand, seem to divide equally between signing and refusing to sign. In this situation, it appears that results are contrary to the hypothetical expectations.

When the results obtained by using a confederate are compared with those obtained under the neutral condition (see Table 2), it is apparent that the effects of the combined confederates upon the Ss' behavior is quite strong. According to this table, 96 per cent of all Ss signed when the assistant signed and 49

TABLE 1. **RESPONSES OF LOW— AND HIGH—PREJUDICE GROUPS TO NEGRO AND WHITE BACKGROUNDS**

| Group | Background Condition | | | | | |
	W—Pos	W—Neg	N—Pos	N—Neg	WN—Pos	WN—Neg
Low prejudice						
Sign	12	3	12	10	24	13
Refuse	0	8	0	4	0	12
p^*		.001		.134		.001
High prejudice						
Sign	10	6	11	7	21	13
Refuse	6	9	1	6	2	15
p^*		.021		.093		.002
Combined						
Sign	22	9	23	17	45	26
Refuse	1	17	1	10	2	27
χ^2		17.02		6.29		24.12
p^*		.001		.02		.001

*Fisher's exact method.

TABLE 2. **ACTION OF SUBJECTS UNDER DIFFERENT BACKGROUND CONDITIONS**

| | Background Condition | | | | | |
| | Positive | | Negative | | Neutral | |
Action of S	N	%	N	%	N	%
Sign	45	96	26	49	37	74
Refuse	2	4	27	51	13	26

Positive–Neutral $\chi^2 = 7.18$, $p = .01$.
Negative–Neutral $\chi^2 = 6.19$, $p = .02$.
Positive–Negative $\chi^2 = 24.12$, $p = .001$.

per cent signed when the confederate refused. These percentages, when compared with the 74 per cent who signed in the absence of a background, lend support to the statement of Helson, Blake, and Mouton (3) that situational variables may be more important in the decision to sign or not to sign a petition than the nature of the petition itself.

D. Discussion

The purpose of the present paper is to explore further some of the implications of the work of Blake and his co-workers in the area of situational and personal factors in conforming behavior. It was assumed that the situational factor of having a Negro or white confederate perform a certain act would influence Ss in accordance with their prejudices. The influence of race of the confederate upon individuals of low and high prejudice was not manifested in this experiment. The results do lend strong support to the position of Helson, Blake, and Mouton (3) that, under certain conditions, situational factors may outweigh personal factors in making decisions about petition signing. In the present study, 22 per cent more Ss signed the petition when the background was positive than when it was neutral, and 25 per cent fewer signed when it was negative. These results are in agreement with those obtained by Helson et al.

The failure of personal factors (level of prejudice) to operate as expected may be a function of the lack of "saliency" of the situation to these factors. In other words, the total situation was nonspecific to the attitudes under consideration. A petition aimed at integrating student housing might be expected to arouse attitudes of prejudice and permit the personal factor to influence the response. Under this condition, personal factors might be expected to outweigh the situational factors. The situation of a Negro petition-bearer and a Negro signing the petition might also be expected to have differential effects upon individuals of high and low prejudice levels.

E. Summary

This paper reports a laboratory study in which Ss observed another student either sign or refuse to sign a petition before being requested to sign the petition themselves. For half of the Ss, the other student (an assistant) was Negro, and for the other half, this individual was white. Both assistants signed or refused to sign the petition according to a prearranged sequence. Attitudes toward Negroes did not appear to play a strong role in this situation. In general, the results indicate that situational factors outweighed personal factors in determining S's reaction to the petition employed in this study.

References

1. Adorno, T. W., Frenkel-Brunswik, E., Levinson, D. J., & Sanford, R. N. The Authoritarian Personality. New York: Harper, 1950.
2. Helson, H. Adaptation-level as a frame of reference for prediction of psychophysical data. Amer. J. Psychol., 1947, 60, 1–29.
3. Helson, H., Blake, R. R., & Mouton, J. S. Petition-signing as an adjustment to situational and personal factors. J. Soc. Psychol., 1958, 48, 3–10.
4. Lefkowitz, M., Blake, R. R., & Mouton, J. S. Status factors in pedestrian violations of traffic signals. J. Abn. & Soc. Psychol., 1955, 51, 704–706.

Conclusions: Take Care of the Company You Keep!

The conclusion reached by Helson, Blake, and Mouton is that the petition signing does not represent the inner convictions of the individual (what I have referred to as "private opinion") but rather the situational factors brought to bear upon the individual.[28] The report by Himelstein and Moore varies the design in that the petition is unloaded (designed not to elicit strong feelings), the race of the confederate is varied, and a different dimension of personality is tapped (prejudice rather than ten-

28. H. Helson, R. R. Blake, and J. S. Mouton, "Petition-Signing as an Adjustment to Situational and Personal Factors," Journal of Social Psychology 58 (1958): 3–10.

dency toward submission). What is remarkable about the experiment is that when the bystander signs the petition, the naive victim is more likely to sign than otherwise. When the bystander refuses to sign the petition, the naive victim is less likely to sign than otherwise. What is even more remarkable is that the influence of this stranger on our victim persists regardless of the race of the stranger, the extent of prejudice of the victim, certain pretested "personality" traits of the victim, or *the content of the petition itself.* In sum, it did not seem to make any difference to a lot of people who the petitioner was, or what kind of people they themselves were, or even what the petition had to say. Significant numbers appear to have been influenced by the action of the stranger. This is the kind of observation which has been made in hundreds of experiments under controlled conditions, with varying degrees of credibility, since Sherif discovered the autokinetic effect in the early thirties.

Milgram's research also provides clear experimental evidence that the kind of private opinion sometimes sought by the survey researcher has little bearing on public behavior. It is, in fact, clear that the subject's *public* opinion may be unrelated to his actions. In some of his later experiments (unlike the one included in Chapter Eight), Milgram had the experimenter take a deliberately aggressive authoritarian role in order to test the "obedience" of subjects. Here is the transcript of one such subject — one who unfailingly obeyed the experimenter and proceeded to the highest shock level on the generator:

> *150 volts delivered.* You want me to keep going?
> *165 volts delivered.* That guy is hollering in there. There's a lot of them [questions] here. He's liable to have [a] heart condition. You want me to go?
> *180 volts delivered.* He can't stand it! I'm not going to kill that man in there! You hear him hollering? He's hollering. He can't stand it. What if something happens to him? . . . I'm not going to get that man sick in there. He's hollering in there. You know what I mean? I mean I refuse to take responsibility. He's getting hurt in there. He's in there hollering. Too many [questions] left here. Geez, if he gets them wrong. There's too many of them left. I mean who is going to take responsibility if anything happens to that gentleman?
> [*The experimenter accepts responsibility.*]
> All right.
> *195 volts delivered.* You see he's hollering. Hear that. Gee, I don't know [The experimenter says: "The experiment requires that you go on."] — I know it does, but that man is hollering in there sir . . .[29]

Not only did this subject persist in behaving contrary to his opinions, but it is important to note that he believed he had drawn straws with the other subject in order to determine which of them would be the learner and which the shock administerer: "There but for the grace of God . . ." Yet, in some ways, Milgram's contribution to this volume is even more persuasive since there is no apparent pressure on the subject to administer the shock. He seems to make the decision pretty much on his own. Recall that he is "in charge" of making the decisions about how much voltage to administer when the "learner" makes a mistake. In effect, Milgram's dia-

---

29. Milgram, "Some Conditions of Obedience and Disobedience to Authority," pp. 268–69.

bolical experiments provide evidence in support of the thesis that sometimes people do naughty (or good) things because of bad (or good) company.

It might be argued that, as in the case of many laboratory experiments, students see through the game. But Milgram's later experiment was with adult males, not with students—nevertheless, it was still defined as an experimental situation. There are, however, field experiments in which controls are imposed upon people engaged in their normal everyday routines—without their knowledge. Lionel Dannick, for example, has demonstrated the extent to which pedestrians will disregard a stoplight when a stranger does so.[30] He found people much more likely to cross against a light when the stranger did and more likely to wait when he did. The decision to act or not to act appears in large part to be determined by the actor's assessment of the immediate situation and only in small part by any inner proclivity or private attitude. Although sex differences are observed by Dannick, they are not great. His controls for age and social class reflect little variation. Dannick's situation is a trivial one, but it does occur during the course of everyday routines for a heterogeneous population who cannot know they are in an experiment. It provides some confirmation that what is observed in the laboratory can also be observed outside. If Milgram's strength lies in the terrible potential consequences of the subject's actions while its weakness lies in the artificiality of the laboratory situation, then Dannick's strength lies in the reality of the situation while his weakness is in the superficiality of the action. Clearly the strengths of the one are the weaknesses of the other and we have another instance of the kind of convergent evidence described when we compared Raven and Gorden in Chapter Eight.

Is all of this merely verification of that defect in American character David Riesman described as "other directedness"? Perhaps, but there is some evidence, albeit scanty, to the contrary. In a study which preceded both of his previously mentioned experiments, Milgram found evidence of social conformity among students in France and Norway.[31] Although Norwegians were considerably more conforming than Frenchmen, both showed a strong tendency to conform to erroneous judgments provided by confederates. Unfortunately, Milgram provides no comparisons with American students under the same experimental conditions. Nevertheless, he does conclude that "the experiment demonstrates that social conformity is not exclu-

---

30. Lionel Dannick, "The Relationship Between Overt Behavior and Verbal Expressions as Influenced by Immediate Situational Determinants" (diss., Syracuse University, 1969). Some of Dannick's work is reported in "Influence of an Anonymous Stranger on a Routine Decision to Act or Not to Act: An Experiment in Conformity," *Sociological Quarterly* 14 (1973): 127–34. Some additional evidence can be found in the experiments conducted by Helson and his colleagues. See Robert R. Blake, Milton Rosebaum, and Rich A. Duryes, "Gift-Giving as a Function of Group Standards," *Human Relations* 8 (1955): 61–73; Monroe Lefkowitz, Robert R. Blake, and Jane S. Mouton, "Status Factors in Pedestrian Violation of Traffic Signals," *Journal of Abnormal and Social Psychology* 51 (1955): 704–06; Anthony N. Doob and Alan E. Gross, "Status of Frustrator as an Inhibiter of Horn-Honking Responses," mimeo, 1966.

31. Stanley Milgram, "Nationality and Conformity," *Scientific American* 215 (1961): 45–51. Some European social scientists have recently been testing Milgram's terrible electrical shocking-machine design with European subjects. Unfortunately, I have been unable to obtain specific references or precise data from these experiments. For example, watching Dutch television in 1971, I saw a film of an experiment conducted by a German psychologist on German students. That film reported that 85 percent of the German subjects applied the maximum voltage under pressure from the psychologist. This is a far higher percentage than is found in Milgram's American experiments.

sively a U.S. phenomenon, as some critics would have us believe." Others have found that foreign students, including Asians, behave just like American students when they are subjects in American experiments.[32] The other-directed man may be less a product of national character, as Riesman would have it, than of human nature. An earlier generation of American sociologists noted a herd-like behavior among crowds under certain conditions. They referred to these conditions generally as "collective behavior" and tended to restrict their observations of human milling, contagious actions, and other cattle-like acts, to situations in which there were no traditional standardized rules for behavior.[33] It appears now that their observation may hold for a far wider range of behavior than they suspected—including such obviously rule-governed situations as pedestrian behavior at street intersections controlled by traffic lights.

If the implications I have drawn from these studies are correct, then it becomes easier to understand not only why people may not always demonstrate consistency between their sentiments and their acts, but also how normal everyday citizens can slaughter other normal everyday citizens—whether on the basis of religion (as is the inclination of Irishmen in Northern Ireland, Vietnamese in Vietnam, and Hindus and Moslems at the time of the Indian partition), or language (as with the French and English in Quebec or the Flemish and French in Belgium), or ethnicity (for example, east and west Pakistanis, blacks and Cape Colored in South Africa, or Indians and blacks in Guiana), or something called "national interests." This last provides the basis for solid German burghers, too old or otherwise unfit for combat duty, to do their patriotic thing to Jews in death camps while, in like manner, American soldiers could do theirs to Vietnamese citizens in their native villages.

Such things need not be matters of life and death. They can be as trivial as crossing a street or crumbling crackers in one's soup. What they share in common is that they are strongly influenced by the actor's definition of the immediate situation—the way he sizes things up. That definition, in turn, seems to be affected in large part by perceptions of what others expect and what others do. During the early sixties, when television quiz shows were the rage in the United States, the great hero of them all was a charming, brilliant young scholar named Charles Van Doren. The shocking discovery that he, in collaboration with those managing the show, was "cheating" led to the demise of the TV quiz show. With the kind of situational explanation proposed here, we can better understand the public cheating in which an otherwise honest scholar found himself gradually entwined on a television quiz program. We can understand it just as we can understand (while simultaneously being appalled) how ordinary American boys can murder Vietnamese civilians. Evidence from the laboratory and from field studies (for example, Raven and Gorden),[34] suggests that once a line of action is initiated, a certain amount of momentum is built up and one action seems to call for the next until the actor finds himself well along a path he never anticipated. Furthermore, it is likely that he also finds himself believing that that is the proper place for him to be.

32. R. B. Zajonc and N. K. Waki, "Conformity and Need Achievement Under Cross-Cultural Norm Conflict," *Human Relations* 14 (1961): 241–50.

33. Herbert Blumer, "Collective Behavior," in *New Outline of the Principles of Sociology*, ed. Alfred McClung Lee (New York: Barnes and Noble, 1946), pp. 167–222.

34. B. H. Raven, "Social Influence on Opinions and the Communication Related Content," *Journal of Abnormal and Social Psychology* 58 (1959): 119–28; R. L. Gorden, "Interaction Between Attitude and Definition."

It is likely that any reader can find in his own experience an example of this type of behavioral and attitudinal inertia. Unless there is a radical revision of the situation, we find that, having been set in motion, we continue to move. A case in point is the moderately liberal professor who, at the urging of his students, and because he believes their cause has merit, agrees to take a couple of turns around the picket line. In rapid succession this simple act leads to a series of confrontations with academic and civil authorities and eventually to the mild professor becoming a *cause célèbre* and a national radical leader. Like Charles Van Doren, he cannot understand how he got into all of this—and neither can his horrified friends and associates. It seems to me that we have an explanatory framework evolving which is based on empirical evidence. It helps us understand such varied phenomena as collective murder, jaywalking, cheating, and the radicalization of liberals. More to our point, it helps us understand why sentiments and acts are frequently unrelated. This is the beginning of a general theory of human behavior that is of some importance and of some use.

The credibility of the folk hypothesis that evil companions cause naughty behavior tends to be confirmed by the available evidence. Both the field studies and the experiments reviewed here provide evidence that a considerable proportion of the variance in human behavior can be explained by efforts (conscious or unconscious) on the part of people to bring their sentiments and acts into line, not with each other, but with what they perceive to be the sentiments and acts of others in the immediate situation. If it is properly reinterpreted, further confirmation can be found in the methodological literature of survey research which was discussed in Chapter Six. It is not my intention to argue that situational constraints explain all, or even most, of the variance found in human behavior. Such constraints do, however, appear to explain significant and frequently large amounts of that variance. The residue can probably be explained by such phenomena as cultural differences, social structural differences (differential location and participation in the society), personality differences (relatively enduring predispositions, and values resulting from effective socialization), biological or genetic differences, by interactions among these sources,* and by idiosyncratic, whimsical, or "accidental" factors. Surely one cannot hope to understand human behavior or social processes without considering how certain types of situations become available at one time rather than another, in one culture rather than another, among some segments of society rather than among others, and how some individuals manage to resist involvement while others do not. Social scientists have vigorously explored such historical, cultural, social structural, and personality dimensions. In contrast, there has been little attention paid to the situational constraints which confront men in the world they never made. This chapter aims to redress that imbalance—to draw attention to social content as well as social context.

---

*At the time I was reading galleys for this chapter, I received the December 1972 issue of the *American Sociological Review* (vol. 37, no. 6). That issue contains an article by one of the leading investigators in this field who provides evidence that both "attitude influence" and "social influence" provide relatively "weak predictive power" regarding the probability of a specific act. The "interaction influence," on the other hand, provides "strong predictive power." The attitudes and actions in this case concerned the legalization of marijuana. See Alan C. Acock and Melvin L. DeFleur, "A Configurational Approach to Contingent Consistency in the Attitude-Behavior Relationship," pp. 714–26.

I think that the social situation is a notion which is different in kind from the constructs "culture," "social structure," and "personality." It is different in that it is an ethnoconcept—one which views behavior from the perspective of the people who are subjects of study. The other concepts are objective or scientific in that they are devices for viewing the behavior of people from the perspective of outsiders (scientists). From this objective perspective the subjects of study become literally objects of study. It seems to me that such abstract forces as culture, social structure, and personality provide little understanding of why people behave as they do in everyday life. Furthermore, unlike the social situation, those concepts are fictions created by the social scientist. None of them exist—except for the social scientist who finds them useful. Unlike the social situation, such concepts are, as some sociologists like to put it, heuristic devices.

There is no culture out there which imposes upon us an imperative to act like one another and differently from those located on other patches of geography; there is no culture other than what the anthropologist has chosen to subsume under that rubric. It is not even clear that culture is an objective concept. It may be viewed as inherently ethnocentric in the sense that it is constructed by an outsider out of what appear to him to be all the odd and funny things that foreigners possess, say, and do. The contemporary urban anthropologist sometimes finds his data compelling him to recognize the limitations of the concept. Elliot Liebow, for example, denies that lower-class life in black ghettos can be understood as mute compliance with cultural imperatives.[35]

The argument regarding personality and social structure is a parallel one. There is no personality in one's head (or wherever it may be) which drives one to act along certain consistent lines which are different from those chosen by one's neighbor because he has a different personality. As was true of culture, there is no personality other than what the psychologist has chosen to subsume under that rubric. Nor is there a social structure in which one finds himself located and which coercively leads him to assume so-called roles and statuses which differentiate him socially from others in the society. There is no social structure other than what the sociologist has chosen to subsume under that rubric. All of these concepts are then inventions, myths, and fantasies which, although sometimes useful, may blind the analyst to the very real constraints imposed by the immediate situation in which the actor finds himself. This is not to deny that such concepts should continue to be used. As I have said, they are heuristic devices. I do not mean to be playful. It is true that when the immediate social situation is controlled experimentally, large amounts of the variance in human behavior remain unexplained. An examination of the data in any of the studies reprinted in this volume shows substantial minorities of stubborn, inner-directed, culturally entrapped (or whatever) subjects. One reason why the so-called ecological fallacy is a fallacy is that even in the areas and among the populations where such phenomena as delinquency or suicide are at their highest rates, most people are neither delinquents nor suicides.

To discard the ideas of culture, social structure, and personality is to ignore their explanatory power. The sociology of knowledge suggests that the gross sociocultural milieu or historical era in which one finds himself has a powerful influence

---

35. Elliot Liebow, *Tally's Corner: A Study of Negro Streetcorner Men* (Boston: Little, Brown and Co., 1967).

over what one is able to think about and how he thinks about it. The skillful and informative use of social structural concepts in the explanatory mode has been demonstrated repeatedly, for example, in Weber's work with religion or Marx's with social class. The great analytic power of the concept of culture when carefully applied is similarly undeniable. Most recently, for example, I have seen it put to work by Murray Wax in his reports on the state of the American Indian.[36] This is in contrast to the naive and frequently stereotyped use of these constructs by the man in the street who explains and excuses all behavior on the grounds of the actor's race, nationality, sex, age, social class, or whatever. This distortion of what his own methods must indicate, occurs, I suppose, as a result of "authoritative" evidence to the contrary provided by social scientists in the mass media.

What is ultimately called for in understanding human behavior is some comprehension of the interaction between action and setting — the ways in which the definition of the immediate situation is mediated by certain preconditioned and predisposing factors. In its simplest form, the problem is, "Under what conditions will what kinds of people define situations differently from other kinds of people under other conditions?" Furthermore, "How do certain situations come to be available at certain times?" Good students and thoughtful critics constantly confront the problem of determinism. To eliminate the notion of helpless, irresponsible individuals relentlessly pushed one way or the other by their culture or personality or social structure is a reasonable goal. But when we suggest a situational sociology are we not substituting a new form of determinism for the older ones? Are we not arguing, from evidence, that men helplessly follow the cues provided in their immediate social situation? Like automatons, they step off the curb following a stranger. Like mindless machines they are programmed to sign or not to sign a petition. Like an army of Frankenstein monsters they kill or maim their fellow men if that seems to be what is called for. This does not seem to me what W. I. Thomas intended when he discussed the definition of the situation. Nor is it what Mead and later Blumer have described in their analyses of the construction of the social act.

Along with Blumer[37] I prefer to believe that man is a situation-assessing, speculative, role-taking animal who considers various lines of action by asking himself, "What if . . . ?" Having tried to put himself in another's shoes, he then acts. But, as E. C. Hughes once asked, "What Other?" How is it possible for the role-taking man of G. H. Mead to inflict pain on his fellow men? Easy! As pathetic as the plight of the experimental subject or the national minority may be, the scientist and the national leader are men of wisdom and authority. If, in assessing the situation, the man in the street must take the role of one at the expense of the other, I suspect his choice is predictable. Fortunately, the prediction will be wrong in a large minority of instances. In every piece of evidence I have seen, no matter how convincing, there remained that large and stubborn minority of research subjects who resisted group pressures toward conformity. It is possible that under the continuous development of social action which occurs in real life (in contrast to experimental situations), this minority may succeed in altering norms and thus alter the majority's definition of the situation. This is one source of social change. But how does it hap-

36. Murray L. Wax, *Indian Americans: Unity and Diversity* (Englewood Cliffs, N.J.: Prentice-Hall, Inc., 1971). For a sampling of Wax's use of the culture concept see his "Kindly Genocide," *The Kenyon Review* 31 (1969): 384–89.

37. Herbert Blumer, *Symbolic Interactionism: Perspective and Method* (Englewood Cliffs, N.J.: Prentice-Hall, Inc., 1969), especially Chapter 1.

pen that some people come to define a situation differently from others and how does it happen that some of these are able to resist the pressures of the majority? Although Mead provides an escape hatch with his somewhat sleazy concept of a "generalized other" (which I read as an underlying notion of the actor's about what people in general think—the ubiquitous "They" in "What will they say if . . . ?"), it seems clear that at this point some of the traditional perspectives of psychology, sociology, and anthropology must be brought into play.

Let me top this closing polemic with an analogy. It seems to me (as someone else once suggested) that all the world *is* a stage. The backdrop and the stage props provide the setting within which the action occurs. But it is the script with its dialogue and its cues which creates the action itself. Culture, personality, and social structure, like the backdrop and props, provide broad suggestions of what range of action seems appropriate. An audience expects different action in a subway scene from what they expect in a bedroom scene, different action in an automobile from what they expect in a bordello, different action in a dining room from what they expect in a jewelry store. Let us ignore, or treat as "deviant," the fact that people occasionally do sleep in subways, make love in automobiles, and have breakfast at Tiffany's. The essential point of the analogue is that even within the restrictions of the backdrop and props, there is an almost infinite number of dramas which may be constructed and played out. Likewise, within one's presumed cultural, personality, and social structural constraints, there are nearly infinite lines of action which can develop. To the extent that this is true, it follows that the gross concepts throw little light on how or why we chose to act and interact as we do. To pursue the analogue, the difference between the revolutionary and the reformer is that, in their efforts to bring about social change, revolutionaries would demand a new set and new props for the stage; reformers, in contrast, would attempt to edit the script.

The image of the tailor-made man—neatly fitted into his culture, hemmed in by his personality, and sewed down by the social structure—the "oversocialized conception of man" as a "judgmental dope," is of limited utility. It is also potentially tragic because of its impact on popular conceptions of the nature of man in society. As long as social science posits an image of the tailor-made man, we are not only incorrect in our perception, but, perhaps of greater consequence, our translation of knowledge into social policy will be couched in terms of creating better controls and constraints—to tailor the man so that he can be counted on to behave himself. When we free ourselves of this deterministic image of the culture-bound, personality-bound, or social structure-bound man and temper it with the interacting, situation-assessing man, the translation into social policy then becomes couched in terms of designing roads to freedom—not to constraint. Everett Hughes reminds us that this is the man W. I. Thomas would have called "creative" and David Riesman calls "autonomous." This man is no automaton, "not a reed blown about by the wind, but a man of many sensitivities who would attain and maintain, by his intelligent and courageous choice of the messages to which he would respond, by the choice of his 'others,' freedom of a high but tough and resilient quality."[38]

38. Everett C. Hughes, "What Other?" in *Human Behavior and Social Processes: An Interactionist Approach*, ed. Arnold M. Rose (Boston: Houghton Mifflin Co., 1962), p. 126. It may be argued that this is a somewhat romanticized notion of man's potentialities—a confusion of what is with what we hope could be. For such a critical statement, couched in sympathetic terms, see Howard J. Ehrlich, "Social Psychology as the End of the Rainbow," *Sociological Quarterly* 11 (1970): 543–44.

11 Stimulus-Response Is for Animals

(Symbols Are for People)

It's What's In Between That Counts

Within what kind of theoretical context can we place the set of data and the interpretations presented in Chapter Ten? In the 1920s, following his remarkable breakthrough in discovering and documenting the conditioned reflex, I. P. Pavlov considered the relationship between his findings with animals and possible generalizations to human behavior. Pavlov, whose brilliant researches have been so distorted by sycophantic followers, was impressed by what he called a "second signal system" in human beings. The physical stimuli to which all animals respond, and which are the focal concern of Pavlov's conditioning experiments, are the "first signals." The "second signals" are primarily *words*: "The word created a second system of signals of reality which is peculiarly ours, being the signal of signals. On the one hand, numerous speech stimuli have removed us from reality. . . . On the other, it is precisely speech which has made us human."[1] It is this symbolic construction of reality, largely through language, which, according to Pavlov, makes it inappropriate to generalize from the behavior of experimental animals to the behavior of human beings. "Of course," he insists, "a word is for man as much a real conditioned stimulus as are other stimuli common to men and animals, yet at the same time it is so all-comprehending that it allows of no quantitative or qualitative comparisons with conditioned stimuli in animals."[2]

Pavlov recognizes that one may, with great pains, create an experimental situation where human beings, like other animals will learn to avoid pushing a red lever because they associate an electric shock with it (and to press a black lever because they associate the receipt of jellybeans with it). This complicated conditioning process is, however, easily bypassed and even thwarted by human subjects. If, as I am about to press a lever, someone whispers in my ear, "press the black one," we have instant conditioning—the second signal system. The "someone" might be a mischievous fellow who says "push the red one," and in either case I might or might not believe him and I might or might not act in accord with his instructions. But, regardless of how I interpret his comment, the fact is that the physical condi-

---

1. I. P. Pavlov, *Conditioned Reflexes: An Investigation of the Psychological Activity of the Cerebral Cortex* (London: Oxford University Press, 1927), p. 357, cited by Dan I. Slobin, "Soviet Psycholinguistics," in *Present Day Russian Psychology*, Neil O'Connor, ed. (Oxford: Pergamon Press, 1967).

2. Pavlov, *Conditioned Reflexes*, p. 407.

tioning process which uses "first signals" has been sabotaged by a different process—one which, if not exclusive to the human race, is employed more extensively and more pervasively by us than any other animal.

The behaviorist's laboratory is an unexpected source for confirmation of the essentially symbolic nature of human behavior. Razran,[3] for example, showed his subjects a list of words while they were eating, conditioning them to salivate at the sight of certain words. One of those words was "style." Having conditioned his subjects, Razran proceeded to introduce a new series of words to them—including both "stile" and "fashion." Even though "stile" is similar to "style" in both appearance and sound, and "fashion" is most dissimilar in these respects, conditioning was, in fact, generalized from "style" to "fashion" and not to "stile." The generalization is semantic—related to invested meaning—rather than dependent upon objective visual or audio clues. Of equal importance is a follow-up experiment conducted by Riess,[4] this time with children as subjects rather than adults. Among children, the generalization was to the homophone rather than to the synonym. It appears that the invisible and inaudible similarity between "style" and "fashion" is one which we must learn to impute and which comes to supersede the less salient sensory similarities: for the child "style" and "stile" resemble one another and "fashion" is unrelated to either. This is not so for the adult, to whom things have come to stand for something other than themselves.

All of this is not to say that, in many respects, human behavior cannot be understood on the same terms as animal behavior. We are animals and we do share with other animals whatever forces may drive them. But there is something else, perhaps a "second signal system," which impinges upon and has great influence in human conduct. It is to this something else, this symbolic quality, that George Herbert Mead directed his attention[5] and which Herbert Blumer has devoted a career to transforming into a different kind of social science.[6] Blumer's contribution to this chapter provides a theoretical link between that Meadian social psychology and the kind of situational sociology which evolved in Chapter Ten. Furthermore, it is rich in methodological implications. Blumer's argument is not that we need to get away from bivariate analysis. Most social scientists would agree with that. His argument is that we need to get away from the very idea of variables, and very few social scientists would agree with that. Let us consider his reasoning.

Blumer's thesis is a familiar one in other contexts. For example, sociologists have traditionally clung to an antireductionist argument (in part, I suppose, out of disciplinary self-preservation) whether it is the classic Durkheimian position that a social fact is a reality *sui generis*, not of a kind with the psychological facts to which some would reduce it, or a more modern C. Wright Mills distinction between private troubles and public issues. An image of the social world as consisting of a set of discrete variables which can be isolated from one another, is, according to Blumer, a form of reductionism. His opening paragraphs are misleading and beside the point he is trying to make. In them he grumbles about using the wrong kind of variables,

3. G. H. S. Razran, "A Quantitative Study of Meaning by a Conditioned Salivary Technique (Semantic Conditioning)," *Science* 90 (1939): 89–90.
4. B. F. Riess, "Genetic Changes in Semantic Conditioning," *Journal of Experimental Psychology* 36 (1946): 143–52.
5. George Herbert Mead, *Mind, Self and Society* (Chicago: University of Chicago Press, 1934).
6. See for example, Herbert Blumer, "Sociological Implications of the Thought of George Herbert Mead," *American Journal of Sociology* 71 (1966): 535–44.

not clearly enough identifying them, the fact that they are historically bound, that they tend to be unstable in their empirical reference (as a result of arbitrary operational definitions), or that they deal with class terms which are tied in with the local conditions they study. In those early pages Blumer considers the prerequisites to the proper application of variable analysis and says that "generic variables are essential to an empirical science. . . ." He points out that most of these problems of variable analysis, although crucial, probably will be overcome. It is not until he finishes what appears to me to be a digression along these lines, that he shifts grounds and challenges variable analysis per se. He begins his basic argument, and the one relevant to our purposes, when he raises the "important question of how well variable analysis is suited to the study of human group life . . . ."

DATA:
Sociological Analysis and the "Variable"
HERBERT BLUMER

My aim in this paper is to examine critically the scheme of sociological analysis which seeks to reduce human group life to variables and their relations. I shall refer to this scheme, henceforth, as "variable analysis." This scheme is widespread and is growing in acceptance. It seems to be becoming the norm of proper sociological analysis. Its sophisticated forms are becoming the model of correct research procedure. Because of the influence which it is exercising in our discipline, I think that it is desirable to note the more serious of its shortcomings in actual use and to consider certain limits to its effective application. The first part of my paper will deal with the current shortcomings that I have in mind and the second part with the more serious question of the limits to its adequacy.

Shortcomings in Contemporary Variable Analysis

The first shortcoming I wish to note in current variable analysis in our field is the rather chaotic condition that prevails in the selection of variables. There seems to be little limit to what may be chosen or designated as a variable. One may select something as simple as a sex distribution or as complex as a depression; something as specific as a birth rate or as vague as social cohesion; something as evident as residential change or as imputed as a collective unconscious; something as generally recognized as hatred or as doctrinaire as the Oedipus complex; something as immediately given as a rate of newspaper circulation to something as elaborately fabricated as an index of anomie. Variables may be selected on the basis of a specious impression of what is important, on the basis

"Sociological Analysis and the 'Variable,' " by Herbert Blumer, from *American Sociological Review*, vol. 21 (1956), pp. 683–90. Reprinted by permission of the author and the American Sociological Association.

of conventional usage, on the basis of what can be secured through a given instrument or technique, on the basis of the demands of some doctrine, or on the basis of an imaginative ingenuity in devising a new term.

Obviously the study of human group life calls for a wide range of variables. However, there is a conspicuous absence of rules, guides, limitations and prohibitions to govern the choice of variables. Relevant rules are not provided even in the thoughtful regulations that accompany sophisticated schemes of variable analysis. For example, the rule that variables should be quantitative does not help, because with ingenuity one can impart a quantitative dimension to almost any qualitative item. One can usually construct some kind of a measure or index of it or develop a rating scheme for judges. The proper insistence that a variable have a quantitative dimension does little to lessen the range or variety of items that may be set up as variables. In a comparable manner, the use of experimental design does not seemingly exercise much restriction on the number and kind of variables which may be brought within the framework of the design. Nor, finally, does careful work with variables, such as establishing tests of reliability, or inserting "test variables," exercise much restraint on what may be put into the pool of sociological variables.

In short, there is a great deal of laxity in choosing variables in our field. This laxity is due chiefly to a neglect of the careful reduction of problems that should properly precede the application of the techniques of variable analysis. This prior task requires thorough and careful reflection on the problem to make reasonably sure that one has identified its genuine parts. It requires intensive and extensive familiarity with the empirical area to which the problem refers. It requires a careful and thoughtful assessment of the theoretical schemes that might apply to the problem. Current variable analysis in our field is inclined to slight these requirements both in practice and in the training of students for that practice. The scheme of variable analysis has become for too many just a handy tool to be put to immediate use.

A second shortcoming in variable analysis in our field is the disconcerting absence of generic variables, that is, variables that stand for abstract categories. Generic variables are essential, of course, to an empirical science — they become the key points of its analytical structure. Without generic variables, variable analysis yields only separate and disconnected findings.

There are three kinds of variables in our discipline which are generally regarded as generic variables. None of them, in my judgment, is generic. The first kind is the typical and frequent variable which stands for a class of objects that is tied down to a given historical and cultural situation. Convenient examples are: attitudes toward the Supreme Court, intention to vote Republican, interest in the United Nations, a college education, army draftees and factory unemployment. Each of these variables, even though a class term, has substance only in a given historical context. The variables do not stand directly for items of abstract human group life; their application to human groups around the world, to human groups in the past, and to conceivable human groups in the future is definitely restricted. While their use may yield propositions that hold in given cultural settings, they do not yield the abstract knowledge that is the core of an empirical science.

The second apparent kind of generic variable in current use in our discipline is represented by unquestionably abstract sociological categories, such as "social cohesion," "social integration," "assimilation," "authority," and "group morale." In actual use these do not turn out to be the generic variables that their labels would suggest. The difficulty is that such terms, as I sought to point out in an earlier article on sensitizing concepts,[1] have no fixed or uniform indicators. Instead, indicators are constructed to fit the particular problem on which one is working. Thus, certain features are chosen to represent the social integration of cities, but other features are used to represent the social integration of boys' gangs. The indicators chosen to represent morale in a small group of school children are very different from those used to stand for morale in a labor movement. The indicators used in studying attitudes of prejudice show a wide range of variation. It seems clear that indicators are tailored and used to meet the peculiar character of the local problem under study. In my judgment, the abstract categories used as variables in our work turn out with rare exception to be something other than generic categories. They are localized in terms of their content. Some measure of support is given to this assertion by the fact that the use of such abstract categories in variable research adds little to generic knowledge of them. The thousands of "variable" studies of attitudes, for instance, have not contributed to our knowledge of the abstract nature of an attitude; in a similar way the studies of "social cohesion," "social integration," "authority," or "group morale" have done nothing, so far as I can detect, to clarify or augment generic knowledge of these categories.

The third form of apparent generic variable in our work is represented by a special set of class terms like "sex," "age," "birth rate," and "time period." These would seem to be unquestionably generic. Each can be applied universally to human group life; each has the same clear and common meaning in its application. Yet, it appears that in their use in our field they do not function as generic variables. Each has a content that is given by its particular instance of application, e.g., the birth rate in Ceylon, or the sex distribution in the State of Nebraska, or the age distribution in the City of St. Louis. The kind of variable relations that result from their use will be found to be localized and non-generic.

These observations on these three specious kinds of generic variables point, of course, to the fact that variables in sociological research are predominantly disparate and localized in nature. Rarely do they refer satisfactorily to a dimension or property of abstract human group life. With little exception they are bound temporally, spatially, and culturally and are inadequately cast to serve as clear instances of generic sociological categories. Many would contend that this is because variable research and analysis are in a beginning state in our discipline. They believe that with the benefit of wider coverage, replication, and the co-ordination of separate studies disparate variable relations may be welded into generic relations. So far there has been little achievement along these lines. Although we already have appreciable accumulations of findings from variable studies, little has been done to convert the findings into generic relations. Such conversion is not an easy task. The difficulty should serve both as a challenge to the effort and an occasion to reflect on the use and limitations of variable analyses.

As a background for noting a third major shortcoming I wish to dwell on the fact that current variable analysis in our field is operating predominantly with

[1]"What Is Wrong with Social Theory?" *American Sociological Review*, 19 (February, 1954), pp. 3–10.

disparate and not generic variables and yielding predominantly disparate and not generic relations. With little exception its data and its findings are "here and now," wherever the "here" be located and whenever the "now" be timed. Its analyses, accordingly, are of localized and concrete matters. Yet, as I think logicians would agree, to understand adequately a "here and now" relation it is necessary to understand the "here and now" context. This latter understanding is not provided by variable analysis. The variable relation is a single relation, necessarily stripped bare of the complex of things that sustain it in a "here and now" context. Accordingly, our understanding of it as a "here and now" matter suffers. Let me give one example. A variable relation states that reasonably staunch Erie County Republicans become confirmed in their attachment to their candidate as a result of listening to the campaign materials of the rival party. This bare and interesting finding gives us no picture of them as human beings in their particular world. We do not know the run of their experiences which induced an organization of their sentiments and views, nor do we know what this organization is; we do not know the social atmosphere or codes in their social circles; we do not know the reinforcements and rationalizations that come from their fellows; we do not know the defining process in their circles; we do not know the pressures, the incitants, and the models that came from their niches in the social structure; we do not know how their ethical sensitivities are organized and so what they would tolerate in the way of shocking behavior on the part of their candidate. In short, we do not have the picture to size up and understand what their confirmed attachment to a political candidate means in terms of their experience and their social context. This fuller picture of the "here and now" context is not given by variable relations. This, I believe, is a major shortcoming in variable analysis, insofar as variable analysis seeks to explain meaningfully the disparate and local situations with which it seems to be primarily concerned.

The three shortcomings which I have noted in current variable research in our field are serious but perhaps not crucial. With increasing experience and maturity they will probably be successfully overcome. They suggest, however, the advisability of inquiring more deeply into the interesting and important question of how well variable analysis is suited to the study of human group life in its fuller dimensions.

Limits of Variable Analysis

In my judgment, the crucial limit to the successful application of variable analysis to human group life is set by the process of interpretation or definition that goes on in human groups. This process, which I believe to be the core of human action, gives a character to human group life that seems to be at variance with the logical premises of variable analysis. I wish to explain at some length what I have in mind.

All sociologists—unless I presume too much—recognize that human group activity is carried on, in the main, through a process of interpretation or definition. As human beings we act singly, collectively, and societally on the basis of the meanings which things have for us. Our world consists of innumerable objects—home, church, job, college education, a political election, a friend, an enemy nation, a tooth brush, or what not—each of which has a meaning on the basis of which we act toward it. In our activities we wend our way by recognizing an object to be such and such, by defining the situations with which we are presented, by attaching a meaning to this or that event, and where need be, by devising a new meaning to cover something new or different. This is done by the individual in his personal action, it is done by a group of individuals acting together in concert, it is done in each of the manifold activities which together constitute an institution in operation, and it is done in each of the diversified acts which fit into and make up the patterned activity of a social structure or a society. We can and, I think, must look upon human group life as chiefly a vast interpretative process in which people, singly and collectively, guide themselves by defining the objects, events, and situations which they encounter. Regularized activity inside this process results from the application of stabilized definitions. Thus, an institution carries on its complicated activity through an articulated complex of such stabilized meanings. In the face of new situations or new experiences individuals, groups, institutions and societies find it necessary to form new definitions. These new definitions may enter into the repertoire of stable meanings. This seems to be the characteristic way in which new activities, new relations, and new social structures are formed. The process of interpretation may be viewed as a vast digestive process through which the confrontations of experience are transformed into activity. While the process of interpretation does not embrace everything that leads to the formation of human group activity and structure, it is, I think, the chief means through which human group life goes on and takes shape.

Any scheme designed to analyze human group life in its general character has to fit this process of interpretation. This is the test that I propose to apply to variable analysis. The variables which designate matters which either directly or indirectly confront people and thus enter into human group life would have to operate through this process of interpretation. The variables which designate the results or effects of the happenings which play upon the experience of people would be the outcome of the process of interpretation. Present-day variable analysis in our field is dealing predominantly with such kinds of variables.

There can be no doubt that, when current variable analysis deals with matters or areas of human group life which involve the process of interpretation, it is markedly disposed to ignore the process. The conventional procedure is to identify something which is presumed to operate on group life and treat it as an independent variable, and then to select some form of group activity as the dependent variable. The independent variable is put at the beginning part of the process of interpretation and the dependent variable at the terminal part of the process. The intervening process is ignored or, what amounts to the same thing, taken for granted as something that need not be considered. Let me cite a few typical examples: the presentation of political programs on the radio and the resulting expression of intention to vote; the entrance of Negro residents into a white neighborhood and the resulting attitudes of the white inhabitants toward Negroes; the occurrence of a business depression and the resulting rate of divorce. In such instances—so common to variable analysis in our field—one's concern is with the two variables and not with what lies between them. If one has neutralized other factors which are regarded as possibly exercising influence on the dependent variable, one is content with the conclusion that the observed change in the dependent variable is the necessary result of the independent variable.

This idea that in such areas of group life the independent variable automatically exercises its influence on the dependent variable is, it seems to me, a basic fallacy. There is a process of definition intervening between the events of experience presupposed by the independent variable and the formed behavior represented by the dependent variable. The political programs on the radio are interpreted by the listeners; the Negro invasion into the white neighborhood must be defined by the whites to have any effect on their attitudes; the many events and happenings which together constitute the business depression must be interpreted at their many points by husbands and wives to have any influence on marital relations. This intervening interpretation is essential to the outcome. It gives the meaning to the presentation that sets the response. Because of the integral position of the defining process between the two variables, it becomes necessary, it seems to me, to incorporate the process in the account of the relationship. Little effort is made in variable analysis to do this. Usually the process is completely ignored. Where the process is recognized, its study is regarded as a problem that is independent of the relation between the variables.

The indifference of variable analysis to the process of interpretation is based apparently on the tacit assumption that the independent variable predetermines its interpretation. This assumption has no foundation. The interpretation is not predetermined by the variable as if the variable emanated its own meaning. If there is anything we do know, it is that an object, event or situation in human experience does not carry its own meaning; the meaning is conferred on it.

Now, it is true that in many instances the interpretation of the object, event or situation may be fixed, since the person or people may have an already constructed meaning which is immediately applied to the item. Where such stabilized interpretation occurs and recurs, variable analysis would have no need to consider the interpretation. One could merely say that as a matter of fact under given conditions the independent variable is followed by such and such a change in the dependent variable. The only necessary precaution would be not to assume that the stated relation between the variables was necessarily intrinsic and universal. Since anything that is defined may be redefined, the relation has no intrinsic fixity.

Alongside the instances where interpretation is made by merely applying stabilized meanings there are the many instances where the interpretation has to be constructed. These instances are obviously increasing in our changing society. It is imperative in the case of such instances for variable analysis to include the act of interpretation in its analytic scheme. As far as I can see, variable analysis shuns such inclusion.

Now the question arises, how can variable analysis include the process of interpretation? Presumably the answer would be to treat the act of interpretation as an "intervening variable." But, what does this mean? If it means that interpretation is merely an intervening neutral medium through which the independent variable exercises its influence, then, of course, this would be no answer. Interpretation is a formative or creative process in its own right. It constructs meanings which, as I have said, are not predetermined or determined by the independent variable.

If one accepts this fact and proposes to treat the act of interpretation as a formative process, then the question arises how one is to characterize it as a variable. What quality is one to assign to it, what property or set of properties? One cannot, with any sense, characterize this act of interpretation in terms of the interpretation which it constructs; one cannot take the product to stand for the process. Nor can one characterize the act of interpretation in terms of what enters into it—the objects perceived, the evaluations and assessments made of them, the cues that are suggested, the possible definitions proposed by oneself or by others. These vary from one instance of interpretation to another and, further, shift from point to point in the development of the act. This varying and shifting content offers no basis for making the act of interpretation into a variable.

Nor, it seems to me, is the problem met by proposing to reduce the act of interpretation into component parts and work with these parts as variables. These parts would presumably have to be processual parts—such as perception, cognition, analysis, evaluation, and decision-making in the individual; and discussion, definition of one another's responses and other forms of social interaction in the group. The same difficulty exists in making any of the processual parts into variables that exists in the case of the complete act of interpretation.

The question of how the act of interpretation can be given the qualitative constancy that is logically required in a variable has so far not been answered. While one can devise some kind of a "more or less" dimension for it, the need is to catch it as a variable, or set of variables, in a manner which reflects its functioning in transforming experience into activity. This is the problem, indeed dilemma, which confronts variable analysis in our field. I see no answer to it inside the logical framework of variable analysis. The process of interpretation is not inconsequential or pedantic. It operates too centrally in group and individual experience to be put aside as being of incidental interest.

In addition to the by-passing of the process of interpretation there is, in my judgment, another profound deficiency in variable analysis as a scheme for analyzing human group life. The deficiency stems from the inevitable tendency to work with truncated factors and, as a result, to conceal or misrepresent the actual operations in human group life. The deficiency stems from the logical need of variable analysis to work with discrete, clean-cut and unitary variables. Let me spell this out.

As a working procedure variable analysis seeks necessarily to achieve a clean identification of the relation between two variables. Irrespective of how one may subsequently combine a number of such identified relations—in an additive manner, a clustering, a chain-like arrangement, or a "feedback" scheme—the objective of variable research is initially to isolate a simple and fixed relation between two variables. For this to be done each of the two variables must be set up as a distinct item with a unitary qualitative make-up. This is accomplished first by giving each variable, where needed, a simple quality or dimension, and second by separating the variable from its connection with other variables through their exclusion or neutralization.

A difficulty with this scheme is that the empirical reference of a true sociological variable is not unitary or distinct. When caught in its actual social character, it turns out to be an intricate and inner-moving complex. To illustrate, let me take what seems ostensibly to be a fairly clean-cut variable relation, namely between a birth control program and the birth rate of a given people. Each of these two variables—the program of birth control and the birth rate—can be given a simple discrete and unitary character. For the program of birth control one may choose merely its time period, or select some reasonable measure such as the number of people visiting birth control clinics. For the birth rate, one merely takes it as it is. Apparently, these indications are sufficient to enable the investigator to ascertain the relations between the two variables.

Yet, a scrutiny of what the two variables stand for in the life of the group gives us a different picture. Thus, viewing the program of birth control in terms of *how it enters into the lives of the people,* we need to note many things such as the literacy of the people, the clarity of the printed information, the manner and extent of its distribution, the social position of the directors of the program and of the personnel, how the personnel act, the character of their instructional talks, the way in which people define attendance at birth control clinics, the expressed views of influential personages with reference to the program, how such personages are regarded, and the nature of the discussions among people with regard to the clinics. These are only a few of the matters which relate to how the birth control program might enter into the experience of the people. The number is sufficient, however, to show the complex and inner-moving character of what otherwise might seem to be a simple variable.

A similar picture is given in the case of the other variable — the birth rate. A birth rate of a people seems to be a very simple and unitary matter. Yet, in terms of what it expresses and stands for in group activity it is exceedingly complex and diversified. We need consider only the variety of social factors that impinge on and affect the sex act, even though the sex act is only one of the activities that set the birth rate. The self-conceptions held by men and by women, the conceptions of family life, the values placed on children, accessibility of men and women to each other, physical arrangements in the home, the sanctions given by established institutions, the code of manliness, the pressures from relatives and neighbors, and ideas of what is proper, convenient and tolerable in the sex act — these are a few of the operating factors in the experience of the group that play upon the sex act. They suffice to indicate something of the complex body of actual experience and practice that is represented in and expressed by the birth rate of a human group.

I think it will be found that, when converted into the actual group activity for which it stands, a sociological variable turns out to be an intricate and inner-moving complex. There are, of course, wide ranges of difference between sociological variables in terms of the extent of such complexity. Still, I believe one will generally find that the discrete and unitary character which the labeling of the variable suggests vanishes.

The failure to recognize this is a source of trouble. In variable analysis one is likely to accept the two variables as the simple and unitary items that they seem to be, and to believe that the relation found between them is a realistic analysis of the given area of group life. Actually, in group life the relation is far more likely to be between complex, diversified and moving bodies of activity. The operation of one of these complexes on the other, or the interaction between them, is both concealed and misrepresented by the statement of the relation between the two variables. The statement of the variable relation merely asserts a connection between abbreviated terms of reference. It leaves out the actual complexes of activity and the actual processes of interaction in which human group life has its being. We are here faced, it seems to me, by the fact that the very features which give variable analysis its high merit — the qualitative constancy of the variables, their clean-cut simplicity, their ease of manipulation as a sort of free counter, their ability to be brought into decisive relation—are the features that lead variable analysis to gloss over the character of the real operating factors in group life, and the real interaction and relations between such factors.

The two major difficulties faced by variable analysis point clearly to the need for a markedly different scheme of sociological analysis for the areas in which these difficulties arise. This is not the occasion to spell out the nature of this scheme. I shall merely mention a few of its rudiments to suggest how its character differs fundamentally from that of variable analysis. The scheme would be based on the premise that the chief means through which human group life operates and is formed is a vast, diversified process of definition. The scheme respects the empirical existence of this process. It devotes itself to the analysis of the operation and formation of human group life as these occur through this process. In doing so it seeks to trace the lines of defining experience through which ways of living, patterns of relations, and social forms are developed, rather than to relate these formations to a set of selected items. It views items of social life as articulated inside moving structures and believes that they have to be understood in terms of this articulation. Thus, it handles these items not as discrete things disengaged from their connections but, instead, as signs of a supporting context which gives them their social character. In its effort to ferret out lines of definition and networks of moving relation, it relies on a distinctive form of procedure. This procedure is to approach the study of group activity through the eyes and experience of the people who have developed the activity. Hence, it necessarily requires an intimate familiarity with this experience and with the scenes of its operation. It uses broad and interlacing observations and not narrow and disjunctive observations. And, may I add, that like variable analysis, it yields empirical findings and "here-and-now" propositions, although in a different form. Finally, it is no worse off than variable analysis in developing generic knowledge out of its findings and propositions.

In closing, I express a hope that my critical remarks about variable analysis are not misinterpreted to mean that variable analysis is useless or makes no contribution to sociological analysis. The contrary is true. Variable analysis is a fit procedure for those areas of social life and formation that are not mediated by an interpretative process. Such areas exist and are important. Further, in the area of interpretative life variable analysis can be an effective means of unearthing stabilized patterns of interpretation which are not likely to be detected through the direct study of the experience of people. Knowledge of such patterns, or rather of the relations between variables which reflect such patterns, is of great value for understanding group life in its "here-and-now" character and indeed may have significant practical value. All of these appropriate uses give variable analysis a worthy status in our field.

In view, however, of the current tendency of variable analysis to become the norm and model for sociological analysis, I believe it important to recognize its shortcomings and its limitations.

It's What's In Between That Counts (Continued)

It is the process of interpretation—of defining the situation—which Blumer believes is overlooked in variable analysis. In Chapter Ten we observed how alterations in the actor's definition of the situation appear to influence his actions or sentiments. The evidence reviewed in Chapter Ten is supportive of Blumer's basic image of human behavior and social processes:

> Our world consists of innumerable objects . . . each of which has a meaning on the basis of which we act toward it. In our activities we wend our way by recognizing an object to be such and such, by defining the situations with which we are presented, by attaching a meaning to this or that event, and where need be, by devising a new meaning to cover something new or different. . . . We can and, I think, must look upon human group life as chiefly a vast interpretative process in which people, singly and collectively, guide themselves by defining the objects, events, and situations which they encounter.

Blumer's image is not restricted to minute interpersonal influences, but is extended to include large organizations, institutions, and social change as well. If, procedurally, in our efforts to analyze human group life, we take this interpretative framework into account, then variable analysis becomes questionable. It does so because it is not the variable as objectively defined by the scientist which exerts influence on the action; to the contrary, it is the actor's interpretation of what that variable means which is related to his action. Clearly, the same variable may be interpreted differently by different categories of people and, sometimes, by different individuals. Outcomes, as we perceive them, are not the consequence of the play of certain objective variables, they are the consequence of the actor's interpretation of such variables or social objects. If this argument seems vaguely familiar, it is because it underlies my discussion of prediction in Chapter Four: the relationship between an "independent" and a "dependent" variable by design ignores the basic interpretative process. In employing that relationship, we blind ourselves deliberately to the locus of the action. What remains is the sometimes useful, but hardly scientific model of human behavior based on input and output alone. As Jordan suggested in Chapter Four, what the scientist wants to know is "how the hell that little black box works." In our quest of understanding, it is indeed what happens in between that counts.

Let me again emphasize that, even though Blumer's examples are all bivariate, this is not an argument against bivariate analysis. Its logic extends to multivariate analysis as well. One can see Blumer's perspective clearly reflected, for example, in Aaron Cicourel's approach to problems of fertility and population control. Cicourel uses gross demographic data to provide preliminary cues for the location of the action. For final cues to problems of population control, Cicourel turns to definitions of the situation by husbands and wives — the actors who are most responsible for making babies.[7] In doing his research, Cicourel treats with respect Blumer's ar-

---

7. Aaron V. Cicourel, "Fertility, Family Planning, and the Social Organization of Family Life: Some Methodological Issues," *Journal of Social Issues* 23 (1967): 57–81. That multivariate analysis is no solution to the problem is evidenced by Wicker's study of the relationship between attitudes toward church and church-related activities. He finds that even when a number of other variables are controlled and collectively taken into account, seventy-five percent of the behavioral variance remains unaccounted for by attitudinal responses. See Alan W. Wicker, "An Examination of the 'Other Variables' Explanation of Attitude-Behavior Inconsistency," *Journal of Personality and Social Psychology* 19 (1971): 18–30.

gument that the "intervening interpretation is essential to the outcome." Variable analysis assumes that the independent variable predetermines its own outcome: the dependent variable. The rhetoric implies as much. But if the meaning is conferred on the variable by the actor, then it is to that semantic process which we must turn if we are to understand what is happening.

Recall that Blumer considers the possibility of treating this intervening interpretive process as a variable in its own right—an intervening variable. This is possible as long as we do not forget that it is this intervening process which is the key to the action. It is not simply a link between the independent and the dependent variables; it is the central subject of research. In terms of our own problem, it then becomes clear that it is inappropriate to view the initial *sentiments* and the ultimate *acts* as the objects of study. The simple relationship between words and deeds, attitudes and behaviors, verbalizations and actions, is no longer the question to which we address ourselves. It becomes, literally, what's in between that counts! Since the mid-sixties there has been, among investigators in this area, a growing awareness of this. Although it remains couched in terms of variable analysis, it is a significant nudge forward. We have begun to concentrate less on the sentiments-acts dichotomy (the input-output model) and more on such intervening processes as "social constraint,"[8] "salience,"[9] "reference groups,"[10] "social distance,"[11] "commitment,"[12] public and private conditions,[13] the opportunity to do the action or express the sentiment,[14] and what might generally be termed actor competence, including both his knowledge of how to behave and his ability to implement that knowledge.[15] Most closely approximating what Blumer intends by the definitional process is Albrecht's work in the early seventies, focusing on the relationship between verbalizations and the expectations of significant others.[16]

Unlike the Blumer article in this chapter, which has no counterpart except in other Blumer articles, our second reprint might have been any one of the above-mentioned studies. We are beginning to understand that the independent variable

8. Gordon H. DeFriese and W. Scott Ford, "Verbal Attitudes, Overt Acts, and the Influence of Social Constraint in Interracial Behavior," *Social Problems* 16 (1969): 493–505; Lyle G. Warner and Melvin L. DeFleur, "Attitude as an Interactional Concept: Social Constraint and Social Distance as Intervening Variables Between Attitudes and Action," *American Sociological Review* 34 (1969): 153–69; James S. Frideres, Lyle G. Warner, and Stan L. Albrecht, "The Impact of Social Constraints on the Relationship Between Attitudes and Behavior," *Social Forces* 50 (1971): 102–12.

9. DeFriese and Ford, "Verbal Attitudes."

10. James M. Fendrich, "Perceived Reference Group Support: Racial Attitudes and Overt Behavior," *American Sociological Review* 32 (1967): 960–70; Alan C. Acock and Melvin L. DeFleur, "A Configurational Approach to Contingent Consistency in the Attitude-Behavior Relationship," *American Sociological Review* 37 (1972): 714–26.

11. Warner and DeFleur, "Attitude as an Interactional Concept."

12. James M. Fendrich, "A Study of the Association Among Verbal Attitudes, Commitment and Overt Behavior in Different Experimental Situations," *Social Forces* 45 (1967): 347–55.

13. Stan L. Albrecht, Melvin L. DeFleur, and Lyle G. Warner, "Attitude-Behavior Relationships: A Re-Examination of the Postulate of Contingent Consistency," *Pacific Sociological Review* (1972): 149–68.

14. See Ehrlich's contribution to this chapter.

15. Ehrlich, ibid.

16. Stan L. Albrecht, "Verbal Attitudes and Significant Other's Expectations as Predictors of Marijuana Use," paper read at the annual meetings of the Rocky Mountain Social Science Association, 1971.

(sentiments) has very little if anything to do with the dependent variable (acts). It is to the complex interpretive process that these studies are turning.

We will consider this new wave of research below. It does not represent the subtle alteration in perspective which Blumer demands. It does, however, begin to focus on what happens in between. According to Blumer, the act of interpretation simply cannot be converted into a variable—intervening or otherwise:

> . . . the question arises how one is to characterize it as a variable. What quality is one to assign to it, what property or set of properties? One cannot, with any sense, characterize the act of interpretation in terms of the interpretation which it constructs; one cannot take the product to stand for the process. Nor can one characterize the act of interpretation in terms of what enters into it—the objects perceived, the evaluation and assessments made of them, the cues that are suggested, the possible definitions proposed by oneself or by others. These vary from one instance of interpretation to another and, further, shift from point to point in the development of the act. This varying and shifting content offers no basis for making the act of interpretation into a variable.

What variable analysis does is to remove or to neutralize (hold constant) the central defining process—and this is not how things happen. Returning again to our own problem, it can be argued that we needed first to confirm the fact that variable analysis is inappropriate. Blumer does concede that there is a legitimate place for and use of variable analysis in studying those areas where the interpretive process is at a minimum. In fact, variable analysis helps us to locate such areas. In like manner, it seems to me that it helps us locate areas where the interpretive process is critical. These are areas where we find the relationship between variables to be highly unstable and to alter radically under different conditions. This is precisely what we do find when we look at evidence which has now accumulated relating sentiments to acts.[17] This is, in part, what I had in mind when I suggested in Chapter Three that perhaps Linton Freeman's proposed moratorium on data collection should be taken seriously. At least, there is little need for further empirical demonstration that sometimes sentiments and acts are in accord and sometimes they are not.

The kind of data which are required is of a very different order. They are data which inform us on the nature of the process which occurs in between. Once we can sort out those instances where sentiments and acts are related from those instances where the relationship is nonexistent or unstable, we can assume that variable analysis may be appropriate for the former group and turn our attention to the unrelated or differentially related instances of which there appear to be very

---

17. For a partial review of such findings see Chapter Three. A more complete and up-to-date review appears in A. Wicker, "Attitudes Versus Actions: The Relationship of Verbal and Overt Behavior Responses to Attitude Objects," *Journal of Social Issues* 25 (1969): 41–78. Wicker points out on the one hand that there seems to be increasing agreement among researchers that situational factors are important in understanding the relationship between attitudes and behaviors, but, on the other hand, there is practically no research which takes them into account.

many. It is in these cases that we need, as Blumer suggests, to study how things come about, rather than the relationship of fragments to one another. This is not an easy undertaking with our present modes of analysis. Let us consider the hypothetical instance where a citizen is asked in an interview if he would act in some manner to assist a stranger whom he observed being mugged. The citizen responds affirmatively. But we cannot check that response against his behavior unless an opportunity arises for him to observe someone being mugged. Ehrlich directs our attention to "opportunity" as an intervening variable, reminding us that not everyone has the opportunity to do what he says he would. Is he inconsistent because he never does as he says since the opportunity does not present itself? That hardly seems reasonable.

Ehrlich also reminds us that even if he does have the opportunity to act, he has to know how to act. That is, he needs to be able to conjure up something to do or else he may end up standing helplessly by as the stranger gets mugged. Is this inconsistent of him? That doesn't seem a reasonable interpretation either. Ehrlich continues to remind us of other intervening factors. The poor fellow, having committed himself verbally and having the opportunity to act and knowing what to do, may still turn out to be incompetent. In his haste to be helpful he may slip and knock himself unconscious or engage in any other amount of well-intentioned but inconsequential bumbling while the mugging is successfully completed. Nor is this the end of what can happen in between. Consider Milgram's observation of a direct relationship between the callousness of a subject administering a shock and his physical remoteness from the "learner" who is getting blasted.[18] From this we might infer that people who say they will help and find themselves in close proximity to the victim are more likely to help than those who are more remotely located from the mugging. A final intervening variable is suggested by an observation by Darley and Latane made under conditions similar to our hypothetical case.[19] Their work suggests that the likelihood of a bystander assisting a stranger in trouble is a function of the number of bystanders. Our respondent who said he would help may find himself observing a mugging along with many other witnesses, and he honestly thinks he should help, and he probably would, except that there are lots of other people who can do it, so it really isn't necessary.

When we come to understand why the person does not act as he talks, the discrepancy is no longer an "inconsistency." The process of exploring the actor's perception of the situation clarifies the actor's logic. The dimensions used in the hypothetical example above were considered as if they occurred in sequence. But in

18. Stanley Milgram, "Some Conditions of Obedience and Disobedience to Authority," *International Journal of Psychiatry* 6 (1968): 259–276. Although there is little doubt about the influence of proximity on behavior, its influence varies under different conditions. In interpersonal situations, Milgram finds an inverse relationship between proximity and callousness. But in intergroup relations, the reverse has been observed. Ransford's data suggest an association between isolation from whites and a willingness on the part of blacks to take violent action. This willingness is confirmed by his few interviews with actual participants in the Watts affair. H. Edward Ransford, "Isolation, Powerlessness, and Violence: A Study of Attitudes and Participation in the Watts Riot," *American Journal of Sociology* 73 (1968): 581–591.

19. J. M. Darley and B. Latane, "Bystander Intervention in Emergencies: Diffusion of Responsibility," *Journal of Personality and Social Psychology* 8 (1968):36–42.

everyday social processes they might appear in almost any order. Furthermore, they would probably criss-cross each other, as well as other dimensions, before any outcome could be determined. Under such conditions it makes no sense to continue asking what is the relationship between sentiments and acts. It becomes necessary to focus on the intervening process. But how does one go about understanding this messy, complicated, unordered process which consists largely of unspoken definitions by the actor? Blumer provides a hint of methodology when he touches on procedures:

> This procedure is to approach the study of group activity through the eyes and experience of the people who have developed the activity. Hence, it necessarily requires an intimate familiarity with this experience and with the scenes of its operation. It uses broad and interlacing observations and not narrow and disjunctive observations.

It is no accident that participant-observation techniques are closely related to symbolic-interactionist theory. If an observer can gain intimate knowledge of the processes of social life as those who live it see them, then he can come to understand this interpretive area in between the independent and the dependent variables. Most other techniques in social science assume a fragmented, variable-laden world which can be understood by hooking up the fragments in an input-output manner. To the extent that Blumer's perception is correct, social science will have to rethink its methodology and manufacture a new set of methods. For under the conditions described by Blumer, variable analysis as we presently understand and employ it is useful only in certain routine, highly stable areas of life. It is true that some objects have a relatively fixed and standardized meaning—they have common shared interpretations. This permits variable analysis in such instances as long as we recognize their transiency: if common meaning can be agreed upon, it can also be redefined. What this seems to me to imply is that our current methods are more likely to be appropriate (a) in small, simple, homogeneous, stable societies and (b) in the study of stable institutionalized forms of social life. In large complex, heterogeneous, changing societies it is unlikely that variable analysis is useful in any but a preliminary manner or in residual areas of social life where consensus survives and change is minimal. Traditional methods may be retained in a future social science as detecting or problem-locating devices, largely exploratory and parameter setting, or for the analysis of the remaining fragments of a once larger consensus.

It is difficult to disagree with Blumer when he insists that "the process of interpretation is not inconsequential or pedantic. It operates too centrally in group and individual experience to be put aside as being of incidental interest." It was the interpretive process which Pavlov identified with language and which he saw as messing things up when, in our research, we treat human beings like other animals. Whether we accept Pavlov's concern for "the word" intervening between stimulus and response, or whether we prefer Blumer's notion of an "interpretive process," makes little difference. What is important is that something happens in between the input and the output and, in attempting to understand human behavior and social processes, it is that something which must become the object of our study.

DATA:
Attitudes, Behavior, and the Intervening Variables
HOWARD J. EHRLICH

Studies on the relation of attitudes and behavior have almost consistently resulted in the conclusion that attitudes are a poor predictor of behavior. The majority of these studies have taken ethnic attitudes as the predictor and some mode of intergroup behavior as the predictand. The summary statement here has usually been of the form that prejudice is a poor predictor of discrimination (Bray, 1950; Brookover and Holland, 1952; DeFleur and Westie, 1958; Fishman, 1961; Killian, 1953; Kutner et al., 1952; LaPiere, 1934, 1936; Linn, 1965; Lohman and Reitzes, 1952; Malof and Lott, 1962; Minard, 1952; Nettler and Golding, 1946; Saenger and Gilbert, 1950).

It is clear that many social scientists concerned with the study of prejudice and intergroup behavior have taken the prevailing interpretations of the evidence of attitude-behavior inconsistency as a premise toward the conclusion that attitude theory has proven inadequate. In his presidential address to the Society for the Study of Social Problems, Deutscher (1966:247) asserts that "no matter what one's theoretical orientation may be, he has no reason to expect to find congruence between attitudes and actions and every reason to expect to find discrepancies between them." DeFleur and Westie (1963:28), for another example, declare a *necessary* inconsistency between verbal scale scores and other overt actions, pointing to "social constraints" or situational norms as the crucial determinants of behavior. Consistency between attitudes and behavior occurs, they argue, "if the normative processes of the groups within which [people] are interacting are consistent."

It is the thesis of this paper that the evidence for inconsistency may be rejected on both methodological and conceptual grounds, and that there is no necessary incompatibility between a theory of attitudes and theories of interpersonal or intergroup behavior. It is my intent, first, to present briefly the major arguments against interpretations of inconsistency, and then to provide a paradigm for the analysis of the attitude-behavior relation. I shall limit my examples to the study of prejudice and intergroup behavior.

Methodological Arguments

From a methodological standpoint it can be argued that attitude measurement, particularly in the domain of prejudice, has been demonstrated to be seriously imprecise and unreliable. Rosenthal (1966), in his review of experimenter error, summarized the effects of the real and perceived ethnicity of experimenters on test and questionnaire performance. From this evidence, it is apparent that the ethnic identity of the researcher significantly biases respondent behavior. Ehrlich (1964) and Ehrlich and Rinehart (1965) have demonstrated that forced-re-

"Attitudes, Behavior, and the Intervening Variables," by Howard J. Ehrlich, from *The American Sociologist*, vol. 4, no. 1 (1969), pp. 29–34. Reprinted by permission of the author and the American Sociological Association.

sponse formats in prejudice scales overstate the degree of prejudice and distort the manifest content of ethnic-group imagery. Fendrich (1967:355) provides a direct test of the effects of the measurement process on predicting intergroup behavior, concluding: "Verbal attitudes can be either consistent or inconsistent with overt behavior, depending upon the way respondents define the attitude measurement situation."

Measurement errors may also be examined in the operations through which the behaviors to be predicted and explained in the attitude-behavior paradigm are measured or assessed. While the operations for attitude-scale construction are relatively well standardized, the operations for observing and recording behavior, particularly in natural settings are generally unstandardized and problem-specific. Further, while the items of attitude scales are presumably a representative set of statements from the attitude domain studied, most behavioral units selected for study have been chosen on a nonsystematic or *ad hoc* basis. It would seem plausible, therefore, to attribute some degree of recorded inconsistency to these less rigorous measures of overt actions in intergroup situations.

It may be, further, that our basic strategy has been wrong. We have generally measured attitudes toward a class of people, but made predictions about a person's behavior toward a specific member of that class (cf. Fishbein, 1966). Certainly a low order of correct predictions may be taken as a special case of the fallacy of ecological correlation (i.e., predicting unit behavior from a knowledge of aggregate relations). Perhaps, more appropriately, we should consider the alternatives: either we measure an attitude toward a specific person and then predict a subject's behavior toward that person, or we measure attitudes toward a class of people and predict a subject's behavior to some (perhaps phenomenologically) representative sample of that class.

On the basis of even these brief and limited methodological arguments, the evidence from past research must be re-examined. The conclusion that verbal attitude expressions are inconsistent with other overt behaviors must be suspended. In reviewing the conceptual arguments, I shall try to show that the conclusion is untenable.

Conceptual Arguments

The conceptual arguments that may be adduced to invalidate interpretations of inconsistency need not be tied to a specific theory of attitudes. The strategy of this presentation is based on the assumption that the most cogent arguments are those which can be easily stated in the language of the current, prevailing attitude theories.

In almost all current theories, attitudes are construed as having a componential structure. Not all the components of an attitude imply behavior. It follows from this that without a direct assessment of the "action potential" of an attitude component, the researcher's inference about the subject's behavior, or intentions, may be phenomenologically naïve. This possibility is illustrated in a study by Kay (1947), who demonstrated that 36 per cent of a sample of presumably anti-Jewish items, drawn from the Levinson-Sanford scale of anti-Semitism, were judged by naïve subjects as friendly or directionally unclear. Predictions of anti-Jewish behavior from these items would probably have displayed high error.

To adopt the argument that not all attitude components imply behavior, it is not necessary to endorse a multidimensional strategy of attitude-theory construction. The argument, from the standpoint of a unidimensional theory, simply becomes: not all attitudes imply behavior. Whatever the other outcomes of these theoretical strategies, they agree in their fundamental statements concerning the relation of attitudes and behavior. Fishbein (1966:213), a leading unidimensional theorist, states his position clearly:

> Because attitude is a hypothetical variable abstracted from the *totality* of an individual's beliefs, behavioral intentions, and actions, toward a given object . . . any given belief, behavioral intention, or behavior, therefore, may be uncorrelated or even negatively correlated with his attitude. Thus, rather than viewing specific beliefs or classes of beliefs and specific behavioral intentions or types of behavioral intentions as part of attitude, these phenomena must be studied as variables in their own right, that, like attitudes, may or may not function as determinants of a specific behavior.

Different scaling models and measurement procedures differentially assess the behaviorally directive components of attitudes. The current major scaling models focus primarily on two attitude components, usually direction and intensity; only the procedure of summated ratings considers both dimensions simultaneously. Where an attitude scale is focused on a single component and where that component has a low action potential, successful prediction should be highly unlikely. Tittle and Hill (1967) provide some confirming evidence. Aside from formal scaling, the two major procedures for measuring prejudice — the stereotype check list and the social-distance questionnaire — similarly tap only a single attitude component. The check list assesses only the salience (typicality) of a stereotype, and that usually in a categorical manner, while social-distance measures provide a report solely of behavioral intentions, usually abstracted from situational reference. Only where these components entail a high directiveness for behavior should a high congruence with behavior be expected.

It may be argued further that the determination of the structure of an attitude at any point in time requires the determination of the interrelations of the components that constitute the attitude. An attitude can be defined as well formed when all of its components achieve some balance and that balanced state persists over time. If this conceptualization is adequate, it follows that reliable predictions of behavior can occur only from well-formed attitudes, or, in the absence of a well-formed attitude, only when the predicted behavior is close in time to the attitude measurement. Even then, it may be the case that the measurement process per se can change the state of a poorly balanced attitude.

Not only does a single attitude comprise several components, but a single attitude object may implicate many attitudes. Predictions of behavior that do not account for all (or at least the major) attitudes evoked by an object will probably be wrong. In a variation on this argument, Rokeach (1967:530) has contended that at least two attitudes are required to make a correct prediction of behavior.

> . . . an attitude may be focused either on an object or on a situation. In the first instance we have in mind an attitude-object, which may be

concrete or abstract, involving a person, a group, an institution, or an issue. In the second instance the attitude is focused on a specific situation, an event, or an activity. To say that a person has an enduring attitude toward a given object is to say that this attitude will, when activated, somehow determine his behavior toward the attitude-object across situations; conversely, to say that a person has an enduring attitude toward a given situation is to say that this attitude will, when activated, determine his behavior toward the situation, across attitude-objects.

It may be that the reported inconsistency between attitude and behavior is a partial result of our naïveté in phenomenological analysis, i.e., our inability to ascertain the intentional meaning of an actor's verbal and nonverbal acts. Without denying the crudities of phenomenological analysis in contemporary social psychology, the fundamental problem may be that our presumed observations of inconsistencies derive from our failure to specify the criteria for judging a consistent or inconsistent response. Campbell (1961:160) provides a graphic illustration of the problem of assessing consistency:

> On an arithmetic test of four items, the child who gets only two items correct is not necessarily regarded as less consistent than the child who gets all right or all wrong. If he gets the two easiest right and the two hardest wrong, he is equally consistent. On intelligence we today think in terms of a continuum, and can conceive of consistent mediocrity. . . . We can regard honesty as something people have in degree, rather than an all-or-none trait. A person of intermediate degree can be just as consistent as a person of extreme position, and his attitude can be determined from his behavior just as well. . . . For intelligence and honesty, we have achieved dimensionality in our thinking. For more emotion-laden topics, such as standing up for civil rights, we have not. If a university president protects a pacifist professor but fires an atheist, we call him inconsistent. If he protects a pacifist and an atheist, but fires a Communist, we accuse him of backing down under pressure. Conceptually, we have the notion of a total non-defendant of professors' rights and a total defender of professors' rights, and lack any concept of genuine mediocrity which would *in consistency* produce defense in a situation of low threshold and firing in another situation with a higher threshold value.

The assessment of consistency is initially contingent on the conditions of adequate measurement and the stability of an attitude. Assuming these conditions, it is then necessary to enumerate the set of obligatory and optional behaviors that comprise the attitude domain. Presumably, this is a highly limited set of behaviors, or at least the obligatory behaviors form a highly limited subset. The number of observations required for a sample of this set or subset of behaviors will doubtless be fixed by the degree to which these behaviors are scalar. The extent to which an individual's verbal and nonverbal behaviors may achieve some level of consistency will then depend upon quasi-logical (probably social-psychological) criteria of contradiction. Such criteria, implicit in everyday behavior, have yet to be made explicit.

Strategy for Research: The Intervening Variables

The search for a more appropriate research strategy must begin with the understanding that the simple question of the consistency of attitudes and behavior is misleading. The correct representation of the problem should take the form: Under what conditions, and to what degree, are attitudes of a given type related to behaviors of a given type? My intent in this section, then, is to identify the social and psychological conditions that intervene between attitudes and behavior. As a matter of intellectual strategy, I shall limit myself here to those variables most directly related to attitude theory. Elsewhere I have attempted to identify the relevant variables of social structure in considering the analogous problem of the relation of role expectations to role behavior (Preiss and Ehrlich, 1966:Chap. 9). Current alternatives may be reviewed in Fishbein (1966) and Himmelstrand (1960).

Clarity

For consistency to occur there has to be a clear way for an attitude to be expressed in behavior. For some attitudes and for some behaviors, the relationship may not be clear. This indeterminacy could appear under a number of possible conditions, the importance of which we shall probably have to ferret out through intensive descriptive research. Williams (1964:329), in discussing the characteristics of behavior in unclear interracial situations, provides a prospectus for research:

> The unfamiliar situation is, by definition, initially one of uncertainty, which is another way of saying that it induces some degree of insecurity. Past experience does not suffice as a guide, and old norms may not lead to the usual results. New situations are likely, therefore, to instigate heightened alertness—including a generalized vigilance toward cues that may indicate what action will lead to what consequences. Under the circumstances of uncertainty and sharpened attentiveness, the individual who first acts with an appearance of decisiveness and confidence is likely to have marked influence. It can and does often happen that the people in leadership positions are themselves confused; for them the situation is not even structured enough to suggest where to turn for clarification. We saw that, in consequence, action on the part of any other participant became disproportionately important in determining their definitions. Confused participants sought indices of how others defined the situation. Since the crucial question in many of these situations was whether or not membership in a particular racial category (Negro) precluded membership in other groups or categories, the first action to be taken by a white was often interpreted by all as an index of acceptance or rejection.

Expressibility

Some attitudes may be clearly expressible only in verbal behavior. Extremely radical, highly unconventional, or strongly antisocial attitudes may in fact have their primary expression in verbal behaviors or in fantasy. Some attitudes may have their expression in sublimated behavior. Attitudes about matters which a person defines, or which are socially defined, as highly intimate may also have their primary expressions in verbal and fantasy behavior. Other expressions may be deliberately concealed from observation.

Disclosure

Related to expressibility is the willingness of a person to disclose his attitude. Under many circumstances, the failure to disclose one's attitude may be neither an attitude-consistent nor an attitude-inconsistent act. In the case of attitudes toward oneself, their disclosure or concealment has indicated such a regular pattern of occurrence that the conditions of disclosure could represent an important class of variables for more general consideration. The research stimulated by Jourard (1964) has confirmed that people vary in their characteristic level of disclosure of self-attitudes. It has also been established, particularly from the work of Altman and Haythorn (1965), that these individual differences are responsive to controlled situational variation both for the number of self-attitude statements disclosed and for their depth of intimacy. Following from this, Graeven (1967) has demonstrated that for thirteen different categories of self-attitude statements and for levels of intimacy associated with each of these categories, all subjects — regardless of their characteristic level of disclosure — reciprocated by category and intimacy the disclosures made by another person. This limited research suggests that reciprocity in the verbal and nonverbal expression of attitudes may be a standard interpersonal tactic as well as a more generalized norm of interpersonal behavior. Thus, it may be hypothesized that attitudes expressible in interpersonal situations may not be disclosed either because others do not express their attitudes or because the actor fails to perceive them. Further, the "race-belief" and the "attitude similarity" hypotheses of Rokeach (1960) and Byrne (1961) suggest an obverse to the disclosure hypothesis: Attitudes expressible in interpersonal situations may not be disclosed when the actor perceives his attitudes as contrary to the attitudes of others in the situation. These disclosure hypotheses will no doubt have to be qualified by considerations of the duration of the situation, among other situational properties.

Perspective and the Definition of the Act

The indeterminate status of the attitude-behavior relation may also be a consequence of perspective. An act consistent from the standpoint of the actor may appear to the observer to be inconsistent. This becomes particularly problematic when an actor deliberately chooses not to act, or when the outcome of an act is contrary to what the actor intended.

Perhaps the most confounding problem of the matter of intent as related to the outcome of an act is that of the social definition of an act. Regardless of the actor's intent, both the scientist as an observer and the actor as an observer of himself must cope with the prevailing social definition. Where the disparity between a personal and social construction of an act is very great, it seems likely that over time an actor may come to question or even redefine his own behavior. The presumed seriousness of this problem has led some social scientists to take the position that a motivational theory must necessarily be a theory of rationalization of behavior (Mills, 1940:906 – 907):

> The aspect of motive which this conception grasps is its intrinsically social character. A satisfactory or adequate motive is one that satisfied the questioners of an act or program, whether it be the other's or the actor's. As a word, a motive tends to be one which is to the actor and to the other members of a situation an unquestioned answer to questions concerning social and lingual conduct. A stable motive is an ultimate in justificatory conversation. The words which in a type situation will fulfill this function are circumscribed by the vocabulary of motives acceptable for such situations. Motives are accepted justifications for present, future, or past programs or acts.

As a theory of motivation, the conspectus of Mills is seriously defective. Nevertheless, the systematic study of vocabularies of motives should lead to a more sophisticated understanding of intentional behavior and self-report. This uniquely sociological perspective furthermore points to three parameters of self-report requiring serious consideration: the strength of prevailing definitions of social acts, the disparity between personal and social definitions of social acts, and the time between an act and the actor's report of his intent, or vice versa.

The sociology of motivational analysis leads us to still another consideration. The same act over time and in different social contexts changes its meaning, i.e., its social definition. Attitude-consistent behavior at one time may be perceived as inconsistent at another time. Yesterday's radical may be today's impediment to progress, though neither his attitudes nor behavior have changed in consistency. Morton Deutsch (1949:49), who calls this the problem of "unrecognized locomotion," describes it:

> To the extent that we do not take cognizance of how changes beyond our control affect our positions in relation to our goals, we are likely to behave in ways which are either inconsistent or irrelevant to our purposes. The incorrect assessment of present position is likely to lead to a faulty perception of the direction to one's goal.

Finally, informal evidence indicates that people sometimes intentionally act in an attitude-inconsistent manner. Such behavior, which may be an important condition for attitude change, may have its basis in either personal curiosity or an attempt to achieve novelty in an unstimulating environment. Inconsistent behavior may also be a primary means by which individuals test themselves and others.

Learning

The discussion so far has focused on the condition of clarity in the relation of attitudes to behavior, where the strategic problems become the determination of an attitude's expressibility and the nexus of intention to act. It is now appropriate to introduce the three assumptions hidden in this discussion. The first of these is the learning assumption. Even where a clear and expressible relation exists between an attitude and behavior, it is not necessary to assume that an actor knows how to behave in a consistent manner. The major determinant of attitude-discrepant behavior may be that an actor has not learned how to express his attitude in action competently. One determinant of the adequacy of such learning may be the level of direct or vicarious experience of the actor, if any, in such behavior situations. Under this condition of no or poor learning, inaction, inappropriate behavior, and sometimes ineffective behavior are defined by the observer as inconsistent acts. Certainly, learning how to behave in a manner consistent with one's attitudes is a primary objective of socialization at all stages of the life cycle.

Accessibility

The second of the assumptions implicit in discussions of attitude-consistent behavior is the assumption of opportunity and access. Knowing how to behave in an appropriate manner is insufficient if the opportunity, access, or perceived access to the opportunity is nonexistent. For example, the study of ethnic intermarriage reveals that the best predictor of intermarriage is the opportunity to intermarry. For Negro-white marriages, for instance, opportunity is partly defined by the proportion of eligible mates, the degree of residential segregation, and the degree of status congruence (Heer, 1966).

Competence

Even knowing what is consistent and having the opportunity to engage in attitude-consistent behavior is only one necessary condition for such behavior. Not only must an actor learn what comprises appropriate behavior, but he must learn how to use his skills and muster his personal resources in order for his actions to be effective. Thus, the third assumption implicit in most past discussions has been an assumption of skill and resource. Patently, individuals vary in the skills they have developed and in the resources they can mobilize for behavior in any given situation. Inferences about behavior, therefore, must take into account such individual differences. An ostensibly inconsistent act may indicate only the actor's deficient skill, his lack of resources, or his inability to organize his resources for effective behavior. It is possible that inferences about behavior and consistency may be biased in the direction of more skillful individuals by the fact that they may emit more behaviors, and/or perform them more confidently and more effectively.

The research strategies indicated so far are of substantial consequence in establishing the attitude-behavior relation. Two widely discussed problems of crucial importance remain: the problem of situational analysis and the problem of multiple-attitude analysis.

Situational Analysis

In the absence of any well-established guidelines for such analysis, it seems reasonable to consider as separate problems those concerned with the structural, primarily physical, characteristics of situations and those concerned with the social dimensions. The focus of structural analysis is, first, the study of the properties of situations and their interrelationships, and second, the study of the relation of these properties to behavior. Barker and his associates (1955, 1963) have developed an extensive language and research operations for structural analysis, but these have not yet had application to the kinds of problems that concern us here. Hall (1963, 1966) has provided systematic procedures for assessing the effects of space on interpersonal behavior, and Sommer (1967) has recently reviewed this developing literature. For the social dimensions of situations, the most well-developed schemes now exist for the analysis of role behavior (e.g., Biddle and Thomas, 1966; Preiss and Ehrlich, 1966) and for the analysis of interaction processes (Borgatta and Crowther, 1965). Although the significance of role playing and role enactment for attitude change has been clearly demonstrated (Sarbin, 1964), attitude theorists have generally ignored role and related theories (and role theorists have generally ignored attitude variables).

Situational characteristics are often given theoretical consideration only if they are *perceived* by the actor, and sometimes they are considered only in terms of the actor's *attitudes* toward them. This strategy may be misleading. It remains to be demonstrated that the actor does, in fact, perceive and have an attitude toward situational properties and that such attitudes are of meaningful behavioral relevance. While many situational variables are invariably perceived, other situational variables of behavioral importance, particularly the structural characteristics, are probably seldom perceived. Whatever the strategy of situational analysis in attitude research, the warrant for its priority should be clear. In the classic formulation of Lewin: behavior is a function of the person and his environment.

Multiple Attitudes

A strategy for research on multiple attitudes is based on the assumptions that for some situations and objects more than one attitude will be evoked and that the behavioral strength of a set of attitudes may be formally determined. The research of Bayton, McAllister, and Hamer (1956), for example, has indicated that attitudes toward social class appear almost as important as race attitudes in determining the stereotypes assigned to Negroes. Triandis (1967) has demonstrated that the expression of behavioral intentions varies across the class, sex, ethnicity, occupation, and belief similarity of the attitude object. For example, behavior toward a Negro female physician may be primarily directed by one's attitudes toward Negroes, toward females, toward physicians, toward any two of these characteristics, or toward all three simultaneously. The development of a calculus of attitudes across attitude objects and situations should seriously be considered as an item of high research priority.

Concluding Remarks

The intervening variables presented here were specifically limited to those directly related to current attitude theories. I began by indicating that not all attitudes are behaviorally expressible, or at least clearly expressible, in interpersonal behavior. Some attitudes are deliberately not expressed in behavior, and I suggested that we examine the interpersonal conditions under which people are willing or unwilling to disclose their attitudes.

The exact behavior that complements a specific attitude is not always clear, and the presumed clarity of an act is itself a consequence of the perspective from which it is evaluated as well as the time that intervenes between act and evaluation. Knowledge of how to act consistently has to be learned, and not all actors will be able to use their knowledge with equal competence. Beyond these conditions, it still remains to be demonstrated that the actor has the opportunity to act appropriately. Finally, I indicated that the actor's failure to act in a manner consistent with a given attitude could be a direct result of other situational constraints or a result of conflict with other relevant attitudes that are more important to the behaviors under analysis.

The specific effects that each of these intervening variables has on behavior remains to be determined. There should be no doubt, however, that the study of these variables and the relation of attitudes to behavior is of strategic significance in the development of social psychology. The question I raised about this relation, in beginning our examination of the intervening variables, is a major instance of the classic problem of social psychology. Under what conditions, how, and to what degree do aspects of social structure and aspects of personality determine interpersonal behavior?

References

Altman, I., and W. W. Haythorn
      1965   "Interpersonal exchange in isolation." Sociometry 28:411–426.
Barker, R. G., and H. F. Wright
      1955   Midwest and Its Children. New York: Harper & Row.
Barker, R. G. (ed.)
      1963   The Stream of Behavior. New York: Appleton-Century-Crofts.
Bayton, J. A., et al.
      1956   "Race-class stereotypes." Journal of Negro Education 25 (Winter) :75–78.
Biddle, B. J., and E. J. Thomas (eds.)
      1966   Role Theory: Concepts and Research. New York: Wiley.
Borgatta, E. F., and B. Crowther
      1965   A Workbook for the Study of Social Interaction Processes. Chicago: Rand-McNally.
Bray, D. W.
      1950   "The prediction of behavior from two attitude scales." Journal of Abnormal and Social
              Psychology 45:64–84.
Brookover, W., and J. Holland
      1952   "An inquiry into the meaning of minority group attitude expressions." American Socio-
              logical Review 17:196–202.
Byrne, D.
      1961   "Interpersonal attraction and attitude similarity." Journal of Abnormal and Social Psy-
              chology 62:713–715.
Campbell, D. T.
      1961   "Social attitudes and other acquired behavioral dispositions," in S. Koch (ed.), Psychol-
              ogy: A Study of a Science, v. 6. New York: McGraw-Hill.
DeFleur, M. L., and F. R. Westie
      1963   "Attitude as a Scientific Concept." Social Forces 42:17–31.
      1958   "Verbal Attitudes and Overt Acts: An Experiment on the Salience of Attitudes." Ameri-
              can Sociological Review 23:677–673.
Deutsch, M.
      1949   "The Directions of Behavior: A Field-Theoretical Approach to the Understanding of
              Inconsistencies." Journal of Social Issues 5:43–51.
Deutscher, I.
      1966   "Words and deeds: social science and social policy." Social Problems 13 (Winter) :
              235–254.

Ehrlich, H. J.
  1964   "Instrument error and the study of prejudice." Social Forces 43:197–206.
Ehrlich, H. J., and J. W. Rinehart
  1965   "A brief report on the methodology of stereotype research." Social Forces 43:564–575.
Fendrich, J. M.
  1967   "A study of the association among verbal attitudes, commitment and overt behavior in different experiment situations." Social Forces 45:347–355.
Fishbein, M.
  1966   "The relationships between beliefs, attitudes, and behavior," in S. Feldman (ed.), Cognitive Consistency. New York: Academic Press.
Fishman, J.
  1961   "Some social and psychological determinants of intergroup relations in changing neighborhoods: an introduction to the Bridgeview study." Social Forces 40:42–51.
Graeven, D. B.
  1967   Reciprocal Self-Disclosure in a Dyadic Situation. M. A. Thesis, University of Iowa.
Hall, E. T.
  1966   The Hidden Dimension. New York: Doubleday.
  1963   "A system of notation of proxemic behavior." American Anthropologist 65:1003–1026.
Heer, D. M.
  1966   "Negro-white marriage in the United States." Journal of Marriage and the Family 28:262–273.
Himmelstrand, U.
  1960   "Verbal attitudes and behavior: a paradigm for the study of message transmission." Public Opinion Quarterly 24:224–250.
Jourard, S. M.
  1964   The Transparent Self. Princeton, N.J.: Van Nostrand.
Kay, L. W.
  1947   "Frame of reference in 'pro' and 'anti' evaluation of test items." Journal of Social Psychology 25:63–68.
Killian, L. M.
  1953   "The adjustment of Southern white migrants to Northern urban norms." Social Forces 32:66–69.
Kutner, B., C. Wilkins, and P. Yarrow
  1952   "Verbal attitudes and overt behavior involving racial prejudice." Journal of Abnormal and Social Psychology 47:649–652.
LaPiere, R. T.
  1936   "Type-rationalizations of group antipathy." Social Forces 15:232–237.
  1934   "Attitudes vs. actions." Social Forces 13:230–237.
Linn, L. S.
  1965   "Verbal attitudes and overt behavior: a study of racial discrimination." Social Forces 43:353–364.
Lohman, J. P., and D. C. Reitzes
  1952   "Note on race relations in mass society." American Journal of Sociology 58:240–246.
Malof, M., and A. Lott
  1962   "Ethnocentrism and the acceptance of Negro support in a group situation." Journal of Abnormal and Social Psychology 65:254–258.
Mills, C. W.
  1940   "Situated actions and vocabularies of motive." American Sociological Review 5:904–913.
Minard, R. D.
  1952   "Race relationships in the Pocahontas coal field." Journal of Social Issues 8:29–44.
Nettler, G., and E. H. Golding
  1946   "The measurement of attitudes toward the Japanese in America." American Journal of Sociology 52:31–39.
Preiss, J. J., and H. J. Ehrlich
  1966   An Examination of Role Theory. Lincoln: University of Nebraska Press.
Rokeach, M.
  1967   "Attitude change and behavioral change." Public Opinion Quarterly 30:529–550.
  1960   The Open and the Closed Mind. New York: Basic Books.

Rosenthal, R.
    1966   Experimenter Effects in Behavioral Research. New York: Appleton-Century-Crofts.
Saenger, G. H., and E. Gilbert
    1950   "Customer reactions to the integration of Negro sales personnel." Public Opinion
            Quarterly 4:57 – 76.
Sarbin, T. R.
    1964   "Role theoretical interpretation of psychological change." Pp. 176 – 219 in P. Worchel
            and D. Byrne (eds.), Personality Change. New York: Wiley.
Sommer, R.
    1967   "Small group ecology." Psychological Bulletin 67:145 – 152.
Tittle, C. R., and R. J. Hill
    1967   "Attitude measurement and prediction of behavior: an evaluation of conditions and
            measurement techniques." Sociometry 30:199 – 213.
Triandis, H. C.
    1967   "Toward an analysis of the components of interpersonal attitudes." Pp. 227 – 270 in C.
            W. Sherif and M. Sherif (eds.), Attitude, Ego-Involvement, and Change. New York:
            Wiley.
Williams, R. M.
    1964   Strangers Next Door. Englewood Cliffs, N.J.: Prentice-Hall.

Looking Forward: Research in the Late Sixties and the Early Seventies

If we were to extend the line of studies analyzed comparatively in our look backward (Chapter Four), the next reasonable point would be provided by James Fendrich's publications in 1967.[20] To the extent that Fendrich's work is typical of what
was happening during the last half of the decade of the sixties, things began to look
up, at least in some respects. This investigator (actually taking his cue from Linn) is
primarily concerned with intervening definitions of the situation, rather than with
what I described in Chapter Four as a primitive straight-line notion of cause and
effect prediction: "In contrast to other studies of verbal attitudes and overt behavior,
this study does not employ a theoretical model that posits there will be a linear one-
to-one association between the independent and dependent variables."[21] Although
he still employs a student sample, they are carefully selected on the basis of their
membership in the university community so that they may be viewed as people
involved in a real world with real consequences outside of the laboratory (e.g., he
excludes freshmen and people who live off-campus). By experimentally altering definitions of the situation, Fendrich introduces a degree of control which was absent
in the earlier studies. His statistical treatment is clean, employing carefully selected
techniques which meet the assumptional requirements of the data. Among the criteria employed in Chapter Four, Fendrich's work is noticeably deficient only in his
use of scales.[22]

Fendrich cites a number of papers published during the late fifties and ear-

---

20. Fendrich, "A Study of the Association Among Verbal Attitudes," and Fendrich, "Perceived Reference Group Support."
21. Fendrich, "A Study of the Association Among Verbal Attitudes," p. 352.
22. His work reflects continuing serious problems in this area. He claims his scales are reliable, but nothing is said about validity. Nor is there any indication of the extent of the cumulative features of the scales or their reproducibility, except for his behavioral scale which does
appear reasonable.

ly sixties, suggesting that the observed discrepancy between attitude and behavior can be explained by the intervening process. He is aware that there is a social situation intervening both when attitude is being expressed and when behavior is being observed, and suggests that the discrepancy may be attributable to the two different situations. It is his intention to manipulate definitions of the situation in order to determine their influence. Note how close Fendrich is moving toward the symbolic interactionist position: "The definition of the situation is used to refer to the respondent's subjective attempt to orient himself to the context in which he finds himself, ascertain his interest, and then proceed to cope with the circumstances."[23] Fendrich provides one situation which he describes as the usual play-like experimental situation. It simply asks white students their attitudes about blacks. The contrasting definition was provided by inducing a degree of "commitment." In this case, subjects were asked to commit themselves to interaction with blacks before responding to the attitude items. Fendrich employs three scales: (1) an "attitude" scale consisting mostly of belief statements with a sprinkling of values, i.e., "ought" statements; (2) a "commitment" scale, consisting of hypothetical expectations or anticipations—behavioral intentions (i.e., "Would you . . . ?"); (3) an "overt behavior" scale ranging from the subjects' expression of willingness to attend an NAACP meeting, through their restatement of such willingness later on the phone, through their actual attendance at such a meeting, to their volunteering for committee work.

Fendrich finds that attitudes explain only a small proportion of the variance in overt behavior (12 percent) while the intervening process of "commitment" accounts for 69 percent of the variance in overt behavior. Further he finds that the two different definitions of the situation he imposed experimentally have markedly different consequences, "producing one set of responses that were consistent with overt behavior and one set of inconsistent responses."[24] Fendrich recognizes that "it is dangerous to assume that participants are willing, but docile subjects in social research, rather, they are active agents who define a social situation and play what they perceive to be the appropriate role." He turns this observation to constructive use in designing his experiment. His other 1967 paper represents a further effort to escape what he calls "theoretical monism"—the idea that "one independent variable can account for all the variance in the dependent variable."[25] In that paper he presents four possible theoretical models relating reference-group behavior to racial attitudes and overt behavior. The one which his data appear to support suggests that reference-group behavior determines both racial attitudes and overt behavior, while racial attitudes simultaneously act as an independent determinant of overt behavior. That paper represents an important movement from description of relationships to explanation of relationships. However, the operations employed by Fendrich in this study reduce the credibility of the conclusions, for reasons the author is well aware of and enumerates. It is interesting that DeFriese and Ford report a field study two years later which confirms the theoretical model proposed by Fendrich, although they are apparently unaware of his paper.

23. Fendrich, "A Study of the Association Among Verbal Attitudes," p. 348. His concept of situational definitions is in line with the W. I. Thomas–G. H. Mead–H. Blumer conception. In fact, he cites Blumer as one of the sources for the perspective introduced in this research (p. 347n). The Blumer article is "Research on Race Relations in the United States of America," *International Social Science Journal* 10 (1958): 403–447.
24. Fendrich, "A Study of the Association Among Verbal Attitudes," p. 354.
25. Fendrich, "Perceived Reference Group Support," p. 960.

DeFriese and Ford analyze survey data on open housing.[26] They solicit from white informants attitudes toward blacks and the influence of certain reference groups. They also solicit signed statements of willingness to endorse or participate in open housing as their behavioral indicator. They find that attitudes and reference-group perceptions both explain about equal amounts of the variance in behavior. They interpret their data as suggesting that attitudes are indeed directly related to behaviors, but so too are reference-group perspectives and it is more expedient to use indices of the latter. Although Fendrich's experimental evidence was weak, this field confirmation provides a degree of convergence which enhances its credibility. I would be remiss if I did not point out that Fendrich is explicit about his clear and heavy debt to both the Linn and the DeFleur and Westie studies which were criticized in Chapter Four. The same is true of DeFriese and Ford. As we move toward the close of this chapter, it should become increasingly clear that it would be an error not to recognize the important contributions made by Linn and DeFleur-Westie, in spite of the somewhat shoddy treatment they received in Chapter Four. As I mentioned then, Linn is typically cited as the beginning of awareness of the salience of intervening variables, and, as we shall see below, DeFleur and his associates have become the major sociological contributors to understanding the relationship between sentiments and acts.

In 1963 DeFleur and Westie suggested that it is possible to view the relationships of attitudes and behaviors as a consequence of a mediating or, as they call it, a latent variable. They considered the possibility of "an intervening variable operating between stimulus and response."[27] This view, however, was rejected on the grounds that it assumes consistency between attitudes and behaviors. Instead, they opted for a probabilistic model, but within a half-dozen years, DeFleur was to return to the exploration of intervening variables, this time via a different route which no longer required the untenable assumption of consistency. Warner and DeFleur, writing in 1969, point out that some students assume a necessary relationship between attitude and behavior while others assume independence between them. But the accumulating data seem not to allow either of these positions; instead, "the results strongly suggest that such interactional concepts as norms, roles, group memberships, subcultures, etc., pose *contingent* conditions which can modify the relationship between attitudes and action."[28]

They are convinced that an adequate theory of attitude must "take into account the intervening situational variables which modify the relationship between attitudes and action." Although this position is a long way from Blumer's insistence that the intervening process is the legitimate and appropriate object of study in itself, it is, nevertheless, a signal improvement over the older stance which searched for a simple relationship between an independent and a dependent variable. The two intervening variables which they seek to control are "social constraint" and "social distance." The former is of particular interest since it would become the theme of a number of studies during the ensuing years. But the idea of social constraint is also interesting because it illustrates some of the problems which result

26. DeFriese and Ford, "Verbal Attitudes."
27. Melvin L. DeFleur and Frank R. Westie, "Attitude as a Scientific Concept," *Social Forces* 42 (1963): 21. See also, Norman C. Weisberg, "On DeFleur and Westie's 'Attitude as a Scientific Concept,'" *Social Forces* 43 (1965): 422–425, and DeFleur and Westie's "Rejoinder" which follows.
28. Warner and DeFleur, "Attitude as an Interactional Concept," p. 154 (italics in original).

from attempts to treat the intervening processes as an intervening variable. In a sense the whole intervening process can be described as one of social constraint, and almost anything that influences the expression of a sentiment or an act can be subsumed under "social constraint": reference groups, significant others, its public or private nature (disclosure), or perceptions of social distance.

Warner and DeFleur borrow their definition of social constraint directly from Durkheim's conception of a collective conscience. This more deterministic Durkheimian perspective brings them into sharp contrast with the more voluntaristic pragmatic perspective of the symbolic interactionist: for example, "Sociologists hold it to be axiomatic that a person acting in relation to others is directly and indirectly compelled to *behave as others expect.*"[29] This has been the dominant sociological perspective, but the symbolic interactionists, reflecting the pragmatic philosophy of the Chicago School, would never choose such a word as "compelled." Blumer, I suspect, would state the "axiom" in a fundamentally different way—something like: "In attempting to construct his line of action, a person must *take into account* the expectations of others." Whether or not the actor properly assesses those expectations, chooses to conform or deviate from them, is capable of carrying through his intentions, and other such contingencies are the stuff out of which inconsistencies between sentiments and acts are made.

These are the kinds of matters which Ehrlich considers in his contribution to this chapter. For the moment, I want only to highlight the fundamental differences between "to be compelled to behave as others expect" and "to take into account what others expect." Central to their research is Warner and DeFleur's notion of the relation between a social-psychological self and "others" in the definition of the social situation. Although they miss it completely, they do skirt very close to Blumer's formulation: ". . . the presence of others, either in the immediate sense or in the actor's psychological definition of the situation, exerts pressure to act in accordance with what those others are perceived to feel as appropriate and desirable conduct."[30] It is the element of a compelling drive to conform which is absent in Thomas' notion of the definition of the situation and Mead's notion of the significant other.

Throughout this volume the dimension of private and public opinions and actions has intruded as a central theme of our discussion (see especially Chapter Ten). It is also the central theme of Warner and DeFleur's 1969 article. What they suggest is that social constraint is a more powerful influence on the expression of an attitude or the performance of an act under public than it is under private conditions. Like Ehrlich, they use the term "disclosure" to refer to what happens when the actor is aware that others will know of his attitude or act. As they put it, how does the actor behave when he knows his behavior is under "surveillance" in contrast to the situation in which he believes his anonymity is preserved? This matter of surveillance is seen by Mayhew in a field study as the major controlling factor in constraining women to abide by the birth control proscriptions of their churches.[31] His logic is that peer-surveillance is provided when people marry co-religionists; the church, in the person of the spouse, is exercising surveillance over sex behavior. On the other hand, women who marry outsiders can practice birth control because

29. Ibid., p. 155 (italics in original).
30. Ibid., p. 155.
31. Bruce Mayhew, "Behavioral Observability and Compliance with Religious Proscriptions on Birth Control," *Social Forces* 47 (1968): 60–70.

of the absence of surveillance by co-religionists. In this sense, Mayhew argues that people comply with their church proscriptions of birth control in accordance with how public (observable) their sex behavior is. He finds that verbal acceptance of the belief — the religious proscription — does not predict high fertility. What does predict fertility differentials is the intervening variable of surveillance of sex behavior by one's own co-religionists. Mayhew's analysis suggests that there are reasonable empirical grounds for considering, as Warner and DeFleur do, this matter of surveillance.

Warner and DeFleur are beginning to focus on the complex intervening process as the molder of eventual outcomes. There is not only a suggestion that the process is a total entity in and of itself, but of equal importance, a recognition that it must be viewed from the perspective of the actor. We have here an awareness of the need for a phenomenological view: ". . . social distance, social constraint, and attitude form a single system of interactional considerations, a *gestalt*, confronting the actor. That is, they are experienced by a subject as a single system of variables impinging upon his decisions concerning acceptance or rejection of the attitude object."[32] What is suggested here is that people may not think of an act in terms of "variables" at all. Rather, they think and act and take into account the totality of the situation as they size it up! Variables may be useful functions for facilitating the scientist's work, but they do not exist in the everyday world of authentic human behavior. Without reviewing the design details of the Warner-DeFleur study, which deals with racial attitudes and behaviors, its most significant feature is that its factorial design allows the analyst to identify sources of variance which derive from the interaction between and among variables. With this design it is no longer necessary to restrict our conception of human behavior as resulting from the action of isolated variables. They are still variables, but at least they are now working in conjunction with each other. The design also encourages the analysts to keep separate the two kinds of consistency and the two kinds of inconsistency identified in Chapter Nine.

Warner and DeFleur do find that the factor of social constraint (the threat of public disclosure) has a powerful effect on both high- and low-prejudiced subjects. Furthermore, that effect is different for these two groups of subjects. The complex interactions they discover seem more closely to approximate what happens in everyday life than the earlier simplistic variable studies:

> . . . high social constraint had a substantial inhibiting effect upon the least prejudiced subjects. Since the requested act was one generally disapproved within relevant norms, the exposure to potential surveillance provided by the condition of high social constraint produced inconsistency between attitudes and action for the least prejudiced subjects. In fact, there was no clear relationship under these conditions between attitude and action. . . . For the most prejudiced subjects, on the other hand, a condition of high social constraint tended to produce substantial consistency between attitudes and action. The general norms surrounding the act, the potential surveillance resulting from high social constraint and the initial attitude all combined to produce a very high level of refusal over compliance. . . . This indicates consistency between negative attitude and rejection of the attitude object.[33]

32. Warner and DeFleur, "Attitude as an Interactional Concept," p. 156.
33. Ibid., p. 164.

Since the publication of that 1969 article, Warner and DeFleur and their associates have for the first time undertaken to extend their research comparatively. In a series of papers they have reported experiments dealing not with attitudes and behaviors of whites toward blacks, but with attitudes and behaviors of students toward marijuana smoking.[34] Their work uniformly reflects an abandonment of the view that a direct relationship necessarily exists between attitudes and behaviors and adopts a concomitant emphasis on the intervening process. It is of considerable interest, that, having abandoned their earlier perspective, they find that there sometimes is a direct relationship—that people do under some conditions act in accord with their sentiments. The conditions under which such concordance might be expected have been illustrated as well as theoretically articulated by Blumer.[35]

Their initial question is, does the knowledge gleaned from studies in the race area hold for other areas too? They believe that it has become evident that, in race relations, the public-private dimension (disclosure) and the subject's perception of what other people think represent important intervening variables in the relationship. The reader who will recall, among other fragments of evidence, the convergence of Gorden and Raven on these matters (see Chapter Eight) will find this a reasonable starting point. By 1972, Albrecht, DeFleur, and Warner are beginning to take a phenomenological perspective in their experiments: ". . . it seems possible that one of the primary sources of error in predicting the effect of disclosure on the attitude-behavior relationship results from a lack of information about the *subject's* definition of the situation. As pointed out long ago by W. I. Thomas, the crucial factor as far as the individual's own response is concerned is not the group's position as such, but his perception of that position."[36] As the researchers begin to treat this position with respect, they must inevitably also begin to move away from concern with variables, and concern with the attitude-behavior relationship, toward an interest in the intervening process as the object of study. This new slant leads them to the observation that it is what's in between that counts. And, in fact, the kinds of information these investigators see as essential data become phenomenological: data is obtained from the vantage point of the subject!

In this research, Albrecht and his associates seek to identify (1) the subject's perception of relevant norms; (2) the subject's perception of relevant reference groups; (3) the subject's perception of the relative importance of those reference groups; and (4) the subject's perception of the normative attitudes of his reference groups toward the issue in question. It seems to me that their central question is, in making an attitude public, to what extent is the actor guided by what he thinks that public thinks? In their terms, "The notion of disclosure must be combined with that of perceptions of the position of significant others to whom disclosure will be made." It is this observation on which the hypotheses of the study are based. Their discussion of reference groups rests on a distinction between what Mead called a

---

34. Stan Albrecht graciously provided me with prepublication copies of three papers which provide the basis for this discussion. Those papers are Albrecht, DeFleur, and Warner, op. cit.; Frideres, Warner, and Albrecht, op. cit.; and Albrecht, op. cit. I encountered Acock and DeFleur as this volume was going to press.

35. For illustrations, see Herbert Blumer, "Public Opinion and Public Opinion Polling," *American Sociological Review* 13 (1948): 547, and our discussion in Chapter Six. The theoretical argument is contained in the Blumer bit reprinted in this Chapter.

36. Albrecht, DeFleur, and Warner, "Attitude-Behavior Relationships," (italics in original).

"generalized other" (the subjects' "perception of what is viewed as acceptable and appropriate in the larger social setting") and "significant others" (specific groups to whom the subject is relatively more or less committed). It is the interrelationships among disclosure, the generalized other, and significant others from which the final set of hypotheses is derived. Their data consist of (1) an attitude scale on marijuana; (2) the subject's estimate of how various reference groups feel about marijuana (family, friends, etc.); (3) the subject's ranking of reference groups in terms of his perception of their influence; (4) the subject's estimates of "more general normative prescriptions" regarding marijuana smoking. Subjects were exposed to two kinds of action situations: (5) they were asked to take a public position on marijuana by signing a petition to legalize it or not to legalize it (the petition was presumably to be published) and (6) they were instructed to take a private position on marijuana by secret ballot.

The investigators controlled for twelve background variables (of which sex seemed to be the only one which made a difference in attitudes toward marijuana) and isolated the two extreme quartiles of their sample. There were seventy-two student subjects in each of the extreme groups. Although there may have been a reasonable doubt about the salience of race issues to some of the student samples in earlier studies, there can be little doubt about the salience of marijuana smoking to student populations in the late sixties and early seventies. It is interesting in view of the elaborate efforts to tap the subjective intervening process, that a very large proportion of the variance in overall behavior is explained by (the same as) the expressed attitude. The little distribution below is adapted from data which appear in the Albrecht, Warner, and DeFleur article:

Overt Behavior

Attitude	Unfavorable	Favorable	Total
Least favorable quartile	57	15	72
Most favorable quartile	15	57	72
Total	72	72	144

Note that each kind of consistency accounts for 40 percent of the subjects.[37] Eighty percent of these students act in accordance with their sentiments. Twenty percent of them do not—10 percent representing each of the two types of inconsistency. The authors remark that this is a stronger direct relationship than has been observed in previous research on race. If we view this study as the kind of preliminary variable analysis which is necessary in order to identify problem areas, then according to the argument in the preceding section of this chapter, the difference may inform us regarding the general stability or institutionalization of attitudes on marijuana in contrast with attitudes on race.

These authors are clearly disappointed that they find no difference in behavior under public and private conditions. This could mean that unlike the race situation, students are not secretive about their attitudes toward marijuana—there may in fact be no discrepancy between public and private attitudes or behavior in

37. The reader should recognize that, with equal marginal totals and with one degree of freedom, the perfect reversal of frequencies in this table is a mathematical artifact. No matter how many subjects fall in a given cell, the other subjects must distribute themselves in this perfect reversal form.

this area. If people are not inclined to be secretive about either their approval or their disapproval of marijuana, then we would obtain the kind of results which appear in this study. Regardless of how the findings are interpreted, they do exist and they are important when compared with the race findings. Although the authors like to think that they have some support for two of their hypotheses, I do not concur. Their data do not permit the rejection of any null hypothesis, nor do they account for an impressive amount of variance—with one exception: there is a direct relationship between the attitude and the act. It seems to me that we have here a situation in which sentiments and acts do coincide. There are also conditions under which they do not.

It is not clear whether the authors understand that in this kind of study one cannot possibly "win" on *all* hypotheses. They are, in effect, playing a zero-sum game. There is only 100 percent variance to begin with and to the extent that one factor explains a bit, there is that much less remaining to be explained. If, in this study, the generalized other (larger social norms) had turned out to be a strong coercive force, then specific significant others (reference groups) could not, mathematically, be so important—and vice versa. Let us pursue the finding that intervening processes seem inoperative in the experimental situations provided in the marijuana study. Recall that, in his contribution to this chapter, Ehrlich insists that "the search for a more appropriate research strategy must begin with the understanding that the simple question of the consistency of attitudes and behavior is misleading. The correct representation of the problem should take the form: Under what conditions, and to what degree, are attitudes of a given type related to behaviors of a given type? My intent . . . is to identify the social and psychological conditions that intervene between attitudes and behavior."[38] It may be of some importance to note that *every potential intervening factor identified by Ehrlich can be ruled out in the study reported by Albrecht, DeFleur, and Warner:* clarity, expressibility, disclosure, perspective, learning, accessibility, and competence.

In another analysis of the same data, Frideres, Warner, and Albrecht[39] find much the same thing—about 80 percent of the subjects behave in accord with their sentiments. This is hardly surprising since they are the same subjects. But in this analysis one important kind of interaction effect does appear. Under private conditions (nondisclosure), when the actor's views are incongruent with the expressed views of others in the situation (confederates), the relationship between the attitude and the behavior decreases substantially. The congruence factor introduced into this study is reminiscent of the modeling effects we have noted from time to time.[40] When a person is aware of how others in the immediate situation feel, he does tend to conform. The complexity of the intervening process, and the manner in which variable analysis may obscure that process, is demonstrated here. Neither disclosure nor social participation appears to have any direct effect on the relationship, but both of these factors have a distinct impact when they are considered in relation to the congruency variable.

38. My own early effort to formulate the question was similar to Ehrlich's: "Under what conditions will people behave as they talk? Under what conditions is there no relationship? And under what conditions do they say one thing and behave exactly the opposite?" (Irwin Deutscher, "Words and Deeds: Social Science and Social Policy," *Social Problems* 13 [1966] :243.)

39. Frideres, Warner, and Albrecht, "The Impact of Social Constraints."

40. See, for example, the bit by Himelstein and Moore in Chapter Ten and related studies such as Lionel Dannick, "The Relationship Between Overt Behavior and Verbal Expressions as Influenced by Immediate Situational Determinants" (diss., Syracuse University, 1969).

One factor which we failed to consider in interpreting the Albrecht-De-Fleur-Warner experiment, was the extent to which the behavioral indicator was equivalent to the attitudinal one. Albrecht pursues this question in a post-interview with the experimental subjects in which he elicits information about their own experience with marijuana.[41] It can be argued that the attitudinal and behavioral situations are more nearly alike when the person asked about marijuana smoking is known to either smoke or not to smoke marijuana, than when the behavioral indicator is voting or signing a petition. Using the previously described indicators along with his self-reports of marijuana use, Albrecht finds "a strong relationship between subject perceptions of the expectations of significant others and their own behavior." In fact, he continues, "the relationship between behavior and interpersonal influence is somewhat stronger than that observed between attitude and action." What he finds is that people who express favorable attitudes toward marijuana but do not use it are in almost every case those who perceive significant others as disapproving.

Before leaving this important set of reports, I want to consider a question related to changing men's minds and changing their behavior. In order to do this, I have reproduced what appears as Table 2 in Albrecht's unpublished manuscript:

Personal Experience with Marijuana

Attitudes Toward Marijuana	Have not used	Have used	Total
Unfavorable*	25	1	26
Favorable	17	16	33
TOTAL	42	17	59

Correct prediction on the basis of attitude — 69.5%
*Albrecht indicates in the original table that the top two quartiles are used for the unfavorable category and the bottom two quartiles for the favorable, otherwise this table is exactly as he presents it.

Notice that Albrecht interprets these data as permitting the prediction of marijuana use on the basis of attitudes toward marijuana. It seems to me that a reverse interpretation is equally plausible. A favorable attitude is clearly not a very good predictor of use and likewise the failure to have used marijuana is not a very good predictor of attitude. However, if we predict that all people with unfavorable attitudes have not used marijuana, we will be nearly perfect in our prognostication. But is it not also true that if we took all marijuana users and predicted that they would have a favorable attitude, our prognosis would also be nearly perfect? It could be argued that 1:26 is better odds than 1:17, but I prefer to think of the cell with the unitary occupant as, for all practical purposes, zero. In other words, regardless of marginal totals, we have something approaching 100 percent predictability either way. I am in fact more persuaded by the logic which suggests that in this case personal experiences are antecedent to expressed attitudes. Regardless of choice in the

41. Albrecht, "Verbal Attitudes and Significant Other's Expectations."

matter of causal direction, what is most striking about this table is not the predictive power of either use or attitude; it is the powerful interaction between these two variables which is most worthy of note. A favorable attitude doesn't tell you much about use, but an unfavorable attitude tells you a great deal. The same observation can be made regarding use.

Whether the problem be one of race or drugs or whatever, it would be unwise to ignore Milton Rokeach's persistent plea that it isn't only intervening variables which must be considered. There is also the whole complex paraphernalia of attitudes, beliefs, and orientations we all carry around with us. It may be that, other things being equal, prejudiced whites will reject blacks as associates, but the facts of life are that other things never are equal. As an example, Rokeach and Mezei present evidence that both high- and low-prejudiced people seek out interaction with people who have beliefs like themselves—regardless of their race.[42] The argument is that since there are lots of different kinds of attitudes operating, why expect any one to be the determinant of behavior? Translated into the terms I have been attempting to use in this chapter, Rokeach is asking that we take into account the whole complex definition of the situation which, in one way or another, culminates in an action.

Other psychologists focus more directly on the intervening process and on situational factors and even on the crucial distinction between public and private expressions. In a summary article published in 1965, Vernon Allen concludes that:

> One of the most important advances in the area of group influence has been the realization that conformity and nonconformity cannot be satisfactorily conceptualized by restricting analysis to the phenotypic level. Two responses which are phenotypically identical may differ in terms of their meaning for the individual, the psychological process which produced them, and in consequences for future behavior.[43]

Allen, too, has reached the conclusion that to establish a relationship between an input variable and an output variable is not a very informative accomplishment. Thus, two people appear to be conforming, let us say, publicly. One has private beliefs which lead him to this public conformity. The other is conforming publicly under some form of social pressure not because of his private beliefs, but in spite of them. These two persons who express the same public opinion certainly cannot be expected to act the same in private and may vary in public depending upon the nature of the perceived social constraints. The reverse is also possible: apparent differences may cloak basic similarities just as apparent similarities can cloak basic differences. It is the application of Allen's logic which makes the demand for a roll call vote in congress such an effective strategy. In Chapter Six we considered the difference in results when congressmen were forced to publicly express their views on a congressional pay raise. That vote was the reverse of one taken secretly only moments before.

The issue of public and private conformity becomes even clearer when we consider Allen's analysis of the Asch-type experiments. Asch had his subjects pro-

42. M. Rokeach and L. Mezei, "Race and Shared Belief as Factors in Social Choice," *Science* 151 (1966) :167–172.

43. Vernon L. Allen, "Situational Factors in Conformity," in *Advances in Social Psychology*, vol. 2, ed. Leonard Berkowitz (New York: Academic Press, 1965), p. 136.

vide judgments on the comparative length of lines in the presence of confederates who, by plan, judge aloud that longer lines are shorter and shorter lines are longer. Unlike the Sherif autokinetic experiments, the Asch model deliberately leads the subjects to accept factually erroneous conclusions by the group. Allen suggests that conformity under these conditions is purely public, with private views not being altered at all. He uses Asch's own interview data as suggesting that "actual change" rarely occurs. Although subjects publicly agree with the group, they remain privately certain that the group is wrong.[44] This issue has been pursued by a pair of scholars in two published reports.[45] Luchins and Luchins readministered the entire set of stimuli (lines) to subjects after they had taken the basic experiment and conformed to the majority. This time the subjects made no objectively incorrect choices. Their second study produced less clear results. Taking the stimuli in private immediately after the experiment, the subjects tended to provide the same erroneous results as they had under social pressure, but one day later these same subjects made no errors.

However we prefer to see them, as intervening variables or an intervening process, it is becoming increasingly apparent that the things which occur in between require attention if we are to understand more fully the sometimes lack of relationship between sentiments and acts. Ehrlich's list, although comprehensive, remains far from complete. For example, he correctly suggests that discrepancies may result from ignorance, lack of logical discipline, or educational deficiency. But he fails to note that, on the other hand, the best educated, logically trained scientists can behave contrary to their beliefs and knowledge. In smoking, for example, there appears to be no relation between knowledge and behavior. There is evidence that certain cancer research scientists who link smoking with lung cancer still maintain their smoking behavior.[46] Baer concludes in his comparison of several types of smokers and nonsmokers that "present smokers who smoked cigarettes only, would like to have stopped smoking, believed they smoked too much, believed in a relationship between smoking and lung cancer, believed in a reduction in life expectancy from smoking. . . ."[47]

What is true of cigarette smokers may be equally true of the inconsistency between knowledge and activity common to many areas of habitual or pleasurable behavior. Such behavior may have known consequences ranging from a high risk of venereal disease to a high risk of accidental death. Psychoanalytic theory might permit us to avoid confronting such knotty problems with notions about self-destructive behavior, a death wish, or other inferential explanations. I suspect, however, that Jeremy Bentham's quaint idea of a hedonistic calculus makes more sense. The smoker continues to smoke against the odds like the reckless driver continues to speed against the odds because both types of behavior are fun. The actors' as-

44. Allen cites as his source, S. E. Asch, "Studies of Independence and Submission to Group Pressure: I. A Minority of One Against a Unanimous Majority," *Psychological Monographs* 70 (1956): whole of no. 417.

45. A. S. Luchins and E. H. Luchins, "On Conformity with True and False Communications," *Journal of Social Psychology* 42 (1955): 283–303, and A. S. Luchins and E. H. Luchins, "On Conformity with Judgments of a Majority or an Authority," *Journal of Social Psychology* 53 (1961): 303–316. These two articles are cited by Allen, "Situational Factors."

46. M. P. Lawton and A. E. Goldman, "Cigarette Smoking and Attitude Toward the Etiology of Lung Cancer," *American Psychologist* 13 (1958): 342.

47. D. J. Baer, "Smoking Attitude, Behavior, and Beliefs of College Males," *Journal of Social Psychology* 68 (1966): 69–70.

sumption is that the long shot will pay off for him. Far from wanting to die, he wants to eat his cake and have it too.

Certainly there are social constraints which intervene between a sentiment and a related act. But to name the process in that manner brings us closer to understanding human behavior and social processes only to the extent that it directs our attention to the proper locus of exploration. It is important that we recognize that it is not input and output or independent and dependent variables or stimulus and response which is our proper concern. It is more likely what's in between that counts. Of all of the reasonable alternatives Ehrlich provides for us in seeking intervening variables, I think that *opportunity* deserves to be singled out for special attention. Perhaps I am influenced by the large impact which that little idea has had in understanding some kinds of juvenile delinquency.[48] The fact is that regardless of all other social, psychological, and physiological forces, we must have an opportunity present before we can behave in a given manner and the absence of such an opportunity severely limits the likelihood of such behavior. Opportunity is, then, a condition which is always salient to human behavior. The absence of opportunity to behave in an approved manner can be illustrated with the results of an educational program for soldiers who are in prison. Imprisoned soldiers who have gone over the hill may well become convinced as a consequence of an educational program that going over the hill is not a reasonable thing to do. They may even honestly intend to refrain from doing so in the future. But when there is trouble at home and they cannot get a leave, they apparently continue to go over the hill — regardless of their good intentions.[49] It can be said that they did not have the opportunity to act according to their intentions. Under such conditions, it is the intervening situation with its lack of opportunity which requires attention.

From my own experiences with public housing I know that many poor people will go to great pains, including considerable degradation, in order to implement their intentions to obtain a public housing unit. People who say they intend to go into public housing do in fact generally apply. To that extent they act in accord with their sentiments. It is also true that these same people generally do not get to live in public housing.[50] To that extent their behavior is not in accord with their sentiments. However, the opportunity is denied these people as a result of factors

48. Richard A. Cloward and Lloyd E. Ohlin, *Delinquency and Opportunity* (New York: The Free Press, 1960).

49. Generally this series of reports on the results of educational programs for imprisoned soldiers shows a remarkable change in attitudes as well as remarkable changes in a wide variety of observable military behaviors. However, 40 percent of these men fail to report back to duty after release. Comparisons between these failures and the successes, on both attitudinal and behavioral items, show no differences. Harry E. Allen, Clifford E. Simonsen, and Harold J. Vetter, "Attitudes and Behavior: A Test," round table discussion at annual meetings of the Ohio Valley Sociological Society, 1971; Clifford E. Simonsen, Harry E. Allen, and Harold J. Vetter, "The 'Purely Military Offender': An Empirical Assessment of Attitudinal and Behavioral Change," paper prepared for presentation at the annual meeting of the Ohio Valley Sociological Society, 1971; Clifford E. Simonsen, Harry E. Allen, Harold J. Vetter, "The 'Military Offender': An Empirical Assessment of Attitudinal and Behavioral Change," paper read at the annual meetings of the Pacific Sociological Association, 1971.

50. Lawrence T. Cagle and Irwin Deutscher, "Housing Aspirations and Housing Achievement: The Relocation of Poor Families," *Social Problems* 18 (1970): 244–256. See also Seymour S. Bellin and Louis Kriesberg, "Relationship Among Attitudes, Circumstances, and Behavior: The Case of Applying for Public Housing," *Sociology and Social Research* 51 (1967): 453–469.

over which they have no control.[51] Note that, once these intervening processes are understood, the discrepancies between sentiments and acts need no longer be viewed as "inconsistent." Our understanding has removed the designation "inconsistent"; it has not, however, removed the discrepancy. The fact is that people sometimes do not do as they say and it is important to be attentive to such discrepancies. Although they may sometimes be more apparent than real, they are sometimes very real. Rather than attempting to explain such discrepancies away as "spurious," it is gratifying to recognize them for what they are and to begin to understand the processes that account for them. That is the function of science.

There is, however, a source of observed discrepancies which is very different from those discussed up to this point. Recall the difficulty I have had in finding appropriate names for the dimensions we have been considering in this volume. By and large it has been implied, for purposes of discussion, that we are exploring the relation between two phenomena (attiudes and behavior, words and deeds, sentiments and acts, etc.). The difficulty in naming these two phenomena reflects much more than an inconvenience; behind that difficulty lies the variety of *different phenomena* which is subsumed under the two gross categories. The confusion which results from this conceptual muddiness has consequences for understanding the relationship between what people say or think or feel and what they do. Although our earlier discussion of language broached this problem, Chapter Twelve will consider in some detail the manner in which conceptual confusion can sometimes lead to attempts to add apples and oranges—can lead to comparing phenomena which are in fact not comparable. In the next chapter we turn to the concrete issue of the building blocks of theory—to the matter of concepts and how they can be a source of confusion as well as a source of clarification.

51. Irwin Deutscher, "The Bureaucratic Gatekeeper in Public Housing," in *Among the People: Encounters with the Poor*, eds. Irwin Deutscher and Elizabeth J. Thompson (New York: Basic Books, 1968), pp. 38–52.

12 Concepts and How Their Confusion Can Mess You Up

Making Distinctions and Connections[1]

At the outset of this book, I insisted on the need to sift information through a double screen before its meaning and credibility could properly be assessed. The first screen concerned methodological credibility as a basis for appropriate discounting and Part II was attentive to that issue. The second screen is a conceptual one. It has been alluded to from time to time since Ajzen and his associates pointed out the distinction between behavioral intention and actual behavior (Chapter Five). It seems appropriate to develop the issue in this part of the book, which is concerned with theory. The problem of conceptual confusion stems from the fact that an individual may simultaneously or sequentially harbor a number of different orientations toward the same social object. It becomes difficult to accumulate comparative knowledge unless it is clear what kinds of orientations are being elicited and observed. This is the problem of conceptual confusion. It implies the need to make more meaningful distinctions in the connotations of words employed in interviews and research instruments. Although, like some of the methodological arguments, it suggests that some observed discrepancies are more apparent than real, it also suggests that there is a large and undifferentiated set of possible relationships between orientations toward the same phenomenon. In this chapter I will concentrate on the confusions which result when we fail to make clear conceptual distinctions.

In my earliest efforts to understand the relationship between what people do and what they say, I complained that we knew so little that I couldn't even find an adequate vocabulary to make the distinction.[2] At that time I was more irritated by the profusion of terms than I was aware of the confusion of concepts. At some point, however, it occurred to me that some of the studies I was attempting to analyze comparatively were dealing with different phenomena (frequently under the same name). It became increasingly clear that behavioral intentions, observed behaviors, and self-reported behaviors are not necessarily all the same. It became equally clear that beliefs, aspirations, norms, values, and knowledge might possibly be unrelated or, at least, differentially related. The distinction between attitude and behavior is vulgar! So too is the distinction between sentiments and acts or any other which implies a dichotomy. There are many kinds of sentimental orientations, possibly as different from each other as each is from the many kinds of action orientations.

Some reputable scholars avoid this issue by classifying, as B. F. Skinner

1. This section is an extension of a paper I read at the annual meetings of the Midwest Sociological Society in 1967: "On Adding Apples and Oranges: Making Distinctions and Connections in Social Science."

2. Irwin Deutscher, "Words and Deeds: Social Science and Social Policy," *Social Problems* 13 (1966): 242.

does, all orientations toward social objects as "behavior."[3] The operant-conditioning psychologists and their sociological counterparts argue that the concept of "attitude" is a useless fiction which can be eliminated from our conceptual repertoire. This is precisely the position Tarter eloquently advocates:

> Recently, I have been drawn more and more consistently to behavioral psychology for the answer to the perplexing attitude-action problem. The answer from this perspective, of course, is that attitudes are just another of the many hypothetical and largely unproductive mental states that behavioral scientists have tried to measure and use in prediction of overt behavior. As a concept, attitudes have had the same ineffective predictive consequences that all the rest of these "inter-state variables" have had. It appears to me that the adoption of this line of reasoning would do much to clarify the attitude-action problem.[4]

Tarter would prefer to discard the "mentalistic" term *attitude*, but he recognizes that this is unrealistic in view of the vested interests and prejudices of social scientists. If some scholars would prefer that everything be seen as "behavior," there are others who suggest that all orientations toward social objects be embraced by the concept of "attitudes."[5] Although both arguments have merit, neither is ultimately very helpful. The sole achievement of this line of reasoning is to rename the study of human interaction as either the study of human behavior or of human attitudes. This is a version of the naming game which the Hughes' have described as sociological exorcism.[6] The creation of euphemisms, epithets, or otherwise relabeling a phenomenon has little scientific import, although it may have social value as in the case of the self-fulfilling prophecy. There is another sense in which it is not very helpful to call everything either behavior or attitudes. Concepts, if they are to be useful and informative, must distinguish among relatively homogeneous categories of phenomena. Otherwise, they cannot facilitate understanding of the relationships among such phenomena. A category makes no sense unless there are at least two of them; it cannot help us make connections when there is nothing left with which to connect. To subsume all orientations toward an object under a single conceptual umbrella is a nominalistic nullification of the problem. It is magic and not science.

It should be clear by now that the concept of a concept being purveyed here is quite different from the operational formulation originally suggested by Bridgman. Bridgman's notion has been widely adopted in the social sciences because it permitted us to avoid embarrassing attempts to understand what was going on in the real world. Instead, Bridgman argues for the creation and study of artificial worlds because they are simpler, clearer, more controllable, and conform to our abil-

3. B. F. Skinner, *Verbal Behavior* (New York: Appleton-Century-Crofts, 1957). Noam Chomsky has provided a thorough critique of this position in his review of Skinner in *Language* 35 (1959): 26–58.

4. Donald E. Tarter, "Attitude: The Mental Myth," *American Sociologist* 5 (1970): 276.

5. Melvin L. DeFleur and Frank R. Westie, "Attitude as a Scientific Concept," *Social Forces* 42 (1963): 17–31. For a discussion of some of the basic problems in the attitude concept see Herbert Blumer, "Attitudes and the Social Act," *Social Problems* 3 (1955): 59–65.

6. See "What's in a Name," Chapter 9 in Everett Cherrington Hughes and Helen MacGill Hughes, *Where Peoples Meet: Racial and Ethnic Frontiers* (Glencoe, Ill.: The Free Press, 1952), pp. 130–44.

ities to measure them: "In general, we mean by any concept nothing more than a set of operations: the concept is synonymous with the corresponding set of operations."[7] It is assumed in this chapter that a concept is synonymous not with a corresponding set of operations, but with the recurring, empirically observable phenomena of everyday life to which it refers, which it identifies, and which it distinguishes from unlike phenomena and relates to like phenomena.

A phenomenological perspective suggests that the scientific definition of concepts is unimportant relative to the definitions employed by the people we are interested in learning about. No effort is made here toward attempting to order a scientific concept of "attitude" or of "behavior." Instead, what is suggested is that a great amount of confusion and misinformation results when we assume that people are providing us with a single datum because we have a name for it. The important variations in definition are those employed by our respondents. This is true not only because people shift perspectives as a result of subtle verbal clues (e.g., "believe," "think," "expect," "like," "approve"), but also because the range, intensity, and intervals respondents customarily employ may differ from the ranges, intensities, and intervals imposed by social scientists in their scaling devices.[8] Occasionally a thoughtful sociologist recognizes this problem. Shalom Schwartz, for example, in his efforts to relate attitudes and behaviors of people regarding the donation of organs for transplanting, writes: "I am now working on a scale to measure sense of moral obligation to serve as a transplant donor. . . . This normative scale runs from -1 'obligation *not* to,' to 0 'no obligation,' through 5 'strong obligation.' This seems closer to the reality of people's natural conceptual scales."[9]

The distinction between covert sentiments and overt acts, although a necessary starting point, remains a first order distinction of the grossest kind. There is a large number of possible cognitive, verbal, and overt action orientations toward the same object whether that object be a black man, a wife, or a political candidate. The extent and direction of covariance among these multiple orientations remains as problematic as the relationship between the components of the basic dichotomy — sentiments and acts. If for no other reason, the fact that the relationships among these various orientations are unknown makes it imperative that we clearly distinguish which of them we are dealing with in our investigations. Although it would be helpful if there were a standard usage of such terms as "values," "norms," "beliefs," "aspirations," "opinions," and the like, this is not the central problem. The problem is to make the necessary distinctions between orientations and to understand what kind of orientation we intend to tap and what kind of orientation our respondents are providing us with.

The two research cases reprinted below help to illustrate my argument. They document what happens when conceptual discrepancies are recognized. What happens is the elimination of a considerable amount of confusion in the comparisons of sets of presumably similar data. The social object in which Hyman Rodman is interested is nonlegal marital unions in Caribbean societies — especially the orien-

7. P. W. Bridgman, *The Logic of Modern Physics* (New York: Macmillan Co., 1927), p. 5 (italics in original).
8. See Nehemiah Jordan, "The 'Asymmetry' of 'Liking' and 'Disliking': A Phenomenon Meriting Further Reflection and Research," *Public Opinion Quarterly* 29 (1956): 315–22. For a partial solution see Robert Hamblin, "Ratio Measurement and Sociological Theory: A Critical Analysis" (St. Louis: Washington University, 1966), mimeograph.
9. Shalom Schwartz, personal communication, September 1969.

tations of members of the lower classes toward such unions. There appears to be consensus regarding the overt behavioral orientation: such unions occur frequently among the Caribbean lower classes. The problem arises when various investigators attempt to assess "attitudes" toward this same object. A rash of contradictory and inconsistent findings are reported. Scanning reports by Rodman, Blake, Simey, Goode, Braithwaite, and Hatt,[10] it is difficult to believe that these social scientists are all talking about the same thing. And, as it turns out, they are in fact not talking about the same thing although they sometimes employ the same name to refer to it. There are many possible sources of explanations for the variance found among these studies, but Rodman has isolated the one which seems to account for a great deal. *He is able to reconcile what appear at first blush to be inconsistent findings by making a simple conceptual distinction.* The second illustration of the way in which meaningful conceptual distinctions can lead to clarification derives from Gunnar Myrdal and is reported by Frank Westie.

10. See Rodman's footnotes 2, 3, and 29 in his contribution to this chapter.

DATA:
Illegitimacy in the
Caribbean Social Structure: A Reconsideration

HYMAN RODMAN

Much theoretical and empirical controversy has centered upon the family in the Caribbean area. One controversial question concerns the values of members of the lower classes in Caribbean societies regarding non-legal marital unions[1] and the illegitimate children born to these unions.[2] There is general agreement on the high rates of illegitimacy and non-legal unions to be found in Caribbean societies,

Hyman Rodman, "Illegitimacy in the Caribbean Social Structure: A Reconsideration," *American Sociological Review*, vol. 31, no. 4 (1966), pp. 673–83. Reprinted by permission of the American Sociological Association and the author. Table 5 from *Backgrounds of Human Fertility in Puerto Rico,* by Paul K. Hatt. Copyright 1952 by Princeton University Press. Reprinted by permission. The following acknowledgment accompanies this article as it was originally published:

"Patricia G. Voydanoff has contributed to this paper as a research assistant and as a critical reader of an earlier draft. In addition, Lloyd Rogler, Constantina Safilios-Rothschild, and John S. Watson have made a number of helpful suggestions, although I have not followed their advice at all points. The research and analysis were supported in part by NIMH grant #MH 08249–01, and by research grants from the Research Institute for the Study of Man and the Welfare Administration, Department of Health, Education, and Welfare, Washington, D.C."

[1]The term, "non-legal marital unions," is used in this paper to refer only to those unions in which the man and the woman are cohabiting. The controversy in the Caribbean data centers on this union, called variously by researchers common-law marriage, concubinage, and consensual union. See Hyman Rodman, "On Understanding Lower-Class Behaviour," *Social and Economic Studies,* 8 (December, 1959), p. 445.

[2]Judith Blake, "Family Instability and Reproductive Behavior in Jamaica," *Current Research in Human Fertility,* Milbank Memorial Fund, New York, 1955, pp. 24–41; Lloyd Braithwaite, "Sociology and Demographic Research in the British Caribbean," *Social and Economic Studies,* 6 (December, 1957), pp. 541–550; Judith Blake, "A Reply to Mr. Braith-

but there is disagreement on whether these patterns of behavior are normative or deviant with respect to the value system of the lower class. It is an intriguing question because, if these patterns are normative, then they are very much at odds with the dominant values of the society, and if these patterns are deviant, then the behavioral patterns within the lower class are very much at odds with the normative patterns. As a result, the Caribbean data have an important bearing upon certain theoretical formulations, and most especially upon the general questions of the development of "deviant" subcultures and the correspondence between behavioral patterns and normative patterns.

Some researchers have taken the position that within the lower class the non-legal marital union and the resulting illegitimate children are the normative patterns, and marriage is rejected or disliked.[3] Blake[4] and Goode[5] have taken the position that the non-legal marital union and the resulting illegitimate children are deviant patterns, and that marriage and legitimate childbirth are normative. In two earlier papers[6] I have suggested that these positions are both only partly correct, and that, as many researchers have recognized,[7] both marriage and the non-legal marital union are normative. The dominant pattern within the lower class can best be described as a "lower-class value stretch" — the normative pattern within the lower class has been stretched so that, in addition to subscribing to the middle-class ideals of marriage and legitimate children, they have also come to subscribe to the pattern of non-legal unions and "illegitimate" children.[8] In this paper I shall present new evidence supporting the position that the value stretch is the dominant lower-class response.

A Review of Goode's Position

In an influential paper Goode reconsidered a number of publications on Caribbean family structure as they bear on the question of the normative status of non-legal marital unions and illegitimacy.[9] The predominant conclusion of the researchers was that non-legal unions and the resulting illegitimate children are normative. However, Goode points to statements in the writings of these same researchers which are supposed to demonstrate that, despite their conclusions that non-legal marital unions and the resulting illegitimate children are normative, they are in actual fact deviant.

Most of the statements that are singled out by Goode[10] are of the follow-

waite," *Social and Economic Studies*, 7 (1958), pp. 234–237; Judith Blake, *Family Structure in Jamaica*, New York: Free Press of Glencoe, 1961; William J. Goode, "Illegitimacy in the Caribbean Social Structure," *American Sociological Review*, 25 (February, 1960), pp. 21–30; Hyman Rodman, "The Lower-Class Value Stretch," *Social Forces*, 42 (December, 1963), pp. 205–215.

[3]T. S. Simey, *Welfare and Planning in the West Indies*, Oxford: Clarendon Press, 1946, p. 183.

[4]Judith Blake, *Family Structure in Jamaica, op. cit.*

[5]William J. Goode, *op. cit.*

[6]Hyman Rodman, "The Lower-Class Value Stretch," *op. cit.*; Hyman Rodman, "On Understanding Lower-Class Behaviour," *op. cit.*

[7]Lloyd Braithwaite, *op. cit.*; Raymond T. Smith, *The Negro Family in British Guiana*, London: Routledge & Kegan Paul, 1956.

[8]Hyman Rodman, "The Lower-Class Value Stretch," *op. cit.*

[9]William J. Goode, *op. cit.*

[10]William J. Goode, *op. cit.*, pp. 24–26.

ing kind—statements to the effect that: (1) non-legal unions and illegitimacy are considered deviant by individuals who are not members of the lower class; (2) the girl in her parents' house who becomes illegitimately pregnant is punished by her parents; (3) non-legal unions are not as stable as legal marriages; (4) most adults eventually do marry; and (5) marriage is preferred to the non-legal union. Yet none of these statements constitutes evidence that the non-legal marital union and the illegitimacy resulting therefrom are considered to be deviant within the lower class.

The first three points need little comment. Obviously, if we are specifically concerned with values of members of the lower class, knowledge about the values of other classes is not directly relevant. If we are concerned with the non-legal union and the resulting illegitimate children, knowledge about attitudes toward illegitimate children who are not conceived within a non-legal union is not directly relevant. And finally, the argument that non-legal unions are less stable than legal marriages does not give us information about the normative status of the non-legal union.

What about the implications of the fact that most adults eventually marry? In Goode's words, "as individuals move through the life cycle, an increasing proportion are actually married, a phenomenon which would be inexplicable if the consensual unions were backed by a set of alternative norms."[11] But consensual or non-legal marital unions are backed by a set of alternative norms, and the explanation for the increasing proportion of married individuals in the older age groups is a simple one. As I have pointed out in an earlier paper, "Legal marriage and a non-legal union are not in opposition, but are, rather, two different types of acceptable marital patterns among the lower classes of the West Indies. . . . This is not to say that these two patterns are equally valued, nor that there are no regularities with respect to when one or the other pattern will be followed."[12] The fluidity of marital relationships that is symbolized by the non-legal marital union makes it possible for lower-class individuals to adapt to the economic uncertainties they face. The lower-class man's occupational and economic problems make it difficult for him to play the breadwinner role with ease; the non-legal marital union provides a flexible relationship within which a marital exchange is possible without the legal bonds of marriage.[13] It is in the later age groups, after a non-legal marital union has stood the test of time, that a marriage may be entered into in order to safeguard the legal rights of the wife and the children to the man's inheritance. Consequently there is good reason for the rising proportion of individuals who are married in the older age groups,[14] even though the non-legal marital union is normative and fulfills important functions within the lower class.

Preferential versus Normative Structure

Perhaps the major defect in the arguments by Goode and Blake is the failure to distinguish between preferential and normative structure. They commit

---

[11]*Ibid.*, p. 24.

[12]Hyman Rodman, "On Understanding Lower-Class Behaviour," *op. cit.*, pp. 448–449.

[13]Hyman Rodman, "Marital Relationships in a Trinidad Village," *Marriage and Family Living*, 23 (May, 1961), pp. 166–170.

[14]A related paper is being prepared to provide further documentation of the reasons presented here for the rising proportion of married individuals in the older age groups.

the fallacy of transforming preferential information into normative information. Information is presented that marriage is "preferred" to the non-legal union, that marriage is the "ideal," that marriage is "superior." This is used to bolster the conclusion that marriage alone is normative and that the non-legal union is deviant. For example, Blake asked the following question in Jamaica: "In general, for people in your position, do you think it is better to marry or just to live with a man (woman)?"[15] She reports that 83 per cent of the men and 83 per cent of the women "choose marriage unreservedly." On the basis of other unspecified questions in the interview she modifies the figure for women so that she can be conservative in her conclusion:

> "74 per cent of the women and 83 per cent of the men unreservedly choose marriage and are consistent in this point of view throughout. The remaining 26 per cent among the women and 17 per cent among the men are ambivalent toward marriage (i.e., choose it with reservations or elsewhere give evidence of ambivalence) with the exception of 3 women and 2 men who are negative."[16]

These data show a strong preference for marriage, but they do not permit the conclusion that "legal marriage is the only true union,"[17] and they tell us very little about the normative status of the non-legal union.

Marriage may very well be the ideal pattern, or the preferred pattern; but to say that the non-legal union is deviant because marriage is preferred is clearly fallacious. It is also possible for the non-legal union to be normative, although less preferred than marriage.

Methodology

There is a basic methodological problem underlying Blake's analysis—she did not ask any questions that would enable her to assess the normative status of the non-legal union.[18] Similarly, in Goode's review of the research literature, he was limited to the statements made by various researchers. His contribution was to single out the apparently confusing statements made about non-legal unions and illegitimacy—some to the effect that they were cultural alternatives to marriage, some that they were preferred to marriage, some that they were less preferred than marriage, and some that they were negatively sanctioned. But there has been no consistent research effort to explore the normative status of the non-legal union and of illegitimacy, and Blake's and Goode's error of considering these behavioral patterns to be deviant is therefore understandable; it is also a bold error, flying in the face of many researchers who have carried out detailed field observations in the Caribbean area.

[15]One could quarrel with the wording here. "For people in your position," coming from a middle-class interviewer, has a patronizing sound, and is perhaps not the best way of getting valid responses. Even more significant is the use of the word "just"—surely a possible indication to the respondent of which response is considered to be more socially desirable by the interviewer.

[16]Judith Blake, *Family Structure in Jamaica, op. cit.,* pp. 118–119.

[17]*Ibid.,* p. 122.

[18]This is not meant as a criticism of Blake's entire book. On the contrary, I gave it a generally favorable review in the *Canadian Journal of Economics and Political Science,* 28 (November, 1962), pp. 622–623.

The controversy was sharply drawn with the publication of Goode's paper in 1960 and Blake's book in 1961. More adequate data on the normative nature of the non-legal union within the lower class were needed in order to re-solve certain questions. On my third field trip to Trinidad, in 1962, I attempted to collect some of the needed normative data. An initial attempt to collect data from respondents in randomly selected households proved unwise because I was ask-ing highly personal questions, including questions about a person's "marital ca-reer." It took only one day of interviewing to demonstrate that respondents were troubled by the presence of others in the household while they were answering the questions. As a result, it was deemed necessary to conduct the interviews in complete privacy.

Through the cooperation of various employers, labor unions, and the Trinidad and Tobago Government, it was possible to arrange for private inter-views with employees at their place of work. The total sample consists of 97 men and 79 women. Of this number, 8 men and 6 women were interviewed in the Unemployment Exchange, and 28 men and 19 women were interviewed from a remote village where the author had done previous field work. As a result of our procedure, we do not have a random sample, and must reserve judgment on the representativeness of the sample; our findings must be taken as tentative. On the other hand, our data are possibly more valid because they are not contaminated by the presence of third parties.[19]

General Findings

A series of questions was asked of the respondents about marriage and non-legal unions (called *living,* in Trinidad). These questions are shown in Table 1 in the order in which they were asked. (Other questions were interspersed). For the total sample, from 21 per cent to 81 per cent are "favorable" to the *living* re-lationship. Forty-three per cent replied favorably to *living* on a majority of the questions they answered; 25 per cent replied favorably on all questions or on all questions but one.

Even though all six questions are getting at the "favorableness" of the respondents to the non-legal union, the great range in the percentages who reply favorably should not come as a surprise. The questions asked were deliberately worded differently, in order to get some idea of the conditions under which a fa-vorable reply is more likely to be given. The most striking result is the distinction between responses to "preferential" questions and to "normative" questions. Questions 1, 4, and 6 are normative—they are getting information about the nor-mative nature of the non-legal union. Questions 2, 3, and 5 are preferential—they are merely getting information on whether marriage or *living* is preferred. It turns out that the three highest percentages favorable to living (81%, 66% and 50%) are

---

[19]Although there is very little information available on the interaction effect of respondent characteristics, interviewer characteristics, and interviewing procedures upon the nature of the research information obtained, a tendency for responses to be biased in the direction of what is considered socially desirable has been noted. It is therefore likely that the figures which were obtained in this study by middle-class interviewers minimize the normative acceptance of non-legal marital unions. Cf. Carol H. Weiss, "Interviewing Low Income Re-spondents: A Preliminary View," paper presented at the American Association of Public Opinion Research meetings, May, 1966.

TABLE 1.　**PER CENT FAVORABLE TO LIVING (NON-LEGAL UNIONS) BY SEX AND CLASS**[a]

Question	Sex	Upper-Lower Class	Lower-Lower Class	Total
1. Is it all right for a man and woman to live together in order to get to know each other's ways before they decide to marry?	Female Male	38　(8) 75 (20)	73 (40) 98 (47)	81 (115)
2. Is it better for a man and woman who are very poor to get married, or is it better for them to live together common-law?	Female Male	0 (17) 15 (34)	16 (57) 37 (57)	21 (165)
3. Do you think that (1) living common-law is better than marriage, (2) that marriage is better than living common-law, or (3) that they both come as the same?	Female Male	12 (17) 31 (36)	19 (57) 38 (57)	28 (167)
4. Do you think that living common-law is a sin or not a sin?	Female Male	24 (17) 61 (36)	36 (56) 63 (60)	50 (169)
5. A man and woman are thinking of getting married: a. One person says they should marry right away, without having sexual intercourse before marriage. b. Another says they should have sexual intercourse before marriage in order to get to know each other's ways. Which do you think is better? (If b) How should they get to know each other—by friending or by living common-law?	Female Male	6 (16) 21 (33)	27 (51) 44 (50)	29 (150)
6. Some people are talking about marriage and living common-law. a. One person says that only *living* is good and that marriage is wrong; b. Another says that only marriage is good and that *living* is wrong; c. Another says that marriage is better but that *living* is also good; d. Another says that *living* is better but that marriage is also good.	Female Male	41 (17) 63 (35)	58 (55) 83 (58)	66 (165)
Favorable to *living* on a majority of the questions answered.	Female Male	18 (17) 45 (36)	28 (57) 65 (59)	43 (169)

Note: Bases of percentages are shown in parentheses. The first question was not added until after some of the interviews had been done. Other variations in N are due to cases in which the information was not ascertained.

[a]Since we do not have a random sample, the use of significance tests is questionable; the discussion in the text is based upon the consistency of the percentage differences. For those prepared to overlook the limitations of our sample, the following results are based upon a $2 \times 2 \times 2$ chi-square test: sex differences in response are significant at the 0.10 level on all six questions; class differences are significant on all questions except (3) and (4); the sex-class interaction is not significant for any of the six questions, while the combined effect of sex and class is significant for all six questions. For a description of the statistical tests used, see J. P. Sutcliffe, "A General Method of Analysis of Frequency Data for Multiple Classification Designs," *Psychological Bulletin*, 54 (March, 1957), pp. 134–137; Hubert M. Blalock, *Social Statistics*, New York: McGraw-Hill, 1960, p. 239.

given in response to the three normative questions, and the three lowest percentages (21%, 28% and 29%) are given in response to the three preferential questions. The predominant response within this lower-class sample is clearly and dramatically that marriage is preferred to the non-legal union, but that the non-legal union is normative. Our results for Trinidad are roughly in accord with Blake's results for Jamaica (cited above); she found approximately 20 per cent of her lower-class respondents "favorable" to the non-legal union on a preferential question.

The same pattern of responses—marriage is preferred, but *living* is normative—is shown in Tables 2 and 3. In these tables the information is presented separately for the three normative questions and for the three preferential questions. (In a number of cases we have information on only two of the questions.) Once again the distinction between the preferential questions and the normative questions is fundamental. Looking at the percentages for the total sample, marriage tends to be "favored" on the preferential questions. On the normative questions *living* tends to be "favored." These data document the fact that it is erroneous to use responses to preferential questions to make inferences about norms. They put the controversy about the Caribbean family in perspective by permitting us to clarify the nature of the normative structure among the lower classes of the Caribbean area.

TABLE 2. PERCENTAGE DISTRIBUTION SUMMARIZING RESPONSES TO THREE "PREFERENCE" QUESTIONS, BY SEX AND CLASS

| | Males | | Females | | |
| | Upper-Lower Class | Lower-Lower Class | Upper-Lower Class | Lower-Lower Class | |
Response Pattern					Total
Prefer marriage on all questions	55	30	82	50	47
Prefer marriage on 2 of 3 questions	24	21	12	32	25
Prefer marriage on 1 of 2 questions	6	9	0	6	6
Prefer marriage on 1 of 3 questions	6	19	6	9	12
Prefer marriage on no questions	9	21	0	3	10
Total	100	100	100	100	100
Number of cases	33	57	17	56	163

TABLE 3. PERCENTAGE DISTRIBUTION SUMMARIZING RESPONSES TO THREE "NORMATIVE" QUESTIONS, BY SEX AND CLASS

| | Males | | Females | | |
| | Upper-Lower Class | Lower-Lower Class | Upper-Lower Class | Lower-Lower Class | |
Response Pattern					Total
Living is normative on all questions	48	61	18	31	44
Living is normative on 2 of 3 questions	14	19	6	14	15
Living is normative on 1 of 2 questions	9	7	17	7	8
Living is normative on 1 of 3 questions	3	10	6	18	11
Living is normative on no questions	26	3	53	30	22
Total	100	100	100	100	100
Number of cases	35	59	17	59	168

The Lower-Class Value Stretch

As suggested in an earlier paper, the lower-class value stretch is a response of members of the lower class to a situation in which circumstances make it difficult or impossible for them to behave in accordance with the dominant values of an open-class society.[20] The following is an elaboration of the assumptions and hypothesized relationships that enter into the theory of the lower-class value stretch.[21]

1. In an open-class society the possibility of mobility is open to all.

2. The values of the dominant social classes (including the possibility of mobility for all) are promulgated to all members of the society.

3. Members of the lower classes have difficulty in behaving in accordance with some of the dominant values because of inadequate resources.

4. Members of the lower classes therefore show more "deviance" from some of the dominant values.

5. As a result, in order to minimize negative sanctions, members of the lower classes are less committed to some of the dominant values than other members of society.

6. Furthermore, some members of the lower classes develop alternative values that are more in accord with their circumstances, so that their actual behavior is likelier to be rewarded. What is deviant from the point of view of the dominant values is normative from the point of view of the alternative values.

7. The development of alternative values is a continuing process; some lower-class members are socialized into accepting them from childhood, others come to accept them later in life, while others never accept them.

8. The major form taken by the system of values that thus develops in the lower class is the "lower-class value stretch":

> By the value stretch I mean that the lower-class person, without abandoning the general values of the society, develops an alternative set of values. Without abandoning the values of marriage and legitimate childbirth he stretches these values so that a non-legal union and legally illegitimate children are also desirable. The result is that the members of the lower class, in many areas, have a wider range of values than others within the society. They share the general values of the society with members of other classes, but in addition they have stretched these values, or developed alternative values, which help them to adjust to their deprived circumstances.[22]

[20]Hyman Rodman, "The Lower-Class Value Stretch," op. cit. This paper was based upon field observations in Trinidad, an extensive review of data on levels of aspiration, and brief reviews of data on the Caribbean and on delinquency.

[21]This formulation has been influenced by George C. Homans, "Bringing Men Back In," American Sociological Review, 29 (December, 1964), pp. 809–818.

[22]Hyman Rodman, "The Lower-Class Value Stretch," op. cit., p. 209. Alternatives to the lower-class value stretch response would be a response in which the lower-class individual retains the dominant values without developing any other values, abandons the dominant values and subscribes to a new set of values, or abandons all commitment to values of any kind in a particular area. Since commitment to a value is a matter of degree it is often difficult to determine whether or not a person is committed to a particular value.

The above assumptions and implied relationships are not new, but they make explicit what has remained largely implicit in the literature — that the value stretch is an important response within the lower classes. It is possible to develop a large number of specific hypotheses to test various portions of the theory of the lower-class value stretch.[23] Hypothesized relationships that stem from points (1) – (4) above are numerous. Are there differences in the rates of mobility in different types of societies? To what extent are the dominant values of society internalized in different segments of that society? Do the rates of "deviance" vary by social class status? These questions have all been phrased as hypotheses and explored in the literature. But the questions that are suggested by points (5) – (8) are relatively new, and have been little explored. In order to formulate testable hypotheses it is necessary to specify which of the dominant values are not in accord with lower-class circumstances, and which alternative values are more in accord with such circumstances. Since tests of the theory depend upon a specification of the relevant values, it is necessary to be explicit about the grounds on which the specified values are or are not in accord with lower-class circumstances. In this paper marriage is specified as a value which is not in accord with lower-class circumstances because it is a legally binding relationship, whereas the lower-class male is frequently unemployed, underemployed, and in poorly paid employment, and accordingly finds it difficult to fulfill his economic obligations within a legally binding relationship. The non-legal marital union is specified as a value which is in accord with lower-class circumstances, in that it provides the partners with a flexible behavioral pattern that may permit them to adapt to such circumstances.[24] As a result, we would expect that the lower the status of a person, the more likely is he to be affected by these value changes. Similarly, since it is the man who is most immediately and directly affected by lower-class occupational circumstances (given the assumption that the man should be the family's breadwinner),[25] we would expect that men are more likely to be affected than women. The following four hypotheses are to be tested:

(1) Social class status is inversely related to the normative acceptance of non-legal marital unions.

(2) Social class status is inversely related to the "value stretch," i.e., to the acceptance of both legal marriage and the non-legal marital union.

(3) Lower-class men show more normative acceptance of non-legal marital unions than do lower-class women.

(4) Lower-class men stretch their values to accept both legal marriage and the non-legal marital union more than do lower-class women.

Hypothesis 1

Although the present study concentrated upon the lower class, it was nevertheless possible to divide the sample into a lower-lower-class group and an

---

[23]Robert R. Bell, "Lower Class Negro Mothers' Aspirations for Their Children," *Social Forces*, 43 (May, 1965), pp. 493 – 500.

[24]For further elaboration of these points see Hyman Rodman, "Marital Relationships in a Trinidad Village," *op. cit.*

[25]Hyman Rodman and Constantina Safilios-Rothschild, "Business and the American Family," in Ivar Berg, ed., *The Business of America*, New York: Harcourt, Brace & World, in press.

upper-lower-class group.[26] A comparison of these two groups indicates that on every normative question in Table 1 (Questions 1, 4, and 6), for males and for females, the lower-lower-class group shows a higher percentage of favorable responses to *living* than the upper-lower-class group. Similarly, the summary information on the three normative questions in Table 3 indicates that *living* is accepted as normative within the lower-lower-class group to a greater extent than within the upper-lower-class group. Among males, 80 per cent within the lower-lower-class group reply that *living* is normative on a majority of the questions, in contrast to 62 per cent within the upper-lower-class group. For females, the comparable figures are 45 per cent and 24 per cent. The hypothesis is therefore validated for this sample on a limited domain of status categories. Comparison with middle-class groups would undoubtedly show even more pronounced value differences.[27]

It can also be seen that the lower-lower-class group gives a higher percentage of favorable responses, both for males and for females, on the three preferential questions. This suggests that there may be an inverse relationship of social class status not only with the normative acceptance, but also with the preferential acceptance, of certain deviant patterns. The latter hypothesis needs to be tested on independent data.

Hypothesis 2

Question 6, in Table 1, was specifically formulated to get information on the lower-class value stretch. A breakdown of the answers to that question is provided in Table 4. An alternative to the value stretch would be the rejection of some dominant value and the acceptance of an alternative value ("*Living* is good and marriage is wrong."). Not a single respondent selected this alternative. Another alternative to the value stretch would be the acceptance of some dominant value and the rejection of an alternative value ("Marriage is good and *living* is wrong."). In the total sample, 34 per cent gave this response, suggesting that it is an important response within the lower classes. A value stretch response [Marriage (*living*) is better but *living* (marriage) is also good"; or the spontaneously mentioned "no difference"] was given by 66 per cent of the respondents in the total sample. Most of these responses, as we would expect from the discus-

[26]Social-class position was determined on the basis of occupation, education and income data, by adapting Hollingshead's technique to the Trinidad material, and using income in some borderline cases (August B. Hollingshead, "Two Factor Index of Social Position," mimeographed, 1957). The upper-lower class consists predominantly of skilled workers, and of semi-skilled workers with comparatively high educational or income levels. The lower-lower class consists of semi-skilled workers with comparatively low levels of education and income, and unskilled workers, private household and service workers. The paper therefore does not deal with social classes as clearly demarcated groups in which the members share an awareness of their collective interests, but with social categories in which the members share a roughly similar position in a status hierarchy. No attempt has been made to determine "category" boundaries on the basis of interaction patterns, or to determine the degree to which there may be an awareness of shared interests. Cf. Dennis Wrong, "Social Inequality without Social Stratification," *Canadian Review of Sociology and Anthropology*, 1 (February, 1964), pp. 5–16.

[27]Nine middle-class respondents were uniformly unfavorable to the non-legal union on all questions. Because of the small number of middle-class respondents, the data on them are not reported.

sion about the normative and preferential data, indicate that "marriage is better but *living* is also good." In other words, the data lend strong support to the existence of the value stretch as the predominant lower-class response.

What about the inverse relationship between social class status and the value stretch response? In Table 4 (cf. Table 1) we see that 83 per cent of the lower-lower-class men, as compared with 63 per cent of the upper-lower-class men give a "stretch" response, while 58 per cent of lower-lower-class women, as compared with 41 per cent of upper-lower-class women give this response. Thus, for both men and women, the lower-lower-class group shows a higher proportion of value stretch responses; the data from this sample validate the hypothesis on a limited domain of status categories.

Hypothesis 3

In response to all of the normative questions in Table 1, as well as to all of the preferential questions, men are more favorable to the non-legal marital union than women, and this holds within both class groups. In addition, in Table 3, we see that men are much more likely than women to state that the non-legal marital union is normative on all questions answered, or on 2 of the 3 questions answered, and this also holds within both class groups. Within the lower-lower-class group, 80 per cent of the men, compared with 45 per cent of the women, accept the non-legal marital union on a majority of the normative questions. Within the upper-lower-class group the figures are 62 per cent for men and 24 per cent for women. Hypothesis 3 is therefore validated—lower-class men do show more normative acceptance of non-legal marital unions than lower-class women.

Hypothesis 4

The data on the value stretch and alternative responses are presented in Table 4 (cf. Table 1, Question 6). It can be seen that men stretch their values to accept both legal marriage and the non-legal marital union to a greater extent than women. This is the case within both class groups. In the lower-lower-class

TABLE 4. **PERCENTAGE DISTRIBUTION OF RESPONSES TO "VALUE STRETCH" QUESTION, BY SEX AND CLASS**

	Males		Females		
Responses to "Value Stretch" Question	Upper-Lower Class	Lower-Lower Class	Upper-Lower Class	Lower-Lower Class	Total
Marriage is good and *living* is wrong	37	17	59	42	34
Marriage is better but *living* is also good	49	48	41	53	49
Living is good and marriage is wrong	0	0	0	0	0
Living is better but marriage is also good	3	12	0	5	7
No difference	11	23	0	0	10
Total	100	100	100	100	100
Number of cases	35	58	17	55	165

Note: See Table 1, question 6 for "value-stretch" question.

group, the value stretch response is given by 83 per cent of the men and 58 per cent of the women. In the upper-lower class group the comparable percentages are 63 and 41. These are the percentages that replied "marriage is better but *living* is also good," "*living* is better but marriage is also good," or "no difference." The hypothesis is therefore validated. for this sample. The value stretch response, however, is not the predominant response of upper-lower-class females in this sample: 42 per cent of the lower-lower-class women and 59 per cent of the upper-lower-class women accept marriage and reject the non-legal marital union.

Further Points of Controversy

Although many of the statements marshalled by Goode from Caribbean researchers to support the argument that the non-legal marital union lacked normative status were easily disposed of, this is not so for all of them. Perhaps the strongest support for Goode's argument is the data that he cites from Hatt's study:

> Two-thirds of both men and women in a national sample of Puerto Rico said that a consensual union is a bad life for a man, and over 80 per cent of the respondents made the same assertion for women. Perhaps a more penetrating test of the normative status of the consensual union may be found in the attitudes expressed about a *daughter* entering a consensual union; only 7.4 per cent of the men and 5.5 per cent of the women admitted that this arrangement would either be "all right" or that "it's up to her; doesn't matter."[28]

Hatt presents the data as normative, and they appear to be normative. It therefore seems that the non-legal union in Puerto Rico is preponderantly considered to be deviant. For our purposes, however, several qualifications must be emphasized: (1) These data are from a national sample, and not from a lower-class sample; (2) Within this national sample several factors have biased the data collected toward groups of higher socioeconomic status;[29] (3) A close examination of the questions that were asked suggests that we must have strong reservations about the presumed "normative" status of the data. A translation of one of the questions into English, and the results, are given in Table 5. It is accurate to conclude from these data, as Goode did, that "two-thirds of both men and women in a national sample of Puerto Rico said that a consensual union is a bad life for a man." However, my more exact translation of portions of Hatt's question, given in italics in the table, raises some questions. In part (1), "to live with a woman without marriage" is not the same as "to live with a woman."[30] In part (4), "a bad life" is not the same as "not a good life." Both of these differences are likely to inflate the reported percentages that consider a "consensual union" to be "bad." More important, however, the initial instructions and part (1) put the

[28]William J. Goode, *op. cit.*, p. 26.
[29]Paul K. Hatt, *Backgrounds of Human Fertility in Puerto Rico*, Princeton, N. J.: Princeton University Press, 1952, pp. 11–17, 20–22.
[30]It should be noted that the Spanish phrase used in this question, *vivir con un hombre sin casarse*, is unlike the phrase used on p. 495, Question 32, dealing with matrimonial status — *viviendo juntos (unión consensual)*. The former phase places the "consensual union" in a comparatively bad light, and is therefore likelier to invite responses that are unfavorable to such a union. See *ibid.*, pp. 60–63, 495–497.

TABLE 5. **PERCENTAGE DISTRIBUTION OF RESPONSES TO A QUESTION CONCERNING ATTITUDES TOWARD CONSENSUAL UNIONS FOR MEN, BY SEX: PUERTO RICO**

Responses	Males	Females
Which of the following statements expresses your feelings best?		
1. To live with a woman is the best possible life for a man. (*To live with a woman without marriage is the best possible life for a man.*)	3.05	2.64
2. It is a good life for a man.	12.75	16.62
3. It does not matter.	16.33	12.57
4. It is a bad life for a man. (*It is not a good life for a man.*)	46.37	45.01
5. It is a very bad life for a man.	21.14	22.91
6. Other answers.	0.36	0.24
Total	100.00	99.99
Number of cases	6,187	7,085

Source: Paul K. Hatt, *op. cit.,* p. 61.

whole question into a preferential context. As a result, each normative condition which follows part (1) is colored by this preferential context, and we simply do not know to what extent the respondents' replies are a reflection of the normative status of the non-legal union or of its preferential status in relation to marriage.

Finally, a word of caution regarding generalizations about "the Caribbean area." Data have been presented on Trinidad, and they have been contrasted with Blake's data on Jamaica, Hatt's data on Puerto Rico, and Goode's general discussion of the data on some ten different territorial or national units within the Caribbean area. Since there may very well be value differences that stem from independent variables such as nationality or community type, it remains to be seen whether the relationships validated in this study stand up once other independent variables are introduced into the analysis.

Theoretical Considerations

It has been seen that both sex and social class are related to the normative acceptance of certain alternatives to the dominant values, and more generally that sex and social class are related to a value stretch response. Specifically, an inverse relationship has been shown between social class status and the normative acceptance of both the non-legal marital union and marriage. In addition, males were shown to have a greater normative acceptance of both the non-legal marital union and marriage than females.

Why should there be such relationships? Perhaps the factor that underlies these relationships is "vulnerability to environmental circumstances." Since the defining attributes that have been used in this paper for social class are occupation, education, and income, members of the lower class are, by definition, low in occupational status, educational status, and income. They have limited economic resources and therefore face greater difficulty in maintaining a marriage relationship. In this sense they are more vulnerable to environmental circumstances, and are likelier to stretch their values. Moreover, within the lower class, if the woman plays the traditional role of housewife, and if the man is expected to be the breadwinner, the major impact of lower-class circumstances falls upon the man. The woman's ability to perform the role of housewife is not as much affected by lower-class membership as is the man's ability to perform the role of breadwinner. In this sense, lower-class men are more vulnerable to environmental circumstances than lower-class women, and they are more likely to stretch their values. If environmental circumstances make performance in accordance with certain dominant values difficult or impossible, then behavior is less likely to be in accordance with these values; commitment to these dominant values is likely to be lessened; alternative values more in accordance with lower-class circumstances are likelier to develop; and we are more likely to find a value stretch.

Several other suggestions immediately come to mind. One is that the existence of the value stretch should show up in other areas where performance in accordance with the dominant values is difficult, such as the area of occupational, income, and educational values.[31] In addition, there may be other independent variables besides social class status and sex that reflect differences in "vulnerability to environmental circumstances," and thus permit further tests of the general relationship.

While there has been agreement about the nature of the behavioral patterns in the Caribbean — high rates of non-legal marital unions and illegitimacy — there has not been agreement about the normative patterns. The data presented on a sample of lower-class respondents in Trinidad offer strong support for one aspect of the theory of the lower-class value stretch: that many members of the lower class share the dominant values and have also stretched these values and developed a set of values unique to themselves.

The data presented in this paper indicate that we do not merely have "deviation from the norm" in the lower classes,[32] but also a stretched system of norms in which the non-legal union is normative. Furthermore, we do not merely have a "lowering of both punishment for deviation and reward for conformity"[33] but also a situation in which the non-legal union is considered to be normative and is positively evaluated (even though it is less preferred than marriage). Perhaps there is a historical sequence for the development of the lower-class value stretch, such that the kind of situation that Goode describes is an interim step on the way to the development of the value stretch. At any rate, the present data for Trinidad clearly point to the value stretch as a major response.

In sum, those who suggest that members of the lower class reject the dominant values and develop alternative values seem from our data to be wrong. Those who suggest that members of the lower class share the dominant values and reject alternative values, also seem to be wrong (although they are documenting an important lower-class pattern). The question about the values that are held in the lower classes is a complex one. In part this reflects the complexity of the social-class structure itself, for we are not dealing with the values of any clearly demarcated group but rather with categories of people who vary on attributes such as occupation, education, and income. The behavioral experiences of these people are not homogeneous; since they are not members of a demarcated group they do not directly exchange solutions to life's problems and share the same values. Nevertheless, the circumstances that are shared toward the lower levels of the class structure do seem to produce certain similarities of behavior and values.

[31]Hyman Rodman, "The Lower-Class Value Stretch," *op. cit.,* pp. 210–212.
[32]William J. Goode, *op. cit.,* p. 30.
[33]*Ibid.*

Most significantly, it has been shown that the lower one goes in the class structure, where the vulnerability to environmental circumstances is greater, the more
likely one is to find stretched values.

DATA:
The American Dilemma: An Empirical Test
FRANK R. WESTIE

Oscar Handlin, in his review article celebrating the recent appearance of the
20th-anniversary of *An American Dilemma*,[1] observes:

> Few serious studies of American society have been more widely read
> than Gunnar Myrdal's social-science classic, *An American Dilemma*. Its
> analysis of the Negro problem in the United States has been a magnet to
> scholars and a catalyst to political groups. Its recommendations have
> helped shape the strategy of every organization interested in legislation
> and in judicial interpretations.[2]

The social impact of the theory cannot be questioned, but the degree to
which it describes empirical events has yet, after 20 years, to be determined. In
the study reported here I have attempted to test empirically the basic propositions,
postulates and assumptions of the dilemma theory.

Many criticisms of the Myrdal theory have appeared in the sociological
literature.[3] Not only did Myrdal and his associates fail to test the dilemma theory,
but the main critics have also failed to test the basic assumptions about the world
of events on which their criticisms are based.[4]

"The American Dilemma: An Empirical Test," by Frank R. Westie, from *American Sociological Review*, vol. 30, no. 1 (1965), pp. 527–38. Reprinted by permission of the author
and the American Sociological Association. The original publication carries the following
acknowledgment: "This study is one of a series supported, at various times, by the Human
Ecology Fund, the Social Science Research Council, and the Graduate School of Indiana
University. The support of these organizations is gratefully acknowledged. The invaluable
assistance and collaboration of Marcia T. Segal, Frederick L. Whitman, and Joseph W. Scott
is greatly appreciated."

[1] Gunnar Myrdal, with the assistance of Richard Sterner and Arnold Rose, *An American
Dilemma*, New York: Harper, 1944.

[2] Oscar Handlin, Review of 20th-Anniversary Edition of *An American Dilemma*, *New York
Times Book Review*, April 21, 1963, p. 1.

[3] Among the more important critiques are Leo F. Crespi, "Is Gunnar Myrdal on the Right
Track?" *Public Opinion Quarterly*, 9 (1945), pp. 201–212; Gwynn Nettler, "A Note on
Myrdal's 'Notes on Facts and Valuations,' Appendix 2 of *An American Dilemma*," *Ameri-
can Sociological Review*, 9 (1944), pp. 686–688; Arnold Rose, Reply to Nettler's "Note,"
American Sociological Review, 10 (1945), pp. 560–562; and the following reviews of *An
American Dilemma*: E. Franklin Frazier in *American Journal of Sociology*, 50 (1945), pp.
455–457; Howard W. Odum, in *Social Forces*, 23 (1944), pp. 94–98; and Kimball Young,
in *American Sociological Review*, 9 (1944), pp. 326–330.

[4] Empirical evaluations of the theory of the American dilemma include Ernest Q. Campbell, "Moral Discomfort and Racial Segregation—An Examination of the Myrdal Hypothe-

The Theory Stated

According to Myrdal,[5] Americans suffer from a basic ambivalence because they embrace, on the one hand, the Christian-democratic tenets of the "American Creed" and, on the other, any number of unChristian and undemocratic valuations defining relations between Negroes and whites. The theory is, essentially, an analysis of how Americans live with themselves in the face of this dilemma.

Myrdal's two basic concepts are *valuations* and *beliefs*. Valuations are conceptions of "what ought to be." Beliefs are conceptions of "what is" or "what was." Beliefs may be bizarre products of the imagination or they may be empirically valid.

Valuations may be placed along a continuum from the most general to the most specific. The American Creed valuations are very general, and their adherents consider them applicable to all Americans if not to all mankind. The valuations defining relations between Negroes and whites, on the other hand, are frequently quite specific, referring to "my kids," "my family," "our school," "our neighborhood," etc. For most Americans, Myrdal avers, the specific valuations are quite inconsistent with the general.

Americans, Myrdal maintains, want to present a rational picture of themselves to the world, but particularly to themselves. Given their desire to maintain an image of themselves as rational creatures on the one hand, and the irrationality inherent in their valuational inconsistencies on the other, Americans are faced with a dilemma. How do they live with themselves under these circumstances? According to Myrdal, they opportunistically call forth beliefs about reality to rationalize their valuation-inconsistencies. These beliefs exist ready-made in the form of culturally shared myths. For example, a particular American agrees with the general valuation in the American Creed which says that Americans ought to work toward achieving greater equality of opportunity for all. The same person also feels that Negroes ought not to go to the same school his children attend (a specific valuation). In order to rationalize this inconsistency, this person calls forth beliefs such as the following: a) "Negroes are inherently less capable intellectually than whites," therefore, b) "Negro children would be frustrated in competition with white children," or, c) "The white children would be held back to the level of the slower Negro children."

sis," *Social Forces*, 39 (1961), pp. 228–234, and R. W. Friedrichs, "Christians and Residential Exclusion: An Empirical Study of a Northern Dilemma," *Journal of Social Issues*, 15 (1959), pp. 14–23. While few investigations have focused specifically on the American dilemma, any number of other studies have important implications for the theory. Perhaps most relevant are those dealing with verbally expressed attitudes and overt acts, e.g., Richard T. LaPiere, "Attitudes vs. Actions," *Social Forces*, 13 (1934), pp. 230–237; Joseph D. Lohman and Dietrich C. Reitzes, "Note on Race Relations in Mass Society," *American Journal of Sociology*, 58 (1952), pp. 240–246; Bernard Kutner, Carol Wilkins and P. R. Yarrow, "Verbal Attitudes and Overt Behavior Involving Racial Prejudice," *Journal of Abnormal and Social Psychology*, 51 (1952), pp. 649–652; Melvin L. DeFleur and Frank R. Westie, "Verbal Attitudes and Overt Acts: An Experiment on the Salience of Attitudes," *American Sociological Review*, 23 (1958), pp. 667–673; Martin Fishbein, "An Investigation of the Relationship Between Beliefs About an Object and Attitudes Toward That Object," *Human Relations*, 16 (1963), pp. 233–240.

[5]This statement of the theory is my own conception of what Myrdal means. The interested reader should consult Appendix I, "The Mechanism of Rationalization" for Myrdal's original statement.

This dilemma may be conceived as existing on a societal level, as a part of culture. Myrdal emphasizes, however, that it ultimately resides in the consciences of particular individuals.

Myrdal's theory contains a number of assumptions about empirical reality which need to be tested. Ralph Turner was probably correct when he observed that

> . . . it does not necessarily follow from the logical contradiction that most people in American society perceive any dilemma here. In fact, the over enthusiastic student of race relations may be distressed to find how many people and groups sincerely feel no disloyalty to democratic ideals in their support of segregation and discrimination.[6]

The empirical questions[7] this study seeks to answer are as follows:[8]

1. Do people endorse such conflicting valuations?
2. Do they recognize the inconsistency involved?
3. Do they, in fact, rationalize this inconsistency, and, if so, do such rationalizations take the form of beliefs?
4. Are psychological mechanisms other than rationalization employed? For example, are conflicting values repressed?
5. Where one or the other of the conflicting valuations is "adjusted" (i.e., changed or qualified), which of the valuations does the respondent alter or qualify, the general or the specific?
6. To what extent are people aware of, or oriented in terms of, the idealistic tenets of democracy and Christianity?

The Form of the Empirical Test

The 103 cases comprising the sample were selected in 1957 from 40 residential blocks in the city of Indianapolis.[9] Within each household, we inter-

---

[6]Ralph H. Turner, "Value Conflict in Social Disorganization," *Sociology and Social Research*, 38 (1954), p. 304.

[7]The research is designed to answer empirical questions rather than test hypotheses *per se;* the questions serve the same basic research purpose without implying the degree of theoretical coherence and guidance hypotheses necessarily presume. See Frank R. Westie, "Toward Closer Relations Between Theory and Research: A Procedure and An Example," *American Sociological Review*, 22 (1957), pp. 149–154.

[8]I have also analyzed the relations between social class and the American dilemma, testing the hypothesis that persons of lower status are less troubled by it. The results will be presented in a separate paper (in preparation).

[9]A living-standard area map constructed by a commercial market analysis agency was used as the sampling base. This map demarcates three living-standard levels in the city. Numbers were assigned to the blocks on each level, and the blocks were selected for the sample through the use of a table of random numbers. The middle- and upper-class areas were combined to obtain a two-class rather than a three-class sample. An equal number of blocks were drawn from the lower living-standard level and the combined middle-upper level. Blocks in which any Negroes were known to reside were excluded from the sample. Within blocks, every nth house was selected, yielding five houses per block. Adjacent houses were used as alternates. For the lower-class sample N = 52; for the upper-class sample N = 51. The more conspicuous sources of bias in this sampling procedure are 1) the use of every nth case within blocks; 2) the selection of an equal number of cases per block; and 3) the use of alternate households, in approximately one third of the cases, according to the interviewer's estimate. Inadequate records on this score made estimation necessary.

viewed either the male head of the household or his spouse, but never both. Since most of the interviewing was done on Saturdays and in the evening, the sex ratio of the sample remained fairly well balanced (53 women and 50 men).

The questionnaire included three forms which were completed by all respondents. Form I, designed to assess *general valuations,* lists ten items designed to assess the degree to which the respondent endorses the general valuations subsumed under the "American Creed" (Table 1). Form II is designed to elicit specific valuations. It consists of ten social distance-type items describing hypothetical but quite plausible situations which permit the respondent to indicate the degree of social distance he prefers to maintain between himself and Negroes. Each item in Form II is matched to an item in Form I in such a way as to maximize the possibility of conflict between the general and specific valuations, and also to enhance the likelihood that respondents would recognize value conflicts where they exist (Table 1). Form III consists simply of spaces to record, at given probe levels, open-ended responses to the value conflicts elicited by the items on Form I and Form II.

In the interview each respondent was first asked to respond (in terms of five degrees of agreement and disagreement) to the items on Form I, then to the items on Form II. He was not permitted to refer back to Form I while completing Form II.

Responses on five probe levels were recorded on Form III:

Probe level−2: Spontaneous remarks made while completing Form I.

Probe level−1: Spontaneous remarks made while completing Form II.

Probe level 0: Replies to the interviewer's request: "Would you now compare your response to question#1 on Form II with your response to question#1 on Form I."

Probe level+1: Responses to interviewer's query: "Any comment?"

Probe level+2: Responses to interviewer's query: "Do you see any contradiction?" (asked only where contradiction existed and where it was *unrecognized* on previous probe levels).

Probe level+3: Responses to interviewer's query: "Any explanation?" (asked only where contradiction existed and was *recognized* on previous probe levels).

The probe levels were used to avoid calling contradictions to respondent's attention, and to determine the extent to which the respondent recognized contradictions without help from the interviewer. Probe +2 was used as a last resort when the respondent failed to recognize the contradictions, where such existed, on all previous levels.[10]

An elaborate system of rules for coding was developed to quantify the open-ended responses elicited at the various probe levels on Form III. Responses were coded not only to indicate whether valuations or beliefs had been volunteered, but also according to type of valuation, type of belief, whether the response was a rationalization, type of rationalization, likelihood of empirical validi-

[10]This procedure was adopted after numerous other techniques were tried. Because of the difficulty involved in developing adequate items and procedures, the total number of pretests far exceeded the number of cases used in the final sample.

ty (in the case of beliefs), etc. This system became so cumbersome as to defeat both statistical analysis and communication of findings. We thus resorted to a simplified code in which responses were classified as *valuations* where they contained any "ought to be" elements whatever, and *beliefs* where they included any statements of "what is," "what was," or conceptions of reality. Responses were also coded according to whether they were explanations of inconsistency or consistency, and the probe level at which each explanation had been evoked was also coded.

Sometimes beliefs and valuations are stated clearly and separately by the respondent, but often they are intertwined in the same remark. Not all statements included elements that could be classified as valuations or beliefs, of course, and such statements were simply rated "unclassifiable" on the valuation-belief dimension. Certain rules were specified for particular types of recurrent responses. For example, statements of *preference* for a "separate but equal" system were coded as valuations while such statements as "Negroes *want* to be separate but equal" were coded as beliefs. The coding was performed by the author and one other sociologist. The reliability of the coding on the valuation-belief dimension was tested by comparing the degree of agreement between the two coders on 27 schedules, including 236 coder-judgments on this dimension. There was agreement in 96 per cent of the judgments.

Results

Table 1 indicates the degree to which the sample as a whole endorsed the specific and the general valuations. Well over half the sample agreed with each of the ten general valuation statements, though agreement is considerably higher on the first seven statements than it is in the last three. The mean percentage agreeing with any given general item was 81. Virtually everyone in the sample (97 per cent or more) agreed that everyone should have equal opportunities to get ahead, that all people should be treated as equals in the eyes of the law, that people should help each other in times of need, that children should have equal educational opportunities and that everyone should be judged according to his own individual worth. Over 90 per cent agreed that everyone should have equal right to hold public office and endorsed the principle of brotherhood among men. Many of those who disagreed with the public office statement (item 5) wanted to append remarks about specific qualifications for public office, such as education or experience, qualifications which do not necessarily imply racial prejudice.

Agreement with Item 8, dealing with public facilities, approximated the mean (83 per cent). Item 9 ("people should be allowed to live where they please") elicited least agreement—only 60 per cent, and Item 10 ("public *recreational* facilities should be open to all") was similar—63 per cent agree. The large difference between the pattern of responses to the first seven items and responses to the last three may be due to the fact that the latter are less abstract than the former, referring to specific situations rather than to general principles, though they are more general than the "specific valuation" items with which they are paired.

Responses to the specific valuations, shown in Table 1, tend to uphold the Myrdal hypothesis. There was considerably less agreement with the specific

TABLE 1. RESPONSES TO EACH GENERAL AND SPECIFIC VALUATION*

General Valuation Statement	Per Cent (n = 103)	Specific Valuation Statement	Per Cent (n = 103)	Discrepancy: Per Cent Agreeing with General minus Per Cent Agreeing with Specific**
1. Everyone in America should have equal opportunities to get ahead.		1. I would be willing to have a Negro as my supervisor in my place of work.		38*
agree	98	agree	60	
undecided	0	undecided	2	
disagree	2	disagree	38	
2. All people should be treated as equals in the eyes of the law.		2. If I went on trial I would not mind having Negroes on the jury.		22
agree	98	agree	76	
undecided	0	undecided	5	
disagree	2	disagree	19	
3. People should help each other in time of need.		3. If a Negro's home burned down, I would be willing to take his family into my home for a night.		35
agree	99	agree	64	
undecided	1	undecided	6	
disagree	0	disagree	30	
4. Children should have equal educational opportunities.		4. I would not mind having Negro children attend the same school my children go to.		19
agree	98	agree	79	
undecided	1	undecided	2	
disagree	1	disagree	19	
5. Everyone should have equal right to hold public office.		5. I believe that I would be willing to have a Negro represent me in the Congress of the U.S.		20
agree	91	agree	71	
undecided	1	undecided	6	
disagree	8	disagree	23	

General valuation			Specific valuation			
6. Each person should be judged according to his own individual worth.			6. I would not mind if my children were taught by a Negro school teacher.			
agree	97		agree	67		30
undecided	1		undecided	8		
disagree	2		disagree	25		
7. I believe in the principle of brotherhood among men.			7. I would be willing to invite Negroes to a dinner party in my home.			
agree	94		agree	29		65
undecided	5		undecided	4		
disagree	1		disagree	67		
8. Public facilities should be equally available to everyone.			8. I would be willing to stay at a hotel that accommodates Negroes as well as whites.			
agree	83***		agree	61		22
undecided	4		undecided	4		
disagree	14		disagree	35		
9. Under our democratic system people should be allowed to live where they please if they can afford it.			9. I would be willing to have a Negro family live next door to me.			
agree	60		agree	35		25
undecided	6		undecided	2		
disagree	34		disagree	63		
10. I believe that all public recreational facilities should be available to all people at all times.			10. I don't think I would mind if Negro children were to swim in the same pool as my children.			
agree	63		agree	38		25
undecided	6		undecided	8		
disagree	31		disagree	54		

*The five response categories—"strongly agree" to "strongly disagree"—were collapsed to form the three categories shown here. ("Undecided" remained the middle category.)

**The percent agreeing with the general valuation is significantly higher than that agreeing with the specific valuation in all ten item pairs (p < .01).

***Percentages do not total 100 due to rounding.

valuations than with the general valuations from which they were derived, in every one of the ten item-pairs (in all cases p < .01).

Agreement with specific valuations was highest on Items 2, 4 and 5 (over 70 per cent). These items refer to Negroes as jurors and congressional representatives, and to school integration. Each refers to a *fait accompli*, to the extent that integration in these areas has been achieved in the community.

At least 60 per cent agreed with Items 1, 3, 6, and 8. Item 1 refers to Negro supervisors on the job, Item 6 with Negro school teachers. For some these too were facts of life as they knew it. Others saw these items as decisions to be made by the administration of the place of employment or the school. They expressed distaste for the idea, but felt they would have to resign themselves to it if it happened.

Item 3 dealt with willingness to take a Negro family whose home had burned down into the subject's own home for the night. The obligation to be charitable seemed very strong and even those who declined to take the hypothetical victims into their own homes said they would contribute money for hotel lodgings or donate food, clothing and furniture.

Item 8 asked whether the respondent would stay in a hotel serving Negroes as well as whites, and the majority said they would. Urban hotels in Indiana do accept Negro guests as they do in most of the northern and border states where the respondents might travel. Once again, they were faced with a question about which they have little choice: hotels in their experience are in fact integrated. Some added that they would not care to stay in a hotel that catered *primarily* to Negroes.

The majority disagreed with Items 7, 9, and 10. Item 7 deals with "social" integration, Item 9 with housing integration and Item 10 with integrated swimming pools. Unlike the other seven items, these deal with close personal contacts over which individuals presumably have some control.

Thus, not only were the more general, abstract American Creed valuations more readily endorsed than specific ones with situational relevance, but the degree to which a given item represents a *fait accompli* for the respondent seems to be a factor in determining whether the majority of the sample accept or reject

TABLE 2. **FREQUENCY OF CONSISTENT AND INCONSISTENT RESPONSES**

	Total Consistent Responses	Agree with Both General and Specific	Disagree with Both General and Specific
Frequency	647	562	85
Per Cent	100	86.9	13.1
Mean per Person	6.3	5.5	.8
	Total Inconsistent Responses	Agree with General, Disagree with or Undecided about Specific	All Others*
Frequency	383	335	48
Per Cent	100	87.5	12.5
Mean per Person	3.7	3.2	.5

*Disagree with general—agree with or undecided about specific; Undecided about general—agree or disagree with specific.

it. This finding supports the "definition of the situation" interpretation of race relations favored by Lohman and Reitzes, Blumer, Killian, Rose and others.[11] Where the formal group structure defines a given action in clear-cut terms and where these definitions are acted out by most of the members, then an individual's valuations (or attitudes, as the case may be) tend to "follow" even though initially he might have preferred a different state of affairs.

Table 2 summarizes the amount of agreement and disagreement for the ten item-pairs. Each person responded to ten item-pairs for a total of 1030 paired responses. Of these, 647 were consistent, the subjects agreeing or disagreeing with both sides of a given item-pair. No dilemma is indicated in these response-pairs. The remaining 383 response-pairs were inconsistent, indicating a potential dilemma. Whether a dilemma exists, however, depends on the respondent's reactions to his own inconsistencies.

Analysis of *response patterns* rather than individuals facilitates statistical treatment of the data where multiple responses are permitted, but it does raise a question as to whether the responses are primarily those of a few exceptionally verbose individuals. The data presented in Table 3 indicate that this is not the case. Relatively few are so consistent in their responses as to be free from the possibility of experiencing a dilemma. Only 13 (12.6 per cent) of the respondents agreed with all ten general valuations and their related specific valuations, and no one disagreed with both the general and the specific valuations in more than five pairs. No respondent agreed with all the general and disagreed with all the specific items. In short, most of the respondents are potentially subject to a dilemma of some sort, though relatively few are subject to it in the majority of areas about which they were questioned.

I have spoken here of "potential" conflict because it is an empirical question whether those who agree with the American Creed valuations and disagree with the specific valuations derived from them do in fact experience a dilemma in a personal sense, as Myrdal maintains. Unless an individual recognizes the contradictions in his responses no dilemma can properly be said to exist for him. Clues as to the extent to which contradictions are recognized appear in Table 4, where open-ended responses are classified according to the point in the interview at which they were made and whether they were spontaneous or elicited under probing. Nearly 60 per cent of all remarks were spontaneous. These people were qualifying their structured responses to Forms I and II or commenting on the statements presented to them for consideration. The bulk of these spontaneous remarks were made while the respondents were completing Form II (specific valuations). Remarks volunteered while completing Form I tended to be situational qualifications that anticipated Form II. It is reasonable to assume that those who made spontaneous remarks clearly experienced contradiction. At this point in the interview the interviewer had given no sign that he saw or was the least bit interested in contradictory responses.

[11]Joseph D. Lohman and Dietrich C. Reitzes, "Note on Race Relations in Mass Society," *op. cit.*, and "Deliberately Organized Groups and Racial Behavior," *American Sociological Review*, 19 (1954), pp. 342–348; Herbert Blumer, "Attitudes and the Social Act," *Social Problems*, 3 (1955), pp. 59–65; Arnold M. Rose, "Intergroups Relations vs. Prejudice: Pertinent Theory for the Study of Social Change," *Social Problems*, 4 (1956), pp. 173–176 and "Inconsistencies in Attitudes Toward Negro Housing," *Social Problems*, 8 (1961), pp. 286–293; and Lewis M. Killian, "The Effects of Southern White Workers on Race Relations in Northern Plants," *American Sociological Review*, 17 (1952), pp. 327–331.

The first explicit probe, "Any comment?" elicited approximately one remark per person, but the more explicit and direct "Do you see any contradiction?" produced an average of 3.5 per person, and the probe "Any explanation?" one or two additional explanatory remarks (Mean = 1.2). Some of those who made remarks only under probing probably do not experience a dilemma but simply recognize contradictions when they are brought to their attention.

Of the 293 inconsistencies noted, respondents admitted approximately 42 per cent (122) and recognized but denied about the same number (125) (Table 5). Nearly 16 per cent of the inconsistencies remained unseen even after explicit probing. (Note that a given respondent may have admitted some inconsistencies, denied others and failed to see still others. References here are to the amount of inconsistency apparent in the responses, not to individuals.)

TABLE 3.   **FREQUENCY DISTRIBUTION OF RESPONSE PATTERNS**

Pattern	\multicolumn{12}{c}{Number of Item-Pairs}
	0	**1**	**2**	**3**	**4**	**5**	**6**	**7**	**8**	**9**	**10**	**Total**
Agree with Both General & Specific	10	8	3	9	7	13	7	16	9	8	13	103
Disagree with Both General & Specific	58	21	15	4	3	2	..	..	..	..	..	103
Agree with General; Disagree with Specific	28	11	16	14	10	6	6	6	3	3	..	103
Agree with General; Undecided, Specific	75	18	7	3	..	..	..	..	..	..	..	103
All Other Patterns	65	26	10	2	..	..	..	..	..	..	..	103

TABLE 4.   **DEGREE OF SPONTANEITY IN OPEN-ENDED REMARKS**

	All Remarks	**Spontaneous**	**Under Probing**
Frequency	1483.5*	884	599.5
Per Cent	100	59.6	40.4
Mean per Person	14.1	8.6	5.8

	Total Number of Spontaneous Remarks	**Form I****	**Form II*****	**After I & II**
Frequency	884	233	399.5	251.5
Per Cent	100	26.4	45.2	28.4
Mean per Person	8.6	2.3	3.9	2.4

	Total Number of Remarks Made Under Probing	**Probe Level +1 "Any Comment?"**	**Probe Level +2 "Any Contradiction?"**	**Probe Level +3 "Any Explanation?"**
Frequency	599.5	116	361	122.5
Per Cent	100	19.4	60.2	20.4
Mean per Person	5.8	1.1	3.5	1.2

*Fractions result from grouping, for coding purposes, the responses of the relatively few people who made ten or more remarks each.
**This column refers to few spontaneous remarks made in response to the general valuation statements.
***This column refers to spontaneous remarks made in response to the specific valuations.

TABLE 5. **TYPES OF REACTIONS OF RESPONDENTS TO THEIR CONSISTENT AND INCON-
SISTENT RESPONSES**

	All Explanations	Explanations of Consistency	Explanations of Inconsistency	
Frequency	1071	274	797	
Per Cent	100	25.6	74.4	
Mean per Person	10.4	2.7	7.7	
	All Inconsistencies	**Admitted**	**Denied***	**Not Seen****
Frequency	293	122	125	46
Per Cent	100	41.6	42.7	15.7
Mean per Person	2.8	1.2	1.2	.4

*In these cases of inconsistency the respondent did in fact respond inconsistently, recognized the "apparent" inconsistency, but denied that his responses were inconsistent.
**These include all instances of inconsistency where the respondent gave no clear-cut evidence of recognizing any inconsistency.

Table 5 presents a rather interesting finding: over 25 per cent of all explanations were not explanations of inconsistency, but rather explanations of *consistency* between general and specific valuations. *Most of these explanations were justifications of democratic responses* (e.g., "It's the only Christian thing to do"). These explanations of consistency were not merely justifications of negative consistency, i.e., disagreement with both the general and specific valuations: 66 per cent of the explanations of consistency were actually made by people whose responses included no negative consistencies.

Myrdal maintains that the value conflicts are rationalized by opportunistically calling forth culturally shared beliefs to explain the apparent contradiction. But a variety of other types of resolutions also occurred.

1. Most conspicuous among these alternatives was the calling forth of new valuations, that is, valuations in addition to those in conflict (e.g., "I don't think Negroes should be in politics").
2. Repression of one or the other of the values in conflict, or of the conflict itself (e.g., the answer "What conflict?" in response to the probe "Do you see any conflict?"). Failure to recognize a conflict could be due to repression or to limited logical abilities or both, but our method does not permit us to distinguish between these.
3. Adjustment of the general valuation as it applies to the respondent (e.g., "I guess I'm not so democratic after all").
4. Limitation of the range of applicability of the general valuation, (e.g., "Brotherhood refers to whites" or, "I wasn't thinking of Negroes at first").
5. Appeal to the doctrine of relativity (e.g., "There are different kinds of brotherhood").
6. Apparent projection of one's own attitudes to others (e.g., "I wouldn't mind having a Negro dinner guest in my home but we must consider the other guests," or, referring to the same situation, "My husband wouldn't like it.") Often the burden of the conflict is shifted to the Negro, "A Negro [juror] would be prejudiced."

7. Compartmentalization of conflicting valuations (e.g., "You can believe in brotherhood and not invite certain people to your home"). This is to be distinguished from repression because in this instance the person is clearly aware of his values on both ends of the continuum, but does not see any necessary connection between the two.

These alternative resolutions of value conflict are sometimes quite difficult to distinguish from each other. In addition, other solutions were offered which, though typically less logical, were frequently more candid than any of those listed (e.g., "He [a Negro] has a right to hold public office, but I just wouldn't vote for him," or, "I'm prejudiced").

To test the Myrdal theory on the most general level, it seemed expedient to ignore many of the subtle differences observed among the response-types listed. Most responses given could be reduced to variations within the general categories beliefs and valuations. The findings in Table 6 clearly indicate that Myrdal's analysis of how people respond to value conflict is limited, for in this sample people invoke valuations as frequently as they do beliefs in attempting to resolve the conflict. *There was no significant difference between the number of beliefs and the number of valuations invoked by respondents in explaining the discrepancies in their responses.* Again the possibility occurs that this finding might be characteristic of a handful of verbose subjects rather than typical. The frequency distribution of beliefs and valuations in Table 7 indicates that this finding is not simply an artifact of method. While 15 subjects invoked more than ten beliefs each, the distribution of the majority in the one-to-ten range is fairly even. Some 84 per cent of the respondents fell within the one-to-ten range and accounted for 66 per cent of the total number (618) of beliefs invoked. The distribution of valuations is quite similar.

Each explanation, whether it involved a valuation or a belief, was in fact a compromise of either the general or the specific standard. Those who are bothered by the conflict must either change or qualify at least one position to resolve the conflict. Table 8 compares the frequency of *adjustments of general valuations* with the frequency of *adjustments of specific valuations*. If a person says, upon recognizing a conflict, "I wasn't thinking of Negroes when I said people should have equal opportunities," this qualifies as an adjustment (i.e., change or qualification) of a general valuation. If, on the other hand, upon seeing the conflict between his endorsement of equal opportunity and his rejection of the idea of a Negro as his supervisor, he says, for example, "Well, I guess it might be all right

TABLE 6.   **BELIEFS VERSUS VALUATIONS: TYPES OF EXPLANATIONS INVOKED BY RESPONDENTS**

	All Explanations*	Beliefs	Valuations
Frequency	1149	618	531
Per Cent	100	53.8	46.2
Mean per Person	11.2	6.0	5.2

*The term "explanation" refers to respondents' open-ended remarks, classifiable as beliefs or valuations, at any probe level. Some respondents made more than one such remark about a discrepancy between a given pair of valuations.

TABLE 7.   DISTRIBUTION OF RESPONDENTS BY NUMBER OF BELIEFS AND NUMBER OF VALUATIONS

Number of Beliefs*	Number of Respondents	Number of Valuations**	Number of Respondents
0	5	0	15
1	9	1	8
2	14	2	7
3	8	3	13
4	10	4	9
5	10	5	6
6	9	6	8
7	4	7	10
8	7	8	6
9	6	9	7
10	6	10	4
11	1	11	2
12	4	12	2
13	3	13	1
14–20	7	14–20	5
	103		103

*Total number of beliefs invoked = 618.
**Total number of valuations invoked = 531.

TABLE 8.   TYPES OF ADJUSTMENT OF CONFLICTING VALUATIONS

	All Adjustments	Adjustment of General Valuations	Adjustment of Specific Valuation
Frequency	1345	248	1097
Per Cent	100	18.4	81.6
Mean per Person	13.1	2.4	10.6

for a Negro to be supervisor if he were unusually qualified," this would be an adjustment of a specific valuation.

In most cases the respondent adjusted the specific valuation so that his disagreement with the specific item did not really seem, to him at least, to violate the precept set forth in the general form. Some adjustments were made in the general valuations, as well, however. Nearly 82 per cent of all responses were adjustments of specific valuations; 18.4 per cent were adjustments of the tenets of the American Creed (see Table 8).

Summary of Empirical Relationships:

1. A substantial majority of the sample subscribe, at least verbally, to the American Creed: the mean per cent of agreement with the ten general valuation statements is 81.1 per cent.

2. Respondents were considerably less likely to endorse the specific valuations than the general valuations; the mean percentage agreeing with the specific valuations was 56 per cent. Thus, as Myrdal emphasizes, a considerable discrepancy exists between specific and general valuations.

3. Respondents tended to recognize the conflict between their general and specific valuations without comment from the interviewer. The majority (59.6 per cent) of explanations of conflict were volunteered spontaneously.

4. There is a tendency to explain consistency as well as inconsistency. Of the total number of "explanations" given by our sample, 25.6 per cent were explanations of consistency.

5. To resolve conflicts between the specific and the general valuations presented to them in the interview, the respondents invoked additional valuations (other than the two in conflict) almost as frequently as they did beliefs.

6. In resolving the dilemma, the general pattern is for the respondent to adjust the specific valuation so that it does not appear to conflict with the general, though some adjustments were also made in the general valuations.

7. When the specific valuations refer to legal, political, and educational relationships, conflict between the general and specific valuations is appreciably less likely. This is due to the fact that non-discriminatory behavior is most likely to be endorsed in these areas.

Interpretations

The possibilities for interpretation in a study such as this are almost infinite. Space limitations make it necessary to ignore many alternative interpretations[12] and to limit analysis to a few of the more significant findings.

Empirical relationship #5 is worthy of discussion. Myrdal theorized that when people find their racial prejudices in conflict with their democratic ideals, they find *logical* ways to deny the conflict. Our findings indicate that people frequently do not follow the type of logical procedure Myrdal expected. Thus, when people who think of themselves as democratic say that they would not want a Negro as their supervisor in their place of work, not all of them invoke a belief such as "Negroes are inherently less capable than whites." Instead, a common reaction is to assert an additional valuation to the ones in conflict, or to repeat, in slightly altered form, one of the valuations in conflict.

A wealth of sociological evidence suggests that in many social situations in America, it is not the person who behaves in a prejudiced manner who is deviant, but rather the non-prejudiced person who refuses to discriminate. Empirical relationship #4 appears to support this contention, for 274 of the explanations were *explanations of consistency*. In other words, many people who endorse the tenets of the American Creed found it necessary to rationalize, explain, or otherwise justify their *democratic* choices regarding specific areas of race relations. Thus, people with no dilemma in Myrdal's sense seem to experience another type

[12]For instance, the relevance of theories of cognitive dissonance is readily apparent. See Leon A. Festinger, *A Theory of Cognitive Dissonance*, Evanston, Ill.: Row, Peterson, 1957, and Jack W. Brehm and Arthur R. Cohen, *Exploration in Cognitive Dissonance*, New York: Wiley, 1962.

of dilemma: a conflict between their endorsement of democratic action and yet *another normative system,* which exists in the majority of American local communities: the system which says that one ought to be prejudiced and one ought to discriminate.

Empirical relationship #6 is of some social significance, though it contradicts neither Myrdal's nor widespread sociological expectations. Myrdal predicts that in the long run the general tenets of the American Creed will win out over the contradictory valuations defining American race relations. We had thought (after pre-tests) that we might find that many people would alter the general to fit the specific. Actually, 81.6 per cent of the "explanations" were adjustments of specific valuations. This suggests that Myrdal's optimism is not unjustified, and lends little support to the fear that people might react to the dilemma by renouncing their allegiance to the democratic tenets of the American Creed. This conclusion must be qualified, however, by the finding that many people feel constrained to justify their egalitarian specific valuations, again suggesting that another, undemocratic normative order co-exists with the more general democratic normative order.

The finding (#7) that conflict is appreciably less when the specific valuation refers to legal, political, and educational institutions (largely integrated in the community studied), is relevant to a number of theories. A most plausible interpretation is that people tend to go along with inter-group arrangements that are *faits accomplis.* Unambiguous democratic definitions of the situation are implied by the fact of integration in these areas, and they may well assume the status of normative imperatives more effective in guiding behavior than the private preferences of those who would prefer less democratic arrangements.

In broadest outline, then, this study supports the Myrdal theory. People do experience a conflict[13] and do try to resolve it. Myrdal does not, however, adequately describe the process whereby people seek resolution.

As a test of Myrdal's theory, this research must be considered preliminary. As a pilot study it supports the Myrdal theory sufficiently to justify test on a nationwide basis. If it is true, as Handlin says, that *An American Dilemma* is "a book that changed American life,"[14] then surely Myrdal's primary theory deserves such a test.

---

[13]An important qualification of the present findings is in order. We do not know 1) whether the conflict our respondents experienced in the interview situation exists for them outside the interview situation, or 2) whether it exists on an affective as well as a verbal or intellectual level. Other-directed, compartmentalizing people responding to the demands of specific situations may not be particularly upset by the fact that what they do in one situation contradicts what is expected in another. As for the nature of the conflict experience, many of our respondents manifested considerable anxiety when the contradiction became apparent to them. I hope one day to combine the techniques used in the present study with those used in a previous study of the relation between autonomic responses and attitudes. A recording of autonomic responses in the conflict situation might reveal the extent to which the conflict is affectively experienced in the interview. Cf. Frank R. Westie and Melvin DeFleur, "Autonomic Responses and Their Relationship to Race Attitudes," *Journal of Abnormal and Social Psychology,* 58 (1959), pp. 340–347.

[14]Review of *An American Dilemma, op. cit.*

On Adding Apples and Oranges

The inconsistent findings discussed by Rodman result from the reports by some investigators "that within the lower class the nonlegal marital union and the resulting illegitimate children are deviant patterns, and that marriage and legitimate childbirth are normative." Rodman points out that no distinction has been made by these analysts between preferential orientations and normative orientations. When we ask people which of two alternatives is "better," we are not asking the same thing as when we ask them if a pattern is considered acceptable. In order to document this observation, Rodman isolates responses from the same people to three "preferential" questions and to three "normative" questions, all referring to the same social object.

> Looking at the percentages for the total sample, marriage tends to be "favored" on the preferential questions. On the normative questions *living* — the alternative arrangement — tends to be "favored." These data document the fact that it is erroneous to use responses to preferential questions to make inferences about norms.

In Rodman's terms, an example of a preferential question is, "Is it better for . . . ?" An example of a normative question is, "Is it all right for . . . ?" To add responses to such questions is indeed to add apples and oranges. They tap different attitudinal dimensions. Furthermore, to expect comparable findings from different studies which employ one or the other type of question, is to expect apples and oranges to add up to something. Perhaps they do add up to something, but the synthetic fruit has about as much basis in reality as a synthesis of different orientations toward the same social object.

Frank Westie provides a second illustration of the way in which meaningful conceptual distinctions can lead to clarification. Contrary to popular distortions, Myrdal did not pose a dilemma between democratic ideology and American discriminatory acts. The distinction he *discovered* and employed as the basic guideline in his analysis of American race relations was between two independent cognitive orientations: valuations and beliefs. I emphasize the word *"discovered"* advisedly. Myrdal did not invent concepts in the manner advocated by Bridgman. He suggested, rather, that in the minds of men there is no necessary relationship between conceptions of what ought to be (valuations) and conceptions of what is (beliefs).

This discovery not only guides Westie's empirical research, but also provides him with a useful device for content analysis of interview probes: " . . . responses were classified as *valuations* where they contained any 'ought to be' elements whatever, and *beliefs* where they included any statements of 'what is,' 'what was,' or conceptions of reality." Although Westie leaves open the question of the extent to which individual Americans experience a "dilemma" as a result of inconsistent valuations and beliefs, his data leave little doubt but what such inconsistencies do occur. Having carefully integrated the distinction discovered by Myrdal into his research instruments, Westie, in the best tradition of cumulative science, builds a new and important discovery on top of it. Contrary to the assumptions of "functional sociologists," "dissonance psychologists," "domino political scientists," and other adherents to balance theories of human behavior, Westie discovers that his respondents feel just as compelled to "explain" consistencies in their choices as they do to explain inconsistencies.

Since "preference" (in Rodman's terms) is frequently directed toward a prejudice orientation in our society, the individual who finds himself agreeing with specific nonprejudiced orientations also finds himself in an awkward position. The more general faith in the platitudes of the democratic ideology are also "preferred." Thus, from one perspective "consistency" means agreeing with both "preferred" positions — specific prejudice and general egalitarianism. This, of course, is not what the social scientist or the logician defines as consistency. *Their* definition of consistency is perceived by respondents as somehow deviant and requiring explanation. In effect, what is "consistent" from one perspective is inconsistent from another.

I have referred above to the simple dichotomous distinctions clarified by Rodman and Westie, as "first order" ones. As I said, the complex interrelationship among various orientations remains a mystery. We do not know what the matrix of such a set of orientations might look like (much less how that matrix itself shifts under varying conditions). We have been inclined to treat such orientations as interchangeable parts in social science research — and sometimes they may be.[11] But, as Rodman and Westie testify, there is evidence that sometimes they are not. Rarely does a research report provide us with an indication of what the matrix of relationships among several of these dimensions might look like. In their analysis of white Brazilian students' responses to queries about Negroes, Bastide and van den Berghe supply one such matrix.[12] In the table below, I have adapted their data by changing some of the titles in the stubs. The authors use the term "stereotype" in reference to subjects' tendency to identify Negroes with a list of stereotyped characteristics. I have changed that caption to "belief" in order to facilitate comparisons with other data in this chapter. Bastide and van den Berghe label responses to a series of "ought" questions as "norms." Again, for purposes of comparability, I have changed their caption to read, "value," in line with the Myrdal-Westie use of that term. They have called responses to a series of questions about interracial behavior "actual behavior." I have changed this to "self-reported behavior." Their final dimension consists of a series of responses to questions about hypothetical behavior put in the conditional form: "Would you . . . ?" I have retained their term, "hypothetical behavior" for this orientation. The numbers are Pearsonian coefficients of correlation, all of which are positive (+):

11. For example, when there is no lack of opportunity and the situation does not change radically, there seems to be a very close relationship between "behavioral intentions" and "overt behaviors." In his study of verbal and overt behavior of church members toward their local churches, Wicker reports that "the correlation between the subjects' pledged contributions and the amounts actually given over 1 fiscal year was .92." When, however, opportunities are blocked, intentions become unrelated to behavior. The first example is from Alan W. Wicker, "An Examination of the 'Other Variables' Explanation of Attitude-Behavior Inconsistency," *Journal of Personality and Social Psychology* 19 (1971): 28–29. An example of what happens when opportunities are blocked can be found in Lawrence T. Cagle and Irwin Deutscher, "Housing Aspirations and Housing Achievement: The Relocation of Poor Families," *Social Problems* 18 (1970): 453–69.

12. Roger Bastide and Pierre van den Berghe, "Stereotypes, Norms and Interracial Behavior in São Paulo, Brazil," *American Sociological Review* 22 (1957): 692. These are the same data which Guttman reanalyzed and which were discussed in Chapter Nine. See Louis Guttman, "A Structural Theory for Intergroup Beliefs and Actions," *American Sociological Review* 24 (1959): 318–28.

	Belief	Value	Self-reported behavior	Hypothetical behavior
Belief	1.00			
Value	.60	1.00		
Self-reported behavior	.25	.51	1.00	
Hypothetical behavior	.37	.68	.49	1.00

These coefficients, based on a sample of 580 "white" Brazilian students, are all unlikely to result from chance alone. For whatever it may be worth, they are all statistically significant in the sense that there is less than a probability of .05 that their difference from no correlation at all (zero) is due to chance. For present purposes, I want only to point out the relative sizes of these relationships. The two largest relationships are found between value (notions of what ought to be) and belief (notions of what is) and between value and hypothetical behavior. The latter is the highest correlation in the matrix and indicates that one could accurately predict nearly half of the responses on one variable from the responses on the other. The two intermediate correlations are with self-reported behavior. Both value and hypothetical behavior can be accurately guessed from self-report responses about 25 percent of the time. The two lowest relationships are with "belief" — self-reported behavior and hypothetical behavior being less likely to be related to belief than any other pair of relationships.

There appears to be a positive, although middling, relationship among these orientations — at least insofar as lighter skinned Brazilians relate to darker skinned Brazilians. Let us consider a similar matrix reflecting the relationship among orientations toward a more mundane situation.[13] Dannick has observed 374 pedestrians either conform to or violate a "don't walk" signal at an intersection. A few blocks away and a few moments later these same persons found themselves confronted with a sidewalk interviewer doing a study of "traffic safety." During the course of the interview a "belief" is elicited: the respondent is asked what most people do when confronted with a stoplight; a "value" is elicited: the respondent is asked what people should do; a self-report is obtained: he is asked what he did the last time he faced a "don't walk" light. The person was also asked what he usually does under those circumstances. I refer to this in the table below as a "norm" although it clearly is not what Bastide and van den Berghe mean by a norm nor is it what Rodman refers to as "normative" in his contribution to this chapter. All of these orientations can be compared with the observed behavior:

13. The following analysis is based on data originally collected by Lionel Dannick. I am grateful to Dannick for supplying me with a deck of his cards and to Victor Theissen for his advice and technical assistance in reanalyzing these data.

	Self-report	Observed behavior	Norm	Belief	Value
Self-report	1.00				
Observed behavior	.82	1.00			
Norm	.35	.29	1.00		
Belief	.06	.09	.23	1.00	
Value	.14	.12	.29	.16	1.00

These, too, are Pearsonian coefficients of correlation and all of them are positive (+). Dannick's 374 cases require a coefficient of .09 before reaching the .05 level of confidence. Anything less than .09 can be considered to differ from zero correlation as a result of chance alone. This is not to say that anything greater than .09 ought to be taken seriously. A correlation of .09 accounts for only eighty-one one-thousandths of the variance. The only relationship of note is that between the observed behavior and the person's own report of that behavior. The next largest relationship is between what the person claims he usually does (norm) and his self-report of what he last did. Beliefs and values appear generally unrelated to anything else including each other. There are three orientations which are common to both the study employing Brazilian student respondents and the one employing American pedestrian respondents. The following table, derived from the other two, facilitates comparisons:

Correlation Between	Brazilian students	American pedestrians
Beliefs and values	.60	.16
Values and self-reports	.51	.14
Beliefs and self-reports	.25	.06

The correlations between racial orientations in Brazil are uniformly higher than the correlations between pedestrian orientations in America. The fact that there are no discrepancies in the ordering of these two sets of coefficients is less important than the fact that there is no apparent contradiction between them other than their absolute size. If one wished to entertain the hypothesis that the relationship between beliefs and values is greater than that between values and self-reports and that both of these are greater than the relationship between beliefs and self-reports, there is no evidence here which suggests the contrary! Furthermore, it would appear from the pedestrian data and a considerable body of evidence on juvenile delinquency, that the highest relationship obtains between observed behavior and self-reported behavior. At the moment, I am not interested in such hypotheses. My purpose is only to indicate the complexity of the relationships found among various orientations toward the same social object.[14]

This chapter has not been concerned with polemics on the proper definition of "attitude." It has been concerned with evidence of the existence of many dimensions of human behavior, the relationships among which are unknown, but which are frequently lumped under a single rubric. Sometimes that rubric is "attitude"; sometimes it is something else. Nor have I been concerned with the annoying lack of uniformity in the symbols assigned to the various orientations subsumed under "attitudes." This is not to deny that it would make our work a bit easier if different scholars would use the terms "value" and "norm" to denote the same things. Standardization of terminology would be helpful but it has little to do with the conceptual problems which plague contemporary social science. Those problems revolve in large part around our inability to identify the distinctions people make in their everyday discourse. Without the conceptual tools which facilitate the making of such distinctions in our research instruments, we find ourselves unable to make the kinds of abstract connections which are the building blocks of theory.

Until we are able to sort out the kinds of orientations toward social objects reflected by our instruments, the possibility of cumulative knowledge is dim. Spurious cumulations, little houses of cards, are of course as possible as they are misleading and dangerous insofar as they have any influence on policy or programs. Such spurious cumulations are possible because they are built on operational definitions—fictions created in the minds of social scientists in order to assure comparability. But it isn't very helpful in understanding human behavior to have at our disposal a mass of comparable irrelevancies. Without a clear understanding of what kinds of orientations our instruments are and are not tapping, it is difficult to know what can be compared with what—what is an apple and what is an orange. Without the ability to make such distinctions we are confronted with the unhappy choice between knowledge limited to the time and place of specific studies or the irrelevant generalizations of operationalists. I would prefer to either of these alternatives, that we continue to identify the various perspectives or orientations people may have toward social objects and proceed to learn how these orientations covary under different conditions.

Summary: A Hatful of Explanations

Why do people sometimes not act in accord with their sentiments? It should be clear by now that there are no grounds for assuming such "consistency" to be a natural or expected state of affairs. The evidence suggests that sometimes they do act as they say and sometimes they do not and sometimes there is no relationship at all. It can be legitimately argued that much of this evidence must be heavily discounted if not discarded on methodological grounds. The observed discrepancy between senti-

14. Charles Perrow has correctly pointed out to me that many of these correlations are very small and the differences not great, so that it may be misleading to order them as I have in these tables. However, if these flimsy data help convince some scholars that little can be taken for granted about the relationships among various orientations, they will have served a useful purpose.

ments and acts (as well as the observed concordance) is sometimes more apparent than real. Our measurement techniques as well as our research designs can produce such findings artifactually. Furthermore, our methodology—the way we think about our procedures—can also result in findings which require reinterpretation: sentiments and acts may represent a continuum—a scale ranging from easiest to hardest expressions—rather than a categorical dichotomy. Technical and methodological analysis may indeed screen out much of the supposed "evidence." It is also true, as our discussion in this chapter suggests, that there are many kinds of sentiments and many kinds of acts and many kinds of indicators of both, and their relationship is obscure. Discrepancies between sentiments and acts sometimes disappear when conceptual clarification is achieved. These explanations all lead to the conclusion that inconsistency may be more apparent than real. So too does the issue of the definition of an "inconsistency." We have seen instances where one man's inconsistency is an other man's congruence.

The conceptual problem is not only confounding because sometimes people try to compare apples and oranges, but because, as Rokeach has argued, an individual's acts are influenced by a number of attitudes rather than any single one.[15] He points out that we not only have attitudes toward objects which may be different from our attitudes toward situations, but we are likely to entertain several attitudes toward any given object or toward any given situation. Rokeach's argument is reflected in Ehrlich's contribution to Chapter Eleven. Its full ramifications can be seen in a concise and comprehensive analysis of the attitudinal dimension by Robert Lauer. Lauer reminds us that attitudes are interdependent and they are multidimensional. He also points to the need to distinguish between attitudes which are central and those which are peripheral, attitudes which are primary and those which are secondary, and, finally, between what he refers to as "extrapolated attitudes" and "existential attitudes." This last dimension is related to subjects' definitions of what constitutes "reality."[16]

The double screen does not sort out everything. When methodological credibility is ascertained and conceptual clarity achieved, it still appears that sometimes men do otherwise than what they say or what they think or what they believe. There is one explanation which appears to be shared by social scientists regardless of their theoretical persuasion. Tarter, an avowed behaviorist, explains the improved predictability of behavior in his own research in terms of the similar stimulus properties present in both the attitudinal measurement and the actual behavioral situation. Jordon, using a Lewinian rhetoric, argues that when the attitudinal field and the behavioral field are similar, there will be concordance and when they are different, there will be a discrepancy. Blumer, the symbolic interactionist, insists that when people define the interview situation in the same manner in which they define the situation in which they are called upon to act, then the words and the deeds will coincide. Otherwise they may not. In his relatively detached summary of literature in this field, Wicker concludes that "the more similar the situations in which verbal and overt behavioral responses are obtained, the stronger will be the attitude-behavior relationship."[17] This broad agreement cannot be ignored. It would seem clear that

15. Milton Rokeach, *Beliefs, Attitudes and Values: A Theory of Organization and Change* (San Francisco: Jossey-Bass Inc., Publishers, 1970).

16. Robert H. Lauer, "The Problems and Values of Attitude Research," *Sociological Quarterly* 12 (1971): 248.

17. Tarter, "Attitude: The Mental Myth," p. 277. Jordan's argument appears in Chapter Six and Blumer's begins to take shape in Chapter Two. The quotation is from Allan W. Wicker, "Attitudes Versus Actions: The Relationship of Verbal and Overt Behavioral Responses to Attitude Objects," *Journal of Social Issues* 25 (1969): 69.

there is a relationship between the actor's definition of the situation in which he speaks and his definition of the situation in which he acts and the extent to which the talk and the action are concordant.

Great emphasis has been placed on subjective definitions by actors during the course of this volume. That is not because I set out to demonstrate the importance of this factor, but because it emerged from my review and analysis of the literature. Evidence from every conceivable source can be brought to bear on the conclusion that men size up a situation in terms of its external features and their internal assessment and *then they act.* They do not simply respond to stimuli; they interpret the scene. Behaviorists such as Tarter would repudiate any internal interpretive process as "mentalistic" and unnecessary and they would hold to an older input-output model of behavior. But it is my impression that they are lonely these days. Most social scientists, regardless of theoretical or methodological differences, are coming to recognize a need to concentrate on the intervening process rather than on the sentiment and the act. In these terms the question "what is the relationship between sentiments and acts" becomes irrelevant. We begin to ask how a variety of events (or factors or characteristics or variables) interact with each other, exerting different kinds of influences under different conditions and eventually culminating in one or another outcome. The focus on what's in between seems to be most promising; it is also most difficult to implement.

Underlying any explanatory mode is the inescapable need to assume that the social act is in a constant state of development and that one cannot expect it to be the same at one point in time as at another or in one situation as in another. Men are flexible — even the most rigid of them! Without such flexibility social survival would be difficult if not impossible. The lack of consistency in human behavior has been an inherent part of the paraphernalia of traditional sociological concepts. The Linton-Parsons structural concept of social roles (like Mead's active verbs, "to take a role" or "to play a role") is a device which permits us to view inconsistent behavior and attitudes as "normal." The problem of understanding the relationship between sentiments and acts need not be seen as a social-psychological or a microsociological one. Blumer spells out potential extensions of his interactionist theory to larger groups and societies. But there are other theoretical clues. W. F. Ogburn's notion of "cultural lag,"[18] for example, can be extended to encompass the sentimental as well as the behavioral and technological elements of a society. If we do this, it becomes possible to see certain peculiar inconsistencies in rapidly changing societies as resulting from a "lag," say, between traditional values and industrial behaviors.

This hatful of explanations would be incomplete without drawing attention to the fact that man is a political animal. The subtlest of psychological and sociological explanations sometimes fail to compare in explanatory power to this superficial quality. People may and do act counter to their sentiments for no better reason than expediency. In ruminating over the fate of idealism among medical students, Becker and Geer put it this way: " . . . when a man's ideals are challenged by outsiders and then further strained by reality, he may salvage them by postponing their application to a future time when conditions are expected to be more propitious."[19] People

18. William F. Ogburn, "Cultural Lag as Theory," *Sociology and Social Research* 61 (1957), reprinted in *William F. Ogburn on Culture and Social Change*, ed. O. D. Duncan (Chicago: University of Chicago Press, 1964), pp. 86–95.

19. Howard S. Becker and Blanche Geer, "The Fate of Idealism in Medical School," *American Sociological Review* 23 (1958): 56.

frequently act in ways which they feel are to their own interests or which will facilitate achievement of ultimate ends regardless of their beliefs or values. This reflects a degree of rationality, but irrationality is also a characteristic of human beings. We may act in ways that we know to be counter to our best interests *and* to our sentiments, for reasons we ourselves are unable to understand. Cigarette smoking among those who believe in the connection with morbidity is one example. Finally, as our earlier discussion of compartmentalization suggests, we may refuse to make any association between orientations which appear to others to be inconsistent.

From time to time, I have alluded to something called a phenomenological approach. What does that mean? How is it different in its practice and consequences from any other kind of approach? Can such an approach be "scientific"? These, and related questions, have important theoretical and methodological implications and merit some consideration in their own right. It is to such questions that we turn in the last chapter.

13

Social Reality as a Social Creature

A Phenomenological Perspective

In the late nineteenth century something called German Idealism began to exert an influence over intellectuals in Northern Europe. It was short-lived—doomed by the massive payoffs of twentieth-century science whose positivism the idealists took issue with. This antiquated idealism is the source of many of the notions I have been discussing in relation to contemporary social science. The idea of "reactivity" derives directly from Kant and is reflected in Heinrich Rickert's insistence that the very act of knowing transforms the object of knowledge.[1] The Austrian psychologist, Franz Brentano built his psychology around the notion of "intention": "Psychical activity 'intends' or is primarily directed upon *objects*. . . . The objects thus intended may exist or not exist, but the fact that they are intended lends them their objective character."[2] It is to Brentano that one pair of social historians attribute the origin of phenomenology in social science. They do, however, allow that it was a student of Brentano's, Edmund Husserl, who established phenomenology under that name as "the descriptive study of consciousness of objects."[3] Since Husserl first applied that name to that activity, we will let it be his, just as we will let "symbolic interactionism" be Herbert Blumer's and "ethnomethodology" be Harold Garfinkel's for the same reason. It does seem to me that these men gave a very specific name (of their own coinage in the cases of Blumer and Garfinkel) to a set of ideas they were proposing. We may disagree with those ideas or modify them or enlarge them, but in so doing we should recognize that what we are talking about is no longer what they were talking about and we ought not to retain the inappropriate label.

This cursory review of the origins of many of the ideas in this volume is based largely on secondary sources. It is intended simply to remind the reader that these notions were not invented yesterday and to give credit where credit seems due. Some well-informed scholars, such as Johan Goudsblom, disagree strongly with my superficial sketch. It is in fact likely that some of my secondary sources have led me astray. Goudsblom has suggested, with some merit, that I am talking not about "phenomenology" in the original sense of that term, but about what

---

1. For a contemporary discussion of the neo-Kantians Rickert, Windelband, and Dilthey, see Lewis A. Coser, *Masters of Sociological Thought: Ideas in Historical and Social Context* (New York: Harcourt Brace Jovanovich, Inc., 1971), pp. 453–55. Coser's treatment is unique in his effort to connect a thinker with his peers, his historical time, and his personal problems. The connection with the notion of reactivity occurred to me as I was reading page 246.

2. Howard P. Becker and Harry Elmer Barnes, *Social Thought from Lore to Science*, vol. II, 2nd edn. (Washington, D.C.: Harren Press, 1952), p. 906.

3. Ibid., p. 906.

Weber called "verstehen." Although Weber's term may be more appropriate and might be acceptable to both symbolic interactionists and ethnomethodologists, Garfinkel has explicitly described his antecedents as phenomenological. Ethnomethodologists think of themselves and are thought of by other sociologists as "phenomenologists." For this reason, I think it would cause more confusion than clarification to change names at midstream. In the preceding paragraph, I urged that we treat labels with due respect. Nevertheless, it is less important what we call the matters we are dealing with than it is to attempt to understand the distinctions, assumptions, and procedures at issue.

I have never been able to make much sense out of Husserl and it is something of a relief to learn from Coser that Karl Mannheim found "Husserl's austere philosophy, centered as it was on the philosophy of mathematics," rather obscure.[4] Albert Salomon suggests that the first student of Husserl's who had any influence on sociology was Max Scheler.[5] It was Scheler, not Mannheim—as some American scholars are inclined to assume—who first wrote on the sociology of knowledge.[6] But it was Alfred Schutz, writing in the early thirties and into the forties, who "has taken seriously the phenomenological method in the original sense of Husserl."[7] It is to Schutz that Garfinkel acknowledges his greatest indebtedness (see footnotes 1 and 2 in Garfinkel's contribution to this chapter). The direct line of descent for ethnomethodology is, then, from Kant to Brentano to Husserl to Schutz to Garfinkel.

Since Descartes, philosophers have been concerned with the problem of knowledge—epistemology, they call it.[8] It is out of that concern that (through Hegel to Marx and Scheler and Mannheim) the sociology of knowledge, as we know it today, eventually emerged. The rationalistic school was laying the groundwork for a super-scientific method that could deal with any kind of knowledge while the counterattack was coming from the more humanistic "idealists" such as Locke and Hume. Comte, the original hard-nosed sociologist, rejected idealism out of hand. For him there is only one way of understanding the rational order of the universe and that is the scientific method. There is only one reality and there is only one way to grasp it, but Kant was not that clear. His distinction between the phenomenal world and the noumenal world is at the bottom of the issue. For Kant both were real and each was different in its knowability.

It is an oversimplification to class Kant as an "idealist" because he reacted against rationalism. Although he does not hold with the positivist position that

4. Coser, *Masters of Sociological Thought*, p. 454.

5. Albert Salomon, "German Sociology," in *Twentieth Century Sociology*, eds. Georges Gurvitch and Wilbert E. Moore (New York: The Philosophical Library, 1945), p. 609. Salomon reminds us that Alfred Vierkand also called his method "phenomenological." Salomon is the only immediate post-World War II sociological historian who, to my knowledge, mentions Alfred Schutz (he spells it Schuetz). Even the more recent encyclopaedic history edited by the Harvard functionalists contains no reference to phenomenology or to Husserl or to Schutz. See, *Theories of Society: Foundations of Modern Sociological Theory*, 2 vols., eds. Talcott Parsons, Edward Shils, Kaspar D. Naegele, and Jesse R. Pitts (New York: The Free Press of Glencoe, Inc., 1961).

6. Barnes and Becker, *Social Thought*, p. 912, conclude that "some hints of *Wissenssoziologie* are to be found as early as 1913. . . . Not until 1924, however, did Scheler make published use of the term *Soziologie des Wissens*."

7. Salomon, "German Sociology," p. 612.

8. I am indebted in this section for a refreshing review of German nineteenth-century epistemology provided by Henry D. Aiken, *The Age of Ideology: The Nineteenth Century Philosophers*, vol. V of *The Great Ages of Western Philosophy* (New York: George Braziller, Inc., 1957).

human understanding passively reflects the inherent nature of things in themselves, as they really are, or whatever, he also rejects the notion that mind itself is the only reality or that mind creates its world. It is because of Kant's acceptance of both noumena and phenomena that it is sometimes difficult to know what position is identified with later groups who call themselves Kantian or neo-Kantian or anti-Kantian. Husserl, for example, took issue with the neo-Kantian dominance in his contemporary German scientific circles. He opted for a phenomenal world and although he may be described as anti-Kantian, it was in fact Kant who provided the option. The basic Kantian idea is that man creates his own history, his own culture, his own self, and these creations have to be understood by methods other than those by which nature can be understood.

I have traced above the intellectual passage of one brand of contemporary phenomenology from Kant to Garfinkel. There is, however, a rather different and considerably older phenomenological tradition in American sociology. It culminates in what Herbert Blumer calls Symbolic Interactionism. Like ethnomethodology, symbolic interactionism is clearly a Kantian derivative. Blumer is explicit about his debt to George Herbert Mead and Mead is equally explicit about his debt to Kant. This makes the tracking problem simple. The strong influence of Kant on Mead's ideas of the relationship between subject and object (the "I" and the "me"), and on the development of the self, can be found throughout his lectures on nineteenth-century philosophy. *Movements of Thought in the Nineteenth Century*[9] begins with the Kantian revolution, moves finally to American pragmatism, and ends with Mead's own social psychology. Mead never lets the reader forget that the issue is realism vs. idealism and, ultimately, that there is little worth bothering with that is "real." The world we must come to understand is a phenomenal world constructed by its actors.

The American pragmatists have always been something of an enigma to me. I am referring here to the Baldwin tradition, carried on by James, Cooley, Dewey, and Mead. The pragmatists were, on the one hand, crassly empirical. They couldn't have cared less what happened in the little black box. If they had a slogan it would have been, "If it works, we'll buy it." Input and output was their game. But that is an incomplete and distorted picture. The pragmatic game, at least as it pervaded the social sciences at the University of Chicago, was almost pure idealism. Mead preached the social construction of the act and a mentalistic psychology in which the important things all happened inside people's heads—in conversations with themselves. I suppose this is why the Chicago school of sociology has always been such a puzzle to me. In its heyday that school produced innumerable descriptive monographs—pure empiricism: the *real* world as only the sociologist could discover it! On the other hand, Mead's symbolism was ever present, manifesting itself, for example, in Thomas' classic "Definition of the Situation" which was to become a widely accepted sociological postulate. Most pervasive was the translation of Mead's "taking the role of the other" into a methodology which demanded that the social world be described from the perspective of the actors in it. Participant observation remains the trademark of Chicago-style sociological research.[10]

9. George Herbert Mead, *Movements of Thought in the Nineteenth Century*, ed. Merritt H. Moore (Chicago: University of Chicago Press, 1936).

10. Gouldner makes an incisive comparison between the Chicago-style and the Columbia–Harvard-style of social research in Alvin W. Gouldner, "Anti-Minotaur: The Myth of a Value Free Sociology," *Social Problems* 9 (1962): 199–213. For a sampling of Chicago-style social re-

This sketch of the nineteenth-century antecedents of contemporary phenomenology in sociology—both symbolic interaction and ethnomethodology—has failed to mention some of the more important and better known of the German idealists. Wilhelm Dilthey, for example, expressed his antipositivism in his emphasis on "meaning" as the crucial element in understanding history. Salomon describes him as the German William James.[11] It was Dilthey who developed the method of "verstehen" which was later to become associated with the name of Max Weber. Dilthey was clearly in the phenomenological tradition, insisting that one had to immerse himself in a phenomenon in order to grasp its meaning. It is equally clear that Weber failed to embrace this tradition, possibly for political reasons. Weber's sociology seems to me one in which men are driven by overwhelming external forces over which they have little or no control. The idea of "verstehen" provided, for Weber, some sort of preliminary familiarization with the phenomenon under study. Weber seems to be conceding that one ought to take a look at and try to make sense out of his object of study before really getting down to the sociological business of studying it. But the real business of sociology is a rational, positivistic one. Weber does recognize the subjective, irrational qualities of humanity, as his essays on values and objectivity indicate.[12] But those same essays reflect his failure to understand that sociologists are people. He recognizes a world populated by irrational, emotional, value-laden human beings. He even suggests that it is these very properties of human nature which may be the most important focus of the sociologist's concern. But he never for a moment allows that the sociologist is also human. He is oblivious to the idea of reactivity and to the constraints suggested by the sociology of knowledge. Both of these ideas were endemic in the intellectual milieu in which Weber grew up. Weber argued that the sociologist, as scientist, is a superman who transcends the value-laden qualities of human nature, and views them objectively from his superior position as detached observer.

If German Idealism survives at all in American sociology, it is thanks largely to Georg Simmel, who has played a much more prominent role than Alfred Schutz. Schutz's link with the American pragmatists, especially Mead and James, is clearly reflected in his footnotes, but Simmel eschewed footnotes. There can be no doubt about the Kantian influence, and Coser suggests that Husserl left traces on Simmel's work. His distinction between the forms of social interaction and their specific content is reminiscent of Kant, and "historical knowledge to Simmel, like the knowledge of nature to Kant, is a product of . . . thinking. It is never given; it has to be created."[13] The impact of Simmel on the Chicago school is reflected from its origins with Robert Park through the works of Louis Wirth and Everett Hughes. Park, who studied under Dewey at Michigan and James at Harvard, was already steeped in the pragmatic philosophy when he spent a semester attending Simmel's lectures. Coser believes this was probably the most important academic semester in Park's life:

search see *Human Behavior and Social Processes*, ed. Arnold M. Rose (Boston: Houghton Mifflin Company, 1962); *Institutions and the Person: Essays Presented to Everett C. Hughes*, eds. Howard S. Becker, Blanche Geer, David Riesman, and Robert S. Weiss (Chicago: Aldine Publishing Company, 1968); *Pathways to Data: Field Methods for Studying Ongoing Social Organizations*, ed. Robert W. Habenstein (Chicago: Aldine Publishing Company, 1970).

11. Salomon, "German Sociology," p. 591.

12. Max Weber, *On the Methodology of the Social Sciences*, eds. Edward Shils and Henry Finch (Glencoe, Ill.: The Free Press, 1949).

13. Coser, *Masters of Sociological Thought*, p. 202.

Park cannot be called a disciple of Simmel but he certainly was deeply marked by his spirit. The index to the *Introduction* [*to the Science of Sociology*] has no fewer than 43 entries for Simmel, more than for any other name. The book contains ten selections from Simmel, again more than from any other author. Park translated Simmel's sparkling and brilliant observations into a more matter-of-fact idiom and merged the German's erudition with the themes of Midwestern progressive thought.[14]

In suggesting that phenomenology in American sociology ultimately took only the forms found in Blumer's symbolic interaction and Garfinkel's ethnomethodology, I have oversimplified. That the influence is almost exclusively through Mead and Schutz is not, however, an oversimplification. Midwestern sociologists, steeped in the Chicago tradition, have used Mead as a basis for a more positivistic sociology foreign to Blumer's phenomenological version. The works of Manfred Kuhn and his students at Iowa is the most striking example, but there are others.[15] In like manner there are sociologists who came under the influence of Schutz during his tenure at the New School and whose phenomenology has nothing to do with Garfinkel's ethnomethodology. Berger and Luckmann provide one clear example, but again, there are others.[16]

The unifying element, the core which permits all of these diverse sociologists to be called "phenomenological," is that they share a perspective on human behavior and social processes. What they have in common is that each of them insists that the proper study of man must attempt to understand the world as its actors do—to view it from their perspective. The phenomenological orientation always sees reality as constructed by men in the process of thinking about it. It is the social version of Descartes' *Cogito, ergo sum*. For the phenomenologist it becomes *Cogitamus, ergo est*—we think, therefore it is! I have done my best to introduce that perspective into this book, not because I am committed to it, but because I believe it can resolve some of the problems plaguing contemporary social science and because it has been neglected. Taking a leaf from Kant, I submit that there are two worlds out there, one of which is objectively perceived by the senses as "real." The other is a world which we create in the process of thinking about it. I refuse to opt for either as the proper perspective for the study of man. It seems to me that there may be some things we can know better one way and some can be better understood the other way.

The fact that we cannot always define reality into existence is evidenced, for example, by the large numbers of people who get killed with "empty" guns. No matter how sincere the definition of the situation, the fact remains that, if there is a bullet in the chamber, there will be empirically observable consequences. And anyone who has ever run out of gas while driving on an isolated stretch of highway is

14. Ibid., p. 374.

15. For an analysis of and many references to Kuhn's work see Charles W. Tucker, "Some Methodological Problems of Kuhn's Self Theory," *Sociological Quarterly* 7 (1966): 345–58. See also Sheldon Stryker, "Conditions of Accurate Role Taking: A Test of Mead's Theory," in Arnold M. Rose, ed., *Human Behavior*, pp. 41–62.

16. Peter L. Berger and Thomas Luckmann, *The Social Construction of Reality: A Treatise in the Sociology of Knowledge* (Garden City, N.Y.: Doubleday, 1966). See also, for example, Alan F. Blum and Peter McHugh, "The Social Ascription of Motives," *American Sociological Review* 36 (1971): 98–109.

well aware that his failure to define the gas tank as empty was utterly ineffective in altering objective reality. It is my impression that Blumer and Garfinkel get around the problem of objective reality in a different way. Neither will allow an objective social world, but both concede that to the extent that subjective definitions become widely shared, they become objectified. For them it is a matter of degree. Garfinkel's basis is Schutz's notion of "typifications" while Blumer's is in Mead's distinction between the symbolic and the nonsymbolic social world. The phenomenological perspective sensitizes us to the centrality of "meaning" and "intention" in human behavior, but the positivistic perspective alerts us to the existence of objectively real consequences as well as socially constructed consequences of human action.

The need for both perspectives can be illustrated in efforts to understand suicidal behavior. There is adequate documentation of the fact that suicide attempters are likely to have very different social and demographic characteristics than suicide completers. The objective fact of killing oneself is, however, not sufficient for making the distinction. In trying to understand the discrepancy between suicidal sentiments and suicidal acts, it becomes necessary to take intentionality into account. The person intent on completing a suicidal act may nevertheless fail if, for example, he believes that four aspirins are a lethal dose or a leap from a third-story window will inevitably kill. Objective reality interferes with his definitions of the situation. To put it more bluntly, his incompetence becomes an intervening variable. The reverse is, tragically, also possible. The individual, symbolically engaging in a "cry for help," as Edwin Schneidman has called it, may end up objectively dead regardless of his intentions otherwise.

The phenomenological perspective manifests itself in a variety of ways in contemporary sociology. In this book it showed itself in the first two chapters as we considered the need, as Mills suggested, to discount research reports as the products of researchers. In Chapter Two our discussion of epistemology and the sociology of knowledge was essentially phenomenological in its argument that ways of knowing are intimately related to the temper of the times. We considered, in Chapter Five, the phenomenological arguments found in analyses by Douglas, Garfinkel, and Kitsuse and Cicourel, that social data is a social product. My quarrel with extreme operationalism in Chapter Five was based on the phenomenological grounds that definitions on which people act are their own definitions and not those imposed by scientists. Scientific definitions are a form of reality created by scientists and are real only for scientists. It follows that only scientists act on such definitions. Men in everyday life behave in accord with their own definitions of reality and it behooves us to be attentive to those definitions.

In Chapter Seven we discussed Cicourel on making sense of the routine grounds of communication and the use of conversations as data. Our discussion of language and social research in that chapter is based on phenomenological grounds. Much of the methodological critique in Part II hangs on the problem of reactivity — of the active role played by the researcher in producing his research results. Those chapters were also concerned about the inability of much of our current research technique to reflect the real world as perceived by its members. To this extent those methodological chapters were phenomenological in their orientation. When we conclude in Chapter Ten that the actor's definition of the social situation becomes central in understanding his actions, we are making a phenomenological conclusion. And our use of Blumer's arguments in Chapter Eleven, along with the analysis of evidence related to the intervening process between sentiments and acts, is explicitly phenomenological. Obviously, I have found this perspective useful in my efforts to understand the relationship between sentiments and acts.

I find it useful in beginning to understand the relationship between what men say and what they otherwise do if—rather than playing objective scientist, rather than trying to develop a theoretical framework within which I can organize their words and their deeds—I take a cue from Garfinkel and treat them as if they were methodologists. What calculus does the man in the street employ in constructing his lines of action? If I can come to see the world as he does, then I can come to understand the relationship between his talk and his action as he does. This seems more effective, as Garfinkel suggests, than assuming that ordinary men are cultural and psychological dopes.[17] Although Blumer's perspective has always seemed persuasive to me, I (like some symbolic interactionists) could not find a technology for research which seemed faithful to that perspective. Garfinkel began to open such technological doors with reports of little studies such as those he modestly submits in his contribution to this chapter. He also explains what he means when he accuses the social scientist of creating a model of man as "a cultural dope." Scheff's essay, which follows immediately after Garfinkel, demonstrates what happens when a scholar takes the abstract notion of "the social construction of reality" and turns it into a concrete research tool.

17. Garfinkel's position on this matter is elaborated in its clearest form, under the prodding of sometimes unsympathetic scholars, in *Proceedings of the Purdue Symposium on Ethnomethodology*, eds. Richard J. Hill and Kathleen Stones Crittenden (Purdue, Ind.: Purdue Research Foundation, 1968).

The Relevance of Common Understandings to the Fact That Models of Man in Society Portray Him as a Judgmental Dope

HAROLD GARFINKEL

For Kant the moral order "within" was an awesome mystery; for sociologists the moral order "without" is a technical mystery. From the point of view of sociological theory the moral order consists of the rule governed activities of everyday life. A society's members encounter and know the moral order as perceivedly normal courses of action—familiar scenes of everyday affairs, the world of daily life known in common with others and with others taken for granted.

This article is a slightly modified version of Harold Garfinkel, "Studies of the Routine Grounds of Everyday Activities," *Social Problems*, vol. 11 (1964), pp. 225–50. It is reprinted with permission of the author and the Society for the Study of Social Problems. The present title was employed by the author as a subtitle in the original version. Pages 226–43 of the original article have been omitted and footnotes two and three have been updated. A full line of ellipsis points is used in the present text to indicate the omission.

The original publication bears the following acknowledgment: "This investigation was supported by a Senior Research Fellowship, SF–81 from the U.S. Public Health Service. I am indebted to Egon Bittner, Craig MacAndrew, Edward Rose, Harvey Sacks, and Eleanor Sheldon for their many criticisms and suggestions."

They refer to this world as the "natural facts of life" which, for members, are through and through moral facts of life. For members not only are matters so about familiar scenes, but they are so because it is morally right or wrong that they are so. Familiar scenes of everyday activities, treated by members as the "natural facts of life," are massive facts of the members' daily existence both *as a* real world and as the product of activities *in* a real world. They furnish the "fix," the "this is it" to which the waking state returns one, and are the points of departure and return for every modification of the world of daily life that is achieved in play, dreaming, trance, theatre, scientific theorizing, or high ceremony.

In every discipline, humanistic or scientific, the familiar common sense world of everyday life is a matter of abiding interest. In the social sciences, and in sociology particularly, it is a matter of essential preoccupation. It makes up sociology's problematic subject matter, enters the very constitution of the sociological attitude, and exercises an odd and obstinate sovereignty over sociologists' claims to adequate explanation.

Despite the topic's centrality, an immense literature contains little data and few methods with which the essential features of socially recognized "familiar scenes" may be detected and related to dimensions of social organization. Although sociologists take socially structured scenes of everyday life as a point of departure they rarely see[1,2] as a task of sociological inquiry in its own right the general question of how any such common sense world is possible. Instead, the possibility of the everyday world is either settled by theoretical representation or merely assumed. As a topic and methodological ground for sociological inquiries, the definition of the common sense world of everyday life, though it is appropriately a project of sociological inquiry, has been neglected. My purposes in this paper are to demonstrate the essential relevance to the program of sociological inquiries of a concern for common sense activities as a topic of inquiry in its own right and, by reporting a series of studies, to urge its "rediscovery."

· ·

Many studies have documented the finding that the social standardization of common understandings, irrespective of what it is that is standardized, orients persons' actions to scenic events, and furnishes persons the grounds upon which departures from perceivedly normal courses of affairs are detectable, restoration is made, and effortful action is mobilized.

Social science theorists—most particularly social psychiatrists, social psychologists, anthropologists, and sociologists—have used the fact of standardization to conceive the character and consequences of actions that comply with standardized expectancies. Generally they have acknowledged but otherwise neglected the fact that by these same actions persons discover, create, and sustain this standardization. An important and prevalent consequence of this neglect is that of being misled about the nature and conditions of stable actions. This occurs

[1] The work of Alfred Schutz, cited in footnote 2, is a magnificent exception. Readers who are acquainted with his writings will recognize how heavily this paper is indebted to him.

[2] Alfred Schutz, *Der Sinnhafte Aufbau Der Socialen Welt* (Wein: Verlag von Julius Springer, 1932); *Collected Papers I: The Problem of Social Reality*, ed. Maurice Natanson (The Hague: Martinus Nijhoff, 1962); *Collected Papers II: Studies in Social Theory*, ed. Arvid Broderson (The Hague: Martinus Nijhoff, 1964); *Collected Papers III: Studies in Phenomenological Philosophy*, ed. I. Schutz (The Hague: Martinus Nijhoff, 1966).

by making out the member of the society to be a judgmental dope of a cultural and/or psychological sort with the result that the *unpublished* results of any accomplished study of the relationship between actions and standardized expectations will invariably contain enough incongruous material to invite essential revision.

By "cultural dope" I refer to the man-in-the-sociologist's-society who produces the stable features of the society by acting in compliance with preestablished and legitimate alternatives of action that the common culture provides. The "psychological dope" is the man-in-the-psychologist's-society who produces the stable features of the society by choices among alternative courses of action that are compelled on the grounds of psychiatric biography, conditioning history, and the variables of mental functioning. The common feature in the use of these "models of man" is the fact that courses of common sense rationalities[3] of judgment which involve the person's use of common sense knowledge of social structures over the temporal "succession" of here and now situations are treated as epiphenomenal.

The misleading character of the use of the judgmental dope to portray the relationship between standardized expectancies and courses of action goes to the problem of adequate explanation as the controlling consideration in the investigator's decision to either consider or disregard the common sense rationalities when deciding the necessary relationships between courses of action, given such problematic considerations as perspectival choice, subjectivity, and inner time. A favored solution is to portray what the member's actions will have come to by using the stable structures — what they came to — as a point of theoretical departure from which to portray the necessary character of the pathways whereby the end result is assembled. Hierarchies of need dispositions, and common culture as enforced rules of action are favored devices for bringing the problem of necessary inference to terms, although at the cost of making out the person-in-society to be a judgmental dope.

How is an investigator *doing* it when he is making out the member of a society to be a judgmental dope? Several examples will furnish some specifics and consequences.

I assigned students the task of bargaining for standard priced merchandise. The relevant standardized expectancy is the "institutionalized one price rule," a constituent element, according to Parsons,[4] of the institution of contract. Because of its "internalized" character the student-customers should have been fearful and shamed by the prospective assignment, and shamed by having done it. Reciprocally, anxiety and anger should have been commonly reported for sales persons.

Sixty-eight students were required to accomplish one trial only for any item costing no more than two dollars, and were to offer much less than the asking price. Another sixty-seven students were required to accomplish a series of six

---

[3]Common sense rationalities are discussed at length in Schutz, "Common Sense and Scientific Interpretation of Human Action," in *Collected Papers I: The Problem of Social Reality*, pp. 3–47 and "The Problem of Rationality in the Social World," in *Collected Papers II: Studies in Social Theory*, pp. 64–88, and in Chapter 8 of Harold Garfinkel, *Studies in Ethnomethodology*, Englewood Cliffs, N.J.: Prentice-Hall, Inc., 1967. The common sense rationalities were used by Egon Bittner to recommend a criticism and reconstruction of sociological interest in mental illness in his "Popular Interests in Psychiatric Remedies: A Study in Social Control," diss., University of California, Los Angeles, 1961.

[4]Talcott Parsons, "Economy, Polity, Money, and Power," dittoed manuscript, 1959.

trials: three for items costing two dollars or less, and three for items costing fifty dollars or more.

Findings. (a) Sales persons can be dismissed as either having been dopes in different ways than current theories of standardized expectancies provide, or not dopes enough. A few showed some anxiety; occasionally one got angry. (b) Twenty percent of the single tries refused to try or aborted the effort, as compared with three percent of those who had been assigned the series of six trials. (c) When the bargaining episode was analyzed as consisting of a series of steps — anticipation of the trial, approaching the sales person, actually making the offer, the ensuing interaction, terminating the episode, and afterwards — it was found that fears occurred with the greatest frequency in both groups in anticipating the assignment and approaching the sales person *for the first try.* Among the single trials the number of persons who reported discomfort declined with each successive step in the sequence. Most of the students who bargained in two or more trials reported that by the third episode they were enjoying the assignment. (d) Most students reported less discomfort in bargaining for high priced than low priced merchandise. (e) Following the six episodes many students reported that they had learned to their "surprise" that one could bargain in standard priced setting with some realistic chance of an advantageous outcome and planned to do so in the future, particularly for costly merchandise.

Such findings suggest that one can make the member of the society out to be a cultural dope (a) by portraying a member of the society as one who operates by the rules when one is actually talking about the anticipatory anxiety that prevents him from permitting a situation to develop, let alone confronting a situation in which he has the alternative of acting or not with respect to a rule; or (b) by overlooking the practical and theoretical importance of the mastery of fears. (c) If upon the arousal of troubled feelings persons avoid tinkering with these "standardized" expectancies, the standardization could consist of an *attributed* standardization that is supported by the fact that persons avoid the very situations in which they might learn about them.

Lay as well as professional knowledge of the nature of rule governed actions and the consequences of breaching the rules is prominently based on just such procedure. Indeed, the more important the rule, the greater is the likelihood that knowledge is based on avoided tests. Strange findings must certainly await anyone who examines the expectancies that make up routine backgrounds of commonplace activities for they have rarely been exposed by investigators even to as much revision as an imaginative rehearsal of their breach would produce.

Another way in which the member of the society can be made a judgmental dope is by using any of the available theories of the formal properties of signs and symbols to portray the way persons construe environmental displays as significant ones. The dope is made out in several ways. I shall mention two.

(a) Characteristically, formal investigations have been concerned either with devising normative theories of symbolic usages or, while seeking descriptive theories, have settled for normative ones. In either case it is necessary to instruct the construing member to act in accordance with the investigator's instructions in order to guarantee that the investigator will be able to study their usages as instances of the usages the investigator has in mind. But, following Wittgenstein,[5] person's actual usages are rational usages in *some* "language game." What is *their*

---

[5]Ludwig Wittgenstein, *Philosophical Investigations,* Oxford: Basil Blackwell, 1959.

game? As long as this programmatic question is neglected, it is inevitable that person's usages will fall short. The more will this be so the more are subjects' interests in usages dictated by different practical considerations than those of investigators.

(b) Available theories have many important things to say about such sign functions as marks and indications, but they are silent on such overwhelmingly more common functions as glosses, synecdoche, documented representation, euphemism, irony, and double entendre. References to common sense knowledge of ordinary affairs may be safely disregarded in detecting and analyzing marks and indications as sign functions *because* users disregard them as well. The analysis of irony, double entendre, glosses, and the like, however, imposes different requirements. Any attempt to consider the related character of utterances, meanings, perspectives, and orders necessarily requires reference to common sense knowledge of ordinary affairs.

Although investigators have neglected these "complex" usages, they have not put their problematic character entirely aside. Instead, they have glossed them by portraying the usages of the member of a language community as either culture bound or need compelled, or by construing the pairing of appearances and intended objects—the pairing of "sign" and "referent"—as an association. In each case a procedural description of such symbolic usages is precluded by neglecting the judgmental work of the user.

Precisely this judgmental work, along with its reliance upon and its reference to common sense knowledge of social structures, forced itself upon our attention in every case where incongruities were induced. Our attention was forced *because* our subjects had exactly their judgmental work and common sense knowledge to contend with as matters which the incongruities presented to them as practical problems. Every procedure that involved departures from an anticipated course of ordinary affairs, regardless of whether the departure was gross or slight, aroused recognition in subjects that the experimenter was engaged in double talk, irony, glosses, euphemism, or lies. This occurred repeatedly in departures from ordinary game play.

Students were instructed to play ticktacktoe and to mix their subjects by age, sex, and degree of acquaintance. After drawing the ticktacktoe matrix they invited the subject to move first. After the subject made his move the experimenter erased the subject's mark, moved it to another square and made his own mark but without giving any indications that anything about the play was unusual. In half of 247 trials students reported that subjects treated the move as a gesture with hidden but definite significance. Subjects were convinced that the experimenter was "after something" that he was not saying and whatever he "really" was doing had nothing to do with ticktacktoe. He was making a sexual pass; he was commenting on the subject's stupidity; he was making a slurring or impudent gesture. Identical effects occurred when students bargained for standard priced merchandise, or asked the other to clarify his commonplace remarks, or joined without invitation a strange group of conversationalists, or used a gaze that during an ordinary conversation wandered "randomly" by time to various objects in the scene.

Still another way of making the person out for a cultural dope is to simplify the communicative texture of his behavioral environment. For example, by giving physical events preferred status one can theorize out of existence the way the person's scene, as a texture of potential and actual events, contains not only appearances and attributions but the person's own lively inner states as well. We encountered this in the following procedure.

Students were instructed to select someone other than a family member and in the course of an ordinary conversation and, without indicating that anything unusual was happening, to bring their faces up to the subject's until their noses were almost touching. According to most of the 79 accounts, regardless of whether the pairs were the same or different sexes, whether they were acquaintances or close friends (strangers were prohibited), and regardless of age differences except where children were involved, the procedure motivated in *both* experimenter and subject attributions of a sexual intent on the part of the other though confirmation of this intent was withheld by the very character of the procedure. Such attributions to the other were accompanied by the person's own impulses which themselves became part of the scene as their not only being desired but their desiring. The unconfirmed invitation to choose had its accompanying conflictful hesitancy about acknowledging the choice and having been chosen. Attempted avoidance, bewilderment, acute embarrassment, furtiveness, and above all uncertainties of these as well as uncertainties of fear, hope, and anger were characteristic. These effects were most pronounced between males. Characteristically, experimenters were unable to restore the situation. Subjects were only partially accepting of the experimenter's explanation that it has been done "as an experiment for a course in Sociology." They often complained, "All right, it was an experiment, but why did you have to choose *me?*" Characteristically, subject and experimenter wanted some further resolution than the explanation furnished but were uncertain about what it could or should consist of.

Finally, the member may be made out to be a judgmental dope by portraying routine actions as those governed by prior agreements, and by making the likelihood that a member will recognize deviance depend upon the existence of prior agreements. That this is a matter of mere theoretical preference whose use theorizes essential phenomena out of existence can be seen by considering the commonplace fact that persons will hold each other to agreements whose terms they never actually stipulated. This neglected property of common understandings has far reaching consequences when it is explicitly brought into the portrayal of the nature of "agreements."

Apparently no matter how specific the terms of common understandings may be — a contract may be considered the prototype — they attain the status of an agreement for persons only insofar as the stipulated conditions carry along an unspoken but understood *et cetera*[6] clause. Specific stipulations are formulated

[6]The et cetera clause, its properties, and the consequences of its use have been prevailing topics of study and discussion among the members of the Conferences on Ethnomethodology that have been in progress at the University of California, Los Angeles, and the University of Colorado since February, 1962, with the aid of a grant from the U.S. Air Force Office of Scientific Research. Conference members are Egon Bittner, Harold Garfinkel, Craig MacAndrew, Edward Rose, and Harvey Sacks. Published discussions of *et cetera* by conference participants will be found in Egon Bittner, "Radicalism: A Study of the Sociology of Knowledge," *American Sociological Review*, 28 (1963), pp. 928–940; Harvey Sacks, "On Sociological Description," *Berkeley Journal of Sociology*, 8 (1963), pp. 1–16; Harold Garfinkel, "A Conception and Some Experiments With Trust . . . ," *op. cit.;* and Chapters 1 and 3 in Garfinkel, *Studies in Ethnomethodology*. Extended studies dealing with coding procedures, methods of interrogation, lawyers' work, translation, model construction, historical

under the rule of an agreement by being brought under the jurisdiction of the *et cetera* clause. This does not occur once and for all, but is essentially bound to both the inner and outer temporal course of activities and thereby to the progressive development of circumstances and their contingencies. Therefore it is both misleading and incorrect to think of an agreement as an actuarial device whereby persons are enabled as of any Here and Now to predict each other's future activities. More accurately, common understandings that have been formulated under the rule of an agreement are used by persons to normalize whatever their actual activities turn out to be. Not only can contingencies arise, but persons know as of any Here and Now that contingencies can materialize or be invented at any time that it must be decided whether or not what the parties actually did satisfied the agreement. The *et cetera* clause provides for the certainty that unknown conditions are at every hand in terms of which an agreement, as of any particular moment, can be retrospectively reread to find out in light of present practical circumstances what the agreement "really" consisted of "in the first place" and "all along." That the work of bringing present circumstances under the rule of previously agreed activity is sometimes contested should not be permitted to mask its pervasive and routine use as an ongoing and essential feature of "actions in accord with common understandings."

This process, which I shall call a method of discovering agreements by eliciting or imposing a respect for the rule of practical circumstances, is a version of practical ethics. Although it has received little if any attention by social scientists, it is a matter of the most abiding and commonplace concern in everyday affairs and common sense theories of these affairs. Adeptness in the deliberate manipulation of *et cetera* considerations for the furtherance of specific advantages is an occupational talent of lawyers and is specifically taught to law school students. One should not suppose, however, that because it is a lawyer's skill, that only lawyers are skilled at it, or that only those who do so deliberately, do so at all. The method is general to the phenomenon of the society as a system of rule governed activities.[7] It is available as one of the mechanisms whereby potential and actual successes and windfalls, on the one hand, and the disappointments, frustrations, and failures, on the other, that persons must inevitably encounter by reason of seeking to comply with agreements, can be managed while retaining the perceived reasonableness of actual socially organized activities.

A small scale but accurate instance of this phenomenon was consistently produced by a procedure in which the experimenter engaged others in conversation while he had a wire recorder hidden under his coat. In the course of the conversation the experimenter opened his jacket to reveal the recorder, saying, "See what I have?" An initial pause was almost invariably followed by the question, "What are you going to do with it?" Subjects claimed the breach of the expectancy that the conversation was "between us." The fact that the conversation was

reconstruction, "social bookkeeping," counting, and personality diagnosis will be found in unpublished papers by Bittner, Garfinkel, MacAndrew, Rose, and Sacks; in transcribed talks given by Bittner, Garfinkel, and Sacks on "Reasonable Accounts" at the Sixteenth Annual Conference on World Affairs, University of Colorado, Boulder, April 11–12, 1963; and in Conference transcriptions.

[7]Insofar as this is true, it establishes the programmatic task of reconstructing the problem of social order as it is currently formulated in sociological theories, and of criticizing currently preferred solutions. At the heart of the reconstruction is the empirical problem of demonstrating the definitive features of "et cetera" thinking.

revealed to have been recorded motivated new possibilities which the parties then sought to bring under the jurisdiction of an agreement that they had never specifically mentioned, and that indeed did not previously exist. The conversation, now seen to have been recorded, thereby acquired fresh and problematic import in view of unknown uses to which it might be turned. An agreed privacy was thereupon treated as though it had operated all along.

The expectancies that make up the attitude of everyday life are constitutive of the institutionalized common understandings of the practical everyday organization and workings of society as it is seen "from within." Modification of these expectancies must thereby modify the real environments of the societies' members. Such modifications transform one perceived environment of real objects into another environment of real objects.

Each of many kinds of modifications of the background of everyday expectancies furnish an area of needed further work. Each modification has as its counterpart transformed objective structures of the behavioral environments that each modification produces. It is disconcerting to find how little we know about these different sets of background expectancies and the different objective environments that they constitute.

One such modification consists of the ceremonial transformation of one environment of real objects into another. Such modifications occur in play, theatre going, high ceremony, religious conversion, convention going, and scientific inquiry. A second modification consists of instrumental transformations of environments of real objects such as occur in experimentally induced psychosis, extreme fatigue, acute sensory deprivation, brain injuries, prefrontal lobotomies, and the use of hallucinogenic drugs. A third transformation consists of neonate learning which quite literally entails the growth of a world and is directed to the production of objective features of the person's environment that "any competent member can see." The growth of the world is necessarily accompanied by the progressively enforced and enforceable compliance of the developing member to the attitude of daily life as a competent societal member's way of "looking at things." A fourth set of modifications are involved in adult socialization, distinguishable from neonate learning by the absence of radically naive expectancies. Other modifications are those of estrangement, which must include the various phenomena intended under the currently popular theme of "alienation," as well as the phenomena of the cultural stranger, of the major and minor forms of mental illness, of the degradation that accompanies charges of criminality and the fates of social incompetence found in mental retardation and old age. Modifications occur through mischief, playful and serious; through the subtle psychopathic effects of aging as one comes to learn that one may sin, cause others harm, and not "pay"; and through the discovery that the common societal orders which in adolescence appear so massive and homogeneous not only have their interstices but depend for their massiveness upon persons' continual improvisations. Finally, there is the modification that consists in the discovery and rationalization of the common sense world through the growth of social science as a social movement.

I have been arguing that a concern for the nature, production, and recognition of reasonable, realistic, and analyzable actions is not the monopoly of philosophers and professional sociologists. Members of a society are concerned as a matter of course and necessarily with these matters both as features and for the socially managed production of their everyday affairs. The study of common sense knowledge and common sense activities consists of treating as problematic phenomena the actual methods whereby members of a society, doing sociology, lay or professional, make the social structures of everyday activities observable. The "rediscovery" of common sense is possible perhaps because professional sociologists, like members, have had too much to do with common sense knowledge of social structures as both a topic and a resource for their inquiries and not enough to do with it only and exclusively as sociology's programmatic topic.

DATA:
Negotiating Reality: Notes on Power in the Assessment of Responsibility
THOMAS J. SCHEFF

The use of interrogation to reconstruct parts of an individual's past history is a common occurrence in human affairs. Reporters, jealous lovers, and policemen on the beat are often faced with the task of determining events in another person's life, and the extent to which he was responsible for those events. The most dramatic use of interrogation to determine responsibility is in criminal trials. As in everyday life, criminal trials are concerned with both act and intent. Courts, in most cases, first determine whether the defendant performed a legally forbidden act. If it is found that he did so, the court then must decide whether he was "responsible" for the act. Reconstructive work of this type goes on less dramatically in a wide variety of other settings, as well. The social worker determining a client's eligibility for unemployment compensation, for example, seeks not only to establish that the client actually is unemployed, but that he has actively sought employment, i.e., that he himself is not responsible for being out of work.

This paper will contrast two perspectives on the process of reconstructing past events for the purpose of fixing responsibility. The first perspective stems from the common sense notion that interrogation, when it is sufficiently skillful, is essentially neutral. Responsibility for past actions can be fixed absolutely and independently of the method of reconstruction. This perspective is held by the typical member of society, engaged in his day-to-day tasks. It is also held, in varying degrees, by most professional interrogators. The basic working doctrine is one of *absolute* responsibility. This point of view actually entails the comparison of two different kinds of items: first, the fixing of actions and intentions, and secondly, comparing these actions and intentions to some predetermined criteria of re-

"Negotiating Reality: Notes on Power in the Assessment of Responsibility," by Thomas J. Scheff, from *Social Problems*, vol. 16, no. 1 (Summer), pp. 3–17. Reprinted by permission of the Society for the Study of Social Problems and the author. The following note of acknowledgment accompanied this article in its originally published form:

"The author wishes to acknowledge the help of the following persons who criticized earlier drafts: Aaron Cicourel, Donald Cressey, Joan Emerson, Erving Goffman, Michael Katz, Lewis Kurke, Robert Levy, Sohan Lal Sharma, and Paul Weubben. The paper was written during a fellowship provided by the Social Science Research Institute, University of Hawaii."

sponsibility. The basic premise of the doctrine of absolute responsibility is that both actions and intentions, on the one hand, and the criteria of responsibility, on the other, are absolute, in that they can be assessed independently of social context.[1]

An alternative approach follows from the sociology of knowledge. From this point of view, the reality within which members of society conduct their lives is largely of their own construction.[2] Since much of reality is a construction, there may be multiple realities, existing side by side, in harmony or in competition. It follows, if one maintains this stance, that the assessment of responsibility involves the construction of reality by members; construction both of actions and intentions, on the one hand, and of criteria of responsibility, on the other. The former process, the continuous reconstruction of the normative order, has long been the focus of sociological concern.[3] The discussion in this paper will be limited, for the most part, to the former process, the way in which actions and intentions are constructed in the act of assessing responsibility.

My purpose is to argue that responsibility is at least partly a product of social structure. The alternative to the doctrine of absolute responsibility is that of relative responsibility: the assessment of responsibility always includes a process of negotiation. In this process, responsibility is in part constructed by the negotiating parties. To illustrate this thesis, excerpts from two dialogues of negotiation will be discussed: a real psychotherapeutic interview, and an interview between a defense attorney and his client, taken from a work of fiction. Before presenting these excerpts it will be useful to review some prior discussions of negotiation, the first in courts of law, the second in medical diagnosis.[4]

The negotiation of pleas in criminal courts, sometimes referred to as "bargain justice," has been frequently noted by observers of legal processes.[5] The defense attorney, or (in many cases, apparently) the defendant himself, strikes a bargain with the prosecutor—a plea of guilty will be made, provided that the prosecutor will reduce the charge. For example, a defendant arrested on suspicion of armed robbery may arrange to plead guilty to the charge of unarmed robbery. The prosecutor obtains ease of conviction from the bargain, the defendant, leniency.

Although no explicit estimates are given, it appears from observers' re-

---

[1]The doctrine of absolute responsibility is clearly illustrated in psychiatric and legal discussions of the issue of "criminal responsibility," i.e., the use of mental illness as an excuse from criminal conviction. An example of the assumption of absolute criteria of responsibility is found in the following quotation, "The finding that someone is criminally responsible means to the psychiatrist that the criminal must change his behavior before he can resume his position in society. *This injunction is dictated not by morality, but, so to speak, by reality.*" See Edward J. Sachar, "Behavioral Science and Criminal Law," *Scientific American*, 209 (1963), pp. 39–45, (emphasis added).

[2]Cf. Peter L. Berger and Thomas Luckmann, *The Social Construction of Reality: A Treatise in the Sociology of Knowledge*, New York: Doubleday, 1966.

[3]The classic treatment of this issue is found in E. Durkheim, *The Elementary Forms of the Religious Life*.

[4]A sociological application of the concept of negotiation, in a different context, is found in Anselm Strauss, et al., "The Hospital and its Negotiated Order," in Eliot Freidson, editor, *The Hospital in Modern Society*, New York: Free Press, 1963, pp. 147–169.

[5]Newman reports a study in this area, together with a review of earlier work, in "The Negotiated Plea," Part III of Donald J. Newman, *Conviction: The Determination of Guilt or Innocence Without Trial*, Boston: Little, Brown, 1966, pp. 76–130.

ports that the great majority of criminal convictions are negotiated. Newman states:

> A major characteristic of criminal justice administration, particularly in jurisdictions characterized by legislatively fixed sentences, is charge reduction to elicit pleas of guilty. Not only does the efficient functioning of criminal justice rest upon a high proportion of guilty pleas, but plea bargaining is closely linked with attempts to individualize justice, to obtain certain desirable conviction consequences, and to avoid undesirable ones such as "undeserved" mandatory sentences.[6]

It would appear that the bargaining process is accepted as routine. In the three jurisdictions Newman studied, there were certain meeting places where the defense attorney, his client, and a representative of the prosecutor's office routinely met to negotiate the plea. It seems clear that in virtually all but the most unusual cases, the interested parties expected to, and actually did, negotiate the plea.

From these comments on the routine acceptance of plea bargaining in the courts, one might expect that this process would be relatively open and unambiguous. Apparently, however, there is some tension between the fact of bargaining and moral expectations concerning justice. Newman refers to this tension by citing two contradictory statements: an actual judicial opinion, "Justice and liberty are not the subjects of bargaining and barter;" and an off-the-cuff statement by another judge, "All law is compromise." A clear example of this tension is provided by an excerpt from a trial and Newman's comments on it.

> The following questions were asked of a defendant after he had pleaded guilty to unarmed robbery when the original charge was armed robbery. This reduction is common, and the judge was fully aware that the plea was negotiated:
>
> Judge: You want to plead guilty to robbery unarmed?
> Defendant: Yes, Sir.
> Judge: Your plea of guilty is free and voluntary?
> Defendant: Yes, Sir.
> Judge: No one has promised you anything?
> Defendant: No.
> Judge: No one has induced you to plead guilty?
> Defendant: No.
> Judge: You're pleading guilty because you are guilty?
> Defendant: Yes.
> Judge: I'll accept your plea of guilty to robbery unarmed and refer it to the probation department for a report and for sentencing Dec. 28.[7]

The delicacy of the relationship between appearance and reality is apparently confusing, even for the sociologist-observer. Newman's comment on this exchange has an Alice-in-Wonderland quality:

[6]*Ibid.*, p. 76.
[7] *Ibid.*, p. 83.

This is a routine procedure designed to satisfy the statutory requirement and is not intended to disguise the process of charge reduction.[8]

If we put the tensions between the different realities aside for the moment, we can say that there is an explicit process of negotiation between the defendant and the prosecution which is a part of the legal determination of guilt or innocence, or in the terms used above, the assessment of responsibility.

In medical diagnosis, a similar process of negotiation occurs, but is much less self-conscious than plea bargaining. The English psychoanalyst Michael Balint refers to this process as one of "offers and responses":

> Some of the people who, for some reason or other, find it difficult to cope with problems of their lives resort to becoming ill. If the doctor has the opportunity of seeing them in the first phases of their being ill, i.e., before they settle down to a definite "organized" illness, he may observe that the patients, so to speak, offer or propose various illnesses, and that they have to go on offering new illnesses until between doctor and patient an agreement can be reached resulting in the acceptance by both of them of one of the illnesses as justified.[9]

Balint gives numerous examples indicating that patients propose reasons for their coming to the doctor which are rejected, one by one, by the physician, who makes counter-proposals until an "illness" acceptable to both parties is found. If "definition of the situation" is substituted for "illness," Balint's observations become relevant to a wide variety of transactions, including the kind of interrogation discussed above. The fixing of responsibility is a process in which the client offers definitions of the situation, to which the interrogator responds. After a series of offers and responses, a definition of the situation acceptable to both the client and the interrogator is reached.

Balint has observed that the negotiation process leads physicians to influence the outcome of medical examinations, independently of the patient's condition. He refers to this process as the "apostolic function" of the doctor, arguing that the physician induces patients to have the kind of illness that the physician thinks is proper:

> Apostolic mission or function means in the first place that every doctor has a vague, but almost unshakably firm, idea of how a patient ought to behave when ill. Although this idea is anything but explicit and concrete, it is immensely powerful, and influences, as we have found, practically every detail of the doctor's work with his patients. It was almost as if every doctor had revealed knowledge of what was right and what was wrong for patients to expect and to endure, and further, as if he had a

---

[8] *Idem.*

[9] Michael Balint, *The Doctor, His Patient, and The Illness,* New York: International Universities Press, 1957, p. 18. A description of the negotiations between patients in a tuberculosis sanitarium and their physicians is found in Julius A. Roth, *Timetables: Structuring the Passage of Time in Hospital Treatment and Other Careers,* Indianapolis: Bobbs-Merrill, 1963, pp. 48–59. Obviously, some cases are more susceptible to negotiation than others. Balint implies that the great majority of cases in medical practice are negotiated.

sacred duty to convert to his faith all the ignorant and unbelieving among his patients.[10]

Implicit in this statement is the notion that interrogator and client have unequal power in determining the resultant definition of the situation. The interrogator's definition of the situation plays an important part in the joint definition of the situation which is finally negotiated. Moreover, his definition is more important than the client's in determining the final outcome of the negotiation, principally because he is well trained, secure, and self-confident in his role in the transaction, whereas the client is untutored, anxious, and uncertain about his role. Stated simply, the subject, because of these conditions, is likely to be susceptible to the influence of the interrogator.

Note that plea bargaining and the process of "offers and responses" in diagnosis differ in the degree of self-consciousness of the participants. In plea bargaining the process is at least partly visible to the participants themselves. There appears to be some ambiguity about the extent to which the negotiation is morally acceptable to some of the commentators, but the parties to the negotiations appear to be aware that bargaining is going on, and accept the process as such. The bargaining process in diagnosis, however, is much more subterranean. Certainly neither physicians nor patients recognize the offers and responses process as being bargaining. There is no commonly accepted vocabulary for describing diagnostic bargaining, such as there is in the legal analogy, e.g. "copping out" or "copping a plea." It may be that in legal processes there is some appreciation of the different kinds of reality, i.e. the difference between the public (official, legal) reality and private reality, whereas in medicine this difference is not recognized.

The discussion so far has suggested that much of reality is arrived at by negotiation. This thesis was illustrated by materials presented on legal processes by Newman, and medical processes by Balint. These processes are similar in that they appear to represent clear instances of the negotiation of reality. The instances are different in that the legal bargaining processes appear to be more open and accepted than the diagnostic process. In order to outline some of the dimensions of the negotiation process, and to establish some of the limitations of the analyses by Newman and Balint, two excerpts of cases of bargaining will be discussed: the first taken from an actual psychiatric "intake" interview, the second from a fictional account of a defense lawyer's first interview with his client.

The Process of Negotiation

The psychiatric interview to be discussed is from the first interview in *The Initial Interview in Psychiatric Practice*.[11] The patient is a thirty-four year old nurse, who feels, as she says, "irritable, tense, depressed." She appears to be saying from the very beginning of the interview that the external situation in which she lives is the cause of her troubles. She focuses particularly on her husband's behavior. She says he is an alcoholic, is verbally abusive, and won't let her work.

[10] Balint, *op. cit.*, p. 216.
[11] Merton Gill, Richard Newman, and Fredrick C. Redlich, *The Initial Interview in Psychiatric Practice*, New York: International Universities Press, 1954.

She feels that she is cooped up in the house all day with her two small children, but that when he is home at night (on the nights when he *is* at home) he will have nothing to do with her and the children. She intimates, in several ways, that he does not serve as a sexual companion. She has thought of divorce, but has rejected it for various reasons (for example, she is afraid she couldn't take proper care of the children, finance the baby sitters, etc.). She feels trapped.[12]

In the concluding paragraph of their description of this interview, Gill, Newman, and Redlich give this summary:

> The patient, pushed by we know not what or why at the time (the children — somebody to talk to) comes for help apparently for what she thinks of as help with her external situation (her husband's behavior as she sees it). The therapist does not respond to this but seeks her role and how it is that she plays such a role. Listening to the recording it sounds as if the therapist is at first bored and disinterested and the patient defensive. He gets down to work and keeps asking, "What is it all about?" Then he becomes more interested and sympathetic and at the same time very active (participating) and demanding. *It sounds as if she keeps saying "This is the trouble." He says, "No! Tell me the trouble." She says, "This is it!" He says, "No, tell me," until the patient finally says, "Well I'll tell you." Then the therapist says, "Good! I'll help you."*[13]

From this summary it is apparent that there is a close fit between Balint's idea of the negotiation of diagnosis through offers and responses, and what took place in this psychiatric interview. It is difficult, however, to document the details. Most of the psychiatrist's responses, rejecting the patient's offers, do not appear in the written transcript, but they are fairly obvious as one listens to the recording. Two particular features of the psychiatrist's responses especially stand out: (1) the flatness of intonation in his responses to the patient's complaints about her external circumstances; and (2) the rapidity with which he introduces new topics, through questioning, when she is talking about her husband.

Some features of the psychiatrist's coaching are verbal, however:

> T. 95: Has anything happened recently that makes it . . . you feel that . . . ah . . . you're sort of coming to the end of your rope? I mean I wondered what led you . . .
>
> P. 95: (Interrupting.) It's nothing special. It's just everything in general.
>
> T. 96: What led you to come to a . . .
>
> P. 96: (Interrupting.) It's just that I . . .
>
> T. 97: . . . a psychiatrist just now? (1)
>
> P. 97: Because I felt that the older girl was getting tense as a result of . . . of my being stewed up all the time.
>
> T. 98: Mmmhnn.
>
> P. 98: Not having much patience with her.

---

[12]Since this interview is complex and subtle, the reader is invited to listen to it himself, and compare his conclusions with those discussed here. The recorded interview is available on the first L.P. record that accompanies Gill, Newman, and Redlich, *op. cit.*

[13] *Ibid.*, p. 133. (Italics added.)

T. 99: Mmmhnn. (Short Pause.) Mmm. And how had you imagined that a psychiatrist could help with this? (Short pause.) (2)

P. 99: Mmm . . . maybe I could sort of get straightened out . . . straighten things out in my own mind. I'm confused. Sometimes I can't remember things that I've done, whether I've done 'em or not or whether they happened.

T. 100: What is it that you want to straighten out?
(Pause.)

P. 100: I think I seem mixed up.

T. 101: Yeah? You see that, it seems to me, is something that we really should talk about because . . . ah . . . from a certain point of view somebody might say, "Well now, it's all very simple. She's unhappy and disturbed because her husband is behaving this way, and unless something can be done about that how could she expect to feel any other way." But, instead of that, you come to the psychiatrist, and you say that you think there's something about you that needs straightening out. (3) I don't quite get it. Can you explain that to me? (Short pause.)

P. 101: I sometimes wonder if I'm emotionally grown up.

T. 102: By which you mean what?

P. 102: When you're married you should have one mate. You shouldn't go around and look at other men.

T. 103: You've been looking at other men?

P. 103: I look at them, but that's all.

T. 104: Mmmhnn. What you mean . . . you mean a grown-up person should accept the marital situation whatever it happens to be?

P. 104: That was the way I was brought up. Yes. (Sighs.)

T. 105: You think that would be a sign of emotional maturity?

P. 105: No.

T. 106: No. So?

P. 106: Well, if you rebel against the laws of society you have to take the consequences.

T. 107: Yes?

P. 107: And it's just that I . . . I'm not willing to take the consequences. I . . . I don't think it's worth it.

T. 108: Mmhnn. So in the meantime then while you're in this very difficult situation, you find yourself reacting in a way that you don't like and that you think is . . . ah . . . damaging to your children and yourself? Now what can be done about that?

P. 108: (Sniffs; sighs.) I dunno. That's why I came to see you.

T. 109: Yes. I was just wondering what you had in mind. Did you think a psychiatrist could . . . ah . . . help you face this kind of a situation calmly and easily and maturely? (4) Is that it?

P. 109: More or less. I need somebody to talk to who isn't emotionally involved with the family. I have a few friends, but I don't like to bore them. I don't think they should know . . . ah . . . all the intimate details of what goes on.

T. 110: Yeah?

P. 110: It becomes food for gossip.

T. 111: Mmmhnn.

P. 111: Besides they're in . . . they're emotionally involved because they're my friends. They tell me not to stand for it, but they don't understand that if I put my foot down it'll only get stepped on.

T. 112: Yeah.

P. 112: That he can make it miserable for me in other ways. . . .

T. 113: Mmm.

P. 113: . . . which he does.

T. 114: Mmmhnn. In other words, you find yourself in a situation and don't know how to cope with it really.

P. 114: I don't.

T. 115: You'd like to be able to talk that through and come to understand it better and learn how to cope with it or deal with it in some way. Is that right?

P. 115: I'd like to know how to deal with it more effectively.

T. 116: Yeah. Does that mean you feel convinced that the way you're dealing with it now . . .

P. 116: There's something wrong of course.

T. 117: . . . something wrong with that. Mmmhnn.

P. 117: There's something wrong with it.[14]

Note that the therapist reminds her *four times* in this short sequence that she has come to see a *psychiatrist*. Since the context of these reminders is one in which the patient is attributing her difficulties to an external situation, particularly her husband, it seems plausible to hear these reminders as subtle requests for analysis of her own contributions to her difficulties. This interpretation is supported by the therapist's subsequent remarks. When the patient once again describes external problems, the therapist tries the following tack:

T. 125: I notice that you've used a number of psychiatric terms here and there. Were you specially interested in that in your training, or what?

P. 125: Well, my great love is psychology.

T. 126: Psychology?

P. 126: Mmmhnn.

T. 127: How much have you studied?

P. 127: Oh (Sighs.) what you have in your nurse's training, and I've had general psych, child and adolescent psych, and the abnormal psych.

T. 128: Mmmhnn. Well, tell me . . . ah . . . what would you say if you had to explain yourself what is the problem?

P. 128: You don't diagnose yourself very well, at least I don't.

T. 129: Well you can make a stab at it. (Pause.)[15]

---

[14] *Ibid.,* pp. 176–182. (Numbers in parentheses added.)
[15] *Ibid.,* pp. 186–187.

This therapeutic thrust is rewarded: the patient gives a long account of her early life which indicates a belief that she was not "adjusted" in the past. The interview continues:

> T. 135: And what conclusions do you draw from all this about why you're not adjusting now the way you think you should?
>
> P. 135: Well, I wasn't adjusted then. I feel that I've come a long way, but I don't think I'm still . . . I still don't feel that I'm adjusted.
>
> T. 136: And you don't regard your husband as being the difficulty? You think it lies within yourself?
>
> P. 136: Oh he's a difficulty all right, but I figure that even . . . ah . . . had . . . if it had been other things that . . . that this probably — this state — would've come on me.
>
> T. 137: Oh you do think so?
>
> P. 137: (Sighs.) I don't think he's the sole factor. No.
>
> T. 138: And what are the factors within . . .
>
> P. 138: I mean . . .
>
> T. 139: . . . yourself?
>
> P. 139: Oh it's probably remorse for the past, things I did.
>
> T. 140: Like what? (Pause.) It's sumping' hard to tell, hunh? (Short pause.)[16]

After some parrying, the patient tells the therapist what he wants to hear. She feels guilty because she was pregnant by another man when her present husband proposed. She cries. The therapist tells the patient she needs, and will get psychiatric help, and the interview ends, the patient still crying. The negotiational aspects of the process are clear: After the patient has spent most of the interview blaming her current difficulties on external circumstances, she tells the therapist a deep secret about which she feels intensely guilty. The patient, and not the husband, is at fault. The therapist's tone and manner change abruptly. From being bored, distant, and rejecting, he becomes warm and solicitous. Through a process of offers and responses, the therapist and patient have, by implication, negotiated a shared definition of the situation — the patient, not the husband, is responsible.

A Contrasting Case

The negotiation process can, of course, proceed on the opposite premise, namely that the client is not responsible. An ideal example would be an interrogation of a client by a skilled defense lawyer. Unfortunately, we have been unable to locate a verbatim transcript of a defense lawyer's initial interview with his client. There is available, however, a fictional portrayal of such an interview, written by a man with extensive experience as defense lawyer, prosecutor, and judge. The excerpt to follow is taken from the novel, *Anatomy of a Murder*.[17]

The defense lawyer, in his initial contact with his client, briefly ques-

---

[16] *Ibid.*, pp. 192–194.
[17] Robert Traver, *Anatomy of a Murder*, New York: Dell, 1959.

tions him regarding his actions on the night of the killing. The client states that he discovered that the deceased, Barney Quill, had raped his wife; he then goes on to state that he then left his wife, found Quill and shot him.

> ". . . How long did you remain with your wife before you went to the hotel bar?"
> "I don't remember."
> "I think it is important, and I suggest you try."
> After a pause. "Maybe an hour."
> "Maybe more?"
> "Maybe."
> "Maybe less?"
> "Maybe."

> I paused and lit a cigar. I took my time. I had reached a point where a few wrong answers to a few right questions would leave me with a client — if I took his case — whose cause was legally defenseless. Either I stopped now and begged off and let some other lawyer worry over it or I asked him the few fatal questions and let him hang himself. Or else, like any smart lawyer, I went into the Lecture. I studied my man, who sat as inscrutable as an Arab, delicately fingering his Ming holder, daintily sipping his dark mustache. He apparently did not realize how close I had him to admitting that he was guilty of first degree murder, that is, that he "feloniously, wilfully and of his malice afore-thought did kill and murder one Barney Quill." The man was a sitting duck.[18]

The lawyer here realizes that his line of questioning has come close to fixing the responsibility for the killing on his client. He therefore shifts his ground by beginning "the lecture":

> The Lecture is an ancient device that lawyers use to coach their clients so that the client won't quite know he has been coached and his lawyer can still preserve the face-saving illusion that he hasn't done any coaching. For coaching clients, like robbing them, is not only frowned upon, it is downright unethical and bad, very bad. Hence the Lecture, an artful device as old as the law itself, and one used constantly by some of the nicest and most ethical lawyers in the land. "Who, me? I didn't tell him what to say," the lawyer can later comfort himself. "I merely explained the law, see." It is a good practice to scowl and shrug here and add virtuously: "That's my duty, isn't it?"
> . . . . . "We will now explore the absorbing subject of legal justification or excuse," I said.
> . . . . . "Well, take self-defense," I began. "That's the classic example of justifiable homicide. On the basis of what I've so far heard and read about your case I do not think we need pause too long over that. Do you?"
> "Perhaps not," Lieutenant Manion conceded. "We'll pass it for now."

18 *Ibid.*, p. 43.

"Let's," I said dryly. "Then there's the defense of habitation, defense of property, and the defense of relatives or friends. Now there are more ramifications to these defenses than a dog has fleas, but we won't explore them now. I've already told you at length why I don't think you can invoke the possible defense of your wife. When you shot Quill her need for defense had passed. It's as simple as that."

"Go on," Lieutenant Manion said, frowning.

"Then there's the defense of a homicide committed to prevent a felony — say you're being robbed —; to prevent the escape of the felon — suppose he's getting away with your wallet —; or to arrest a felon — you've caught up with him and he's either trying to get away or has actually escaped." . . . . .

. . . . . "Go on, then; what are some of the other legal justifications or excuses?"

"Then there's the tricky and dubious defense of intoxication. Personally I've never seen it succeed. But since you were not drunk when you shot Quill we shall mercifully not dwell on that. Or were you?"

"I was cold sober. Please go on."

"Then finally there's the defense of insanity." I paused and spoke abruptly, airily: "Well, that just about winds it up." I arose as though making ready to leave.

"Tell me more."

"There is no more." I slowly paced up and down the room.

"I mean about this insanity."

"Oh, insanity," I said, elaborately surprised. It was like luring a trained seal with a herring. "Well, insanity, where proven, is a complete defense to murder. It does not legally justify the killing, like self-defense, say, but rather excuses it." The lecturer was hitting his stride. He was also on the home stretch. "Our law requires that a punishable killing — in fact, any crime — must be committed by a sapient human being, one capable, as the law insists, of distinguishing between right and wrong. If a man is insane, legally insane, the act of homicide may still be murder but the law excuses the perpetrator."

Lieutenant Manion was sitting erect now, very still and erect. "I see — and this — this perpetrator, what happens to him if he should — should be excused?"

"Under Michigan law — like that of many other states — if he is acquitted of murder on the grounds of insanity it is provided that he must be sent to a hospital for the criminally insane until he is pronounced sane."
. . . . .

. . . . . Then he looked at me. "Maybe," he said, "maybe I was insane."

. . . . . Thoughtfully: "Hm. . . . Why do you say that?"

"Well, I can't really say," he went on slowly. "I — I guess I blacked out. I can't remember a thing after I saw him standing behind the bar that night until I got back to my trailer."

"You mean — you mean you don't remember shooting him?" I shook my head in wonderment.

"Yes, that's what I mean."

"You don't even remember driving home?"

"No."

"You don't remember threatening Barney's bartender when he followed you outside after the shooting—as the newspaper says you did?" I paused and held my breath. "You don't remember telling him, 'Do you want some, too, Buster?' ?"

The smoldering dark eyes flickered ever so little. "No, not a thing."

"My, my," I said blinking my eyes, contemplating the wonder of it all. "Maybe you've got something there."

The Lecture was over; I had told my man the law; and now he had told me things that might possibly invoke the defense of insanity. . . .[19]

The negotiation is complete. The ostensibly shared definition of the situation established by the negotiation process is that the defendant was probably not responsible for his actions.

Let us now compare the two interviews. The major similarity between them is their negotiated character: they both take the form of a series of offers and responses that continue until an offer (a definition of the situation) is reached that is acceptable to both parties. The major difference between the transactions is that one, the psychotherapeutic interview, arrives at an assessment that the client is responsible; the other, the defense attorney's interview, reaches an assessment that the client was not at fault, i.e., not responsible. How can we account for this difference in outcome?

Discussion

Obviously, given any two real cases of negotiation which have different outcomes, one might construct a reasonable argument that the difference is due to the differences between the cases—the finding of responsibility in one case and lack of responsibility in the other, the only outcomes which are reasonably consonant with the facts of the respective cases. Without rejecting this argument, for the sake of discussion only, and without claiming any kind of proof or demonstration, I wish to present an alternative argument; that the difference in outcome is largely due to the differences in technique used by the interrogators. This argument will allow us to suggest some crucial dimensions of negotiation processes.

The first dimension, consciousness of the bargaining aspects of the transaction, has already been mentioned. In the psychotherapeutic interview, the negotiational nature of the transaction seems not to be articulated by either party. In the legal interview, however, certainly the lawyer, and perhaps to some extent the client as well, is aware of, and accepts the situation as one of striking a bargain, rather than as a relentless pursuit of the absolute facts of the matter.

The dimension of shared awareness that the definition of the situation is negotiable seems particularly crucial for assessments of responsibility. In both interviews, there is an agenda hidden from the client. In the psychotherapeutic interview, it is probably the psychiatric criteria for acceptance into treatment, the

[19]*Ibid.*, pp. 46–47, 57, 58–59, and 60.

criterion of "insight." The psychotherapist has probably been trained to view patients with "insight into their illness" as favorable candidates for psychotherapy, i.e., patients who accept, or can be led to accept, the problems as internal, as part of their personality, rather than seeing them as caused by external conditions.

In the legal interview, the agenda that is unknown to the client is the legal structure of defenses or justifications for killing. In both the legal and psychiatric cases, the hidden agenda is not a simple one. Both involve fitting abstract and ambiguous criteria (insight, on the one hand, legal justification, on the other) to a richly specific, concrete case. In the legal interview, the lawyer almost immediately broaches this hidden agenda; he states clearly and concisely the major legal justifications for killing. In the psychiatric interview, the hidden agenda is never revealed. The patient's offers during most of the interview are rejected or ignored. In the last part of the interview, her last offer is accepted and she is told that she will be given treatment. In no case are the reasons for these actions articulated by either party.

The degree of shared awareness is related to a second dimension which concerns the format of the conversation. The legal interview began as an interrogation, but was quickly shifted away from that format when the defense lawyer realized the direction in which the questioning was leading the client, i.e., toward a legally unambiguous admission of guilt. On the very brink of such an admission, the defense lawyer stopped asking questions and started, instead, to make statements. He listed the principal legal justifications for killing, and, in response to the *client's* questions, gave an explanation of each of the justifications. This shift in format put the client, rather than the lawyer, in control of the crucial aspects of the negotiation. It is the client, not the lawyer, who is allowed to pose the questions, assess the answers for their relevance to his case, and most crucially, to determine himself the most advantageous tack to take. Control of the definition of the situation, the evocation of the events and intentions relevant to the assessment of the client's responsibility for the killing, was given to the client by the lawyer. The resulting client-controlled format of negotiation gives the client a double advantage. It not only allows the client the benefit of formulating his account of actions and intentions in their most favorable light, it also allows him to select, out of a diverse and ambiguous set of normative criteria concerning killing, that criterion which is most favorable to his own case.

Contrast the format of negotiation used by the psychotherapist. The form is consistently that of interrogation. The psychotherapist poses the questions; the patient answers. The psychotherapist then has the answers at his disposal. He may approve or disapprove, accept or reject, or merely ignore them. Throughout the entire interview, the psychotherapist is in complete control of the situation. Within this framework, the tactic that the psychotherapist uses is to reject the patient's "offers" that her husband is at fault, first by ignoring them, later, and ever more insistently, by leading her to define the situation as one in which she is at fault. In effect, what the therapist does is to reject her offers, and to make his own counteroffers.

These remarks concerning the relationship between technique of interrogation and outcome suggest an approach to assessment of responsibility somewhat different than that usually followed. The common sense approach to interrogation is to ask how accurate and fair is the outcome. Both Newman's and Balint's analyses of negotiation raise this question. Both presuppose that there is an objective state of affairs that is independent of the technique of assessment. This is quite clear in Newman's discussion, as he continually refers to defendants who are "really" or "actually" guilty or innocent.[20] The situation is less clear in Balint's discussion, although occasionally he implies that certain patients are really physically healthy, but psychologically distressed.

The type of analysis suggested by this paper seeks to avoid such presuppositions. It can be argued that *independently* of the facts of the case, the technique of assessment plays a part in determining the outcome. In particular, one can avoid making assumptions about actual responsibility by utilizing a technique of textual criticism of a transaction. The key dimension in such work would be the relative power and authority of the participants in the situation.[21]

As an introduction to the way in which power differences between interactants shape the outcome of negotiations, let us take as an example an attorney in a trial dealing with "friendly" and "unfriendly" witnesses. A friendly witness is a person whose testimony will support the definition of the situation the attorney seeks to convey to the jury. With such a witness the attorney does not employ power, but treats him as an equal. His questions to such a witness are open, and allow the witness considerable freedom. The attorney might frame a question such as "Could you tell us about your actions on the night of ———?"

The opposing attorney, however, interested in establishing his own version of the witness' behavior on the same night, would probably approach the task quite differently. He might say: "You felt angry and offended on the night of ———, didn't you?" The witness frequently will try to evade so direct a question with an answer like: "Actually, I had started to. . . . " The attorney quickly interrupts, addressing the judge: "Will the court order the witness to respond to the question, yes or no?" That is to say, the question posed by the opposing attorney is abrupt and direct. When the witness attempts to answer indirectly, and at length, the attorney quickly invokes the power of the court to coerce the witness to answer as he wishes, directly. The witness and the attorney are not equals in power; the attorney used the coercive power of the court to force the witness to answer in the manner desired.

The attorney confronted by an "unfriendly" witness wishes to control the format of the interaction, so that he can retain control of the definition of the situation that is conveyed to the jury. It is much easier for him to neutralize an opposing definition of the situation if he retains control of the interrogation format in this manner. By allowing the unfriendly witness to respond only by yes or no to

[20]In his Foreword the editor of the series, Frank J. Remington, comments on one of the slips that occurs frequently, the "acquittal of the guilty," noting that this phrase is contradictory from the legal point of view. He goes on to say that Newman is well aware of this, but uses the phrase as a convenience. Needless to say, both Remington's comments and mine can both be correct: the phrase is used as a convenience, but it also reveals the author's presuppositions.

[21]Berger and Luckman op. cit., p. 100, also emphasize the role of power, but at the societal level. "The success of particular conceptual machineries is related to the power possessed by those who operate them. The confrontation of alternative symbolic universes implies a problem of power—which of the conflicting definitions of reality will be "made to stick" in the society." Haley's discussions of control in psychotherapy are also relevant. See Jay Haley, "Control in Psychoanalytic Psychotherapy," *Progress in Psychotherapy*, 4, New York: Grune and Stratton, 1959, pp. 48–65; see also by the same author, "The Power Tactics of Jesus Christ" (in press).

his own verbally conveyed account, he can suppress the ambient details of the opposing view that might sway the jury, and thus maintain an advantage for his definition over that of the witness.

In the psychiatric interview discussed above, the psychiatrist obviously does not invoke a third party to enforce his control of the interview. But he does use a device to impress the patient that she is not to be his equal in the interview, that is reminiscent of the attorney with an unfriendly witness. The device is to pose abrupt and direct questions to the patient's open-ended accounts, implying that the patient should answer briefly and directly; and, through that implication, the psychiatrist controls the whole transaction. Throughout most of the interview the patient seeks to give detailed accounts of her behavior and her husband's, but the psychiatrist almost invariably counters with a direct and, to the patient, seemingly unrelated question.

The first instance of this procedure occurs at T6, the psychiatrist asking the patient, "what do you do?" She replies "I'm a nurse, but my husband won't let me work." Rather than responding to the last part of her answer, which would be expected in conversation between equals, the psychiatrist asks another question, changing the subject: "How old are you?" This pattern continues throughout most of the interview. The psychiatrist appears to be trying to teach the patient to follow his lead. After some thirty of forty exchanges of this kind, the patient apparently learns her lesson; she cedes control of the transaction competely to the therapist, answering briefly and directly to direct questions, and elaborating only on cue from the therapist. The therapist thus implements his control of the interview not by direct coercion, but by subtle manipulation.

All of the discussion above, concerning shared awareness and the format of the negotiation, suggests several propositions concerning control over the definition of the situation. The professional interrogator, whether lawyer or psychotherapist, can maintain control if the client cedes control to him because of his authority as an expert, because of his manipulative skill in the transaction, or merely because the interrogator controls access to something the client wants, e.g., treatment, or a legal excuse. The propositions are:

1a. Shared awareness of the participants that the situation is one of negotiation. (The greater the shared awareness the more control the client gets over the resultant definition of the situation.)

b. Explicitness of the agenda. (The more explicit the agenda of the transaction, the more control the client gets over the resulting definition of the situation.)

2a. Organization of the format of the transaction, offers and responses. (The party to a negotiation who responds, rather than the party who makes the offers, has relatively more power in controlling the resultant shared definition of the situation.)

b. Counter-offers. (The responding party who makes counter-offers has relatively more power than the responding party who limits his response to merely accepting or rejecting the offers of the other party.)

c. Directness of questions and answers. (The more direct the questions of the interrogator, and the more direct the answers he demands and receives, the more control he has over the resultant definition of the situation.)

These concepts and hypotheses are only suggestive until such times as operational definitions can be developed. Although such terms as offers and responses seem to have an immediate applicability to most conversation, it is likely that a thorough and systematic analysis of any given conversation would show the need for clearly stated criteria of class inclusion and exclusion. Perhaps a good place for such research would be in the transactions for assessing responsibility discussed above. Since some 90 percent of all criminal convictions in the United States are based on guilty pleas, the extent to which techniques of interrogation subtly influence outcomes would have immediate policy implication. There is considerable evidence that interrogation techniques influence the outcome of psychotherapeutic interviews also.[22] Research in both of these areas would probably have implications for both the theory and practice of assessing responsibility.

Conclusion: Negotiation in Social Science Research

More broadly, the application of the sociology of knowledge to the negotiation of reality has ramifications which may apply to all of social science. The interviewer in a survey, or the experimenter in a social psychological experiment, is also involved in a transaction with a client—the respondent or subject. Recent studies by Rosenthal and others strongly suggest that the findings in such studies are negotiated, and influenced by the format of the study.[23] Rosenthal's review of bias in research suggests that such bias is produced by a pervasive and subtle process of interaction between the investigator and his source of data. Those errors which arise because of the investigator's influence over the subject (the kind of influence discussed in this paper as arising out of power disparities in the process of negotiation), Rosenthal calls "expectancy effects." In order for these errors to occur, there must be direct contact between the investigator and the subject.

A second kind of bias Rosenthal refers to as "observer effects." These are errors of perception or reporting which do not require that the subject be influenced by investigation. Rosenthal's review leads one to surmise that even with techniques that are completely non-obtrusive, observer error could be quite large.[24]

The occurrence of these two kinds of bias poses an interesting dilemma for the lawyer, psychiatrist, and social scientist. The investigator of human phenomena is usually interested in more than a sequence of events, he wants to know why the events occurred. Usually this quest for an explanation leads him to deal with the motivation of the persons involved. The lawyer, clinician, social psychol-

[22]Thomas J. Scheff, *Being Mentally Ill*, Chicago: Aldine, 1966.

[23]Robert Rosenthal, *Experimenter Effects in Behavioral Research*, New York: Appleton-Century Crofts, 1966. Friedman, reporting a series of studies of expectancy effects, seeks to put the results within a broad sociological framework; Neil Friedman, *The Social Nature of Psychological Research: The Psychological Experiment as Social Interaction*, New York: Basic Books, 1967.

[24]Critics of "reactive techniques" often disregard the problem of observer effects. See, for example, Eugene J. Webb, Donald T. Campbell, Richard D. Schwartz, and Lee Sechrest, *Unobtrusive Measures: Nonreactive Research in Social Science*, Chicago: Rand-McNally, 1966.

ogist, or survey researcher try to elicit motives directly, by questioning the partici-pants. But in the process of questioning, as suggested above, he himself becomes involved in a process of negotiation, perhaps subtly influencing the informants through expectancy effects. A historian, on the other hand, might try to use docu-ments and records to determine motives. He would certainly avoid expectancy effects in this way, but since he would not elicit motives directly, he might find it necessary to collect and interpret various kinds of evidence which are only indi-rectly related, at best, to determine motives of the participants. Thus through his choice in the selection and interpretation of the indirect evidence, he may be as susceptible to error as the interrogator, survey researcher, or experimentalist—his error being due to observer effects, however, rather than expectancy effects.

The application of the ideas outlined here to social and psychological research need to be developed. The five propositions suggested above might be used, for example, to estimate the validity of surveys using varying degrees of open-endedness in their interview format. If some technique could be developed which would yield an independent assessment of validity, it might be possible to demonstrate, as Aaron Cicourel has suggested, the more reliable the technique, the less valid the results.

The influence of the assessment itself on the phenomena to be assessed appears to be an ubiquitous process in human affairs, whether in ordinary daily life, the determination of responsibility in legal or clinical interrogation, or in most types of social science research. The sociology of knowledge perspective, which suggests that people go through their lives constructing reality, offers a framework within which the negotiation of reality can be seriously and construc-tively studied. This paper has suggested some of the avenues of the problem that might require further study. The prevalence of the problem in most areas of hu-man concern recommends it to our attention as a substantial field of study, rather than as an issue that can be ignored or, alternatively, be taken as the proof that rigorous knowledge of social affairs is impossible.

It Makes a Difference

Some sociologists, perched on the leading edges of contemporary methodology, tend to view the issues we have been discussing in this chapter on "theory" as es-sentially a "methodological" matter.[18] The grandiose quality of an idea like "the so-cial construction of reality" is whittled down to size by Scheff in his contribution to this chapter as he moves from an easily recognizable instance of negotiating "what really happened" (the case of copping a plea) to the less apparent but equally plausi-ble case of negotiating a medical diagnosis—defining in a way satisfactory to both physician and patient what is "really" the nature of the illness. From the phenom-enological perspective it becomes essential to learn how members of the society provide satisfactory accounts for what is happening. This is the root of Blum and McHughes' analysis of members' ascriptions of motives[19] and of Scott and Lyman's

18. Derek Phillips, for example, sweeps the phenomenological perspective into a section on "Participant Observation Techniques" in his chapter entitled "Alternate Methods of Data Collection." See, Derek L. Phillips, *Knowledge from What: Theories and Methods in Social Research* (Chicago: Rand McNally and Co., 1971), pp. 128–40.

19. Blum and McHugh, "The Social Ascription of Motives."

analysis of the conditions under which members feel called upon to account for their actions (rather than assuming that they can be taken for granted) and their further delving into the nature of what constitutes a satisfactory account within the methodological rules of the man in the street.[20] This seems to me to neatly bolster and supplement Campbell's discussion of high hurdles and low hurdles in Chapter Nine. For if the man in the street does in fact define some situations as "easy" to talk about but "difficult" to perform, then Campbell's argument becomes more viable than if we have to assume that the scientist must define what is "easy" and what is "hard."

Let us consider what difference a phenomenological perspective makes in the work of the social scientist. The differences I shall discuss tend to be somewhat overlapping—perhaps because the opposite views they represent are each relatively coherent. They also tend to be stated in either-or terms for expository purposes. In fact, many of these "differences" can be viewed as matters of relative degree of emphasis rather than as absolute dichotomies. For purposes of contrast I will compare a phenomenological approach with the more traditional positivistic approach in social science. Again, this is a device for present purposes only. We have already seen the variety of peoples and activities which can be subsumed under the phenomenological rubric; this variety is even greater within a "traditional positivistic" rubric.

We began differentiating the two views of the study of man by noting their major differences in perspective: the phenomenologist seeks to understand the social world from the point of view of the actors in it. The positivistic scientist, rather than attempting to discover the actors' categories, creates his own scientific categories and employs them for making sense out of the behavior of others. The phenomenologist sees man as an active creator of his own social world—fitting together his lines of action as he assesses and defines situations. The scientist, in contrast, tends to explain man's behavior in terms of passive reaction to external forces—he responds to stimuli. The scientist is "objective." He is outside of and separate from the behavior he studies. He is detached and value free. In contrast, the phenomenologist takes the position that in order to understand human behavior one must be or must have been a part of. It is necessary to take the role of the other—to walk in his shoes—in contrast to maintaining a scientific distance from one's subjects.

It follows that the phenomenologist would employ a basically inductive method in building knowledge. He begins with minute observations of particular events and builds up from there, perhaps creating theories about more general events from his little observations. The positivistic scientist, on the other hand, needs broad scientific theories as a starting point for testing his little empirical observations. He moves out deductively from general theories, verifying them with specific observations. The scientist works in an atomistic world where parts can be dissected and understood in themselves, with knowledge accumulating as more and more parts are catalogued. The phenomenologist cannot work with such "variables" because he sees them as making sense only in context—only in relation with their setting—only as a *gestalt*. For the scientist one discovers the whole by summing up the individual parts; not so for the phenomenologist, who sees the whole as something different from the sum of its parts. The scientist who experiments with his

20. Marvin B. Scott and Stanford M. Lyman, "Accounts," *American Sociological Review* 33 (1968): 46–62.

variables, trying to understand their relationship with one another, views with some contempt the phenomenologist who has regressed into ancient mysticism with questions about "meaning" and "intentions." The phenomenologist is essentially a social semanticist while the positivist is concerned with syntactics.

Consistent with these two sets of views is the further distinction between process, as emphasized by the phenomenologist, and structure, as emphasized by the positivist. The Hegelian idea of "becoming" is central to the phenomenological perspective. Human behavior is a social process—constantly reforming, reshaping, redirecting itself. The positivistic scientist's emphasis on input and output or on independent and dependent variables makes no sense to the phenomenologist since he sees all of the important things as happening "in between." From the phenomenological perspective, to slice up time makes as little sense as slicing a social situation into component variables. The phenomenological focus on process assumes that change is the normal state of affairs in human social life. The positivistic focus on being (in contrast to becoming) assumes that stability or balance is the normal state of affairs.

This idealized set of distinctions carries with it a methodological paraphernalia. The phenomenologist must study social life as it is found in its natural milieu, while the behaviorist may isolate bits and pieces or simulate them for study in isolation. The phenomenologist must in one way or another and to some degree use his subjective knowledge as a member of society while the positivist attempts to isolate himself personally in order to preserve his objectivity. The phenomenologist is inclined to make observations through time, while the positivist can observe a slice of time as easily as he can a slice of behavior. The phenomenologist must attempt to discover the categories used by ordinary men—the scales they carry around with them are the only legitimate scales for the phenomenologist. The positivist creates his own categories—builds with his own logic, scales which he then tests and applies on his subjects. For the phenomenologist the empirical world provides the raw materials out of which theory may be constructed bit by bit. The positivist applies reason and logic, developing an overarching scheme which seems to make sense and then testing, modifying, and altering this scheme in the empirical world.

The phenomenologist must preserve the essential subjectivity of human behavior by subtly entering into it, while the positivist must objectify human behavior and make it measurable. His definitions must be operational not only because that makes them "scientific" (i.e., the social construction of the scientist), but because such definitions have objective measurement explicitly built into them. By now it should be clear that the only measurement which makes sense to the phenomenologist is the measurement employed by the people he studies. The scientist may be satisfied to measure color along a light spectrum or heat with a thermometer. But the phenomenologist must be attentive to the color categories people themselves act in terms of or the manner in which the man in the street defines "hot" and "cold." The warm beer and cold soup about which a truck driver may complain in a roadside diner make no sense at all to the positivist. His thermometer indicates that the warm beer is many degrees colder than the cold soup. To the scientist the truck driver is being unreasonable in his complaints. To the phenomenologist the categories of warm and cold are as defined by that member of society (and it is a shared definition, not an idiosyncratic one). It is his definitions which determine his actions. Finally, Blumer's critique of variable analysis is a purely phenomenological argument, implying that the proper object of research is the intervening process and not the irrelevant independent and dependent variables.

The phenomenologist might take the skeptical view that the "scientist" is ethnocentric in his attempts to impose his perception of reality on everyone else. The scientist can in turn argue that his perception of reality is as good as anyone else's and that it is shared by a large scientific community and that it permits the accumulation of knowledge in a manner which is hardly possible if we allow to everyman his own definition of the situation. Both views are well endowed with their own cultish adherents, but the essential pragmatic question is, What use is it all? The kinds of evidence and arguments which have appeared throughout this volume should bear witness to my own catholicism on this matter. Whatever contributes to my understanding, in whatever small way, of the relationship between sentiments and acts, is admissible as evidence. Such an eclectic stance sometimes creates problems of inconsistency in basic assumptions, but I believe these can be compartmentalized in the same manner as we compartmentalize the variety of perspectives which impinge upon us in our everyday life. For my part I will draw from whatever compartment in which I may find a tasty morsel, although I must take care not to incur indigestion from mixing pickles and ice cream at the same moment. I am not, however, at all adverse to eating pickles and ice cream at the same meal—each put to good use in its proper place. If, in the course of this volume, I appear to have overemphasized a phenomenological view, it is more an act of compensation than an act of faith.

There are matters which ought not to be confused with the issue we have been discussing. The ancient functionalist debate in sociology is not central here. A self-styled functionalist may as well be a phenomenologist as a positivist and may have strong objections to either position. For example he may take a static rather than a process view of social life (positivistic), but he may also insist that a society is a *gestalt* with all of its parts intimately interrelated with each other (phenomenological) so that any interference with a part automatically upsets the whole system. It is, in fact, possible to undertake a positivistic form of phenomenology—in spite of the use I made of these two for purposes of contrast. I have referred to the work of such symbolic interactionists as Manford Kuhn and Sheldon Stryker. These men have attempted to apply positivistic science to phenomenological theory. One of the great strengths in the variety of contributions made by Arnold Rose was his eclecticism. He could be passionately loyal to the Chicago school and to symbolic interaction on the one hand, but he could also put to work whatever methods based on whatever assumptions were required to meet his necessary research goals.

It would also be an error to assume that such versions of phenomenology as ethnomethodology and symbolic interaction are the same. Their strongest adherents become almost violent in their contempt for each other. Much of this reflects the cultish quality of both schools, but there are also very real differences. The ethnomethodologists see themselves as a new discipline—a radical perspective on human behavior and its study. The symbolic interactionists see themselves as part of an old and respectable tradition in sociology and see their mission as the revitalization of a discipline gone stale. Out of this difference emerges a different view of the history of social science. The ethnomethodologist is likely to argue that there is no literature worth reading—that the journals are loaded with irrelevancies, that history begins with ethnomethodology. The anti-intellectual overtones of this argument seem horrendous to the more traditional scholars of the symbolic-interactionist school.

For the purist of either school there is also a basic methodological difference. The symbolic interactionist immerses himself in the world he studies—wallows in it. The ethnomethodologist, however, if he is to take note of the taken-for-granted rules which guide the behavior of members of the world of study, must maintain sufficient distance so that he does not come to take those rules for granted like everyone else. He must maintain the detachment necessary to make explicit the rules which participants implicitly accept. The emphasis on rules results in a somewhat more deterministic, somewhat less volitional view of man than is found among the symbolic interactionists. The latter tend to see free men constructing their lines of action in terms of their own definitions of the situation. The rule-guided man of the ethnomethodologist is not quite that free. In effect ethnomethodology may be viewed as the study of microsocial structure, in contrast with symbolic interaction which is a social psychology. Traditionally in sociology we have been inclined to view the study of little interactions as "social psychology" and the study of big systems as "social organization" or "social structure." But as Garfinkel is prone to remind us, little interactions may be highly structured and, as Blumer is prone to remind us, big systems can operate as symbolically as little ones.

Fiddling with People's Lives

Although, on the surface, this book may appear to be a harmless quest for knowledge about the relationship between people's sentiments and their actions, that quest clearly implies knowledge about *changing those sentiments and those actions*. It is an easy jump to apply such knowledge to the design and evaluation of programs which plan to intervene in and alter ongoing social processes. It is at this point that we begin fiddling with people's lives and need to consider the consequences of such knowledge: who will use it for what purposes? I concur with the sentiment that it is "difficult to imagine a truth that mankind as a whole is better off not knowing."[21] But knowledge can hardly be divorced from the uses to which it may be put.

As social scientists we have responsibility for encouraging and working for social change. There is no question about that. The question is "change for what and for whom and why?" The typical social–science-fiction future, projected by novelists, is one where, having learned how to alter man's sentiments and his actions, that knowledge is imposed ruthlessly in order to achieve an accommodating uniformity in society. Men are manipulated and adjusted so that they behave themselves. This is, in fact, a not unreasonable future to project. But it is not the only one. Marx's dream became Stalin's reality, but it did not have to. One of our themes in this volume has been that man constructs his lines of action and that he can do so intelligently or stupidly, with knowledge or with ignorance, benignly or maliciously. He is not, as Dennis Wrong has reminded us,[22] a helplessly socialized robot responding automatically to whatever stimuli are thrust at him. He is rather a man such as the one described by Everett C. Hughes — a man who is creative and who is autonomous.[23] He is a man who achieves his freedom through his ability to make intelligent choices among his many "others" and to interpret the situations in which he finds himself, in ways that create a reality, the social meaning of which we could all share: a good life in a good world.

21. Robert A. Gordon, "Letter: Amongst Competent Sociologists?" *American Sociologist* 4 (1969): 249–50. Gordon's letter is in response to a letter of my own. See, "Letters: On Social Science and the Sociology of Knowledge," *American Sociologist* 3 (1968): 291–92.

22. Dennis H. Wrong, "The Oversocialized Conception of Man in Modern Society," *American Sociological Review* 26 (1961): 183–93.

23. Everett C. Hughes, "What Other?" in Arnold M. Rose, ed., *Human Behavior*, pp. 119–27.

No one is more profoundly convinced than myself of the inadequacy of my intellectual powers, even if they were far superior to what they are, to undertake such a vast and noble work. But, although the task is too great for a single mind or a single lifetime, yet one man can state the problem clearly, and that is all I am ambitious of doing.

August Comte, *Cours de philosophie positive*, 1830

---

[1]References for entries in this index are to be found in the text and the reprinted selections. For references to persons cited in the text footnotes, see the Index which begins on page 367.

Index (Notes)[1]

A

Acock, Alan C., 240, 256, 276
Adams, R. N., 42
Aiken, Henry D., 325
Albrecht, Stanley L., 93
Allen, Harry E., 93, 127, 282
Angell, Robert Cooley, 36
Arnold, W. J., 199
Aronson, E., 151

B

Baer, D. J., 49
Baldwin, James M., 326
Barnes, Harry Elmer, 324, 325
Bastide, Roger, 47, 213
Becker, Howard P., 324, 325
Becker, Howard S., 8, 65, 150, 163, 327
Bellin, Seymour S., 93, 282
Berkowitz, Leonard, 280
Blackman, Sheldon, 221
Blake, R. R., 153, 238
Blum, Alan F., 328
Blumer, Herbert, 272, 285
Bodine, George E., 43, 60
Bogden, Robert, 147
Bouman, L., 151
Brayfield, A., 49, 60, 64
Breen, Leonard Z., 49
Bridgman, P. W., 128
Brody, Charles R., 201
Brogi, David, 204
Brookover, W., 47
Brown, Julia, 12
Bunker, John P., 115
Butler, Donald C., 221

C

Cagle, Lawrence, 45, 59, 93, 127, 148, 282, 317
Campbell, Donald T., 22, 40, 94, 109, 133
Cannell, C. F., 151
Cantor, A., 151
Caro, Francis G., 113
Cassetta, Rhonda K., 106
Chomsky, Noam, 285

Cicourel, Aaron, 63, 115
Clancy, Kevin J., 151
Cloward, Richard A., 282
Cochran, William G., 96
Coleman, John R., 153
Colombotos, John, 151
Cook, Stuart W., 45
Corwin, Ronald G., 148
Coser, Lewis A., 324
Crane, Wilder W., 63, 159
Crittenden, Kathleen Stones, 65, 330
Crockett, D. M., 49, 60, 64
Cronbach, L. J., 109
Cumming, Elaine, 49

D

Dalton, Melville, 3
Dannick, Lionel I., 49, 148, 278
Dean, Lois, 48
DeFleur, Melvin L., 93, 240, 256, 285
Defriese, Gordon H., 93, 256
DeJong, G., 12
Denny, Reuel, 201
Diekema, A. J., 42
Dilthey, Wilhelm, 324
Dohrenwerd, Barbara Snell, 151
Dohrenwerd, Bruce P., 151
Donahue, W., 49
Doob, Anthony N., 238
Drabek, Thomas E., 197
Duncan, O. D., 61, 322
Duryes, Rich A., 238

E

Ehrlich, Howard J., 93, 243, 256
Eisenhart, C., 93
Empey, Lamar T., 60
Erikson, Jon, 222
Erickson, Maynard, 60
Erickson, Milton, 199
Etzioni, Amitai, 130, 199

F

Faris, Robert E. L., 61
Faulkner, J. E., 12

[1]All entries in this index are references to persons cited in the footnotes which accompany the original text, and do not include those which accompany the reprinted selections. For references to persons discussed in the text and selections, see the general Index which begins on page 360.

1 2 3 4 5 6 7 8 9 10 11 12 13 14 15 16 17 18 19 20 21 22 23 24 25   78 77 76 75 74 73